DYING: Faci

DYING: Facing the Facts

Third Edition

Edited by

Hannelore Wass, Ph.D.
University of Florida

Robert A. Neimeyer, Ph.D.
University of Memphis

Taylor & Francis
Publishers since 1798

USA	Publishing Office:	Taylor & Francis 1101 Vermont Avenue, N.W. Suite 200 Washington, D.C. 20005–3521 Tel: (202) 289–2174 Fax: (202) 289–3665
	Distribution Center:	Taylor & Francis 1900 Frost Road Suite 101 Bristol, PA 19007-1598 Tel: (215) 785-5800 Fax: (215) 785-5515
UK		Taylor & Francis Ltd. 4 John St. London WC1N 2ET Tel: 071 405 2237

Dying: Facing the Facts, Third Edition

1 2 3 4 5 6 7 8 9   BRBR   0 9 8 7 6 5

This book was set in Times Roman by Graphic Composition. The editors were Christine Williams, Holly Seltzer, and Deborah Klenotic; the prepress supervisor was Miriam Gonzalez. Cover design by Michelle M. Fleitz. Printing and binding by Braun-Brumfield, Inc.

A CIP catalog record for this book is available from the British Library.
∞ The paper in this publication meets the requirements of the ANSI Standard Z39.48-1984 (Permanence of Paper)

Library of Congress Cataloging-in-Publication Data

Dying: facing the facts / edited by Hannelore Wass and Robert A. Neimeyer.—3rd ed.
    p.   cm.—(Series in death education, aging, and health care)
  Includes bibliographical references and indexes.
    1. Death. 2. Thanatology. I. Wass, Hannelore. II. Neimeyer, Robert A., date.
  III. Series.
  HQ1073.D93   1995
  306.9—dc20   94-44886
                                                     CIP

ISBN 1-56032-285-3 (case)
ISBN 1-56032-286-1 (paper)
ISSN 0275-3510

Contents

Contributors

DAVID E. BALK, Ph.D.
Department of Human Development and
  Family Studies
Kansas State University
Manhattan, KS 66506

JEANNE QUINT BENOLIEL, R.N., Ph.D
University of Washington
Seattle, WA 98195

STEPHEN CONNOR, Ph.D.
Hospice of Central Kentucky
Elizabethtown, KY 42702

LESLEY F. DEGNER, R.N., Ph.D.
St. Boniface General Hospital Research
  Center
351 Tache Avenue
Winnipeg, Manitoba R2H 2A6
Canada

ROBERT FULTON, Ph.D.
Department of Sociology
University of Minnesota
Minneapolis, MN 55455

MICHAEL C. KEARL, Ph.D.
Department of Sociology and
  Anthropology
715 Stadium Drive
Trinity University
San Antonio, TX 78210

DENNIS KLASS, Ph.D.
Department of Religion
Webster University
St. Louis, MO 63119

MARCIA LATTANZI-LICHT, R.N., M.A.
Comprehensive Psychological Service
1526 Spruce Street, Suite 301
Boulder, CO 80302

ANTOON A. LEENAARS, Ph.D.
880 Ouellette Avenue, Suite 806
Windsor, Ontario N9A 1C7
Canada

JOHN D. MORGAN, Ph.D.
Department of Philosophy
King's College, Western Ontario
  University
London, Ontario N6A 2M3
Canada

ROBERT A. NEIMEYER, Ph.D.
Department of Psychology
University of Memphis
Memphis, TN 38152

KAREN E. PETERSON, Ph.D.
1320 S. Dixie Highway, #1150
Coral Gables, FL 33146

THERESE A. RANDO, Ph.D.
Therese A. Rando Associates, Ltd.
33 College Hill Road, Bldg. 30A
Warwick, RI 02886

NELDA SAMAREL, R.N., Ed.D.
Department of Nursing
William Paterson College of New Jersey
Wayne, NJ 07470

SHERYL SCHEIBLE WOLF, J.D.
University of New Mexico, School of Law
1117 Stanford NE
Albuquerque, NM 87131

JUDITH M. STILLION, Ph.D.
Department of Psychology
Western Carolina University
Cullowhee, NC 28723

DAVID VAN BRUNT
Department of Psychology
University of Memphis
Memphis, TN 38152

ROBERT M. VEATCH, Ph.D.
Kennedy Institute/Ethics
Georgetown University
Washington, DC 20057

HANNELORE WASS, Ph.D.
Department of Educational Psychology
University of Florida
Gainesville, FL 32611

ARTHUR ZUCKER, Ph.D.
Department of Philosophy
Ohio University
Athens, OH 45701-2979

Preface

Since the first edition of *Dying: Facing the Facts* was published 15 years ago, thanatology—the study of death and dying—has emerged as a recognized field of study, as well as something of a cultural phenomenon. While the roots of the contemporary "death awareness" movement reach back to the work of pioneering thanatologists in the 1950s, a widespread and abiding concern with death in the medical and social sciences and related disciplines is a comparatively recent development. Indeed, serious research and scholarship in such areas as bereavement and death attitudes among children and adults was still in its infancy at the time of the first edition, and such critical topics as euthanasia, funeral reform, hospice care for the dying, and the changing definition of death in view of advances in medical technology were just beginning to press themselves to the forefront of our social consciousness. The ensuing decade witnessed continued research on basic issues, as well as still greater social foment in the form of enhanced concerns for global human survival, prompting us to revise and update *Dying* in 1988 to encompass these developments. Now, six years later, the burgeoning literature in core thanatological disciplines combined with new death-related threats to our society and our species (e.g., the AIDS pandemic) have prompted us to undertake a third revision of the volume, with the aim of providing an authoritative and high-level discussion of the cluster of perspectives, data, and issues that comprise the contemporary field of death studies.

Our objectives in the current edition are threefold. First, we have attempted to offer the reader the most current knowledge available in thanatology—knowledge grounded in empirical research, solid scholarship, and compassionate caregiving. To achieve this objective, we have provided thorough revisions of previous cornerstone chapters and invited a talented cadre of new contributors to expand coverage of previously neglected or inadequately represented areas. Second, we have tried to reflect the complex interdisciplinary character of the field of death and dying, to which nursing, medicine, psychology, family studies, sociology, education, philosophy, law, religion, the humanities, and even political science have all made substantial contributions. Much of the vitality of the field at its current state of development is owed to the interdisciplinary nature of this effort to understand the multifaceted phenomena of death and dying within the unique theoretical and applied frameworks provided by these various fields of study. Yet within this multidisciplinary context, we have tried to give thematic continuity to the volume by emphasizing those foci of thanatological thought that have perhaps the most immediate implications for research and practice, namely, those concerned with psychosocial and clinical aspects of the field. Thus, our third objective was to highlight the psychological and therapeutic dimensions of thanatology, while still paying close attention to those larger social, cultural, and political structures and processes that reciprocally influence the individuals who live (and die) within them. To accomplish this, we have in some instances reassigned previous chapters to authors with clinical as well as scholarly expertise and have invited others to contribute new chapters emphasizing a caregiving perspective.

As editors of the third edition, we obviously continue to believe that serious readers are well served by having the experts speak directly and authoritatively to them. We are fortunate to have been joined in this effort by an outstanding set of contributors consisting both of pioneers in thanatology, as well as younger leaders who are beginning to shape the future of the discipline. As in the previous editions, both the content and form of the book reflect our goal of producing a sophisticated but readable examination of issues surrounding death and dying for the serious student and professional. For this reason, we have emphasized substance over style, omitting cartoons, photographs, or other supplemental materials in the text in order to devote space to scholarly discussion of the various topics. Nevertheless, we have tried to avoid technical jargon as much as possible. This book, then, is intended primarily for advanced undergraduate or graduate students and professionals and may be useful as a primary textbook as well as a reference.

In a sense, the organization of the book follows a pattern of development from the general to the specific, moving from broad examinations of death systems from the vantage point of various cultural, historical, and disciplinary perspectives, through a detailed consideration of several substantive areas of research and practice, to critical examinations of pressing issues regarding death that we now face on both individual and societal levels. In part I, Kearl opens with a sweeping and novel reconstruction of political theory along thanatological lines. Analyzing those means by which states and cultures symbolically harness the power of death for their own ends (e.g., by manipulating the death anxieties of the populace, granting their members various forms of symbolic immortality, and exercising a monopoly on the legitimate use of deadly force), he provides the scholarly basis for a detailed critique of political practices that lead to racial and gender inequalities in death rates and more flagrant expressions of power including genocide. Morgan extends this macroscopic view through his review of historically significant death orientations in Western culture and his sustained examination of our death system, that distinctive matrix of ideas, traditions, acts, omissions, people, and positions that shape our current understandings of what it means to be mortal. He finds that our current relationship to death in Western societies is influenced by social and cultural forces (e.g., our diminished contact with death, our accentuated sense of self, and our assumed control over nature) that may have both beneficial and deleterious consequences, muting our affective consciousness of death on an individual level. Together, these two chapters set a broad historical context within which the reader can place the more specialized concerns of later contributors.

Part II represents the core of the book, offering detailed surveys of the "data" of death, dying, and bereavement as they relate to different phases of our encounter with death as an abstract possibility and concrete reality. It proceeds from consideration of individuals' attitudes toward death, to the process of dying and its contexts, to responses to loss and death, and finally, provides a survey of major topics in the field from a life span developmental orientation. Neimeyer and Van Brunt begin by reviewing the voluminous empirical literature on attitudes toward death with a special focus on death-related fears and anxieties. After guiding the reader toward a more sophisticated understanding of the strengths and limitations of existing means of studying death attitudes, they evaluate what is known about the causes, correlates, and consequences of death anxiety and death acceptance.

Samarel then provides a clinically grounded and sometimes moving discussion of the dying process, both from the standpoint of dying individuals in their final moments and from the perspective of the family and friends who must negotiate the process with them. She concludes with specific recommendations winnowed both from the literature and from her own clinical experience as a nurse attempting to humanize the dying process. However individualized dying might be, it cannot be understood except in a social context. For those of us in "first world" countries that have been shaped by the forces of urbanization, secularization, and technological sophistication, this context has become increasingly institutional. In the next chapter in this section, Quint Benoliel and Degner examine the "new forms of dying" that have arisen in modern hospitals, forms often marked by isolation of patients and an emphasis on *cure* over *care*. This leads them toward an examination of the various patterns of patient-staff communication that are typical of institutional settings, and finally toward an analysis of the conflicting values embodied in institutions for those who work in them versus those who die in them. In part as a response to the shortcomings of these traditional institutions, hospices have evolved to provide more adequately for the palliative care of the dying, as well as to attend to their unique psychosocial and spiritual needs. Lattanzi-Licht and Connor survey the evolution of hospice care as an alternative to the constraints of institutional dying note its still problematic relation to more conventional medical institutions and problems related to public perception of their purposes. In addition, they provide representative illustrations of its holistic orientation in caring for the unique needs of patients and their families.

One measure of an individual's preparedness for death is the existence of a last will and testament well in advance of one's final hours. Scheible Wolf provides a lucid and practical discussion of the complex legalities of death, including the role of the last will and testament, will substitutes, the probate process, and rules of inheritance. She also discusses regulations surrounding disposal of the body, with a special emphasis on organ donation and funeral regulation. This latter topic leads to the broader consideration of the contemporary funeral provided by Fulton. Construing the funeral in dramaturgical, sociological, psychological, and anthropological terms, he presents it as a rite of both separation (from the deceased) and integration (of the community) and analyzes both its functional and dysfunctional aspects.

Of course, the funeral is only the first phase in the process of adjustment to an often deeply personal loss for the survivors. The next two chapters examine bereavement, with an emphasis on its psychological and spiritual dimensions. In her comprehensive discussion of grief and mourning, Rando reviews five major theories of loss and explicates the tasks or processes of accommodation these imply for the bereaved individual. She then delineates seven requirements for appropriate mourning and outlines the causes and treatment of mourning that becomes complicated. Klass supplements this coverage of loss in his subsequent contribution on the spiritual dimensions of grieving, anchoring his discussion not only in religious and philosophic scholarship, but also in his ongoing ethnographic study of a chapter of The Compassionate Friends, an international support group for parents who have lost a child. From this vantage point he critiques those theories of loss that presume that the mourner must psychologically detach from the deceased, instead arguing that cultivating a continuing relationship with an inner representation of the one who has died can provide a powerful source of solace for the living.

Finally, our treatment of the basic "data" on death concludes with two chapters that place many of the foregoing topics in a life span developmental perspective. Concentrating on death in the lives of children and adolescents, Wass highlights the ironic relationship of young people to death in contemporary American culture. On the one hand, young people are more "protected" from (natural) death than at any other time in human history, while at the same time they are bombarded with death-related imagery by the media and increasingly, confronted with the very real threat of death in the form of interpersonal violence. In addition, she amplifies themes encountered in other chapters by teasing out the distinctive features of children's conceptions of death, death anxieties, ways of mourning, and risk of suicide. Stillion's concluding chapter in this section extends this developmental view by considering the changing role of death in adult life. Anchoring her discussion in the demography of death in the United States and other countries, she goes on to provide a unique generational perspective that suggests that different cohorts of adults have characteristic ways of construing death, and by implication, life itself. Because exposure to death increases in both frequency and intensity across the course of adulthood, leading inevitably toward our own cessation, she argues that coping with the deaths of those we love and coming to accept our own mortality are perhaps the paramount issues of adult development.

Part III of the book addresses a cluster of death-related issues and challenges that confront us at both a societal and individual level. Peterson opens this section with a thorough and sometimes poignant consideration of the AIDS pandemic, examining its etiology, epidemiology, symptomatology, treatment, and prevention. She argues that a sober appraisal of the threat of the disease and the difficulties faced by HIV-prevention efforts must be leavened with hope and even humor as we contend with the grim realities that AIDS poses for all of us, regardless of age, sex, gender, sexual preference, or nationality. Leenaars follows this with a broad analysis of a second "epidemic" that affects all ages and ethnic groups—suicide. Beginning with a unique historical perspective on the role of suicide in Western philosophic and cultural traditions, he then concentrates on the demography of self-destruction and the sociological and psychological conditions that give rise to it. In particular, Leenaars emphasizes the emotional and cognitive factors that predispose persons in crisis to seek suicide as a solution, and he sketches the goals of treatment and prevention of this uniquely human tragedy.

The concluding two chapters in this section tackle thorny issues raised by the efficacy of life-sustaining medical technology. In the first of these, Zucker examines pressing questions concerning the right to die, euthanasia, and physician-assisted suicide from the standpoint of moral theory. His analysis leads him to the heart of medical and legal ambiguities surrounding the very definition of life and death and the problems and prospects of various forms of patient self-determination. These critical definitional themes are amplified by Veatch in the closing chapter of this section. Veatch outlines both the continuities and disconti-nuities in the criteria used to define the end of life, as we move from gross struc-tural or functional criteria to increasingly sophisticated neurological criteria for identifying the transition to death. Veatch argues convincingly that, far from being abstruse philosophical or medical questions, negotiating such definitions is criti-cal to developing an informed public policy that recognizes the legitimate limits of medical intervention.

Finally, we close the volume with a few personal reflections on the complex character of contemporary thanatology, framing some issues and recommenda-tions that deserve greater attention by scholars, researchers, policymakers, and practitioners. The volume concludes with a brief resource bibliography compiled by Wass and Balk, listing recent and classic books, journals, dissertations, audio-visual media, and organizational resources that should be of value to both death educators and readers interested in learning more.

Altogether, in this third edition of *Dying: Facing the Facts* we have tried to present current thinking and state-of-the-art knowledge in a balance of major thrusts. We have sought to provide coverage of a broad range of death-related topics with in-depth examination of the core psychosocial and caregiving issues they entail. In this, we have attempted to balance scholarship and application and have tried to present the data on death and dying within broader disciplinary con-texts that render them intelligible. We hope that the resulting volume will inform and stimulate readers to explore further this challenging and exciting field and perhaps to reflect more deeply on the relevance of death to their own lives.

Hannelore Wass
University of Florida

Robert A. Neimeyer
University of Memphis

Preface to the Second Edition

Since the first edition of *Dying: Facing the Facts* was published, the field of thanatology has expanded and crystallized. In response to these changes, this second edition has also evolved, both in its editorship and its scope. Joining Hannelore Wass, an educational psychologist and editor of the original volume, is Felix M. Berardo, a sociologist, and Robert A. Neimeyer, a clinical psychologist. We have tried to contribute the unique expertise of our respective disciplines in our dual roles as authors and editors. We hope that our efforts, together with those of the other contributors, have resulted in a book that reflects the multidisciplinary character of thanatology, achieves scholarly rigor, and attains our goal of presenting state-of-the-art knowledge of the broad range of topics selected for inclusion in this volume. Of the 17 contributors to this edition, five are psychologists, five are sociologists, four are philosophers or medical ethicists, and the remaining three are specialists in nursing, law, and chemistry, respectively.

To meet our objectives, some changes in the range and organization of topics in the first edition were necessary. Of the 18 chapters in the current volume, 13 are newly written and the remaining five have been thoroughly revised. New chapters address topics that were omitted in the first edition, such as suicide, the experience of dying, death anxiety, and problems in studying death, as well as issues that have gained salience over the past several years, such as life preservation and global survival. Inevitably, the addition of these chapters required the deletion of others covered in the original edition. Most of these deletions were made reluctantly. Two highly literate introductory chapters providing an overview of the first edition have been replaced by a single, much briefer one. The chapter on the funeral industry has been deleted. Three other chapters, on death and the elderly, death education, and the physiology of dying, have been deleted with some regret, although whenever possible, related material has been assimilated into the reorganized chapters. Most notably, the material in the original chapter on social and psychological aspects of dying has been considerably expanded and is now discussed in three separate chapters. In spite of these changes, we have retained the organizational scheme of the first edition, combining the chapters into three major groupings: I. Problems and Perspectives; II. Data: The Facts of Dying and Death; and III. Challenge: Meeting the Issues of Death.

Finally, we should note that both the content and form of the book reflect our decision to produce a readable, but sophisticated, examination of thanatological issues suitable for the serious reader. For this reason, we have emphasized substance over style, omitting illustrations and other supplementary materials in the text proper in order to devote the space to a scholarly discussion of the various topics. Nonetheless, we have tried to avoid technical jargon as much as possible, in order to ensure the accessibility of the book to specialists and nonspecialists alike.

We have provided review questions at the end of each chapter and listed some suggested activities and a variety of additional resources, including selections from literature and the arts in the appendixes. We hope the reader will find these helpful and stimulating.

In conclusion, this second edition of *Dying: Facing the Facts* attempts to present up-to-date knowledge and current thinking in the field of thanatology. We hope that it will both inform and sensitize the reader to the complexities surrounding the human experience of death and dying in contemporary western societies.

Hannelore Wass
Felix M. Berardo
Robert A. Neimeyer

Preface to the First Edition

Why add another book on death and dying to the many volumes that have already been written on the subject? This question must be asked today by anyone who thinks of writing in the field. The primary motivation to proceed with this book was the conviction that there is a need for a volume that focuses on the *basic facts of death* and that presents them comprehensively and in a systematic manner. Much information has emerged over the past few decades from the efforts of researchers, scholars, clinicians, and practitioners in various death-related disciplines and professional fields. This information can be found scattered in various journals and other publications but has not been brought together in one book. Nine chapters, almost two-thirds of this book, are devoted to the discussion of the facts of death.

A second objective was to provide a volume that is structured with *logic and cohesion,* leading from A to B to C. Such a structure is achieved, I believe, by using a simple basic assumption, namely, that we as individuals as well as a society have problems with death and dying, and if our aim is to solve them, we must first clearly identify these problems, then consider all the facts, and use this information in trying to find solutions. Therefore in designing the book, while keeping the discussion of the facts of death as the main focus, I recognized the need to offer a clear statement of the problems we have with respect to dying and death. Moreover, these problems had to be placed within a larger framework, that is, they had to be treated within a broad sociocultural and historical context to provide valid perspective. Thus in Part One the first two chapters introduce and define the problems of death-related attitudes and behaviors in our society and their manifestations and consequences. These chapters probe deeply and do not retreat from presenting complexities and ambivalence. They attempt to capture the problems in the process of change in a changing society. Oversimplification was avoided for the simple reason that it is of little value to those who seriously seek solutions. In Part Three, four chapters dealing with current issues and controversies are included. These chapters give an indication of the efforts by leaders in the field to grapple with contemporary controversies about death and dying. I feel they will stimulate thought as well as inform and thereby help the reader work through the problems and face the facts. In order to further unify the book, I have written a short introduction to each chapter, in which the chapter is discussed in the overall context of the book as a whole.

The contributors have made every effort to write in a straightforward manner, avoiding technical language whenever possible. I hope the reader will recognize that the simplicity of style did not interfere with maintaining high standards of scholarship. Contributors representing the broad spectrum of relevant fields (such as philosophy, psychology, psychiatry, medicine, nursing, sociology, anthropology, law, and education) have drawn upon existing knowledge and in many instances communicated new information and thought they generated in their respective areas.

In designing this volume, I envisioned it to become a comprehensive basic text for the serious student, whether he or she is an undergraduate student, a professional in the field, a parent, or simply an interested person. It should be mentioned that a number of the contributors to this volume have written their own books in the field of death and dying or are in the process of doing so. Their willingness to expend time and energy to write for this book is evidence that such a book is needed. Several contributors have written their chapters while carrying the burdens of personal tragedy, such as a terminally ill child or spouse, the death of a parent, or personal illness. Their dedication and commitment is deeply appreciated.

This book, then, delineates the problems related to dying and death that confront individuals and society as a whole. It presents in systematic fashion the facts of death as we now know them. I hope this book will stimulate the reader's interest and motivation to apply these facts toward achievement of solutions of the problems concerning dying in our society today and that this will be true for the reader who is a student or professional in regular contact with the dying and their families, as well as for the reader who seeks his or her own confrontation with death in an existential way in order to be better able to define life purposes and goals. It should help the reader achieve a clearer sense of self within a larger order. In sum, I hope the reader will find this a compact, comprehensive, and current volume of personal and professional value.

Hannelore Wass

Part One

Contexts and Perspectives

Chapter 1

Death and Politics:
A Psychosocial Perspective

Michael C. Kearl

Underlying the kaleidoscope of death perspectives presented in this book are hints of a multidisciplinary core. Indeed, into the family of deterministic theories in the social sciences—those paradigms that feature some central force underlying the human condition, such as sociobiology in biology, psychoanalytic theory in psychology, communications and transportation determinism in technology studies, and materialism in sociology and anthropology—has arrived thanatology, perhaps the most unifying of the lot.

For thanatologists, the roots of civilization are bound up with humans' first awareness of their own mortality. With social evolution, we learned that death was the fate of not just individual life forms, but of entire species and genuses. We learned that the passage from existence to nonexistence was not the fate of just life, but also of mountains, planets, stars, galaxies, and, according to the Big Bang eschatology, eventually the entire universe. This appreciation of the prospect of meaningless nothingness was to motivate only the human animal. And the essence of this motivation was to be like no other: transcendence.

Each academic discipline has broken down death into various constituent parts. For instance, philosophers consider the distinctive fears of meaninglessness, self-extinction, extinction with insignificance, and incompleteness. Psychologists have broken down the dying process into the experiences of pain; fears of the unknown; regret; and, of course, the emotional stages of Kübler-Ross. They have broken down the bereavement experience into phases of grief work. Among disciplines focusing on death on a societal or cultural level, one research tradition has been to determine how social systems themselves break down death into distinctive dreads. For instance, one may investigate how religions mold death anxiety into fear of agonizing hell or undesirable reincarnation as a means of obtaining moral obedience or how secularization and the rise of contemporary medicine have shifted cultural death anxiety from fear of postmortem judgment to fear of the dying process. As will be developed, how these anxieties are focused determines, at the individual level, the nature of the rituals people use to manage them; at the social level, the distribution of power; and at the cultural level, the nature of the death ethos.

For thanatologists in these more macroscopically oriented disciplines, there were many lessons to be learned during the spring of 1993: the burning of the Waco, Texas, compound of the Branch Davidian cult; the dedication of the United States Holocaust Museum in Washington, DC; and heated Congressional debates over whether the United States should intervene in the civil war in former Yugoslavia, whether women should serve in military combat roles, and whether there should be a federal health care system. Although these events were apparently coincidental, what they were publicly dramatizing was the ascendency of civil religion over all matters of life and death. In Waco, the state reaffirmed its monopoly over legitimate violence. In Washington, DC, the state demonstrated its power to rescue from oblivion the memories of the millions politically selected to die. And in Congress, the state determined the degree that premature deaths would occur due to combat and disease.

Well over half the federal budget is devoted to

- Refining the instruments of death (e.g., the military),
- Preventing death (e.g., environmental control and cleanup, and paying for nearly one third of the nation's health care bill), and
- Assisting those most likely to die (between the 1960s and 1980s, the portion of the federal budget spent on those 65 or older increased from 15% to 28%, and 25–35% of Medicare expenditures go to the 5–6% of enrollees who die during the year [Callahan, 1987].

This ascendancy of the state as the most powerful social agency against death has a host of implications. For thanatological determinists, political structures of power are seen ultimately to be collective efforts to control death, either unleashing it against our enemies or harnessing it at home. With modernization, most premature death occurs because of man-made (hence avoidable) causes. Concurrently, and not unrelatedly, modern political regimes have become the social institution providing the cultural rituals related to death control and death transcendence. It is not so much Eisenhower's military–industrial complex, but rather a *medical–military–industrial complex,* that has evolved as the skeletal structure of the social organism. During the 1980s, military and health care employment were the major sources of job growth in the United States, creating one in four new jobs (Greenhouse, 1993). As will be argued, political systems are replacing religions as the mechanism by which death beliefs and fears are shaped and used for social control.

A PARADIGM FOR A SOCIAL PSYCHOLOGY OF DEATH

People's ideas and fears of death are not innate but rather are learned from their social and cultural environments. Thus to study such matters as the psychology of dying or grief separate from individuals' social, cultural, and historical contexts is analogous to conducting an ethological study in a zoo. The resultant agenda for some of the more sociologically inclined social psychologists and historians has been to map the influences of separate institutions (e.g., religion, the mass media, families, and the military) on individuals' death-related fears and motivations and to relate historical changes in their relative power to distinctive cultural orientations to death (e.g., Ariès 1974, 1981).

Extreme among these researchers are the thanatological determinists (i.e., Bauman, 1992; Becker, 1973; Harrington, 1977; Kearl, 1989) who argue that social power concentrates in the institution that is best able to harness death's power ritually. Such harnessing occurs through giving meaning to death's occurrence, reminding individuals of their mortality, helping them to outlive their contemporaries, and providing opportunities for transcendence over death.

Death and the Problem of Meaning

Arguably, the central accomplishment of any culture is its capacity to give symbolic order and meaning to human mortality. A culture's death system (Kastenbaum & Aisenberg, 1972) or death ethos (Geertz, 1973) strongly conditions the behaviors of the living. It determines such widely ranging phenomena as a people's militancy and suicide rate, their willingness to take risks, their fears of or hopes for reincarnation and resurrection, their willingness to receive organ transplants or to purchase life insurance, their preference for burial or cremation, their attitudes toward capital punishment and abortion, and their conceptualizations of good deaths. So great is the power of an ethos—the construction of meaning erected against the terror of death—that various social agencies seek to harness its energy as a method of social control.

Canetti asked, "How many people will find it worth while living once they don't have to die?" (cited by Bauman, 1992, p. 6). The power of death derives, in part, from that fact that it is a catalyst that, when put into contact with any cultural order, precipitates out the central beliefs and concerns of a people. Experimental demonstrations of this cultural chemistry come from tests of Becker's (1973) thesis that death anxiety intensifies allegiance to moral codes. Rosenblatt, Greenberg, Solomon, Pyszczynski, and Lyon (1989) found that when reminded of their mortality, people reacted more harshly toward moral transgressors and became more favorably disposed to those who upheld their values. In one experiment (Greenberg et al., 1990), for instance, 22 municipal judges were given a battery of psychological tests. In the experimental group, 11 judges were told to write about their own death, including what happens physically and what emotions are evoked when they think about it. When asked to set bond for a prostitute on the basis of a case brief, those who had thought about their death set an average bond of $455, whereas the average bond set by the control group, who had not been asked to write about their own death, was $50. The authors concluded that when awareness of death is increased, in-group solidarity intensifies, out-groups become more despised, and prejudice and religious extremism escalate. It is for this reason that regimes attempt to monopolize collective death awareness and to focus its energies toward political ends; examples are Hussein's coverage of civilian casualties during the Persian Gulf War and the United States's and former Soviet Union's development of military–industrial complexes during the Cold War, when

fear of nuclear annihilation was great (e.g., Boyer, 1985). Any breech in this monopoly, such as the martyrization of antiregime victims in Northern Ireland and
South Africa, portends political change.

Being Forced To Think Unwanted Thoughts and
the Power of Disgust

It was a result of having been routinely forced to contemplate their own mortality
that our ancestors were, indeed, a more moralistic lot than we. Death's omnipres-
ence forced them to come to terms with their inevitable limits. Theirs were generations of character, the products of pain and tragedy. But as death, at least death
due to natural causes, began to recede from everyday life (Ariès, 1974), there
arose during the 20th century the coinciding processes of heightened individualism, featuring excessive narcissism (Lasch, 1979); the self-esteem and self-
fulfillment movements; sexual licentiousness; pornographic death (Gorer, 1955/
1965); and moral relativism (Rigney & Kearl, 1994). Although the causal role of
death's changing character in these cultural phenomena remains a matter of debate, their cognitive correlations within Americans' minds is an empirical fact
(Kearl & Harris, 1981–82).

Wegner (1989) experimentally demonstrated that telling people not to think
certain thoughts resulted in their becoming obsessed with these thoughts. Undoubtedly, death's contemporary status as a taboo topic for everyday discourse
relates to Americans' appetite for violence and pornographic death. But what
about forcing individuals to think unwanted thoughts—the thoughts that they are
not the center of the universe, but rather powerless and insignificant beings; that
their contributions are basically meaningless in the total scheme of things; and
that their fate is only death? What power accrues to those individuals or institutions that bring up these unwanted thoughts?

In describing the nature of the sacred that "communifies" or attracts individuals into groups, Bataille (1938/1988) argued that the essence of the force is that
which disgusts:

The social nucleus is, in fact, taboo . . . untouchable and unspeakable; from the outset it
partakes of the nature of corpses, menstrual blood, pariahs. . . . Early human beings were
brought together by disgust and by common terror, by an insurmountable horror focused
precisely on what originally was the central attraction to their union. (p. 106)

These repulsive aspects of the sacred, responsible for the very origin of culture,
Bataille argued, are denied by contemporary society. On this point, Bataille
is partially wrong, as evidenced by the dedication of the Holocaust Museum in
the United States, the collective memories triggered by newsreel footage of the
concentration camp liberations and of the nuclear devastation of Hiroshima
and Nagasaki, and the evening news coverage of starvation in Somalia and ethnic
cleansing in the former Yugoslavia. The lesson given is that disgusting death now
typically occurs because of political, not natural, reasons.

The Bonding Power of Death

It is for the reasons above that death has the ritual power that it does and funerals and ritual sacrifices are nearly universal practices. Of all phenomena, death most demands attention, ripping individuals out of their everyday, automatic routines. As Blauner (1966) noted, death's sword is double-edged: "The very sharpness of its disintegrating potential demands adaptations that can bring higher levels of cohesion and continuity" (p. 394).

Nowhere is death's power to invigorate life greater than during war. Reflecting on his experiences as a journalist at the front in World War II, Andy Rooney observed that people normally live at 50% and only in war does that experience total 100% (ABC News, 1987). As described by Captain John Early, a former Rhodesian mercenary who served with the U.S. Army in Vietnam,

This is really going to sound strange, but there's a love relationship that is nurtured in combat because the man next to you—you're depending on him for the most important thing you have, your life, and if he lets you down you're either maimed or killed. If you make a mistake the same thing happens to him, so the bond of trust has to be extremely close, and I'd say this bond is stronger than almost anything, with the exception of parent and child. It's a hell of a lot stronger than man and wife—your life is in his hands, you trust that person with the most valuable thing you have. (Dyer, 1985, p. 104)

Capitalizing on the Desire To Survive Contemporaries

Beyond death's challenge to the meaning of life and its ability to bring together individuals, an additional social psychological assumption entails the morbid satisfactions derived when death comes to others. As Canetti (1960/1973) noted, "The moment of survival is the moment of power" (p. 227). Others' deaths give meaning to our own success, evidence of our progress in our quest for immortality, and feelings of superiority. "The desire for a long life which plays such a large part in most cultures really means that most people want to survive their contemporaries" (Canetti, p. 249). As shall be shown, it is for these reasons that international life expectancy and infant mortality "box scores" have assumed the political significance they have.

In the extreme, Canetti (1960/1973) argued, this survival drive leads to murder. When legitimated by religion or political regime, the demons of war are cognitively unleashed. Observed Bauman (1992),

The cynicism with which the wish of survival is inevitably, though self-ashamedly, infused, comes blatantly into the open during war—that socially sanctioned, legitimate murder; the declared purpose is then "to limit our casualties," . . . "Kill, so that you and your beloved shalt not be killed." Declaration of war means suspension of the guilt and shame that the wish of survival spawns at "normal" times. (p. 34)

Transcendence Through Symbolic Immortality as
the Central Motivation

Becker (1973) argued that being able to stand out and be remembered, to excel
according to the standards of all and within the framework of social constraints,
is what life is all about. Structure is what makes life's games possible in the first
place and what ultimately gives them meaning. The structure of the baseball
game, for instance, determines players' roles and the standards against which their
performances are judged. Over time, certain players, for example, Willie Mays
catching a ball over his shoulder in the deep outfield and Babe Ruth pointing in
the direction of his forthcoming home run, come to define the parameters and
the possibilities of their position. These role-defining individuals, these cultural
standards of how biography and society can be fused, become immortalized in
eponyms, legend, art, statistics, and halls of fame.

It is important that individuals believe that this meaning-generating life structure is something eternal, that society existed before their births and will continue
to exist after their deaths. The seeds of civilization begin when, for instance, parents begin feeding their children before themselves and discover (because behavior normally precedes its ideological justification) their obligation to the survival
of the sociocultural order.

THE POLITICALIZATION OF PREMATURE DEATHS

What is the significance of the federal government's monitoring of what Americans eat, drink, breathe, wear, and drive; requiring that health warnings be affixed
to cigarette packs and safety warnings to buckets and extension ladders; financing
weather satellites to predict severe storms, monitoring systems to predict earthquakes, and feasibility studies of the use of nuclear weapons against threatening
asteroids; and spending billions of dollars to perfect instruments of death (i.e.,
military weapons)? By deconstructing death into the things that kill us and then
attempting to eradicate these things, modern political systems have become the
master agents of social control. As Canetti (1973/1985) noted, the "efforts of
individuals to ward off death gave rise to the monstrous structure of power" (p.
280).

Among the stories surfacing with the fall of the Soviet Bloc were reports of
how East German physicians drowned very premature babies in buckets of water
and then officially recorded the deaths as abortions ("Former East German Hospital," 1992). *Der Spiegel* claimed the reason was to bolster East Germany's live
birth statistics. National statistics on life expectancy and standardized rates of
infant mortality, homicide, suicide, cancer deaths, and executions have become
interpreted as international "box scores." These death statistics measure not only
countries' levels of cultural and economic development, but also the adequacy
and legitimacy of their political regimes. Among other things, these figures reflect

Social Progress and Cultural Humanitarianism Between 1915 and 1990, the U.S. infant mortality rate dropped from 99.9 to 9.1 deaths for every 1,000 births. However, by the early 1990s, the United States ranked behind 22 other nations in preventing infant deaths. In fact, so damaging had the statistics become that in 1988 a Public Health Service proposal to examine the relationship between reductions in government antipoverty programs and increasing infant mortality rates was turned down by the White House Office of Management and Budget (Walters, 1988).

Inequalities of Race and Ethnicity As Figure 1 shows, death reveals the full extent of the inequality of life due to race. It may be noted, for instance, that the mortality rates of African American men and women ages 25–64 exceed those of their white counterparts even when education is controlled. Among those with 4 or more years of education in 1986, the mortality rate of black men was more than twice that of white men. It may also be seen that in 1989 the homicide rate of black women was more than 4½ times that of white women, and that black men were nearly 7½ times more likely to be murdered than were white men. Racial inequality is further demonstrated by the 4-year decline in African Americans' life expectancy during the late 1980s, the twofold difference between blacks' and whites' infant mortality rates (in 1991, 17.6 deaths per 1,000 live black births vs. 7.3 deaths per 1,000 live white births), and the 59% longer wait of African Americans for kidney transplants and the 89% higher rate of bypasses for whites. In the former Soviet Union, ethnic resentments were fueled by extreme inequalities in infant mortality rates, ranging from 60.1 deaths per 1,000 births in Karakalpak and 53.3 deaths per 1,000 births in Turkmenia to 18.9 deaths per 1,000 births in the Russian Republic and 11.0 deaths per 1,000 births in Latvia.

Gender Inequalities Although approximately 105 boys are born for every 100 girls worldwide, the 1990 Chinese census revealed a ratio of 111.3 to 100. Only infanticide can account for the missing 5% of infant girls (30 million), indicating gross inequality in men's and women's cultural status (Kristof, 1991).

Civic Stability and Cultures of Violence The United States ranks third in the world in crude homicide rates, following only the Bahamas and Ecuador (Reiss & Roth, 1993). Over the course of the Persian Gulf War, 376 Americans died in the campaign; 4 times as many persons were murdered in New York City alone in that time span (Gergen, 1991). From World War II until the early 1960s, homicide rates generally declined; thereafter, they began increasing dramatically, 122% just between 1963 and 1980. Following a decline in the late 1970s and early 1980s, the murder epidemic accelerated after 1985, particularly for young and African American males. By the end of the decade, the homicide rate of American males ages 15–24 years was 4–73 times that of other industrialized countries, with firearms being involved in three fourths of the killings. In the nation's capital during the early 1990s, 1 in 440 black male teens was being murdered each year.

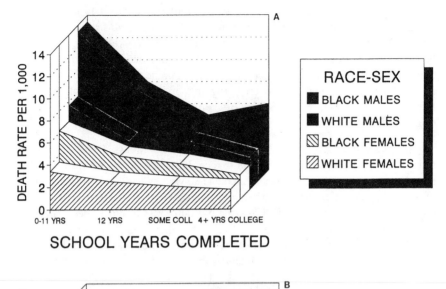

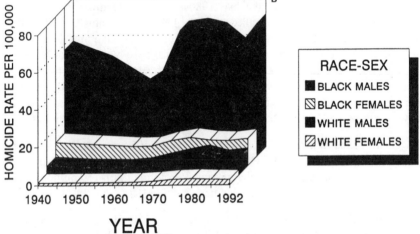

Figure 1 The inequality of death in the United States. (a) Mortality rates of the 25–64 years old by education, race, and sex in 1986. (Adapted from information appearing in *The New England Journal of Medicine, 329,* 103–109, "The increasing disparity in mortality between socioeconomic groups in the United States, 1960 and 1986," by G. Pappas, S. Queen, W. Hadden, and G. Fisher, 1993.) (b) Homicide rates (per 100,000) of black and white males and females, 1940–1992. (Source: U.S. Bureau of the Census, 1987, 1992.)

POLITICAL DECONSTRUCTIONS OF DEATH FEARS

As the overarching basis of social solidarity has shifted from kinship to tribe to religion and finally to nationalism, political legitimacy has increasingly become bound up with mortality control.

Bauman (1992) explained how the modern strategy for managing death entails *deconstructing mortality*, that is, breaking down the insoluble issue of death into the specific problems of safety and disease, which are "soluble in principle." According to Bauman, "Fighting death may stay meaningless, but fighting the causes of dying turns into the meaning of life" (p. 140).

The first stage of the deconstruction of death is the political acknowledgment or definition of a lethal threat. Throughout the 19th century, lethal threat was invariably defined in terms of militaristic or criminal perils. At the turn of the century, however, the federal government began intervening to effect various forms of public safety, including the purity of foods and drugs, transportation security, fire-retardant infant clothing, reduced air and water pollution, and the prevention of electromagnetic and nuclear radiation. Interestingly, as evidenced by warnings of radiation exposure, ozone depletion, and lethal microbes, these singled-out agents of death have, over the course of the century, become increasingly invisible. As a result, citizens have become increasingly dependent on state-supported experts to identify the forces that kill them.

With the explication of these fears have arisen politically sponsored rituals of death avoidance and control, such as the highly publicized victories over polio and smallpox. When effective, these rituals provide the public with a sense of control over the dangerous and unpredictable forces of chaos. Social and psychological tensions are relieved as attention is redirected from the uncontrollable aspects of crisis situations to ritual details (Turner, 1969; van Gennep, 1909/1961). Even if these rituals fail, as when a battle against some lethal disease founders or a killer earthquake occurs without warning, the source of failure can always be blamed on organizational defects and not on the culture's inability to ward off death. In 1984, for instance, a U.S. District Court judge ruled that the National Oceanic and Atmospheric Administration was liable for the deaths of three lobstermen who drowned off the Massachusetts coast because forecasters were negligent in not predicting the fierce storm (Associated Press, 1984). In sum, death fears are inhibited not only by socially attacking the things that kill us but also by politically monitoring and controlling those agencies responsible for our war against death.

Political Control over Deaths in the Workplace

On an average day, 17 American workers are killed in on-the-job accidents (Associated Press, 1994). Many more die from the long-term effects of exposure to radiation, mercury, coal dust, lead, asbestos, benzene, vinyl chloride, PCB, and hundreds of other known lethal substances (Magnuson, 1985). A study conducted in the mid-1970s by the Institute of Occupational Safety and Health reported that one out of four workers is exposed to some substance thought to be capable of causing death. Given the short-term incentives of capitalism, it is typically cheaper to pay for killed workers than to invest in safety and antipollutant equipment (Berman, 1979). Eula Bingham, the executive director of the Occupational Safety and Health Administration, observed that "a particular American form of suicide is holding a steady job" (cited by Lens, 1979, p. 50).

Furthermore, as a result of massive industrialization, work-related death is no longer confined to the workplace and its workers. It now emanates to surrounding neighborhoods and counties—as our experiences at Love Canal and Three Mile Island attest—and even to neighboring countries, as is the case of acid rain.

Over the past century, the U.S. government has created a host of statutes and regulatory agencies to maintain its death avoidance contract with its citizens. In addition to controlling the safety of the workplace, political involvements have expanded into the safety of the products and services produced. The rituals of recalling defective automobiles, overseeing the purity of foods and drugs, dictating the use of fireproof fabrics for infant wear, reducing and enforcing the speed of highway travel, and requiring cigarette warning labels all dramatize the government's campaign against the things that kill us.

Political Accountability for a Risk-Free Environment

Because most premature death is nowadays manmade, there is a shared sense that such deaths are avoidable and therefore controllable. Judging from the spate of laws requiring warning labels on 5-gallon buckets (so children will not fall in them and drown), stepladders (30% of the price of which goes to cover potential liabilities; metal extension ladders now carry 37 warnings and instructions), and even balloons, ours is becoming risk-free culture. This ethos has even been tapped into by Madison Avenue, as evinced by a 1993 Minolta copier ad with the headline "Maybe The Best Way To Handle Risk Is To Avoid It Altogether."

Instead of generating moral doubt, premature death is now perceived to be something avoidable, being caused by the failure to heed warnings (i.e., against smoking), an inadequate lifestyle (i.e., poor exercise habits or, in the case of AIDS, one's sexual preferences), or the "underconsumption of clinical care" (Illich, 1975, p. 38). In other words, the individual is generally to be blamed.

THE POLITICAL MONOPOLIZATION OF VIOLENCE

Historically, the state's central function was the maintenance of order through its monopoly over the use or threat of force. This was evident in the fall of several communist regimes during the late 1980s. In Rumania, for instance, Nicolae Ceausescu used his security forces to crack down on tens of thousands of protesters. The Rumanian state radio declared a state of emergency in western Rumania, where protests were ended with an invasion by Rumanian army tanks, helicopters, and armored vehicles in which hundreds of unarmed civilians were killed or wounded. Ceausescu said the army had been forced to restore order after the unrest caused by those wanting to destroy "the construction of socialism in Rumania" (Bohlen, 1989).

According to modernization theory, with social evolution, the exercising of political control through physical coercion and threats of death cancels out whatever claims to legitimacy a regime may have. But death fears remain part of the equation of control. The following is a brief consideration of the political induction of premature death (and control through their associated fears) through genocide, capital punishment, and militarism.

Genocide

Consolidation of political power too often entails directing violence against one's own people. Under conditions of extreme poverty; political unrest; authoritarian leadership; virulent nationalism; and prejudice against a particular class, religious group, or ethnic minority, this violence can lead to genocide (Staub, 1989).

During the 20th century, we have witnessed government-sponsored mass murder in Turkey, where in 1915 more than 1.5 million Armenians were exterminated; in the former Soviet Union, where between 1932 and 1933 some 6 million Ukrainians starved to death as a result of a deliberate famine induced by Stalin in his quest for collectivization; in such developing nations as Argentina, Cambodia (where perhaps 40% of the population perished during the 1970s), and Iraq; and, of course, in Nazi Germany, where more than 6 million Jews, gypsies, homosexuals, and infirm persons were exterminated.

Young survivors are particularly affected by such catastrophic events. In a study of 40 Cambodian teenagers who endured the Khmer Rouge death camps of the late 1970s, Kinzie and his associates (Kinzie, Fredrick, Ben, Fleck & Karls, 1984; Kinzie, Sack, Angell, Manson, & Rath, 1986) found a host of psychological problems, including recurrent nightmares, inability to concentrate, depression, self-pity, and a pessimistic outlook on life. Two thirds suffered from "survivor's guilt," the deep remorse for having lived when other family members died.

Capital Punishment

Between 1608 and 1992, nearly 18,550 individuals were executed in the United States (estimates of Watt Espy, cited by Clines, 1992). By late 1992, some 2,636 convicts awaited this ultimate punishment, more than at any one time before. According to the 1992 report of Amnesty International, only three countries executed more individuals than the United States (Greenberg, 1993). These countries were China (1,050+), Iran (775), and the former Soviet Union (195).

The United States remains one of the few developed nations of the world to continue this ritual of retribution. The reasons for this involve the nation's extreme individualism (and absence of common moral code), its militaristic history, the racial and ethnic heterogeneity of its population (and the social tensions generated by huge influxes of immigrants), and the extreme gap between its haves and have nots. Most important is America's culture of violence and guns, dramatized in its most widely known genre of epic folklore: the taming of the Wild West.

Since World War II, support for capital punishment has roughly mirrored the nation's homicide rates, dramatically declining from the early 1950s until the mid-1960s, when only 42% favored execution, and thereafter increasing. By the late 1980s, nearly 8 of 10 Americans favored the death penalty for persons convicted of murder.

Numerous arguments have been made against the continuing practice of gassing, electrocuting, hanging, shooting, or giving lethal injections to those who commit society's most grievous crimes. Opponents point out the punishment's failure as a deterrent, the risk of error, the preclusion of any chance for rehabilitation, the capriciousness of the law as practiced across states, the law's legitimation of violence and vengeance, and the tendency to discriminate against minorities. For example, although African Americans comprise about 12.1% of the U.S. population, they made up nearly 40% of those executed between 1976 and 1990 (Associated Press, 1990). Among those convicted of murder, black persons who kill whites are several times more likely (e.g., 43 times more likely in Florida between 1973 and 1977) to receive the death sentence than black persons who kill another black, but, since 1945, only one white person has been executed for killing a black.

Despite these arguments, the execution ritual continues. In 1992, there were 31 executions in the United States, the most since 1962. Unable to control the illegitimate violence, the state directs public attention to the gruesome ritual destruction of its perpetrators (Weisberg, 1991). To manage the collective sense of moral indignation and need for justice when such premature deaths occur, perhaps the state must ritually respond or else acknowledge (and risk loss of legitimacy) its inability to control death. From this perspective, the required mental competency of the individual being executed exists not so that he can be held accountable for his actions, but so that he understands the humiliation associated with this ritual of social vengeance.

The Evolution of Death Fears Due to Military Actions

Endings prompt reflections. With the fast-approaching conclusion of the most militaristically lethal century known to our species, we find ourselves increasingly haunted by memories of the tens of millions who died for reasons of political ideology or matters in the "national interest." The cultural, sociological, and psychological consequences for those European and Asian nations where modern war has been waged are only beginning to be gauged.

When considering the tensions between the needs of individuals (e.g., survival, belonging, and esteem) and the needs of social systems (e.g., social integration and unselfish cooperation between members), social scientists have increasingly appreciated how conflict with outside groups energizes collective solidarities. Coser (1956) argued that social conflicts (especially if they are frequent and relatively low in intensity) can promote innovation and creativity, release hostilities before severe polarization occurs between groups, increase normative regulation, increase awareness of realistic issues, stimulate coalitions among related groups, and produce a heightened sense of in-group identity. When group members die because of conflict, the dynamics of martyrization are unleashed, sacralizing the group's cause.

With the advent of total war and the evolution of the military–industrial complex, fears of death at the hands of some enemy have translated into not only trillions of dollars spent in the name of defense, but also amplified political power. Political loyalties and global stability have been obtained through threats of both collective death and, with the advent of thermonuclear weapons, collective extinction. The psychological and cultural impacts of exterminism, the continuing fear of mutually assured nuclear annihilation, have been detailed by numerous observers (e.g., Boyer, 1985; Lifton, 1967, 1979; Weart, 1988). Lifton and Faulk (1982), for instance, defined nuclearism as "the embrace of the bomb as a new 'fundamental,' as a source of 'salvation' and a way of restoring our lost sense of immortality" (p. 87). According to Ungar (1992), the bomb became the answer to the culmination of the "Great Collapse," the 20th century's final extinguishment of

faith in moral progress and the belief in a providential history. . . . [Its] transcendent power embodied one of the most critical attributes of a deity: dominion of life and death, the power to preserve or to deny the future. . . . Not only could it remove the threat posed by totalitarianism, but it seemed capable of securing the future, of assuring historical continuity to Western democracies and values. Finally, it afforded the promise of a utopian future, one based on (nothing more than) cheap and abundant energy. (p. 3)

Fearing the worst from their Soviet counterparts, the American government harnessed its ingenuity to design an increasingly terrifying arsenal of conventional, nuclear, biological, and chemical weaponry. Serious study was given to such devices as antimatter and brain bombs and gamma-ray lasers. Even the use of radiation from nuclear bombs as an instrument of terror was explored by military planners (Wald, 1992). Fear of a nuclear holocaust was to become the unwanted thought *par excellence*. More recently, in the late 1980s, 70% of U.S. programs in research and development and testing and evaluation were defense related, and nearly 40% of all American engineers and scientists were involved in military projects.

Recent declassifications and investigations of the American nuclear program reveal that political and military officials intentionally lied to the American public about the effects of open-air atomic blasts (Gallagher, 1993) and the safety of nuclear weapons plants. The degree to which such revelations of the government's complicity in the deaths of its own citizens are related to increasing voter apathy and distrust of Washington remains to be investigated.

Modern Uses of Death for Political Control

In democratic countries, it is rarely acceptable for a government to use the threat of violence against its citizenry as a form of social control. Unable to control their people by force, governments now control how they think. (It is for this reason that the United States has such an advanced public relations industry.) Given the aforementioned relationship between having to think unwanted thoughts about death and how death thoughts trigger group loyalty and moral feelings, matters of death invariably are part of the politically structured thought processes.

With social evolution, political control increasingly is legitimated by regimes' ability to focus public attention on specific causes of death and to direct collective resources toward their elimination. Increasingly, these causes have been understood in medical terms.

HEALTH AS A CITIZEN'S RIGHT: THE POLITICAL ECONOMY OF MEDICINE

Political power now resides in the medical establishment as well as in the military establishment. By 1992, health care accounted for more than 14% of the total economic output in the United States, up from 6% three decades earlier, with a tab soon to exceed one trillion dollars a year (Pear, 1991, 1993).

In modern states, death is becoming increasingly confined to the older segment of the population that has lived full and completed lives, and citizens now feel entitled to live their biblical three score and ten years. In the United States, more than 80% of all deaths occur among individuals 65 and older; in contrast, in developing countries, 30% of all deaths occur among children under the age of 5, two thirds of whom die from four easily remedied causes (Parsons, 1990). This ritual nature of medicine, observes Illich (1975), is "structured to foster the belief that natural extinction from peaceful exhaustion is the birthright of all men" (p. 25).

Like the military establishment, one key to medicine's success is its ability to absorb and integrate large numbers of individuals from all levels of the social hierarchy in the name of death avoidance. During the 1980s, this institution produced jobs at a rate three times faster than the growth of the population (one out of four new jobs in New York City) and provided work for 37 of every 1,000 Americans by 1989 (Freudenheim, 1990).

Symbolizing the government's involvement in the quasi-religious goals of universal health and prolongevity, eleven national institutes of health were established to spearhead society's attack on death and diseases (e.g., the National Cancer Institute; the National Institute of Neurological and Communicative Disorders and Stroke; the National Institute on Aging; and, as of 1992, even the Division of Alternative Medicines). In a climate of fear of AIDS, federal spending per AIDS fatality reached 13 times that per cancer fatality by the early 1990s. Such social organization and investment enhance the legitimacy of both medicine and the political order while increasing professional exploitation (Illich, 1975, p. 28).

At the close of the century, medical involvement in the war against death has not stopped with the control of viruses, bacteria, and lethal genes. In 1984, U.S. Surgeon General C. Everett Koop defined homicide as an epidemic, stating, "Violence is every bit a public health issue for me and my successors in the century as smallpox, tuberculosis, and syphilis were for my predecessors in the last two centuries" (cited by Meredith, 1984, p. 43). The disease metaphor is politically significant: If death fears are beyond political control, such as in the violent subcultures of America's inner cities, they may shift individuals' loyalties to the alternative social systems that kill them.

Americans' faith that medical science will provide a cure for anything that ails them, including old age and violence, has led to the increasing politicalization of death. Hard-won medical victories have led not only to rising expectations, but also to further problems. Consider the rising expectations and social class resentments of those unable to afford artificial or transplanted organs or of a public led to believe that their financial contributions will enable a cure to be found, only to find years later that little progress has been made. Such disappointments have far-reaching economic and political implications.

POLITICAL CONTROL OVER TRANSCENDENCE OPPORTUNITIES

With the rise of the state and the concomitant decline of religion in the West, both collective transcendence and individual transcendence over death have become political responsibilities. Through state-sponsored historical observations (e.g., the American Bicentennial), holidays (e.g., Memorial Day), Presidential Proclamation Days, museums, postage stamps, monuments, namings of buildings and parks, national cemeteries, and bureaucratic archives, governments preserve the memories of dead citizens, even if their names are forgotten, as with the Tomb of the Unknown Soldiers). Through political–legal control over rules of inheritance, governments assist in the perpetuation of family names and estates—even socialist regimes have always limited estate taxes. By so deconstructing and extending immortality, polities create a sense of continuity with past and future generations while simultaneously addressing their citizens' needs to preserve their "postselves" (Schmitt & Leonard, 1986).

Ritual demonstrations of the immortality-bestowing power of political regimes occur in communist and democratic states alike. In the United States, for instance, there were much-publicized Congressional debates over the restoration of citizenship to Robert E. Lee and Eugene V. Debs in the 1970s and over making Martin Luther King's birthday a political holiday in the 1980s. In the Soviet Union during the 1980s, charges of treason against Bolshevik revolutionaries executed during Stalin's purges were cleared, and Boris Pasternak was posthumously reinstated into the Soviet Writers' Union. Immortality can also be obliterated, as the memories of some are consigned to political purgatory. Such was the fate of some of the leaders of the 1956 Hungarian revolution (including former prime minister

Imre Nagy), who, after being hanged and buried, had their cemetery plots bull-dozed and left unmarked by the Moscow-controlled government in Budapest. And such is becoming the fate of Brezhnev and Stalin, whose names and memorials are being stripped from cities, streets, parks, and buildings in the former Soviet Union.

In addition to managing individuals' immortality, political regimes are in the business of preserving the transcendence of the collective whole. Interestingly, the conclusion of the Cold War has not dampened exctinctionist fears, on which promised political transcendence depends. Nuclear weapons remain symbols of political salvation as fears of devastating asteroids are publicized (along with the extinction stories of the dinosaur, one facet of the millennialist motif of contempo-rary American culture). Furthermore, the scale of environmental devastation re-sulting from the unleashing of the nuclear genie is so great (estimated in 1988 to exceed $100 billion, a price tag comparable to the entire Apollo program or ten times the cost of the Manhattan Project) that, again, it can only be tackled at the collective political level. The rituals of cleaning up the millions of gallons of radioactive waste spilt at the Hanford plutonium plant in Washington State, the millions of curies of fallout from atmospheric tests in Nevada, and the pounds of plutonium dust around the Rocky Flats weapons plant address these extinctionist fears. As the environmental movement grows, the preservation of the planet for future generations may well become the next holy cause of regimes.

Finally, with the rocketry produced during the Cold War, the United States launched a new means of ensuring the symbolic immortality of the human spe-cies. The two Voyager spacecraft now leaving the solar system for their tour of infinity will continue to pass stars long after our total extinction is brought about by the supernova of the sun.

HOW DEATH IDEOLOGIES ARE INTERWOVEN
WITH PUBLIC MORALITIES

Before concluding, it is worth appreciating how thoroughly public moralities sur-rounding death issues have been interwoven with political ideology. Consider the following correlations that Rigney and Kearl (1994) found between their measure of moral relativism and attitudes toward abortion, euthanasia, and suicides of the terminally ill. Analyses were based on the 1988 General Social Survey conducted by the National Opinion Research Center (1994).

The primary dimension in Rigney and Kearl's (1994) schema involved moral ambiguity/certainty, that is, the social actor's degree of perceived confidence in the existence of clearly defined and applicable standards of right and wrong. This dimension was measured by responses, on a scale ranging from *strongly agree* to *strongly disagree,* to the following statement: *"Right and wrong are not usually a matter of black and white. There are many shades of gray."* The second dimension involved moral individualism/communalism, that is, individuals' perceptions of the appropriate locus of moral judgment. Do people regard judgments of right and wrong as primarily personal and individual decisions, or are such judgments perceived as primarily communal and hence externally binding on a community's members with or without their consent? This dimension was measured through responses, from *strongly agree* to *strongly disagree,* to the following statement: *"Morality is a personal matter and society should not force everyone to follow one standard."* From these two questions, the typology of moral types shown in Figure 2 was constructed.

As is evident from the first three columns of Table 1, with increasing relativism, individuals were significantly more likely to favor abortion, the right of the terminally ill to commit suicide, and physician-assisted euthanasia. These items are, in fact, three of the five components of Kearl and Harris's (1981–82) Ideology of Death scale. They found that people whose scores were on the most permissive end of this scale were most likely to condone homosexual lifestyles, to favor the legalization of marijuana, to consider it acceptable for a man and woman to have sexual relations before marriage, to disagree that a woman's place is in the home, to not believe in life after death, and to be divorced.

When modeling the determinants of individuals' positions on the Ideology of Death scale, the relativism scale exerted significant influence even when its most-cited predictors were taken into account. With individuals' death ideology as the dependent variable in a regression model, the partial correlation of relativ-

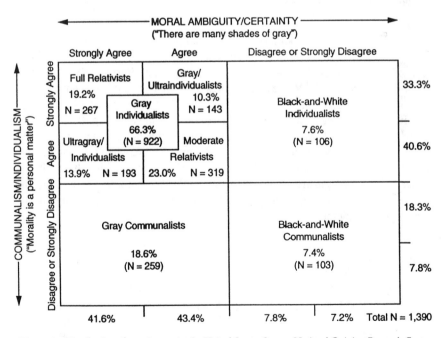

Figure 2 Distribution of moral types in the United States. Source: National Opinion Research Center 1988 General Social Survey (Rigney & Kearl, 1994). Reprinted by permission of the *Journal of Social Philosophy.*

Table 1 Attitudes of Moral Types Toward Selected Death Issues and
Where They Place Themselves on the Political Spectrum

Moral type	Euthanasia should be allowed[a] (% Agree)	Right to suicide if incurable[b] (% Agree)	Abortion on demand[c] (% Agree)	Political views[d] (Mean score)
Full relativists	84	70	51	3.84
Ultragray/individualists	74	54	50	3.92
Gray/ultraindividualists	72	59	38	4.00
Moderate relativists	74	54	32	4.06
Gray communalists	64	46	33	4.15
Black-and-white individualists	51	35	15	4.45
Black-and-white communalists	34	23	16	4.78
Total sample	69	52	37	4.11
Pr (x^2=0)	<.001	<.001	<.001	<.001

Source: 1988 NORC General Social Survey (N = 1,481).

[a]"When a person has a disease that cannot be cured, do you think doctors should be allowed by law to end the patient's life by some painless means if the patient and his or her family request it?" (yes or no)

[b]"Do you think a person has the right to end his or her own life if this person has an incurable disease?" (yes or no)

[c]"Do you think that a woman should have the right to an abortion if she wants it for any reason?" (yes or no)

[d]"I'm going to show you a 7-point scale on which the political views that people might hold are arranged from extremely liberal to extremely conservative. Where would you place yourself on this scale?" (1 = *extremely liberal*, 2 = *liberal*, 3 = *lean liberal*, 4 = *moderate*, 5 = *lean conservative*, 6 = *conservative*, 7 = *extremely conservative*)

[e]Chi-square analyses were performed on data from Questions 1–3; an analysis of variance was performed on Question 4.

ism (beta = $-.28$ for a 7-point scale) remained potent compared with education (beta = .24 for a 20-point scale), religiosity (beta = .23 for a 4-point scale), and political ideology (beta = $-.13$ for a 7-point scale). Intriguingly, unlike the Ideology of Death scale, Rigney and Kearl's measure of relativism is unrelated to education, religiosity, and age.

Finally, as evident in the rightmost column of Table 1, Rigney and Kearl found a clear linear relationship between moral relativism and where individuals placed themselves on the political spectrum. Furthermore, when individuals' political positions were used as the dependent variable in an equation that included education, age, religiosity, moral relativism, and death ideology as independent variables, only individuals' age and death ideologies turned out to be significant (and equal) predictors.

CONCLUSION

Existing in the social sciences are dual tendencies to maximize and to minimize death's potency in shaping the psychologies, philosophies, moralities, and activities of individuals and social systems. In this chapter, the former perspective is taken. First, a social psychological paradigm now emerging in thanatology, which gives death anxieties a key role in modeling how personal motivations become meshed with social processes, is outlined. From this perspective, the ways in which political systems deconstruct people's fear of death and hope for immortality as a means of social control are examined.

As Lukacs (1993) observed, "Nationalism, mass nationalism, was the main political and social phenomenon of the twentieth century" (p. 41). Bound up with the rise of nationalism was the emergence of civil religion, which uses many of the ideological and ritual techniques traditionally used by religion to harness death's power, ensuring that it works for and not against the social order. Instead of bringing anomie and chaos, death anxieties become the building blocks of civilization and political solidarities alike.

As a result of technological and social evolution, individuals are increasingly dying after living full and completed lives. If death does come prematurely, it typically is understood to occur because of manmade (and hence supposedly avoidable) reasons. Concurrent with the rising nationalism and secularization of the 20th century, the meaning of death has become increasingly politicized. As a result, instead of worshipping the forces that kill us (Harrington, 1977), modern political regimes ritually isolate and attack them in what has become their war against death. So central, in fact, are death orientations to core cultural belief systems that in one study (Rigney & Kearl, 1994), Americans' attitudes toward abortion, euthanasia, and suicide were among the key predictors of their positions on spectrums of moral relativism–absolutism and political liberalism–conservatism.

REFERENCES

ABC News. (1987, April 9). The summer of 1944: Liberation summer. (A. Westin and A. Potter, Directors and Producers), *Our world*. New York: ABC News.

Ariès, P. (1974). *Western attitudes toward death*. Baltimore: Johns Hopkins University Press.

Ariès, P. (1981). *The hour of our death*. New York: Knopf.

Associated Press. (1984, December 22). Judge: Weathermen liable in storm deaths. *S. A. Express-News*, p.1.

Associated Press. (1991, September 30). 40% on death row are black, new figures show. *The New York Times*, p. A12.

Associated Press. (1992, February 16). Former East German hospital "drowned" premature babies. *San Antonio Light*, p. A9.

Associated Press. (1994, April 15). 17 American workers a day died on the job during the 80's. *The New York Times*, p. A8.

Bataille, G. (1988). Attraction and repulsion I: Tropisms, sexuality, laughter and tears (B. Wing, Trans.). In D. Hollier (Ed.), *The college of sociology (1937–39)* (pp. 103–112). Minneapolis, MN: University of Minnesota Press. (Original work published 1938)

Bauman, Z. (1992). *Mortality, immortality and other life strategies*. Stanford, CA: Stanford University Press.

Becker, E. (1973). *The denial of death*. New York: Free Press.

Berman, D. (1979). *Death on the job*. New York: W. W. Norton.

Blauner, R. (1966). Death and social structure. *Psychiatry, 29,* 378–394.

Bohlen, C. (1989, December 21). Ceausescu blames "fascists" for uproar in Rumanian city. *The New York Times*, p. 12.

Boyer, P. (1985). *By the bomb's early light: American thought and culture at the dawn of the atomic age*. New York: Pantheon.

Callahan, D. (1987). *Setting limits: Medical goals in an aging society.* New York: Simon & Schuster.

Canetti, E. (1973). *Crowds and power* (C. Stewart, Trans.). New York: Continuum. (Original work published 1960)

Canetti, E. (1985). *The human province* (J. Neugroschel, Trans.). London: Deutsch. (Original work published 1973)

Clines, F. X. (1992, November 18). The grim list of those put to death. *New York Times,* p. A10.

Coser, L. A. (1956). *The functions of social conflict.* Glencoe, IL: Free Press.

Dyer, G. (1985). *War.* New York: Crown.

Freudenheim, M. (1990, March 5). Job growth in health care soars. *New York Times,* p. D1.

Gallagher, C. (1993). *American ground zero: The secret nuclear war.* Cambridge, MA: MIT Press.

Geertz, C. (1973). *The interpretation of cultures.* New York: Basic Books.

Gergen, D. (1991, October 7). Death on our footsteps. *U.S. News & World Report,* p. 98.

Gorer, G. (1965). The pornography of death. In *Death, grief, and mourning in contemporary Britain* (pp. 192–199). London: Cresset Press. (Original work published 1955)

Greenberg, J. (1993, June 2). Death row, U.S.A. *New York Times,* p. A19.

Greenberg, J., Pyszczynski, T., Solomon, S., Rosenblatt, A., Veeder, M., Kirkland, S., & Lyon, D. (1990). Evidence for terror management theory II: The effects of mortality salience on reactions to those who threaten or bolster the cultural worldview. *Journal of Personality and Social Psychology, 58,* 308–318.

Greenhouse, S. (1993, April 26). Changes in spending on military and health would slow growth. *New York Times,* p. A15.

Harrington, A. (1977). *The immortalist.* Millbrae, CA: Celestial Arts.

Illich, I. (1975). The political uses of natural death. In P. Steinfels & R. M. Veatch (Eds.), *Death inside out: The Hastings Center report* (pp. 25–42). New York: Harper & Row.

Kastenbaum, R., & Aisenberg, R. (1972). *The psychology of death.* New York: Springer.

Kearl, M. (1989). *Endings: A sociology of death and dying.* New York: Oxford University Press.

Kearl, M., & Harris, R. (1981–82). Individualism and the emerging "modern" ideology of death. *Omega, 12,* 269–280.

Kinzie, J. D., Fredrick, R. H., Ben, R., Fleck, J., & Karls, W. (1984). Posttraumatic stress disorder among survivors of Cambodian concentration-camps. *American Journal of Psychiatry, 141,* 645–650.

Kinzie, J. D., Sack, W. H., Angell, R. H., Manson, S., & Rath, B. (1986). Psychiatric effects of massive trauma on Cambodian children. *Journal of the American Academy of Child Psychiatry, 25,* 370–376.

Kristof, N. (1991, June 17). A mystery of China's census: Where have the girls gone? *The New York Times,* pp. A1, A7.

Lasch, C. (1979). *The culture of narcissism: American life in an age of diminishing expectations.* New York: W. W. Norton.

Lens, S. (1979, November). Dead on the job: Steady work can be a suicide trip. *The Progressive,* pp. 50–52.

Lifton, R. (1967). *Death in life: Survivors of Hiroshima.* New York: Random House.

Lifton, R. (1979). *The broken connection: On death and the continuity of life.* New York: Touchstone Books.

Lifton, R., & Falk, R. (1982). *Indefensible weapons: The political and psychological case against nuclearism.* Toronto, Ontario, Canada: Canadian Broadcasting Corporation.

Lukacs, J. (1993, January). The end of the twentieth century. *Harper's Magazine,* pp. 39–58.

Magnuson, E. (1985, October 14). A problem that cannot be buried. *Time,* pp. 76–77.

Meredith, N. (1984, December). The murder epidemic. *Science 84,* 43–48.

National Opinion Research Center. (1994). *General social surveys 1972–1993.* (J. A. Davis, Principal Investigator, and T. W. Smith, Senior Study Director and Co-Principal Investigator). Storrs, CT: Roper Center for Public Opinion Research.

Pappas, G., Queen, S., Hadden, W., & Fisher, G. (1993). The increasing disparity in mortality between socioeconomic groups in the United States, 1960 and 1986. *New England Journal of Medicine, 329,* 103–109.

Parsons, D. (1990, September 29). U.N. summit: The plight of the world's children. *New York Times,* p. 6.

Pear, R. (1991, April 17). Darman forecasts dire health costs. *The New York Times,* p. A14.

Pear, R. (1993, January 5). Health-care costs up sharply again, posing new threat. *The New York Times,* pp. A1, A7.

Reiss, A. J., Jr., & Roth, J. A. (Eds.). (1993). *Understanding and preventing violence.* Washington, DC: National Academy Press.

Rigney, D., & Kearl, M. (1994). A nation of gray individualists: Moral relativism in the United States. *Journal of Social Philosophy, 25,* 20–45.

Rosenblatt, A., Greenberg, J., Solomon, S., Pyszczynski, T., & Lyon, D. (1989). Evidence for terror management theory: I. The effects of mortality salience on reactions to those who violate or uphold cultural values. *Journal of Personality and Social Psychology, 57,* 681–690.

Schmitt, R., & Leonard, W. II. (1986). Immortalizing the self through sport. *American Journal of Sociology, 91,* 1088–1111.

Staub, E. (1989). *The roots of evil: The psychological and cultural origins of genocide and other forms of group violence.* New York: Cambridge University Press.

Turner, V. (1969). *The ritual process: Structure and anti-structure.* Chicago: Aldine.

Ungar, S. (1992). *The rise and fall of nuclearism: Fear and faith as determinants of the arms race.* University Park, PA: Pennsylvania State University Press.

U.S. Bureau of the Census. (1987). *Statistical abstract of the United States: 1988.* Washington, DC: U.S. Government Printing Office.

U.S. Bureau of the Census. (1992). *Statistical abstract of the United States: 1993.* Washington, DC: U.S. Government Printing Office.

van Gennep, A. (1961). *The rites of passage* (M. B. Vizedom & G. L. Caffee, Trans.). Chicago: University of Chicago Press. (Original work published 1909)

Wald, M. L. (1992, November 19). Early U.S. nuclear weapons plan weighed use of radioactive mists. *New York Times,* p. A15.

Walters, R. (1988, June 2). Knot in information line. *San Antonio Express-News,* p. 6B.

Weart, S. (1988). *Nuclear fear: A history of images.* Cambridge, MA: Harvard University Press.

Wegner, D. (1989). *White bears and other unwanted thoughts: Suppression, obsession, and the psychology of mental control.* New York: Viking.

Weisberg, J. (1991, July 1). This is your death. *The New Republic,* pp. 23–27.

Chapter 2

Living Our Dying and Our Grieving: Historical and Cultural Attitudes

John D. Morgan

Death, the cessation of biological functions, is a fact. Although age-specific death rates have changed over the centuries, the most elementary datum has not. Death is still one per customer, and one for every customer. But, whereas death is a fact, something that happens to us, dying is primarily an activity. With the possible exception of those who die suddenly and without warning, dying is something we *do*.

We are not born with our attitudes toward dying and bereavement, the way we are born with our needs for food, drink, and sex. Attitudes (attitude being defined as a more or less enduring readiness to behave in a characteristic way [Kalish 1978]) are no different from other attitudes. We are socialized into them by our culture, which the Spanish philosopher Jose Ortega y Gasset (1944) has defined as the "ideas by which we live" (p. 70).

In this chapter, the death culture in North America in the closing decade of the 20th century is examined. Dying and grieving are not absolutes; they are realities we live in the manner in which our culture teaches us. This living of dying and grieving has been called a *death system* (Kastenbaum & Aisenberg, 1972). There are ways of looking at death, dying, and bereavement other than the ways we have learned, however. These other ways are present to modest degrees in our own culture, but they are not dominant; in other cultures, they have been and still are dominant. It is shown in this chapter that death cultures differ because of four major factors—life expectancy, exposure to death, perceived control over the forces of nature, and understanding of what it means to be an individual person. It is also shown that death cultures are not static. North America's death culture, for example, changed after World War II and changed again after the 1960s as a result of courses and books much like the one in which this chapter is included (Irwin & Melbin-Helbers, 1993).

A DEATH SYSTEM

The term *death system* was coined by Kastenbaum and Aisenberg (1972) to describe the manner in which people live their dying. A death system is cognitive, affective, and behavioral (Corr, 1979)—that is, it teaches us what to think about death, how to feel about it, and what to do with regard to it. The death system is the sum total of the persons, places, ideas, traditions, acts, omissions, emotions, and statements that we think or make about death. In other words, it is the total picture of death, dying, and bereavement we have at any given time. Our expectation that we will live to our middle or late 70s is part of our death system. Our hesitation in discussing death with children is a component of our death system. The awkwardness we feel at a funeral visitation because we do not know what to say is part of our death system. The death system is "the total range of thought, feeling, and behaviour that is directly or indirectly related to death" (Kastenbaum & Aisenberg, pp. 191–192).

Persons, places, and things that represent death or bereavement to us are part of our death system. Whereas some places, such as a cemetery or funeral home, are consistently identified with death, there are other places, such as the emergency room in a hospital, the neonatal intensive care unit, and some churches, that have a death purpose for only a few moments but may be linked to death in a person's mind for a long time. The same is true of people. As an obvious example, funeral directors are almost always associated with death. However, we associate others with death on the basis of our experience. For example, a nurse, physician, or clergyperson spends little of his or her time doing death-related work, but to the members of a bereft family, that person will be associated with death for a long time. This *halo effect* may also apply to inanimate things. A car, for example, is not necessarily related to death. But for the family of an accident victim, the car will forever have death overtones.

Traditions in speaking and behaving with regard to death are also important parts of our death system. We often speak of someone's "passing away," "going to God," or having "expired." This inability to speak of death without circumlocutions is part of our death system. It is estimated that children see tens of thousands of deaths on television, from the realistic deaths on news broadcasts to the absurdly fictional deaths and resurrections on cartoons, and many nursery rhymes have a death content, yet it is rare that parents will take a child to visit a terminally ill patient or to a funeral. This "protection" of children from death is a part of our death system. We hospitalize our dying persons for many reasons, ranging from the fact that there are fewer adults at home today to care for the dying to the fact that most people would not be able to provide the complicated care that is sometimes needed. The effect of such hospitalization is that dying persons are cared for by professionals rather than by their family. Once a person has died, we allow other service providers to prepare the body, arrange visitation and funeral services, and make the final disposition of the body. This professionalization of death (Fulton, Markusen, Owen, & Scheiber, 1978) is a part of our death system. Sending flowers, arranging religious remembrances, and donating money to charitable organizations in the name of the deceased are other traditions that shape our consciousness of death, as does the publishing of obituaries in the newspaper.

Roles also play an important part in our death system. Physicians sign death certificates, nurses wash the body and take it to the hospital morgue, funeral directors prepare the final viewing and disposition of the body, and clergypersons give the eulogy or offer prayers. In other cultures and eras, the dying person and the bereaved have had well-defined roles. They knew what they were supposed to do because they saw it practiced by their parents and grandparents. This is less true in our death system.

We must realize that not everyone thinks and acts the way we do about death. We have our way of thinking, willing, acting, avoiding, fearing, crying, and supporting that differs from that of other times and places. Our 20th century North American death system is the network of our personal, social, religious, philosophical, and psychological approaches to handling death.

THE FOUR FACTORS THAT SHAPE A DEATH SYSTEM

Because death systems are cultural, they change as key factors of the culture change. Specifically, a death system is shaped by two categories of factors: factual and theoretical (Kastenbaum & Aisenberg, 1972). The factual elements are our exposure to death and life expectancy. The theoretical factors are the control we perceive ourselves to have over the forces of nature and our sense of what it means to be a person.

Factual Factors

Exposure to Death   Our experience of death and bereavement is the first factor that influences our understanding of death. If a person has not experienced the loss of a significant other, his or her death attitudes will be limited. Attitudes toward funerals are a good illustration of this. Many persons speak of funerals as a waste of money or a ripoff. Usually, however, this critique is made by people who have had little personal experience with death. After people have received the support that comes from a thoughtfully planned and executed funeral, their attitude changes. Thus their individual death system has changed, or, more accurately, their experience now allows a fuller participation in the death system. There is evidence that attitudes toward death also change as a consequence of near-death experiences (Greyson, 1992).

Inexperience regarding death is not universal, even in North America. The child of a funeral director or emergency room physician grows up with a greater exposure to death than do most other children. A hospice volunteer is much more conscious of the fragility of life than is a butcher, baker, or candlestick maker.

Life Expectancy   Exposure to death is related to life expectancy. A baby born in North America can be expected to live to his or her middle or late 70s. One of the consequences of longevity is that because the child's relatives will probably have a similar life span, the child is likely to have little or perhaps even no exposure to the death of a significant other until his or her 20s or 30s. There are many places in the world, even today, where this is not the case. In many places where war, starvation, and violence predominate, a child grows up with the realization that persons die and often die young. Our current innocence of death was unheard of even 50 years ago. Our grandparents had a different understanding of the fragility of life. The vast majority of our ancestors were intimately acquainted with death. At the time of Plato (5th century B.C.E.), the average life expectancy was 20 years; it was 33 at the time of St. Aquinas and St. Anselm (12th century C.E.). At the time of William James, the beginning of this century, the average life expectancy was no more than 40 years (Lerner, 1970). These figures do not imply that people did not live to advanced years in prior eras. We know that Socrates, Plato's teacher, was 70 when he died, for example. What is implied is that so many children died in the first two years of life and so many women died in childbirth that the average life expectancy was low.

Theoretical Factors

Perceived Control over the Forces of Nature   On the theoretical level, our attitudes toward death are shaped by our view of the world and our place in it. Our understanding of the physical universe is important in our death attitudes. If we believe that we are impotently subject to the laws of nature, our death attitudes will differ from those who believe they have significant control over the forces of nature. In North America, the dominant attitude is that nature exists for us to use and control. Other cultures do not share that view. Even in North America, the First Nation peoples believe that they are an integral part of nature and that their prime mandate is to respect nature, rather than use it. Those who live in the flood plain of Bangladesh or the shadow of Mount Pinatubo have a different perception of their control over nature than do we who move about in climate-controlled cars, offices, and homes. If we believe that we can be protected from nature, we will have less respect for nature's power over human life.

Perception of What It Means To Be a Human   The second theoretical factor that affects our understanding of death is our perception of what it is to be a human. In a culture such as ours that emphasizes the uniqueness of the individual and individual rights, persons have a different orientation toward death than do people in a culture that emphasizes that the individual is a part of a whole, be it a religious (Kapp, 1993) or political (Marx & Engels, 1845/1980, p. 155) whole, or sees the individual as not having any meaning at all. Although the distinction between an individual (one member of the species) and a person (a unique, rational individual) goes back to the 6th century Roman philosopher Boethius (trans. 1978), the full implications of that distinction have been realized only in the 20th century. It would be a mistake to assume that everyone places the same value on individual uniqueness that we do.

ARIÈS'S CLASSIFICATION OF DEATH SYSTEMS

Some ways in which our perception of death differs from that of others have been pointed out, but it would be helpful at this point to take a more formal look at other death systems so that we can understand our own better. As a result of his study of the literature of different periods as well as his examination of tombstones, the French historian Philippe Ariès has postulated that attitudes toward death over the centuries have not been merely statements about individuals' fears, hopes, and expectations, but are indications of a person's awareness of him- or herself and his or her degree of individuality (Ariès, 1981). In other words, our attitudes about death and bereavement are our predictions about life for ourselves and the whole race. Ariès claimed that these attitudes are reducible to four basic orientations: *"tamed death," "the death of the self," "the death of the other,"* and *"death denied."*

Tamed Death

All living beings become old like a garment, for the decree from of old is, "you must surely die!" Like flourishing leaves on a spreading tree which sheds some and puts forth others, so are the generations of flesh and blood: one dies and another is born. Every product decays and ceases to exist, and the man who made it will pass away with it. (Ecclesiastes, VII, 1–8, *New Jerusalem Bible*)

Ariès (1981) dated the period that he called *"tamed death,"* reflected in the foregoing quotation from Ecclesiastes, from the early to the late Middle Ages but argued that it is in reality the unnoticed death orientation throughout ancient history. This attitude, held by most cultures throughout all periods of history and found even in our own time, dominated until the late Middle Ages.

The main characteristic of this death orientation, as may be observed in the passage from Ecclesiastes, is familiarity with death. Because life was, as Hobbes (1651/1952) described in the 16th century, "solitary, poor, nasty, brutish and short" (p. 85), people were constantly exposed to death. The very fact that one survived into one's 30s or 40s indicated wisdom, and as a result one was treated as a sage (Lerner, 1970). In this yet-untamed world, violence, as evidenced by skulls marked from blows, was the usual cause of death. Death was a familiar, even if not always welcome, neighbor.

There were both positive and negative effects of this nearness to death. An affective consciousness of death made life more precious (Feifel & Branscomb, 1973), but because people were ignorant of most of its causes, death still appeared mysterious, and it mostly affected the young and other vulnerable segments of the population (Corr, 1979). Given the prospect that the adult years would be so limited (Ariès, 1981), childhood's irresponsibility did not last long. Kinship groups were important because of their relatively long endurance; families were large because fertility was society's protection against the ravages of death; early marriages were necessary because there was not time for courtship; reduced emotional ties between parents and offspring resulted from the high mortality rate among children; there was a large proportion of orphans and young widows in the population; and religious or otherworldly explanations of death were frequent and public features of daily life (Corr, 1979).

The view of the person in the tamed-death orientation was that found in the *Epic of Gilgamesh,* written approximately 2,000 years before the present era: Death is the lot of the human race.

For when the Gods created man, They let Death be his share, and life Withheld in their own hands. Gilgamesh, fill your belly—Day and night make merry, Dance and make music day and night. . . . Look at the child that is holding your hand, And let your wife delight in your embraces. These things alone are the concern of men. (*Epic of Gilgamesh,* trans. 1964, p. 105)

By examining the philosophical and religious traditions of the ancient and medieval world, we can get a picture of the average person's perception of death. The basic theme is found in Ecclesiastes: "There is a time to be born and a time to die" (Ecclesiastes, III, 1). Both the Hebrew Bible and Christian revelation stressed not only that the individual is mortal, but indeed that "all existence must be perceived as futile, as death-directed" (Bailey, 1978, p. 245). In the 16th century, the French essayist Montaigne (1588/1952) wrote, "we may die at any moment of the slightest cause; rather than be surprised, we should expect death everywhere. If we can conquer our fear of death, we can face all the tribulations of life with equanimity" (p. 34). This stoicism in the face of death has been the predominant theme of philosophy in the West from Heroditus (Gutmann, 1978) through Epicurus and Seneca, to Spinoza. Stated in terms of Erikson's psychology, a stoic philosophy provided persons with more ego integrity and thus lessened their fear of death (Goebel & Boeck, 1987).

The main consequence of the presence of death was acceptance of the inevitable, producing what Levine (1991) recently called "conscious dying" (p. 68). Death was not simply a possibility in a remote future—death was the dominant fact of life. In addition, the nonprofessionalization of death meant that persons cared for each other to a greater extent. Care for the dying and funeral arrangements were the tasks of the immediate family, unlike today, when families have the sense that there is nothing they can do for their dying. "Handling funeral arrangements for a friend is a deeply emotional experience. It forces us to think about our spiritual relationships, and to put into perspective our physical relationships" (Carlson, 1991, p. 8).

The prevailing view of the period was that only the dying person could tell how much time he or she had left (Ariès, 1981). Custom prescribed that death was to be marked by a ritual ceremony in which the priest would have his place, but as only one of the participants. The leading role went to the dying person him- or herself. Having bade farewell, the dying person calmly commended his or her soul to God:

Once he has assumed this position (lying on his back with his hands folded on his chest), the dying man can perform the last acts of the ceremony. He begins with a sorrowful and sober recollection of the things and people he has loved and a brief account of his life, reduced to essential things. (Aries, p. 14)

The dying presided over the affair with hardly a misstep, for s/he knew how to conduct him/herself, having witnessed so many similar scenes (Ariès, 1978).

Sudden death, which did not give one the opportunity to put one's physical and spiritual affairs in order, was considered a curse. A sudden death in a life already short was considered vile, ugly, and frightening, a "thing that nobody dared talk about" (Ariès, 1981, p. 11). The Litany of the Saints, a prayer said often throughout the church year, had an invocation "to preserve us from a sudden death." This prayer seems less useful to us in the light of the chronic debilitative diseases we are dealing with in the closing days of the 20th century, but to people in the 10th–14th centuries, whose life spans were short, the prospect of a sudden death was terrifying.

Death was perceived to be not a purely isolated act. Death was celebrated by a solemn ceremony whose purpose was to express the individual's solidarity with his or her family and community (Ariès, 1981). A death was not only a personal drama but an obligation of the community, which was responsible for maintaining the continuity of the race (Corr, 1979). The community, weakened by the loss of one of its members, had to recover its strength. Rituals had the effect of bringing the community together for reestablishment (Ariès, 1981). The facility with which this happened was a test of the community (Tuchman, 1984).

Community integrity was stretched almost beyond the possibility of reintegration during the 14th century in Europe. The Black Plague killed one third of the population (Hertz, cited by Kastenbaum & Aisenberg, 1972). In Avignon, 400 died daily; in Pisa, 400; in Vienna, 600. One gets a sense of the calamity by considering that Paris had 800 deaths a day out of a population of only 100,000. Even in today's society, with our hospitals, funeral directors, and cemeteries, none of our cities of 100,000 could handle 800 deaths a day (Goldscheider, 1978). Persons died without either religious (the last rites) or legal (a will) formalities. Burials were haphazard, further contributing to the spread of the disease.

One man shunned another. . . . Kinsfolk held aloof, brother was forsaken by brother, oftentimes husband by wife; nay what is more, and scarcely to be believed, fathers and mothers were found to abandon their children to their fate, untended, unvisited as if they had been strangers. (Tuchman, 1984, p. 97)

This is the period Goldscheider (1971) described as "uncontrolled mortality." The disruption of the social order persisted for nearly a century. Land titles were meaningless, as was government. One can readily see why the church chose the requiem (from the Latin for "rest") as the dominant prayer for the dead. The understanding of life after death as a state of repose or peaceful sleep became the most tenacious attitude toward death (Ariès, 1981), found in the writings of the Pythagoreans, Plato, and Aristotle (Gutmann, 1978).

In sum, in the *tamed-death* orientation toward death, mortality was calmly accepted as part of the meaning of being human. Attention was focused almost entirely on this world and its activities, the activities of a responsible life in a community called to serve God.

Death of the Self

Perchance he for whom this bell tolls may be so ill as that he knows not it tolls for him; and perchance I may think myself so much better than I am, as that they who are about me and see my state may have caused it to toll for me, and I know not that. . . . No man is an island, entire of itself; every man is a piece of the continent, a part of the main. . . . Any man's death diminishes me because I am involved in mankind, and therefore never send to know for whom the bell tolls; it tolls for thee. (Donne, 1624/1985, p. 440)

According to Ariès (1981), in the period from approximately the 12th to the 15th century, the individual became conscious of him- or herself as distinct from the community. This distinction had its ramifications in people's awareness of death. Whereas the tamed-death orientation emphasized personal and community familiarity with death and the community's ability to integrate the loss of a member, the attitude toward death from 1100 to 1400 emphasized the death of the self— one's own personal death. In this period flourished the genre of writing called *ars moriendi*, or "the art of dying"—little manuals on dying that were meant to guide the reader's behavior on this occasion of some importance to him or her (Copenhaver, 1978).

There was a relationship between this newly discovered idea of life as a biography and a judicial conception òf the world. It was believed that each moment of life would be weighed someday in a solemn hearing, before all the powers of heaven and hell (Ariès, 1981). Dominant themes of the period were judgment, resurrection for the just, and damnation for the wicked. "No one among the people of God is assured of his salvation, not even those who have preferred the solitude of the cloisters to the profane world" (Ariès, p. 101). Aware of his or her uniqueness, the strong individual of the later Middle Ages could not be satisfied with the peaceful but passive conception of eternal rest; he or she would survive as a full person, even if this required splitting into two parts: a body and an immortal soul that was released by death. The concept of the immortality of the soul was an important aspect of this period. The person, as we perceive the concept, is rendered apart at death to a fate known only by faith.

Eleventh-hour conversions were prayed for by both the individual and his or her family. St. Augustine, Bishop of Hippo in the fourth century of the Christian era and known for his classics *Confessions* (written in 397 C.E.) and *The City of God* (written in 426 C.E.), is quoted as saying, "Lord, give me chastity—but not yet" (Augustine, 397/1952, p. 42). This idea is consistent with the period of which Ariès spoke. Dostoevsky's (1880/1952) portrayal of the eleventh-hour conversion of a thief is also consistent with this orientation. Wills regained predominance, especially those that arranged for prayers for the deceased as he or she met God (Ariès, 1981). People believed that such arrangements brought merit before God, which would guarantee salvation. Consciousness of their sinfulness had the twofold effect of making people fear hell and inspiring them to do good works. The Latin poem *Dies Irae—Day of Wrath—*dates to this period.

Death was perceived as the last act of a private, unique drama. It was the dying person's duty to be master over his or her death and to create an appropriate scene. Cyrano de Bergerac's farewell to Roxanne is an example of a death in which the central character has staged his or her death to be consistent with his or her lifestyle and values (Rostand, 1930). Elaborate tombs, often depicting praying figures, became common and were even placed in cathedrals (Ariès, 1981).

In this second of Ariès's (1981) orientations—*death of the self*—death was no longer quite the welcomed friend it was in the earlier period. Death was recognized as the end of the individual person as he or she was known—but there was a hope for continuity in another form after death. However, the fear of hell and the sense of one's unworthiness made death a fearsome reality.

Death of the Other

"Ah!" returned the man, with relish, "he'll be drawn on a hurdle to be half hanged, and then he'll be taken down and sliced before his own face, and then his inside will be taken out and burnt while he looks on, and then his head will be chopped off, and he'll be cut into quarters. That's the sentence." (Dickens, 1859/1952, p. 409)

Up to now, humanity's death orientation had proceeded from the perception of death as a universal and common destiny to the view of death as a personal and specific biography. In the 19th century, both of these perspectives receded in favor of a third sense, the death of the other (Ariès, 1981). The fear of, and fascination for, death was transferred from the self to the other, the other usually, but not necessarily, being the loved one. Although public death did not occur as often as in previous eras, there was a fascination with the death of others. What the survivors mourned was no longer the fact of dying but the physical separation from the beloved (Ariès, 1981). Death was seen as the last act of a relationship.

The art of the period reflects the sundering of relationships and the promise of reunion in the next life. For example, the death of the other was a dominant theme in opera. Perhaps the best example is the death of Mimi in *La Boheme*. The fourth act is dominated not by Mimi's slipping away, but by Rudolfo's grief at her death. Whereas the images of the beyond in the earlier eras included eternal sleep, glorious heaven, and damned hell, in the 19th century, the next world became the scene of the reunion of those separated by death.

Death was not always idealized as a romantic ending, however. This was also the period of the French Revolution.

Interestingly, few wills were written at the time, as though it would be a breach of trust to write a will when one had loved ones to carry out one's wishes. In the 18th and 19th centuries family affection was considered more solid than the last will and testament (Ariès, 1978).

This *death-of-the-other* orientation anticipates much of our experience of bereavement today. The person is composed of a unique history of relationships, illustrated in contemporary bereavement literature. Lindemann's (1944) classic study of bereavement revealed five common elements of grief: bodily distress, psychological preoccupation with the deceased person, feelings of guilt, loss of the ability to feel anything emotionally, and disorientation. If life means relationship, the bereaved person has *literally* lost a part of him- or herself. Persons are composed not only of body parts, but also of history and relationships. The bereaved person is wounded as truly as if blood were dripping from torn flesh. This loss of the other was first reflected in the 19th century.

OUR DEATH SYSTEM

Three different orientations toward death, dying, and bereavement have been discussed. Although they are not our own attitudes, they are sufficiently close that we can recognize their importance. Indeed, each of us from time to time has conceived of death as a familiar guest, as the last act of a personal drama, and as the sundering of an important relationship. The above outline shows Kastenbaum and Aisenberg's (1972) thesis that the death system—or death attitude—is a consequence of longevity and exposure to death as well as a culture's predominate view of nature and what it means to be a human. Until fairly recently, the predominately held position was that persons were subject to the forces of nature and the will of God. One took one's self-definition from this viewpoint.

Precisely because our exposure to death has changed, as has our life expectancy, our view of our place in nature, and our self definition, our death system has changed. The North American death system has changed from calm acceptance in the pre-World War II years to denial in the postwar years and has changed again since then. In a symbiotic relationship, our death system changes our attitudes toward other things, and our attitudes toward other things change our death system. For example, although cigarette smoking has always been recognized as a cause of poor health, including heart disease and cancer, until fairly recently our prevalent attitude toward smoking has been one of laissez faire. The acceptance of death as a result of cigarette smoking was a part of the North American death system after World War II. As a result of increasing death awareness, as well as increased knowledge of the dangers of smoking, our attitudes have changed and we no longer tolerate smoking in public places without complaint. Our present trends toward the use of cremation and funerals without visitation will reshape our death system in the next few years. We must now examine how these same elements create our own death system and indicate the adequacy of our culture's view of death.

Life Expectancy

Almost two-thirds of the 2 million persons who will die in the United States this year will be 65 years of age or older, although this age group represents only 9 percent of the total population. Children under the age of 15, on the other hand, account for 29 percent of the total United States population, but only 5.5 percent of the total deaths. This is in sharp contrast to the mortality statistics in 1900, for instance, when proportionally, far more children died. At that time children under the age of 15 accounted for 34 percent of the population—approximately the same proportion as today—but this age group accounted for 53 percent of the total deaths. In the same year, persons aged 65 and over accounted for 4 percent of the total population, and 17 percent of all deaths. (Fulton & Fulton, 1971, p. 91)

Earthquakes in Mexico, volcanic eruptions in the Philippines and Central America, and chemical and nuclear disasters in India and Russia indicate that even our age is subject to uncontrolled mortality. However, these events create headlines because they are unusual. Ours is a period of increased longevity and predictable age-specific death rates due to better sanitation, food supplies, and medical care. The discovery that contagious diseases could be prevented, and sometimes eliminated, through inoculation (Thomas, 1979) neutralized the effects of diseases that killed most of the population in earlier times. Consequently, today it is reasonable to assume that mothers will not die from infections in childbirth and that children will live to maturity.

In the early 1900s, there were approximately 17 deaths per 1,000 live people, whereas today there are fewer than 8. This means that although we have more deaths numerically, we have proportionately fewer deaths occurring in our everyday experience (Pine, 1986). The very old constitute the fastest growing segment of the population. Four fifths of those over 65 years of age have one or more living children, about half have great-grandchildren, and 1 in 10 has a child who is already over 65 (Kowalski, 1986).

Women outlive men, as they always have. The age-adjusted mortality rate, which fell 26% for elderly men between 1940 and 1980, dropped 48% for elderly women in the same time period (Kowalski, 1986). Comparisons of men and women with similar lifestyles, such as a monastery of men and a convent of women, both leading lives of quiet prayer, show that the women still outlive men (Goldscheider, 1978). However, today the gap is closing. This seems to be because of the increased number of women holding jobs that previously were held only by men. These range from the dangers involved in construction work and military activity and the stress-related death of the executive.

Although death rates have improved in the population as a whole, the benefits have not been shared equally. In North America, race, poverty, and poor education are predictors of early death. In 1986, the mortality rate from heart disease for blacks was 1.3 times that of whites (Navarro, 1991). Among Native Americans, the high incidence of alcoholism is a potent source of mortality. From 1983 to 1988, the percentage of individuals with an annual income over $60,000 whose activity was limited because of a chronic condition declined, whereas among those with incomes less than $10,000, the percentage increased (Navarro, 1991). Poor or poorly educated persons have higher death rates than wealthy or better educated persons, and these differences increased from 1960 to 1986 (Pappas, Queen, Hadden, & Fisher, 1993). This is as true of Canada with its socialized medicine as it is in the United States with entrepreneurial medicine. No doubt, the causes are related to the limited possibilities open to the poor. In better neighborhoods, persons accept the fact that they will see physicians and can afford to purchase vegetables, fruits, and protein substances.

In general, the poor experience high mortality rates at young ages and from communicable diseases, while the middle class, especially males, experiences high mortality rates in the older ages and from degenerative diseases. The working class appears to experience the lowest mortality rates (Lerner, 1970).

Longevity progressed until our own century when it peaked in the United States in 1915 at 54.5 years. The great flu epidemic [in 1918] was a setback, but longevity returned and increased to 69.6 years in 1967. (Lerner, p. 9)

Because the birth rate has slowed, we will see proportionally more deaths. The percentage of the population over age 65 will increase and, with it, the likelihood of death. For example, the incidence of Alzheimer's disease has increased in recent years. It is estimated that 90% of the population will have this disease if they do not succumb to other diseases first.

Today's elderly tend to be retired and live physically and psychologically removed from their children and grandchildren. Medical technology not only makes possible the prolongation of life, but also is the basis for repeated and often extended separations of the chronically ill or dying persons from the family. The disengagement of the aged from their families prior to their death means that their death may have little effect on the family's day-to-day life (Fulton & Fulton, 1971), depriving the elderly of traditional family assistance (Fulton, 1986). For example, Riley and Foner (cited by Fulton & Fulton, 1971) reported that a disproportionate number of deaths occur among elderly patients recently committed to an institution. Frequently, professional caregivers experience grief at the loss of a patient and react as bereaved survivors themselves. Attending caregivers often find themselves participating in the emotional support of patients under their care (Fulton, 1978).

The effect of our increased life span is lessened consciousness of and respect for death. The community no longer thinks it necessary to defend itself against a nature that has been domesticated once and for all by the advance of technology. Because we no longer have a strong sense of community, we have abandoned responsibility for the organization of life (Ariès, 1981). The community in the traditional sense of the word, persons coming together with common interests to live their lives in common, has been replaced by atomized individuals. Long life, rather than personal salvation, has become the goal. Fulton et al. (1978) said that for two millennia, such sacred texts as the *I Ching,* the *Tibetan Book of the Dead,* the *Egyptian Book of the Dead,* and the *ars moriendi* literature of the West served as guidebooks for the passage of the soul. Today, however, our focus is on the need to comfort the dying person and to offer assistance to the grieving survivors.

Exposure to Death

As Fulton (1978) said, the very appearance of death has changed. We now do not admit that a death has occurred until we have technological proof. "Death has moved from the moral order to the technological order" (Cassell, 1978, p. 121). The increased life span and the decline of diseases of childhood and rise of diseases of longevity have had the effect of increasing the number of deaths that occur in hospitals. Hospitals have become increasingly important as medicine has become more specialized. In earlier days, the physician's primary role was to encourage life's own recuperative powers to regenerate the body and, as Ramsey (1970) stated, to "care [only] for the dying". As the medical field has increasingly broken down into specialties, it has become more difficult for one physician to do everything. With increased specialization, the setting of medical practice has changed. Medicine is practiced less often in the doctor's office or the patient's home than in hospitals. Today at least 75% of persons die in hospitals. The consequence of this is that dying is now seen by fewer people than it was previously. We do not have the mass deaths that once were viewed on streets, and we do not have persons dying at home.

Not only do we see fewer deaths, but with the increased mobility of North American society, we scarcely even see the aged. Few of us live within 500 miles of our place of birth. Consequently, we and our children do not see the aging process taking place. The elderly who still live in their homes are not visited on a regular basis. More and more often, the elderly live in senior homes or retirement villages where they are seen only by other elderly or by professionals (Fulton et al., 1978). Consequently, death seems to be not a gradual process but a telephone call in the night. The dead are seen at the funeral home, but dying is not seen. As a result, we have no role models either for our own dying process or for expressing grief at the time of another's death.

The medicalization of death has had the effect of our entire culture's accepting the medical profession's view of death. The medical profession has defined its role as curing, researching, and teaching. Persons who become physicians are bright, hard-working self-starters. The death of a patient may be the first time in the young physician's life he or she meets a problem that will not respond to his or her enterprise. Death becomes viewed as defeat (Parsons, Fox, & Lidz, 1973). Doctors, when questioned, state that their goals are to accompany the patient in his or her illness, yet the reality is that they view "mere" accompanying as failure (Family, 1993). Feifel, Hanson, Jones, and Edwards (1967) confirmed that the fear of death was a consideration in the choice of a medical career. Physicians were more afraid of death than were physically sick or healthy normal groups, despite the finding that 63% of the physicians stated that "they were *now* less fearful of death than heretofore" (Feifel et al., p. 201).

Sense of the Self

All of us have had occasion to fill out resumes and application forms. This is standard practice in our complex and organized world. We tell the person who reads our resume our name, age, cultural and linguistic background, physical characteristics, educational background, work experience, perhaps our parentage, perhaps our medical history. Depending on the extent and complexity of our resume, the reader may know a great deal about us. Yet we would distinguish between knowing about us and knowing us. We believe that there is a self hidden within each of us that no resume or application blank captures. All resumes are objective—answers are in terms of absolute categories. But the person is a subject.

The person is not only a subject, but a unique one. Never before in the history of the universe did this person exist; never again will he or she exist. Several years ago, when the World's Fair was held in New York City, the Vatican gave permission for Michelangelo's masterpiece "The Pieta" to be brought for exhibit. There was general concern for the safety of the statue in transport. Luckily, no disasters occurred. However, Michelangelo made several copies of the statue. The statue is, in that sense, replaceable. More fundamentally, the statue is a piece of marble that is replaceable fundamentally, although the accidental characteristics that the artist gave to it could be replaced only with difficulty. The death of any individual person is a greater loss. There is no fundamental or accidental way of replacing the person. A person is a once-in-the-lifetime-of-the-universe event. This uniqueness of the person—the realization that never before in the history of the human race has this person existed, and never again will he or she exist—is what Becker (1973) referred to as "the ache of cosmic specialness" (p. 4).

William James (1879/1959a) has said that the word "good" fundamentally means "destined to survive" (p. 13). When an individual says that something is good, he or she implicitly affirms that the thing ought to exist. The effect of our self-awareness is the following enigma: *I am. I am good. Yet I shall die.* This awareness is, in the words of James, "the worm at the core of our pretensions to happiness" (cited by Becker, 1973, p. 15). Perhaps the human situation is best summarized in the line that Becker (1973) quoted from Malraux: "It takes sixty years of incredible suffering and effort to make such an individual, then he is good only for dying" (p. 269).

Our society speaks about the sanctity of life and death with dignity. However, the sanctity of life does not exist outside the religious context of North American culture. In spite of lower church attendance, ours remains a religious culture. By religion is meant a person's sense that he or she is part of a whole and has a responsibility to that whole. The religious attitude also entails a sense that we belong to a history that makes our individual lives more meaningful. If we believe that the universe came from the hand of a loving creator—as do all the great religious traditions—then we must ask, Why is the world the way it is? Why do pain and evil exist? Or, in the words of Rabbi Kushner (1983), "Why do bad things happen to good people?" One answer is that the gift of life must be acknowledged and developed. Life is precisely the gift by which the creative will of God is to be carried out. It is a gift from God that places on the individual the obligation to use for the good of the human community and, in accepting the reality of human limitation, the obligation to surrender the gift of life by the acceptance of death (Parsons et al., 1973, p. 5).

The idea of life as a gift is important to this discussion of death. Obviously, life is a gift in the sense that no one ever earned it. There is, however, a deeper meaning. Life is also a gift in the sense in which we identify "gift" with "talent." We speak of a person's having a gift for languages or for music. What we mean is that there is a talent that is being developed and amplifies this person and all around him or her. There is a sense of responsibility to acknowledge the gift, to develop it, and to be thankful for it. The religious view is that life is a gift in this sense, that each person has a special status in creation.

Death ultimately is the proof that no matter what powers humans have or develop, we still are not God (Parsons et al., 1973, p. 7). If James (1907/1959b) was right that good means "destined to survive," then death is nature's way of telling us that we are not absolutely good. Death gives meaning to our lives because it is the act by which we complete the task for which we were born (James, 1907/1959b).

Control over Nature

What might be called the North American world view or philosophy of life is ambivalent. On one hand, we espouse the uniqueness of the individual person; on the other hand, we are a continent of doers, and we admire people who can get things done, even if getting things done might infringe on our respect for individual persons. As Cohen (1962) has stated, "American worship of business is not merely the worship of the dollar but rather worship of the active life" (p. 30). This has given us one of the highest standards of living in the world. We transplant organs, build malls and domed stadiums to protect us from the elements, and repair satellites and telescopes in space. We emphasize this aspect of our culture even when there might be a high human cost. An examination of some of our cliches reveals this emphasis: "It's the bottom line that counts"—"It's the cost of doing business"—"You can't make an omelette without breaking a few eggs."

This orientation toward getting things done is what is known as *pragmatism,* the fundamental philosophy of North America. The word *pragmatism* comes from the Greek *pragma,* meaning "action," and stresses that an idea is meaningful only if it is useful (James, 1879/1959a, p. 152). Philosophical disputes are examined to see if the answer will make any concrete difference in getting something done. If not, the answer, no matter what it is, is deemed meaningless. Theoretical knowledge is valuable only to the extent that it has some possibility of application. The same criterion of practicality is applied to such questions as the existence of God, the existence of a soul or spiritual nature, and questions of life after death. Perhaps the epitome of pragmatism is shown by a funeral home in California, where a drive-up window is provided for mourners so they can view the remains and sign the book without leaving their cars (Whalen, 1990).

There is no aspect of our lives that has not been touched by the engineering progress of North America. We transmit words and pictures instantaneously via radio, telegraph, television, and facsimile. Closed-circuit television has allowed greater surveillance of both persons and property. Computer linkups have created enormous databases that give us access to information in a way never before imagined. At the push of a button, we can be informed of the books, monographs, articles, and other references that have been published on almost any topic. We can check fingerprints and records. As a result primarily of labor contracts, the average worker today has health and other insurance programs that guarantee a standard of living undreamed of before. Dental care, prescriptions, and hospital care are perceived today to be rights, rather than privileges. The same is true of education and care of the aged. Old-age pensions such as Social Security provide a basic, if not always adequate, guarantee of a retirement period that is relatively free of care for the basic necessities. Few cultures are as "progress" oriented as ours.

After two centuries of conquering problems, we are convinced that we can conquer all problems. One of the biggest obstacles to the environmental movement is our implicit belief that, given enough time, we can solve all problems. We do not need to conserve or recycle. Our belief is that the universe is raw material for our dreams. Few would openly express the belief that we will eradicate death, but it is a hope in the back of the minds of many (Goldscheider, 1971). Today, death is viewed as something that does not have to happen when it does happen and "the idea is being entertained that it is remotely conceivable that for a very significant minority, that death eventually won't need to happen at all" (Fulton et al., 1978, p. 11).

Death Denied

Death is a slap in the face of the American Dream. Death refuses to die. Thus our North American death system, which is a result of our limited exposure, which is a result of our high life expectancy, is a tension between our pragmatism and our religiosity, between our conviction that we can do anything and our respect for life as a unique gift.

We know that death exists. In our lifetime, more deaths have occurred than in the history of the human race (Corr, 1979). We have lived in the shadow of nuclear destruction, which Feifel (1990) has called our possible common epitaph. We even accept the abstraction of our own death. Indeed, there is evidence that college students think about death more often than did their grandparents (Lester, 1993). But we do not have an *affective consciousness* of death. We do not seem to take seriously that death is the end of our possibilities, the collapse of our space and time (Flynn, 1987). As death is removed from daily consciousness, it appears to be less appropriate (Corr, 1979), creating more complicated grief (Rando, 1993). Ariès (1981) called our orientation to death *death denied.* Perhaps it is better called *death rejected.* We see our ambivalence, especially in dealing with children. "The idea that children die is an insult to our sense of appropriateness, is traumatic and guilt-provoking, and taxes our emotions. The idea that children feel grief is also difficult for us to accept; we want to keep the child away from pain" (Wass, 1987, p. 495).

The AIDS epidemic is cornerstone to our death system. In AIDS we have persons dying who are usually significantly younger than the death date anticipated for their age cohort. Many of them contracted AIDS because they engaged in practices that they believed were consistent with their personal needs and views of reality. For the most part, these young persons are bright and well educated and believe that AIDS is a form of genocide for their community (Lévy & Nouss, 1993). Thus the AIDS epidemic calls into question our presuppositions about the reasonableness of the universe in which we live, creating greater death anxiety and depression (Hintze, Templer, Cappelletty, & Frederick, 1993). Death for many people today is a barrier to life's meaning, rather than a transformation (Ross & Pollio, 1991).

HOW EFFECTIVE IS OUR DEATH SYSTEM?

Weisman (1978) listed the following as characteristics of an appropriate death: being relatively free of pain, experiencing little suffering, experiencing minimal emotional impoverishment, operating on as high a level as possible, recognizing and resolving residual conflicts, and satisfying remaining wishes consistent within present plight and ego ideal. Finally, we should be able to yield control to others in whom we have confidence and to have the option of seeking or relinquishing significant people (Weisman, 1978). If we had an appropriate death system, we would have the appropriate death that Weisman described. In other words, an integrated death system would enable individuals "to think, feel and behave with respect to death in ways that they might consider to be effective and appropriate" (Kastenbaum & Aisenberg, 1972, p. 193).

A valuable death system is one that contributes to our psychological growth as well as alleviating our fears of death and bereavement, so that we can get on with other aspects of living (Kastenbaum & Aisenberg, 1972). As Parsons et al. (1973) indicated, an ideal death would be a coincidence of the meaning of the words "His work is done" for both the dying patient and the physician. The patient is ready to go, whereas the physician not only has done the best to save the patient's life, but has complemented these efforts by facilitating a dignified and meaningful death.

There is substantial evidence that the violence, as well as addiction and poverty, that grows daily is the result of our refusal to take seriously the human reality of death (Leviton, 1991). Violence, "a nightmare spectacle taking place on a planet that has been soaked for hundreds of years in the blood of all its creatures" (Becker, 1973, p. 283), exists in spite of the fact that for millennia the great religions have taught that we are responsible for each other and are to see the Creator in the least of our neighbors. Apart from religion, philosophical systems have agreed with Kant (1785/1949) that one ought never to use another person as a means. Violence, according to Becker (1973), is "a symbolic solution of a biological limitation" (p. 99). It is easy to believe that one is master of one's own life when one holds someone else's fate in one's hands (Becker, 1975). To feel more in control of one's own fate, one takes action against those one views as a threat (Feifel, 1971). Hatred of groups leads to a violence whose purpose is "to cleanse the earth of tainted ones" (Becker, 1975, p. 111).

Once we have reached the age at which we can ignore our parents' wishes, each facet of our lives is controlled by ourselves. We decide when and what we eat. We decide whether we will go to school or work on a given day or whether we will resign from a job or quit school. We decide whether we go to church and which one it will be. We decide whether we shall marry and whom and where. We can today decide with great accuracy whether and when we will have children. We decide when to terminate a marriage. We decide whether we shall smoke or engage in other life-threatening behavior. The professionalization of death, however, has meant that we have turned over to others the important decisions at the end of life. The dying person is deprived of his or her death. For thousands of years, the individual was lord and master of his or her death and the circumstances surrounding it. Today this has ceased to be so (Ariès, 1978).

CONCLUSION

How North Americans live their dying in the latter days of the 20th century has been described. The death awareness movement has made significant progress in bringing death back into our consciousness and therefore making it more human (Feifel & Morgan, 1986), but in many ways our life is no different from that of the peasant in the 14th century. The peasant missed a fully human life because he or she was inundated with death. We do not live fully because we reject death (Kastenbaum & Aisenberg, 1972). We accept the fact that to live fully in an economic manner we must budget our resources. Time is our most important and most limited resource, but we act as though no economizing were necessary. Our fear of the human reality of death causes us to live not as though there is no tomorrow, but as though there are always tomorrows. Consequently, we miss the opportunity to live fully.

REFERENCES

Ariès, P. (1978). The reversal of death. In R. Fulton, E. Markusen, G. Owen, & J. L. Scheiber (Eds.), *Death and dying: Challenge and change* (pp. 52–57). Reading, MA: Addison-Wesley.
Ariès, P. (1981). *The hour of our death.* New York: Knopf.
Augustine, St. (1952). *Confessions. Great Books of the Western World.* Chicago: Britannica. (Original work published 397)
Bailey, L. (1978). Death in Western thought: 1. Death in biblical thought. In W. T. Reich (Ed.), *Encyclopedia of Bioethics* (Vol. I, pp. 243–246). New York: Free Press.

Becker, E. (1973). *The denial of death*. New York: Free Press.

Becker, E. (1975). *Escape from evil*. New York: Collier Macmillan.

Boethius. (1978). Contra eutychen. In F. J. Coplestone (Ed.), *A history of philosophy: Vol. II. Medieval philosophy, Augustine to Scotus*. Westminster, England: Newman.

Carlson, L. (1991, September/October). Caring for our own dead. *Utne Reader*, pp. 79–81.

Cassell, E. J. (1978). Dying in a technological society. In R. Fulton, E. Markusen, G. Owen, & J. L. Scheiber (Eds.), *Death and dying: Challenge and change* (pp. 121–126). Reading, MA: Addison-Wesley.

Cohen, M. R. (1962). *American thought: A critical sketch*. New York: Collier.

Copenhaver, B. P. (1978). Death: IV Western religious thought: 4. Death in the Western world. In W. T. Reich (Ed.), *Encyclopedia of bioethics* (Vol. I, pp. 253–255). New York: Free Press.

Corr, C. A. (1979). Reconstructing the face of death. In H. Wass (Ed.), *Dying: Facing the facts* (pp. 5–42). Washington, DC: Hemisphere.

Dickens, C. (1952). *A tale of two cities*. London: Oxford University Press (Original work published 1859)

Donne, J. (1985). *The complete English poems of John Donne* (C. A. Phtrides, Ed.). London: Dent. (Original work published 1624)

Dostoevsky, F. (1952). The brothers Karamazov. In *Great books of the Western world* (Vol. 52). Chicago: Encyclopedia Britannica. (Original work published 1880.)

Epic of Gilgamesh. (1964). Baltimore: Penguin.

Family, G. (1993). Projected image and observed behaviour of physicians in terminal cancer care. *Omega, 26*, 129–136.

Feifel, H. (1971). The meaning of death in American society. In B. R. Green & D. P. Irish (Eds.), *Death education: Preparation for living* (pp. 3–14). Cambridge, England: Schenkman.

Feifel, H. (1990). Psychology and death: Meaningful rediscovery. *American Psychologist, 45*, 537–543.

Feifel, H., & Branscomb, A. B. (1973). Who's afraid of death? *Journal of Abnormal Psychology, 81*, 282–289.

Feifel, H., Hanson, S., Jones, R., & Edwards, L. (1967, September). Physicians consider death. Paper presented at the 75th Annual Convention of the American Psychological Association, Washington, DC.

Feifel, H., & Morgan, J. D. (1986). Humanity has to be the model. *Death Studies, 10*, 1–9.

Flynn, T. (1987). Dying as doing: Philosophical thoughts on death and authenticity. In M. A. Morgan & J. D. Morgan (Eds.), *Thanatology: A liberal arts approach* (pp. 199–206). London, Ontario, Canada: King's College.

Fulton, R. L. (1978). Anticipatory grief, stress, and the surrogate griever. In R. L. Fulton, E. Markusen, G. Owen, & J. L. Scheiber (Eds.), *Death and dying: Challenge and change* (pp. 241–245). Reading, MA: Addison-Wesley.

Fulton, R. (1986). Foreword. In T. A. Rando (Ed.), *Loss and anticipatory grief* (pp. ix–xv). Lexington, MA: Lexington Books.

Fulton, R., & Fulton, J. (1971). A psychosocial aspect of terminal care: Anticipatory grief. *Omega, 2*, 91–100.

Fulton, R., Markusen, E., Owen, G., & Scheiber, J. L. (Eds.). (1978). *Death and dying: Challenge and change*. Reading, MA: Addison-Wesley.

Goebel, B. L., & Boeck, B. E. (1987). Ego integrity and fear of death: A comparison of institutionalized and independently living older adults. *Death Studies, 11*, 193–204.

Goldscheider, C. (1971). *Population, modernization and social structure*. Boston: Little, Brown.

Goldscheider, C. (1978). The social inequality of death. In R. Fulton, E. Markusen, G. Owen, & J. L. Scheiber (Eds.), *Death and dying: Challenge and change* (pp. 98–102). Reading, MA: Addison-Wesley.

Greyson, B. (1992). Reduced death threat in near-death experiences. *Death Studies, 16*, 523–536.

Gutmann, J. (1978). Death: III Western Philosophical Thought. In W. T. Reich (Ed.), *Encyclopedia of bioethics* (Vol. 1). New York: Free Press.

Hintze, J., Templer, D. I., Cappelletty, G. G., & Frederick, W. (1993). Death depression and death anxiety in HIV-infected males. *Death Studies, 17,* 333–341.

Hobbes, T. (1952). The leviathan. In *Great books of the Western world.* Chicago: Encyclopedia Britannica (Vol. 23). (Original work published 1651)

Irwin, H. J., & Melbin-Helbers, E. B. (1993). Enhancement of death acceptance by a grief counselling course. *Omega, 25,* 73–86.

James, W. (1959a). Sentiment of rationality. In A. Castell (Ed.), *Essays in pragmatism by William James* (pp. 3–36). New York: Hafner. (Original work published 1879)

James, W. (1959b). What pragmatism means. In A. Castell (Ed.), *Essays in pragmatism by William James* (pp. 141–158). New York: Hafner. (Original work published 1907)

Kalish, R. A. (1978). Attitudes toward death. In W. T. Reich (Ed.), *Encyclopedia of Bioethics* (Vol. 1). New York: Free Press.

Kant, I. (1949). *Fundamental principles of the metaphysics of morals* (T. K. Abbott, Trans.). Indianapolis, IN: Bobbs-Merrill. (Original work published 1785)

Kapp, M. B. (1993). Living and dying in the Jewish way: Secular rights and religious duties. *Death Studies, 17,* 267–276.

Kastenbaum, R., & Aisenberg, R. (1972). *The psychology of death.* New York: Springer Publishing Company.

Kowalski, N. C. (1986). Anticipating the death of an elderly parent. In T. A. Rando (Ed.), *Loss and anticipatory grief* (pp. 175–186). Lexington, MA: D.C. Heath.

Kushner, H. (1983). *Why do bad things happen to good people?* New York: Avon.

Lerner, M. (1970). When, why and where people die. In O. G. Brim, H. E. Freeman, S. Levine, & N. A. Scotch (Eds.), *The dying patient* (pp. 5–29). New York: Russell Sage.

Lester, D. (1993). College students' attitudes toward death as compared to the 1930's. *Omega, 26,* 219–222.

Levine, S. (1991, September/October). Conscious dying: It all begins with conscious living. *Utne Reader,* pp. 66–74.

Leviton, D. (1991). *Horrendous death, health, and well-being.* Washington, DC: Hemisphere.

Lévy, J. J., & Nouss, A. (1993). Death and its rituals in novels on AIDS. *Omega, 27,* 67–74.

Lindemann, E. (1978). Symptomatology and management of acute grief. In R. Fulton, E. Markusen, G. Owen, & J. L. Scheiber (Eds.), *Death and dying: Challenge and change* (pp. 221–228). Reading, MA: Addison-Wesley.

Marx, K., & Engels, F. (1980). The German ideology. In L. Stevenson (Ed.), *The study of human nature* (pp. 136–163). New York: Oxford University Press. (Original work published 1845)

Montaigne, M. (1952). Essays. In *great books of the Western world* (Vol. I). Chicago: Encyclopedia Britannica. (Original work published 1588)

Navarro, V. (1991, April 8). The class gap. *The Nation,* pp. 436–437.

Ortega y Gasset, J. (1944). *Mission of the university.* New York: W. W. Norton.

Pappas, G., Queen, S., Hadden, W., & Fisher, G. (1993). The increasing disparity in mortality between socioeconomic groups in the United States, 1960 and 1986. *New England Journal of Medicine, 329,* 103–109.

Parsons, T., Fox, R. C., & Lidz, V. M. (1973). The "gift of life" and its reciprocation. In A. Mack (Ed.), *Death in American experience* (pp. 1–49). New York: Schocken.

Pine, V. R. (1986). An agenda for adaptive anticipation of bereavement. In T. Rando (Ed.), *Loss and anticipatory grief.* Lexington, MA: D.C. Heath.

Ramsey, P. (1970). *The patient as person.* New Haven, CT: Yale University Press.

Rando, T. (1993). The increasing prevalence of complicated mourning: The onslaught is just beginning. *Omega, 26,* 43–60.

Ross, L. M., & Pollio, H. R. (1991). Metaphors of death: A thematic analysis of personal meanings. *Omega, 23,* 291–307.

Rostand, E. (1930). *Cyrano de Bergerac.* Paris: E. Sasquelle.

Thomas, L. (1979). *The medusa and the snail.* Toronto, Ontario, Canada: Bantam.

Tuchman, B. W. (1984). *A distant mirror: The calamitous 14th century.* New York: Knopf.
Wass, H. (1987). Teaching the facts of death: A living issue. In M. A. Morgan & J. D. Morgan (Eds.),
      Thanatology: A liberal arts approach (pp. 495–508). London, Ontario, Canada: King's College.
Weisman, A. (1978). An appropriate death. In R. Fulton, E. Markusen, G. Owen, & J. L. Scheiber
      (Eds.), *Death and dying: Challenge and change* (pp. 193–194). Reading, MA: Addison-Wesley.
Whalen, W. J. (1990). How different religions pay their final respects. *U.S. Catholic, 55* 29–35.

Part Two

Data: The Facts of Death and Dying

Chapter 3

Death Anxiety

Robert A. Neimeyer
David Van Brunt

Of all things that move man, one of the principal ones is his terror of death.

Becker (1973)

Traditionally, when poets, philosophers, and scientists have contemplated the human encounter with death, they have taken for granted that it is an encounter marked by terror, fear, or at least uneasiness (Choron, 1974). Although this assumption of the universality of the fear of death is not itself universal, it has clearly dominated Western thought on death. Thus, with the emergence of the death awareness movement in the 1950s, it was not surprising that the study of death anxiety would come to occupy a prominent place in the books and articles generated by the movement.

This chapter surveys this now voluminous literature, in an attempt to winnow out of the profusion of reports those "facts" about death anxiety that have been fairly well established. A few remarks on the growth of this literature over the last 35 years are offered first, to place this effort in perspective, and the methods commonly used to study death attitudes are briefly sketched. As the reader will see, even this brief examination points up certain crucial conceptual and methodological problems that have limited thanatologists' ability to study the human encounter with death. Is death anxiety conscious or unconscious? Is it a single, global fear or a multifaceted concept, encompassing such distinctive reactions as the fear of nonexistence, the fear of eternal punishment, and the fear of experiencing the painful death of oneself or another? Is the absence of death anxiety synonymous with death acceptance, and is the latter construct itself multidimensional? A consideration of these questions will lead to a critical appraisal of the validity of the techniques used to operationalize the concept of death anxiety and related attitudes toward death.

In the next and longest section of the chapter, the results of empirical research on the correlates of fear of death are presented. For the sake of clarity, they are organized under two general headings: (a) demographic and situational factors and (b) personality characteristics. Counterbalancing this emphasis on the "trait" of death anxiety, consideration is also given to the modification of death anxiety,

This chapter is an update of the chapter entitled "Death Anxiety" in the second edition of this book. Although hundreds of additional studies have been published since the 1988 review, few substantial changes have occurred in the overall character or emphases of this literature. For this reason, we have retained much of the outline of the previous chapter, adding elaboration, contradiction, and revision where appropriate. Readers interested in a more systematic and detailed review of research and measurement issues concerning death attitudes are encouraged to consult Neimeyer (1994b).

particularly through death education. The chapter concludes with recommendations that could help make future research more progressive.

AN OVERVIEW OF THE LITERATURE

From its inception, thanatology (the study of death and dying) has been a multidisciplinary field, including contributions by philosophers, sociologists, physicians, nurses, psychologists, anthropologists, lawyers, educators, theologians, and
even political scientists and art historians. In contrast to this trend, research on
death anxiety has been conducted mainly by psychologists, with occasional contributions from other social scientists and medical professionals. Perhaps for this
reason, the resulting literature has shown an increasing concern with methodological issues, often at the expense of broader social, cultural, philosophical, and
applied perspectives that might enhance the pertinence of the findings. But at least
if assessed in quantitative terms, this concentration of effort has been fertile: To
date, approximately 1,000 articles have appeared that focus on death anxiety or
the closely related constructs of death fear, threat, and concern. In actuality, this
figure is likely a conservative estimate of the number of published studies. In
scientometric research, searches that rely on computer databases generally access as little as 50% of the relevant literature on a given topic, as Durlak
and Riesenberg (1991) found in their recent meta-analysis of the literature on
death education.

Figure 1 depicts the growth in this literature over the last four decades. As
may be seen, death anxiety became a topic of psychological interest in the late
1950s, although a handful of pioneering studies had appeared before then. Methodologically, these early studies tended to rely on projective methods (e.g., the
tabulation of death themes in Thematic Apperception Test [TAT] stories) and
simple face-valid questionnaires. In the mid-1960s, the volume of reports began
to increase, coincident with the rising popular interest in the topic of death, as
reflected in the appearance of Kübler-Ross's (1969) *On Death and Dying*. But a
publication explosion in this literature did not occur until the mid-1970s, peaking
at 70 articles per year in 1987. Interestingly, the impetus for this dramatic growth
of the literature appeared to be the development of the first validated and widely
available instruments designed specifically for the direct assessment of death fear
(Collett & Lester, 1969; Lester, 1967), threat (Krieger, Epting, & Leitner, 1974),
and anxiety (Templer, 1970). Both in the shape of the growth curve and in the
apparently facilitative role played by methodological advances, the evolution of
the death anxiety literature closely parallels the development of other specialty
areas in psychology (Neimeyer, 1985b) and science generally (Mulkay, 1980).

At the high point of interest in death attitudes in the late 1970s, several
authors undertook reviews to integrate (Pollak, 1979), criticize (Simpson, 1980),
and give direction to (Kastenbaum & Costa, 1977) the burgeoning literature. Together, these reviews provide an adequate overview of the methodological limitations and substantive findings of the research through 1977, and they are relied

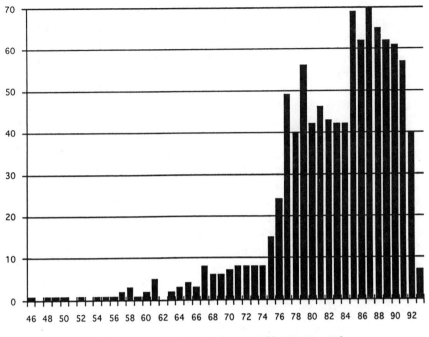

Figure 1   Number of publications on death anxiety by year, 1946–1992 (*N* = 986).

on in this chapter for coverage of the older literature. But as shall be shown, recent years have produced programmatic research on certain instruments, populations, and issues that were only dimly foreshadowed 18 years ago.

As death anxiety research moved into the 1980s, there was a plateauing of interest followed by another surge of growth and eventual decline. It is difficult to determine any single cause of the second surge of interest in the mid 1980s, but possibilities include continued development and validation of assessment tools for measuring death attitudes; the expansion of leading journals, such as *Death Studies,* that publish relevant literature; the emergence of professional organizations, such as the *Association for Death Education and Counseling,* that promote the presentation of research on death and loss, and a heightened public awareness of such global threats to survival as nuclear proliferation (Dodds & Lin, 1992; Gerber, 1990; Keefe, 1992) and the AIDS pandemic (Bivens, Neimeyer, Kirchberg, & Moore, 1994; Hayslip, Luhr, & Beyerlein, 1991; Hintze et al., 1994). The apparent decline in publication in recent years likely reflects the frequent lag time between publication and citation in common indexing sources.

In part because of its sheer volume, the literature on death fear is diffuse in its publication outlets as well as in its content. This wide dispersion in publication tends to delimit the impact of the conceptual and methodological advances that do occur in the field, helping to perpetuate the theoretical and empirical problems discussed in the next two sections.

THE PROBLEM OF DEFINITION OF DEATH ANXIETY

It might seem obvious that the study of any topic must start with a clear definition of what is to be investigated. Yet in spite of this, definitional problems have plagued the field of death anxiety from the beginning. The first and most persistent of these difficulties concerns the term *death anxiety* itself. In the opinion of earlier reviewers, such as Kastenbaum and Costa (1977), much of the confusion in the literature on death attitudes can be traced to this "careless interchange of 'fear' and 'anxiety,' each of which implies different approaches to measurement" (p. 233). For example, if fear represents a more realistic reaction to a specific danger, whereas anxiety refers to a more neurotic response that is out of proportion to any actual external hazard (Choron, 1974), a questionnaire measuring fear of death might contain questions about the pain of dying or one's reactions to witnessing the death of another, whereas an instrument measuring death anxiety might inquire about reactions to more abstract factors, such as apprehension about the state of nonbeing that death may represent.

As persuasive as these arguments may be, a distinction between fear and anxiety is not compelling on conceptual or practical grounds. Theoretically, the distinction has always received its strongest support from the psychoanalytic camp, who link the experience of anxiety with the expression of unconscious conflicts. As the influence of the psychodynamic model has waned, this theoretical basis for the distinction between fear and anxiety has become less secure. More important, fear and anxiety are seldom differentiated in the construction of instruments assessing apprehension about death, making the concepts essentially equivalent in practice. But this argument does not imply that *no* theoretical distinctions can be made among varieties of death concern. Indeed, some defensible distinctions—between threat and anxiety and between death fear and death acceptance, for example—are implicit or explicit in the sections on measurement below. The general point is that terminological distinctions may be valid, but only if they are suitably and consistently operationalized.

LEVELS OF DEATH ANXIETY AND THE PROBLEM OF MEASUREMENT

The Denial of Death?

It has become almost cliché to say that ours is a death-denying society. As applied to individuals, this assertion strongly implies that however much people may profess to accept the reality of their death at a conscious level, at an unconscious level they remain terrified of its occurrence (Becker, 1973; Firestone, 1994). Obviously, obtaining support for this contention would require that measurement strategies tap death fears at conscious and nonconscious levels. But although there may be important senses in which people do deny the psychological reality of their deaths, direct evidence for the ubiquitous denial of death anxiety is remarkably sparse.

A large-scale study conducted by Warren and Chopra (1979b) provides an interesting perspective on the question of whether people deny the reality of their death. Administering a face-valid survey on death attitudes to 749 Australian respondents, Warren and Chopra discovered that although only 9% of their sample described themselves as "fearful" when reflecting on their own death, fully 30% reported some variety of negative emotional reaction (e.g., discouragement, depression, or purposelessness). Perhaps the most reasonable conclusions to draw from such findings are that (a) a substantial number of people do not deny feeling apprehensive about death and (b) the determinants of denial, when it does occur, deserve further study. The few methodologically sound studies of denial of death fear that have been conducted support this view. For example, in a study that is notable for the sophistication of its sampling procedures, Nelson (1979) found a modest negative correlation between death anxiety denial and occupational and educational status among 699 Virginia residents. Although such studies indicate that denial does exist and is associated with certain personal or social factors, they have not established that it masks a deeper level of unconscious death anxiety.

In sum, the little research that is available raises more questions than it answers about the nature and extent of death anxiety denial. Certainly, it remains possible that the denial of death anxiety may sometimes be linked to repression, as suggested in the psychoanalytic literature (Firestone, 1994), and evidence of this is discussed in the section on personality factors below. But in order to understand more clearly the results of the broader literature, it is first necessary to review the various direct and indirect means of assessing death orientation that have been used to date.

Indirect Methods of Assessing Death Orientation

One of the important consequences of researchers' assuming that people deny their death fear was that indirect methods for assessing death anxiety were devised. Thus, by studying fantasies, reaction times, or physiological responses to death stimuli, researchers attempted to circumvent subjects' tendencies to deny or otherwise distort their "true," possibly unconscious, emotional reactions. Two fairly distinct kinds of indirect assessment have resulted, the first based on projective testing and the second on experimental reaction time and word association tasks.

Projective Methods   One of the most influential early traditions in personality assessment was based on the projective hypothesis, the assumption that individuals project their own conflicts by seeing in ambiguous stimuli those emotional issues that are most central to their own personalities. Thus, a subject who told a story that contained allusions to death in response to the vague drawings presented in the TAT was assumed to have an anxious preoccupation with death issues.

Although such projective methods were relatively common in the early years of death anxiety research (Rhudick & Dibner, 1961), they have since fallen largely into disfavor because of their dubious reliability and validity (Wass & Forfar,

1982). When projective materials such as TAT cards are used in contemporary research, they are typically used in conjunction with another, better validated instrument, providing a "cross-validation" of the results of the TAT (Ungar, Florian, & Zernitsky-Shurka, 1990), or they are used to assess populations (e.g., children) whose conceptions of death may be difficult to access through the usual verbal means (Tamm & Granqvist, in press). One example of the projective approach to assessment in contemporary research is the work of Feifel and Nagy (1980, 1981). These authors used a battery of tests in an attempt to measure different "levels" of death anxiety experienced by more than 600 persons who varied in their level of risk-taking behavior. At a "conscious" level, subjects were asked to rate their personal fear of death on a 5-point scale. At a "fantasy" level, they were instructed to select an image that best represented their view of death. These projective images were then classed as positive (e.g., a soft pillow) or negative (e.g., a devouring tiger). It was assumed that this fantasy task circumvented the respondents' defensive or intellectualized conception of death. Finally, as a "below the level of awareness" measure, they administered a color/word interference task that is described in Experimental Tasks.

The results, however, did not clearly support the independence of these three levels. Instead, conscious and fantasy measures were found to be significantly more correlated with one another than either was with the nonconscious measure (Feifel & Nagy, 1981), a result that has been replicated by Epting, Rainey, and Weiss (1979). In fact, Rigdon (1983) provided evidence that direct ratings and imagery measures actually form a single factor, which he termed "conscious death fear." Thus, the key assumption of projective methods—that they disclose emotional conflicts of which the respondent is unaware—does not seem to be clearly supported by present data.

Although the case for unconscious death denial and the rationale for projective methods have both weakened in recent years, it may still prove to be interesting to investigate death fantasies as phenomena in their own right, irrespective of whether they offer glimpses of unconscious death anxiety. An example of well-conducted research of this type is the work of Tamm and Granqvist (in press), who studied a stratified sample of 431 Swedish schoolchildren ages 9–18. Using a sophisticated content-analytic scheme for categorizing the imagery in children's drawings of death, they discovered that biological concepts tended to dominate the responses of younger age groups, whereas metaphysical conceptions emerged in the work of older children. Boys were found to have more violent and personified death concepts than girls, who depicted death in more emotional terms. Presumably, the relatively low frequency of religious imagery in their sample reflects the secular emphasis of Swedish culture, suggesting the possibility of using the relatively culture-fair medium of children's drawings to conduct cross-cultural developmental studies of death-related imagery. Tamm and Granqvist's tendency to stay relatively close to the data in interpreting their findings, eschewing unwarranted assumptions about the children's unconscious conflicts, represents a salutary trend evident in recent studies.

Experimental Tasks   A second set of indirect measures of death anxiety has been derived from classical laboratory tasks administered under highly controlled circumstances. In such tasks, subjects are presented both death-related words and neutral words and are asked to read them aloud, associate to them, or identify the color of ink in which they are printed. The number of errors made, the time required to react, or the degree of physiological arousal displayed in responding to the death words as opposed to the neutral words supposedly reflects the degree of "perceptual defensiveness" or anxiety that the death words aroused in the subject (Alexander & Alderstein, 1958).

Like the projective methods, these indirect experimental methods have largely been abandoned in recent work, mainly because of their failure to demonstrate sufficient reliability or validity (Kastenbaum & Costa, 1977). Although further refinement of these measures may be worth pursuing, most available data do not support the conclusion that they tap a theoretically consistent nonconscious level of death fear (Rigdon, 1983). Despite the fact that research using these older experimental procedures has been discouraging, it may nonetheless be worthwhile to investigate the relevance to the study of death-related concepts and schemas of newer cognitive science measures using highly accurate computer-administered procedures. For example, implicit memory tasks, such as lexical decision or perceptual identification procedures, could enable investigators to measure the accessibility of death concepts or reactivity to death stimuli while bypassing conscious processing. A useful general discussion of these procedures has been provided by Roediger (1990), although their specific application to the study of death-related schemas remains to be explored.

Direct Measures of Death Orientation

Although death anxiety has been conceptualized by some authors as a multilevel phenomenon requiring a multilevel assessment, most "authors of death scales . . . have assumed, at least implicitly, that death anxiety, like death fear, is a conscious experience" (Wass, Corr, Pacholski, & Forfar, 1985, p. 188). In keeping with this assumption, most researchers have used fairly direct measures of death attitudes, ranging from the occasional interview and text-based measure to the ubiquitous questionnaire.

Interviews   The use of interviews to assess death anxiety, although still infrequent, has made some gains in popularity over the last decade. But because interview methods have been devised for a host of practical and theoretical reasons, they vary widely in their format, length, structure, and demonstrated validity. Perhaps the simplest interview method consists of simply reading aloud a brief, forced-choice questionnaire and asking the interviewee to respond verbally rather than in writing. This method has been used to administer Templer's (1970) Death Anxiety Scale (DAS) to populations who require special assistance, such as the elderly (Given & Range, 1990; Sanders, Poole, & Rivero, 1980).

At the opposite extreme, some investigators have coded unstructured verbalizations to open-ended prompts, on the rationale that death concern can best be assessed by simply encouraging people to talk freely and then listening carefully to their responses. A good example of this approach is the work of Fry (1990), who conducted a study to elucidate the concerns of the homebound elderly about death and dying. In a two-stage interview process, subjects were first given an open-ended question about their death concerns and then were given a semistructured interview to elaborate those concerns. Results were coded with very high interrater reliability into the categories emotional security, personal safety, sensory loss, self-regulation behaviors, social support, and avoidance behaviors. Some common themes in the homebound elderly were the idea of dying alone, being forgotten after death, and the uncertainty of life after death. Coping mechanisms such as prayer and social support were also identified. Such an approach clearly possesses advantages over a forced-choice questionnaire, although the usefulness of the responses hinges on the establishment of trust and rapport between the interviewer and interviewee.

Finally, it is noteworthy that the validity and reliability of interview procedures are not often considered. Yet there is no apparent reason for believing that spoken responses to questions about death anxiety are anymore exempt from concerns about consistency or accuracy than are written answers to the same questions. One can easily imagine how interview situations could subtly influence a respondent's answers, yet there have been no investigations into this source of bias in the death anxiety area.

The one interview method whose validity and reliability have been extensively scrutinized is the Threat Index (TI), a measure introduced by Krieger, et al. (1974). Founded in personal construct theory, the TI procedure requires respondents first to compare and contrast such situations as "your father dying while trying to save someone from drowning," "three children dying when a tornado hits their school," and "your own death, if it were to occur at this time in your life." For example, interviewees might respond that the first situation is "purposeful," whereas the last two are "meaningless." In the second step, respondents are asked to describe themselves and their own death in these terms. Instances in which the self is described by one construct pole (e.g., "purposeful") and death by the opposite (e.g., "meaningless") are taken to indicate threat. The higher the number of such splits, the more threatened subjects are assumed to be by the prospect of their own mortality. A description of this structured interview procedure has been provided by Neimeyer (1994a).

Considerable evidence supports the validity of this index of death threat. For example, individuals who scored low in threat reported that they were more able to accept death and to conceive of their personal mortality (Krieger et al., 1974). Moreover, death constructs elicited by the TI procedure appear to be more meaningful to respondents than a list of semantic differential dimensions (Neimeyer, Dingemans, & Epting, 1977), and the score on the instrument seems to be free of social desirability bias (Krieger, Epting, & Hays, 1979). However, because of the substantial amount of time required to administer this (or any other) in-depth interview protocol, recent studies have relied on more convenient questionnaire forms of the measure.

In summary, a variety of interview methods of assessing death orientation have been explored over the last 15 years, adding breadth, detail, and flexibility to the study of death attitudes. If used in conjunction with established coding schemes, such methods warrant more frequent application.

Text-Based Measures   A recent innovation in the assessment of death attitudes is the development of text-based measures, which elicit the respondent's own conceptualizations of death for subsequent coding by the investigator. The Revised Twenty Statement Test (R-TST; Durlak, Horn, & Kass, 1990) is a case in point. In the R-TST, subjects are asked to provide 20 open-ended responses to the question "What does your own death mean to you?" These responses are coded by the investigator using 10 mutually exclusive content categories (e.g., positive, negative, neutral; religious, impact on others). Evidence of the R-TST's interrater reliability is promising, as is evidence of its test–retest reliability, suggesting that the themes identified in subjects' responses are consistent over time.

A second example of a text-based method has recently been provided by Holcomb, Neimeyer, and Moore (1993). Soliciting narrative descriptions to the question "What does death mean to you?", these investigators first segmented the narratives of more than 500 individuals into discrete construct units (e.g., "Death to me is *something to be resisted*; it *makes no sense*"). These constructs were then coded using a reliable content-coding dictionary developed by Neimeyer, Fontana, and Gold (1984), consisting of 25 nonexclusive categories (e.g., Negative Evaluation and Purposelessness), and the resulting scores were related to respondents' demographic characteristics and death attitudes as measured by other instruments. Among the more interesting patterns to emerge was the finding that respondents who professed a coherent "personal philosophy of death" viewed death as more purposeful, expected, and involving some form of continued existence, whereas those without such a philosophy wrote narratives that implied a negative evaluation, low acceptance, and low understanding of death.

Unique advantages of both of these text-based methods include the minimal constraints they pose for the subject, their amenability to the coding of transcribed interviews as well as written material, and their ability to assess idiosyncratic aspects of death attitudes not assessed by standard questionnaires. In view of these advantages, such measures deserve greater exploration in future studies.

Questionnaires   Alternative research methods continue to be used, but the dramatic increase in research on death anxiety over the last 20 years owes almost entirely to the use of questionnaire measures of death orientation. In fact, more than 95% of the published studies to date have relied on some form of direct questionnaire. Because the study of death anxiety has become almost synonymous with the use of a relatively small number of instruments, it is crucial to consider precisely what these instruments measure before moving on to consider the correlates and consequences of death anxiety identified in this literature.

DEATH ANXIETY OR DEATH ANXIETIES?

Exactly what do we fear if we fear death? From quite early on in the death aware-ness movement it was recognized that this was a complex question. Choron (1974), for example, argued for a distinction among varieties of death fear. Grounding his discussion in Western philosophy, he distinguished among fear of what happens after death (e.g., eternal punishment), fear of the event of dying (e.g., the pain and indignity involved), and fear of ceasing to be (e.g., extinction and loss of the activities that make up life). Thus, at a theoretical level, Choron believed death anxiety to be multidimensional, a view endorsed by subsequent theorists (e.g., Mount, 1983).

Still, it is not clear on the basis of theory alone what dimensions are being measured by particular death attitude questionnaires. It therefore becomes essen-tial to distinguish between the *theoretical* dimensionality of a given questionnaire and its *empirical* dimensionality. The former refers to what it purports to measure and the latter, to what it actually does measure. For example, many death orienta-tion questionnaires that were assumed by their originators to measure a single construct (general death anxiety) appear, on closer scrutiny, to tap a number of distinct dimensions. In this section, the dimensionality of four of the more im-portant death attitude questionnaires is discussed to illustrate these issues and to pave the way for a discussion of the impact of situational and personality variables on death anxiety.

Concern about the empirical dimensionality and validity of death anxiety in-struments dates from the earliest reviews of the literature and has continued since that time. Perhaps the bluntest of these criticisms was voiced by Simpson (1980), who concluded that "research on death . . . is often logically and methodologically shoddy and has produced discrepant and contradictory results. This has been due to . . . the appalling lack of critical rigor that allowed too much indifferent or sloppy work to be published too easily" (p. 139). This critical sentiment has been counterbalanced by optimistic claims that inconsistencies in the literature will be clarified as greater attention is paid to the various components of death anxiety (Keller, Sherry, & Piotrowski, 1984).

A close examination of the current literature suggests that these mounting criticisms have had an effect. A much smaller proportion of recent studies have relied on unvalidated instruments, although other design problems persist in these studies and are addressed below. Moreover, as the field has progressed, early in-struments that treated death anxiety as a unidimensional concept have been sup-plemented by others that are explicitly multidimensional. A psychometric review of the six best validated measures of death attitudes, complete with instruments and scoring keys, has recently been provided by Neimeyer (1994b). Some of these measures are discussed below to give the reader some idea of their strengths and limitations.

The Death Anxiety Scale

Developed by Templer (1970), the DAS has been used in roughly 60% of the studies published in the last 10 years. Much of the reason for the scale's popularity lies in its simplicity. The DAS consists of 15 short statements (e.g., "I am very much afraid to die" and "I am often distressed by the way time flies so very rapidly"), which the respondent endorses as true or false. The number of responses indicative of a negative reaction is taken as a measure of death anxiety.

A certain degree of construct validation for the DAS has been provided by its moderate correlations with other measures of death fear (Lonetto & Templer, 1986). Reliability estimates on the DAS have also been moderately high (.8) over periods of 3 weeks (McMordie, 1978; Templer, 1970). Estimates of its internal consistency, on the other hand, have been more equivocal in both Australian and Canadian samples (Schell & Zinger, 1984; Warren & Chopra, 1978).

In terms of the DAS's dimensionality, the low internal consistency of Templer's (1970) original version of the instrument strongly suggests that it measures more than one dimension of death attitude. A number of studies using factor analysis, a statistical method for determining the underlying dimensions in a set of data, tend to support this claim (e.g., Gilliland & Templer, 1985; Lonetto, Fleming, & Mercer, 1979; Martin, 1982). Across these studies, which collectively included more than 2,500 subjects, the DAS tended to produce three to five factors that generally include: (a) a general death anxiety dimension, (b) a factor focusing on thoughts and talk of death, (c) a cluster of items bearing on the subjective proximity of death, and (d) a factor suggesting fear of pain and suffering. Thus, although the DAS was proposed as a theoretically unidimensional questionnaire, it is clearly empirically multidimensional. This state of affairs led Durlak (1982) to recommend that the use of the instrument be discontinued, because the scores it yields are uninterpretable. For example, a group of retirees and teenagers might obtain the same mean score on the DAS, but the former might do so by scoring high on the "subjective proximity to death" factor, whereas the latter might do so by scoring high on the "fear of physical alterations" dimension. The conclusion that the two groups have similar death anxieties would clearly be unwarranted.

In response to these limitations, some subsequent investigators have attempted to improve the DAS's internal consistency and precision (McMordie, 1978). The most promising of these second-generation instruments is the Revised Death Anxiety Scale (RDAS), constructed by Thorson and Powell (1994). In its current form, the RDAS consists of 25 statements, some of which are reverse scored (e.g., "I am not worried about ever being helpless") to reduce response bias. Respondents agree or disagree with each item on a 5-point Likert scale. Thorson and Powell (1992) reported that the RDAS has good internal reliability and displays meaningful relationships with measures of intrinsic religious motivation. In view of its increased sensitivity over that of its predecessor, the RDAS deserves greater study and application.

The Threat Index

Originally introduced in a structured-interview format in 1974, the TI was eventually adapted to a paper-and-pencil format to promote its use in research (Krieger et al., 1979; Neimeyer et al., 1977). Like the interview format of the TI, the paper-and-pencil version of the instrument assesses threat by measuring the subject's tendency to construe the self and death on contrasting poles of a sample of constructs (e.g., "static" vs. "changing"). Unlike the interview form, it circumvents the need to elicit constructs from the subject by providing a standardized set of dimensions used most frequently by subjects in earlier studies. As a result, it is easily administered in group settings and requires far less time to complete than the original. Complete instructions for the instrument have been provided by Neimeyer (1994a).

Although the interpretation of the threat score derived from the index has been questioned (Chambers, 1986), the developers of the TI have defended its validity on both logical and empirical grounds (Neimeyer, 1986; Neimeyer & Moore, 1989). For example, Krieger et al. (1979) found that respondents showed a strong tendency to rate something they found very "comfortable" the same as they would rate themselves and to contrast both with ratings of a personally "terrifying" event. This finding supports the construct validity of the split configuration as a measure of threat. Further evidence of the TI's construct validity has been provided by Rainey and Epting (1977), who found that death education students and persons who had made arrangements for the disposal of their bodies after death had lower threat scores than did relevant control groups. Other studies have demonstrated the convergence of the TI with established death anxiety instruments (e.g., Dattel & Neimeyer, 1990; Epting et al., 1979; Neimeyer & Dingemans, 1980; Tobacyk & Eckstein, 1980), providing evidence of the concurrent validity of the measure. Moreover, the TI appears to have high test–retest reliability over periods of up to 3 months (Krieger et al., 1979: Neimeyer et al., 1977; Rainey & Epting, 1977). Unlike the DAS, it also displays strong internal consistency (Krieger et al., 1979; MacInnes & Neimeyer, 1980; Moore & Neimeyer, 1991; Rigdon & Epting, 1985). Although this suggests that the TI is more uniform and hence more interpretable than the DAS, of at least equal importance is its performance in factor-analytic studies that assess its empirical dimensionality.

The most ambitious of the studies designed to determine the TI's factor structure was conducted by Moore and Neimeyer (1991). Using state-of-the-art confirmatory factor-analytic procedures, they were able to identify and confirm an empirically derived factor structure for a 25-item version of the instrument and found acceptable reliability for the Global Threat factor, as well as for three subfactors of the scale: Threat to Well-Being, Uncertainty, and Fatalism. At this point, the TI appears to be the most extensively researched instrument for the assessment of death attitudes available in the literature, leading some reviewers to consider it a model for future research (Prichard & Epting, 1992; Simpson, 1980).

The Hoelter Multidimensional Fear of Death Scale

The Multidimensional Fear of Death Scale (MDFODS; Hoelter, 1979; Neimeyer & Moore, 1994) has been used in relatively few studies since its development in 1977. But it deserves mention because it represents the best current attempt to construct a genuinely multidimensional measure of death anxiety on empirical grounds. It consists of eight independent subscales, each containing six items with which respondents indicate the extent of their agreement. The factors (and representative items) are as follows: Fear of Dying ("I am afraid of dying very slowly"), Fear of the Dead ("I dread visiting a funeral home"), Fear of Being Destroyed ("I do not want to donate my eyes after I die"), Fear for Significant Others ("I sometimes get upset when acquaintances die"), Fear of the Unknown ("No one can say for sure what will happen after death"), Fear of Conscious Death ("I am afraid of being buried alive"), Fear for Body after Death ("The thought of my body decaying after I die scares me"), Fear of Premature Death ("I am afraid I will not have time to experience everything I want to"). In Hoelter's (1979) study, these dimensions emerged from a factor analysis of a larger sample of items administered to 395 American students. They have, however, been largely replicated in a subsequent study of Australian adults by Walkey (1982).

Other data reported by Long (1985) limit the generalizability of these findings, however. Translating the original MFODS into Arabic, Long administered the scale to 84 Saudi Arabian men temporarily living in the United States. In contrast to the previous studies, he found that the best factor solution produced only three dimensions of death anxiety, including General Fear of Dying and the Dead, Fear for Significant Others, and Fear of Premature Death. The extremely high religious orthodoxy scores obtained by the sample suggested that several of the fear dimensions posited by Hoelter (1979) (e.g., Fear of Being Destroyed and Fear of Conscious Death) may be entirely inapplicable to a devout Islamic respondent. At a methodological level, these results are a reminder that even empirically constructed instruments should not be assumed to be generalizable to cultures that contrast sharply with those on which they were based.

Although the majority of research on the MFODS has been concerned with replicating its unique factor structure, preliminary data regrading its validity and reliability are also promising. Acceptable levels of internal consistency for the various subscales have been reported (Hoelter, 1979; Walkey, 1982), and Neimeyer and Moore (1994) have found good test–retest reliability coefficients for the overall measure, with slightly lower, but still acceptable, coefficients for the component subscales. These investigators have also established a measure of convergent validity for the MFODS with both the TI and straightforward self-report of death concern. In summary, the MFODS holds considerable promise as a psychometrically sound, multidimensional measure of various facets of death fear and should prove an attractive choice for future researchers.

The Death Attitude Profile–Revised

An exhaustive review of measures of death attitudes is beyond the scope of this chapter, but at least one other instrument should be mentioned, particularly because its focus on *death acceptance* counterbalances the uniform emphasis on negative responses to death assessed by the foregoing questionnaires. In constructing the Death Attitude Profile–Revised (DAP–R), Wong, Reker, and Gesser (1994) premised their work on the existential assumption that acceptance of personal mortality did not necessarily imply an absence of death fear. Thus, in a series of studies (Gesser, Wong, & Reker, 1987; Wong et al., 1994), they devised a well-constructed measure of death attitudes ranging from negative to positive and provided validational support for the instrument.

In its revised form, the DAP–R consists of 32 items (e.g., "I see death as a release from the burden of this life") rated on 7-point scales of agreement. Items cluster into five empirically distinguishable subscales: Fear of Death/Dying (having negative thoughts and feelings about death as a state and dying as a process), Approach Acceptance (viewing death as a passage to a satisfying afterlife), Escape Acceptance (seeing death as an alternative to a painful existence), Neutral Acceptance (understanding death as a reality that is to be neither feared nor welcomed), and Death Avoidance (a defensive attempt to keep thoughts of death out of one's consciousness). Internal consistency, test–retest reliability, and convergent validity were found to be acceptable. A further possible advantage of the DAP–R is its relevance to the study of death attitudes among the elderly, insofar as preliminary data suggest that older adults tend to express greater acceptance of death as a form of escape from a burdensome life and also higher levels of approach acceptance, envisioning death as a transition to a blissful afterlife, than do middle-aged adults (Wong et al., 1994). The growing interest in researching quality-of-life issues among the elderly should lead to greater use of the DAP–R.

Summary

Thanatological research has been characterized by a diversity of methods, which have gradually begun to capture some of the complexity of the human encounter with death. Some of the demographic and personal factors that influence that encounter are discussed in the remainder of this chapter.

EMPIRICAL CORRELATES OF DEATH ANXIETY
Demographic and Situational Factors

A great deal of research in the last 20 years has focused on the relationship between demographic variables and death anxiety, owing largely to the ease with which such variables as age and sex can be measured. Ironically, however, few of these studies have been designed primarily to test demographic hypotheses. Instead, most researchers have simply made passing reference to differences between demographic groups while pursuing other questions of greater interest to them. As a consequence, a diffuse and largely atheoretical literature has grown up in the area, leaving unanswered many important questions about the impact of such variables on death anxiety. This is less true of the recent research on such situational variables as health status or experiences with death, where testing of a priori hypotheses is more common. This section is a review of the research on the most important of these variables, and the reader is referred to the previous version of this chapter (Neimeyer, 1988) for a more adequate discussion of the older literature.

Gender In his review of the death anxiety literature through 1977, Pollak (1979) noted that the majority of the earlier work indicated that women reported more death fear than did men and that virtually all of the remaining studies demonstrated no differences between the sexes. Research conducted since that time reinforces and provides a more refined view of this possible gender difference in death fear.

Not surprisingly, the instrument most commonly used in more recent research has been the DAS, and the most commonly studied subject group is college students. Much of the work using this measure with this population supports the conclusion that women feel more anxiety about death than do men (e.g., Davis, Bremer, Anderson, & Tramill, 1983; Davis, Martin, Wilee, & Voorhees, 1978; McMordie, 1978; Sadowski, Davis, & Loftus-Vergari, 1979). Moreover, there is some indication that this sex difference is not simply an American phenomenon: It has been generalized to samples of Irish and Canadian students (Lonetto, Mercer, Fleming, Bunting, & Clare, 1980), as well as Australian and Malaysian respondents (Schumaker, Barraclough, & Vagg, 1987). Other studies using the DAS have found sex differences in death anxiety in demographically varied samples, including rural southern high school students (Young & Daniels, 1980) and elderly (Sanders et al., 1980). Using the Lester Fear of Death Scale and the R-DAS, respectively, Neimeyer et al. (1977) and Thorson and Powell (1994) corroborated this view.

However, the literature is far from unequivocal regarding whether girls and women have more negative attitudes toward death. For example, Neimeyer and his associates found no differences between men and women in death threat, as measured by the TI, in either college student (Neimeyer et al., 1977) or adult (Neimeyer & Dingemans, 1980; Neimeyer & Neimeyer, 1984) samples, and Eggerman and Dustin (1985) reported similar negative results with the TI in a study of physicians. Other researchers using rather different methods also have found no sex difference in death anxiety. Conte, Weiner, and Plutchick (1982) found that men and women scored similarly on their Death Anxiety Questionnaire, an instrument for which they provided some preliminary validational evidence, and

Viney (1984) was unable to detect any gender differences in her interview-based study of nearly 800 ill and healthy adults. Similarly, Wong et al. (1994) found no difference between the sexes on the death anxiety factor of their scale and in fact reported that women experienced higher approach acceptance and escape acceptance than did men. Although these conflicting studies call into question the robustness of a sex difference in death concern, they are fairly uniform in indicating the direction of this difference when it does occur.

Although the existence of a gender difference in death anxiety measures is fairly clear, its explanation is not. One hypothesis is that the discrepancy in death anxiety scores simply reflects women's greater tendency to admit having troubling feelings (Stillion, 1985). This emotional-expressiveness hypothesis receives indirect support from the fact that studies in which sex differences were found tended to use the DAS or similar feeling-oriented questionnaires, whereas those in which no such differences were found often used more cognitive measures, such as the TI. In an attempt to evaluate this rationale empirically, Dattel and Neimeyer (1990) administered both the more affect-oriented DAS and more thought-oriented TI to a racially and occupationally diverse group of adults, along with well-validated measures of self-disclosure and social desirability. They reasoned that if a gender difference could be accounted for by women's greater emotional expressiveness, any difference that would emerge on the DAS should disappear once social desirability and self-disclosure were statistically controlled. As predicted, women outscored men on the DAS but not on the TI. However, this gender difference persisted even after social desirability and self-disclosure were taken into account, casting doubt on the adequacy of the emotional-expressiveness hypothesis as an explanation of women's greater report of death anxiety.

An alternative interpretation of this persistent trend is provided by the recent finding that men attempted to avoid thoughts of death and dying to a greater extent than did women (Wong et al., 1994), suggesting that men may deal with intrusive thoughts of their mortality more defensively than women deal with theirs. However, this plausible explanation remains to be evaluated in controlled studies.

Whatever explanation is put forward for the gender difference in death anxiety, it seems clear that it would have to be quite general, insofar as evidence suggests that the greater death anxiety of females may extend to Eastern as well as Western cultures (McMordie & Kumar, 1984).

Age   Curiously, the influence of age on adults' death anxiety was ignored until relatively recently. While much remains to be learned about the maturation of death attitudes beyond adolescence, an outline of significant shifts in death concern across the life span has begun to emerge. Kalish's (1977) elegant study of more than 400 California residents provides a point of departure for this literature. Conducting door-to-door surveys of various ethnic communities, Kalish found that the elderly members of all ethnic groups thought about death more often but were less anxious about it than were respondents at earlier stages in the life cycle.

Across ethnic categories, approximately 10% of the elderly respondents reported fearing death, compared with 25% of the middle-aged and 40% of the young respondents. This general pattern has been replicated in a sophisticated sociological study of 699 Virginia residents conducted by Nelson (1979), who found that age was negatively correlated with death avoidance, fear, and reluctance to interact with the dying as measured by a multidimensional inventory. The greater death anxiety of younger respondents has also been demonstrated in other studies using a variety of instruments (Neimeyer, 1985a; Robinson & Wood, 1984; Stevens, Cooper, & Thomas, 1980; Thorson & Powell, 1994), including investigations of more specific populations, such as rehabilitation clients (Johnson, 1980) and medical students (Eggerman & Dustin, 1985; Thorson & Powell, 1990b).

The relationship between age and death concern may not be linear, however. In a carefully conducted study, Gesser et al. (1987) administered the Death Attitude Profile to 50 respondents in each of three age groups: young (18–25), middle-aged (35–50), and elderly (60+). As they predicted, general fear of death and dying displayed a curvilinear relationship with age, such that death anxiety was relatively high in the young, peaked in middle adulthood, and was minimal in old age. Subsequent research (Thorson & Powell, 1994) has identified particular sources of anxiety for younger respondents (e.g., decomposition, pain, helplessness, and isolation) and for older adults (loss of control and the existence of an afterlife). Future use of multidimensional scales could help clarify discrepant findings resulting from the use of unidimensional scales with diverse populations.

As with sex differences in death anxiety, the general negative correlation between age and death fear is more obvious than its explanation. For example, the more positive attitude toward death and dying in the elderly could reflect the diminished quality of elderly persons' health and lives; their greater religiosity; their more extensive experience in having worked through the deaths of parents, peers, and partners; or the fact that their expectation to live a certain number of years has been met. Thorson and Powell (1988) remarked that the age-related differences in death anxiety they observed could support the claim that older adults resolve fears about their mortality as they review their lives. Alternatively, they suggested that older subjects may have simply accumulated enough unpleasant life events over the years to make dying seem less traumatic. Although the finding that the elderly show greater escape acceptance of death supports this view (Wong et al., 1994), there is not yet enough evidence to provide a secure interpretation of older respondents' lower death concern.

A second topic that deserves research attention concerns variations in death anxiety within the elderly population. For example, although nursing home residents may generally experience less fear of dying than younger persons (Devins, 1979), there is some evidence that the old old (75+) in such institutions may become more death anxious than their young-old (60–75) fellow residents (Mullins & Lopez, 1982). This resurgence of fear of death may possibly reflect an exacerbation of anxieties about the pain involved in dying or about the subjective proximity of death, rather than fear of the state of death per se. This would seem to be a plausible hypothesis, given that death anxiety in this group was heightened for residents with diminished functional ability or subjective health.

A study of the concerns of 178 homebound elderly (Fry, 1990) sheds further light on the concerns of the vulnerable old. Using a semistructured interview and factor analysis to determine the categories of elderly subjects' fears, Fry coded the results into the categories emotional insecurity, personal safety, sensory loss, self-regulation behaviors, social support, and avoidance behaviors. The principle concerns appeared to be physical pain and loss and the risk to personal safety. Other themes were self-esteem needs, the fears that they would be easily forgotten after they died and that they would die alone, and the uncertainty of life after death. Investigators who wish to study such age effects across the life span would do well to consider the use of interview as well as questionnaire techniques, as Wass and Forfar (1982) suggested.

Occupation   Much of the current research on the relationship between death concern and occupation extends Feifel, Hanson, Jones, and Edwards's (1967) finding in the late 1960s that physicians and medical students, relative to other groups, displayed exaggerated death anxiety. This led to the conjecture that medical practitioners may actually select their professions in part to assuage their own fear of death, by symbolically conquering it in their daily efforts. However, attempts to replicate this finding have produced negative or equivocal results (Pollak, 1979). For example, Howells and Field (1982) administered simple Likert scales of fear of personal death and dying and apprehension about the dying of others to 178 medical students and a comparable number of social science students. They found no significant differences between the groups. Similarly, Neimeyer, Bagley, and Moore (1986) detected no differences between allied health professionals enrolled in death education courses and their classmates on either the DAS or the subscales of the Collett–Lester Fear of Death Scale. Likewise, DePaola, Neimeyer, Lupfer, and Fielder (1992) were unable to support predictions that nursing home personnel have higher levels of death concern than do demographically matched controls. Indeed, nursing staff displayed significantly *less* fear on two dimensions of the MFODS (Fear of the Dead and Fear of Significant Others Dying), perhaps as a function of their daily exposure to death in the nursing home environment. Thus, current data do not support the earlier contention that medical professionals are significantly more apprehensive about death and dying than are comparison groups.

Of course, the fact that the average health care worker is not unusually anxious about death does not negate the possibility that at least some facets of death are distressing to many health care workers. For instance, in their nursing home study, DePaola et al. (1992) found that staff reported greater anxieties than did controls on the MFODS factor Fear of the Unknown. A second study by Field and Howells (1985) clarified the specific death concerns common among medical students. Surveying 98 students on what aspects of death they found most disturbing, Field and Howells found that 84% expressed worry about dying themselves, especially fears of pain and loss. Ninety-one percent indicated that they worried about someone close to them dying, stressing the emotional impact that such bereavement would have on them. Seventy-six percent shared concerns about interacting with terminal patients, particularly in terms of their own awkwardness in communicating with the dying. Across domains, it was striking that most of the fears these students expressed referred more to themselves than to others who would be affected. This finding might reflect the students' stage of life rather than their chosen profession, however, because it has been found that one of the more distasteful aspects of death for older physicians is their inability to provide for their dependents (Warren & Chopra, 1979a).

Of course, these analyses of health care workers' death attitudes leave unanswered the more critical question of how such personal concerns might influence their professional behavior. Perhaps the most critical question of all concerns the effect of a health care professional's death attitudes on his or her direct patient care. For instance, Eakes (1985) administered the DAS to 159 nursing home personnel and found that those who were more anxious about death also held more negative attitudes toward the aged, and this finding was replicated in the DePaola et al. (1992) study. It remains to be established whether such attitudinal negativity is subtly expressed in nurse–patient interaction. In the case of physicians, the data are even more provocative. For example, some studies have reported that medical caregivers who are highly threatened by the prospect of their own death are likely to consider more factors before deciding whether to inform a terminal patient of his or her diagnosis (Eggerman & Dustin, 1985) and may even prolong heroic treatment during a patient's final days in the hospital (Schulz & Aderman, 1979). Given the real-world relevance of such findings, these results deserve replication.

A more limited literature has begun to address the death attitudes of occupational groups outside the medical professions. Amenta (1984) compared the death anxiety scores of volunteers who withdrew from a hospice program before serving 1 year with those who continued to work with the dying patients. As predicted, the dropouts had significantly higher DAS scores than did the persisters, suggesting one possible criterion for future volunteer selection. However, programmatic research by Robbins (1992, 1994) suggests that volunteer performance may be predicted less by death anxiety than by *death competency,* conceptualized as skill in managing death-related situations, irrespective of one's personal discomforts. After first establishing the reliability and validity of her Coping with Death measure, composed of items such as, "I am familiar with funeral prearrangement" and "I can communicate with the dying," Robbins administered this scale and a measure of perceived self-efficacy specific to hospice work to a large sample of hospice trainees, medium- and long-term hospice volunteers, and controls. She found no differences among the groups on the DAS but discovered that the experienced volunteers scored higher than controls on Coping with Death and that all hospice volunteers outscored the controls in death self-efficacy.

Neimeyer and Dingemans (1980) examined the death orientation of another paraprofessional group—suicide prevention volunteers. Administering a full battery of death attitude measures to workers at a crisis center and nonvolunteer controls, they found the suicide interventionists to have greater anxieties about their own deaths but not about the deaths of others. Moreover, this appeared to represent a self-selection effect, because novice and veteran interventionists did not differ on any of these dimensions. However, a subsequent attempt by Neimeyer and Neimeyer (1984) to replicate this finding using the DAS actually produced the opposite results, with suicide interventionists scoring lower than demographically similar controls. Thus, there is no clear evidence that volunteers who work with people who are threatening to take their lives are more anxious about death than comparison groups. Moreover, it is questionable whether interventionists who are more fearful of death are less skillful than those who are less fearful, because the latter study found no correlation between the DAS and a validated and reliable test of suicide counseling skills (Neimeyer & MacInnes, 1981; Neimeyer & Pfeiffer, 1994).

Recent research has extended this attention to the death attitudes of counselors to a group of caregivers who must contend not only with the inevitability of client death, but also with concerns about their own vulnerability—namely, HIV-negative gay men who work with others who have AIDS. Administering the TI and MFODS to a large sample of such caregivers (the AIDS-involved group), to noninvolved and noninfected gay men, and to a third group who had tested seropositive, Bivens et al. (in press) discovered that those in the AIDS-involved group actually experienced less death threat, as well as less fear of premature death, than their healthy but uninvolved counterparts.

Findings are equivocal concerning the death attitudes of funeral directors relative to other professionals. Rockwell (1981) presented evidence that funeral directors and psychiatrists may have lower DAS scores than psychologists and suicidologists, but these results failed to attain statistical significance. Similarly, Schell and Zinger (1984) reported that funeral directors' scores on the DAS were comparable to those of funeral service students and lower than those of a group of university students. However, a reexamination of their data suggests that the apparently lower scores of the funeral directors may reflect the much lower percentage of women in that sample than in the student group, a confound that the authors did not acknowledge.

One of the few clear-cut occupation-related differences in death anxiety that has been reported in the literature is between firefighters and police officers on the one hand and college faculty and business students on the other (Hunt, Lester, & Ashton, 1983). The former groups showed more apprehension about their own dying than did the latter, but the groups did not differ in concern about the deaths of others. This finding, however, is in need of replication.

In summary, a good deal of research has now been conducted on the death attitudes of people employed in various death-relevant work settings. However, a review of the literature suggests that a distinction be made between *death-exposure* occupations and *death-risk* occupations in future research. The former include professions that bring the professional in contact with the deaths of others (e.g., medicine; nursing; and suicide, grief, and AIDS counseling), whereas the latter represent careers in which the professional's own life may be in jeopardy (e.g., law enforcement, firefighting, and active military service). Current evidence indicates that whereas workers in death-risk occupations may experience elevated death anxiety, members of death-exposure professions do not and, in fact, may display unique competencies in responding to the challenges of death and loss. However, it remains true that a certain percentage of the latter do express a heightened fear of death, and data are beginning to suggest that this may adversely affect the quality of care they provide to patients. This issue may rank as the most important area for further research in vocational studies of death attitudes.

Health Status Despite the intuitive importance of the topic, relatively little research had been conducted on the relationship between physical illness and death anxiety before 1988. This relationship had been studied by Mullins and Lopez (1982), who found that nursing home patients who reported worse health and diminished functional ability scored higher on the DAS regardless of their age. In another study, Kureshi and Husain (1981) found that smokers outscored nonsmokers on the DAS, indirectly reinforcing the conclusion that perceived health has an impact on death concern.

Two additional studies qualify the interpretation of these results, however. In the first, Robinson and Wood (1984) compared 100 subjects, divided equally among the following groups: (a) healthy individuals, (b) persons having routine medical checkups, (c) persons with rheumatoid arthritis, (d) persons with diabetes, and (e) persons with cancer. In contrast to the earlier studies, the investigators found no differences among the various subject groups on the TI, the DAS, or the Collett–Lester Fear of Death Scale (Lester, 1994). However, they did find a significant relationship between various dimensions of death anxiety and personality variables, as discussed later. In the second study, Viney (1984), compared large numbers of patients and nonpatients using the Gottschalk interview-based measure of death anxiety. She found that (a) ill persons displayed higher death concern than did well persons, (b) surgical patients were more anxious about death than were other patients, (c) acutely ill patients were more fearful of death than were chronically ill patients, and (d) people who received treatment in their own homes were less apprehensive than those who were treated in the hospital. But still more interesting was the finding that patients' expression of death anxiety may have been adaptive insofar as it was associated with positive affect and mastery as well as a certain amount of anger and uncertainty. In nonpatient groups, on the other hand, it was related only to anger and negative affect.

In response to the AIDS pandemic, a number of research groups have begun to study the distinctive death concerns of HIV-positive individuals and the factors that mediate them. For example, Catania, Turner, Choi, and Coates (1992) used a longitudinal design in studying the relationship of AIDS to death anxiety. Following a sample of 529 gay men, they examined help-seeking behaviors, HIV status, and death anxiety at 6-month intervals for 3 years. They observed that the subjects turned more to peers than to family in times of need but that family support was negatively related to level of death anxiety. Catania et al. suggested that in symptomatic men, nearness to death may initiate a process that allows a higher level of family support that asymptomatic or HIV-negative gay men do not have. However, these conclusions are qualified by Hintze et al.'s (1994) somewhat discrepant findings that higher levels of death anxiety in HIV-infected men were associated not only with greater medical deterioration, but also with greater family awareness of the diagnosis. At a minimum, these results should caution against the simple assumption that all families can function as a source of support when given full disclosure of a member's condition. Finally, Bivens et al. (in press) found that HIV-positive men were generally less threatened by the prospect of their inevitable death than were their HIV-negative, uninvolved counterparts. The HIV-positive group did, however, report greater fear of premature death, which might be seen as a realistic appraisal of the threat to their longevity posed by the disease process.

Experience with Death   Tokunuga (1985) has provided a useful review of the relatively small empirical literature on the effect of bereavement on death attitudes. He concluded, "With varying degrees of certainty these studies reach the same conclusion: suffering the death of a close friend or relative has little or no effect upon survivors' feelings about their own impending mortality" (Tokunuga, p. 272). In line with this conclusion, various researchers (e.g., Neimeyer et al., 1977; Pratt, Hare, & Wright, 1985) were unable to discover any relationship between personal experience with bereavement and death concern. One exception to this general trend is the findings of Meshot and Leitner (1994), who studied the long-term effects of parental loss during adolescence in a group of young adults. They found that the loss group showed less apprehension on a personalized, but not a standard, measure of death threat, but they also had a greater need to be noticed and included by others.

Other aspects of experience with death have also been investigated, beyond bereavement per se. For example, Brent, Speece, Gates, Mood, and Kaul (1991) found that a greater range of death-related experiences (personal, professional, and educational) fostered a more positive attitude toward care for the dying patients in a group of more than 400 nursing students. They noted that direct contact with death and dying had the greatest positive effect on attitudes.

A second factor likely to have a sustained impact on one's death attitudes is a near death experience, a profound and sometimes transcendental experience reported by about one third of people who have been close to death. Studying nearly 300 individuals who (a) had had a near-death experience, (b) had had a brush with death without a near-death experience, or (c) had had no brushes with death, Greyson (1992) found that the first group clearly differed from the latter two in showing less death concern as measured by the TI. Moreover, the depth or richness of the near-death experience was negatively correlated with death threat, such that individuals who had had the most intensely transcendental experiences were the least threatened by the prospect of their own deaths in the future. Studies of loss and other intensely personal forms of encounter with death are important to the study of death attitudes, insofar as they begin to elucidate critical determinants of death attitudes in our personal biographies.

Personality Factors

The literature that has emerged on the relationship between personality factors and death anxiety, although not necessarily more extensive than that on demographic correlates, tends to be somewhat more systematic. For the sake of convenience, the term *personality* is interpreted broadly, to include factors ranging from religious orientation, to psychopathology, to general lifestyle. No commitment to an individualistic conception of these variables is implied by this classification.

Social Desirability   Reviewing the research on the psychology of death conducted through the late 1970s, Kastenbaum and Costa (1977) observed that the influence of a social desirability set on reports of death anxiety had been neglected as an area of study. They strongly recommended that future investigators examine whether respondents were modifying their answer to questionnaire items in what they believed to be a socially approved direction. Such examinations have now been conducted for several of the major instruments used in the area. For example, no relationship has been found between the Marlow–Crowne Social Desirability Scale and the TI in either its interview or its paper-and-pencil form (Dattel & Neimeyer, 1990; Krieger et al., 1979). In contrast, the Collett–Lester Fear of Death Scale tends to suffer from a social desirability confound (Lester, 1994), as does the DAS, at least in its original version (Dattel & Neimeyer, 1990; Martin, 1982). To the extent that future investigators continue to rely on confounded measures, these findings suggest that such instruments should be paired with a social desirability measure and the influence of this extraneous variable controlled through covariance methods before results are interpreted.

Religious Belief   Studies of the relationship between religion and death concern began with attempts to establish simple group differences between subjects classed according to religious belief. In general, studies that have included only a simple face-valid measure of religiosity have produced equivocal results (e.g., Krieger et al., 1974; Neimeyer et al., 1977; Pratt et al., 1985; Wagner & Lorion, 1984). At best, the relationships found between these direct, unidimensional assessments of religiosity and death fear have seldom been robust, even when they attained statistical significance (Lonetto et al., 1980; Young & Daniels, 1980).

Investigators who have adopted a more refined view of religiosity have reported more complex results. Rigdon and Epting (1985), for instance, administered the TI and Collett-Lester scale to 95 college students and learned that those who experienced less death fear and threat were more likely to express a stronger belief in an afterlife, to report more frequent church attendance, and to engage in more religious reading. But work by Downey (1984) suggests that the relationship between religious belief and death anxiety may not be a simple linear one. He administered a well-constructed religiosity scale along with Boyar's Fear of Death Scale to a sample of 237 middle-class men and found no significant relationship between death fear and either religious affiliation or self-rated religiosity. Instead, he discovered a curvilinear relationship, such that men who were moderately religious felt more death anxiety than did either those who were believers or those who were nonbelievers. This implies that ambivalence of belief, rather than religiosity per se, is the critical variable affecting apprehension about dying. This interpretation is broadly compatible with Ingram and Leitner's (1989) findings that death threat was inversely correlated with religious orthodoxy and fanaticism and was positively correlated with a degree of religious ambivalence.

In a similar vein, Thorson and Powell (1990a) measured intrinsic religiosity (placement of faith in the center of one's life) as opposed to mere assessments of religious affiliation or church membership. They found that both age and intrinsic religiosity were associated negatively with death concern. In a separate factor-analytic study (Thorson & Powell, 1991), the authors examined the factors of death anxiety and religiosity among the elderly. They concluded that the older adults who had a high degree of intrinsic religiosity may have largely solved their existential problems and were looking forward to a life after this one—they were concerned that there is an afterlife, but it was not an issue that troubled them greatly. After the concern over an afterlife was accounted for, their fears of death were essentially the same as everybody else's. Bivens et al.'s (in press) work with gay and bisexual men at variable proximities to AIDS suggests that intrinsic religiosity may also ameliorate fears of death in this population, especially fears connected to an afterlife.

But religious beliefs also may have their drawbacks, as suggested by a study conducted by Florian and Kravetz (1983). These investigators administered the Fear of Personal Death Scale to 178 Israeli Jews, along with an established measure of religious practice. Although moderately religious respondents scored higher on some dimensions of death fear (e.g., concern over the consequences of one's death for one's family and friends), highly religious subjects scored higher on others (e.g., fear of punishment in the afterlife). Thus, it appears that more and less religious persons may have qualitatively, as well as quantitatively, different anxieties about death.

Even if a stable relationship between strength of religious conviction and death fear is beginning to be identified, its meaning is open to interpretation. For example, although religious belief may genuinely assuage death anxieties, it may also simply help repress them, because they may be incompatible with one's verbalized belief in a benign god. Kuzendorf (1985) has examined this issue in a fascinating study, where a series of face-valid questions concerning fear of death was administered to 50 college students under two conditions—when they were in a normal state of consciousness and when they were in a hypnotically induced trance. In the trance state, students were instructed to let their subconscious minds automatically write true answers to the same death anxiety questions they were asked when conscious. As predicted by the repression hypothesis, fear of inexistence was greater under hypnosis, and this effect was especially pronounced among students who had consciously professed a belief in an afterlife. This raises the possibility that some varieties of religious belief may merely suppress, rather than extinguish, fears about one's mortality.

Finally, it should be mentioned that religion may have other effects on people's attitudes toward death, aside from affecting their simple positivity or negativity. For example, Feifel and Nagy (1981) found that the more religious members of a diverse group of men displayed more consistent attitudes toward death, as measured by their multilevel assessment of death fear. This finding was reinforced by Neimeyer et al.'s (1986) finding that believers in an afterlife had more coherent and less uncertain understandings of death-related situations, irrespective of the positivity of these understandings. Thus, future work on the psychology of religion could include more sophisticated assessments of the structure of belief systems about death, which may vary considerably within as well as between members of particular denominations. Research in this area might also be broadened to include secular as well as religious "philosophies of death," which may be equally important in shaping individuals' emotional evaluations of their own mortality (Holcomb et al., 1993).

Maladjustment Because death fear, threat, and anxiety are by definition distressing, it is logical to ask whether they are related in any systematic way to other forms of psychological distress. A good deal of research has focused on this topic in the last 15 years, and the resulting evidence suggests a relationship between conscious death anxiety and broader maladjustment.

At a general level, Howells and Field (1982) administered a neuroticism scale and a measure of death anxiety to more than 300 medical and social science students and discovered a low but positive correlation between the two measures. These findings were reinforced by Loo's (1984) similar results with an undergraduate sample. Moreover, Vargo and Black (1984) found that the DAS correlated negatively with personality measures of well-being, self-control, and tolerance in a group of first-year medical students. Westman and Brackney (1990) studied the relationships among the neuroticism indices of the 16 Personality Factor Questionnaire (16 PF), denial, and the concept of death. Fear of death was associated with denial of death and proneness to guilt, but no relationship was found between fear of death and impulsivity or anxiety. Thus, these studies point to an association between death anxiety and neurotic symptoms, a finding that is compatible with the older literature in this area (Pollak, 1979).

Recent research has also established a connection between death concerns and more specific expressions of psychopathology. Not surprisingly, given the term *death anxiety* itself, much of this work has concentrated on a possible link to state and trait anxiety. In general, this research has indicated that subjects with exaggerated death anxiety (e.g., Conte et al., 1982; Gilliland & Templer, 1985; Hintze et al., 1994; Lonetto et al., 1980) fear (Loo, 1984), and threat (Tobacyk & Eckstein, 1980) also obtain higher scores on traditional anxiety scales, particularly those that assess its more characterological forms.

However, research indicates that the link between maladjustment and death concern also extends to a range of other forms of distress. For example, Amenta and Weiner (1981a) found that more death-anxious hospice workers displayed more frustration, suspiciousness, and guilt proneness, and Hintze et al. (1994) found depression to be a significant predictor of death anxiety in an HIV-infected population. But it is noteworthy that the pattern of association between fear of death and other psychological disorders may vary with the population being studied. This is illustrated by the factor-analytic work of Gilliland and Templer (1985), who found that general and death anxiety both loaded on the same factor in a normal population, but were sharply distinguished in a psychiatric comparison group. In the latter group, death anxiety was clearly separable from depression and anxiety, but it accounted for only 5% of the variation in this more disturbed group.

In some cases, the relationship between psychopathology and death anxiety can be methodologically problematic. Levin (1990), for example, conducted a sophisticated form of factor analysis on the dimensions of psychological disturbance assessed by the Minnesota Multiphasic Personality Inventory as related to the DAS, and found a very broad relationship between psychopathology and the primary factor derived from the DAS. In contrast, pure death anxiety emerged as only a minor factor of the latter instrument, raising doubts about its adequacy as a measure of death-specific attitudes. These results indirectly support the importance of examining the factor structure of commonly used measures, rather than assuming that their title adequately reflects their content.

Finally, the link between death anxiety and depression raises the possibility that death attitudes may play a role in suicidal behavior. To date, researchers have failed to find a consistent connection between death threat and suicide ideation, but this has remained a badly underinvestigated area. In a recent correlational study, D'Attilio and Campbell (1990) noted a significant relationship between scores on the DAS and the Suicide Probability Scale, suggesting that subjects who reported greater death anxiety had greater suicide risk. These results are less than definitive, however, insofar as both heightened suicidality and death anxiety may be the consequence of a third, unmeasured variable, such as psychological perturbation (see Chapter 14). Because suicide represents a tragic form of elective death, elucidating the relationship between death attitudes and self-destruction should be given greater priority in future work.

Self-Actualization   Just as interest has increased in the connection between death anxiety and maladjustment, interest has grown in the possible link between minimal death anxiety and optimal functioning. The occasional studies that addressed this issue prior to the late 1970s supported the view that more competent individuals with a greater sense of purpose in life experience less death anxiety (Pollak, 1979).

More recent research adds considerable weight to this conclusion. Several studies have been consistent in pointing to a negative correlation between measures of death fear and anxiety and high scores on such indices of self-actualization as the Purpose In Life Test (Amenta & Weiner, 1981b; Rappaport, Fossler, Bross, & Gilden, 1993), self-esteem scales (Davis et al., 1983; Davis et al., 1978), and various subscales of the Personal Orientation Inventory (Lester & Colvin, 1977; Vargo, 1980). Similar findings have emerged even when investigators initiated the study with contrary hypotheses. For example, Aronow, Rauchway, Peller, and DeVito (1980) administered the DAS and seven self-relevant measures to 117 college students to test the prediction that individuals who highly value themselves would be more afraid of death. Contrary to expectation, subjects who reported greater well-being scored lower on the DAS than did more self-devaluing subjects. Thus, the tendency of more actualized individuals to express minimal fear of death is one of the more extensively replicated findings in the literature.

One coherent line of research in this area stems from the work of Neimeyer and Chapman (1980). Basing their argument on existential philosophy, they hypothesized that individuals whose life projects were incomplete and whose current identities were discrepant with their ideals would show greater fear of death than would their more actualized peers. To test this hypothesis, they derived a self–ideal discrepancy measure from the TI and compared it to scores on the other death anxiety scales taken by 101 non-college-educated adults. As predicted, they found that subjects with less self–ideal discrepancy scored lower on the DAS and on the Death of Self and Death and Dying of Others subscales of the Collett–Lester scale. The only dimension of death concern on which the more and less actualized respondents did not differ was Dying of Self, an aspect of death anxiety that might be more related to apprehension about the pain of dying.

A replication of this study was performed by Wood and Robinson (1982). Administering the same questionnaires to an undergraduate sample, they found that highly actualized respondents scored lower on the Collett–Lester scale but not on the DAS. Moreover, of the Collett–Lester subscales, only Dying of Self failed to correlate with level of actualization, again fitting the pattern that Neimeyer and Chapman (1980) found. But Wood and Robinson also found that within the high-actualization group, subjects who were also more "integrated" (i.e., showed more compatibility or less threat in their construing of self and death) scored even lower on the Collett–Lester scale and DAS than did the equally actualized but less integrated comparison group. This suggested an additive hypothesis, with both factors contributing to the prediction of the individual's level of death anxiety. A follow-up test of this hypothesis provided support for this view (Robinson & Wood, 1983).

In a dramatic test of the robustness of the effect of actualization on death concern, Robinson and Wood (1984) then tested a group of 100 adult subjects, who varied in health status from quite healthy to seriously ill (e.g., diabetes and cancer). Perhaps counterintuitively, they found that health status was unrelated to level of death fear or anxiety. Actualization, on the other hand, correlated with scores on the DAS, as well as both the Death of Self and Dying of Self Collett–Lester scale. However, they were unable to demonstrate an additive effect between actualization and integration, contrary to their previous findings. A subsequent test of the additive hypothesis conducted by Neimeyer (1985a) also failed to uncover any interaction between the two variables in predicting death anxiety, although each was significantly related to different aspects of death fear. In combination, these studies reinforce the conclusion that actualization may be a powerful determinant of death anxiety, more powerful even than level of physical health or illness.

Temporal Orientation Compared with the relatively well-researched areas of religiosity, maladjustment, and self-actualization, other personality factors have received less attention in the thanatology literature. This is exemplified by the work on the relationship between temporal orientation and death anxiety. Reviewing the older literature in this area, Pollak (1979) concluded that anxious preoccupation with death was linked to tendencies to live in the past rather than the future, to eschew experimentation and change, and in general to choose safety over novelty in life. The few relevant studies that have been conducted in the last 15 years add little in the way of elaboration or qualification to this picture. Vargo and Batsel (1981) replicated the finding that subjects with less death anxiety adopt a more present orientation than those with greater death fears, and Neimeyer et al. (1986) reported that individuals with a greater personal fear of death and dying on the CL tended to "postpone" death cognitively by projecting a longer life expectancy. On the other hand, Joubert (1983) could establish no relationship between subjective acceleration of time and death anxiety as measured by the DAS. Thus, the relatively scant evidence that has accumulated suggests that death anxiety may be related more to a broader temporal orientation to past, present, and future than to a moment-to-moment sense of time passing, although this conclusion clearly stands in need of more empirical support.

A recent study in this area by Rappaport et al. (1993) is as interesting for its methodology as for its conclusions. To study the relationship between awareness of death and the subjective feeling of experienced time, they administered the DAS, the Purpose In Life Test and the Rappaport Time Line (RTL) to a group of 58 residents of a retirement community who were an average age of 73. The RTL procedure required subjects to represent their life in spatial terms on a 24-inch paper strip, marking that point on the time line that represented "the present," enclosing the point within brackets to represent their sense of the present, and then marking past and present important experiences on either side of the bracket. The investigators used these data to calculate subjects' *temporal extension* into the past (number of years from the "present" bracket to the first experience noted) and future (years from the "present" bracket to the last experience listed). They also scored the RTL for past, present, and future *temporal density* (number of events listed within each time zone). As hypothesized, temporal density in the present was found to correlate with death anxiety, which in turn correlated with diminished purpose in life. However, the predicted negative correlation between death anxiety and temporal extension failed to emerge, a finding that could be attributed to reliance on the DAS as a measure of death concern, the reduced future extension that reasonably could be expected in this elderly sample, or other confounding factors. Although the RTL procedure is new and hence has been used in few studies to date, it may be a feasible tool to use in studying life and death attitudes with other populations, such as children and adolescents, individuals experiencing midlife crises, and the severely ill.

Repression Thanatological interest in repression has waned somewhat, because direct questionnaires have attained virtual methodological hegemony in the death anxiety literature. But in line with the older literature (Pollak, 1979), there remains a lingering suspicion among researchers that low scores on death anxiety questionnaires may be obtained by subjects with repressive or defensive personality styles. This possibility has been given credence by a handful of studies. Tobacyk and Eckstein (1980) administered the TI and a repression–sensitization scale to more than 100 students and found that those with lower threat scores also scored as more extreme repressors. Using the DAS, Kane and Hogan (1985) found similar results in a group of physicians. Both of these studies offer at least correlational support for the proposition that reduced death anxiety may be a function of a defensive personality style aimed at avoiding, rather than confronting, threatening stimuli.

Two experimental studies also have examined the repression–death anxiety link. The first, by Handal (1980), involved 159 female college students in a hypothetical life-or-death problem-solving task under group and individual conditions. He discovered that subjects with low death anxiety performed better in the latter but not the former condition and interpreted this as evidence that they effectively repressed extraneous stimuli under the "simpler" instructional set. The more parsimonious interpretation—that the poorer showing of the group with a high degree of death anxiety reflected the disruptive effects of anxiety—was not entertained. Consequently, the conclusion that low scorers were repressors remains dubious, although the study does represent one of the few attempts to use a genuine experimental design in this area.

The second experiment, by Kuzendorf (1985), yielded clearer conclusions. As noted earlier in the discussion of the relationship between religiosity and death concern, Kuzendorf used hypnotic suggestion to instruct subjects to write automatically their true reactions to death anxiety questions and discovered that greater anxiety was revealed than when the same subjects completed a normal test-taking set. To the extent that the trance state permitted Kuzendorf to circumvent his subjects' usual defenses in responding to questions about their fears of inexistence, this study raises important questions about the interpretation of low death anxiety scores. At a methodological level, it suggests that future researchers need to distinguish between individuals who express little death anxiety as a result of repressing their death fear and those who are genuinely unafraid of their mortality. At a theoretical level, it could be seen as supporting Firestone's (1994) conceptualization of freedom from death anxiety as a consequence of a defensive, but life-inhibiting style. Because this issue goes to the heart of the study of death anxiety—whether death anxiety is a "good" or "bad" thing—the link between death anxiety and repression deserves more sophisticated study.

CHANGES IN DEATH ANXIETY AS A RESULT OF DEATH EDUCATION

As Warren (1982) observed, many death education programs have at least implicitly adopted the reduction of death anxiety as a primary goal, and this goal has occasionally been met. Tobacyk and Eckstein (1980), for instance, were able to demonstrate that a semester-long undergraduate thanatology course produced a greater decrease in death threat than did unrelated course work, even though death education students had lower TI scores than controls at the outset. But even in studies in which an antianxiety effect has been found, it has not necessarily generalized across instruments. For example, Rosenthal (1983) administered both the DAS and an independent 3 factor scale to a class of death education students and controls before and after their 5-week courses. She found that, across time, thanatology students showed reduced death avoidance, disengagement, and death fear on the 3 factor inventory but no comparable changes on the DAS. This suggests that when changes in death anxiety result from educational experiences, they may be limited in their generality.

Perhaps a more common finding is that such interventions have no predictable impact on death attitudes at all. Several studies of interventions as diverse as brief death awareness exercises (Rigdon & Epting, 1985), professional workshops (McClam, 1980), counseling groups (Bohart & Bergland, 1979), and behavior therapy (Testa, 1981) have failed to produce any mean change in death threat and anxiety in their experimental groups. But the failure to detect a *mean* effect in these studies cannot be taken as evidence that the interventions had *no* effect. This point was vividly illustrated in a study by Rainey and Epting (1977), who found that although students' average score on the TI did not change across the course of a semester of death education, the *variance* of their scores increased threefold. No such change occurred in control group subjects. In other words, death education seemed to destabilize students' construing of themselves in relation to death, but whether this resulted in their experiencing increased or decreased death threat was a highly individual matter. The reality of negative (i.e., anxiety-provoking) outcomes should be taken seriously, because some researchers have actually reported that death fears were aggravated by death education (Wittmaier, 1980), especially in sensitive medical contexts (Hayslip & Walling, 1985; Mullins &

Merriam, 1983). It may be that students with higher levels of self-efficacy in dealing with death may be better prepared to benefit from, rather than be traumatized by, death education efforts (Robbins, 1994).

In examining death education curricula, it is helpful to draw a distinction between courses that are didactic and those that are primarily experiential in nature (Durlak, 1978). In a quantitative review of this area, Durlak and Reisenberg (1991) analyzed 47 studies of death education published between 1975 and 1987. Typical didactic programs were primarily based on reading and lectures and used audiovisual aids as a part of a classroom activity. Experiential programs typically involved visiting cemeteries or mortuaries, witnessing interviews with the terminally ill, and engaging in role play or other personal awareness exercises. Results were coded for separate outcome domains, described as affective, cognitive, personality, and behavioral change. In general, cognitive and behavioral changes were moderately large across types of educational intervention, whereas the affective impact of interventions varied as a function of program type. In comparing the two styles of death education, Durlak and Reisenberg observed that the experiential groups generally produced a modest decrease in death fears and anxieties, whereas the didactic groups tended to show an increase in discomfort with death. The reader interested in an enlarged understanding of the *functions* of death attitudes and factors that facilitate their educational modification is encouraged to consult Durlak's (1994) thoughtful analysis of the topic.

The variability of findings through the years suggests that the anxiety reduction model of death education may be inadequate to deal with the complex personal meanings with which different persons shroud death. Examined from a different angle, the findings also remind us of the limits of our understanding of death anxiety and the factors that influence it. Although much has been learned about death anxiety and its correlates, perhaps the most important lessons concern the limitations of the research conducted to date. As a constructive response to these shortcomings, a few observations are given to guide future research in this area.

SUMMARY AND RECOMMENDATIONS
FOR FUTURE RESEARCH

A fair evaluation of the current state of death anxiety research yields a more optimistic conclusion than did similar evaluations written 15 years ago. As a result of the increase in both the quality and quantity of this literature, more is known about the demographic and situational correlates of death anxiety. There is now ample evidence that women express more fear of personal death than men do, although the explanation for this sex difference is not clear. In addition, we are beginning to realize that death orientation is anything but stable across the course of adult development and instead shifts into increased comfort with mortality in later life, at least among relatively healthy respondents. There are also data indicating that although the pursuit of death-exposure professions such as medicine does not necessarily predict the level of death fear, individuals with exaggerated anxiety about death may enact their professional roles differently than their less anxious co-workers, perhaps to the detriment of their patients. Conversely, at least some professionals and volunteers who successfully work with the dying show reduced death fear and greater death competency. Fear of death may be enhanced in other occupations, however, especially those that entail actual death risk to the worker. Interestingly, health status does not seem to be a potent predictor of death anxiety, perhaps because of the individualized ways in which people adapt to illness.

Substantial numbers of studies have also established connections between personality factors and attitudes toward death. In general, individuals with strong intrinsic religious beliefs tend to report less death anxiety, although the extent to which this is the result of repression is difficult to estimate. Good evidence now supports the view that fear of death is often associated with other forms of psychological maladjustment, particularly anxiety and depression. Conversely, the more self-actualized people are, the more comfortable with their mortality they are likely to be. The literature also hints that a person's apprehension about his or her eventual death is associated with a tendency to "postpone" its occurrence cognitively and to focus instead on past or present events.

Finally, we are starting to recognize that people's fears of death are not easily altered by even well-intentioned educational interventions, although such programs may be more effective at stimulating cognitive or behavioral change. In fact, there is evidence that death education may sometimes arouse death anxiety rather than dampen it. The current movement to discriminate between the effects of various didactic and experiential interventions is encouraging, however. Studies of death education should sensitize thanatologists to the complex and poorly understood processes by which people develop their personal philosophies of life and death in response to relevant life experiences.

Despite this substantial literature, many of even the best researched areas contain unanswered questions. To a large degree, this reflects certain persistent methodological inadequacies in the study of death anxiety. For the sake of clarity, these can be addressed in terms of *regressive* and *progressive* trends in the literature, as summarized in Table 1. For example, many researchers continue to rely on small, easily accessible samples, which limit the generalizability of their findings to a broader population. In contrast, a growing number of investigators have begun to recruit large, often community-based samples and control groups (Brockopp, King, & Hamilton, 1991; DePaola et al., 1992; Viney, Henry, Walker, & Crooks, 1991), sometimes using sophisticated stratified sampling techniques (e.g., Kalish, 1977). The latter approach not only permits more confident generalization of results, but also enables meaningful comparisons of subgroups of respondents within the larger design.

Past research has also been regressive at the level of research design. Too many researchers seem to perform studies on an opportunistic basis, making too little contact with the extant literature and hence doing little to advance what is already known. In contrast, several investigators (Neimeyer, 1994a; Thorson &

Table 1   Regressive and Progressive Trends in Research on Death Attitudes

Aspect of research	Regressive	Progressive
Sampling techniques	Small, idiosyncratic samples	Substantial, generalizable samples
	Convenience sampling	Systematic (e.g., stratified) sampling
Design	Shotgun studies	Programmatic studies
	Correlational designs	(Quasi-)experimental designs
Instrumentation	Unidimensional assessment	Multidimensional assessment
	Focus on anxiety	Focus on broader range of attitudes
Analysis	A priori clustering of items	Factor-analytic clustering of items
	Correlational designs	Multiple regression analysis
Hypothesis generation	Intuitive	Theory guided
	Socially irrelevant	Socially significant

Powell, 1994; Wong et al., 1994) have conducted a series of programmatic studies that address basic methodological and substantive issues in a more progressive fashion, building on what is known and reaching forward toward that which remains obscure. Particularly when such studies make use of more sophisticated experimental or quasiexperimental designs (Firth-Cozens & Field, 1991), they hold promise of extending thanatologists' understanding of the causes and consequences of death anxiety.

As this review indicates, there has been a general shift in the last 15 years from a regressive reliance on unvalidated, unidimensional assessments of death concerns toward the more consistent use of validated, reliable measures that tap multiple aspects of death anxiety. However, investigators still tend to focus preemptively on negative death attitudes (e.g., anxiety, fear, and threat), rather than on a fuller range of responses (e.g., death acceptance or death-related coping skills). The recent development of psychometrically sound measures of the latter variety (e.g., Robbins, 1994; Wong et al., 1994) should stimulate more broad-based and progressive research.

The bulk of death anxiety research has also been constrained by an apparent lack of analytical sophistication, lending to the continued (but diminishing) use of a priori groupings of items to measure some presumed facet of death fear (e.g., fear of death vs. fear of dying). However, more investigators have begun to make appropriate use of more sophisticated factor-analytic procedures to construct instrument subscales, sometimes using state-of-the-art confirmatory techniques (Moore & Neimeyer, 1991). Less progress has been made in other aspects of data analysis, with simple correlation procedures between pairs of instruments still representing the modal choice of investigators, even when more elaborate multiple regression designs (Bivens et al., 1994; Frazier & Foss-Goodman, 1988; Robbins, 1989) would be more informative.

Finally, too many researchers continue to test only intuitively plausible hypotheses, rather than grounding investigations in coherent theories of death anxiety, be they philosophical, psychological, or sociological in orientation (see

Tomer, 1994, for an excellent summary of these perspectives). Similarly, most studies are regressive in the sense that they are irrelevant to the more pressing problems of living with death, as detailed elsewhere throughout this book. However, there are encouraging signs of increasing social or real-world relevance in this literature, as researchers begin to study the beneficial emotional impact of such psychosocial interventions as hospice care for the dying (Hendon & Epting, 1989) and offering elderly patients a measure of choice in nursing home placement (Thorson, 1988).

As scientific research on the psychology of death enters its fifth decade, thanatologists are presented with the opportunity to base their future work not only on the findings of the accumulated studies, but also on a keener appreciation of their limitations, so that the fifth decade of research will be stronger than the preceding four. How to understand death is one of the most ancient and persistent questions that human begins have framed. If reasking this question in the context of current psychological research is to yield fresh answers, then thanatologists need to be as systematic and articulate in their questioning as possible.

REFERENCES

Alexander, I. E., & Alderstein, A. M. (1958). Affective responses to the concept of death in a population of children and early adolescents. *Journal of Genetic Psychology, 93,* 167–177.

Amenta, M. M. (1984). Death anxiety, purpose in life and duration of service in hospice volunteers. *Psychological Reports, 54,* 979–984.

Amenta, M. M., & Weiner, A. W. (1981a). Death anxiety and general anxiety in hospice workers. *New England Journal of Medicine, 49,* 962.

Amenta, M. M., & Weiner, A. W. (1981b). Death anxiety and purpose in life in hospice workers. *Psychological Reports, 49,* 920.

Aronow, E., Rauchway, A., Peller, M., & DeVito, A. (1980). The value of the self in relation to fear of death. *Omega, 11,* 37–44.

Becker, E. (1973). *The denial of death.* New York: Macmillan.

Bivens, A. J., Neimeyer, R. A., Kirchberg, T. M., & Moore, M. K. (in press). Death concern and religious belief among gays and bisexuals of variable proximity to AIDS. *Omega.*

Bohart, J., & Bergland, B. W. (1979). The impact of death and dying counseling groups on death anxiety in college students. *Death Education, 2,* 381–391.

Brent, S. B., Speece, M. W., Gates, M. F., Mood, D., & Kaul, M. (1991). The contribution of death-related experiences to health care providers' attitudes toward dying patients: I. Graduate and undergraduate nursing students. *Omega, 23,* 249–278.

Brockopp, D. Y., King, D. B., & Hamilton, J. E. (1991). The dying patient: A comparative study of nurse caregiver characteristics. *Death Studies, 15,* 245–258.

Catania, J. A., Turner, H. A., Choi, K.-h., & Coates, T. J. (1992). Coping with death anxiety: Help-seeking and social support among gay men with various HIV diagnoses. *AIDS, 6,* 999–1005.

Chambers, W. V. (1986). Inconsistencies in the theory of death threat. *Death Studies, 10,* 165–175.

Choron, J. (1974). *Death and modern man.* New York: Macmillan.

Collett, L. J., & Lester, D. (1969). The fear of death and the fear of dying. *Journal of Psychology, 72,* 179–181.

Conte, H. R., Weiner, M. B., & Plutchik, R. (1982). Measuring death anxiety: Conceptual, psychometric and factor analytic aspects. *Journal of Personality and Social Psychology, 43,* 775–785.

Dattel, A. R., & Neimeyer, R. A. (1990). Sex differences in death anxiety: Testing the emotional expressiveness hypothesis. *Death Studies, 14,* 1–11.

D'Attilio, J. P., & Campbell, B. (1990). Relationship between death anxiety and suicide potential in an adolescent population. *Psychological Reports, 67,* 975–978.

Davis, S. F., Bremer, S. A., Anderson, B. J., & Tramill, J. L. (1983). The interrelationships of ego strength, self-esteem, death anxiety and gender in undergraduate college students. *Journal of General Psychology, 108,* 55–59.

Davis, S. F., Martin, D. A., Wilee, C. T., & Voorhees, J. W. (1978). Relationship of fear of death and level of self-esteem in college students. *Psychological Reports, 42,* 419–422.

DePaola, S. J., Neimeyer, R. A., Lupfer, M. B., & Fiedler, J. (1992). Death concern and attitudes toward the elderly in nursing home personnel. *Death Studies, 16,* 537–555.

Devins, G. M. (1979). Death anxiety and voluntary passive euthanasia. *Journal of Consulting and Clinical Psychology 47,* 301–309.

Dodds, J., & Lin, C. D. (1992). Chinese teenagers' concerns about the future: A cross-national comparison. *Adolescence, 27,* 481–486.

Downey, A. M. (1984). Relationship of religiosity to death anxiety in middle aged males. *Psychological Reports, 54,* 811–822.

Durlak, J. A. (1978). Comparison between experiential and didactic methods of death education. *Omega, 9,* 57–66.

Durlak, J. A. (1982). Using the Templer scale to assess "death anxiety": A cautionary note. *Psychological Reports, 50,* 1257–1258.

Durlak, J. A. (1994). Changing death attitudes through death education. In R. A. Neimeyer (Ed.), *Death anxiety handbook: Research, instrumentation, and application* (pp. 243–260). Washington, DC: Taylor & Francis.

Durlak, J. A., Horn, W., & Kass, R. A. (1990). A self-administering assessment of personal meanings of death: Report on the revised Twenty Statements Test. *Omega, 21,* 301–309.

Durlak, J. A., & Riesenberg, L. A. (1991). The impact of death education. *Death Studies, 15,* 39–58.

Eakes, G. G. (1985). The relationship between death anxiety and attitudes toward the elderly among nursing staff. *Death Studies, 9,* 163–172.

Eggerman, S., & Dustin, D. (1985). Death orientation and communication with the terminally ill. *Omega, 16,* 255–265.

Epting, F. R., Rainey, L. C., & Weiss, M. J. (1979). Constructions of death and levels of death fear. *Death Education, 3,* 21–30.

Feifel, H., Hanson, S., Jones, R., & Edwards, L. (1967, September). *Physicians consider death.* Paper presented at the 75th Annual Convention of the American Psychological Association, Washington, DC.

Feifel, H., & Nagy, V. T. (1980). Death orientation and life-threatening behavior. *Journal of Abnormal Psychology, 89,* 38–45.

Feifel, H., & Nagy, V. T. (1981). Another look at fear of death. *Journal of Consulting and Clinical Psychology 49,* 278–286.

Field, D., & Howells, K. (1985). Medical students' self-reported worries about aspects of death and dying. *Death Studies, 10,* 147–154.

Firestone, R. W. (1994). Psychological defenses against death anxiety. In R. A. Neimeyer (Ed.), *Death anxiety handbook: Research, instrumentation, and application* (pp. 217–241). Washington, DC: Taylor & Francis.

Firth-Cozens, J., & Field, D. (1991). Fear of death and strategies of coping with patient death among medical trainees. *British Journal of Medical Psychology, 64,* 263–271.

Florian, V., & Kravetz, S. (1983). Fear of personal death: Attribution, structure and relation to religious belief. *Journal of Personality and Social Psychology, 44,* 600–607.

Frazier, P. H., & Foss-Goodman, D. (1988). Death anxiety and personality: Are they related? *Omega, 19,* 265–274.

Fry, P. S. (1990). A factor analytic investigation of home-bound elderly individuals' concerns about death and dying, and their coping responses. *Journal of Clinical Psychology, 46,* 737–748.

Gerber, L. A. (1990). Integrating political-societal concerns in psychotherapy. *American Journal of Psychotherapy, 44,* 471–483.

Gesser, G., Wong, P. T. P., & Reker, G. T. (1987). Death attitudes across the life-span: the development and validation of the death attitude profile. *Omega, 18,* 113–128.

Gilliland, J. C., & Templer, D. I. (1985). Relationship of death anxiety scale factors to subjective states. *Omega, 16,* 155–167.

Given, J. E., & Range, L. M. (1990). Life satisfaction and death anxiety in elderly nursing home and public housing residents. *Journal of Applied Gerontology, 9,* 224–229.

Greyson, B. (1992). Reduced death threat in near-death experiencers. *Death Studies, 16,* 523–536.

Handal, P. J. (1980). Individual and group problem solving and type of orientation as a function of high, moderate, and low death anxiety. *Omega, 10,* 365–377.

Hayslip, B., Luhr, D. D., & Beyerlein, M. M. (1991). Levels of death anxiety in terminally ill men: A pilot study. *Omega, 24,* 13–19.

Hayslip, B., & Walling, M. L. (1985). Impact of hospice volunteer training on death anxiety and locus of control. *Omega, 16,* 243–254.

Hendon, M., & Epting, F. R. (1989). A comparison of hospice patients with other recovering and ill patients. *Death Studies, 13,* 567–578.

Hintze, J., Templer, D. I., Cappelletty, G. C., & Frederick, W. (1994). Death depression and death anxiety in HIV-infected males. In R. A. Neimeyer (Ed.), *Death anxiety handbook: Research, instrumentation, and application* (pp. 193–200). Washington, DC: Taylor & Francis.

Hoelter, J. W. (1979). Multidimensional treatment of fear of death. *Journal of Consulting and Clinical Psychology, 47,* 996–999.

Holcomb, L. E., Neimeyer, R. A., & Moore, M. K. (1993). Personal meanings of death: A content analysis of free-response narratives. *Death studies, 17,* 299–318.

Howells, K., & Field, D. (1982). Fear of death and dying among medical students. *Social Science and Medicine, 16,* 1421–1424.

Hunt, D. M., Lester, D., & Ashton, N. (1983). Fear of death, locus of control and occupation. *Psychological Reports, 53,* 1022.

Ingram, B. J., & Leitner, L. M. (1989). Death threat, religiosity, and fear of death. *International Journal of Personal Construct Psychology, 2,* 199–214.

Johnson, J. C. (1980). Death anxiety of rehabilitation counselors and clients. *Psychological Reports, 46,* 325–326.

Joubert, C. E. (1983). Subjective acceleration of time: Death anxiety and sex differences. *Psychological Reports, 57,* 49–50.

Kalish, R. A. (1977). The role of age in death attitudes. *Death Education, 1,* 205–230.

Kane, A. C., & Hogan, J. D. (1985). Death anxiety in physicians: Defensive style, medical specialty, and exposure to death. *Omega, 16,* 11–22.

Kastenbaum, R., & Costa, P. T. (1977). Psychological perspectives on death. *Annual Review of Psychology, 28,* 22–249.

Keefe, T. W. (1992). The human family and its children under the nuclear addiction. *International Social Work, 35,* 65–77.

Keller, J. W., Sherry, D., & Piotrowski, D. (1984). Perspectives in death: A developmental study. *Journal of Psychology, 116,* 137–142.

Krieger, S. R., Epting, F. R., & Hays, L. H. (1979). Validity and reliability of provided constructs in assessing death threat. *Omega, 10,* 87–95.

Krieger, S. R., Epting, F. R., & Leitner, L. M. (1974). Personal constructs, threat, and attitudes toward death. *Omega, 5,* 299–310.

Kübler-Ross, E. (1969). *On death and dying.* New York: Macmillan.

Kureshi, A., & Husain, A. (1981). Death anxiety in intrapunitiveness among smokers and nonsmokers: A comparative study. *Journal of Psychological Research, 25,* 42–45.

Kuzendorf, R. G. (1985). Repressed fear of inexistence and its hypnotic recovery in religious students. *Omega, 16,* 23–33.

Lester, D. (1967). Fear of death of suicidal persons. *Psychological Reports, 20,* 1077–1078.

Lester, D. (1994). The Collett–Lester Fear of Death Scale. In R. A. Neimeyer (Ed.), *Death anxiety handbook: Research, instrumentation, and application* (pp. 45–60). Washington, DC: Taylor & Francis.

Lester, D., & Colvin, L. M. (1977). Fear of death, alienation and self-actualization. *Psychological Reports, 41,* 526.

Levin, R. (1990). A reexamination of the dimensionality of death anxiety. *Omega, 20,* 341–349.

Lonetto, R., Fleming, S., & Mercer, G. W. (1979). The structure of death anxiety: A factor analytic study. *Journal of Personality Assessment, 43.*

Lonetto, R., Mercer, G. W., Fleming, S., Bunting, B., & Clare, M. (1980). Death anxiety among university students in Northern Ireland and Canada. *Journal of Psychology, 104,* 75–82.

Lonetto, R., & Templer, D. I. (1986). *Death anxiety.* Washington, DC: Hemisphere.

Long, D. D. (1985). A cross-cultural examination of fears of death among Saudi Arabians. *Omega, 16,* 43–50.

Loo, R. (1984). Personality correlates of the Fear of Death and Dying Scale. *Journal of Clinical Psychology, 40,* 120–122.

MacInnes, W. D., & Neimeyer, R. A. (1980). Internal consistency of the Threat Index. *Death Education, 4,* 193–194.

Martin, T. O. (1982). Death anxiety and social desirability among nurses. *Omega, 13,* 51–58.

McClam, T. (1980). Death anxiety before and after death education: Negative results. *Psychological Reports, 46,* 513–514.

McMordie, W. R. (1978). Improving measurement of death anxiety. *Psychological Reports, 44,* 975–980.

McMordie, W. R., & Kumar, A. (1984). Cross-cultural research on the Templer/McMordie Death Anxiety Scale. *Psychological Reports, 54,* 959–963.

Meshot, C. M., & Leitner, L. M. (1994). Death threat, parental loss, and interpersonal style. In R. A. Neimeyer (Ed.), *Death anxiety handbook: Research, instrumentation, and application* (pp. 181–191). Washington, DC: Taylor & Francis.

Moore, M. K., & Neimeyer, R. A. (1991). A confirmatory factor analysis of the Threat Index. *Journal of Personality and Social Psychology, 60,* 122–129.

Mount, E. (1983). Individualism and fears of death. *Death Education, 7,* 25–31.

Mulkay, M. (1980). The sociology of science in east and west. *Current Sociology, 28,* 1–184.

Mullins, L. C., & Lopez, M. A. (1982). Death anxiety among nursing home residents: A comparison of the young-old and the old-old. *Death Education, 6,* 75–86.

Mullins, L. C., & Merriam, S. (1983). The effects of a short-term death training program on nursing home staff. *Death Education, 7,* 353–368.

Neimeyer, R. A. (1985a). Actualization, intergration and fear of death: A test of the additive model. *Death Studies, 9,* 235–250.

Neimeyer, R. A. (1985b). *The development of personal construct psychology.* Lincoln, NE: University of Nebraska Press.

Neimeyer, R. A. (1986). The threat hypothesis: A conceptual and empirical defense. *Death Studies, 10,* 177–190.

Neimeyer, R. A. (1988). Death anxiety. In H. Wass, F. Berardo, & R. A. Neimeyer (Eds.), *Dying: Facing the facts* (2nd ed., pp. 97–136). Washington, DC: Hemisphere.

Neimeyer, R. A. (1994a). The Threat Index and related methods. In R. A. Neimeyer (Ed.), *Death anxiety handbook: Research, instrumentation, and application.* (pp. 61–101). Washington, DC: Taylor & Francis.

Neimeyer, R. A. (Ed.) (1994b). *Death anxiety handbook: Research, instrumentation, and application.* Washington, DC: Taylor & Francis.

Neimeyer, R. A., Bagley, K. J., & Moore, M. K. (1986). Cognitive structure and death anxiety. *Death Studies, 10,* 273–288.

Neimeyer, R. A., & Chapman, K. M. (1980). Self/ideal discrepancy and fear of death: The test of an existential hypothesis. *Omega, 11,* 233–240.

Neimeyer, R. A., & Dingemans, P. (1980). Death orientation in the suicide intervention worker. *Omega, 11,* 15–23.

Neimeyer, R. A., Dingemans, P., & Epting, F. R. (1977). Convergent validity, situational stability and meaningfulness of the Threat Index. *Omega, 8,* 251–265.

Neimeyer, R. A., Fontana, D. J., & Gold, K. (1984). A manual for content analysis of death constructs. In F. R. Epting & R. A. Neimeyer (Eds.), *Personal meanings of death* (pp. 213–234). Washington, DC: Hemisphere.

Neimeyer, R. A., & MacInnes, W. D. (1981). Assessing paraprofessional competence with the Suicide Intervention Response Inventory. *Journal of Counseling Psychology, 28,* 176–179.

Neimeyer, R. A., & Moore, M. K. (1989). Assessing personal meanings of death: Empirical refinements in the Threat Index. *Death Studies, 13,* 227–245.

Neimeyer, R. A., & Moore, M. K. (1994). Validity and reliability of the Multidimensional Fear of Death Scale. In R. A. Neimeyer (Ed.), *Death anxiety handbook: Research, instrumentation, and application* (pp. 103–119). Washington, DC: Taylor & Francis.

Neimeyer, R. A., & Neimeyer, G. J. (1984). Death anxiety and counseling skill in the suicide interventionist. *Suicide and Life-Threatening Behavior, 14,* 126–131.

Neimeyer, R. A., & Pfeiffer, A. M. (1994). Evaluation of suicide intervention effectiveness. *Death Studies, 18,* 127–162.

Nelson, L. D. (1979). Structural conduciveness, personality characteristics and death anxiety. *Omega, 10,* 123–133.

Pollak, J. M. (1979). Correlates of death anxiety: A review of empirical studies. *Omega, 10,* 97–121.

Pratt, C. C., Hare, J., & Wright, C. (1985). Death anxiety and comfort in teaching about death among preschool teachers. *Death Studies, 9,* 417–425.

Prichard, S., & Epting, F. R. (1992). Diversity from simplicity: A review of the Threat Index. *Omega, 25,* 249–257.

Rainey, L. C., & Epting, F. R. (1977). Death threat constructions in the student and the prudent. *Omega, 8,* 19–28.

Rappaport, H., Fossler, R., Bross, L., & Gilden, D. (1993). Future time, death anxiety, and life purpose among older adults. *Death Studies, 17,* 369–399.

Rhudick, P. J., & Dibner, A. S. (1961). Age, personality, and health correlates of death concern in normal aged individuals. *Journal of Gerontology, 16,* 44–49.

Rigdon, M. A. (1983). Levels of death fear: A factor analysis. *Death Education, 6,* 365–373.

Rigdon, M. A., & Epting, F. R. (1985). Reduction in death threat as a basis for optimal functioning. *Death Studies, 9,* 427–448.

Robbins, R. A. (1989). Gender and sex-role stereotypes in scales of death concern. *Death Studies, 13,* 579–591.

Robbins, R. A. (1992). Death competency: A study of hospice volunteers. *Death Studies, 16,* 557–569.

Robbins, R. A. (1994). Death competency: Bugen's Coping with Death Scale and Death Self-Efficacy. In R. A. Neimeyer (Ed.), *Death anxiety handbook: Research, instrumentation, and application* (pp. 149–165). Washington, DC: Taylor & Francis.

Robinson, P. J., & Wood, K. (1983). The Threat Index: An additive approach. *Omega, 14,* 139–144.

Robinson, P. J., & Wood, K. (1984). Fear of death and physical illness. A personal construct approach. In F. Epting & R. A. Neimeyer (Eds.), *Personal meanings of death* (pp. 127–142). Washington, DC: Hemisphere.

Rockwell, F. P. A. (1981). Death anxiety: Comparison of psychiatrists, psychologists, suicidologists and funeral directors. *Psychological Reports, 49,* 979–982.

Roediger, H. L. (1990). Implicit memory: Retention without remembering. *American Psychologist, 45,* 1043–1056.

Rosenthal, N. R. (1983). Death education and suicide potentiality. *Death Education, 7,* 39–51.

Sadowski, C. J., Davis, S. F., & Loftus-Vergari, M. C. (1979). Locus of control and death anxiety: A reexamination. *Omega, 10,* 203–210.

Sanders, J. F., Poole, T. E., & Rivero, W. T. (1980). Death anxiety among the elderly. *Psychological Reports, 46,* 53–56.

Schell, B. H., & Zinger, J. T. (1984). Death anxiety scale means and standard deviations for Ontario undergraduates and funeral directors. *Psychological Reports, 54,* 439–446.

Schulz, R., & Aderman, D. (1979). Physicians' death anxiety and patient outcomes. *Omega, 9,* 327–332.

Schumaker, J. F., Barraclough, R. A., & Vagg, L. M. (1987). Death anxiety in Malaysian and Australian university students. *Journal of Social Psychology, 128,* 41–47.

Simpson, M. A. (1980). Studying death: Problems of methodology. *Death Education, 4,* 139–148.

Stevens, S. J., Cooper, P. E., & Thomas, L. E. (1980). Age norms for the Templer's Death Anxiety Scale. *Psychological Reports, 46,* 205–206.

Stillion, J. M. (1985). *Death and the sexes.* Washington, DC: Hemisphere.

Tamm, M. E., & Granqvist, A. (in press). The meaning of death for children and adolescents: A phenomenographic study of drawings. *Death Studies.*

Templer, D. I. (1970). The construction and validation of a death anxiety scale. *Journal of General Psychology, 82,* 165–177.

Testa, J. (1981). Group systematic desensitization and implosive therapy for death anxiety. *Psychological Reports, 48,* 376–378.

Thorson, J. A. (1988). Relocation of the elderly: Some implications from the research. *Gerontology Review, 1,* 29–36.

Thorson, J. A., & Powell, F. C., (1988). Elements of death anxiety and meanings of death. *Journal of Clinical Psychology, 44,* 691–701.

Thorson, J. A., & Powell, F. C. (1990a). Meanings of death and intrinsic religiosity. *Journal of Clinical Psychology, 46,* 379–391.

Thorson, J. A., & Powell, F. C. (1990b). Medical students' attitudes towards aging and death: A cross-sequential study. *Medical Education, 25,* 32–37.

Thorson, J. A., & Powell, F. C. (1991). Constructions of death among those high in intrinsic religious motivation: A factor analytic study. *Death Studies, 15,* 131–138.

Thorson, J. A., & Powell, F. C. (1992). A Revised Death Anxiety Scale. *Death Studies, 16,* 507–521.

Thorson, J. A., & Powell, F. C. (1994). A Revised Death Anxiety Scale. In R. A. Neimeyer (Ed.), *Death anxiety handbook: Research, instrumentation, and application* (pp. 31–43). Washington, DC: Taylor & Francis.

Tobacyk, J., & Eckstein, D. (1980). Death threat and death concerns in the college student. *Omega, 11,* 139–155.

Tokunuga, H. T. (1985). The effect of bereavement upon death related attitudes and fears. *Omega, 16,* 267–380.

Tomer, A. (1994). Death anxiety in adult life: Theoretical perspectives. In R. A. Neimeyer (Ed.), *Death anxiety handbook: Research, instrumentation, and application* (pp. 3–28). Washington, DC: Taylor & Francis.

Ungar, L., Florian, V., & Zernitsky-Shurka, E. (1990). Aspects of fear of personal death, levels of awareness, and professional affiliation among dialysis unit staff members. *Omega, 21,* 51–67.

Vargo, M. (1980). Relationship between the Templer Death Anxiety Scale and the Collett-Lester Fear of Death Scale. *Psychological Reports, 46,* 561–562.

Vargo, M. E., & Batsel, W. M. (1981). Relationship between death anxiety and components of the self-actualization process. *Psychological Reports, 48,* 89–90.

Vargo, M. E., & Black, W. F. (1984). Psychosocial correlates of death anxiety in a population of medical students. *Psychological Reports, 54,* 737–738.

Viney, L. L. (1984). Concerns about death among severely ill people. In F. R. Epting & R. A. Neimeyer (Eds.), *Personal meanings of death* (pp. 143–158). Washington, DC: Hemisphere.

Viney, L. L., Henry, R. M., Walker, B. M., & Crooks, L. (1991). The psychosocial impact of multiple deaths from AIDS. *Omega, 24,* 151–163.

Wagner, K. D., & Lorion, R. P. (1984). Correlates of death anxiety in elderly persons. *Journal of Clinical Psychology, 40,* 1235–1241.

Walkey, F. W. (1982). The Multidimensional Fear of Death Scale: An independent analysis. *Journal of Consulting and Clinical Psychology, 50,* 466–467.

Warren, W. G. (1982). Personal construction of death and death education. *Death Education, 6,* 17–28.
Warren, W. G., & Chopra, P. N. (1978). Some reliability and validity considerations on Australian data from the Death Anxiety Scale. *Omega, 9,* 293–299.
Warren, W., & Chopra, P. (1979a). Physicians and death: Some Australian data. *Medical Journal of Australia,* March, 191–193.
Warren, W. G., & Chopra, P. N. (1979b). An Australian survey of attitudes to death. *Australian Journal of Social Issues, 14,* 134–142.
Wass, H., Corr, C. A., Pacholski, R. A., & Forfar, C. S. (1985). *Death Education II: An annotated resource guide.* Washington, DC: Hemisphere.
Wass, H., & Forfar, C. S. (1982). Assessment of attitudes toward death. *Measurement and Evaluation in Guidance, 15,* 210–220.
Westman, A. S., & Brackney, B. E. (1990). Relationships between indices of neuroticism, attitudes toward and concepts of death, and religiosity. *Psychological Reports, 66,* 1039–1043.
Wittmaier, B. C. (1980). Some unexpected attitudinal consequences of a short course on death. *Omega, 10,* 271–275.
Wong, P. T., Reker, G. T., & Gesser, G. (1994). Death Attitude Profile–Revised. In R. A. Neimeyer (Ed.), *Death anxiety handbook: Research, instrumentation, and application* (pp. 121–148). Washington, DC: Taylor & Francis.
Wood, K., & Robinson, P. J. (1982). Actualization and the fear of death: Retesting an existential hypothesis. *Essence, 5,* 235–243.
Young, M., & Daniels, S. (1980). Born again status as a factor in death anxiety. *Psychological Reports, 47,* 367–370.

Chapter 4

The Dying Process

Nelda Samarel

Death, although written about by scientists and sages throughout time, is an abstract concept that may be defined clinically but remains an existential mystery. The *process of dying,* however, is less abstract. The process of dying is known because (a) it can be witnessed and (b) it can be described by those who are actually involved in it. A process is a "series of actions, changes, or functions that bring about an end or result" (Morris, 1979, p. 1043). As a process, dying takes place over time.

The purpose of this chapter is to give the reader an understanding of the actions, changes, and functions of the dying process through an exploration of selected theories and models of dying and examination of the empirical data. The experiences of dying individuals and of health care providers who care for the dying are presented, followed by some suggestions that may assist with the process. Finally, because everyone is engaged in the dying process, a discussion of how we may live with dying concludes the chapter.

THEORY AND DATA ON COPING WITH DYING

In an attempt to understand this universal phenomenon more fully, many authors have described the dying process in terms of psychosocial perspectives. Some of the better known research-based theories explain dying in terms of contexts of awareness (Glaser & Strauss, 1965), trajectories (Glaser & Strauss, 1968), phases (Pattison, 1978), stages (Kübler-Ross, 1969), appropriateness (Weisman, 1984), and responses to challenges (Shneidman, 1977).

Contexts of Awareness

Kastenbaum (1989) has cited sociologists Glaser and Strauss's (1965) field study on "awareness concepts" as one of the most influential contributions to the understanding of the social context of dying. Glaser and Strauss obtained their data through direct observation of the communication patterns of dying patients in a variety of public and private hospitals and through interviews with nursing students. They observed four basic types of awareness contexts: closed awareness, suspected awareness, mutual pretense, and open awareness.

In *closed awareness,* the patient does not recognize that he or she is dying, but everyone else does. Family and health care professionals join in a conspiracy to keep the secret by preventing communication to the patient of information that may lead to a realization that death is a prospect. If the patient begins to ask questions about his or her condition, the family and staff improvise explanations to distract the patient or explain away new symptoms or developments in the illness. As the patient becomes increasingly ill, the explanations become unconvincing and the relationships become strained as family and staff remain on guard in an effort to protect their secret. Although closed awareness causes great tension and is deceitful, five structural conditions lead to its occurrence: (a) Most patients are unfamiliar with the signs of impending death; (b) physicians are reluctant to tell patients that death is probable; (c) families often wish to shield or protect the patient; (d) the health care system is organized so that medical information is not disclosed; and (e) everyone is engaged in the conspiracy of silence, so the patient has no one with whom to speak.

In *suspected awareness,* the patient suspects what others know and attempts to verify the suspicion that he or she is dying by luring or tricking the family and staff into spilling the beans. The patient's suspicion is often aroused by changes in others' attitudes and behaviors, a change in medical treatment, and a noticeable deterioration of his or her condition. In this situation, the health care providers usually prefer to allow the patient to realize on his or her own that death is impending, rather than tell the patient this. This often results in the staff's avoiding answering the patient's direct questions about his or her condition. Suspicion, an inherently unstable state, usually yields to either mutual pretense or open awareness.

Mutual pretense is the best known and yet most subtle of the awareness contexts. Although all the players in this game (patient, family, and staff) are aware that the patient is dying, all continue to act as if this were not so. The pretense is continued, often with great effort, through a mutual conspiracy of silence on the topic of death. Occasionally, the patient may offer cues that signify that he or she understands death is impending. However, staff and family are unwilling to speak the truth. This results in the "Let's pretend" game, in which all players are aware of the others' knowledge but do not openly admit it and instead keep up the pretense that the patient will recover. This becomes a ritual in which all players must continually play their roles in every interaction. Mutual pretense is useful in helping the staff keep a safe emotional distance from the dying patient and in giving some patients more privacy, dignity, and control. It may, however, result in alienation.

Open awareness exists when everyone involved knows the patient is dying and acknowledges the fact in interactions. Open awareness allows the patient to complete the necessary tasks associated with dying, such as bringing relationships to closure, reflecting on his or her life, and coping with psychological problems such as fears and regrets. Although the open awareness context is preferable to the other three, it may be the most difficult because of the many questions and problems it presents the family and staff. For example, the family needs to decide whether the patient should be made aware of all facets of the situation, including the details of the prognosis. Would such knowledge cause depression or possibly suicide? Although open awareness frees the family and staff from the strain of maintaining the script that is necessary for closed awareness and mutual pretense, it presents the burden of continually facing work with the dying individual.

Glaser and Strauss (1965), pioneers in the introduction of these concepts in the mid-1960s, argued that it is essential to understand the awareness context in which an interaction takes place because of its effect on the interplay among patient, family, and staff. They maintained that all involved persons' words and actions are guided by what they know. Although a shift toward open awareness has been encouraged by the development of the hospice movement since the 1970s, it is not always possible or desirable to maintain an entirely open awareness. Some patients, family members, or health care providers may not be prepared to function in an open awareness context because of high anxiety, limited communication ability, or a characterological tendency to use denial as a defense mechanism.

Weisman (1972) argued that denial is healthy and necessary for many individuals and described three orders, or degrees, of denial. First-order denial is denial of the facts of the illness. Patients at this level of denial are said to hear what they want to hear about the diagnosis and illness. Usually, first-order denial is short-lived. Second-order denial is the denial of implications; that is, the patient accepts the diagnosis and the facts of the illness but does not accept the implications. Third-order denial is denial of extinction. Patients accept their diagnosis and its implications but resist the conclusion that the illness is incurable and will result in death. Because interpersonal dynamics constantly change, as does the progression of the dying process, situations need to be constantly analyzed from the standpoint of the awareness context in order to determine the most effective way the process may be managed.

Dying Trajectories

Glaser and Strauss (1968), along with Benoliel (1987–88), also studied dying as a process that occurs over time. Being a process, dying may take a variety of trajectories. All trajectories take time and have a certain shape through time. For example, the trajectory may plunge straight downward; may move slowly and steadily downward; may vacillate slowly, moving slightly up and down before plunging downward; or may move downward, plateau, and then plunge rapidly downward toward death.

The dying trajectory may be lingering, expectedly quick, or unexpectedly quick. In a *lingering trajectory,* gradual decline occurs over a long period and requires custodial care. Examples include patients in nursing homes or those with chronic degenerative illnesses. Often, the lingering patient is viewed by the staff or family as ready to die, a perception the patient does not necessarily share. The *expected quick trajectory* is associated with a different pattern of care, specifically, with prompt and effective action designed either to save lives (e.g., the patient who is admitted after a major physiological insult, such as an acute myocardial infarction) or to keep the patient as comfortable as possible (e.g., the patient with metastatic lung cancer). The *unexpected quick trajectory* results in an emergency situation, as, for example, in the case of a patient's appearing stable after an uneventful recovery from surgery and then suddenly deteriorating and dying.

Certainty and time yield four types of dying trajectories: (a) certain death at a known time (e.g., late-diagnosed metastatic cancers), (b) certain death at an unknown time (e.g., a chronic fatal illness such as amyotrophic lateral sclerosis), (c) uncertain death at a known time when certainty will be established (e.g., successful radical surgery for cancer but the existence of the threat of recurrence), and (d) uncertain death at an unknown time when the question will be resolved (e.g., multiple sclerosis or another chronic disease of uncertain outcome).

It is important to recognize that dying trajectories are perceived rather than actual courses of dying. The way in which patients, families, and health care providers perceive dying trajectories may have a profound impact on the ways in which patients live their lives and on the care they receive. For example, the uncertainty associated with the third and fourth of the foregoing trajectories is difficult to live with and may result in heightened anxiety for the patient and family. The health care provider's belief that a quick and certain death (first trajectory) awaits a patient may result in a decision for less aggressive medical care for that patient, even though recovery may still be a possibility. Moreover, expected certain trajectories may result in a sense of hopelessness. Heightened anxiety in the case of an uncertain trajectory, a decision for less aggressive medical care in the case of a quick and certain trajectory, and hopelessness in the case of a certain trajectory may occur despite the reality that these trajectories are merely perceived expectations and may in fact be inaccurate.

Appropriateness of the Personal Experience

Weisman (1984) described the concept of *appropriate death* as a style of dying that is adaptive to each specific person. In describing this concept, Weisman (1974) stressed respect for each individual's personality and values in the unique definition of what may be appropriate for him or her. Individuals must live their own life and death in a manner consonant with their own pattern of living and dying and their own definition of life and death and within their own context.

Obviously, appropriate death for one person might be unsuitable for another. . . . What might seem appropriate from the outside might be utterly meaningless to the dying person himself. Conversely, deaths that seem unacceptable to an outsider might be desirable from the inner viewpoint of the patient. (Weisman, 1972, p. 37)

Although particular patterns of appropriate death differ among individuals, appropriate deaths do have the following common characteristics: reduced conflict, compatibility with the individual's ego ideal, preservation or restoration of continuity of significant relationships, consummation of basic instincts, and fulfillment of fantasy. The most desired condition, of course, is not always met, but it may guide the health care professional in assisting the person through the dying process.

Shneidman (1977) maintained that it is imperative to understand the ways in which dying individuals have lived through and experienced previous stressful life events in order to understand how they respond to the *challenges inherent in the dying process*. How individuals behaved during earlier life crises will give significant clues to how they will behave during dying. In other words, people die in the same way that they live. The situation (dying) may be extraordinary, but the psychosocial variables that influence it, such as personality traits and coping history, are long established. Similar to Weisman, then, Shneidman asserted that individuals respond to dying in unique ways.

In a phenomenological study, Paige (1980) interviewed 5 terminally ill patients to ascertain their needs and experiences. Consistent with Shneidman and Weisman, she found that each related to the dying experience in a unique way and made sense of the experience in light of previous life patterns. The dying process was experienced differently by each as "a responsibility," "a resignation," "an act," "anguished courage," and "a challenge.' Although perceptual similarities were noted for all, their unique experiential patterns, the meanings of their personal experiences of their illnesses, markedly differentiated their response to the dying process.

Making sense or meaning of the experience is a critical factor in successful coping with the dying experience. Individuals with severe or life-threatening illnesses often search for meaning in what is happening to them and develop images of the illness (Viney, 1989). The images people create may be laden with emotions, such as anger, uncertainty, anxiety, helplessness, depression, or isolation. Conversely, the images may resonate with humor, competence, interpersonal involvement, or opportunity. Viney (1989) contended that individuals respond not to the illness per se, but to its image and that, to communicate in a meaningful way with a patient, health care providers must understand the meaning or image the illness holds for the patient.

Stages of Dying

Perhaps the best known and most influential of the pioneers describing the neglected needs of dying individuals is psychiatrist Elisabeth Kübler-Ross (1969), who postulated five stages of dying. Her book *On Death and Dying* has been translated into more languages than the Bible and has been the most instrumental publication in changing people's attitudes and behavior toward dying persons. Kübler-Ross developed her stage theory of dying on the basis of interviews with more than 200 dying patients. The five stages (denial, anger, bargaining, depression, and acceptance) refer to the person's successive mental and emotional responses to dying.

Denial ("No, not me"), the first response to learning that one is terminally ill, is an attempt to negate or escape from the idea of one's own death. Most individuals experience partial and temporary denial. The second stage, *anger* ("Why me?"), often characterized by envy, rage, and resentment, is often difficult for family and for health care professionals who may be the target of the anger. This stage is stimulated by fear and frustration. In *bargaining* ("Yes, me, but . . ."), the third stage, the terminally ill person attempts to forestall the inevitable by making a deal with the doctor, family, God, or fate if permitted to live somewhat longer. At this point in the dying process, the person recognizes the prognosis but is still attempting to modify the outcome. *Depression* ("Yes, me" grieving) is associated with the ultimate future loss of life and may be characterized by fatigue, loss of function, feelings of guilt, and fear of dying. The dying person realizes that bargaining is of no use and becomes sorrowful and withdrawn. The final stage, *acceptance* ("Yes, me"), signifies the end of the struggle. Rather than accompanied by a happy or serene feeling, acceptance is often associated with a voidness of all feeling. These stages are not rigid; neither are they mutually exclusive. Moreover, hope is associated with all stages, even with depression and with acceptance. Indeed, Kübler-Ross asserted that when hope is gone, death follows shortly.

Kübler-Ross's significant contribution to the death awareness movement has not been without its problems, many of which have been created by the naive ways in which her theory has been accepted and applied. Kastenbaum (1991), Corr (1993), and others have attempted to provide systematic critiques of the shortcomings and strengths of Kübler-Ross's work. The following are problems inherent either in the theory or in its widespread acceptance:

1   There is no clear evidence for the existence of the five stages. Shneidman (1977) cautioned against accepting the universality of Kübler-Ross' stages, maintaining that terminally ill persons are a complex cluster of affective states that are related to their total personality and ways of approaching life. Pattison (1977) expressed reservations about applying generalizations to dying persons, urging that each terminally ill person should be considered a unique individual. Corr (1993) asserted that individuals cope with living and dying "in far richer, more variegated, and more individualistic ways" (p. 73) than the stage-based theory allows. There have been no attempts to refine the stages and test the theory.

2   If the stages do, in fact exist, there is no evidence that dying individuals actually move through them in a linear fashion. Weisman (1974) wrote that the staging of dying is artificial and that no recognized succession of emotional stages exists. He suggested three phases of dying, later described by Pattison (1978).

3   The stage-based theory is founded entirely on interviews conducted within the confines of clinical practice and interpreted by one person who made no reported attempts to establish intrarater or interrater reliability. The research has not been replicated, and the theory has not been tested. Furthermore, the small sample for these observations was highly selective. Although the data generated by these interviews are invaluable, the limitations of the method have not been acknowledged. Conclusions have been widely accepted without benefit of further research to validate these data.

4   The stage theory is descriptive in nature but has been treated as prescriptive. That is, some health care professionals have abused the theory by attempting to force patients to move from one stage to the next according to an imposed schedule. Moreover, the prescriptive view of the dying process interprets the final

stage of acceptance as the universally desired outcome for all dying individuals. It is interesting that this expectation exists despite Kübler-Ross's repeated assertions that progression through the various stages is not necessarily linear and may not be rushed and that not all people experience all stages.

5   General application of such a theory negates individuality related to the illness, treatment effects, preexisting personality factors, sociocultural factors, and environmental factors. Often, negation of individuality and the uniqueness of a patient's dying experience acts as a shield for health care providers, protecting them against intimate interactions with their terminally ill patients.

Kübler-Ross provided a theory that is invaluable in the care of dying patients. It describes a variety of psychological and behavioral responses to dying, all of which are considered normal. Also, it recognizes the great variation of possible responses throughout the course of the dying process. Most important, Kübler-Ross was a pioneer in focusing on the human, rather than biomedical, aspect of dying, encouraging the health care provider to help through compassionate listening. Unfortunately, in an effort to simplify Kübler-Ross's stage theory, professionals have often interpreted it as a universal and fixed sequence of stages through which all patients move. Moreover, in the oversimplification of her theory, her message of compassion has often been misunderstood or omitted. It is fascinating that the concept of hope, which is essential to Kübler-Ross's theory, has been consistently omitted from its references and descriptions. Hope is discussed in Maintaining Hope.

Phases of the Living–Dying Process

Pattison (1978) described dimensions of a "living–dying" process that includes three clinical phases. In the *acute crisis phase,* in which the illness is first learned of, the patient may experience immobilization, alterations in consciousness, and feelings of inadequacy, anxiety, and fear and may exhibit pathological defenses. It is during the acute crisis phase that peak anxiety is experienced. Pattison maintained that reduction of the anxiety through crisis intervention and emotional support moves the person toward more appropriate responses to living–dying. The *chronic living–dying phase* is the longest in duration and may be experienced through integration or disintegration. In this phase, patients experience progressive fears associated with dying: fear of suffering and pain, the unknown, loneliness, sorrow, and regression; and fear of loss of body, self-control, and identity. Because we cannot deal simultaneously with all these fears, it is essential to determine which is occurring at any time and to deal with it. Pattison argued that when assisted in working through the fears associated with the chronic living–dying phase, the patient may experience a "healthy," or appropriate, death. The *terminal phase* begins when the dying person begins to withdraw and proceeds to the point of death. Although expressed almost exclusively in terms of dealing with fears, Pattison's phases of living–dying take into account both the subjective viewpoint of the dying person and objective observations of the person's coping mechanisms.

Testimony from Dying Patients

The literature on the experiences of dying patients has been of increasing interest to health care providers. This literature differs from that on near-death experiences, in which individuals who have been brought back from clinical death describe the event. The literature on the experiences of the dying, consists of health care providers', most often nurses', reports of the phenomena they have witnessed while caring for their dying patients.

Callanan and Kelley (1992) noted several recurring themes in their care of more than 200 terminally ill patients and their families. Quite often, as persons near death, they will speak, within their own frames of reference, of preparation for travel. For example, the businessman may fret about needing to find his passport, while the sailing buff may ask about the tides. This theme is consistent with the concept of death as a passage or journey and with the notion of hospice care, which actually has its roots as an inn or way station for weary travelers.

The most prevalent theme observed by Callanan and Kelley (1992) was the dying person's being accompanied by another who has already died. Most often, the dying recognize a relative or close friend who has previously died; occasionally, they speak of angels or religious figures. Schoenbeck (1993) offered a beautiful anecdote regarding an elderly dying woman seen by her granddaughter to be conversing with her long-dead husband. After this "conversation," she announced with great serenity to her granddaughter that Grandpa had stopped by to tell Grandma not to be afraid and that she would be joining him soon. He also said that he would be guiding her on her journey among beautiful gardens. She shortly drifted off to sleep, her fact tranquil and calm; she died a short while later.

As an example from this author's experience, one imminently terminal man, asleep in his hospital room, awoke with a start, became quite alert, and called the author to his bedside. He said that, while asleep, he had "seen" two angels who would be with him when he was ready "to go." Several days later, he serenely pointed to a corner of the ceiling and matter-of-factly announced, "There they are, the angels. They've come for me." He took one final breath and closed his eyes. Needless to say, this was a dramatic event that this author may not have believed had not a nursing colleague been present to confirm this most amazing experience. The message here, according to Callanan and Kelley (1992), is that the dying person is not alone.

Factors That Influence the Dying Process

Kastenbaum (1991) identified several variables that may influence the experience of dying, specifically, age, gender, interpersonal relationships, and the nature of the disease and treatment environment.

Age The intellectual grasp of death being related to developmental level and extent of life experiences, chronological *age* may affect a person's comprehension of dying and death. The dying process for a mature adult with a well-developed cognitive structure and diverse life experiences will vary considerably from that of a young child, who may not comprehend the nature of death. An example this author's experience clearly illustrates the influence of age on the experience of dying. A young child who had been diagnosed with cancer and given a prognosis of less than 6 months began to question her future when the pain from her bone metastases interfered with her ability to walk. She struggled to understand the concept of death but could not easily move beyond the fear of being alone, that is, without her parents. Her major concern was who would take care of her. Age further influences the dying process in terms of the degree of control the patient has over the situation. The young cancer patient understandably had little opportunity to participate in the decision-making process regarding her treatment and therefore attempted to exercise control over the situation in other ways. For example, she would refuse to respond to adults' attempts to make conversation at times, indicating that *she* would be the one to decide when and if conversation would be initiated, emphatically declaring in response to a statement or question, "Not now! We'll talk after the cuckoo [clock] strikes!" Age also influences the patient's perception of others and of the ways he or she is treated. Although this child was clearly in the terminal phase of inoperable cancer, the treatment team found it difficult, if not impossible, to make the final decision to terminate treatment, as is often the case in the treatment of young children. In American culture, which greatly values youth, it is often difficult to reconcile the death of a child. Conversely, advancing age may result in a less aggressive treatment protocol.

Gender Kastenbaum (1991) suggested that *gender* affects the dying experience because of the difference in life roles for men and women and the resulting difference in values. A man who is facing a life-threatening illness may be concerned with financial provisions for his family, whereas a woman facing impending death may be more concerned with family integrity. However, changing gender role patterns and lifestyles in recent years may reduce the influence of gender on the dying experience. More and more women are entering the workforce, with the result that their interests are shifting to their careers as well as their home and family or to their careers to the exclusion of a family. Likewise, some men's focus is shifting toward the home and child care. These changing gender roles may result in more androgynous personal identities and therefore a decreased influence of gender on life experiences, including dying.

Interpersonal Relationships The quality of *interpersonal relationships* is related to length of survival and to quality of remaining life, with individuals who have poor interpersonal relationships experiencing greater distress with the dying process (Kastenbaum, 1991). This is entirely consistent with the increasing volumes of research literature on the influence of social support on cancer patients' outcomes. Vachon (1994) suggested that effective social support affects long-term outcome by enhancing coping, allowing the person to avoid the negative emotional and behavioral sequelae of life-threatening illness. She further suggested that social support from family, friends, and health care professionals may act to enhance patients' compliance with medical regimes, having a direct relationship with disease outcome.

Nature of Disease and Treatment Environment   The nature of the *disease and treatment environment* critically influences the experience of dying (Kastenbaum, 1991). Individuals die of a particular cause in a particular place. For example, a degenerative lung condition that is associated with respiratory distress and is being treated in a hospital is likely to cause more alarming symptoms for the patient than is a home death due to chronic kidney failure, which may cause increasing lethargy as death approaches.

Religion and Culture   A person's attitudes and beliefs about life, living, and death, as shaped by religion and culture, also influence his or her dying process. For example, a person who believes that death signifies the end of all life as we know it may have a profound fear of the dying process and of death. Conversely, a person who believes in an afterlife or in reincarnation may fear the anticipated separation from loved ones but not the dying process or death. The profoundly different fears of these two individuals will influence the ways in which they respond to the dying process and the ways in which health care providers can assist them through the process. Having a faith, too, influences the experience of dying. In one study (Samarel, 1991), a hospice nurse commented,

At the end, those [patients] with a faith—it really doesn't matter in what, but a faith in something—find it easier. Not always, but as a rule. I've seen people with faith panic and I've seen those without faith accept it [death]. But, as a rule, it's much easier [for those] with faith. (pp. 64–65)

THE END OF THE DYING TRAJECTORY
The Dying Individual's Experiences

Physiological Experiences   In addition to the physiological signs specifically related to his or her pathology, the dying patient experiences physiological signs indicative of impending death (Kozier & Erb, 1987), as shown in Table 1. It is important to note that all these signs may not and, most probably will not, be present in any one patient. Interventions to assist the patient are palliative. Although a detailed discussion of how the physiological needs of the patient facing impending death may be met is beyond the scope of this chapter, suggestions for palliative intervention are included in Table 1. In general, interventions need to meet physiological challenges associated with pain control, personal hygiene needs, relief of respiratory difficulty, movement, nutrition and hydration, elimination, and sensory changes. The physiological signs of *imminent* death include dilated and fixed pupils; inability to move; loss of reflexes; weaker, more rapid pulse; Cheyne-Stokes respirations; noisy breathing ("death rattle"); and lowered blood pressure.

Psychological and Spiritual Experiences   In addition to the emotions discussed earlier (denial, fear, depression, etc.), one of the most remarkable signs of impending death is an increasing *disengagement* from the world of the living. Patients who are aware of their terminal illness and have accepted their impending death gradually disengage, or separate, from the world of the living. In the last few days or, in some cases, weeks, dying persons, in an attempt to pull away from loved ones, often seem to withdraw into themselves for increasingly long periods of time. Indications of disengagement include less verbalization, rejection of others, and increased sleep. Often, patients appear to be totally distracted by inner thoughts or work. Terminally ill individuals who are in the process of disengaging prefer not to be disturbed, but would rather have the opportunity to continue their separation. Occasionally, they will clearly communicate this, as the following case of a 63-year-old retired nurse with metastatic breast cancer illustrates.

"Selma" was lying motionless in bed, very white and very still, with her eyes open, sad, and pensive. Her husband of 40 years entered the room, kissed her forehead, sat in the chair next to her bed, and attempted to take her hand in his. Selma looked startled for a moment, apparently not having heard him enter the room. She withdrew her hand from his and said gently, almost pleadingly, "Not now." She then closed her eyes, as if to temporarily shut out the world, and continued with her private thoughts. Selma clearly was in the process of disengaging and needed time alone to continue the process.

Other disengaging patients are not as gentle as Selma in communicating their need to be alone with their thoughts. Seven-year-old "Amy" knew she was dying of neuroblastoma. She had spoken about leaving her family and going to be with her grandpa and her dog, both of whom had died before her. During the last 6 days of her life, Amy spent more and more time lying quietly in her living room; her eyes remained closed while her family went on with life all around her. During those quiet times, Amy's mother or father occasionally knelt beside her bed and attempted to take her small hand in their own or touch her forehead. Amy very clearly communicated that she did not want to be disturbed at those times. She would whine loudly and withdraw her hand or would turn her head away, shouting, "Leave me alone!"

Disengagement appears to be a private experience that terminally ill persons refrain from sharing. From the comments that patients have shared with this author, however, it seems that the process may involve one or two separate tasks, performed either singly or in combination. The first is introspection and reflec-

Table 1 Physiological Signs Indicative of Impending Death and Palliative Interventions

Physiological sign	Resultant symptoms	Interventions for palliation
Loss of muscle tone	Diminished body movement; Relaxation of facial muscles (i.e. sagging jaw)	Support the patient in a position of comfort with pillows and towels. Change positions whenever necessary (every 1–2 hr but not waking the patient if he or she is asleep) to maintain comfort.
Dysphasia	Difficulty speaking	Do not ask frequent, unnecessary questions that require complex answers. If the patient is able to write, provide pen and paper. Be patient, allowing the patient time for self-expression. Do not leave the patient alone with no means to summon assistance (provide the patient with a bell or other means to summon assistance if it is necessary for you to leave the room temporarily).
Dysphagia	Difficulty swallowing Pooled secretions Drooling	Position the patient sitting or side-lying to facilitate drainage of saliva. When providing fluids, use a straw to prevent aspiration (cutting the straw in half often makes it easier to use). When the patient is no longer able to sip through a straw, provide fluids using a syringe *without the needle*, being sure to aim the syringe into the patient's cheek, not in the center of mouth (to avoid aspiration). Provide frequent mouth care, using soft gauze to moisten the lips.
Decreased gastrointestinal activity	Nausea Flatus Abdominal distention Constipation	Position the patient comfortably, side-lying if possible. Using a clockwise motion, gently massage the patient's lower abdomen.
Decreased sphincter control	Urinary and rectal incontinence Diminished sensation	Check frequently for incontinence and keep skin clean and dry. Use extreme care when positioning and handling the patient.
Sluggish circulation	Cyanosis and mottling of extremities Cold skin (progressing from feet to hands, ears, and nose)	Maintain sufficient warmth. Massage gently, using slow strokes. Assist the patient in visualization of increased circulation and warming of extremities.
Changes in vital signs	Decreased blood pressure Slowed and weak pulse Shallow, irregular respirations (may be rapid or abnormally slow)	Try to reach a balance in positioning the patient for optimal comfort (keeping the head of the bed elevated may facilitate breathing but may decrease circulation to the brain).
Sensory impairment	Blurred vision Impaired (hypersensitive or hyposensitive) taste and smell	Identify yourself when approaching the patient. When handing any item to the patient, place the item directly in his or her hands, being sure the patient is gripping the item. Keep unpleasant odors to a minimum.

tion—the life review. One patient said, "I'm getting my mental and emotional house in order." The second task, as noted in the earlier discussion of Callanan and Kelley's (1992) findings is to prepare for travel or being accompanied.

Preparation for dying seems to involve a *transition* that is not done without effort—physical, emotional, and spiritual. It is important not to interrupt the progression of this effort. That is, when caring for a terminally ill patient, family and health care providers must be aware of the patient's need for solitude and must respect it. This must be carefully explained to family members, who may feel rejected if they do not understand that the disengagement process is normal.

Equally as important as recognizing and respecting the dying patient's need for disengagement is recognizing the patient's need not to be abandoned. The *fear of abandonment* is understandable, considering that dying is something that is done alone, with loved ones left behind. It is necessary, therefore, to reach a balance whereby the terminally ill have both their need for disengagement and their need not to be abandoned met. Interventions designed to accomplish this balance of care are discussed later.

The Health Care Provider's Experiences

In early studies of nurses caring for terminally ill patients, researchers observed that these nurses tended to avoid the terminally ill, exhibited high levels of anxiety when confronted with imminent death, and displayed exaggerated levels of objectivity and detachment as a self-protective coping mechanism (Samarel, 1989a). These nurses, however, were all general-duty nurses observed more than 2 decades ago and were neither cognitively nor affectively prepared for their work with the dying. Nursing care of the terminally ill is particularly demanding and stressful, especially when there is a lack of theoretical preparation, staff development, and interpersonal skills appropriate for this care. In a more recent study (Samarel, 1991), hospice nurses who were prepared cognitively and affectively for their work with the dying and who had developed personal philosophies of living and dying were observed consistently to meet their patient's needs in a caring and supportive manner. This was accomplished, too, with a surprisingly low stress level for staff, as evidenced by the fact that many of the observed hospice nurses had been caring for terminally ill patients for more than 5 years and claimed that they enjoyed their work immensely.

The key to the nurses' effectiveness in this study was a combination of three things: education for terminal care, development of a personal philosophy of living and dying, and mutual support. The education took the form of staff development designed to strengthen interpersonal skills and instruct on the needs of the terminally and their families. The personal philosophies ensured that each nurse had confronted death on a personal level and did not feel especially threatened by his or her own death. The mutual support, received through scheduled support groups and through informal daily camaraderie, served to alleviate stress.

Naturally, nurses do find it difficult at times to care for their dying patients.

This is especially so when patients appear to suffer. One hospice nurse admitted that sometimes it was difficult to do this kind of work:

Sometimes we laugh a lot. But it relieves tension. And sometimes I think I just don't feel anything anymore. But then I find myself crying for no apparent reason. (Samarel, 1989b, p. 135)

But there are also high points, or peak experiences, in caring for the dying. The following description of one nurse's experiences with a patient at the moment of death poignantly reflects much more than an acceptance of death. It reflects an appreciation of life, of which death is the final part:

It became very still. Not quiet, but still. But it was as if a lot was happening. There was almost a presence felt in the room. And it wasn't bad [that the patient was dying]. It felt calm, peaceful, and okay. No, it was more than okay. It was right and it was beautiful. And, all of a sudden, I felt the same kind of joyful tears that I felt when I saw my first baby born in nursing school. Then I realized that, at that very moment, he [the patient] had died. Death seemed to be the same miracle as birth was. (Samarel, 1991, p. 72)

Being present at the moment of death was, for this nurse, what Maslow (1971) called a peak experience, a "transient moment of self-actualization" (p. 48). Peak experiences are personal events that are profound, joyous, blissful, transcendent, illuminating, mystical, or ecstatic and result in one's feeling different about oneself or the world. The experience described by this nurse, an experience triggered by a patient's death, contained these characteristics.

Peak experiences are, according to Maslow (1971), components of the self-actualization process, the process of becoming all one can be. Accompanying a person at the moment of death may be a powerful means of learning and growing toward self-actualization.

Rather than viewing "this kind of work" as difficult, then, it is possible to experience it as an opportunity for personal growth (Samarel, 1991). According to Dossey, Keegan, Guzzetta, and Kilkmeier (1988), dying "can truly be a transformation—a time of remembering, of growth, and of peaceful completion of this life" (p. 381).

CARING FOR THE DYING

Family members and health care providers so often strive unsuccessfully to assist terminally ill individuals in their final passage. Their efforts may be unsuccessful for two reasons. First, the efforts may be uninformed. Helping an individual during the final stages of the dying trajectory requires knowledge of the physiological, emotional, and spiritual needs inherent in the process. It is only by making a knowledgeable (educated) assessment of the dying person's unmet needs that the family and care providers can formulate a plan to meet those needs. Often, however, both family members and health care professionals seek to alleviate *their own* pain, rather than that of the dying person. This is an unintentional projective process that results from a lack of awareness. In addition to educating themselves as to the needs of the dying, family members and caregivers must overcome yet another obstacle in order to be of optimal therapeutic value in this effort.

Personal Beliefs about Death

Pattison (1978) argued that before health care professionals may help others in the dying process, they must examine their own attitudes toward death. That is, if they are to relate to another who is dying, they first must understand their own attitudes toward dying in general and their own death in particular. Do we fear death? Or do we view death as a part of life?

In a study of hospice nurses caring for dying patients, this author described the necessity of nurses' giving thought to the issues of life and death in their personal life before they could provide care for others who are dying (Samarel, 1991). Each nurse in the study had reflected on the personal meaning that death held for her. Some expressed an ambivalence; some verbalized thoughts of a life beyond, of God, and of heaven. They spoke of the presence or absence of emotions connected with their own death, and those that felt emotions identified them as anger, sadness, and resentment.

Despite the differences in personal feelings regarding death, there were two recurring themes expressed by these nurses: loneliness, that is, leaving loved ones behind and dying alone, and overcoming the personal fear of dying and death. They believed that, unless one overcomes any personal fear associated with death, it is not possible to assist another through the process. Furthermore, each nurse expressed a personal and unique idea of a good death. A good death was identified as being comfortable and in no pain, dying in one's sleep, being alert and dying consciously, feeling peaceful, having family present, having all affairs in order, and so on. Regardless of what they felt about their own death or the death of loved ones, the nurses believed, it was essential that they acknowledge and identify these feelings. They may then be "bracketed" and placed aside *as their own personal feelings,* differentiated from the patient's feelings and resultant needs. Only after they had dealt with their personal thoughts and feelings about death could they be of therapeutic value in assisting others in their passage. One nurse summarized,

A good death is whatever the particular patient wants and needs, For instance, if a patient has to resolve certain issues with a family member and does so, that is a good death for that patient. Or if they want to be asleep and are, that is a good death. But to be asleep is not for everyone. . . . A good death is, in essence, defined by each patient. (Samarel, 1991, p. 71)

And so the health care provider's idea of a good death is not projected as the patient's idea. Once it is recognized that each patient must define (verbally or nonverbally) for him- or herself what a good death is and how the dying process should proceed, the health care provider may provide assistance in facilitating that process. This is entirely consistent with Weisman's (1984) notion of appropriate death. What is important to keep in mind is to be alert for cues or signals of this definition, because some individuals may not clearly communicate their definition of a good death.

Interventions

Interventions with dying patients need to address five goals: (a) maintaining a meaningful quality of life, which includes maintaining physical and emotional comfort; (b) coping with a deteriorating physical condition; (c) confronting relevant existential and spiritual issues, which includes fostering and maintaining self-worth and self-esteem, security, dignity, self-confidence, acceptance of losses, and hope; (d) planning for surviving family members; and (e) letting go. The interventions described in the following sections are directed toward these goals.

Pain Management   Maintenance of physical comfort has been briefly discussed earlier. Pain management, however, is so important that it must be discussed separately. For persons dying of cancer, pain may be a reality or it may be a fear for the future. Unfortunately, cancer and pain are still closely related in the minds of many patients. It is beyond the scope of this chapter to discuss the pharmacological methods of pain relief. Suffice it to say that, with the variety of analgesics and medication delivery systems currently available, it is unnecessary and unjust for anyone to suffer needlessly. Nonpharmacological methods of pain management are addressed below in the discussion of complementary interventions.

There are emotional and spiritual components, as well as physical components, to the experience of pain. Angell (1982) has said, "Pain is soul destroying. No patient should have to endure intense pain unnecessarily." The word *pain* comes from the Greek *poine,* meaning "punishment." This is not surprising, considering that patients who are experiencing prolonged and severe pain often perceive their experience as a punishment. This is especially true of children, as evidenced by a comment made by a child regarding her severe bone pain from metastasized cancer:

I must be a bad girl. I don't know what I did that was wrong, but I'm really bad. Otherwise I wouldn't have cancer and I wouldn't hurt so much.

This child had carried that thought with her for an unknown period of time. Had it not been for a casual comment made to her mother, this child's interpretation of pain as punishment may have accompanied her to her death. Thankfully, her mother was given the opportunity to reinforce to her daughter that she was not a bad girl; that she was, in fact, a very good girl; and that cancer is an illness that many good children get. The attitude change in that child was remarkable. It was as if she had a burden lifted. This case underscores an extremely important aspect of caring for terminally ill persons, regardless of whether they are in pain or not: effective communication.

Facilitating Effective Communication   Open communication among the dying, their families, and health care providers is essential for the well-being of all concerned. Too often, however, open and honest communication is something that is taken for granted and yet not achieved. Consider the following example of a conversation between a hospice nurse, Kate, and her patient, Mack, a 62-year-old hospitalized man who was terminally ill with metastatic brain cancer. They were speaking about Mack's wife, Adele.

Mack: We [he and Adele] are pretty much alone. We really don't have anyone but each other.

Kate: That must be really difficult for you. You love each other very much. [Tears well up in Mack's eyes, and he looks down.]

Kate: Have you told her?

Mack: Told her what?

Kate: That you love her.

Mack: Those things are really hard to say. And, anyway, she knows how I feel about her. She knows how much I love her.

Kate: [Gently] Yes, I'm sure she does. But I believe you will both feel a lot better if you talk about those things. It's important, you know. I understand that it's really hard to say some things, especially when you are not accustomed to. But I think you will both feel a whole lot better if you talk to each other about what is going on and about how you are feeling.

Mack: I'll give it some thought. Maybe you can help me. It's really so hard. (Samarel, 1991, p. 33)

Obviously, this man had not thought to communicate his feelings of love to his wife. Such words are often painful to verbalize because they bring people face-to-face with the reality of the present situation. Later that same day, when the patient's wife was visiting, he used the call bell to summon the nurse. Upon entering the room, she saw the patient and his wife silently seated next to each other at the window.

Mack: [To Kate] Oh, I hope I wasn't disturbing you. But I wanted to thank you for talking with me this morning. [To Adele] Kate and I had quite a conversation this morning. [He turns back to Kate and looks searchingly at her.] Didn't we?

Kate: Yes, we did. [To Adele] Your husband was talking about how difficult this whole thing is for both of you. And about how much he cares for you. [To Mack] Isn't that so?

Mack: [Looking down, with tears rolling down his cheek] Sometimes it's so hard to talk about the things that matter most. [Adele takes a tissue from her purse and clutches it in her lap.]

Mack: Talking with Kate today made me realize how much I really love you. I
         think that's probably the hardest part of this whole thing.
         [Adele] gets up from her chair and kneels in front of her husband, taking
         both his hands in hers, looks up at him silently.]
Mack: Oh, God [He begins weeping.]
         [Adele rests her head in his lap and places her arms around his hips,
         weeping.]
Mack: [Placing his hands gently on Adele's hair] I *do* love you, you know.
         (Samarel, 1991, p. 35)

In facilitating an open expression of feelings between this terminally ill patient
and his wife, this nurse made it possible for them to do what would have been
otherwise impossible. Every interaction with their terminally ill patients gives
health care providers the opportunity not only to have open and honest communication with these patients, but also to facilitate this type of communication between the patients and their families.

Counseling and Therapy   Emotional support in the form of empathetic
understanding, clear and honest communication, and acknowledgment of feelings
is, ideally, provided to all terminally ill patients by family members and/or health
care providers. In addition, counseling provided by mental health nurses, social
workers, psychologists, and psychiatrists may be more focused, intensive, and
structured. According to Rainey (1988), terminally ill patients may manifest emotional dysphoria, changes in mental status, characterological problems, or severe
interpersonal conflict that may require psychosocial support services. Types of
psychosocial services range from informal peer support groups to formal structured psychotherapy.

Support groups designed to help patients adapt to terminal illness are based
on the premise that terminally ill patients benefit from contact with other such
patients through mutual social support. According to Samarel and Fawcett (1992),
the social support literature clearly demonstrates that informal support from fellow patients, family members, and the health care team is a powerful influence
on adaptation. In fact, a great proportion of the women in Samarel and Fawcett's
research on the effect of participation in a support group on adaptation to breast
cancer stated that one of the most significant benefits they obtained from their
participation in the groups was knowing they were not alone with their problem.
Many groups offer much more than peer support; they are facilitated by professionals who are prepared to provide expert information and guidance. Examples
of groups that offer both support and education for individuals with cancer and
their families are I Can Cope and Make Today Count, programs sponsored by the
American Cancer Society.

Individual and family psychotherapies are more intensive interventions than
support groups and may be needed by some individuals and families to help meet
the challenges of terminal illness. Psychotherapy may be suitable for many terminally ill patients, but it is particularly recommended for those more vulnerable

patients with difficulties in coping. According to Christ (1991), vulnerable patients include those who live alone or have few friends; children, young adults, and those over age 75; the financially stressed; parents of dependent children; patients who have suffered multiple life stresses; members of families characterized by high levels of conflict; and patients with other concurrent personal or family illness. Unfortunately, many patients who are considered to be at low psychological risk and appear resilient actually have numerous psychological problems and could benefit from individual or family therapy. These patients are often not offered needed psychological services.

According to Shneidman (1978), individual and family psychotherapy for terminally ill patients differs from therapy for people for whom life expectancy is not an issue. Rainey (1988) summarized these differences in terms of goals, rules, focus, process, and patient identity. Because the overriding goal in therapy for the terminally ill is emotional comfort, the uncovering of hidden issues may be omitted. In assisting the patient to achieve emotional comfort within the limited time available, the therapist may suspend some of the traditional rules of psychotherapy. For example, *the therapist may take a more active role in moving the patient along toward the goal, rather than allowing the patient to work through old issues and develop his or her own solutions.* According to Rainey, "working through is a luxury for those who have time to live" (p. 151). In such a relationship, *the terminally ill person is permitted to set the pace. That is, the therapist does not force confrontation of issues, keeping in mind the overriding goal of emotional comfort.* Moreover, there is no move toward termination of the therapeutic relationship, which, in this situation, occurs naturally at the patient's death.

The involvement of the patient's family is an essential part of the therapeutic process. Family members are valuable sources of important information about the patient. Moreover, because the family's integrity may be seriously challenged by the life-threatening illness, the family members themselves may be in need of active assistance from the therapist. Inasmuch as the survivor becomes the patient, the therapist needs to establish a rapport with and be available for the family of the dying person.

What is important to keep in mind regarding counseling and therapy is to be aware of cues that such services are needed and, once need is recognized, to make the appropriate referrals.

Maintaining Hope Kübler-Ross (1969) found that hope was an essential aspect underlying the entire dying process. All of the dying persons with whom she worked expressed hope until the end of their lives. In fact, Kübler-Ross found that, when hopelessness was expressed, death followed within 24 hr. Fanslow (1981) maintained.

Anyone can live with the fact that he has an incurable disease, but no one can live with the thought that he, as a person, is hopeless. (p. 253)

Often, family members and health care professionals believe that to help a terminally ill patient maintain hope, it is necessary to lie about the prognosis of the disease, thereby betraying a trusting relationship. Kübler-Ross (1969) asserted that it is possible to allow a dying person to maintain hope without lying about the seriousness of the illness. The health care provider who is asked by a dying patient whether he or she thinks a remission is possible, may say, "Remission is a possibility." This reply enables the patient to maintain hope for remission, unrealistic though it may be, without stating that remission is probable.

As a result of her extensive work with hospice patients, Fanslow (1981) has identified what she calls the "hope system" of many dying persons, that is, the four phases that dying patients' hope goes through as they progress through the dying trajectory: the hope for a cure ("I hope that whatever I have is curable"); the hope for successful treatment ("I hope that my tumor can be completely removed by surgery"); the hope for prolongation of life ("I hope to live longer so that, perhaps, a cure may be found"); and, finally, the hope for a peaceful death.

In this author's experience, the focus of patients' hope may change from extended life to other things. For example, the patient may hope to remain free of pain or may hope that there will be no burdens, such as unaffordable funeral expenses, left with the family. To assist the dying person to maintain hope, caregivers must know for what the person is hoping. This sounds elementary and unnecessary to discuss, but how often has a health care provider said to a dying person, "Tell me what it is you are hoping for"? The response to this question may be surprising. Often, the patient has not yet thought about what it is that he or she is hoping for and will welcome an opportunity for reflection. Such an interaction empowers the patient, who is given the opportunity to bring to consciousness a positive hope that may yet be achieved; it empowers the family and the health care provider who may be given the opportunity to help the patient achieve the expressed hope.

For example, when asked, "What is it that you are hoping for?", one terminally ill patient, a 43-year-old mother of three teenagers, replied,

> What I was really hoping for was that I could live long enough to see the three of them [her children] spend some time together as friends. You know, without fighting. But I guess that can't happen at their ages. And I know I won't be around too much longer.

Often, family members want desperately to be of assistance but feel helpless and inadequate. When this woman's children learned, through the hospice nurse, of their mother's hope, they were amazed at how simple it was to fulfill. And it was empowering for them to be able to provide tangible assistance to their terminally ill mother.

Once an individual stops expressing hope, family members and health care providers need to accept the hopelessness.

Being Present   Being truly present enhances the value of the caregiver's interactions with the terminally ill patient (or, for that matter, anyone). Being truly present means that the caregiver is with the person physically, emotionally, and spiritually, focusing his or her attention on the present time, in the present place, with the present person. To be truly present is to be in the here and now. This means listening with ears, eyes, mind, and heart. It means not entertaining any extraneous thoughts while with someone—not thinking that it may be too warm in the room, that the day has been particularly stressful, etc. In other words, to be truly and sincerely present, the caregiver needs to suspend thought temporarily to stop the inner dialogue of the mind and give full attention to the present situation.

Whether being present is achieved through speaking, listening, touching, sharing, or silence, it always involves sincerity and requires practice. This does not mean that those caring for the terminally ill need to be superhuman. What it does mean is that the health care provider, or anyone else who wishes to communicate on a deeper and more caring level, simply needs to be fully attentive to the moment. A full attention, or a true presence, is felt on many levels. Sensitive individuals, and especially children and those who are dying, can sense and relate to a true and complete presence by relaxing physically and emotionally and feeling free to express themselves. A complete presence, too, will ease any sense of abandonment that the dying may be experiencing.

Assisting the Passage   When death is imminent, it is often appropriate to assist the dying in their final passage. In the dying person who is responsive, a need for assistance may be apparent in his or her facial expression, gesture, or verbalization. The unresponsive patient, too, may have needs for assistance, although he or she is unable to express them.

This thought seems foreign to most individuals in Western cultures. After all, how can we who are living assist a person to die, to go where we may not? It is true that the dying cannot be accompanied on their entire journey, but presence and support can be offered throughout most of the process.

The most important way in which caregivers may assist the dying in the final transition from life to death is to assure them that they are not abandoned, as previously discussed, and to provide them with a sense of peace. Peace means freedom from all pain—physical, emotional, and spiritual; it is a profound sense that all is well with the world. Peace is the most valuable gift caregivers may give to the dying.

A sense of peace may be conveyed despite the presence of physical discomfort (not severe distress) and unfinished business. As death becomes imminent, it seems as if the need for peace supersedes all other needs. To be able to give peacefulness to another, however, the caregiver must feel peace within him- or herself. To find that peace, the caregiver must be still, be present in the moment, and accept the moment. To accept the moment means to accept death without fear. If the caregiver is fearful, the dying person will sense this. Therefore, to be helpful to the dying, health care providers must reconcile death in themselves. Only after they have done this can they assist the dying, whether they are responsive or unresponsive, to find peace.

In this author's experience, the following approach to conveying a sense of peace to a dying person, adapted from a combination of methods developed by Dora Kunz and Cathleen Fanslow, has been quite effective.

1 Sit with the patient and hold one of his or her hands firmly, to provide the physical feeling of security;

2 Gently affirm your presence and the fact that the patient is not alone;

3 Mentally project your own sense of peace, visualizing (discussed in the next section) that peacefulness flowing from your heart, through your arms and hands, through the patient's hand and arm, to his or her heart; and

4 When appropriate, slowly and gently release the patient's hand.

This may be taught to family members, who often hover helplessly near, wishing they could be of use but not knowing what to do.

Complementary Health Care Interventions

A complementary health care intervention is a nontraditional, holistic intervention that is offered in addition to, not instead of, traditional health care. Complementary health care practices have been increasing in popularity and have been found to be useful in the care of the dying, possibly because of the holistic focus—the focus on body, mind, and spirit—of the dying process. Health care providers are not expected to be experts in all these modalities. It is helpful, however, for them to be familiar with a variety of modalities in order to guide the patient and family in finding sources of support for their use. The following list of complementary health care practices is by no means all inclusive; these modalities are simply ones that this author has found useful in her own practice with dying persons.

Meditation Meditation, a means of focusing and concentrating attention, requires physical and mental stillness for 10–20 min, during which time the individual sits or lies in a comfortable position with his or her eyes closed. There are many forms of meditation, but the ones most commonly used are focusing on one's breathing and repeating a word or phrase. Meditation has been used effectively to assist patients with cancer (U.S. Congress, 1990). It may be taught to the dying person and is effective in helping him or her to relax, decrease the feeling of discomfort, and increase the duration and effectiveness of pain medication. It also helps dying persons increase their awareness of the emotional and spiritual aspects of their beings, increasing the likelihood of achieving peace.

Visualization Imagery or visualization, the creation of positive mental images, is usually preceded by progressive muscle relaxation. It has been taught to patients with cancer by Simonton, Matthews-Simonton, and Creighton (1978) and Siegel (1986). The patients found visualization easy to learn and satisfying to use. An example of patients' use of visualization from this author's experience is the case of a 52-year-old man with metastatic lung cancer who was distraught about leaving his 10-year-old son without a father. He was asked to visualize his son as surrounded by a white light that symbolized all the good in the universe and to practice this visualization for 2 min each day for a week. One week later, he said it was remarkable how much his anxiety about his son had eased. He said he knew that his little boy would do fine "afterward" (after the patient died). Moreover, this patient said he was now able to spend time with his son, whereas before he used the visualization he could not be with the boy because he was afraid of becoming too emotional and scaring him.

As just mentioned, visualization may also be used by the family or health care provider to achieve a sense of peace. Fanslow (1981) suggested that family members and health care providers use visualization to bathe the patient in a white or blue light to decrease their anxiety and assist the patient with the transition.

Therapeutic Touch Therapeutic touch, first described by Krieger (1973) and more recently by Macrae (1988), "has been identified as one of the most effective therapeutic modalities for the dying person" (Igou, 1984). Therapeutic touch is derived from the ancient practice of the laying on of hands, but it is not done within a religious context and does not require that either the practitioner or the patient profess a faith or belief. It consists of several steps taken by the practitioner:

- Assuming a meditative state of awareness and mentally making the intention to help the patient;
- Using the hands to assess the patient's energy flow and needs; and
- Using the hands to repattern the patient's energy field.

The beneficial effects of therapeutic touch on patients' experiences of serious illness include increased relaxation, reduced pain and anxiety, and increased positive mood (Heidt, 1990; Samarel, 1992).

Caring: The Essential Component

Regardless of which interventions health care providers use when caring for dying persons, the component required to make any of them effective is caring. Caring is an interactive process that helps another person grow toward self-actualization (Samarel, 1991). In true caring, devotion is present and is manifested by total attention and acceptance of obligations. The ingredients of caring include knowledge, alternation of activity and inactivity, patience, honesty, trust, humility, hope, courage, and selflessness. Caring includes

those human acts and processes which provide assistance to another individual or group based on an interest in or concern for that human being, or to meet an expressed, obvious, or anticipated need. (Leininger, 1980, p. 136)

Caring denotes concern, devotion, and commitment and is expressed more nonverbally than verbally. The deep caring required to help dying patients must embrace the spiritual dimension. If health care providers are to care truly for the dying, they must face the reality of their own death; this enables them to establish a bond with their dying patients.

One of the most basic and honest ways to communicate caring to the dying is to use touch as a conscious and deliberative act. Caring through touch is particularly important for those terminally ill patients who may be experiencing sensory impairment, such as visual or hearing deficits. A caring touch conveys presence, understanding, and compassion. In a truly caring interaction, the dying patient and caregiver come together through the dynamics of an honest and open human relationship, regardless of the brevity or length of that relationship. The interaction affects both the dying patient and the caregiver, with both gaining something of value as a result of the relationship.

LIVING WITH DYING: MANAGING SERIOUS ILLNESS

From the moment of birth, all persons are engaged in the dying process. However, most people do not consider themselves to be dying and seldom, if ever, think about their own death. Once an individual comes face to face with a serious illness whose outcome is usually death, life changes. Once there is a diagnosis of cancer, for example, the eventuality of death becomes more personal.

Stages of Illness

When an individual receives the diagnosis of a potentially life-threatening illness, whether the threat is real or perceived, the person responds in a variety of ways. Previous work with patients with cancer (Adams, 1991; Samarel & Fawcett, 1992; Samarel, Fawcett, & Tulman, 1993) has indicated that individuals respond to the threat of serious illness according to stages, similar to the stages of dying described by Kübler-Ross (1969). Naturally, as with Kübler-Ross's stages, these are not mutually exclusive and are not necessarily experienced in a linear and orderly sequence. Moreover, not all individuals experience all stages. The following description is a generality that may be helpful in identifying an individual's current psychosocial health care needs.

Shock and disbelief, described by Engel (1964) as a stage of grief, is often the initial response to the diagnosis. The individual is stunned and refuses to accept or think about the diagnosis. After shock and disbelief, there may be active denial; anger; bargaining; depression; and, finally, acceptance of the reality of the diagnosis. It is during these stages that the person actively gives thought to and comes to terms with the possibility of his or her own dying. This is usually more difficult for individuals who have not previously thought about death and for those for whom the thought of death is frightening.

Before coming to terms with death, however, the patient must deal with the reality of the illness. This means gathering information, making treatment choices, and accepting the possibility of future lifestyle limitations.

Strategies of Coping

Patients faced with life-threatening illness need to develop new coping skills to deal effectively with the treatment and with the life changes the illness causes (Viney, 1989). Patients' development of these skills depends on how they perceive, or image, the illness. Illness may be imaged as a fight or challenge, an opportunity, an insurmountable obstacle, or a punishment (Viney, 1989). Responses to these images may vary, as do the images themselves. The nature and balance of the responses, or coping strategies, may be examined on a continuum ranging from adaptive to ineffective.

Even when a person images his or her life-threatening illness as a challenge, the balance of responses may lead to ineffective coping. Many patients, unfortunately, become fixated in the area of information gathering and treatment choices. An example from this author's experience is a woman who had an excellent prognosis (95% survival, according to statistics) after treatment for Stage I breast cancer but had not yet returned to work 2 years after diagnosis. She reported that she was too busy fighting her illness, although no medical treatment was currently indicated or received. She spent an inordinate amount of time reading all the current literature about breast cancer, speaking with many "knowledgeable" individuals to obtain more information, and continually trying a variety of new techniques to ensure her future health. These techniques included special diets, megavitamin regimes, physical and mental exercises, music and dance therapy, and acupressure. In addition, she regularly attended several area support groups. This woman was making a career of her breast cancer; it had become her life. This was an ineffective coping strategy that made it difficult, if not impossible, for her to move along and live her life in a healthy and enjoyable manner.

Ineffective coping is also illustrated in the actions of Michael, diagnosed with multiple sclerosis in his early 30s. Michael was determined to "beat this disease," the progression of which seemed relentless despite his efforts, which included megavitamins, acupuncture, and various healing modalities, as well as successive consultations with medical specialists. He read everything he was able to find about his disease. Needless to say, Michael found it necessary to stop working due to a combination of the progression of his illness, which rendered him partially disabled, and the time required for his new career focus, fighting multiple sclerosis. During the next 10 years, Michael became increasingly self-centered and bitter about his life. He was unable to think about anything other than his illness and his failure to control it. In his late 40s, Michael found a tumor on his knee, finally diagnosed as bone cancer. After a course of chemotherapy, he experienced a brief remission. It was during this time that a dramatic change in occurred in Michael's image of his illness, resulting in the development of more effective, or adaptive, coping strategies. It seemed that the bitterness that was for so long a part of Michael dissipated and he began to reach out to people whom he thought needed his assistance. He offered to accompany a neighbor to a clinic appointment when she was nervously awaiting the results of previous medical testing; he invited another neighbor, alone during his birthday, to his apartment to share some cake and conversation; and he began asking others about their lives. Although Michael continued to take care of himself and fight for his health, his life took on more of a balance as his focus widened to include other people. Michael never recovered from his multiple sclerosis or cancer, but when he died 18 months later he was at peace and left behind many new friends who had shared in his meaningful life.

Many patients with whom this author has worked have indicated that after accepting their diagnosis, dealing with the reality of the illness, and coming to terms with the reality of eventual death, they made a conscious decision about how they would live with their illness and whether the illness would have a positive or negative influence on their lives.

How can a potentially life-threatening illness have a positive aspect? Kaye (1991) noted that the Chinese character for *crisis* is a combination of two words: *danger* and *opportunity*. With the diagnosis of a life-threatening illness, the dangers are obvious and the idea that anything beneficial could ever result from such an event is ludicrous. The true challenge of such a situation, according to Kaye, is for people to use the experience in a positive way, extracting from it what they have learned and applying those lessons to every area of their life. There are advantages to coming to terms with mortality. When we learn to understand our deepest feelings, we may become more complete and compassionate human beings, changing our perspective on life in general. This change is manifested in an improved ability to communicate, enhanced relationships with other people, and feelings of empowerment. Resolution of previous issues, such as low self-esteem, may occur and enrich the rest of our life. Moving past the danger of life-threatening illness permits us to take full advantage of opportunities provided by the crisis experience.

Group support may help patients with life-threatening illness share positive possibilities with each other. Through mutual social support, patients may be encouraged to make the decision to allow their experience of illness enrich their life, rather than pull it down. Peer support, when it is carefully guided in a positive way by trained and experienced health care professionals, can be invaluable in helping patients live with dying.

Living the Decision

Once a person decides to make a potentially life-threatening illness a life-enriching experience, three outcomes are possible, none of which is final. The first is *recurrence* of the illness, requiring that the patient go through the entire process again. This means that, for the most part, the person again experiences the stages of illness, the development of coping mechanisms, and the decision-making process as to the way in which the new illness will influence his or her life. In the case of recurrent illness, the fact that the patient is experienced in dealing with the illness may be of benefit or harm. The benefit lies in the development of coping methods that may have been strengthened by the previous episode. The harm lies in the fact that recurrence is a new crisis, and, according to crisis theory (Aguilera & Messick, 1985), crises are cumulative. The second possible outcome is a *fading of the memory and experience* of the enrichment. When this occurs, the positive life changes that have been brought about by the illness are not sustained, and the patient returns to his or her previous habits and lifestyle. The third possible outcome is the person's maintenance of his or her commitment to the decision to allow the experience of the illness to influence life positively. Every day requires that the person renew the commitment to allow his or her life to be enriched by the experience.

Understanding the process of dying is a formidable challenge. Although it is possible to explore and critique related theory and to examine the empirical data, the fact that all humans are a part of this process every day of their lives imparts a large degree of subjectivity to the exploration of dying. This subjectivity, however unscientific it may seem, provides caregivers with the opportunity, and in fact implores them, to be a part of this process for their patients, providing the presence and caring that so enrich human interaction.

REFERENCES

Adams, M. (1991). Information and education across the phases of cancer care. *Seminars in Oncology Nursing, 7,* 105–111.

Aguilera, D., & Messick, J. (1985). *Crisis intervention: Theory and methodology* (5th ed.). St. Louis, MO: Mosby.

Angell, M. (1982). The quality of mercy [Editorial]. *New England Journal of Medicine, 306,* 98–99.

Benoliel, J. Q. (1987–88). Health care providers and dying patients: Critical issues in terminal care. *Omega, 18,* 341–364.

Callanan, M., & Kelley, P. (1992). *Final gifts: Understanding the special awareness, needs, and communications of the dying.* New York: Poseidon Press.

Christ, G. (1991). Principles of oncology social work. In A. I. Holleb, D. J. Find, & G. P. Murphy (Eds.), *American Cancer Society textbook of clinical oncology* (pp. 594–605). Atlanta, GA: American Cancer Society.

Corr, C. A. (1993). Coping with dying: Lessons that we should and should not learn from the work of Elisabeth Kübler-Ross. *Death Studies, 17,* 69–83.

Dossey, B. M., Keegan, L., Guzzetta, C. E., & Kilkmeier, L. G. (1988). *Holistic nursing: A handbook for practice.* Rockville, MD: Aspen.

Engel, G. L. (1964). Grief and grieving. *American Journal of Nursing, 64,* 93–98.

Fanslow, C. A. (1981). Death: A natural facet of the life continuum. In D. Krieger (Ed.), *Foundations for holistic health nursing practices: The renaissance nurse* (pp. 249–272). Philadelphia: J. B. Lippincott.

Glaser, B. G., & Strauss, A. L. (1965). *Awareness of dying.* Chicago: Aldine.

Glaser, B. G., & Strauss, A. L. (1968). *Time for dying.* Chicago: Aldine.

Heidt, P. R. (1990). Openness: A qualitative analysis of nurses' and patients' experiences of therapeutic touch. *Image: The Journal of Nursing Scholarship, 22,* 180–186.

Igou, J. F. (1984). Current issues and future directions. In S. H. Schraff (Ed.), *Hospice: The nursing perspective* (pp. 153–168). New York: National League for Nursing.

Kastenbaum, R. (1989). Awareness of dying. In R. Kastenbaum & B. Kastenbaum (Eds.), *Encyclopedia of death* (pp. 24–27) Phoenix, AZ: Oryx Pres.

Kastenbaum, R. (1991). *Death, society, and human experience* (4th ed.). New York: Macmillan.

Kaye, R. (1991). *Spinning straw into gold: Your emotional recovery from breast cancer.* New York: Simon & Schuster.

Kozier, B., & Erb, G. (1987). *Fundamentals of nursing* (3rd ed.). Menlo Park, CA: Addison-Wesley.

Krieger, D. (1973). The relationship of touch with the intent to help or to heal to subjects' in-vivo hemoglobin values: A study in personalized interaction. In *Proceedings of the Ninth American Nurses' Association Research Conference.* New York: American Nurses' Association.

Kübler-Ross, E. (1969). *On death and dying.* New York: Macmillan.

Leininger, M. M. (1980). Caring: A central focus of nursing and health care services. *Nursing and Health Care, 1,* 135–143, 176.

Macrae, J. (1988). *Therapeutic touch: A practical guide.* New York: Knopf.

Maslow, A. (1971). *The farther reaches of human nature.* New York: Viking Press.

Morris, W. (1979). *The American heritage dictionary of the English language.* Boston: Houghton Mifflin.

Paige, S. D. (1980). *Alone into the alone: A phenomenological study of the experience of dying.* Unpublished doctoral dissertation, Graduate School of Nursing, Boston University, Boston, MA.

Pattison, E. M. (1977). *The experience of dying.* Englewood Cliffs, NJ: Prentice-Hall.

Pattison, E. M. (1978). The living-dying process. In C. A. Garfield (Ed.), *Psychological care of the dying patient* (pp. 133–168). New York: McGraw-Hill.

Rainey, L. C. (1988). The experience of dying. In H. Wass, F. M. Berardo, & R. A. Neimeyer (Eds.), *Dying: Facing the facts* (2nd ed., pp. 137–157). Washington, DC: Hemisphere.

Samarel, N. (1989a). Caring for the living and dying: A study of role transition. *International Journal of Nursing Studies, 26,* 313–326.

Samarel, N. (1989b). Nursing in a hospital-based hospice unit. *Image: Journal of Nursing Scholarship, 21,* 132–136.

Samarel, N. (1991). *Caring for life and death.* Washington, DC: Hemisphere.

Samarel, N. (1992). The experience of receiving therapeutic touch. *Journal of Advanced Nursing, 17,* 651–657.

Samarel, N., & Fawcett, J. (1992). Enhancing adaptation to breast cancer: The addition of coaching to support groups. *Oncology Nursing Forum, 19,* 591–596.

Samarel, N., Fawcett, F., & Tulman, L. (1993). The effects of coaching in breast cancer support groups: A pilot study. *Oncology Nursing Forum, 20,* 795–798.

Schoenbeck, S. B. (1993). Exploring the mystery of near-death experiences. *American Journal of Nursing, 93*(5), 43–46.

Shneidman, E. S. (1977). Aspects of the dying process. *Psychiatric Annals, 8,* 25–40.

Shneidman, E. S. (1978). Some aspects of psychotherapy with dying persons. In C. A. Garfield (Ed.), *Psychological care of the dying patient* (pp. 201–218). New York: McGraw-Hill.

Siegel, B. S. (1986). *Love, medicine, and miracles.* New York: Harper & Row.

Simonton, O. C., Matthews-Simonton, S., & Creighton, J. L. (1978). *Getting well again.* New York: Bantam.

U.S. Congress, Office of Technology Assessment. (1990). *Unconventional cancer treatments.* Washington, DC: U.S. Government Printing Office.

Vachon, M. L. S. (1994). Psychosocial variables: Cancer morbidity and mortality. In I. B. Corless, B. B. Germino, & M. Pittman (Eds.), *Dying, death, and bereavement: Theoretical perspectives and other ways of knowing* (pp. 135–155). Boston: Jones and Bartlett.

Viney, L. L. (1989). *Images of illness* (2nd ed.). Malabar, FL: Robert E. Krieger.

Weisman, A. D. (1972). *On dying and denying: A psychiatric study of terminality.* New York: Behavioral Publications.

Weisman, A. D. (1974). *The realization of death.* New York: Aronson.

Weisman, A. D. (1984). *The coping capacity: On the nature of being mortal.* New York: Sciences Press.

Chapter 5

Institutional Dying: A Convergence of Cultural Values, Technology, and Social Organization

Jeanne Quint Benoliel and Lesley F. Degner

Death and dying are experiences known to all human societies. How people manage these important social transitions is determined by the values and beliefs that govern their society, the level of technology available, and the types of death they most commonly encounter. Sudden death has always been a part of the human condition. Prolonged dying by large numbers of people is a phenomenon of the 20th century brought about by the appearance of urban industrial systems of existence and increased life expectancy.

DEATH, CULTURE, AND CAREGIVING PRACTICES

Cross-cultural studies of societal practices for coping with death reveal several common customs: the use of priests or special functionaries at funeral ceremonies; isolation or separation of the bereaved from other members of society; and final ceremonies that bring the mourning period to an end after a culturally prescribed period of weeks, months, or sometimes years (Rosenblatt, Walsh, & Jackson, 1976). Cultural configurations also determine the customs followed in the care of the sick, including the places set aside for ill persons and those about to die. In hunting-and-gathering societies, the role of shaman or witch doctor—responsible for driving out the demons or other causes of illness—was commonly filled by a man, and the role of caregiver of the sick was filled by a woman (Downs, 1971).

Special institutions for the care of sick persons probably did not appear until agriculture replaced hunting and gathering as the major change in the lifestyle of human living. This change in lifestyle set the stage for the emergence of civilization, complex social and hierarchical institutions, and specialized occupations of many kinds. The evidence available suggests that the earliest hospitals—whether in ancient Egypt, Buddhist India, or Judaic Palestine—were associated with temples or other institutions concerned with religious beliefs and practices. Military operations also fostered the appearance of hospitals, as is shown in historical documents describing the Roman Empire (Rosen, 1963).

INSTITUTIONS FOR DYING: A PRODUCT
OF CIVILIZATION

In Western society, the history of caregiving institutions reflects a succession of powerful cultural influences: Christianity resulted in caregiving's being seen as a religious obligation, industrialization led to the creation of state-managed public services, and science has resulted in a technologization of care.

After the fall of Rome, caregiving institutions in Europe developed as manifestations of Christian values, and they were managed and run by religious communities. The hospital in medieval times provided services for the elderly, indigent, and infirm as well as the sick and was a center committed to medical care, philanthropy, and spirituality (Rosen, 1963).

In the later Middle Ages, industrialization, urbanization, and the Reformation contributed to a secularization of European societies. Responsibilities once assumed to be religious became the province of the state or community, and public institutions were created to meet the needs of the sick and the poor. New demands for services were created, and the old philanthropic institutions gave way to hospitals and other institutions designed for special purposes—the treatment of small pox, venereal disease, mental illness, and so on (Rosen, 1963).

During this period, physicians came to be associated with hospitals on a regular basis. From the 17th century on, hospitals increasingly came to be defined as places for the treatment of disease. The ties between physicians and hospitals were strengthened by the appearance of science and the application of the scientific method to the study of the human body and its ills. In time, the focus of the hospital became limited to sick people with *treatable* diseases. Persons with chronic, incurable, and terminal diseases were relegated to almshouses, poorhouses, and other public institutions, and these settings came to be seen as undesirable places where persons with limited means did their dying (Knowles, 1973).

Although hospitals came to be seen as places to treat disease, well into the 20th century the death-preventing capabilities of medical treatments were negligible. In fact, mortality rates in hospitals were high, predominantly because of infection and cross-contamination (Knowles, 1973). It is also worth noting that across these centuries of change, the majority of deaths occurred outside of institutions, taking place in private homes, on the streets, and close to the daily lives of the people.

THE NEW CULTURE OF THE 20TH CENTURY

In the 20th century, a combination of changing societal values, expanding technology, and population pressures has altered the nature of living and dying in profound ways. People's attitudes and behaviors in relation to death and dying have been affected by the secularization of society, the dominance of science over medical practice, and the pressure of an expanding population.

Separation of Dying from the Human Existence

As the culture of Western society changed from a religious orientation toward life and death to a perspective dominated by the values of science, trade, and business, the act of dying underwent changes such that control over its management shifted progressively from the dying person to the family and eventually to the physician and the hospital team (Aries, 1974, 1981). The rise of science has been accompanied by a progressive decline in religious belief, and the fear of death has emerged as society's most pervasive attitude (Toynbee, 1968). Direct experience with death and dying has disappeared for many members of society as new professions have been created to take care of the many death-related tasks associated with an expanding population. Responsibility for the management of dying has shifted from the family to the larger society, and the necessary actions related to death have become bureaucratized, as is true of many other activities essential to the ongoing flow of human affairs.

The perception of death as a supernatural phenomenon has been replaced by the perception of death as natural—and thus capable of being conquered by human ingenuity and the application of societal resources for all classes of society (Illich, 1976). With this shift in values, ordinary people's direct experience with death and dying as human transitions has decreased, with the result that people have little opportunity to learn how to handle themselves in these situations. The pattern of "protecting" the dying person by not talking about the fatal disease has replaced the traditional religious obligation of informing the dying person so that preparation for death could be completed. Changes in attitudes and practices have led to the tendency to withhold diagnostic and prognostic information from the individual with a terminal illness.

Influence of Science and Applied Technology

The influence of science and technology on Western societal attitudes and practices increased steadily between 1700 and 1900, paving the way for the takeover of society by applied technology that has occurred in the 20th century. By the turn of the century, human existence had already been altered by secularization, urbanization, and industrialization as these affected work, family, and lifestyle possibilities. However, these changes were minor compared to what the next 90 years would bring. The creation of mass transportation has resulted in a mobile society. The development of mass communication has radically increased the flow of information and knowledge, facilitating a movement toward industrialization of the world.

Contributing to these changes in the United States has been the creation of an assembly-line model of work production that operationalizes the historical values of hard work, pragmatism, control over nature, and action and has made the products of technology readily accessible to ordinary members of society. On the other side of the coin, the assembly-line model encourages a depersonalization of work through fragmentation of the tasks to be done, leading to monotony in many people's daily lives. The assembly-line model has come to be applied to service agencies as well as to factories, and the one-to-one, provider–client relationship has given way to the provision of social, educational, and health care services by multiple workers (Benoliel, 1978).

Science's Dominance over Medical Practice

The influence of science on medicine has come about in two ways. First, scientific discoveries such as x-ray and radiation have led to the direct application of technology to methods of diagnosis and treatment. Second, the creation of a scientific method, known as the *biomedical model* of disease, for applying the reductionist principles of the physical sciences to the study of disease has led to an objectification of the doctor–patient relationship and a disregard for the social and behavioral factors that affect illness. The expansion of knowledge has led to the development of specialized fields of medical practice, often centered in hospitals. This means that patients receive services from many doctors instead of one. The movement of medical schools into universities has increased the scientific community's control over medical education, and the hospital has become as much a medical laboratory for the study of disease as a setting for patient care (Ebert, 1986).

Since 1945, the biomedical model of disease has been the dominant influence in the practice of medicine and the education of its practitioners. In this model, disease is defined as physical and biochemical deviations from established norms, and the body is treated as a broken machine subject to recovery through replacement or repair of defective body parts. In Engel's (1977) view, this belief system has become a cultural imperative on the American scene—that is, all members of society are influenced to some extent by these beliefs. Within such a framework, an expansion of the life-saving ethic and a deployment of resources into life-prolonging activities can be understood as socially adaptive mechanisms to resolve the uncertainties surrounding disease and to control death, now defined as the enemy. More and more, hospitals have come to be designed and organized for the purpose of controlling death (Benoliel, 1978).

The industrialization of disease management and death control has moved rapidly since the end of World War II, with the result that the hospital has become a technical life-saving establishment. In the United States, this change has been facilitated by the government's aggressive movement into financial support for biomedical research and by social legislation that has expanded the availability of health care services to certain high-need members of society. Medical research has produced a variety of life-sustaining and supporting procedures and machines, and new paramedical occupations have been developed to implement the specialized functions created by the new technology. Research programs at medical schools are now influenced by what the government will fund and by the government's selection of the university-affiliated hospital as the most favorable environment for biomedical research (Ebert, 1986).

With the invention of kidney dialysis machines, respirators, transplant surgeries, and other life-prolonging techniques, has come the demand for their use, and hospital administrators have reorganized the use of staff and space to accommodate this demand (Ebert, 1986; Knowles, 1973; Raffel, 1984). Between 1960 and 1970, a variety of critical care settings developed, all emphasizing medical control over death (Hilberman, 1975). By 1981, there were intensive care units in 95% of acute care hospitals in the United States, providing an estimated 66,000 beds for adults and 8,000 beds for children and infants (Knaus, Draper, & Wagner, 1983). Training programs have been developed to prepare nurses and other workers for coping with the demands of this highly technical work, and nurses in hospitals have increasingly found their daily activities dominated by the pressures and stresses of life-saving medical activities (Benoliel, 1975). Thus over a very short span of years, the hospital has become a setting in which dying is a technologized experience, and the influence of science has led to new forms of dying.

NEW FORMS OF DYING

For much of the history of humankind, the death of children was commonplace. At the beginning of the 20th century, the loss of one or more children in a family was not unusual, and these deaths often occurred at home. However, progressive control over the communicable diseases resulted in a decline in childhood deaths to the extent that by the early 1960s, the death of a child, especially from an infectious disease, was a rare occurrence that carried a special poignancy. Although children do die today of cancer, poisons, and accidental injuries, the number of child deaths is small compared with the number of adult deaths, and people's reactions to the loss of a child are disproportionately intense.

Effects of Increased Life Expectancy

Over the same span of 60 years, increased life expectancy in the adult population created a new social phenomenon—large numbers of people living to be 70 years of age or older. This rise in the number of elderly persons changed the character of dying by making chronic illness and the deteriorations of aging the primary causes of death in Western societies. As a result of this change, the relatively short time it took to die when death was usually caused by acute infectious processes was replaced by prolonged dying over a period of weeks, months, or sometimes years.

In the 1970s, a social problem of serious dimensions was identified when it became clear that the number of elderly persons over the age of 80 was increasing faster than the number of people over 65 in general. This old-old segment of the population contains large numbers of frail, elderly people with limited capacity to take care of themselves who need caregiving services. Improvements in the modern medicine's life-saving capabilities have meant that for many older people, dying, rather than living, is the stage being prolonged. Thus, the technical advances capable of postponing death have brought negative as well as positive consequences to the quality of living for many people, perhaps especially for the elderly. With the advent of antibiotics and other chemotherapeutic agents, pneumonia, once known as the old man's friend, no longer functions easily as a "friend" of those who were ready to die (Gruenberg, 1977).

Effects of Life-Saving Medical Procedures

The use of new life-saving techniques and procedures also keeps alive persons who in previous eras would have died at an early age. New populations in need of special services and institutional care appeared. For example, children with Down's syndrome, long known to have a high susceptibility to respiratory infection, have had an increase in life expectancy greater than that of the general population. This outcome resulted from the application of medical techniques to physical defects that formerly led to death in the first year of life. In addition, the prevalence of severely retarded people in general is growing rapidly, resulting in a demand for special institutions capable of providing services to those with limited capability to care for themselves (Gruenberg, 1977).

In a similar way, medical technology has been found to be capable of keeping alive many newborn infants with severe congenital deformities or other physical problems, as well as premature infants whose vulnerability to early death was traditionally high. Special settings for the intensive treatment of high-risk infants and children are now commonplace in medical center hospitals. Physicians and nurses in these settings daily face the tensions of work that puts them in constant contact with dying babies (Benoliel, 1975).

Medical technology has also made possible the prolongation of life with chronic diseases that once would have led to early death. The discovery of insulin by Banting and Best in 1922, for example, has meant that children with insulin-dependent diabetes mellitus no longer are subject to dying from ketoacidosis and the uncontrolled metabolism of carbohydrates and fats. However, living into adulthood requires that they fight the vascular complications of diabetes that are prone to appear in the middle and late years (Gruenberg, 1977). People with chronic kidney failure are able to have their lives extended by spending part of their time attached to kidney dialysis machines, but their living styles are radically altered by the requirements of this time-consuming medical regimen.

Although advances in medical technology have made it possible for many people with these and other chronic diseases to live longer, they often have to spend part of that time in the hospital being treated for complications and acute exacerbations of illness (Strauss et al., 1984). For many people, prolongation of life with chronic disease has meant struggling through periods of near death, not just an extension of time. Although generally perceived as a place for sustaining life, the hospital is also the place in which people die and other people care for them during the dying process.

INSTITUTIONAL DYING: NURSING HOMES AND HOSPITALS

Statistics on where dying occurs are difficult to obtain. In 1988 in the United States, 58.8% of deaths occurred in hospitals or medical centers, 16.4% of deaths occurred in other institutions, 4.4% of deaths were classified as dead on arrival (DOA), and 20.4% of deaths occurred in other places (National Center for Health Statistics, 1991). These results suggest that for many persons, the final period of living takes place in hospitals, but the length of time involved and the setting are not completely clear.

Institutional dying takes many different forms, with particular types of dying associated with different types of settings. Each pattern of dying is determined by an interplay of several factors: the physical state of the person who is dying, the social and spatial arrangements of the setting, the patterns of social interaction around and with the dying person, the patient's defined state, the methods of treatment and caregiving provided, the availability of advocates or allies for the dying person, and the number and types of caregiving personnel involved.

Dying in a Nursing Home: The Forgotten Ones

In the United States, the nursing home industry expanded rapidly after World War II to meet a growing demand for institutional services for the incapacitated elderly. Nursing homes and other custodial institutions became places for the prolonged dying of individuals with low social value, and they effectively served to remove these reminders of death from the view of other members of society. This segregation of the elderly can be viewed as a direct reflection of the youth-oriented, death-denying American culture.

The allocation of resources to these institutions appears to coincide with the low value accorded its occupants and, according to Vladek (1980), the failure of public policy to provide mechanisms for caregiving to an aging population. The typical nursing home resident is an 80-year-old white widow or spinster who has relatively limited means and three to four chronic ailments; the average length of stay is 2.6 years, with 30% of discharges being due to death (Vladek, 1980). Often, the people hired for positions of direct patient care are both poorly trained and poorly paid, and the work itself is hard (Kayser-Jones, 1981). The situation is one that encourages the practice of patient abuse, sometimes contributing to a patient's death (Stannard, 1973).

Although many people sent to nursing homes are undergoing a prolonged process of dying, observation in the 1960s of nursing home staff in interaction with their elderly clients revealed very little open discussion about death (McGinity & Stotsky, 1967). When an institution must provide services for a large number of confused and physically disabled elderly patients, the work of keeping them bathed and fed and mobile is organized in regimented ways, removing many of the personal touches that elderly people enjoy. In a study of one nursing home, Kayser-Jones (1981) observed that staff members used a variety of depersonalizing practices with the patients: (a) scolding patients and calling them by their first names, (b) routinizing care and preventing personal choices, (c) providing little protection against theft of personal belongings or personal harm, and (d) showing insensitivity to patients' feelings and a lack of compassion and kindness.

Dying in a Hospital: Complexity and Variability

In previous centuries, the treatments available to patients in hospitals were the symptomatic treatments and comfort measures commonly classed as nursing care. In the 20th century, highly specialized and technical medical procedures have become the dominant form of therapy, and hospital services have changed to accommodate this development. During the 20 years immediately after the end of World War II, urban hospitals became intricate multipurpose social structures designed to accommodate the pressures of three interrelated goals: research, instruction, and patient services.

Dominated by the continually growing influence of the biomedical model of disease, the practice of medicine has come to be structured and organized around the primacy of the cure ethic. Life-saving procedures and machines have become increasingly important in the daily activities of physicians, and the solo practice of a general practitioner has given way to a group practice provided by specialists. Heavily influenced by these changes in medical practice, work in hospitals is now organized around the diagnosis and treatment of disease. The focus of nursing work has been altered by the pressures of medical technology and the demands for attention to activities that maintain control over death. As the day-to-day activities of physicians, nurses, and other hospital workers have come to center on the primacy of life-saving tasks, services to meet the human needs of patients and families have become tangential and secondary. These changes have appeared not because the various professional groups lack concern, but because the work to be done has been organized for the purpose of saving lives, and the dying patient represents failure.

The primacy of the goal of cure over the goal of care has institutionalized the secular value of control over death and facilitated the objectification of the practitioner–patient relationship (Engel, 1977). Despite the appearance of mental health concepts and knowledge about the psychological needs of patients and families, the education of new practitioners in nursing is strongly influenced by the power of death control and is relatively ineffective in preparing them for the psychosocial aspects of caring for dying patients and their families (Quint, 1967). Yet their work in hospitals brings them face to face with the dilemmas of care and cure, and sometimes they find themselves having to choose between personal and professional values. In addition to dehumanizing death the technologizing of death has added greatly to the stresses and strains of hospital work.

Hospital Work, Dying Patients, and Caregiving

A major outcome of the specialization of medicine has been the appearance of special-purpose hospital units organized specifically for the treatment of particular groups of patients. Reaching its peak in 1965, this influence has been most powerfully experienced in university-affiliated teaching hospitals through the ready availability of federal research monies (Ebert, 1986). It has shifted the focus of hospital services away from generalized medical–surgical care toward highly specialized treatments of special groups—patients with heart attacks, burns, cancer, trauma, or birth defects (Benoliel, 1978; Hilberman, 1975). Although mainly concerned with life-saving activity, the staff in these settings must also provide services for patients who die there. The death work in different settings in the hospital is regularized around several interrelated elements: (a) the types of dying most characteristically found there, (b) the types of death-related tasks expected of the workers, (c) the primary emphasis regarding the work to be done, (d) the frequency of death and dying, and (e) the staff's preparation for and experience in the tasks they must perform.

Specialization and technology have complicated the business of caregiving by increasing the number of people required to get the work done. Strauss, Fagerhaugh, Suczek, and Wiener (1985) described the organization of medical work in hospitals as including five kinds of work that shape the characteristics of illness trajectories and the essential tasks to be done. *Machine work* relates to the invention, servicing, and use of various technologies to diagnose and treat diseases and other ailments. In some settings, such as the coronary care unit, a great deal of time and effort must be given to monitoring both the machines and the patients. *Safety work* is closely related to machine work in that attention must be given to judging whether a given technology is harmful to patients. However, safety work also involves attention to the effects of medical treatments and other procedures on patients' well-being. It also means assessing and monitoring clinical hazards in the work environment, including the competency of various personnel, and developing safety measures and routines (Strauss et al., 1985). *Comfort work* consists of activities geared toward the relief of pain and discomfort. *Sentimental work* refers to a variety of interpersonal activities that facilitate interacting with patients, building their trust, maintaining composure, supporting their identities, and controlling their awareness of their illness states. *Articulation work* relates to the coordination of all other forms of work to serve the patient's best interests, but it is highly susceptible to disruption for a variety of personal, interpersonal, and organizational reasons. Patients can suffer harm when articulation work is impossible to achieve, but all patients suffer some disarticulation in today's complex hospitals because of the number of people involved (Strauss et al., 1985).

Communication with patients, family members, and other providers is a central component of caregiving in hospitals. In a study of dying in hospitals in 1965, Glaser and Strauss found some common problems in social relationships and personal experiences of staff, regardless of differences in the characteristics of the settings. These problems included (a) a tendency for the staff to avoid open conversations with dying patients about their dying, (b) communication difficulties among the staff associated with differences in expectations and failures in the flow of information, and (c) strong emotional reactions to difficult choices and decisions. Depending on how the death work was organized, these problems sometimes led to explicit role conflicts and interpersonal difficulties involving patients, families, and members of the unit. Glaser and Strauss (1965) and Sudnow (1967) noted that the more routinized and regularized a unit's death work was, the more the disruptive effects of death were minimized and controlled.

Hospital Care in The 1970s

In the 1960s, a death awareness movement arose in the United States as something of a counterculture against the death-avoiding practices of the 20th century (Benoliel, 1978). Professional and lay literature dealing with many complex issues related to death and dying proliferated in the 1970s. The public's interest in finding alternatives to hospitalization was demonstrated in the creation of hospices for terminal care, demands for new legislation permitting consumer participation in decisions about the use of life-prolonging methods, and a burgeoning of voluntary groups devoted to helping people with various life-threatening disorders and situations. Professional interest in creating alternative forms of care for dying people commonly took the form of federally funded demonstration projects, such as the Minnesota home care program for children with leukemia (Martinson et al., 1978).

The death awareness movement influenced hospital practices in several ways. It legitimized the medical care of the dying patient and permitted the introduction of palliative care services and hospice units into established hospitals (Wilson, Ajemian, & Mount, 1978). It stimulated a variety of workshops and other educational activities to prepare physicians, nurses, and other health care providers for work that involved them with dying patients and their families (Benoliel, 1982). These teaching efforts did not refocus the goals of the health care system, but they did sensitize a number of providers to the complexities of collaboration in death work.

Others attempted to bring about changes in the institutions themselves. Nursing organizations attempted to counteract the depersonalizing influences of institutional routines by sending well-prepared nurses to institutions to assist patients and families with the situationally derived stresses and strains that hospitalization often brings. These nurses were known by a variety of different names, such as *clinical specialist* or *nurse practitioner,* and their achievements were variable, depending on whether their activities were perceived as nonthreatening or threatening by physicians, other nurses, and other members of the institutional staff (Benoliel, 1977). In some settings, the introduction of clinical nurse specialists led to discord between the medical and nursing staffs, but in other settings, it paved the way for the creation of new services, for example, a procedure for providing regular support to grieving spouses of patients hospitalized in a coronary care unit (Dracup & Breu, 1977).

In the 1970s, the work of caregiving in hospitals was greatly influenced by a range of ethical and legal problems associated with the use of advanced biomedical technology. Serving as an exemplar of the problem was the case of Karen

Quinlan, which highlighted the question of parents' right to make a surrogate decision for their child to discontinue active medical treatments (Regan, 1980). These ethical and legal concerns added to the complexity of decision making in terminal care and to the tensions of decision makers. Legal issues, in particular, put pressure on physicians to do everything possible in the way of treatment to avoid the possibility of being sued for malpractice. Analysis of records of patients who died in one teaching hospital showed that the majority had been designated "no code" (no use of active cardiopulmonary resuscitation) and as having conditions labeled by their physicians as grim or terminal. Yet the medical treatment orientation was overwhelmingly toward the use of life support maintenance and active cardiopulmonary resuscitation (Mumma & Benoliel, 1984–85).

Hospital Care in the 1980s and 1990s

In the 1980s, the ethical and legal issues over treatment decisions expanded to include the appropriateness of discontinuing fluids and nutrition for terminally ill patients or those who requested it, the exemplar case of which was Elizabeth Bouvia (Kane, 1985). In addition, the cost of hospitalization became a major political issue, and the appearance of AIDS created a variety of personal, social, and political problems.

In 1950, the average cost of hospital care was about $15.62 a day and $126.52 for the total hospital stay. By 1982, the average cost per day had increased to $327.37, and the average cost for a hospital stay was $2,500.52 (Raffel, 1984). This change was directly related to an overall increase in health care expenditures in the United States: The proportion of the gross national product accounted for by health expenditures shifted from 4.4% in 1950 to 10.5% in 1982. Also of importance, the government assumed increased responsibility for the payment of health care expenditures, and beginning in 1965, an increased proportion of these funds were spent on personal health services (Benoliel & Packard, 1986). Using data for 1968, Mushkin and DiScullio (1974) estimated that about one fourth of all Medicare hospital costs were spent on the care of aged dying patients, and they argued that terminal illness claimed a significant share of hospital resources. Through secondary analysis of cost data from several studies, Scitovsky (1984) showed that the large proportion of costs at the end of life was due not so much to intensive treatment of terminal patients as to the cost of ordinary medical care for very sick patients.

In an effort to contain Medicare costs of hospitalization, the Health Care Financing Administration initiated a prospective payment system based on 467 diagnosis-related groups (DRGs) to control the amount of money available to hospitals for different types of medical cases. The DRG system does not take into account variations in severity of illness within groups, and hospitals that treat a disproportionately large share of severely ill patients can be disadvantaged financially when DRGs are not adjusted for severity of illness (Horn, Sharkey, Chamber, & Horn, 1985). Some analysts have suggested that hospitals may be biased toward upgrading the classification of severity in order to obtain more reimbursement (Redelmeier & Fuchs, 1993). Such cost containment strategies do not bode well for the dying patient who requires intensive, but low-technology institutional care.

In 1981, AIDS was identified as an HTLV-III viral infection that increased the vulnerability of infected persons to fatal opportunistic diseases and an early death (Centers for Disease Control [CDC], 1985). The National Commission on Acquired Immune Deficiency Syndrome estimated in 1991 that the population of HIV-infected individuals was at least one million. From a few diagnosed persons living with AIDS in United States in 1981 has grown an estimated population of 151,000–225,000 people diagnosed with AIDS in 1993, according to the CDC (1990). The CDC (1993) reported that in 1990, 25,188 deaths resulted from HIV infection and that this figure was 14% higher than the previous year. This epidemic has created a form of dying that involves much suffering and frequent hospitalizations, making problems for insurance companies, which must foot the bill—in 1990 estimated to be $85,333 for the lifetime care of the average AIDS case (Hellinger, 1991).

The epidemic has also created tensions for health care providers, who are concerned about their safety when in contact with AIDS victims. These concerns have not lessened in spite of evidence that HIV is not easily transmitted in the workplace (O'Donnell & O'Donnell, 1988). The CDC's development of universal precautions against infection has been one approach to reducing these fears, but such procedures can prevent only about 40% of needlestick and mucous membrane exposures to HIV (Elmslie, Mulligan, & O'Shaughnessy, 1988). For the first time in recent decades, health personnel have had to confront the possibility that providing care could potentially result in their own death.

DIFFERENT TYPES OF HOSPITAL DYING

The term *dying trajectory* was coined by Glaser and Strauss (1968) to refer to dying as a social process created and modified by the decisions and actions of the people involved. According to this definition, dying is a process that takes time— sometimes only a few minutes but more often days and weeks. As a social process, dying can be described by the pattern of events that serve as markers of the patient's movement toward death. These events function as indicators of the degree of certainty that death is forthcoming at a predictable or unpredictable time.

In the simplest form of the dying trajectory, all persons involved have the same perceptions regarding the speed and certainty of death's arrival and share the same outlook on the proper activities to perform during the final period of life. However, the dying trajectory is usually much more complicated, because the people involved have different perceptions regarding whether the patient is actually dying. Many communication difficulties associated with dying result directly from the difference in perceptions of what is taking place (Glaser & Strauss, 1965, 1968).

Three types of dying trajectory are commonly observed in hospitals: (a) a lingering pattern of dying, (b) a quick trajectory leading to expected death, and (c) a sudden trajectory leading to unexpected death. The different types are characteristically associated with particular types of hospital units, and they typically produce different types of staff activity. The actual social process of dying in any one situation, however, reflects a convergence of cultural values and individual choices as well as organizational structure, available technology, and medical treatment goals.

The Emergency Room: DOA and Sudden Death

Emergency rooms are designed and organized for the rapid treatment of accidental injury and sudden critical illness. The problems brought in for treatment range from simple cuts and bruises in one person to massive and extensive injuries in a large group of people. Workers in emergency rooms in large metropolitan areas often are exposed to death and near death in their most unpleasant forms. The work requires them to help victims of homicide, fire, hit-and-run accidents, child abuse, suicide, and other forms of violence and destruction. The quick trajectory leading to expected death is a common pattern in these settings.

When patients are admitted in critical condition, emergency room work requires rapid evaluation of the problem and rapid initiation of action in a context of incomplete information and uncertainty. The work is organized to implement immediate life-saving activity and to meet the challenge of preventing death. Because of the intense focus on medical treatment activities during an emergency situation, little time is available for contacts between staff members and waiting family members. The nature of emergency work in combination with the limited time for contacts between families and the staff contributes to communication difficulties and stressful circumstances for both (Benoliel, 1977).

Using *observations* of family members' experiences in an emergency room in relation to the sudden death of a relative or friend, Jones (1978) identified the sequence of their experiences as follows:

1 Arriving and searching for information,
2 Waiting,
3 Being notified of death,
4 Viewing the body,
5 Signing papers,
6 Concluding the process.

About half of the respondents reported the experience to have been handled well because staff members took time to provide explanations, notified them of the death in a warm and concerned manner, and remained with them when they viewed the body. The other half reported feelings of anger, frustration, confusion, and emptiness as remnants of their unsatisfactory contacts with emergency staff.

The traditional emergency room is organized to offer emergency medical treatments but not the crisis intervention services that patients, families, and staff need to cope with the psychosocial crises associated with sudden death. Hess (1970) observed that the staff behaviors that appeared to be callous to the outside observer came in time to be understood as necessary coping mechanisms for dealing with difficult choices, decisions, and patient situations. The need for crisis intervention services in emergency settings or emotional support training for emergency staffs has been recognized and met in several hospitals (Hess, 1970; Jensen, 1973; Jones, 1978).

Hooked to Machines: Dying in the Intensive Care Unit

Critical care settings are typically organized to prevent the occurrence of death in patients whose physical conditions can suddenly worsen, thereby moving them rapidly onto the trajectory toward sudden death. Some of these settings deal only with special problems, such as coronary care or extensive burns. Others provide services for a range of medical and surgical conditions and treat both children and adults. Some settings offer care for only a few patients; others are designed to accommodate large numbers of critically ill patients.

Regardless of their size and established purpose, critical care settings are organized and structured to maximize the application of life-sustaining medical technology. Nurses in critical care settings tend to be highly committed to life-saving goals, and their activities are organized around the primacy of preventing death. Their work often involves tending the machines that monitor patients' conditions or assisting patients to maintain their vital functions (Strauss et al., 1985). These nurses must maintain constant vigilance to pick up early cues that something is wrong, and they are ever ready to move into rapid action when an emergency takes place. Their situation has been compared to that of soldiers serving in an elite combat team, because they are never able to remove themselves from the stresses of battle (Hay & Oken, 1972).

Because the critical care setting is organized to prevent death, it is spatially arranged so that the doctors and nurses can easily maintain observation of all the patients in it. Thus patients' need for privacy is superseded by the need for constant vigilance, and contacts with patients are made mainly for the implementation of technical tasks and the performance of medical procedures. Relationships between patients and providers center on life-saving activities, and contacts are frequently short because the staff are responsible for many patients. The unit regulations are commonly designed to minimize disruption of the staff's activities by controlling the family's presence at the bedside, and the staff's disclosure of information to the family is likely to be minimal and controlled.

These structural and organizational conditions create a depersonalizing situation for many patients. Those who recover from their critical states ordinarily remain in the intensive care unit for only a short period of time. Others who remain in serious condition may be kept there at length. Those who die there generally end their lives attached to all manner of life-prolonging apparatus, and often death occurs after intensive heroic activity by the staff. Dying in the intensive care unit is one of the new rituals of transition in a technologically sophisticated society, and it makes the central participant something of an object.

Although outsiders tend to view the doctors and nurses in the intensive care unit as detached and unfeeling people, the reality is that work in these settings results in many situational and psychological stresses. Staff members are faced with frequent exposure to death and dying; daily contact with unsightly patients; heavy workloads; the operation of intricate machinery; and the challenge of communicating in a stressful situation among themselves and with their patients and their patients' families (Benoliel, 1975). The work is easiest when patients are comatose. It becomes more complex when patients are alert and young, have likeable personalities, or stay long enough for the staff to become attached to them. Among the coping mechanisms doctors and nurses use to adapt to the pressures of work in the intensive care unit are detachment, increased activity, and humor (Swanson & Swanson, 1977). Yet even these adaptive mechanisms cannot protect them completely from feelings of sadness, anger, and frustration as they confront the daily uncertainties of their work or the feeling of having been negligent when they make errors in judgment or lack needed supplies at a time of emergency.

The context of critical care is one of recurring crises involving patients, families, and members of the hospital staff in complicated and tension-producing interactions and decisions. Often, mechanisms evolve for the maintenance of an emotional order of composure and constraint in the face of these difficulties. Yet the people involved cannot help but be personally affected by the stresses of the situation and the difficult task of maintaining composure in the face of conflicting pressures (Glaser & Strauss, 1965).

In and Out: The Prolonged Dying of the Cancer Patient

Although patients with cancer occasionally end their days on an intensive care ward, they are more likely to die on a general medical–surgical unit or one designed specifically for the care of cancer patients. Typically, patients dying of cancer have been undergoing treatment for some time, and many have been in and out of the hospital several times before arriving for the final stay. This history of several hospitalizations means that dying cancer patients and hospital staff have already established a level of involvement that makes efforts at detachment difficult to maintain.

Sometimes the end of a lingering trajectory lasts only a day or two. The patient is usually brought to the hospital to die because the family cannot manage the situation at home. Sometimes, the dying cancer patient is sent from a nursing home where the staff are unable to provide care during the final period of dying. In either case, the patient is clearly known to be dying, and the treatment usually consists of comfort measures and symptomatic support. For the staff, the situation usually entails watchful waiting and is easiest to perform when the patient is comatose. Far more difficult for all concerned is the situation of a fully alert dying patient who is capable of initiating conversation that may be awkward or unsettling. Equally upsetting is the family that has not come to terms with the forthcoming death and insists on active life-saving treatment even though its use is to no avail.

Very difficult for the patient and staff alike is the prolonged hospital dying of a person with far advanced cancer, particularly when the patient is not to know the diagnosis and prognosis (Benoliel, 1977; Glaser & Strauss, 1965). When either the physician or the family makes the judgment that the patient is not to know of his or her prognosis, the nurses feel trapped and frequently handle the situation by minimizing their contacts with the dying patient. The result for the patient is social isolation, often brought about by well-intentioned relatives who believe they are offering "protection" by preventing the dissemination of bad news. The consequence is that the person facing death is effectively barred from bringing closure to his or her life by communicating personal wishes and participating in decisions about the context of dying.

Cancer is notably a tension-producing disease, and many of the difficulties encountered in the hospital are tied to problems in communication associated with the progression of disease. Patients with advanced cancer have high levels of anxiety associated with fears of painful dying and abandonment by other people, and they often reach out for opportunities to express their fears and concerns. The problem is that other people find it difficult to listen to these expressions of concern, because the situation triggers a variety of distressing feelings, including helplessness, anger, guilt, sadness, and depression. Family members and staff alike protect themselves by using many behaviors designed to control strong emotional reactions (Glaser & Strauss, 1965; Strauss et al., 1985).

These problems of communication can be compounded by the physical changes associated with advancing cancer and the difficulty of helping the patient achieve a comfortable death. One of the most difficult problems encountered on a cancer unit is the patient whose pain is not amenable to control. In this situation, tension is high and interpersonal conflicts among the staff are frequent. The feeling of helplessness is intense when little can be done to help the patient, and the resulting tension can sometimes permeate the atmosphere of the entire ward.

The problem for the staff working on cancer wards is that they are functioning in a setting in which dying is an ever-present but not necessarily acknowledged process. Cancer units typically have patients who are at different stages of cancer and are undergoing different kinds of oncological treatments, and the doctors and nurses constantly interact with patients and families at different points on the living–dying timetable. Constant uncertainty about the future and tension about the present affect patients and staff alike, and their interactions are molded to permit control over the underlying stresses.

The Patient Whose Family Cannot Let Go

One of the most tension-producing problems encountered by nurses in the hospital is the situation of the patient whose family insists on life-saving activity when the patient is clearly on the trajectory toward death. This situation happens most commonly when the trajectory has been precipitated suddenly (e.g., by an accident or heart attack) and the members of the family are not prepared for the shocking possibility of death. Often, the physicians and nurses are aware of the seriousness of the person's condition soon after his or her arrival at the hospital, but the decision to discontinue active medical treatment may be delayed until the family has had time to agree with this recommendation.

Usually, the trajectory of dying in these situations is 1 or 2 days at most. The process of dying can be extended, however, if the patient is attached to life-support machines that keep the vital physiological systems functioning and the family cannot agree to discontinue the treatment. Both the family and the staff are faced with the interpersonal complexities of maintaining composure and control in a context of uncertainty and tension. When this form of dying extends for a long period of time, the nursing staff carries the burden of care, a task made additionally burdensome if members of the family withdraw from contact with the patient.

There are also occasions when a member of the family, most commonly a spouse, cannot face up to the possibility of death during prolonged dying and insists on the patient's receiving active medical treatment. If the patient is young, the staff are often in sympathy with the fight for life, and active participation in treatment provides a mechanism for counteracting prevailing feelings of helplessness. If the patient is elderly, the nurses are likely to view the choice as somewhat inappropriate, particularly if the patient has indicated on previous occasions the wish not to have life prolonged.

The undercurrent of unspoken and unresolved feelings and tensions associated with this type of dying makes it one of the most problematic in hospital work. It is evidence of the lack, in many hospitals, of effective services for helping families cope with the complex personal and social problems to which the process of dying gives rise.

The Special Poignancy of Dying Children

In some hospitals, a child's dying is a rare occurrence, and staff members are unprepared for the stresses and strong feelings that this difficult problem provokes. In other hospitals, it is fairly common for children to die, and the staff cope with these same stresses and feelings on a regular basis. In the first instance, staff members react in a manner similar to that of people in general, and they frequently cope by recounting the events of the dying over and over again. In the second case, staff members are likely to have developed a number of routines for distancing themselves from the stresses.

As is true when adults are dying, nurses and doctors are better able to keep themselves detached when the child is in a coma. When the child is alert and capable of interactions, contacts include conversation as well as treatment, and withdrawal from involvement is difficult to achieve. The care of a dying child is always affected by the reactions and behaviors of his or her parents, and many of the difficulties described by hospital staff are associated with the problem of relating to parents living under continuing stress. Bluebond-Langner (1978) found that the majority of terminally ill children learned they were dying before death became imminent but participated in a game of mutual pretense with their parents and the staff. This pretense allowed the parents and caregivers to play their reciprocal roles and maintained the sentimental and social order without disruption, but the children came to see their role as supporting others.

Hospital settings that provide services for large numbers of dying or potentially dying children carry their own special poignancy, because the children cannot help but be aware of the deaths of other children. In fact, Bluebond-Langner (1978) observed that dying children learned to define themselves as dying through watching what happened to children who had died before them.

Some kinds of dying are distressing to witness because of their effects on the body, as in the case of massive burns (Mannon, 1985; Seligman, 1977). Others are distressing because they drag on or serve as reminders of certain tragic aspects of the human condition. Providing care for dying children is a difficult task for probably the majority of physicians and nurses. It triggers both a sense of professional failure and strong personal reactions associated with the loss of a child (Suarez & Benoliel, 1976).

NEGOTIATIONS, DECISIONS, AND ADAPTATIONS TO DYING

Just as styles of living have been diversified in the 20th century, so too have styles of dying. For the most part, dying has been removed from public view into the private realm of institutions. At the same time, its characteristics as a social and interpersonal process have become more variable. Medical technology and cultural values have interacted with new causes of dying to create new rituals of transition. Under the influence of industrialization, dying has changed from a tribal or familial ritual to an organizational procedure governed by bureaucratic rules and dominated by the influence of health care providers.

Death Information and Communication

Many patients who enter the hospital are not defined as dying. The labels used by staff for defining patients are based on their perception of the stability of the illness process. These labels include *well, acutely ill, chronically ill, high risk of dying, dying,* and *dead* (Martocchio, 1980). Assignment of these labels by doctors and nurses is a process, not a single event, and a new label is given when the illness process is perceived to have changed. In a study of adult patients on medical and surgical wards, Martocchio (1980) observed four patterns of living–dying that culminated in death:

peaks and valleys—a swinging back and forth between apparent wellness and high risk of dying,

descending plateau—periods of relative stability of illness interspersed with periods of apparent deterioration,

downward slope—a fairly rapid downward movement toward death, and

gradual slant—a gradual, rather than rapid, movement toward the end.

Different labels were assigned to patients at different points during the various dying trajectories, and these labels influenced the patterns of communication among patients, family members, and health care providers. The shift from the label *high risk of dying* to the label *dying* took place through processes of negotiation by which different interactants became aware of a change in the patient's status. Although patients were infrequently told directly that they were going to die, they picked up clues about their futures from changes in the behaviors of others (Martocchio, 1980). On a cancer ward, McIntosh (1977) noted that patients who wanted confirmation about their conditions had to take the initiative in seeking information from physicians. On a burn unit, Mannon (1985) observed that patients picked up a lot of information about their futures from physicians' comments during weekly grand rounds. He also noted that when the staff began to be certain that death was forthcoming, they made efforts to predict the length of the trajectory and to prepare families for what was coming.

Information Exchange and Life–Death Decisions

Degner and Beaton (1987) found that hospital staff also sought confirmation of the dying label through negotiations with others. Doctors and nurses exchanged information through face-to-face interaction or through written comments on patients' records. Sometimes disagreements arose among staff because the nurses wanted clear messages about the dying state, but the physicians continued to speak in terms of high risk of dying. Sometimes physicians were loath to make a clear designation because they were waiting for new information on which to make a decision. Often, the context was one of uncertainty, rather than certainty, about the patient's condition. The decision to label a patient as dying is not made lightly, given the life-saving values of medical practitioners. Degner and Beaton observed that physicians' processes of decision making in life–death situations involved calculations of various pros and cons:

- The risks versus benefits of treatment,
- Whether the patient's condition was getting better or getting worse,
- The advantages versus disadvantages of a treatment in relation to the work order on the ward,
- The disruptive versus nondisruptive effects of a treatment choice on the sentimental order,
- The costs versus benefits of a given treatment, and
- Quality-of-life considerations.

It is clear that treatment decisions are affected by a variety of personal, social, and organizational factors. All participants in the situation engage in their own calculations regarding whether a patient is dying, but clear information from physicians can make an important difference in the dying experience of the patient and the family and the caregiving practices of other providers. It is clear to nurses that the *dying* label has been applied when the physician writes a "no code" order and specifies "palliative care only." One problem is that in many settings there are many physicians involved in a patient's care. In hospital units with large numbers of physicians, disagreements among them can lead to conflicting orders and problems for the nurses in communicating with families about the reality of what is happening. Such actions have been found to contribute to confusion for families and to make it difficult for them to give up active medical treatment (Mannon, 1985).

Movement toward labeling the patient as dying requires some consensus among the various people involved and working agreements among them about boundary rules and subject matter appropriate for discussion. Once consensus has been reached that the patient is dying, the rules related to the goal of getting well are relaxed, and the rules related to dying comfortably are accepted. The latter usually include a relaxation of visiting hours, permission for families to sleep over, and minimal attention to therapeutic medical regimes (Martocchio, 1980). This shift in focus permits the patient and family to adapt to the experience of dying.

Patients' and Families' Adaptations to Dying

Martocchio (1980) found that dying patients in the hospital indicated their personal awareness of dying in a number of ways. Some turned to religion and its special meaning for them. Others described and interpreted their dreams. Others talked about particular symbols that signified the meaning of life and death to them. Martocchio identified two patterns of patients' adaptation to the knowledge that they were dying. *Relief from uncertainty* was a response characterized by a searching for closure either through religion or coming to terms with the universe. It was observed most commonly after a lingering illness. *Escape* was a response characterized by an attitude of resignation and efforts to get away from loneliness and despair. It was most often observed in the downward slope trajectory.

Families also showed certain adaptive patterns once the dying trajectory was clear, according to Martocchio (1980). *Permission to die* was a pattern of adaptation characterized by the family's openly offering consolation to the dying person and giving the message that continuing to fight to live is no longer necessary. *Invitation to die* consisted of an acknowledgment to the dying person, usually after a long and debilitating illness, that giving up and letting go was all right. *Relabeling as nonperson* was an adaptive pattern in which the family members no longer perceived the dying patient as a person. This pattern was observed when the patient was no longer able to communicate, the noncommunicative state was persistent, and the timetable for dying was unpredictable.

Although initially the physician has great power over information and other factors that affect the social experience of dying in the hospital, the ongoing processes of living, working, and dying are shaped by the actions and transactions of all participants in the experience. These interpersonal negotiations are intricate and subject to change. The outcomes for dying patients as persons are quite variable and depend greatly on the choices and actions of their families and physicians and nurses.

INSTITUTIONAL DYING: A CHANGING
SOCIAL PROBLEM

The nature of dying in the 1990s is understandable when it is viewed as another reflection of the secularization and technologization of Western societies. The secularization and technologization of death have resulted in a range of complex problems, including the allocation of scarce resources to the living and the dying and the dehumanizing effects of applied technology on the experiences of people whose lives are ending.

Values in Conflict

Even though dying has become a phenomenon largely controlled by organizational goals, it also continues to be a singular experience in the personal and interpersonal lives of those for whom forthcoming death carries significant meaning. The problematic nature of some types of institutional dying can be explained, at least in part, as a collision between two systems of values.

From the perspective of the organization and its workers, services for dying people are a portion of the work to be done and the tasks to be accomplished. The tasks associated with dying need to be regularized and routinized to maximize efficiency and to assist the staff in the maintenance of sentimental and social control (Glaser & Strauss, 1965; Sudnow, 1967). The problem is that dying is also a human transition with significant meanings in the cultural, social, and personal spheres. The tasks associated with this definition of dying have to do with bringing closure to life in an acceptable manner and completing unfinished business with persons who are important. The values at issue here are particularistic, having much to do with the dying person's relationships to nature, other people, and the community.

The institutions that provide patient care in the United States have been organized around the primacy of the life-saving ethic, and the emphasis placed on control over death has impeded the development of person-oriented services (Benoliel, 1978). The bulk of health care resources has been allocated to high-technology and biomedical research centered on the diagnosis and treatment of disease. Medicare coverage also supports the biomedical model, providing coverage for hospitalization but little for nursing home care (Benoliel & Packard, 1986). Society's investment in high-technology medical care has fostered a public attitude of expecting too much from technology. There is now a simplistic expectation that early diagnosis of any disease can lead to cure (Jennett, 1985). To date, investment in caregiving services for an aging population at risk has been comparatively minimal.

Costs, Technology, and Aging

Current evidence suggests that the use of high-technology health care procedures burdens as well as benefits people and is very expensive. Knaus, Draper, and Wagner (1983) performed a prospective study of 1,987 consecutive admissions to an intensive care unit over a 30-month period and identified 74 patients with severe acute and chronic problems who represented 40% of the admissions but received 80% of the resources. Of this group, 80% were dead before they left the hospital, and 92% were dead within 6 months after hospitalization. On the basis of this and other analyses, Knaus et al. argued that (a) there is little evidence the intensive care unit has improved either the survival rate or the quality of life for many patients and (b) the intensive care unit is a highly inefficient use of medical resources.

The 1990s have been characterized by growing public awareness of finite resources and the high cost of medical care. In 1984, about 11% of the gross national product in the United States was spent on health, and roughly one third of this went to the care of those over the age of 65. Elderly persons make more use of hospitals and nursing homes than do younger persons, and the cost of their hospitalization is greater. In 1981, the average annual per capita expenditures for hospitalized elderly persons were $1,381, compared with $392 for hospitalized young and middle-aged persons (Davis, 1986). High administrative costs have been targeted as the reason for the higher cost of hospitalization in the United States than in other countries, such as Canada (Redelmeier & Fuchs, 1993).

Many questions have been raised regarding the effect of high-technology medicine on living and dying. Verbrugge (1984) made a case that mortality rates have fallen, with one consequence being that elderly persons are living longer with the progressive disabilities of chronic disease. Avorn (1986) argued that society needs to rethink the relationship between medicine and death and questioned whether additional medical care is necessarily in the patient's best interests. Callahan (1986) argued that the high cost of medical care in combination with an aging population has created a serious moral problem vis-à-vis the allocation of health resources disproportionately to the illness needs of the elderly.

Over the past 40 years, institutional dying in the United States has been shaped by two societal forces: (a) the powerful influence of high-technology medicine on the characteristics of hospitals and (b) the paucity of attention paid to the social as well as health needs of an aging population. The care needs of elderly persons require different kinds of services than intensive medical care and custodial placement without concern for personal wishes.

An effort to change social policies to reflect a concern for basic human values is demonstrated in the rise of the hospice movement. Yet the power of scientific medicine and a worship of technology still permeate society, making the introduction of change very difficult. People still look to physicians for miraculous ways of curing them from their ills, and this image is perpetuated through the influence of the mass media. The push for cost containment means that fewer governmental resources will be available for the caregiving needs of vulnerable groups, and cost containment will undoubtedly influence the characteristics of institutional dying in the future. Whether the future will bring a balance between technology and humanism remains to be seen, but, whatever the outcome, it will show in the services available to those who are dying.

REFERENCES

Aries, P. (1974). *Western attitudes toward death.* Baltimore: Johns Hopkins University Press.

Aries, P. (1981). *The hour of our death.* New York: Knopf.

Avorn, J. L. (1986). Medicine, health, and the geriatric transformation. *Daedalus, 115,* 221–225.

Benoliel, J. Q. (1975). The realities of work. In J. Howard & A. L. Strauss (Eds.), *Humanizing health care* (pp. 175–183). New York: Wiley.

Benoliel, J. Q. (1977). Nurses and the human experience of dying. In H. Feifel (Ed.), *New meanings of death* (pp. 124–142). New York: McGraw-Hill.

Benoliel, J. Q. (1978). The changing social context for life and death decisions. *Essence, 2*(2), 5–14.

Benoliel, J. Q. (Ed.). (1982). *Death education for the health professional.* Washington, DC: Hemisphere.

Benoliel, J. Q., & Packard, N. (1986). Nurses and health policy. *Nursing Administration Quarterly, 10*(3), 1–14.

Bluebond-Langer, M. (1978). *The private worlds of dying children.* Princeton, NJ: Princeton University Press.

Callahan, D. (1986). Adequate health care and an aging society: Are they morally compatible? *Daedalus, 115,* 247–267.

Centers for Disease Control. (1985, May 10). Update: Acquired immunodeficiency syndrome— United States. *Morbidity and Mortality Weekly Report, 34,* 245–248.

Centers for Disease Control. (1990, November 30). HIV prevalence estimates and AIDS case projections for the United States: Report based upon a workshop. *Morbidity and Mortality Weekly Report, 39,* 1–31.

Centers for Disease Control. (1993, January 7). Advance report of final mortality statistics, 1990. *Morbidity and Mortality Weekly Report, 41,* 1–15.

Davis, K. (1986). Aging and the health-care system: Economics and structural issues. *Daedalus, 115,* 227–246.

Degner, L. F., & Beaton, J. I. (1987). *Life–death decisions in health care.* Washington, DC: Hemisphere.

Downs, J. F. (1971). *Cultures in crisis.* Beverly Hills, CA: Glencoe Press.

Dracup, K. A., & Breu, C. S. (1977). Strengthening practice through research utilization. In *Communicating nursing research* (Vol. 10, pp. 339–353). Boulder, CO: Western Interstate Commission for Higher Education.

Ebert, R. H. (1986). Medical education at the peak of the era of experimental medicine. *Daedalus, 115,* 55–81.

Elmslie, K., Mulligan, M., & O'Shaughnessy, M. (1988). Occupational exposure to the human immunodeficiency virus among health-care workers in Canada. *Canada Diseases Weekly Report, 14–43,* 197–200.

Engel, G. L. (1977). The need for a new medical model: A challenge for biomedicine. *Science, 196,* 129–136.

Glaser, B. G., & Strauss, A. L. (1965). *Awareness of dying.* Chicago: Aldine.

Glaser, B. G., & Strauss, A. L. (1968). *Time for dying.* Chicago: Aldine.

Gruenberg, E. M. (1977). The failures of success. *Milbank Memorial Fund Quarterly, 55,* 3–24.

Hay, D., & Oken, D. (1972). The psychological stresses of intensive care nursing. *Psychosomatic Medicine, 34,* 109.

Hellinger, F. J. (1991). Forecasting the medical care costs of the HIV epidemic: 1991–1994. *Inquiry, 28,* 213–225.

Hess, G. (1970). Health care needs inherent in emergency services Can they be met? *Nursing Clinics of North America, 5,* 243–249.

Hilberman, M. (1975). The evolution of intensive care units. *Critical Care Medicine, 3,* 159–165.

Horn, S. D., Sharkey, P. D., Chamber, A. F., & Horn, R. A. (1985). Severity of illness within DRG's: Impact on prospective payment. *American Journal of Public Health, 75,* 1195–1199.

Illich, I. (1976). *Medical nemesis.* New York: Random House.

Jennett, B. (1985). High technology medicine: How defined and how regarded. *Milbank Memorial Fund Quarterly, 63,* 141–173.

Jensen, D. (1973). Crisis resolved: Impact through planned change. *Nursing Clinics of North America, 8,* 735–742.

Jones, W. H. (1978). Emergency room sudden death: What can be done for the survivors? *Death Education, 2,* 231–248.

Kane, F. I. (1985). Keeping Elizabeth Bouvia alive for the public good. *Hastings Center Report, 12*(6), 5–8.

Kayser-Jones, J. S. (1981). *Old, alone and neglected.* Berkeley: University of California Press.

Knaus, W. A., Draper, E. A., & Wagner, D. P. (1983). The use of intensive care: New research initiatives and their implications for national health policy. *Milbank Memorial Fund Quarterly, 61,* 561–583.

Knowles, J. H. (1973). The hospital. In *Life and death and medicine* (pp. 91–100). San Francisco: Freeman.

Mannon, J. M. (1985). *Caring for the burned: Life and death in a hospital burn center.* Springfield, IL: Charles C. Thomas.

Martinson, I. M., Armstrong, G. D., Geis, D. P., Anglim, M. A., Gronseth, E. C., MacInnis, H., Kersey, J. H., & Nesbitt, M. E. (1978). Home care for children dying of cancer. *Pediatrics, 62,* 106–113.

Martocchio, B. C. (1980). *Living while dying.* Bowie, MD: Robert J. Brady.

McGinity, P. F., & Stotsky, B. A. (1967). The patient in the nursing home. *Nursing Forum, 6,* 238–261.

McIntosh, J. (1977). *Communication and awareness in a cancer ward.* New York: PRODIST.

Mumma, C. M., & Benoliel, J. Q. (1984–85). Care, cure, and hospital dying trajectories. *Omega, 15,* 275–288.

Mushkin, S. J., & DiScuillo, A. (1974). Terminal illness and incentives for health care usage. In S. J. Mushkin (Ed.), *Consumer incentives for health care* (pp. 183–216). New York: PRODIST.

National Center for Health Statistics. (1991). *Vital statistics of the United States, 1988, Vol. II, Mortality, Part A* (DHHS Publication No. PHS 91-1101). Washington, DC: U.S. Government Printing Office.

National Commission on Acquired Immune Deficiency Syndrome. (1991). *America living with AIDS: Transforming anger, fear, and indifference into action.* Washington, DC: U.S. Government Printing Office.

O'Donnell, L., & O'Donnell, C. (1988). Hospital workers and AIDS: Effect of inservice education on knowledge and perceived risks and stresses. *New York State Journal of Medicine, 87,* 278–280.

Quint, J. C. (1967). *The nurse and the dying patient.* New York: Macmillan.

Raffel, M. W. (1984). *The U.S. health system: Origins and functions* (2nd ed.). New York: Wiley.

Redelmeier, D. A., & Fuchs, V. R. (1993). Hospital expenditures in the United States and Canada. *New England Journal of Medicine, 328,* 772–778.

Regan, T. (Ed.). (1980). *Matters of life and death.* Philadelphia: Temple University Press.

Rosen, G. (1963). The hospital: Historical sociology of a community institution. In E. Freidson (Ed.), *The hospital in modern society* (pp. 1–36). New York: Free Press.

Rosenblatt, P. D., Walsh, R. P., & Jackson, D. A. (1976). *Grief and mourning in cross-cultural perspective.* Minneapolis, MN: Human Relations Area Files Press

Scitovsky, A. A. (1984). The high cost of dying: What do the data show? *Milbank Memorial Fund Quarterly, 4,* 591–608.

Seligman, R. (1977). The burned child. In E. M. Pattison (Ed.). *The experience of dying* (pp. 245–251). Englewood Cliffs, NJ: Prentice-Hall.

Stannard, C. I. (1973). Old folks and dirty work: The social conditions for patient abuse in a nursing home. *Social Problems, 20,* 329–342.

Strauss, A. L., Corbin, J., Fagerhaugh, S., Glaser, G. B., Maines, D., Suczek, B., & Wiener, C. L. (1984). *Chronic illness and the quality of life* (2nd ed.). St. Louis: Mosby.

Strauss, A. Fageraugh, S., Suczek, B., & Wiener, C. L. (1985). *Social organization of medical work.* Chicago: University of Chicago Press.

Suarez, M., & Benoliel, J. Q. (1976). Coping with failure: The case of death in childhood. *Issues in comprehensive pediatric nursing* (pp. 3–15). New York: McGraw-Hill.

Sudnow, D. (1967). *Passing on: The social organization of dying.* Englewood Cliffs, NJ: Prentice-Hall.

Swanson, T. R., & Swanson, M. J. (1977). Acute uncertainty: The intensive care unit. In E. M. Pattison (Ed.), *The experience of dying* (pp. 119–137). Englewood Cliffs, NJ: Prentice-Hall.

Toynbee, A. (1968). Traditional attitudes toward death. In A. Toynbee, A. K. Mant, N. Smart, J. Hinton, S. Yudkin, E. Rhode, R. Heywood, & H. H. Price (Eds.). *Man's concern with death* (pp. 59–94). London: Hodder and Stoughton.

Verbrugge, L. M. (1984). Longer life but worsening health? Trends in health and mortality of middle-aged and older persons. *Milbank Memorial Fund Quarterly, 62,* 475–519.

Vladek, B. C. (1980). *Unloving care: The nursing home tragedy.* New York: Basic Books.

Wilson, D. C., Ajemian, I., & Mount, B. M. (1978). Montreal (1975)—The Royal Victoria Hospital palliative care service. *Death Education, 2,* 3–19.

Chapter 6

Care of the Dying:
The Hospice Approach

Marcia Lattanzi-Licht and Stephen Connor

The word *hospice* was used in medieval times to refer to a place where travelers could find rest and shelter on their journey. Religious orders historically maintained hospices, offering care for the soul of the weary or ill. In the 19th and 20th centuries, the Irish Sisters of Charity began to use the word *hospice* to refer to homes for dying patients (Saunders, 1978). Eventually, hospices offered medical care, particularly care for the very ill and dying. The words *hospital, hostel, hotel,* and *hospice* all derive from the Latin *hospitus,* meaning "a place in which guests are received." The themes of hospitality and caring for those in need are common to all the modern derivations.

Today's hospice is not a place; it is a coordinated interdisciplinary program of pain and symptom control and supportive services for terminally ill persons and their families. A hospice program addresses physical, emotional, social, and spiritual needs. Hospice care is at the same time a new and old, practical and symbolic service. It is a return to a more human, family-oriented philosophy of care aimed at controlling symptoms and improving the quality of life for individuals with a terminal illness.

THE ORIGIN OF HOSPICE CARE

Hospice programs in their current form are designed to attend to the needs of a population that has often been isolated, ignored, or abandoned. Dame Cicely Saunders developed the present approach to care of the dying. In 1967, she founded St. Christopher's Hospice in London, and to this day she remains a strong voice for the needs of dying persons and their families. The story of her efforts to bring about better care for the dying is a personal one. In 1948 she grew close to David Tasma, a 40-year-old man who had escaped the Warsaw ghetto and was dying of cancer. They discussed a vision of care that would alleviate physical distress and offer personal human contact, creating opportunities for death with peace and dignity. When Mr. Tasma died, he left Dr. Saunders 500 pounds sterling to begin the establishment of this new type of care, a legacy that led to the creation of St. Christopher's Hospice.

The spread of hospice programs in the United States has resulted from many grassroots efforts of communities wishing to develop volunteer home care services. Hospice programs developed in the early to mid-1970s. The first program began delivering services in 1974 in New Haven, Connecticut. Dr. Sylvia Lack, along with a committed group of other founders, established a model for hospice programs in the United States. Since 1974, more than 1,900 hospice programs have been established in the United States. In 1975, Dr. Balfour Mount initiated the Palliative Care Unit at the Royal Victoria Hospital in Montreal, Quebec. The pioneering efforts in Canada adapted the British hospice model to the setting of the university teaching hospital.

Hospice programs in North America have been based on the values and practices of the hospice programs in England. Hospice programs in the United States have been further shaped by gaps in the health care system as well as by the nature of the communities in which they are located. A major initial emphasis was on home care services.

Today, hospice programs exist in various forms throughout the world (Harris & Finlay-Jones, 1987). In the Western world, the hospice movement is widely seen as incorporating a more appropriate philosophy and approach to caring for the dying than may be found in hospitals. In spite of the slightly different approaches used, all hospice programs retain the vital basic principles taught at St. Christopher's.

The Need for Hospice Care

The subject of death is particularly unpleasant for medical personnel. Health care professionals are taught to cure and often see death as a failure. The dying person, in effect, becomes a deviant in the medical subculture (Wheeler, 1973), subject to health care professionals' avoidance and fears. Medical personnel can give up and actually avoid or spend less time with the dying patient and his or her family. One of the rewards of hospice work for health care professionals is the redefinition of medical success from curing to caring.

Whereas in earlier eras dying was a process attended to by family and friends, by the mid-1970s, 70% of deaths occurred in institutions such as hospitals and nursing homes (Veatch, 1976). The trend for deaths to occur in hospitals means that dying people are isolated from all that is familiar to them and are spending the last period of their life in a place that offers them limited understanding and few choices (Hinton, 1963).

As a result of the increasingly impersonal and bureaucratic nature of health care, the terminally ill are often "processed" by external systems with little regard for personal needs or wishes (Kastenbaum, 1980). Advances in technological interventions and the institutionalization of death have distanced families from the care of a family member with a terminal illness and increased their levels of distress. Care is often fragmented, and both the dying person and family members lose their roles in decision making.

In addition, whereas treatment advances for malignant diseases have lengthened the life span for some, they have simply increased the time of ill health and dependence for others. Hospice care has become an option for those who do not want to die in a hospital. Family members caring for their loved one at home can feel less guilt and self-recrimination at the time of bereavement (Schulz, 1978).

Also, involvement in the actual physical caregiving can be very therapeutic (Hine, 1979).

The Growth and Development of Hospice Care

More than an alternative form of care, hospice care was seen originally as a movement for change in the health care system. Two groups were aware of gaps in the range of services available to address the needs of dying persons and their families. Interested consumers from communities and health care professionals who were familiar with the inadequacies and limitations of the existing system collaborated to form an unusually powerful base for the evolution of hospice care.

Another unique aspect of the development of hospice care is its rapid spread and evolution. The rapid growth of hospice care meant that rules and regulations, accreditation, and licensure were often a step behind the process. As a result, the early years of hospice care witnessed a freer, more personalized program development, born out of individual community needs and resources. There was also little reimbursement potential, and early hospices relied heavily on voluntary efforts. Consumers had fewer protections from unqualified providers and perhaps limited services (Kilburn, 1988).

It is notable that one of the long-range goals in the development of hospice care was "to incorporate hospice care philosophies and principles into the fabric of the nation's health care system" (Rezendes & Abbot, 1979). Corr and Corr (1985) strongly emphasized that hospice care is a philosophy, not a facility, and that hospice principles can be applied in diverse ways. Their experience led them to believe that hospice principles are applicable not only to terminally ill cancer patients, but also to individuals coping with other terminal conditions, chronic illnesses, or bereavement.

THE HOSPICE CARE APPROACH

Pioneers in the field of hospice care, such as Dame Cicely Saunders and Dr. Sylvia Lack, worked to define and develop the care innovations that distinguish hospice care as well as the values on which they are based. An emphasis on *quality of life* is central to the philosophy of hospice care. The hospice approach recognizes that at some point diseases can be beyond curative efforts and a different type of treatment and care is then required. The *defining components* of the hospice approach are as follows:

1   The *patient and family* are the unit of care.

2   A comprehensive, holistic approach is taken to meet the patient's physical, emotional, social, and spiritual needs, including major attention to effective *symptom control and pain management.*

3   Care is provided by an *interdisciplinary team,* which includes medical supervision and use of volunteers.

4   The patient is kept at home or in an inpatient setting with a homelike environment where there is *coordination and continuity of care.*

5   In addition to regularly scheduled home care visits, *services are avail-able* on a 24-hr, 7 day-a-week, on-call basis.
6   The focus of care is on *improving the quality of remaining life,* that is, on palliative, not curative, measures.
7   *Bereavement follow-up* services are offered to family members in the year after the death of their loved one.

Philosophy and Values of Hospice Care

The National Hospice Organization (NHO), an organization incorporated in 1978, is dedicated to creating a national forum for hospice care issues, including standard setting and education. In *The Standards of a Hospice Program of Care* (1993b), the NHO defines the "Hospice Philosophy":

Hospice provides support and care for persons in the last phases of incurable disease so that they may live as fully and as comfortably as possible. Hospice recognizes dying as part of the normal process of living and focuses on maintaining the quality of remaining life. Hospice affirms life and neither hastens nor postpones death. Hospice exists in the hope and belief that through appropriate care, and promotion of a caring community sensitive to their needs, patients and their families may be free to attain a degree of mental and spiritual preparation for death that is satisfactory to them. Hospice offers palliative care to terminally ill people and their families without regard for age, gender, nationality, race, creed, sexual orientation, disability, diagnosis, availability of a primary caregiver, or ability to pay. (p. iii).

The values that this philosophy incorporates are values of individual worth and importance and an approach of advocacy rather than prescriptive paternalism. It is recognized that not all dying persons and their families desire or need hospice care. The needs of the individual and family and their request for care are important elements, along with the coordination of care, which includes working with the dying person's primary physician.

A major tenet of hospice care is that the dying individual and his or her family should be offered choices. One of the significant choices that increases the sense of control for the dying person and the family is the option for care to be given at home if circumstances allow. Home care was the original experience and emphasis of hospice in the United States. Inpatient care is now part of the hospice continuum of care, but it is used only when necessary.

The Evolution of Hospice Care

In the 20 years since the first hospice program began, there has been a rapid proliferation of hospice programs across the United States. In 1992 there were 1,935 hospices identified in the NHO's annual census. The growth in the number of patients served by hospice programs in the past 5 years has been substantial (see

Figure 1). In 1992, 37% of all people who died of cancer in the United States were under the care of hospice programs. Although people with AIDS have had difficulty using hospice care because of their youth and hope for survival, 31% of AIDS patients who died in the United States in 1992 received hospice care.

Hospice programs not only are growing in number, but are growing in size. In 1992, 21% of the hospice programs in the United States had budgets in excess of $1 million. Initially some hospice programs were concerned about becoming Medicare certified, but Medicare reimbursement is now a major source of funding for hospice programs. In 1992, 72% of American hospice programs reported being certified or having certification pending.

Hospice programs in the United States are still predominantly non-profit organizations. Only 5% of programs report being for profit, and 6% are run by the government. An independent hospice corporation is the model for 40% of hospice programs, 37% are a division of a hospital, and 21% are a division of a home health agency.

In 1992, 53% of the hospice patients in the United States were men, 68% of whom were 65 or older. Of the women, 72% were over 65. There was still a preponderance of Caucasian patients (85%) among admissions, with 9% of patients being African American, 3% being Hispanic, 1% being Native American, and 2% being another race. The majority (63%) of hospice patients were married, although only 55% of them lived with their spouse. Twenty percent of the patients lived with their children, 10% with a significant other, and 5% with parents. A full 10% of hospice patients had no primary caregiver.

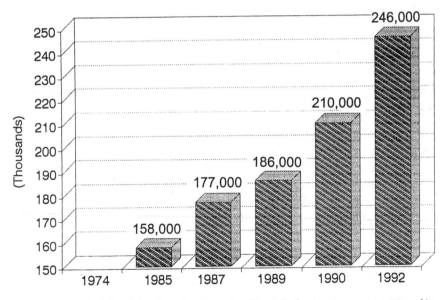

Figure 1   Growth of the U.S. hospice patient population. (Note: The first hospice program was started in 1974, but the first National Hospice Organization census was not conducted until 1985.)

The growth of hospice care is remarkable given that it has been seen as a consumer's movement (Callan, 1979), a grassroots movement (Longest, 1980), a reaction to deficits in the medical care system (Finn Paradis & Cummings, 1986), and even a counterculture trend (Munley, 1983). Russell (1989) pointed out that hospice programs, with their popular roots, rapidly gained the government's interest and attention, changing from a grassroots movement to a structure within the bureaucracy.

The Dying Person's Needs

The time of dying can involve an exaggeration and intensification of the needs and fears that are in many ways basic to the human experience.

To be in pain, dependent, . . . in a state of isolation from one's family, to lose authority to influence the course of one's life—these exigencies can be more threatening than death. (Koenig, 1973)

Death itself cannot be conquered, but the fears that are part of the experience of dying can be addressed (Pattison, 1977). Hospice care directly addresses the fears of suffering and pain, loss of self-control, loss of identity, loneliness, sadness, and of the unknown.

Summarizing the literature, Schulz (1978) said there is a consensus on the three major needs of the terminally ill person:

1 The need to control pain;
2 The need to retain dignity and the feeling of self-worth, and
3 The need for love and affection.

As this list shows, the needs of dying persons are basic human needs, differing only in their intensity, which is caused by the disequilibrium of the dying process. By attending to patients' primary physical symptoms and needs, hospice workers create the potential for other higher order needs to be addressed. The emphasis on pain and symptom control is a hallmark of hospice care. The attention to the dying person's needs is approached with a philosophy of advocacy that respectfully invites the dying person and the family to define their needs and the care they desire. The hospice approach is to *meet the dying person and family where they are.* Rather than offering a predetermined package of services, the dying person and family members discuss their needs and resources and choose from the menu of available services.

The Interdisciplinary Team

The goal of providing holistic care demands involvement from a variety of disciplines able to address not only the dying person's physical needs, but also his or her psychological, emotional, and spiritual needs. Work in an *interdisciplinary team* context implies more than a multidisciplinary collection of individuals focused on a task. Interdisciplinary teams are not just engaged in shared, common goals; the members assume that collectively they can offer care by actively engaging with and learning from each other. There is less competition and more collaboration because individuals are asked to expand their roles and share responsibility with the person most able to meet the care objectives. Volunteers are included as respected members and often contribute valuable insight and input not available to the professionals involved. Overall care is coordinated by the dying person's primary physician. In addition, the hospice team typically includes a nurse, nursing aide, chaplain, counselor or social worker, and pharmacist. Hospice program administrators are important team members who may or may not attend the team meetings. Other team members may be involved as needed, such as a physical or occupational therapist, music therapist, psychiatrist, dietitian, and massage or relaxation therapist.

Typically, the interdisciplinary team holds weekly meetings to discuss the plan of care for the dying persons and families the hospice program serves. Problem solving and information sharing are two main goals of the interdisciplinary team meeting. In addition, the meeting is an opportunity for hospice team members to receive supervision and support designed to help them cope with the stresses involved in caring for the dying.

Members of the interdisciplinary team, including volunteers, also attend a training program in which they are presented information on the principles of hospice care, the concerns of the dying, funeral preparations, and coping with grief and bereavement. Most training programs encourage participants to explore their own experiences with death and grief and to gain perspective on the motivations, values, beliefs, and meaning that sustains them in their work. Schneider and Kastenbaum (1993) found that hospice volunteers typically have strong religious values and rely frequently on nondogmatic and personal praying as a way of coping with the stresses involved in the care of the dying. Hospice workers seem to have unique competencies for dealing with death in their own lives as well as in the lives of patients (Robbins, 1994).

Family Members' Needs

Although death is a very personal experience, it is also a central experience in a family's life. Family members are a person's greatest resource for intimacy, acceptance, support, and rewarding relationships. Family relationships can also be conflicted and complicated by differing personalities and needs. In facing the death of a loved one, family members are asked to put that person's needs first and, if possible, to offer physical care and support. The family members, as well as the dying person, all struggle with a sense of loss of control, a loss of power, and an awareness of personal vulnerability in the face of death. In addition, the demands of physical caregiving are considerable, particularly for the primary caregiver, the person responsible for organizing and/or delivering the physical care.

In identifying the conditions that can contribute to an "appropriate death," Weisman (1972) cited warm, personal relationships and open communication as two of the most important elements. Hospice care enhances and facilitates these elements whenever possible. Efforts are geared toward creating opportunities for open communication between the dying person and family (Pattison, 1977). Often, the hospice nurse, home health aide, volunteer, or social worker acts as a buffer, mediating between the dying person and the primary caregiver or other family members. The presence of outside resource persons can help reduce the considerable tension and distress the family is experiencing.

Early in the hospice involvement, the dying person may be interested in social interaction and conversations with the hospice nurse or volunteer. Hospice workers are often able to relate to the dying person as a unique individual, without focusing on the disease or the person's past. The nurse or volunteer can become, in effect, a *transition object,* a person to whom the patient has not had an ongoing attachment and who will not be painful to lose. It is often easier for the dying person to be with a stranger than to be with family, because the eventual separation will not have a major impact.

As the dying person begins to withdraw, shifting away from people and turning inward toward the self, family members are in greater need of reassurance and support. At this point, the hospice team members increase their efforts to give family members information on what to expect as death approaches. The time close to death is a time of intensified need for the family members.

CASE ILLUSTRATION:

Mr. Owens, a 64-year-old businessman, was in the terminal stages of metastatic prostate cancer. He was cared for by Karen, his 33-year-old middle daughter, who lived nearby. Karen expressed concern at her father's lack of activity, and at the fact that he was spending considerable time in bed. The hospice nurse caring for Mr. Owens asked him to rank the level of his pain at several points in the day. Using a 10-point scale on which $1 = low$ and $10 = high,$ with specific descriptors for each level, Mr. Owens typically rated his pain at 3–4, indicating considerable discomfort. The hospice nurse contacted Mr. Owens's physician and over the next few days focused on helping Mr. Owens and Karen monitor his pain and titrate the around-the-clock medication dosage. Both the hospice nurse and home health aide found that Mr. Owens was slightly resistant to increasing the amount of pain medication and occasionally delayed or skipped a dose. Mr. Owens's pain continued at a level of 2–3 for several more days.

The hospice nurse mentioned her concern over Mr. Owens's level of pain and lack of activity at the interdisciplinary team meeting. A priority for hospice pain management is to break the cycle of pain and help the patient achieve a self-monitored level of 0–1 on the 10-point scale of pain control. The hospice chaplain inquired about Mr. Owens's cultural and religious background. The interdisciplinary team suggested that the nurse and home health aide talk with Mr. Owens and Karen about any beliefs or experiences that might be interfering with his use of pain medication.

Several days later, Mr. Owens told the home health aide about a favorite uncle with a chronic illness who had become addicted to pain medication that was withdrawn and changed several months prior to his death. The painful family memories around that experience and his own stoic nature were prohibiting Mr. Owens from managing his own pain. After several talks with the hospice nurse, Mr. Owens agreed to take his pain medication more faithfully, and his pain level stayed consistently low.

A visit by the hospice social worker helped Karen deal with her frustrations about caring for her father and their difficulty in communicating. A volunteer was enlisted to stay with Mr. Owens for 2–3 hr twice a week to give Karen time to run errands, exercise, or see friends. With his pain under control, Mr. Owens enjoyed visits from his work associates and friends as well as from the hospice volunteer. He spent several hours a day on a chaise lounge on his porch, and visited with friends and read there. The hospice interdisciplinary team later reflected on the valuable lessons in understanding reasons for resistance to pain medication, and in supporting the dying person's need to make choices and decisions that are a reflection of his or her person's life.

THE DELIVERY OF HOSPICE SERVICES
Preponderance of Cancer Patients

In the early years, most hospice programs in the United States cared almost exclusively for cancer patients. This came about as a result of a limited ability to determine prognosis in the noncancer patient population. If a determination could not be made as to when a patient would die, it would be difficult to admit him or her to a hospice program. This bothered many in the hospice movement, because it was clear that there were many other dying persons who were not being served. The advent of the AIDS crisis forced the issue with many hospice programs. To respond to the needs of so many people dying of AIDS, hospice programs were obliged to change their admission criteria to include patients with nonmalignant terminal illness. It was then reasoned that if people with AIDS could be admitted to hospice programs, services should be expanded to others as well, including those with motor neuron diseases, severe pulmonary disease, congestive heart failure, cardiovascular disease, and a variety of other less common terminal conditions.

At present, almost all hospice programs admit patients with a variety of terminal illnesses. On average, 22% of the patients in hospice programs have a terminal illness other than cancer. In spite of this, the issue remains a difficult one for hospice programs, because patients with illnesses other than cancer tend to be difficult to manage and often become chronic patients who have to be discharged from the program. This raises ethical difficulties when, for instance, after discharge, the individual deteriorates. The intensive support and improved quality of life provided by a hospice program give some patients further reason to live. It is important to note that hospice programs are generally not geared to provide chronic care, another prominent gap in the health care system in the United States. The intensive efforts necessary for good hospice care are difficult to maintain for long periods. Also, the emotional preparation for death cannot be accomplished if death is only a distant possibility.

Concentration on the Elderly

In 1992, 68% of male and 72% of female hospice patients were over the age of 65 (NHO, 1992). It is only natural that hospice programs would focus their energy on the elderly, because they are the ones most likely to be dying. There is generally a correlation between increasing age and decreasing fear of death (Neimeyer, 1988). The elderly, having lived their lives, are less likely to want to do everything possible to prolong it. The reverse is true for the young, who have yet to live their lives. Willingness to enroll in a hospice program is greatly influenced by one's perception of hope. As much as hospice care stresses living and quality of life, patients perceive that entering a hospice program means accepting the reality that death is near.

Locus of Care

Care in the home has been the focus of hospice programs in the United States since their beginning. This is a curious development, considering that the founders of the modern hospice movement in England devoted their efforts almost exclusively to the creation of inpatient facilities for the dying. It is perhaps a reflection of American history that we would want to do what they did, only differently, putting our own stamp on hospice care. Besides, Americans cherish their homes almost above all else. At a practical level, the operating expenses are much less for a home care program.

Concurrently the English are now trying to move away from expensive inpatient care toward the creation of in-home hospice services, while American hospice programs, frustrated over a lack of inpatient facilities, are moving toward a variety of inpatient options.

Currently, hospice patients spend an average of 64 days in their homes (NHO, 1992). This includes a growing number of residents of skilled nursing facilities (SNFs) who are admitted to hospice programs. The hospice program views the SNF as the patient's home and delivers services just as it would to a patient at home. In addition to the patient's family, the SNF staff are enlisted in caregiving, either as hired caregivers or sometimes as the patient's family. In spite of the limitations of the environment, hospice care needs to be available to people in SNFs, because a significant portion of the dying population reside there.

As hospice programs reach more and more of the terminally ill, they are finding more people who are not able to be safely cared for at home. At first, most hospice programs refused to serve those without primary caregivers. As time has progressed, hospice program administrators have realized that those without support are often the ones who need help the most. As hospices have reached out to these clients, they have had to face new problems. Admitting them to an acute care inpatient facility with no plan for discharge creates serious financial problems for the hospice and the facility. Usually, these clients do not require the skilled care that is provided at an SNF and have to wait long periods for a bed in a custodial nursing home. If they can afford to hire in-home primary caregivers, care works out well. However, this can be quite expensive.

Admission to a residential care facility works for some clients. However, once clients become nonambulatory and unable to do self-care, they usually have to be discharged. An alternative being pursued by many hospice programs in the United States is the creation of a residential facility that can retain patients until they die. This type of facility has been approved by a number of states. In California, it is referred to as a *congregate living health facility*. In other states, it is called a *hospice residence facility*. The push to develop these programs resulted from the problems hospice programs have encountered in caring for people living with AIDS. Because they are usually denied admission to SNFs, they are often housed in acute care hospitals at great expense. An AIDS residence is very cost-effective for people with AIDS who have no one to care for them.

Adult Hospice Day Care

A number of hospice programs have begun to explore the provision of adult hospice day care. This type of care is especially effective when the patient's caregivers are under stress as a result of having to work, their own health problems, strain from long-term caregiving, and so on. The day care operation is "a day out and a day off" (Corr & Corr, 1992a), offering a day out for the patient and a day off for the caregiver.

Adult day care offers the patient an opportunity to interact with others facing terminal illness. It can involve people in a hospice program sooner than they might otherwise have considered. Hospice staff have more frequent contact with both the patient and family, and volunteers play a vital role in the operation. If financing can be arranged, adult hospice day care can be an effective component in the hospice continuum of care.

Some hospice programs have tried to combine all types of inpatient care—acute, skilled, and residential—under one roof. This has been problematic for general acute care because physicians are reluctant to do rounds outside the hospital setting, and many states require that extensive facilities be built that are never likely to be used by the hospice program. In addition to the expense, there are many obstacles in states' process of approving health care plans and granting certificates of need, not to mention the political obstacles in being perceived as a competitor by other hospitals.

Hospice Care for Children

More and more hospice programs are expanding their services to children. At present, 90% of hospice programs accept children as patients. The death of a child is psychologically devastating. Emotional support and good symptom management are paramount (Armstrong-Dailey, 1991). Of course, parents find it extremely difficult to end their attempts to find a cure for their child.

A number of hospice programs have developed specific pediatric hospice programs to respond to the unique needs of children. In many cases, admission requirements have been made more flexible to accommodate continuation of treatment. Expressive therapy services have become more common in work with both children who are patients and their siblings and with children whose parents are dying. Programs for grieving children are also becoming a more common part of hospice bereavement services. In spite of their initial reluctance, hospice programs are accepting the challenge of working with children facing life-threatening illness (Corr & Corr, 1992b). The NHO has recommended that all terminally ill patients have a right to receive hospice care, regardless of their age (NHO, 1993).

CASE ILLUSTRATION:

Michael was the first-born child of the Andersons. For the past 2 years he had been treated for acute leukemia at a major metropolitan area children's hospital. Now, just weeks after Michael's 13th birthday, the Andersons were told that all treatment possibilities were exhausted and that Michael would probably die within 2–3 weeks. Emotionally devastated, his parents began to make plans for taking Michael home to care for him until he died. The staff of the children's hospital assisted the Andersons in planning for taking Michael home, reassuring them that if at any point they felt unable to care for Michael at home, they could return to the hospital.

The hospital social worker contacted the hospice program serving the area where the Andersons lived, and the hospice nurse who specialized in pediatric care made an initial visit to Michael and his parents while he was still in the hospital. After consulting with the hospital staff, the hospice nurse met again with the Andersons to discuss Michael's care at home. The following morning, Michael was discharged and taken home by his parents. The hospice nurse visited them at their home that day and showed them how to provide physical care for Michael to increase his comfort. In addition, she discussed what they might expect in their care of Michael.

In the days that followed, the hospice nurse visited the Andersons daily. Mr. and Mrs. Anderson were distressed and in need of reassurance and support. Mrs. Anderson's mother and Mr. Anderson's sister both came in from out of town to stay with and support the family. Neighbors and other family members were helping provide meals and other tangible support. A hospice volunteer helped with the grocery shopping and offered companionship to Michael's younger sister, Ann. Two of Michael's friends and Ann spent time with him playing computer games and watching movies.

Fifteen days after the Andersons took Michael home, he died with his mother and father at his side. They had called the hospice nurse earlier that evening and she was with the family for several hours while Michael was dying. The Andersons planned Michael's funeral with the help of their minister, and both the hospice nurse and volunteer attended the service.

In the weeks that followed, the hospice nurse and volunteer each visited the family for a final time and complimented the parents on their excellent care of Michael. A volunteer with the hospice bereavement service visited the Andersons 3 weeks after Michael's death. She listened as they recounted the experience of caring for Michael and talked with them about difficulties they were experiencing since his death. She left some brief written materials that described the grief process. In addition, she left them a flier that described a support group for parents who had experienced the death of a child.

The hospice bereavement volunteer continued to phone the Andersons periodically and visited them three other times during the following year. For 5 months after Michael's death, the Andersons attended an 8-week support group for bereaved parents and occasionally attended the group's monthly meetings. Ann attended a group for siblings that met at the same time as the parents' group.

HOSPICE TODAY AND TOMORROW: CURRENT ISSUES FOR HOSPICE PROGRAMS IN THE UNITED STATES

In the last 10 years, hospice programs have gone from being primarily small, volunteer, home-based programs to mature, professional-dominated organizations that serve large numbers of dying patients both in the home and in a variety of inpatient settings.

The vehicle for this growth has been the availability of Medicare and Medicaid benefits to hospice patients. These benefits have allowed hospices to deliver more services to some patients but have limited access to hospice care for others. In the early years of hospice care in the United States, there was a belief that whatever type of care a dying patient wanted should be provided. Because services were provided by volunteers at no charge, reimbursement and the cost of treatment were not significant factors. Patient choice was a foremost value. It was generally believed that if patients were accurately educated about their condition and prognosis, they would choose not to pursue extensive curative treatments.

In 1982, Congress created a Medicare benefit for hospice care. This was the only new benefit added to the Medicare program during the Reagan administration, and it represented an extraordinary bipartisan effort.

Hospice care reimbursement was "sold," in part, to the Congress as a cost-effective program. Hospice programs would keep dying patients at home and out of the hospitals and discourage them from pursuing expensive futile treatments. In return, hospice programs would receive adequate reimbursement for the care they provided at home, and the patients would be kept comfortable through good symptom management.

Palliative Care

The definition of palliation has evolved considerably in recent years. Whereas 10 years ago a hospice program might have viewed radiation therapy as aggressive treatment, it is now seen as a frequent and effective treatment for symptoms such as bone pain. Similarly, many cancer chemotherapies are now part of hospice plans of treatment. If they are used to help reduce or control a physical or emotional symptom, then they fit this newer description of palliation. The NHO (1993) has suggested the following definition for palliation:

Palliative care is defined by hospice as treatment which enhances comfort and improves the quality of a patient's life. The goals of intervention are pain control, symptom management, quality of life enhancement, and spiritual/emotional comfort for patients and their primary care support. Each patient's needs are continuously assessed and all treatment options are explored and evaluated in the context of the patient's values and symptoms. (p. 12)

The assumption that, if properly educated, dying patients will opt to discontinue aggressive treatment runs into many difficulties. There are substantial numbers of patients who, when faced with this choice, decide to go for even a slim chance at recovery. The reasons for this are often valid. The presence of hope in a dying person should not be viewed as unhealthy. Most people need something to hang onto when faced with tragedy. Dying persons may have important unresolved issues to address, or they may be terrified at the prospect of loss of self. They might be young or middle-aged and feel that they are being robbed of the opportunity for a full life span. Whatever the reason, it goes against the fundamental belief in the patient's right to make treatment choices when a hospice program refuses to serve a dying patient who is not ready to die.

Admission Considerations

Until recently, hospice programs limited admissions to patients who agreed to a conservative form of palliative care that included only the least invasive forms of treatment. Many programs would not provide treatments such as intravenous fluids, parenteral medication administration, chemotherapy and radiation, gastric feeding, and other "aggressive" procedures. The patient who wanted cardiac life support or could not decide whether to forego resuscitation might be denied hospice services.

There were several reasons for these admission limitations. First, aggressive procedures were not seen as being palliative or contributing to the patient's comfort, and, second, they were often quite expensive. Moreover, the staff at many hospice programs lacked competence in performing some of these procedures. Finally, because hospice care is usually paid for on a set per-day payment rate, the hospice program is responsible for paying for all treatment related to the terminal condition. This put hospice programs at some financial peril if they accepted a patient who wished to continue to pursue aggressive treatment.

Some of the more successful hospice programs in the United States have realized that limiting patients' treatment choices is ultimately counterproductive to success in delivering hospice care to as many dying patients as need services. Removing obstacles to admission and allowing patients greater choice of treatment have led to more cooperative relationships between hospice programs and the medical community. Physicians are more likely to refer a patient to a hospice program if hands are not tied regarding what treatment to order for the patient.

This arrangement works well for large hospice programs and those in communities where there is a balanced practice of oncology. The number of patients who want expensive treatments is offset by the number of patients who demand few treatments and services. Smaller hospice programs and those near research centers where new treatment protocols are encouraged find it much harder to accept all treatments in the hospice care plan.

Some hospice programs in this situation have had to be more flexible in how they respond to the needs of dying patients in the community. If a patient does not fit the model of the hospice Medicare benefit, these programs have had to find other ways of continuing to serve the patient. After all, hospice programs were serving patients long before there was such thing as reimbursement. Some programs see these patients at no charge, and others get reimbursement for parts of their service by getting dually certified as both a hospice and a home health agency and billing for professional visits made. In this case, the hospice program is not responsible for paying for all the treatments the patient receives.

Cost-Effectiveness

A larger number of studies have been done on the cost-effectiveness of hospice care. The results of these studies have been equivocal. Some researchers have reported no or questionable savings, whereas others have found substantial savings. A large, randomized, controlled trial of hospice care provided at a Veteran's Administration hospital found no difference in treatment costs between hospice and conventional care patients (Kane et al., 1984).

The National Hospice Study funded by the Health Care Finance Administration (Mor, Greer, & Kastenbaum, 1988) revealed that home-care-based hospice programs' treatment costs were lower than the costs of conventional care regardless of length of stay and hospital-based hospice programs' treatment costs were lower than conventional-care costs only for patients with lengths of stay of less than 2 months. These results may have been affected by selection bias, however.

The results of a study of the effect of the hospice program on Medicare Part A expenditures during the first 3 years of the program reported that Medicare saved $1.26 for every dollar spent on hospice care. However, these estimated savings may have been overstated as a result of persistent selection effects (Birnbaum & Kidder, 1992). Patients who elected hospice care may have been predisposed to use less institutional care than conventional-care patients.

Still, most studies have shown some positive effects of hospice care on the experience of dying patients. No studies have shown patients to be worse off for using hospice care. Perhaps the variations in findings reflect differences in the quality of hospice care offered throughout the United States. It is important to remember that the main reason for creating hospice programs was to improve the care of dying individuals, not to save health care dollars.

Cost Concerns and Treatment Choices

When the hospice Medicare benefit was created in the early 1980s, no one expected that hospice programs would become responsible for paying for so much treatment. The field of oncology has grown immensely in recent years. There are more treatments available now that were not developed 10 years ago. Overall survival in the cancer patient population has not improved much, but progress has been made in the treatment of certain malignancies, such as testicular cancer, lymphomas, and leukemia.

Unfortunately, having sold their services as reducing treatment use and costs, hospice programs can hardly go back to Congress now and ask that they be excused from having to pay for the most expensive treatments. The issue of deciding who gets aggressive treatments with minimal chance of response is one that is bigger than hospice care. Society will have to grapple with the ethical issues that are created by refusing some patients access to treatment. To start with, the medical profession will have to begin by developing practice guidelines that are flexible enough to assist the clinician in knowing when to suggest withdrawal of treatment.

Of course, physicians are human too, so much of the motivation for continuing to offer treatment lies in doctors' difficulty in accepting the death of a patient. Often, it is the physician's difficulty with his or her own mortality that motivates the continuing quest for a cure beyond the limits of current medical practice.

Being Outside the Mainstream of Health Care

In the 20 years that hospice care has existed in the United States, palliative care has not been brought into the mainstream of the health care system. Although perhaps medical professionals are more aware of what they should be doing in the care of dying patients, they still are not doing it. The popularity of Dr. Jack Kevorkian's physician-assisted euthanasia campaign says a lot about the unmet needs of dying patients in the mainstream health care system.

Many people involved in the early days of hospice care sincerely believed that if the hospice movement did its job well, in 20 years it would no longer need to exist. It was believed that the public and the medical establishment would embrace the hospice movement's values and methods and palliative care for the dying would become a routine part of medical practice. Why hasn't this happened?

The answer to this question is complex, but it seems to boil down to two main factors. The first is the human factor. In spite of the progress made in death awareness since Elizabeth Kübler-Ross's pioneering medical school workshops in Chicago in the 1960s, avoidance of the reality of natural death pervades American society. Unnatural death, however, remains a fascination to the public, perhaps as a way of ignoring the inevitable approach of disease and old age.

The aversion to facing death carries over from the public to the medical profession. Many physicians and nurses enter the field seeing death as the enemy to be conquered. Anxiety about their own personal deaths can be bound up in their ongoing and noble efforts to preserve life. The debate about abortion rights had spilled over into the debate about end-of-life decisions. Many antiabortion activists equate efforts to allow natural death with euthanasia. In spite of their strong stand against euthanasia, hospice programs have been perceived as part of an effort to focus on the right to die rather than the value of life.

With so much debate going on about life-and-death issues, it is surprising that the public is still poorly educated about hospice care. In a recent Gallup poll (NHO, 1992), 9 out of 10 people said they preferred to be cared for and to die in their home, and 3 out of 4 were very interested in hospice care when it was described to them. However, when presented with the term *hospice,* 22% of those who were interested in the services hospice programs provide said they were unlikely to choose it because they were unfamiliar with it.

The second reason for hospice care's lack of integration into the mainstream health care system is that hospice programs have not won over the leaders of the medical profession. Hospice care is still viewed by many as an alternative to traditional care. Most important, there is little research being done in the United States on palliative and supportive care. The medical profession values research on the latest advances in curing illness and the latest technology that may be to treat illness. Palliative care deemphasizes cure and minimizes technological interventions. The work done by hospice programs is considered unimportant, something done by physicians who lack the ability to explore the "frontiers" of medicine.

In the United States, there has been resistance to the notion that palliative care should be a recognized subspecialty. In contrast, hospice programs in the United Kingdom have been embraced by the medical establishment. Recently, the Royal College of Physicians accepted palliative medicine as a recognized specialty, and a significant number of career posts are being established. The difference is the dedicated involvement of many highly regarded physicians who are conducting ongoing research on the intricacies of palliative medicine. Palliative care is a broad field that addresses the relief of a variety of physical, psychological, and spiritual symptoms; palliative medicine is the medical component of that care. A considerable body of knowledge on palliative medicine has accrued that is not readily available or accepted in the United States.

At present, the most training in palliative care an American medical school student can expect is approximately one lecture during 4 years of schooling. Small wonder that the care of the dying in the United States is still generally poor and occasionally horrible.

Future Issues for Hospice Programs in the United States

What can be done to improve the acceptance of hospice care in the United States? There are a number of areas where progress needs to be made. A sustained effort at conducting credible research on symptom management is needed. Most of this research needs to be conducted by physicians who are well regarded in the profession. Government support for this effort in the form of National Institutes of Health grants needs to be sought by the NHO. Hospice programs must overcome their resistance to applying scientific measurement methods and allow more patients access to their services.

The current possibility of health care reform in the United States poses both opportunities and risks for the hospice movement. The growth in hospice care that has come from Medicare reimbursement could be lost if hospice care is not part of the new basic benefit package. It is most likely that hospice care will be seen as part of the solution to the health care crisis. Twenty-eight percent of the Medicare budget is spent in the last year of life, half of that in the final 2 months (Lubitz & Riley, 1993). Hospice care is the only viable alternative to expensive attempts at prolongative treatment for dying patients.

If patients are to be served by hospice programs, greater cooperation is needed from physicians. It is unlikely that physicians' perception of hospice care will change until palliative medicine gains recognition as a legitimate medical pursuit. Because there is already an overabundance of specialists in the United States, the creation of a palliative medical specialty seems unlikely. One possible approach would be the creation of a diploma in palliative medicine that could be awarded to a physician after completion of a yearlong self-study course.

The challenge for all providers in the new health care system will be to provide the highest quality of care the most efficiently. How will hospice programs prove that what they offer is better than conventional care? The hospice community must discover how to more accurately describe the outcomes of its care in terms that relate directly to quality of services as well as to quality-of-life measures. Hospice programs need to describe consistently how well their care controls pain and other symptoms.

A national database is needed that can show how hospice programs stack up against other providers on indices such as percentage of patients dying at home, amount of hospital use, quality of symptom management, and patient and family satisfaction. In addition, hospice programs must continue to demonstrate that their care is cost-effective by substituting care in the home for hospitalization.

If hospice programs are to continue to grow as the health care system changes, their services will have to be at a consistently high level of quality. Hospice programs still vary considerably in the quantity and quality of services they deliver. The quantity and quality of services a program offers depends mainly on the level of community support the program receives, the competency of the staff, and whether the program participates in the Medicare and Medicaid hospice benefit. The latest edition of the NHO's *Standards of a Hospice Program of Care* (NHO, 1993) comprehensively describes what ought to be available in a quality hospice program. All hospice programs should strive to meet these standards; however, there is no enforcement other than program self-evaluation. The National League for Nursing has a hospice accreditation program, but few hospice programs have shown interest in participating.

The Joint Commission on Accreditation of Healthcare Organizations (JCAHO) discontinued their hospice accreditation program in 1990 because of its high cost and a lack of participation by the hospice community. The JCAHO plans to begin offering hospice accreditation again in 1995 through the Accreditation Program for Home Care. More hospice programs would participate in accreditation if governmental "deemed status" for hospice certification can offer approval for Medicare reimbursement. Accreditation may be one of the main factors in determining who receives payment in *the new health care system.*

What is happening to the hospice field is similar to what other social movements have experienced. A process of redefinition is occurring that has taken a dynamic, creative concept of care and codified it so that it is no longer what it was. It has become a more narrowly defined service with fewer components and described characteristics. This outcome is not necessarily bad, given that it was an adaptation necessary for the survival of hospice care. Had this not happened, anyone could claim to provide hospice care and do as he or she pleases. This would confuse the public, who are already unclear about what the word *hospice* means.

Hospice programs must be careful not to become so rigid that they are unable to accommodate creative solutions to the needs of the dying people they were originally intended to serve. If hospice programs serve only those who are easy to care for or who meet strict admission criteria, the spirit of caring that has made the movement special will be lost and hospice care will be just another cog in the great health care machine.

The essence of hospice care is that it gives highly personalized attention to a dying person and his or her family. Perhaps the uniqueness of this approach is conveyed in the words of Dame Cicely Saunders:

> You matter because you are you.
> You matter to the last moment of your life,
> and we will do all we can,
> not only to help you die in peace,
> but also to live until you die. (Hodder & Turley, 1989, p. 5)

REFERENCES

Armstrong-Dailey, A. (1991). Hospice care for children, their families, and health care providers. In D. Papadatou & C. Papadatos (Eds.). *Children and death* (pp. 225–229). Washington, DC: Hemisphere.

Birnbaum, H. G., & Kidder, D. (1992). What does hospice cost? *American Journal of Public Health, 74,* 689–697.

Callan, P. J. (1979). The hospice movement [Editorial]. *Journal of the American Medical Association, 241,* 600.

Corr, C. A., & Corr, D. M. (Eds.). (1985). *Hospice approaches to pediatric care.* New York: Springer Publishing Company.

Corr, C. A., & Corr, D. M. (1992a). Children's hospice care. *Death Studies, 16,* 431–450.

Corr, C. A., & Corr, D. M. (1992b). Adult hospice day care. *Death Studies, 16,* 155–172.

Finn Paradis, L. F., & Cummings, S. B. (1986). The evolution of hospice in America toward organizational homogeneity. *Journal of Health and Social Behavior, 27,* 370–386.

Harris, R. D., & Finlay-Jones, L. M. (1987). Terminal care in Australia. *The Hospice Journal, 3*(1), 77–90.

Hine, V. H. (1979). Dying at home: Can families cope? *Omega, 10,* 175–187.

Hinton, J. (1963). The physical and mental distress of the dying. *Quarterly Medical Journal, 32,* 1–10.

Hodder, P., & Turley, A. (1989). *The creative option of palliative care.* North Fitzroy, Victoria, Australia: Melbourne City mission.

Kane, R. L., Wales, J., & Bernstein, L., (1984). A randomized controlled trial of hospice care. *Lancet, 1,* 890–894.

Kastenbaum, R. J. (1980). Toward standards of care for the terminally ill. In R. A. Kalish (Ed.), *Caring relationships: The dying and the bereaved.* Farmingdale, NY: Baywood.

Kilburn, L. (1988). *Hospice operations manual.* Arlington, VA: National Hospice Organization.

Koenig, R. (1973). Dying vs. well-being. *Omega, 4,* 181–194.

Longest, B. B., Jr. (1980). Delivery prospers in diversity. *Hospitals, 54*(7), 91–94.

Lubitz, J. & Riley G. (1993). Trends in Medicare payments in the last year of life. *The New England Journal of Medicine, 328,* 1092–1096.

Mor, V., Greer, D., & Kastenbaum, R. (1988). *The hospice experiment.* Baltimore: Johns Hopkins University Press.

Munley, A. (1983). *The hospice alternative.* New York: Basic Books.

National Hospice Organization. (1992). Poll says hospice leads. *Hospice, 3*(3), 4.

National Hospice Organization. (1993a). *1992 Provider census data.* Arlington, VA: Author.

National Hospice Organization. (1993b). *Standards of a hospice program of care.* Arlington, VA: Author.

Neimeyer, R. A. (1988). Death anxiety. In H. Wass, F. Berardo, & R. Neimeyer (Eds.), *Dying: Facing the facts,* 2nd ed. New York: Hemisphere.

Pattison, E. M. (Ed). (1977). *The experience of dying.* Englewood Cliffs, NJ: Prentice-Hall.

Rezendes, D., & Abbott, J. (1979). Hospice movement: Way stations for the terminally ill. *Perspective on Aging, 8.*

Robbins, R. A. (1994). Death competency: Bugen's Coping with Death Scale and death self-efficacy. In R. A. Neimeyer (Ed.), *Death anxiety handbook: Research, instrumentation, and application* (pp. 149–165). Washington, DC: Taylor & Francis.

Russell, G. (1989). Hospice programs and the hospice movement: An investigation based on general systems theory. *The Hospice Journal, 5*(3/4), 23–49.

Saunders, C. M. (1978). *The management of terminal disease.* London: Edward Arnold.

Schneider, S., & Kastenbaum, R. (1993). Patterns and meanings of prayer in hospice caregivers: An exploratory study. *Death Studies, 17,* 471–485.

Schulz, R. (1978). *The psychology of death, dying, and bereavement.* Reading, MA: Addison-Wesley.

Veatch, R. M. (1976). *Death, dying, and biological revolution.* New Haven, CT: Yale University Press.

Weisman, A. D. (1972). *On dying and denying.* New York: Behavioral Publications.

Wheeler, A. L. (1973, April). *The dying person: A deviant in the medical subculture.* Paper presented at the annual meeting of the *Southern Sociological Society,* Atlanta, GA.

Chapter 7

Legal Perspectives on Planning for Death

Sheryl Scheible Wolf

Most people have at least a vague idea of what they would like done with their belongings and their bodies upon death. Their primary concerns often center around providing for their family or friends and ensuring that funeral arrangements do not impose unnecessary burdens on their survivors. Some people may also wish that their lives not be prolonged once meaningful existence is no longer possible. In death, as in life, legal restrictions may frustrate the achievement of their goals. Failure to prepare for death in light of the current law may not only thwart an individual's intentions, but cause considerable delay and expense for family members and other survivors. It is critical, therefore, to plan for the practical aspects of death and to make arrangements that will be legally enforceable.

THE IMPORTANCE OF LEGAL COUNSEL

The legal restrictions concerning death have been established to assure that the deceased person's genuine intentions are carried out, to safeguard family members and the public at large, and to provide an efficient and orderly system of distributing property and disposing of bodies. Much of the law regulating the disposition of property and the body originated in previous centuries and no longer reflects contemporary policies and family composition. In recent years, however, considerable legal reform has been proposed for updating the law relating to death to reflect modern values and policies and to remove outdated obstacles in order to effectuate the individual's intent (Waggoner, Wellman, Alexander, & Fellows, 1991).

The states control most of the law involving death, and considerable variation exists among them. While a number of uniform laws have been promulgated in an attempt to standardize state law (Uniform Probate Code [U.P.C.], 1990), not all state legislatures have adopted them. When a uniform law is enacted at the state level, legislative bodies frequently alter some provisions to accommodate the perceived needs and policies of their own state; thus, even "uniform" laws may vary from state to state.

In general, the law of the state where a person resided at the time of death controls disposition of the body and of property. Real estate, however, is governed by the law of the state where the property is located. Therefore, the laws of several states may have an impact on a particular individual's estate planning. In addition, certain federal laws, which are applicable nationwide and preempt state laws, also must be considered.

Although general legal principles govern the planning for death, it is important that individuals seek local legal advice in order to comply with the relevant law and to ascertain whether the necessary documents have been properly executed to ensure implementation of the individual's desires without unnecessary complications. Attorneys specializing in probate law and estate planning have expertise in developing individualized plans, implementing the precise verbal formulas, and foreseeing contingencies that might otherwise be overlooked. An estate plan should be reviewed periodically because its effect may be altered by changes in the law; by alterations in the family through births, deaths, divorces, and adoptions; and by variations in financial circumstances and assets.

DISPOSITION OF PROPERTY
The Probate Process

Upon death, the financial and business affairs of the deceased person, or decedent, must be concluded; debts, taxes, and funeral and administrative expenses must be paid; and then remaining assets are distributed to those entitled to them. The legal mechanism for accomplishing these functions is the probate process, which is administered by the appropriate state court. Property that the decedent owns at death comprises the probate estate, which is managed by a personal representative. The personal representative is referred to as an *executor* if designated by the decedent's will or an *administrator* if appointed by the court. Traditionally, the terms *executrix* and *administratrix* were applied if the personal representative was female, but these terms have been largely replaced by gender-neutral terms.

The personal representative may be required to post a bond to ensure that he or she properly performs the required duties. Those duties include inventorying and collecting assets; notifying parties with claims; paying debts, expenses, and taxes; winding up business affairs; arranging for the preparation of documents; distributing the decedent's remaining property to the appropriate people; and preparing a final accounting and closing the estate (Waggoner et al., 1991). The personal representative usually retains an attorney to assist in the estate administration. The personal representative and the attorney are entitled to fees, which may be calculated as a percentage of the estate's value and are often regulated by law. These fees, along with court costs, can make the probate process expensive as well as time consuming.

Intestacy

Property owned by a decedent that is not transferred by a valid will is distributed pursuant to the laws of intestacy. Intestacy statutes in every state designate, in order of preference, those relatives who are entitled to the decedent's property as heirs. Unless a person falls within an explicit statutory category as an heir, he or she is not entitled to share in the intestate estate.

The details of intestacy statutes vary considerably among states, although they tend to follow general patterns. All states designate a surviving spouse and the decedent's direct descendants, or *issue*, as heirs, to the exclusion of other relatives. The spouse and issue share the estate in proportions prescribed by statute. While the decedent's own children have priority over more distant issue, if a child of a decedent has predeceased the parent, that child's children or other descendants receive the share as representatives of their parent (U.P.C., 1990, § 2-103). When the decedent is not survived by any issue, some states give the surviving spouse the entire estate, whereas others apportion the estate between the spouse and the decedent's living parents.

When a person dies leaving no surviving spouse or descendants, the property usually passes to the decedent's ancestors and issue of deceased ancestors. In most states, parties related to the decedent through his or her parents have superior rights to those related through a more distant ancestor, such as a grandparent (U.P.C., 1990, § 2-103). In a number of states, parties who are related to the decedent through ancestors more distant than grandparents are not considered heirs (U.P.C., 1990, § 2-103); in other states, any relative may qualify. When no one qualifies as an heir, property *escheats*, or passes to the state (U.P.C., 1990, § 2-105).

Except for surviving spouse, only parties related to a decedent through bloodlines (*consanguinity*) generally are considered heirs; persons related by marriage (*affinity*), such as in-laws and stepchildren, or by informal relationships, such as cohabitants, foster children, or friends, are excluded from the intestacy statutes. Currently, legally adopted relatives have the same status as biological relations (U.P.C., 1990, § 2-114). Persons born outside of marriage, formerly considered illegitimate, are now treated the same for inheritance purposes as marital children, provided that paternity can be proven according to the state's evidentiary standards (U.P.C., 1990, § 2-114). Persons related by the half-blood, that is, who share one, but not both, parent or other ancestor of the decedent, are treated the same as those related by the whole-blood in most states (U.P.C., 1990, § 2-107).

Wills

As a general principle, a person is free to leave his or her property to anyone by executing a valid will, a formal legal document that is probated through the court system. A person who withholds a will from probate may be subject to criminal or other penalties.

Every state has statutory formalities for executing wills, which must be strictly complied with in most states (McGovern, Kurtz, & Rein, 1988). Although the statutes governing wills, like the intestacy statutes, vary considerably among states, many states recognize wills that were validly executed in another state (U.P.C., 1990, § 2-506). The strict, formal requirements are imposed to ensure that the writer of a will, the *testator,* realizes the importance of the act; to protect against fraud or other improper actions of others; and to provide evidence at probate to ensure that the document truly represents the testator's intentions (McGovern et al., 1988). A document that does not properly comply with the statutory formalities has no legal effect, and the estate will pass by intestacy.

In general, any adult of "sound mind" may dispose of property by will. A will is invalid if the testator lacked mental capacity or if another person unduly influenced the testator to the extent that the will does not represent the testator's true intentions. Parties who would receive the testator's estate if the will is invalidated, such as the intestate heirs, may initiate a will contest, a legal action challenging the validity of a will.

A formal will must be attested to and signed by at least two witnesses, often according to a prescribed ceremony. The witnesses may be required to appear at the probate procedure and testify that the will was properly executed. Although a number of states have relaxed their statutory qualifications for witnesses, a person who will benefit from the will should not be a witness because some states disqualify an interested witness from receiving all or a portion of a gift given to the witness in the will (McGovern et al., 1988).

Although all states recognize and prefer formal wills, rather ironically, approximately half the states also permit handwritten, unwitnessed wills, known as *holographic wills*. However, even where holographic wills are recognized, they should be used with caution because individual state requirements for holographic wills vary. Printed or typed words, rather than those written in the testator's own hand, may be struck out or may render the entire instrument inoperative. Specific information, such as the date, may be required, and some states require that a holographic will be found in a particular location at the testator's death (N.C. Gen. Stat, 1953, § 31-3.4). In addition, a handwritten document may be questionable as to whether it was actually intended to be a will or was merely a statement of future intentions, a memorandum for a later will, or other writing (McGovern et al., 1988). An ambiguous writing does not constitute a valid will and is ineffective to transfer the decedent's property. Furthermore, language is interpreted according to its legal meaning, and imprecision may frustrate the testator's intentions. Because of the hazards involved, it is advisable to avoid holographic and form wills and to seek professional legal assistance to ensure that a will is effective.

The testator retains complete ownership and control over his or her assets during lifetime, and a will may be totally or partially revoked at any time before the testator's death, provided that the testator has the requisite mental capacity and the intention to revoke. Wills may be revoked by physical acts specified by statute, such as burning, cutting, or tearing (U.P.C., 1990, § 2-507). The appropriate acts must be performed by the testator personally or by another at the testator's direction and in the testator's presence (U.P.C., 1990, § 2-507). Other physical actions are ineffective to constitute revocation. Because physical acts may be ambiguous, revocation by a subsequent writing that conforms with the formalities required for executing a will is preferable (McGovern et al., 1988). A later valid will may revoke an earlier will, either expressly or by its inconsistency with the terms of an earlier will. The most recent valid will controls disposition of the decedent's property.

A will that has not been revoked properly will be given legal effect at the testator's death. Even though the actual document itself may not exist, its terms may be proved by other competent evidence, usually a copy of the original will. The safest method of revoking a will is to execute a new will that expressly states that all previous wills are revoked (Haskell, 1987).

In many states, once a will has been validly revoked either by a subsequent written instrument or by physical act, it may not be revived and given legal effect. A new will or a new execution ceremony is required.

Specific provisions of a will may be altered by a *codicil,* an additional or supplementary formal document. A codicil leaves the earlier will intact except for the changes and avoids the expense of having an entirely new will prepared.

Certain events in the testator's life may implicitly revoke all or part of a will. For example, in most states, gifts to a former spouse are automatically revoked if the testator divorces (U.P.C., 1990, § 2-802). Historically, a testator's subsequent marriage revoked all or a portion of an earlier will, and this still holds in some states today (Waggoner et al., 1991). Accordingly, a person experiencing important family changes should seek legal advice to determine whether a new will or codicil should be prepared.

In a will, a testator may give specific gifts of identifiable assets to various parties and general gifts of certain sums of money that are to be paid from the overall assets of the estate. Assuming that the testator wants the entire estate to be distributed pursuant to the will, a residuary clause should be included to transfer any remaining property, or *residue,* of the estate to one or more beneficiaries.

Because a will has no legal effect until the testator dies, only the property owned at death will be transferred by the will, and changes in the testator's estate between the time the will is prepared and the time of death may alter its effect. For instance, if the testator sells or gives away assets expressly referred to in the will, the beneficiary of a specific gift will not receive a substitute gift. Even if the item was unintentionally destroyed or stolen, the intended beneficiary of the asset usually will not receive a substitution, such as insurance proceeds or a replacement item. Instead, the new assets will be used to satisfy general gifts or will become part of the residue (U.P.C., 1990, § 2-606).

Furthermore, the estate may have insufficient assets to pay the testator's debts and administrative expenses and to satisfy all gifts. Unless the testator specifies which gifts should be consumed first, the state's statutory *order of abatement* determines payment preferences, and the testator's favored beneficiaries may receive a smaller share of the estate than what the testator intended (U.P.C., 1990, § 3-902).

Similarly, if a will beneficiary dies before the testator, the gift is said to *lapse,* meaning the gift fails. Lapsed gifts become part of the residue of the estate; if the will does not contain a residuary clause or if the residuary gift fails, the lapsed gift is distributed to the decedent's intestate heirs. Most states have an antilapse statute that preserves lapsed gifts for a deceased beneficiary's issue, but most antilapse statutes apply only to beneficiaries who are close relatives of the testator (Waggoner et al., 1991).

Exceptions to the Rules of Inheritance

Heirs or will beneficiaries who receive gifts from the decedent during his or her lifetime may have the value of the gift subtracted from the share they receive upon the testator's death. Many states now require written proof that the testator intended that result (U.P.C., 1990, §§ 2-109, 2-609). Furthermore, an heir or will beneficiary may choose to reject a gift or inheritance and may disclaim or renounce it according to a statutory procedure (U.P.C., 1990, § 2-801).

An heir or will beneficiary may be disqualified from sharing in the estate because of certain improper actions. For example, most states prohibit a person who wrongfully and intentionally killed the decedent from financially benefiting, and the property the killer would otherwise have inherited passes as if the killer had predeceased the decedent (U.P.C., 1990, § 2-803). Also, a few states bar parties who abandoned or failed to support a dependent spouse or child from receiving a portion of that spouse's or child's estate (Dukeminier & Johanson, 1990).

Protecting Family Members

In general, individuals are free to leave their property to whomever they wish and may completely disinherit their heirs by executing a valid will. Nonetheless, wills leaving significant gifts to persons outside of the decedent's family, including nonmarital cohabitants and same-sex partners, are particularly susceptible to challenge by disappointed relatives (Rein, 1984–85).

Most states also protect the decedent's surviving spouse from disinheritance. Eight states—Arizona, California, Idaho, Louisiana, Nevada, New Mexico, Texas, and Washington—traditionally have safeguarded spouses through community property law, a system of property ownership that regards marriage as an economic partnership. In 1985, Wisconsin effectively became a community property state when it enacted the Uniform Marital Property Act (1983), which adopts principles comparable to community property law. Under community property law, each spouse obtains an equal, undivided ownership interest in certain property acquired by either of them during marriage, which is classified as community property. Each spouse may also own separate property, which typically consists of assets owned before marriage and property received individually through gift or inheritance during marriage. Upon the death of one spouse, the surviving spouse is entitled to his or her one-half share of all the community property assets (Waggoner et al., 1991). The decedent spouse may dispose of his or her one-half share of the community property and all of his or her separate assets by transferring them by will. If the decedent spouse dies intestate, the surviving spouse typically inherits a portion of the decedent's property as an intestate heir (U.P.C., 1990, § 2-102A).

In states without community property law, ownership of property acquired during marriage generally is attributed to the spouse who earns the funds for its acquisition. Upon death, a spouse may dispose of his or her own property, and the surviving spouse could be left destitute, especially if the survivor was not employed outside the home. To protect the possibility of disinheritance, most states historically permitted a widow to receive *dower,* a lifetime interest in a portion of certain real estate owned by her husband during their marriage. A surviving husband was eligible for a similar, although not identical, interest, known as *curtesy.* Today, state laws treat spouses of either gender equally, and most have abolished both dower and curtesy (Haskell, 1987).

The majority of states have replaced dower and curtesy with a statutory *elective share* (Haskell, 1987). The elective share allows a surviving spouse, regardless of need, to demand a minimum portion of the decedent spouse's estate. The size of the elective share varies among states, but, often, the surviving spouse is entitled to one third to one half of the estate if he or she has been left a smaller portion or nothing in the decedent's will (Haskell, 1987). The current Uniform Probate Code determines the size of a spouse's elective share on a sliding scale, according to the length of marriage. It also requires consideration of certain assets transferred by the decedent spouse before death as well as of the financial resources of the surviving spouse (U.P.C., 1990, § 2-201).

In most states, surviving spouses and sometimes minor children of the decedent are further protected by entitlements to certain types of property. These frequently include personal belongings and household articles, portions of the decedent's unpaid wages, rights to the family home, and support allotments from the estate during the probate process (U.P.C., 1990, §§ 2-402, 2-403, 2-404).

Unlike the preferential treatment afforded surviving spouses, virtually every state permits a testator to leave nothing, not even the proverbial one dollar, to children or other relatives, regardless of their age, actual financial condition, or physical dependency. Most states, however, afford limited protection to the decedent's children to safeguard them from inadvertent disinheritance. Statutory provisions allow specified children to demand a portion equal to their intestate share if they were not intentionally omitted from the parent's will (U.P.C., 1990, § 2-302). Often, these statutes apply only to children who were born or adopted after the final will was prepared. The statutes generally apply equally to the testator's children born outside of marriage (U.P.C., §§ 2-109, 2-302). A child born alive to a decedent's spouse within 9 lunar months of the testator's death is presumed to be the testator's child and acquires the same inheritance rights as other children. The best practice is to acknowledge all the testator's children in the will and either expressly provide for or disinherit them (Haskell, 1987).

Minor children or incapacitated adult relatives raise additional considerations. A living parent will normally be designated the natural guardian of a minor child, responsible for the child's physical care and custody, but a parent should also appoint a guardian in his or her will, in the event both parents die before the child reaches adulthood (U.P.C., 1990, § 5-202). The guardian of a child will not necessarily be entitled to manage and control the child's property, however, and a will should also designate a person to act as conservator for the child's assets (U.P.C., 1990, § 5-401). If no guardian or conservator is nominated by will, the court will appoint one, which may be more costly and administratively cumbersome. Some states severely restrict the custodian's investment and use of the child's property (Fratcher, 1960). Gifts to or inheritances by incapacitated adults raise similar issues.

Careful estate planning may eliminate many of these potential problems. The Uniform Transfers to Minors Act (1983) authorizes a custodianship to be created for the property of a minor, and trusts may be useful for assuring the financial care of children, the elderly, or handicapped individuals. Most states also authorize direct payment of relatively small gifts directly to a minor's legal guardian on behalf of the child.

Will Substitutes

To avoid the expense and delay of the probate process, a person planning for the disposition of property upon death may decide to transfer many or most assets during life to keep them out of the probate estate. While absolute lifetime gifts are often inappropriate because of the obvious reason that the donor loses the use and benefit of the property during life, a variety of transfers recognized by many states laws allow a person to retain most of the ownership rights to assets during life but still keep those assets out of the probate estate. Because such transfers, when effective, are functionally equivalent to transfers made by will, while avoiding the probate process, they are commonly referred to as *will substitutes.* Unlike a will, however, which can transfer all the testator's property by one document, will substitutes usually are *asset specific,* meaning that each asset must be transferred in a separate transaction (Waggoner et al., 1991).

Without professional legal guidance, a will substitute may fail, resulting in the asset's passing through the probate estate and possibly to someone other than the intended recipient. For example, revocable or conditional gifts are, in general, legally ineffective (Burke, 1993). Promises to make gifts in the future are unenforceable, (Burke, 1993), and transfers of real estate (land and the structures thereon) require delivery of a valid deed. A deed that is intended to become operative only upon the owner's death is invalid (Dukeminier & Johanson, 1990). Although some deeds may permit the owner to retain use and possession of the property until death and then immediately confer the right to possession to another party, precise legal language must be used to effectuate the transaction (Dukeminier & Johanson, 1990).

Another common will substitute is the transfer of property into a form of co-ownership known as a *joint tenancy with right of survivorship.* Under this legal arrangement, two or more parties are given equal rights to the property in question during their mutual lifetimes. When one co-owner dies, his or her ownership interest dissolves, leaving nothing to pass through his or her probate estate. Thus, the survivors' interests automatically expand to include the remaining ownership rights, and the last surviving co-owner becomes the sole owner of the property (Haskell, 1987). The joint tenancy with right of survivorship is frequently created with respect to land, but it may be used for other types of property. The disadvantage of a joint tenancy with right of survivorship is that the original property owner must give equal access to the co-owners in order to achieve the desired result at death (Haskell, 1987). Any one co-owner may terminate a joint tenancy during life and obtain a separate fractional share of the property. Also, joint tenancy ownership subjects the property to claims of any of the co-owner's creditors (Haskell, 1987).

About 20 states recognize a special form of joint tenancy for married couples, known as a *tenancy by the entirety*. The tenancy by the entirety may not be unilaterally dissolved by either spouse, and the property may be shielded from the creditors of either spouse, although the legal implications vary considerably among the states (Haskell, 1987).

Life insurance policies are a common form of will substitute (Haskell, 1987). All states recognize the contractual agreement between a policyholder and an insurance company to pay money to a specified beneficiary upon the death of the insured. Contingent beneficiaries are usually designated to receive the insurance proceeds if the primary beneficiary predeceases the insured. Insurance proceeds may also be paid into a trust or to the insured's estate, but the proceeds may be subject to probate if they are paid into the estate.

Many varieties of life insurance are available, including those that provide lifetime benefits for the insured. Insurance policies allow the insured considerable flexibility over the value of the policy during life and the power to change beneficiaries before death (Haskell, 1987). Money paid directly to a beneficiary of a life insurance policy generally is not accessible to the creditors of the deceased.

Although insurance contracts are useful will substitutes, other types of contractual agreements to transfer property on a person's death are not as uniformly enforceable. For example, a bank account or stock certificate containing a designation that the assets are "payable on death" to another are not effective in some states (Waggoner et al., 1991). Multiple-party bank accounts, however, are highly regulated by state law. By using specific terms, a person may set up an account that gives the depositor complete lifetime ownership and control of the funds and, on death, automatically transfers ownership to another without probate (U.P.C., 1990, § 6-201). In recent years, many states have enacted statutes that validate "payable on death" designations on a wide variety of contractual documents (U.P.C., 1990, § 6-101).

One of the most effective and flexible types of will substitutes is the trust (Waggoner et al., 1991). Any type of property may be placed in a trust, although some assets, such as liquid, income-producing resources, are more suitable than others. The owner of the property (the *settlor* or *grantor* of the trust) may reserve extensive use and control over the property during life. On the settlor's death, the trust property is distributed to designated beneficiaries without becoming part of the probate estate (*Farkas v. Williams,* 1955). Alternatively, the trust may be continued to provide for the care and support of others, according to its terms.

In a trust arrangement, the settlor transfers assets to a trustee with directions regarding the management and distribution of the property. The settlor may be the trustee during life, with a successor trustee designated to take over at the settlor's death or incapacity. Alternatively, a third party, often an officer of a trust company or a bank, may be appointed trustee. The trustee has a legal duty to use the trust property for the beneficiaries and only under the terms provided in the trust document or imposed by the law (Haskell, 1987). A settlor may expressly reserve the right to revoke or amend the terms of the trust, including the power to change or add beneficiaries (Waggoner et al., 1991).

The trustee may be directed to distribute the trust property upon the settlor's death or may be instructed to continue management of the property and distribute designated portions of the income and principal to beneficiaries in the future. A trust may be useful to ensure the continued management of the property and a source of income for minor children, the elderly, or the incapacitated. A trust can continue for several generations of beneficiaries before it is terminated and the remaining assets are distributed. The settlor can tailor the terms of the trust to suit individual desires and may give the trustee discretion to vary the management and distribution of the trust as contingencies arise. Whereas private trusts are restricted in duration by law (Haskell, 1987) trust for recognized charitable purposes may continue indefinitely (Haskell, 1987). Trusts are often considered the most flexible type of will substitute.

A trust created during the settlor's lifetime to act as a will substitute is frequently referred to as a *living trust* or an *intervivos trust.* Trusts may also be established in a will, in which case they are known as *testamentary trusts.* Assets may be transferred by will to a preexisting trust, using a technique referred to as a *pour-over will* (U.P.C., 1990, § 2-511). Use of a testamentary trust or a pour-over will does not avoid probate, however, but is primarily intended to provide professional management and postpone outright distribution of assets until sometime after the settlor's death.

Valid will substitutes are effective ways of legally circumventing the formalities required for wills and for avoiding probate, but they may not be entirely effective for achieving other goals. For example, many jurisdictions today include certain assets transferred to a trust or by other will substitutes in a surviving spouse's elective share (U.P.C., 1990, § 2-202). Some states also allow the decedent's creditors to reach assets transferred by will substitutes in certain circumstances (Waggoner et al., 1991). Furthermore, despite a common misconception, the use of will substitutes usually does not result in significant tax advantages.

Taxes

Death taxes are imposed in two general forms: estate tax and inheritance tax. Estate taxes are assessed on the transfer from the decedent to another; inheritance taxes are levied on the individual recipient. Both types of tax generally are paid from the estate before the remaining assets are distributed to heirs or beneficiaries. The federal estate tax applies uniformly throughout the United States, regardless of which state controls the probate of the decedent's estate. Most states also impose their own death taxes, in the form of either an estate or inheritance tax.

The federal tax law also assesses a gift tax on lifetime transfers. Because the Internal Revenue Code (I.R.C.) was revised to unify the federal gift and estate taxes nearly two decades ago (Tax Reform Act of 1976), the total amount of lifetime gifts and transfers at death is calculated and taxed uniformly, resulting in diminished tax advantages from transferring property before death (Waggoner et al., 1991). However, the current federal gift tax allows individuals to make tax-free lifetime gifts of $10,000 per year to an unlimited number of recipients; married couples jointly can give $20,000 a year to each recipient without tax consequences (I.R.C., 1984, §§ 2503, 2513). Another advantage to lifetime gifts may exist when property is expected to increase in value, because gift and estate taxes are both calculated on the value of the asset at the time of transfer (I.R.C., 1984, §§ 2031, 2512). And while neither gifts nor inheritances are taxable to the recipient for income tax purposes, the recipient may receive later tax advantages by receiving appreciated property at the donor's death, rather than during the donor's lifetime (Waggoner et al., 1991). Lifetime transactions that act as will substitutes and avoid probate, however, are taxed as estate assets whenever the transferor retains any of the many enumerated types of lifetime interests in the property, including income or use of the property or a right to change beneficiaries (Waggoner et al., 1991).

Contrary to popular belief, death taxes should not be of great concern to people of moderate wealth. Currently, only estates greater than $600,000, including the value of taxable lifetime gifts and excluding various allowances, are subject to the federal estate tax (I.R.C., 1984, §§ 2010, 2502). Any amount of property may be given to qualifying charities without tax consequences (I.R.C., 1984, §§ 2055, 2522). Similarly, an unlimited marital deduction allows a person to transfer property tax free to a surviving spouse (I.R.C., 1984, §§ 2056, 2523); however, the tax is merely deferred, and any such property still owned by the surviving spouse at the time of his or her death will be taxable in that spouse's estate.

Because of the complexity and constant revision of the tax laws, a person who anticipates tax consequences on death should procure expert tax advice in order to maximize tax savings.

DEFINING LIFE AND DEATH

Legal definitions of life and death are sometimes ambiguous and may not correspond to contemporary societal values. An individual is considered to be a legal *person* for inheritance and property rights retroactively from the time of conception if he or she is later born alive (U.P.C., 1990, § 2-108). Similarly, a person can recover damages for prenatal injuries (Romney & Duffy, 1990). *Life* is defined differently for purposes of recognizing the competing interest of a woman to obtain an abortion, however. In the landmark 1973 case *Roe v. Wade* (410 U.S. 113), the Supreme Court concluded that a fetus did not have an overriding protected interest until "viability," which the Court held occurred during the third trimester of pregnancy. In 1989, however, in *Webster v. Reproductive Health Services* (492 U.S. 490), the Court upheld a Missouri statute that contained a legislative declaration that a fetus has protectable interests in life, health, and well-being from the moment of conception and declared that the state may have an interest in protecting human life before viability. While affirming the central principles of *Roe v. Wade,* which forbade states from preventing women from making their own ultimate decisions to obtain an abortion before viability, the Supreme Court has recently rejected the trimester analysis. It concluded that viability is "the time which there is a realistic possibility of maintaining and nourishing a life outside the womb" (*Planned Parenthood of Southeastern Pennsylvania v. Casey,* 1992, p. 2816). Thus, states now have greater freedom to regulate abortion.

Uncertainty also exists at the other end of the spectrum, in determining when life has ended. Until the 1960s, death was defined as "the cessation of life; the ceasing to exist; defined by physicians as a total stoppage of the circulation of blood, and a cessation of the animal and vital functions consequent thereon, such as respiration, pulsation, etc." (*Black's Law Dictionary,* 1968, p. 488). Although state law varies, the Uniform Determination of Death Act (1980), which had been adopted by 30 states and the District of Columbia by 1993, provides that

An individual who has sustained either (1) irreversible cessation of circulatory and respiratory functions, or (2) irreversible cessation of all functions of the entire brain, including the brain stem, is dead. A determination of death is to be made in accordance with acceptable medical standards. (§1, p. 1)

What statutes defining death do not do, however, is legislate the extent to which various life-extending medical treatments must be used to prolong life. Postponing death once no reasonable likelihood of recovery exists may not only frustrate the individual's wish to die with dignity, but can financially and emotionally overwhelm the patient's family and place an unnecessary burden on medical resources (Janzen, 1984). Although medical treatment cannot be authorized without a patient's consent, a patient who is unconscious, incapacitated, or underage cannot legally refuse treatment or consent to withdrawal from life-support systems already in place. Despite individual rights to privacy and freedom of choice, countervailing public interests in preserving life, preventing suicide, ensuring the integrity of the medical profession, and protecting family members may conflict with those rights (Janzen, 1984).

To reconcile these conflicting interests, most states have enacted legislation, often known as a *right-to-die, natural-death,* or *death-with-dignity* act, which allows a competent person to execute an advance-directive document, frequently referred to as a *living will.* These documents express the person's intention to decline life-prolonging or extraordinary treatment when death is imminent. The

Uniform Rights of the Terminally Ill Act (1989) similarly confer broad powers on the individual to make an advance declaration regarding the withholding or withdrawal of treatment and relieves third parties from liability for honoring the person's declaration. In the absence of such legislation, similar documents may be useful, although not legally binding, to clarify the patient's wishes.

Although the specifics of right-to-die laws vary among states, the living will must usually be witnessed by two people unrelated to the declarant and without potentially conflicting interests. The document is revocable. A physician who fails to comply with the living will or refuses to transfer the patient to a doctor who will may be subject to sanctions (Uniform Rights of the Terminally Ill Act, 1989).

Recent federal legislation now requires health care providers to provide all adult patients with information regarding their rights under state law to refuse treatment and to formulate advance directives (Social Security Act, 1988). The individual's medical record must be documented as to whether the person has executed an advance directive. Facilities may not discriminate against an individual on the basis of the existence of such a directive and must comply with state law in respecting the individual's stated wishes (Social Security Act, 1988).

An additional option recognized in many states is *durable power of attorney* for medical decisions, in which the individual (*principal*) designates another person to act as his or her agent or representative in consenting to or refusing medical care (U.P.C., 1990, § 5-501). Although the traditional power of attorney was used primarily to authorize another to act in financial and business transactions and automatically terminated on the death or incapacity of the principal, the durable power expands that concept to allow the agency to continue when the principal has lost the legal capacity to make his or her own decisions. Of course, the person using a durable power of attorney for health care matters, must be sure to give the agent precise and detailed instructions.

In the absence of a legally binding advance directive, a court action may be necessary to decide whether treatment of an incompetent person or minor may be terminated. Judicial determinations have focused on ascertaining what the patient would most likely have chosen had he or she been competent and whether the judgment of a third party, such as a parent, guardian, or physician, may be substituted for the patient's consent (*In re Quinlan*, 1976; Kadish, 1992). The court in *In re Quinlan* (1976) suggested that a hospital ethics committee may make these decisions in appropriate cases, rather than require the frequently prolonged process of litigation in court. By 1990, an estimated 60% of hospitals in this country had established bioethics committees (*In re Guardianship of L.W.*, 1992).

In *Cruzan v. Director of Missouri Dept. of Health* (1990), the U.S. Supreme Court held that a state law requiring clear and convincing evidence of a comatose patient's wishes was not unconstitutional. The Court did *not,* however, hold that a state is required to apply such a stringent standard. Under this standard of proof, the Court refused to order the withdrawal of feeding and hydration tubes that had kept the patient Nancy Cruzan alive but in a vegetative state after an automobile accident. Upon rehearing in a Missouri state court, the judge found that the standard had been met, ordered the removal of the tubing, and allowed Nancy Cruzan to die (Waggoner et al., 1991).

Allowing a person to die naturally by withholding treatment in accordance with the person's wishes may be viewed as *passive euthanasia* (Tecklenburg, 1982). *Active euthanasia,* or *mercy killing,* on the other hand, may result in criminal or civil liability. In *State v. Forrest* (1987), a son was convicted of first-degree murder and sentenced to life in prison for shooting his terminally ill father in the head. Similarly, in *Gilbert v. State* (1986), a 75-year-old man was convicted of first-degree murder after he shot his wife who was suffering from osteoporosis, Alzheimer's disease, and arthritis and had been crying and pleading to die.

Another variation of active euthanasia, physician-assisted suicide, recently has drawn national attention, centering around Dr. Jack Kevorkian. Dr. Kevorkian was arrested on more than 15 charges of assisting terminally ill patients to commit suicide but was never convicted, although he was ordered to desist (Zischerk, 1991). A number of states have enacted legislation to prohibit assisted suicide, although few cases have been successfully prosecuted for facilitating the suicide of a terminally ill patient (Geltzer, Andrews, & Mariner, 1989).

DISPOSITION OF THE BODY

The relative legal freedom afforded an individual with respect to property does not extend to the disposition of his or her own body. The decedent's body is not property in any conventional sense of the word and does not become part of the decedent's estate (Scarmon, 1991–92). The right to control one's own body, like other legal rights, ends at death, and any remaining rights pass to living persons.

The law reflects society's deep respect for human life and extends to the treatment of bodily remains after life has ended. Unfortunately, while attempting to protect people from the unreasonable or harmful acts of others and themselves, legal restrictions may disregard the individual's wishes relating to life and death.

Disposing of the Body

Once death has occurred, immediate arrangements must be made for disposing of the deceased's body. Family members and close friends may be emotionally unprepared to make the many necessary decisions for funeral arrangements. During life, a person can specify funeral and burial directions to simplify the responsibilities of survivors. Considerations include whether the body should be buried or cremated; whether funeral home visitation, a memorial service, or religious ceremony is desired; the type of casket to be used and whether it should be open or closed; the nature of any obituary; and whether to request that gifts be made to a specific charity in lieu of flowers (Roybal, 1984). Unless the decedent's close relatives agree with the arrangements, however, there is little certainty that the decedent's predeath plan will be implemented. Traditional law has never recognized a right to decide the disposition of one's own body; rather, the closest relatives (usually a spouse, child, parent, or other household member) have a right and a corresponding duty to bury the deceased in an expeditious and appropriate manner (Scarman, 1991–92).

Although the courts have asserted that the individual's expressed intentions should be respected to the extent that is proper and reasonable, they have often balanced those intentions against any conflicting wishes of the survivors (American Jurisprudence, 1965). Similarly, a decedent's instructions for a nonrelative to decide on funeral and burial arrangements may be overridden by the surviving family members. Because a court may consider a written document more persuasive evidence of the decedent's wishes should a dispute arise (American Jurisprudence, 1965) it is advisable to give a copy of funeral and burial instructions to someone who is likely to be available when death occurs and to discuss the arrangements with family members to obtain their concurrence in advance (Marshall, 1982). A will typically is not read until after disposal of the body, so a separate writing containing funeral plans is preferable.

Cremation has become a less expensive and more accepted option, selected in approximately 15% of all deaths in 1987 (Micheli, 1988). Recently, a few states have enacted statutes that allow individuals to make binding decisions regarding cremation (Texas Code, 1992, § 711.002).

Anatomical Gifts

Despite other restrictions on disposing of the body, individuals have considerable freedom in donating their bodies or specific organs for legitimate medical purposes. In the past, medical research and teaching depended on the bodies of prisoners and paupers and other unclaimed bodies (Marshall, 1982). Although a shortage of corpses for medical purposes has always existed, an increased demand far exceeding the supply has developed since medical advances have been made in the area of organ transplantation (Crown, 1982).

Gifts of anatomical parts at death provide the primary source of transplant organs. During life, vital organs may not be donated because of criminal prohibitions against suicide and homicide (Weissman, 1977). The federal National Organ Transplantation Act (1984) banned the sale of human organs in 1984 and established $50,000 fines and imprisonment for violations. Similarly, informed-consent issues and the health risks of surgical procedures restrict lifetime donation of nonessential organs (Weissman, 1977).

Many types of organs, such as corneas, pituitary, glands, and skin, can be stored in organ banks until needed (Crown, 1982). Other vital organs, such as livers, hearts, and kidneys, must be transplanted immediately to avoid tissue deterioration that may be harmful or fatal to the recipient (Crown, 1982). Therefore, predeath authorization is preferable in order to avoid delay.

No obligation to contribute organs has ever existed. Absent evidence of the deceased's opposing wishes, the closest relatives traditionally have been authorized to make anatomical gifts. Organ donations, especially for transplantation, may alleviate the family's sense of loss and can make the death seem less meaningless (Crown, 1982).

By the early 1970s, all states had enacted some version of the Uniform Anatomical Gifts Act (1987). The act permits an individual to direct organ donation without the consent of surviving relatives. In practice, however, physicians generally refuse a donation when the family objects (Weissman, 1977). The act allows any competent adult to donate specific organs, prosthetic devices, or the entire body to any hospital, physician, medical or dental school, or storage facility to be used for education, research, therapy, or transplant. Only organs that meet necessary requirements of age and physical condition are removed, and nonstorable organs are accepted only if compatible donees are available. Although practice varies among facilities, when only some organs are removed, the body generally is returned to the family for burial (Crown, 1982). When remains are donated for research, some institutions cremate or bury locally, whereas others return the remains or ashes to the family if desired (Quay, 1984).

The Uniform Anatomical Gifts Act contemplates a short, simple statement in a separate document or in a will, even if the will has not yet been probated. Most states provide Uniform Donor Cards, and forms are commonly available documents, such as drivers' licenses and senior citizens' cards. Most widely distributed forms contain insufficient space for specific instructions, but they sometimes include a provision for repudiating donation. The form requires two witnesses. The donor must be competent at the time the form is executed, but mental capacity need not be proven at death.

When a donor card has not been signed or cannot be found, the act permits specified family members to consent to anatomical gifts, absent a contrary expression of intention by the deceased before death. If the designated family members are unavailable, some states permit local officials to authorize donations. Little formality is required for obtaining the consent of a family member, who can authorize by telephone, telegraph, or other recorded device without witnesses (Uniform Anatomical Gifts Act, 1987). This provision has been criticized for failing to protect the rights of the deceased and the family adequately, because genuine informed consent may be unlikely when the request for donation is made almost simultaneously with the notification of death (Quay, 1984). However, if a request is made before death, the family's hope for the patient's recovery, however unrealistic, may be destroyed (Weissman, 1977).

In a recent Gallup poll, 73% of Americans said they would be very likely to donate the organs of their loved ones, whereas only 27% said they would want their own organs taken (Lehman, 1985). Only a small proportion of the population has executed donor cards, however. For example, of approximately 170 kidney transplants performed at one teaching hospital, about 100 of those kidneys were removed from some 60 bodies, none of which carried a donor card (Quay, 1984). Relatedly, many potential donors have gone undiscovered and their organs wasted because hospitals, police personnel, or paramedics failed to discover donor cards because of the nature and time constraints of their duties. If the current organ shortage is to be alleviated, appropriate personnel must be instructed to conduct an immediate and thorough investigation to identify donors, and the public must be made aware of the simple procedure available for making an anatomical gift. The Uniform Anatomical Gifts Act requires hospitals to inquire upon admission whether patients are organ or tissue donors and to record such information. Recent federal legislation facilitates organ donation by regulating organ procurement organizations and authorizing funding (National Organ Transplant Act, 1984).

Registries have been established for facilitating the distribution of certain vital organs. A national computerized system, the Living Bank, is accessible to all hospitals to help match organs with persons awaiting transplants (Crown, 1982).

Although the Uniform Anatomical Gifts Act has been successful in increasing the supply of organs available for transplant, the demand continues to exceed the supply. Routine, nonconsensual removal of organs is presently illegal. Furthermore, if only specified body parts have been donated, removal of additional organs is forbidden. Some commentators have advocated a reversal of the current law, dictating compulsory removal of critical organs (Dukeminier, 1970), which would assert a policy priority of favoring the living over the dead. Mandatory and involuntary removal of anatomical parts may be an unjustified interference with the religious freedom and privacy rights of the survivors, however (Weissman, 1977). An alternative policy would presume consent to organ donation, absent express objection, a practice followed by most European countries (Weissman, 1977).

Funeral and Burial Practices

American funeral and burial practices are largely a product of a religious and legal heritage developed in early England, where the ecclesiastical or church courts controlled matters relating to death (Marshall, 1982). Proper services and burial were considered necessary to ensure that the deceased would attain peace in the afterlife (Marshall, 1982). Before burial, the body was regarded as the vessel of the soul and, as such, was entitled to special care and respect. A churchyard burial was crucial, and the bodies of persons deemed unworthy of a Christian burial were often donated for medical research (Marshall, 1982).

Despite its rejection of the English ecclesiastical courts, American law adopted the English law's general attitudes toward death. A person's religious beliefs notwithstanding, American courts have concluded that a body deserves extraordinary treatment. The courts, however, have experienced difficulty in formulating precise rules, as a 1905 opinion of the Georgia Supreme Court illustrates:

Death is unique. It is unlike aught else in its certainty and its incidents. A corpse in some respects is the strangest thing on earth. A man who but yesterday breathed and thought and walked among us has passed away. Something has gone. The body is left still and cold, and is all that is visible to mortal eye of the man we knew. Around it cling love and memory. Beyond it may reach hope. It must be laid away. And the law—that rule of action which touches all human things—must touch also this thing of death. It is not surprising that the law relating to this mystery of what death leaves behind cannot be precisely brought within the letter of all the rules regarding corn, lumber and pig iron. And yet the body must be buried or disposed of. If buried, it must be carried to the place of burial. And the law, in its all-sufficiency, must furnish some rule, by legislative enactment or analogy, or based on some sound legal principle, by which to determine between the living questions of the disposition of the dead and the rights surrounding their bodies. (*Louisville & N.R. Co. v. Wilson*, 1905, p. 25).

Such indefiniteness regarding disposition of the body remains apparent in the law today.

Funeral and burial procedures in the United States now are largely a matter of religious and social custom (Quay, 1984), rather than legal concern. If the decedent has not left binding funeral and burial instructions, surviving family members must dispose of the body in a timely and appropriate manner. The law forbids the mishandling, desecration, or sale of a body, and the survivors have a right to recover damages from a party who deliberately or negligently mistreats or improperly deals with a body. For example, in *Carney v. Knollwood Cemetery Assn.* (1986), the Ohio Court of Appeals held that relatives may sue for negligent infliction of emotional distress and punitive damages when an ancestor's remains were disinterred and thrown in the refuse. Similarly, in *Christensen v. Pasadena Crematorium of Altadena* (1990), the California Court of Appeals recognized a claim for negligent mishandling of a corpse when employees of a crematorium piled corpses in a van for transport to the facility where, after removing and selling the deceaseds' gold fillings, they cremated 30–40 bodies at one time and returned indistinguishable ashes to the family members.

Furthermore, the law attempts to protect the survivors, who are often in a diminished emotional state, from unfair or deceptive practices by the businesses and industries that provide funeral and burial goods and services.

Regulation of the Funeral Industry

Because of its relationship to the public welfare, the funeral industry is subject to regulation by state and local governments and is supervised by state agencies. Undertakers and embalmers may be required to be licensed and may need to meet certain educational, training, and skill criteria (American Jurisprudence, 1968). Funeral professionals may be subject to discipline for failure to comply with sanitation requirements, for unprofessional or incompetent conduct, or for unfair sales or pricing techniques (American Jurisprudence, 1968). Solicitation of business and advertising often are limited or prohibited. Funeral insurance and preneed contracts for funeral services are legal, but they are regulated because of the potential for fraud, the uncertainty of the time for performance, the possibility that the company may be out of business at the time of death, and the risk that the survivors may be unaware of the plan (American Jurisprudence, 1965).

The funeral industry provides merchandise and services to more than 2 million American families a year. Funerals typically cost about $3,500, but may exceed $10,000 (Micheli, 1988). Often, because the parties arranging a funeral are emotionally distraught and must act promptly, they are not initially concerned with the cost of what may be one of their most expensive lifetime purchases (Roybal, 1984). To protect the vulnerable public from sales pressure and deceptive or fraudulent business practices, the Bureau of Consumer Protection of the Federal Trade Commission began investigating the funeral industry in the early 1970s (Roybal, 1984). As a result, federal regulations, collectively known as the Funeral Rule, were enacted in 1984 (Funeral Industry Practice, 1985). The Funeral Rule requires full disclosure of the costs of funeral goods and services and orders the sale of individual items as well as complete packages. The individual costs of items such as flowers, death notices, hearses and limousines, pallbearers, guest registers, and other services must be disclosed. Pricing information for caskets and outer burial containers must be revealed, and customers must be advised of legal and cemetery requirements regarding necessary products (Funeral Industry Practice, 1985).

The funeral rule prohibits funeral providers from falsely claiming that expensive products are necessary for cremation. The provider must inform the consumer when embalming is not legally required and may not inaccurately characterize the preservative effect of any items (Funeral Industry Practice, 1985). Because consumers are provided full information regarding alternatives and prices, they can select only what they want and need (Roybal, 1984).

Health and Safety Regulations

The rights of the survivors are further restricted by legal regulations designed to protect public health and sensitivities. State and local regulations often control the location and operation of funeral homes and mortuaries to ensure sanitation and to prevent the spread of contagious or infectious disease (American Jurisprudence, 1968). Funeral homes sometimes are prohibited in residential areas or near hospitals to shield neighbors and patients from the constant reminder of death (American Jurisprudence, 1968). Local boards of health may require a burial permit, and states or municipalities may restrict the sites of cemeteries (American Jurisprudence, 1968).

Embalming may be mandated when the body will not be disposed of immediately and refrigeration is not available (Roybal, 1984). Transportation of corpses is regulated, and in extreme circumstances the body may be buried at sea or where it is presently located (American Jurisprudence, 1965). Many localities require a certification of death to provide health data and to compile vital statistics (American Jurisprudence, 1985).

In some areas, crematory ashes may not be scattered over land or water (Roybal, 1984). Once buried, a body may not be disinterred or exhumed except for extraordinary reasons and then only upon court order. Disinterment usually is ordered only when necessary for evidence in a criminal case, such as to prove that a person accused of killing the decedent could not have done so in the manner alleged (American Jurisprudence, 1965). Occasionally, exhumation is authorized in private lawsuit, for instance, to prove the cause of death for an insurance claim (American Jurisprudence, 1965) or to prove paternity (*Batcheldor v. Boyd*, 1992). Permission for disinterment or exhumation is less likely to be granted as the time from death lengthens. Any disinterment or exhumation must be properly performed, both for health reasons and for respect for the family members (American Jurisprudence, 1965). Unauthorized interference with the body or the grave site may subject the violator to both criminal and civil liability (American Jurisprudence, 1965).

Police Intervention

When a person dies of unnatural causes, by violence or accident, the body may be made available to the appropriate police authorities for evidentiary and record-keeping purposes. The coroner or public medical examiner is authorized to view the body and conduct an autopsy; if criminal conduct or suicide is suspected or if public health may be affected, an autopsy may be performed over the objections of the deceased's family in extreme circumstances (American Jurisprudence, 1985).

The coroner is a public officer of the county, often a licensed physician, whose duties are fixed by statute. The coroner is liable for misconduct, such as conducting an autopsy in bad faith or engaging in transactions indicating a conflict of interest, such as selling funeral supplies (American Jurisprudence, 1985).

In suspected criminal cases, the coroner may call an inquest to determine whether death resulted from criminal acts and to assist in prosecuting the person responsible. The inquest is a preliminary investigation, not a trial, which may involve calling witnesses to testify so that the coroner, and sometimes a jury, can advise whether a criminal action should be prosecuted. The inquest results in the issuance of a death certificate or other official report stating the cause of death and other relevant information, not a conclusion of guilt or innocence, although in some localities the coroner is authorized to issue warrants for arrest (American Jurisprudence, 1985).

CONCLUSION

Effective planning for death can only be accomplished within the existing and often intricate legal structure. Only by planning within the confines of the current law can a person feel reasonably secure that his or her wishes will be carried out and that family and friends will be provided for adequately, with minimal expense, delay, and distress. Relevant financial information should be compiled, and adequate instructions should be left easily accessible to reduce the unavoidable practical problems that arise on one's inevitable death.

REFERENCES

American Jurisprudence. (1965). *Dead bodies* (2nd ed., Vol. 22). Rochester, NY: Lawyers Cooperative.

American Jurisprudence. (1968). *Funeral directors and embalmers* (2nd ed., Vol. 38). Rochester, NY: Lawyers Cooperative.

American Jurisprudence. (1985). *Coroners* (2nd ed., Vol. 18). Rochester, NY: Lawyers Cooperative.

Batcheldor v. Boyd, 423 S.E.2d 810 (N.C. Ct. App. 1992).

Black's law dictionary (4th ed.). (1968). St. Paul, MN: West.

Burke, B. (1993). *Personal property* (2nd ed.). St. Paul, MN: West.

Carney v. Knollwood Cemetery Assn., 214 N.E.2d 430 (Ohio Ct. App. 1986).

Christensen v. Pasadena Crematorium of Altadena, 271 Cal. Rptr. 360 (Ct. App. 1990).

Crown, J. L. (1982). Anatomical gift form. *Probate and Property, 11,* 9–12.

Cruzan v. Director of Missouri Dept. of Health, 497 U.S. 261 (1990).

Dukeminier, J. (1970). Supplying organs for transplantation. *Michigan Law Review, 68,* 811–866.

Dukeminier, J., & Johanson, S. M. (1990). *Wills, trusts, and estates* (4th ed.). Boston: Little, Brown.

Farkas v. Williams, 125 N.E.2d 600 (Ill. 1955).

Fratcher, W. F. (1960). Powers and duties of guardians of property. *Iowa Law Review, 45,* 264–335.

Funeral Industry Practice (Funeral Rule), 16 C.F.R. § 453 (1985).

Geltzer, R., Andrews, L., & Mariner, W. (1989). Report on conference: National conference on birth, death, and law. *Jurimetrics Journal, 29,* 403–542.

Gilbert v. State, 487 So.2d 1185 (Fla. Ct. App. 1986).

Haskell, P. G. (1987). *Preface to wills, trusts, and administration.* Mineola, NY: Foundation Press.

In re Guardianship of L. W., 482 N.W.2d 60 (Wis. 1992).

In re Quinlan, 355 A.2d 647 (N.J. 1976), *cert. denied* 429 U.S. 922.

Internal Revenue Code, Title 26 of the United States Code (1984).

Janzen, P. S. (1984). Law at the edge of life: Issues of death and dying. *Hamline Law Review, 7,* 431–462.

Kadish, S. (1992). Letting patients die: Legal and moral reflections. *California Law Review, 80,* 857–888.

Lehman, B. (1985, May 6). A gift of life: How should it be given? *Boston Globe,* p. 41.

Louisville & N.R. Co. v. Wilson, 51 S.E. 24 (Ga. 1905).

Marshall, J. R. (1982). Testamentary rights of bodily disposition. *Law Notes, 18,* 31–36.

McGovern, W. M., Kurtz, S. F., & Rein, J. A. (1988). *Wills, trusts, and estates.* St. Paul, MN: West.

Micheli, R. (1988, December). Paying for the big chill: Arranging for a funeral could be your biggest outlay in a year. *Money Magazine,* p. 143.

National Organ Transplantation Act, 42 U.S.C. § 274 (1984).

N.C. Gen. Stat. § 31-3.4 (1953).

Planned Parenthood of Southeastern Pennsylvania v. Casey, 112 S.Ct. 2791 (1992).

Quay, P. M. (1984). Utilizing the bodies of the dead. *St. Louis University Law Journal, 28,* 889–927.

Rein, J. (1984–85). An ounce of prevention: Grounds for upsetting wills and will substitutes. *Gonzaga Law Review, 20,* 1–68.

Roe v. Wade, 410 U.S. 113 (1973).

Romney, M. C., & Duffy, D. (1990). Medicine and law: Recent developments. *Torts and Insurance Law Journal, 25,* 351–368.

Roybal, E. R. (1984). *A guide to funeral planning* (Comm. Pub. No. 98–166). Washington, DC: U.S. Government Printing Office.

Scarmon, M. (1991–92). Brotherton v. Cleveland: Property rights in the human body—are the goods oft interred with their bones? *University of South Dakota Law Review 37,* 429–449.

Social Security Act, 42 U.S.C. § 1395cc (f) (1988).

State v. Forrest, 362 S.E.2d 252 (N.C. 1987).

Tax Reform Act of 1976, Pub. L. No. 94–455, § 1902, 90 Stat. 1805 (1976).

Tecklenburg, N. (1982). Medico-legal implications of "orders not to resuscitate." *Catholic University Law Review, 31,* 515–537.

Texas Code Ann., § 711.002 (West 1992).

Uniform Anatomical Gifts Act, 8A U.L.A. 3 (1993).

Uniform Determination of Death Act, 12 U.L.A. 384 (1975 & Supp. 1994).

Uniform Marital Property Act, 9A U.L.A. 97 (1987).

Uniform Probate Code 8B U.L.A. 1 (1991 & Supp. 1994).

Uniform Rights of the Terminally Ill Act, 9A U.L.A. 109 (1989).

Uniform Transfers to Minors Act, 8B U.L.A. 497 (1991 & Supp. 1994).

Waggoner, L. W., Wellman, R. V., Alexander, G. S., & Fellows, M. L. (1991). *Family property law.* Westbury, NY: Foundation Press.

Webster v. Reproductive Health Services, 492 U.S. 490 (1989).

Weissman, S. I. (1977). Why the uniform anatomical gifts act has failed. *Trusts and Estates, 116,* 264–267, 281–282.

Zischerk, F. (1991). Michigan's proposed assisted suicide legislation: Strong public policy or legislative rhetoric? *University of Detroit Mercy Law Review, 69,* 33–53.

Chapter 8

The Contemporary Funeral: Functional or Dysfunctional?

Robert Fulton

THE DRAMATURGY OF DEATH

Burial of the dead is an ancient practice among humans. From paleolithic times to the present, humans have responded to the death of their fellow humans with solemnity and ceremony. Not only has the event of death evoked a religious awe, but also its threat to the survival of communal life has engendered fear, and its disruption of family life has aroused sorrow. The vehicle through which these reactions to death have been expressed has been the funeral. The funeral traditionally has served as

- a ceremony acknowledging a death,
- a religious rite,
- an occasion to reassure and reestablish the social group,
- a commemoration, and
- a ritual of disposal.

The dramaturgical celebration of death and its significance for the individual and society have long attracted the interest of scholars. Different authors have emphasized the function of ritualized behavior in promoting and maintaining the emotional well-being of the individual as well as the social cohesion and structural integration of the group (Bendann, 1930; Durkheim, 1954; Evans-Pritchard, 1965; Gluckman, 1962; Goody, 1962a; Habenstein & Lamers, 1963; Hertz, 1960; Malinowski, 1984; Mandelbaum, 1959; Puckle, 1926; Radcliffe-Brown, 1965; Van Gennep, 1961).

Malinowski (1984), for instance, viewed ceremonies associated with death as a part of the sacramental institution of religion that bestowed on individuals the gift of mental integrity, a function that he believed was also fulfilled with regard to the whole group. He saw funerary customs as powerful counteracts to the centrifugal forces of fear, dismay, and demoralization. He believed they had the potential to provide the most powerful means of reintegrating a group's weakened solidarity and reestablish shaken morale.

Radcliffe-Brown (1965) and Durkheim (1954) emphasized the role of ritualized behavior in promoting and maintaining social forms. Durkheim, for example, spoke of ceremony as being a collective expression of sentiment and interpreted certain attitudes and rituals as "objectified sentiments." On the other hand, Van Gennep (1961) assigned the greatest importance to the rituals associated with death because he found that funeral rites, which had as their express purpose the incorporation of the deceased into the "world of the dead," were characteristically the most elaborate.

About the same time, Mandelbaum (1959) examined death rites in five widely diverse cultures. His research not only contributed new insights regarding death rituals, but also identified more clearly their role and meaning in our changing world. Mandelbaum concluded that funeral ceremonies serve "manifest" as well as "latent" functions. Manifest functions are those activities associated with mortuary rites that are most readily apparent, such as the disposal of the body, assistance to the bereaved, public acknowledgment of the death, and declarations and demonstrations of the group's continued viability. Mandelbaum characterized latent functions, on the other hand, as funeral customs that include the economic and reciprocal social obligations that are remembered and reenacted at the time of a death. The role thus taken by a participant in a funeral reflects his or her position in society and reaffirms the social order. Other latent functions identified by Mandelbaum were the obligations and restrictions placed on all members of the deceased's family with regard to attire, demeanor, food, and social intercourse. Such observances, he noted, serve to identify and demonstrate family cohesion. Still another latent function of the funeral that Mandelbaum identified was the acknowledgment and affirmation of the extended kinship system in which members of the larger family console the survivors and frequently share in the expenses of the ceremony.

Mandelbaum (1959) argued that participating in the funeral ceremony, the procession, the exchange of food, and the mourning and keening gave the mourner the sense of being part of a larger social whole, just as the order of precedence in the conduct of the ceremony is a reminder that there are structure and order in the social system. Finally, Mandelbaum concurred with Van Gennep (1961) that the funeral is a "rite of passage," because, Mandelbaum noted, it not only reaffirms the participant's belief in the immortal character of human existence, but also marks the end of life and the separation of the dead from the living.

CEREMONY: FUNCTIONAL AND DYSFUNCTIONAL

The question is, however, whether the funeral (as described by Mandelbaum and others and based, as their analyses were, on non-Western or preindustrial societies) is relevant for a modern nation state. Is the funeral a functional ceremony in today's urban, industrial world? Does it meet the needs of contemporary men and women? These are not new questions, yet, they are still being asked. Indeed, they need to be asked—perhaps now more than at any time in history.

The funeral can be dysfunctional. Geertz (1957) described a funeral in Java in which the insistence on traditional practices served to disrupt, rather than restore, the sense of community. He reported that traditional rites, which were suited to an agricultural village and folk milieu, caused much dissention and confusion among villagers when practiced in town, where the economic, social, and political orientations were different from those of the village.

Mandelbaum (1959) provided the example of the Kota, for whom the traditional funeral ceremony actually aggravated the sorrow of the mourner and provoked social discord. At one stage of the Kota funeral—what is termed the "dry funeral"—there is a juncture when all Kotas who are present at the ceremony come forward one by one to give a parting bow of respect to the relics of the deceased. Over time, Mandelbaum reported, this moment had become a time of great tension and conflict, because violent quarrels often broke out. Although the occasion was ostensibly one to mark social unity, the kin of the deceased often tried to prevent members of opposing factions within Kota society from performing this gesture of respect, implying that such persons were not true Kotas. Despite such friction, the ceremony was typically concluded with as much show of social unity as was possible through the help of neutral persons. But, as Mandelbaum observed, "a ritual action which symbolizes concord has frequently triggered a good deal of discord" (p. 213).

There is a further point to consider: the level of social organization. What may be an operative and functional ritual at one level of social life, for example, the community, may not be functional for, or congruent with, human aims and purposes at another level of social life, for example, the nation. This is illustrated by the death of Mr. Tom Mboya, Kenya's Minister of Defense and a member of the Luo tribe, by assassination by a member of the Kikuyu tribe in 1969. His death resulted in the subsequent deaths of more than a dozen fellow citizens among the Luo and Kikuyu tribes and the destruction of hundreds of thousands of dollars worth of property. The English journal *The Economist,* reported at the time that never in the history of Nairobi had there been such disturbance and loss of life as that which followed the memorial service held in Mboya's honor in Nairobi (*The Economist,* Aug. 9, 1969, p. 240).

In Kenya, it is a family obligation to see that the deceased is returned to his village and buried on his father's land with only members of the tribal community in attendance. Thus the Kikuyu were excluded from taking part in Mr. Mboya's funeral not only because they had been held responsible for his death, but also because it is traditional for the tribes to exclude all but their own from funeral ceremonies. There was the possibility, therefore, that upon the death of Mr. Jomo Kenyatta, then Prime Minister of Kenya and a member of the Kikuyu tribe, there would be civil strife in Kenya, strife of such magnitude that the national aspirations of Kenya could well have been threatened. It was highly possible that his mourners would exclude the Luo (who are the second strongest political party and the second largest tribe in Kenya) from participation in the ceremonies. Indeed, they might have held the Luo responsible for the death itself. If the national state of Kenya survived Kenyatta's death, it would only be because the Kikuyu and the Luo recognized that the state had to take priority over tribal traditions and ambitions.

In 1978, Prime Minister Kenyatta died a natural death. His funeral took place amid great mourning but without incident. This was mainly due to the fact that extraordinary efforts were taken to make his funeral as public and as symbolic of the nation as possible. The British government intervened directly. It took charge of all the funeral arrangements and went so far as to provide the use of Winston Churchill's funeral coach in order to dramatize the international significance of the event.

In contrast, the U.S. experience with death at the national level in recent decades has been a study in the functional qualities of the funeral. The sudden and unexpected assassinations of President John F. Kennedy, Senator Robert Kennedy, and Dr. Martin Luther King came as successive shocks to the body politic and were sorely felt.

To review the events following the assassination of President Kennedy is to recall a period of social and political turmoil unparalleled since the assassination of President Lincoln in 1865. At that time, the country bordered on panic as rumors of conspiracy and intrigue swept through the Capital and across the nation. The attempted assassination of other members of Lincoln's cabinet gave substance to those fears and placed the country on a war alert.

A repeat performance of that turmoil occurred in the hours and days following President Kennedy's death in 1963. At the same time that the nation was plunged into grief and mourned his death, it was alive to reports and rumors of conspiracies both from the political left and right. The assassination of Lee Harvey Oswald, President Kennedy's alleged assassin, by Jack Ruby, before a nationwide television audience, only aggravated the fears of the nation as it compounded the tragedy.

The state funeral that was held for President Kennedy was the most widely viewed ceremony in history. It is estimated that half a billion people throughout the world watched the funeral on television ("Kennedy Is Laid To Rest," 1963). In attendance, in addition to President Kennedy's immediate family, personal friends, and colleagues, were dignitaries from all branches of the government, representatives from the various political parties, and the heads of state or their personal representatives of 90 nonbelligerent countries. President Kennedy's funeral served to declare not only that he was dead, but also that order had been restored to the country and that the nation was secure in its relations with most other nations of the world.

The funeral of President Kennedy was followed in numbing succession by the funerals of Dr. Martin Luther King and Senator Robert Kennedy in 1968. Like President Kennedy's assassination, their violent deaths threatened social and political disruption throughout the nation. In particular, the murder of Dr. King, one of the country's most celebrated and revered leaders in the peaceful attempt to integrate white and black America, was little short of cataclysmic in its import. It precipitated racial disturbances across the country, resulting in the deaths of more than a score of citizens, both black and white, as well as the destruction of hundreds of millions of dollars worth of property ("They Came To Mourn," 1969). Dr. King's death removed the strongest voice of moderation from America's racially antagonistic society. Despite this fact, however, and the fact that his assassin was a white man, his funeral included many prominent white political and social leaders. In effect, his funeral testified to the nation as well as to the world that the followers of Dr. King were determined to remain true to his philosophy of nonviolence and to his dream of a racially mixed nation free of prejudice and discrimination. In his funeral Dr. King's survivors saw an opportunity to bind the wound that his death had inflicted on the body politic.

Death evokes powerful emotions that need to be vented or calmed. This was made evident with the assassinations of President Kennedy, Dr. King, and Senator Kennedy. The country grieved their deaths; Americans mourned openly not only as individual citizens but also as a community. They participated in three funerals to which the whole world paid heed.

Public evidence of private reactions to President Kennedy's death is available. Thirty-nine surveys (Bureau of Social Science Research, 1966; Greenberg & Parker, 1965; Wolfenstein & Kliman, 1965) were conducted after his assassination. Although the studies were manifestly different in design and intent, certain common reactions were discernible in all of the participants. These reactions are best represented by the findings of the Nation Opinion Research Center in Chicago (Sheatsley & Feldman, 1964), which polled a representative national sample of 1,400 adults within a week of the assassination. The findings of the study were as follows:

1 Preoccupation with the death was almost total.

2 Nine out of ten respondents reported experiencing one or more physical symptoms, such as headache, upset stomach, tiredness, dizziness, or loss of appetite.

3 Two thirds of the respondents felt very nervous and tense during the 4 days.

4 A majority of the respondents confessed to feeling dazed and numb.

5 Most respondents—both men and women—cried at some period during this time.

6 The event was compared most often to the death of a parent, close friend, or relative.

7 There was a tendency to react to the assassination in terms of personal grief and loss, rather than political or ideological concern or anxiety about the future.

As the researchers noted, the reactions of the American people during the 4 days after the death of President Kennedy followed a well-defined pattern of grief; the President's funeral channeled that grief and gave it poignant expression. This study supports the conclusion that the funeral of President Kennedy was functional in that it served society's formal needs and, at the same time, provided a vehicle for the expression of private as well as public grief.

The value of public rites for the dead was seen most recently after the explosion of the space shuttle Challenger in January 1986, in which the entire crew, including the first teacher to travel in space, was killed. Witnessed on national television, the Challenger's sudden, unexpected explosion shocked the nation at the same time that it wrenched the emotions of millions of eager and excited schoolchildren. Studies conducted after the disaster (Brabeck & Weisgerber, 1988; Kubey & Peluso, 1990) found essentially the same emotional reactions that were engendered by President Kennedy's assassination. Almost half the respondents reported crying or feeling like crying and feeling better after talking to others, and those who informed others about the disaster reported stronger emotional reactions than those who did not. There was virtually no difference in the cognitive or emotional responses of boys and girls to the disaster. Importantly, the nation was able to apply the findings and recommendations of the Kennedy studies in dealing with children's grief reactions and, from all accounts, was largely successful in palliating the emotional impact of the disaster.

Mortuary rituals, then, may be a functional or a dysfunctional set of activities, depending on place and circumstance. The funeral of Prime Minister Kenyatta had the potential to do Kenya profound injury, given Kikuyu philosophy and tribal tradition. But for the United States, the funerals of President Kennedy, Senator Kennedy, and Dr. King and the national as well as local ceremonies arranged for the crew of the Challenger were beneficial with respect to the American public's emotional and social needs.

In America, however, as in Kenya and Java, funeral ceremonies or other mortuary rites or symbols, such as monuments and memorials, can also evoke conflicting emotions and arouse social strife. Two memorials honoring the dead in the United States have provoked intense controversy and generated acrimonious debate in recent years: the Vietnam Veterans Memorial and the AIDS Memorial Quilt.

The Vietnam Veterans Memorial, which stands in Constitution Gardens in the nation's capital, honors the men and women of the U.S. Armed Services who died in the Vietnam War. The memorial consists of two triangular-shaped, black granite walls, which are 10 feet high at their vertex and approximately 246 feet in length. The two walls form a wide angle, pointing to both the Washington Monument and the Lincoln Memorial, between which they are situated. The names of more than 58,000 people who gave their lives or who remain missing are inscribed on the walls in the order in which they were killed or reported missing.

The Vietnam War—a war that was ultimately lost—was the longest and most bitterly protested war in the history of the United States. From 1959 to 1975, approximately 2.7 million Americans served in the war zone, of whom 300,000 were wounded and 75,000 were permanently disabled. An additional 1,200 combatants remain missing or unaccounted for (National Park Service, 1984).

The Vietnam Veterans Memorial was conceived as a means to promote the reconciliation of the country after the profound divisions caused by the war. Because Vietnam had been America's "most controversial and politicized war" (Scruggs & Swerdlow, 1985, p. 80), the planners of the memorial had wanted it to "symbolize the experience of the Americans who fought [there]" (Scruggs &

Swerdlow, 1985, p. 80). For many, however, the memorial was an insult to the country and a "black gash of shame" (Scruggs & Swerdlow, 1985, p. 81). Despite continued public attacks against the proposed memorial from various groups, including some Vietnam veteran groups, and the continuing prospect that different government agencies would prevent its construction, support for the memorial continued to come from people from all walks of life. The demand for the memorial ultimately prevailed, and with the private donations of more than 650,000 citizens—men, women, and children—the Memorial was dedicated on November 13, 1982, in the face of a threat to blow it up. Later, a life-size sculpture depicting three American soldiers in Vietnam, symbolizing their devotion and patriotism, as well as a 60-foot flagstaff were added to the site. This realistic sculpture has in turn evoked its own controversy, but it is the Vietnam Memorial that stands as one of America's most emotionally challenging and contemplative national monuments.

It could be said that the AIDS Memorial Quilt also commemorates those who died in a war—a war against a virus that is yet far from being over. The idea for the AIDS Quilt began in San Francisco in 1985. In a candlelight service, participants covered the walls of the Federal Building with placards bearing the names of those who had died in the AIDS epidemic. Subsequently, a gay activist, Cleve Jones, envisioned in the patchwork effect of the placards the design of a quilt. Using spray paint, he made the first panel for a quilt for his best friend, who had recently died. In the spring of 1987, the Names Project was organized with the intention to display the Quilt on the Mall in Washington, DC, as a conscience call to the American government to acknowledge the seriousness of the epidemic and as a public expression of grief for all those who had died. When laid out on the Washington Mall in the fall of that year, the Quilt consisted of 1,920 panels, each 3 × 6 feet, each unique in design and sentiment. The power of the Quilt, in part, is in its sheer size—which dramatizes the enormity of the epidemic—while allowing the viewer, at the same time, to experience the profound impact of a single, human death.

The Quilt has been exhibited nationally and internationally and includes panels from more than 25 countries, uniting people around the world in their grief in a most singular way.

But the Quilt is more than a memorial that evokes remembrance: it also bears witness to the courage of surviving family members and friends, who prepare the panels, to identify themselves in the face of a disease that has been stigmatized because of its initial association with homosexuality. The Quilt confronts the homophobia in America as well as the resistance of a large segment of the American public to accept the reality of the epidemic. It thus serves as an educational and political statement as well as a therapeutic exercise for an epidemic that has been described as "the defining crisis of [the present] generation" (Sturken, 1992, p. 66). Its exhibition has allowed for a collective experience of sharing and remembering in the midst of a government that has underplayed the epidemic and a heterosexual public that does not believe it is at risk for the disease.

Unlike other memorials to the dead, the Quilt keeps pace with the ever-growing number of casualties. As of this writing, the Quilt consists of more than 24,000 panels and covers (with its walkway) 16 acres of ground, or 15 football fields, yet it represents only 13% of all those in the United States who have died thus far from the disease. (It may interest the reader to know that the materials used in this unique memorial include such items as a 100-year-old quilt, afghans, Barbie dolls, burlap, buttons, car keys, carpet, champagne glasses, condoms, corduroy, corsets, cowboy boots, cremation ashes, credit cards, curtains, dresses, feather boas, first-place ribbons, fishnet hose, flags, fur, gloves, hats, human hair, jeans, jewelry, jockstraps, lace, lamé, leather, love letters, Mardi gras masks, merit badges, mink, motorcycle jackets, needlepoint, paintings, pearls, photographs, pins, plastic, quartz crystals, racing silks, records, rhinestones, sequins, shirts, silk flowers, studs, stuffed animals, suede, taffeta, tennis shoes, vinyl, and wedding rings [*Quilt Facts,* 1993]).

As the epidemic has spread, panels representing heterosexual men and women as well as children have been added to the Quilt. As a result, controversy has arisen in the gay community regarding the overall purpose of the memorial. Whereas the Names Project leadership has attempted to have the memorial include all those who have died from AIDS, others insist that the memorial should reflect the public emergence and political militancy of the gay community. In the general public, however, there has been little controversy over the Quilt. Although some panels have been vandalized and the Quilt has been called a "v.d. blanket" and a "fag scam," the memorial has for the most part been well received. It has been featured on television shows, on film, as the subject of a book, as well as in innumerable newspaper articles. The Quilt has received a nomination for the Nobel Peace Prize, and some of its panels have been deposited in the Smithsonian Institute.

Whatever the future of the AIDS epidemic—and at this writing, it continues to hold the United States, as well as the world, in its ever-tightening grip—the AIDS Quilt has profoundly altered American society. Not only has it brought into question the nature of the social codes and traditional ideas of morality in America, but the reality of the Quilt has served to challenge the traditional social and political distance between the gay and heterosexual communities. Most important, the Quilt speaks to the issues of human life, human love, and human loss. Like the Vietnam Memorial, the AIDS Memorial Quilt is not only a roll call of the dead, but also a call to the living to put an end to the carnage.

But what of the role of funerary ritual or memorialization for the average American whose life has been touched by neither the Vietnam War nor the AIDS epidemic? What can be said about the funeral of the ordinary man, woman, or child who dies an ordinary death? Is it also beneficial? The question is more than academic, in view of the fact that criticism of the conventional funeral and funeral director has been strident over the past three decades. The funeral has been charged with being pagan in origin and ostentatious in practice, and the funeral director has been characterized as one who exploits the dead at the expense of the living (Mitford, 1963).

AMERICAN FUNERAL PRACTICES AND ATTITUDES TOWARD FUNERALS

In the past 35 years, this author has conducted three nationwide surveys (Fulton 1961, 1965, 1971) on the issues and attitudes surrounding mortality in the United States. An overview presents the major findings.

Study 1: The Clergy's Negative Attitude Toward Funerals

The first study (Fulton, 1961) was a survey of the attitudes of clergy ($N = 1647$) toward funerals and funeral directors in the United States. Clerical criticism of the funeral director and of funeral practices was both widespread and intense. Among the different reasons the clergy gave for their negative appraisal, two stand out. First, they charged funeral directors with dramatizing the presence of the body while ignoring the spiritual dimension of death and, second, they accused funeral directors of taking undue advantage of the bereaved. A third reason was left unstated but was nevertheless implicit in the clergy's criticism: The profession conflates American funeral customs with those of other cultures and religions and thus represents paganism. Specifically, the study showed that the Protestant clergy (more so than their Catholic colleagues) were troubled by contemporary funeral practices and by the increasing prominence of the funeral director in the overall conduct of the funeral. Some clergy were rankled by the funeral profession's designation of funeral establishments as chapels and by what they perceived as encroachment on their role.

These developments have led some members of the clergy to label the contemporary funeral as pagan and to describe the expenses associated with it as conspicuous waste. It has also led some of them to promote what they term the "simplified" funeral, to advocate cremation, or to recommend that monies usually spent on elaborate display be donated to public charities or scientific research.

Study 2: Influence of Religious Affiliation on Americans' Attitudes Toward Funerals

In the second study (Fulton, 1965), the attitudes of the American public ($N = 1722$) toward death, funerals, and funeral directors were surveyed. The respondents included persons who were members of the funeral reform or Memorial Society movement. Like the clergy study, this survey showed that negative and critical attitudes toward contemporary funeral rites and practices were held by segments of the public. The survey showed, however, that these attitudes were not shared equally; criticism of the contemporary funeral varied by religious affiliation, education, occupation, income, and geographical region.

The majority of the respondents in the survey were favorably disposed toward the funeral director and present-day funeral practices. They saw the funeral director as a professional person or one who combined a professional service with a business function, and they viewed the funeral as providing a meaningful emotional experience for the bereaved.

Members of the memorial societies, however, expressed views strongly divergent from those of the general public. They believed the funeral director primarily conducted a business and offered the public no professional service whatsoever. The majority of members expressed unfavorable opinions on both funeral directors and funeral costs. In addition, a majority of the respondents did not believe that the purposes of a funeral were, in fact, served by contemporary ceremonies. Only 25% of the memorial society respondents believed that funerals serve the emotional needs of the bereaved in any way, and 16% perceived the traditional funeral as performing no useful function at all. Consistent with these findings, the memorial society members were the strongest advocates for cremation or the donation of the body to medical programs and scientific research and for simplification or abandonment of the ritual and ceremony of the funeral.

Of interest is the social profile of the average memorial society member. Members of memorial societies generally reported higher educational and professional levels than did nonmembers. They also reported an average annual income twice that of the average American family. They reported being the least religious, or the least religiously affiliated, of those interviewed.

On the whole, the study showed that responses toward funeral directors and funerals varied with religious affiliation. Religious affiliation, or its absence, was the key factor influencing the various attitudes expressed. Simply stated, favorable opinions on funerals and funeral directors were most often expressed by Catholics, followed by Protestants, Jews, nonaffiliated respondents, and Unitarians. The order was reversed with respect to critical attitudes toward funerals and funeral directors. Unitarians were the most critical, followed by Jews, nonaffiliated respondents, Protestants, and Catholics. Regionally, the most favorable attitudes toward funerals and funeral directors were expressed by residents from the central sections of the country, and the least favorable views were expressed by respondents residing along the Atlantic and Pacific coasts.

Study 3: Emergent Variability in Contemporary Funeral Practices

The third study (Fulton, 1971), sought to determine the character of contemporary funeral practices in the United States. A questionnaire was mailed to the membership of the National Funeral Directors Association as well as to the membership of the Jewish Funeral Directors Association. In all, 14,144 questionnaires were mailed. One out of four (24.6%) of the funeral directors polled returned the questionnaire, for a total of 3,474 replies.

In many important aspects, the results of the third study confirmed those of the previous two. The 1971 study, however, went beyond mere confirmation. It showed that the funeral in contemporary America represents different things to different people. Although what might be called the traditional funeral—a public service with a public viewing and a public committal service—characterizes almost all of the great central portion of the United States and is the predominant practice everywhere else, it is nevertheless subject to modification and change. New rituals and practices for disposing of the dead, as well as for coping with death, are emerging. Emergent variability is a fact in funeral dramaturgy, as it is throughout all of society. Change is at work not only in the mode of disposal of the dead, but also in every aspect of funeralization, from the type of funeral establishment constructed, to the emotional climate in which the funeral is conducted, to the meaning(s) imputed to death itself.

The significance of the findings from the three studies is best understood when the findings are placed in the larger context of American life and ideology. A funeral does not take place in a vacuum. Rather, the results of the studies can be understood to mirror what society as a whole has been experiencing since World War I—a shift in its religious beliefs and values related to death and dying.

Factors Contributing to Americans' Changing Attitudes Toward Funerals

American Religious Ideology   First, let's consider the basic religious tenets of the majority of Americans who are heir to the Judeo-Christian tradition. According to this doctrine, human beings are creatures of God and have been formed in His image. Because of their fall from grace, however, humans are born in sin and therefore spiritually flawed. Death is the consequence of that sin and is a necessary experience for all individuals if they are to be restored to their prior state of grace. In American society, the funeral has been an instrument of this theology, and its ritual has served to dramatize such beliefs for the living at the same time that it effected a liturgy for the dead.

This sacerdotal perception of human life, however, is not shared by everyone. The idea entertained today by a great number of Americans is, rather, that death is not the wages of sin and that it need not even be as certain as taxes. Also, it is no longer an unquestioned belief, on the part of many, that life is necessarily a gift from God. The papal encyclical *Humanae vitae,* restating the Church's opposition to birth control in 1968, created a storm of protest and debate in the country that has had almost no precedent (*Humanae vitae,* 1969). Protests, petitions, and pronouncements by clergy and laity alike, of many different faiths and persuasions, questioned or openly opposed the papal edict. The same year, moreover, saw the first successful heart transplant in the United States, the continued progress toward kidney and other organ transplants, and increased speculation regarding the unlimited possibilities of medical technology to extend life. The religious, moral, and legal arguments surrounding such practices and prospects and their implications for the future are only now beginning to take definite form. One thing appears clear: Humankind persists in its refusal to accept the inevitability of death and with death, as with life, seeks to be the final judge.

Demography   A second factor influencing Americans' changing perspective on death is the demographic aspects of life and death. This year, approximately 1% of the U.S. population, or more than 2 million persons, will die (U.S. Bureau of the Census, 1990). More than 70% of these deaths will occur among persons age 65 or older. Moreover, more than 80% of these deaths will take place outside the home, in a hospital, hospice facility, or a nursing home. The number of persons over the age of 65 is now 31 million, or 12% of the population (U.S. Bureau of the Census, 1990). In contrast, 27.5 million persons, approximately one fourth of the population, are children under 15 years of age. Children, however, account for only 4% of all deaths. This is a dramatic reversal in mortality statistics compared with the 1920s, when the mortality rate was highest for children (U.S. Bureau of the Census, 1960). As a matter of fact, contemporary American youth could almost be called the first death-free generation in the history of the world. That is, statistically, a family in the United States has only a 1 in 20 chance of having a death occur among its immediate members within a 20-year span. The implications of these statistics cannot be overlooked. Americans' conception of death and expectations as to who will die, as well as their view of what constitutes an appropriate response to a death, are colored by these basic demographic facts.

Economic Concerns   A third factor among the myriad social and cultural influences changing Americans' attitudes toward death is the detrimental impact that inflation can have on the private household economies of millions of American families. Several million families are headed by widows, the majority of whom live on fixed incomes consisting of Social Security or other retirement benefits (Berardo, 1968). Regardless of provisions made beforehand, the expense of death cannot help but be a source of anxiety and concern. Such concern, moreover, is deepened by a fourth factor: the changing character of the American home.

Family   Over the past several generations, the structure of the average American family has changed from a large, extended family to a small, nuclear group. As a consequence, it is more mobile, socially as well as geographically, than ever before. It is child oriented rather than adult oriented and relatively more individualized than integrated. That is, the young, contemporary family is less a part of a rural community or a neighborhood than it used to be; increasingly, the family exists as a disengaged unit in an anonymous urban environment. As already mentioned, death is increasingly an experience of the aged, most of whom are retired from work, free of parental obligations, and frequently outside of the main current of family life. Moreover, although medical advances have made it possible to prolong the life of the elderly, this is often at the cost of hospitalization or other institutional care, further separating the elderly from their families. Familial ties and friendships are loosened by such separations, and emotional and societal bonds are weakened. Not the least consequence of this development is the fact that great numbers of the elderly live alone and, as research shows, die alone as well (Fulton & Gupta, 1974). The disengagement of the aged from society prior to their deaths means that their dying has little impact on the round of life.

As noted earlier, the death of a leader such as President John F. Kennedy, Senator Robert Kennedy, or Dr. Martin Luther King can seriously disrupt the functioning of a modern society. Their deaths wrenched the social and political life of the United States. For the average family, it is either the death of someone in his or her middle productive years or the death of someone young and unfulfilled that will have a comparable effect. Because the elderly are less relevant to the functioning of modern society, their deaths do not compel the same degree of attention. Like the late General MacArthur's "old soldier," they do not die, but rather "fade away."

Changing Values   The belief that the funeral is a meaningful rite for the dead has been seriously challenged in the United States in recent years. In a society in which only half of the population is affiliated with a church and the social and spatial mobility of its citizens is great, the religious, emotional, and economic obligations that a funeral has traditionally imposed on a family are seen by many today as inappropriate. Increasingly, the funeral is for that member of the family who is least functionally relevant to it. In a society that is predisposed toward the young and healthy as well as that which is practical and economical, an elaborate funeral for an elderly relative strikes the average citizen as extravagant.

Advocacy of memorial services in which the body is absent and the promotion of cremation as a form of human disposition are contemporary attempts to resolve these vexing issues.

THE FUNERAL AS A PIACULAR RITE

What of the funeral, then, in the face of these trends and developments? Sixty thousand years ago, as the archaeological discovery at Shanidar, Iraq, has shown, humans buried their dead with ceremony (Solecki, 1971). They did so, given the evidence, because they believed in an afterlife. The question is, Are paleolithic funeral practices still relevant or functional for contemporary humans?

Although burial or entombment of the dead is not universal, it is practiced in many different societies and has served to signify the belief in immortality: the belief that a person assumes a spiritual state after mortal death. It has been believed since time immemorial that the funeral is the ritual by which this transition is accomplished.

The funeral, however, is not like other rituals or ceremonies, which are festive or joyous (e.g., Thanksgiving or Christmas) or mark cyclical or progressive events (e.g., New Year's Eve or a birthday). The funeral is, to use an anthropological term, a *piacular rite*. That is, it is a ceremony that attempts to atone or make amends for a presumed wrongdoing. Piacular rites deal with those aspects of social life that are stigmatized or that result in defilement. They are ceremonies that are intended to remove the onerous blemish that has been cast on the individual or group by a wrongful act of commission or omission. Death, as already mentioned, is perceived within the Christian tradition as punishment for human sin. By definition, a human corpse is evidence of that sin and is thus spiritually unclean. Religious authority for this view can be found in the Old Testament, where it states that the Lord said to Moses, "Speak to the priests, the sons of Aaron, and say to them that none of them shall defile himself for the dead among his people" (Leviticus 21:1, Revised Standard Version) and further commanded the chief priest "not to approach a corpse even that of his father or mother for fear of defiling himself" (Leviticus 21:11, Revised Standard Version).

It was the anthropologist Van Gennep (1961) who observed that funeral rites were the most extensive and elaborate of all human ceremonies—in other words, the most costly. Arguably, the reason for the inordinate expense of the funeral is the fact that its main function is expiation. But the funeral is also, by definition, obligatory. It is imposed on the community by the fact that humans die and by society's cultural and/or religious interpretations of death. Simply put, people have no control over deaths, yet at the same time they believe that to die is evidence of human culpability. Thus, on one hand, the excessiveness of the funeral reflects the desire to be exonerated from sin and to free the spirit from corrupting flesh, but, on the other hand, people's aversion toward the corpse reflects their fear of religious defilement. Herein lies the paradox: the historical impulse to conduct an elaborate and ostentatious ceremony for the disposition of a human body that is feared and dreaded.

This paradox can also be observed in the place funerals have in society as well as in the form they assume. Although the funeral is indeed an ancient and time-honored ceremony that is observed around the world, it demonstrates a wide variety of forms. This is due to the fact that it is highly subjective in its individual configuration. This can be readily seen in the United States, where a variety of funeral options, or what might be called customized funerals, are available. This historic volatility is also evidenced in the dramatic changes that have taken place with respect to the funeral since World War II: the virtual disappearance of such traditional funeral practices as the wearing of widows weeds and the black hat band, tie, and arm band; the black hearse; and the funeral wreath on the door of the home of the deceased. In addition, cremation is becoming a preferred mode of disposition in certain regions of the United States. Mourners' participation in funerals is also increasing with friends and relatives contributing poetry readings, songs, musical offerings, and eulogies to the ceremony and, even, in some instances, designing a complete service that may or may not contain a religious component.

The volatility and variability of funeral practices are not limited to the United States. Anthropologists have long observed that among different aboriginal peoples as far removed from each other as North America and South Africa, funeral practices are subject to wide variation and change, even among groups who are in close proximity to each other and who share the same cultural heritage (Kroeber, 1927). This may be due to the fact that the funeral is the least regarded of all public ceremonies, even though it is one of the most necessary (as far as the disposition of the body is concerned) and the most costly. It may also be due to the idiosyncratic or personal element of funerals. That is, individual survivors are typically allowed to introduce personal components into the funeral, which promotes the instability that has been observed. Because the funeral fundamentally represents the negative side of mortal life and is an obligation, reluctantly assumed, it is like no other ceremony in social life. Moreover, social etiquette historically has generally required the avoidance of any discussion of death, including the problems of widowhood, grief and mourning, the cemetery, or the functions of the embalmer or mortician, except as he or she may be the object of humor or censure. As a result, the public recognition of these changes has been rarely reported or their implications for social life clearly understood.

Today, the belief in immortality and the piacular obligations of the funeral are contrary to the philosophical and ideological beliefs of a large segment of the American public. Many people do not believe there is a life after death or that it is necessary or felicitous to consume the resources of the living for the doubtful benefit they may have for the dead. For a growing number of people, the most desirable procedure is the simplest and one that involves as little material expense as possible—the immediate disposition of the body with no public ceremony (Fulton, 1971).

But, as has been noted, social scientists have recognized that there are important aspects of the funeral other than the expression of a belief in immortality or the dramaturgical incorporation of the dead into an afterlife. It is important to consider these aspects and their place and function in contemporary society.

THE FUNERAL AS A RITE OF INTEGRATION AND SEPARATION

As well as being a rite of incorporation, the funeral is a rite of separation and integration. The funerals of President Kennedy, Dr. King, and Senator Kennedy, as well as that of Mr. Mboya, demonstrated the tripartite nature of the funeral. The dramaturgy of those funerals expressed the belief that the world will go on, that the survivors will continue to live, that social order will prevail, and that society will continue to believe in the justice and mercy of God. But the funeral is also a drama that says that someone has been lost through death. As such, it focuses attention on the survivors, and to the degree that it does so it is a rite of separation as well.

Psychologically, the loss of a significant person by death constitutes a crisis situation for the survivor. Medical and behavioral science experts have found that such loss evokes powerful emotions that need to be given proper expression

(Ciocco, 1940; Cox & Ford, 1964; Frederick, 1961; Fulton, 1973; Holmes & Rahe, 1967; Kraus & Lilienfeld, 1959; Parkes, 1964, 1965; Rahe, McKean, & Arthur, 1967; Rahe, Meyer, Smith, Kjaek, & Holmes, 1964; Rees & Lutkins, 1967; Stern, Windkur, Graham, & Graham, 1961; Wretmark, 1959).

Several authors (Bowlby, 1963; Lindemann, 1944; Kübler-Ross, 1969; Weisman, 1972; Young et al., 1963) have claimed that acceptance of the separation or permanent loss of a significant other is an exceedingly difficult task to achieve and that many persons never recover from permanent loss or ever wholly accept, or indeed ever admit to, the death of a loved one.

How can people be taught to accept permanent loss? Two leading British psychiatrists, John Bowlby and C. Murray Parkes (1970), have pointed out that a major component of acute grief is the denial that a death or a separation has occurred. The value of the tasks and rituals surrounding a death, they argued, is that they gradually bring home to the bereaved person the reality of the loss that has been sustained. As they observed,

Drawing the blinds, viewing the body, attending the funeral service, lowering the coffin into the grave all serve to emphasize the finality and the absoluteness of death, and make denial more difficult. (Bowlby & Parkes, p. 198)

The ritual of the funeral, when it is responsive to the survivors' psychological needs, can aid in the ventilation of profound emotions and help facilitate the normal dissolution of grief. Viewing the dead potentially allows this dissolution to take place.

True, there are elements of disguise in the cosmetic preparation of the body for the funeral. But such prettifying of the corpse is no more the basis of a funeral ceremony than the use of cosmetics or a veil is the basis of a wedding. The masking of the ravages of an illness or injury is functional to the extent that it assists the grieving survivors to move from shocked denial to acceptance of the death. As Emily Dickinson would have us remember, "The truth must dazzle gradually, or else every man be blinded."

The events leading up to the interment or cremation of the body are those in which the survivors are invited to gather together, acknowledge the death, share in the grief, participate in the mourning rites, and witness the final disposition of the body. The funeral must be understood in terms of this dramaturgical denouement: The deceased has been forever removed from the living community.

IS THE FUNERAL BENEFICIAL?

The question remains, If the funeral is a rite of integration and separation, is it beneficial? The answer to that question depends on the individual survivor and the circumstances surrounding a death. For some survivors, the loss of an elderly relative is an occasion for the barest acknowledgment of the death and the most expeditious disposal of the body. In such instances of what could be called "low-grief" death, loss can be slight and grief muted. The sudden, unexpected death of a child or a young husband, on the other hand, may be perceived as premature and unjust and denied or resented by the survivors. Such a death could be termed a "high-grief" loss. The social and emotional needs of the family, friends, or community in such instances are infinitely greater and the problems of the survivors potentially more extensive than in the case of low-grief loss. On the other hand, "no-grief" may be felt by a relative who is privately relieved or gratified by a death, and "improper grief" may be experienced by a person who is not allowed to mourn publicly (e.g., a man who was a companion of a homosexual man who died of AIDS but is prohibited from attending the funeral by the deceased's family). Care must be taken, therefore, not to define too narrowly what funeral rites or behaviors are appropriate for the bereaved. Insensitivity and inadequate social acknowledgment of the intensity or absence of grief and the social expectations of the bereaved can serve to aggravate their difficulties. For instance, when members of the clergy perceive the funeral as a rite of passage only and describe death as a spiritual victory to be celebrated, they ignore the fact that a death may represent the separation of a husband from a wife or a father from a daughter and that, as with any irrevocable separation, the survivor may experience a profound sense of loss. Reaction to human loss should never be dismissed or denigrated. I am sure that this is the insight John intended when he stated that "Jesus wept" (John 11:35, Revised Standard Version) upon hearing of the death of his friend Lazarus.

Mourning is the intersection of grief (a psychological drama) and bereavement (a social fact) where loss through death finds expression. The successful orchestration of this public process facilitates healing at the same time that it allows for the expression of private grief. The funeral thus provides the setting in which both private sorrow and public loss can be both expressed and shared. Fulcomer (1942) concluded, after reviewing the cases of 72 bereaved subjects, that the bereaved person's responses are positively affected if he or she realizes or believes that other persons are also mourning. In other words, "Sorrows tend to be diminished by the knowledge that another sorrows with us" (Shand, 1914, p. 341). Likewise, after their 4-year case analysis of 68 bereaved persons, Glick, Weiss, and Parkes (1974), concluded that even though the survivor frequently has mixed feelings, the tasks and activities associated with the ceremonies of leave-taking meet profound human needs. They observed, however, that many survivors found it difficult to view the corpse. But as they and Kübler-Ross (1969) and others have noted, viewing is a way for many to confront the death of their loved one. Glick et al. quoted one widow as remarking, "I didn't believe he was dead until I saw him in the casket" (p. 110).

Loss through death can be a crisis situation. Studies show, though, that survivors display a wide range of responses and varying capacities to adjust to a death. Prolonged maladjustment, as characterized by mental and physical ailments as well as the increased consumption of alcohol and sedatives, is all too common. However, a study at the University of Minnesota (Fulton & Gupta, 1974) and the studies of Mole (1974) and Glick et al. (1974) show that, apart from family and friends, relatively few survivors contact health care persons after a death. Yet, the evidence strongly suggests that many persons are in need of much more support than they receive from their closest family members or friends. The Minnesota study showed, for example, that only 15% of a sample of 362 widows and widowers reported receiving professional health care contact or support after their bereavement.

The funeral, as a rite of separation and integration, requires of funeral directors that they, too, be cognizant of and sensitive to the social and emotional needs of the families they serve. They must believe, as must the survivors, that the funeral is more than a commercial transaction.

In this connection, it is important to note that, in addition to this author's own work (discussed earlier), both the study of Binger et al. (1969) at Langley-Porter Institute and the Harvard Bereavement Study of Glick et al. (1974) found that the funeral director played a valuable social role. Binger et al. reported, for instance, that 15 of the 20 families they interviewed "expressed positive feelings toward the mortician or funeral director" (p. 417). They observed that funeral directors' "experience with grief reactions makes them skilled in offering solace to grieving families" (p. 417).

Since the first version of this chapter was written in 1978, an increasing amount of research has appeared that supports the contention that bereaved individuals typically find their interaction with funeral directors to be a supportive and helpful experience. In Khleif's (1975) study of some general populations and studies of widows and widowers by Winn (1981), Carey (1979), and Liberman and Borman (1982), as well as the studies of bereaved parents by Cook (1981, 1983) and Anglim (1976), the majority of respondents rated their funeral directors as somewhat or very helpful or supportive. In two studies of the widowed, moreover, the majority of widows and widowers described their spouse's funeral as helpful to their adjustment (Liberman & Borman 1982; Winn, 1981).

The different studies now available show that the contemporary funeral can be functional to the extent that it recognizes the separation and integration issues associated with death. Given the newfound understanding of the social and psychological dimensions of loss and grief, the funeral should be perceived more as a rite of separation and integration than as a rite of incorporation. To do so would acknowledge not only the social and personal values to be derived from such an approach to the funeral, but also the decreasing relevancy of the funeral as a piacular rite. In appreciating this subtle but, nevertheless, significant shift in emphasis, we will do ourselves and our fellow citizens a considerable service.

Of course, in addition to being competently and adequately served, people must be protected from malpractice. They must also have freedom of choice. Ultimately, a person's relationship with a funeral director is based on trust.

There is increasing scholarly evidence that a funeral is a ceremony of value for the mourner, just as competent funeral directors often are of assistance to the bereaved.

American society is experiencing rapid social change, particularly in its attitudes toward death and death practices. Society is presently in the process of defining and redefining grief, bereavement, and loss, to say nothing of the meaning of death itself. Comparable issues loom with respect to the elderly and the dying. The role of the funeral director is an emergent one.

It would be beneficial if the funeral director would come to be seen as a participant in the community's mental health network. This view would support those practices that historically have served human needs, strengthen the mental health movement within funeral service itself, and play a positive role in helping with the multiple burdens of bereavement. Perhaps, most of all, treating funeral service personnel like other professional and paraprofessional caregivers would express trust in the good intentions of others. To do so might be to remove, finally, the admonition *Caveat emptor* (Let the buyer beware) that has been held over the funeral director's head since time immemorial. That warning might be replaced with the historic medical directive *Primum non nocere* (Above all, do no harm), an admonition to which we might all pay more heed.

The dramaturgy of death compels the recognition that a death has occurred. In a society in which many people respond to the death of another by turning away, the funeral is a vehicle through which recovery from the crisis of bereavement can be initiated. The funeral is also a ceremony that recognizes the integral worth and dignity of a human being. It is not just a sociological statement that a death has occurred; it also proclaims that a life has been lived.

CONCLUSION

What does the future hold for the funeral? The funeral, as well as every other social ceremony or practice invented by human beings, is subject to change. Mourning rites and funeral customs are not carved in concrete and do not exist in a vacuum. They are contained, rather, within a cultural context that they define even as it defines them. American funeral customs and practices have been evolving since colonial days, as a result of both internal and external social forces.

The last two decades have witnessed not only appreciable changes in traditional funeral practices—the white pall of the Catholic funeral mass and the emergence of the humanistic funeral—but also extensive public criticism of funeral practices. Such criticism led, in the late 1970s, to the direct intervention of the government. The Federal Trade Commission ultimately effected legislation that required funeral directors to abide by rules of conduct and business procedures that more closely protected the public's interest. Change can also be observed in the public's behavior as well. In San Francisco, Los Angeles, New York, and other major cities across the United States, upwards of 25% of deaths now go unreported in the obituary columns of the daily newspapers (McReavy, 1980).

Of more immediate significance is the manner of disposition of the dead that is now practiced in almost one sixth of all deaths in San Diego County, California. Upon the declaration of a patient's death, the body is removed to the hospital morgue; an organization called Telephase is notified; the body is picked up at the morgue and enclosed in a rubberized bag; it is transported in an unmarked station wagon to a crematorium; the body is cremated, and the ashes are placed in a cardboard or plastic container for storage, dispersal, or delivery to a designated recipient; the legal survivor is later billed. Similar practices are occurring in other cities across the country in which the body of the deceased is disposed of by means of cremation and no memorial service or public or religious observances of any kind are held.

Cremation with or without memorialization, as an alternative form of disposition, is on the increase across the country. Although the prevalence of the practice still varies considerably, from approximately 13% of all deaths in Minnesota to more than 40% of all deaths on the Pacific coast, there is little doubt that with the Catholic Church's conditionally lifting its ban on cremation, the practice will continue to gain in public acceptance.

Another, more serendipitous factor may come in to play—AIDS. AIDS is not contagious in the normal course of human interaction, but the fear that it has generated among the American public may lead to mandatory changes not only in American funeral customs, but also in many other social customs. Only time will tell whether AIDS will have the same relative impact on contemporary society and the funeral that the Plague had during the successive centuries that it ravaged the populations of Europe.

Parsons (1963), the distinguished American sociologist, believed that the emergent changes that have been observed in contemporary funeral practices are the result of the convergence of the social, industrial, and medical trends that have characterized the United States since the turn of the century. Advocacy of change in funeral practices, he argued, was natural and to be expected in a society that strives to achieve order, practicality, efficiency, and economy in all facets of life. Blauner (1966), another American sociologist, was even more direct in his analysis. He argued that the dramatic changes that have occurred in society, particularly the profound demographic shifts, have resulted in a situation in which the majority of persons who die are those who are no longer central to the stream of life. Their deaths have little consequence for the social order. Under such circumstances, Blauner contended, the American funeral should be expected not only to continue to change significantly, but also eventually to "wither away."

There is some evidence to support Blauner's (1966) contention that funeral customs, as presently practiced in the United States, could wither away. A study of 558 bereaved persons conducted by the Center for Death Education and Research at the University of Minnesota (Owen, Fulton, & Markusen, 1982) showed that the death of an elderly parent is appreciably less disruptive emotionally, less debilitating, and socially less significant than is the death of either a spouse or a child. To be sure, adult children of the study (average age = 48) did mourn the loss of their parent—in some instances, profoundly—but, as a group, their responses were markedly different from the other two groups.

The study showed, for instance, that, compared with the bereaved parents and spouses, the bereaved adult children reported the least amount of change in such postdeath indexes of adjustment as crying, depression, anorexia, insomnia, smoking, drinking, and hallucinations. They also reported the least amount of physical illness after their bereavement. Moreover, they were the least expressive of their respective losses. That is, they were the least likely to conduct traditional funeral rites, the least likely to view the body, and the least likely to observe the anniversary of the death.

The study showed, further, that the group of adult children who had experienced the death of a parent were less likely than the group of parents who had lost a child and the group of bereaved spouses to be affected by and preoccupied with memories of the death of the deceased. Finally, the adult children were less likely than the other groups to be more appreciative of life, to be helpful toward others, to enjoy life or their families more, or to be warm toward other persons after the death. On the other hand, the adult children reported more personal guilt and more hostility toward others after the death than did the other survivors (Owen, Fulton, & Markusen, 1982).

The constellation of feelings and behaviors demonstrated by the adult children of the study after the death of an elderly parent could be described as diminished or transitory grief followed by limited postdeath activities. Although the sample of adult children in the study was admittedly small, their diminished grief may be an indication of a diminishing of interpersonal relationships that promises to grow more pronounced in the years ahead. Like the tip of an iceberg, the responses of the adult children suggest the magnitude of the changes that lie hidden below the surface of social intercourse. Although the tip in no way reveals the iceberg's actual proportions, it does indicate the iceberg's presence.

It is important to recognize that the mature adult child need not experience the grief reaction or profound sense of loss that characterized the responses of the parents and spouses in the Minnesota study. In modern society, the elderly are often defined differently from other age groups. They "have had their life." It is only "normal" and "natural" that they die.

The following cases taken from the study (Owen et al., 1982) are illustrative:

Case A. The respondent, a 45-year-old male construction worker, had the primary responsibility of attending to his 79-year-old father who died a lingering death from emphysema. The father had planned in advance that his body should be cremated with no service of any kind. The son complied with his wishes. The respondent and one brother took "the last ride" with his father from the funeral home to the crematorium. He looked into the furnace, which he regretted for a time. Later he drove alone to a nearby lake where he scattered his fathers ashes. At one point in the interview, after the respondent had denied experiencing any of the ordinary grief symptoms, the interviewer asked him what had helped him adjust to his loss. He replied by saying, "There was no adjustment required. I don't consider myself bereaved." When the interviewer asked him why he had chosen not to view the body, he said that he would have, "had the person been especially close, like a wife or a child."

Case B. The respondent, a 42-year-old banker, described his feelings following the death of his 81-year-old mother. She had developed pneumonia following a five month confinement in a nursing home. He acknowledged no symptoms of grief but admitted that he felt angry with his mother's physician. He believed that the doctor had gone to "extreme efforts to maintain her life after she developed pneumonia."

Case C. The respondent, a 51-year-old life insurance agent, was interviewed six months following the death of his 87-year-old father. The interviewer observed: "There was no evidence that the son was experiencing any of the ordinary grief symptoms." Both the respondent and his father were members of memorial societies, and the disposition of the body was by cremation. The respondent indicated that his father was nearly blind and had been in declining health. He could not think of any way in which his father's death had affected his life or the life of his family. His father felt it was most important to "work out details in advance to spare the survivors." When the respondent was asked what had helped him adjust to his loss, he responded that "there really wasn't any adjustment necessary; after all, he was 87 and we all have to go sometime." (pp. 31–33)

Minimal rites acknowledging the death of a socially disengaged, elderly person may make sense at the personal level. Funerals, it is said, are for the living, and if the living are not seriously affected by the death of a family member, the need for a traditional rite of passage may not be felt. A funeral, however, has traditionally had other functions besides disposing of a corpse or publicly acknowledging a death. As a social ceremony, it serves to bring together the community. As such, it serves as an important vehicle of cultural transmission. The contemporary impulse to preclude funerals from society or to exclude children from funerals can also have unintended consequences. In addition to cutting children off from direct expressions of love, concern, and support at this time of family crisis, it may deprive them of the opportunity to learn about life's most basic fact—death. The social meaning and intrinsic value of human life itself, moreover, may be implicitly denied by the failure to acknowledge our mortality.

REFERENCES

Anglim, M. A. (1976). Reintegration of the family after the death of a child. In I. Martinson (Ed.), *Home care for the dying child: Professional and family perspectives* (pp. 144–167). New York: Appleton-Century-Crofts.

Bendann, E. (1930). *Death customs: An analytical study of burial rites.* New York: Knopf.

Berardo, F. (1968). Widowhood status in the United States: Perspectives on a neglected aspect of the family life cycle. *The Family Coordinator, 17,* 191–203.

Binger, C. M., Ablin, A. R., Feuerstein, R. C., Kushner, J. H., Zoger, S., & Mikkelsen, C. (1969). Childhood leukemia: Emotional impact on patient and family. *New England Journal of Medicine, 8,* 414–418.

Blauner, R. (1966). Death and social structure. *Psychiatry, 29,* 378–394.

Bowlby, J. (1953). Some pathological processes engendered by early mother-child separation. *British Journal of Psychiatry, 99,* 265–256.

Bowlby, J. (1963). Childhood mourning and its implications for psychiatry. *Journal of the American Psychoanalytic Association, 11,* 500–541.

Bowlby, J., & Parkes, C. M. (1970). Separation and loss within the family. In E. J. Anthony & C. Koupernik (Eds.), *The child in his family* (pp. 197–216). New York: Wiley.

Bowman, L. E. (1959). *The American funeral: A study in guilt, extravagance and sublimity.* Washington, DC: Public Affairs Press.

Brabeck, M. M., & Weisgerber, K. (1988). Responses to the Challenger tragedy: Subtle and significant gender differences. *Sex-Roles, 19,* 9–10.

Bureau of Social Science Research. (1966). *Studies of Kennedy's assassination.* Washington, DC: Author.

Carey, R. G. (1979). Weathering widowhood: Problems·and adjustment of the widowed during the first year. *National Reporter, 2,* 1–5.

Center for Death Education and Research. (1971). *A compilation of studies of attitudes toward death, funerals and funeral directors.* Minneapolis, MN: University of Minnesota.

Ciocco, A. (1940). On the mortality in husbands and wives. *Human Biology, 12,* 508–531.

Cook, J. A. (1981). Children's funerals and their effect on familiar grief adjustment. *National Reporter, 4,* 1–2.

Cook, J. A. (1983). A death in the family: Parental bereavement in the first year. *Suicide and Life-Threatening Behavior, 13,* 42–61.

Cox, P., & Ford, J. R. (1964). The mortality of widows shortly after widowhood. *Lancet, 1,* 163–164.

Durkheim, E. (1954). *The elementary forms of religious life.* London: Allen and Unwin.

Evans-Pritchard, E. (1965). *Theories of primitive religion.* Oxford, England: Clarendon Press.

Fulcomer, D. M. (1942). *The adjustive behavior of some recently bereaved spouses: A psychosociological study.* Unpublished doctoral dissertation, Northwestern University, Evanston, IL.

Fulton, R. (1961). The clergyman and the funeral director: A study in role conflict. *Social Forces, 39,* 317–323.

Fulton, R. (1965). The sacred and the secular. In R. Fulton (Ed.), *Death and identity* (pp. 89–105). New York: Wiley.

Fulton, R. (1971). Contemporary funeral practices. In H. C. Raether (Ed.), *Successful funeral service practice* (pp. 216–235). Englewood Cliffs, NJ: Prentice-Hall.

Fulton, R. (Ed.). (1973). *Bibliography on death, grief and bereavement 1945–1973* (3rd ed.). Minneapolis, MN: Center for Death Education and Research.

Fulton, F., & Gupta, V. (1974). *Psychological adjustment to loss.* Unpublished manuscript, Center for Death Education and Research, University of Minnesota, Minneapolis, MN.

Frederick, J. F. (1961). The physiology of grief. *Dodge Magazine, 63,* 8–10.

Geertz, C. (1957). Ritual and social change; A Javanese example. *American Anthropologist, 59,* 32–54.

Glick, I. O., Weiss, R. S., & Parkes, C. M. (1974). *The first year of bereavement.* New York: Wiley.

Gluckman, M. (1962). Rituals of rebellion in South-East Africa. In M. Gluckman (Ed.), *Essays on the ritual of social relations* (pp. 1–35). New York: Humanities Press.

Goody, J. (1962a). *Death, property and the ancestors: A study of the mortuary customs of the Lo Dagaa of West Africa.* Stanford, CA: Stanford University Press.

Goody, J. (1962b). Religion and ritual: The definitional problem. *British Journal of Sociology, 12,* 142–164.

Greenberg, B. S., & Parker, E. B. (Eds.). (1965). *The Kennedy assassination and the American public: Social communication in crisis.* Stanford, CA: Stanford University Press.

Habenstein, R. W., & Lamers, W. M. (1963). *Funeral customs the world over.* Milwaukee, WI: Bulfin.

Harmer, R. M. (1971). Funerals, fantasy and flight. *Omega, 2,* 127–135.

Hertz, R. (1960). *Death and the right hand.* Glenco, IL: Free Press.

Holmes, T. H., & Rahe, R. H. (1967). The Social Readjustment Rating Scale. *Journal of Psychosomatic Research, 11,* 213–218.

Humanae vitae. (1969, July 30). *The New York Times,* pp. 1, 20.

Kennedy is laid to rest on an open slope in Arlington National Cemetery. (1963, November 26). *The New York Times,* p. 2.

Khleif, B. (1975). The sociology of the mortuary: Attitudes to the funeral, funeral director and funeral arrangements. In O. Margolis et al. (Eds.), *Grief and the meaning of the funeral* (pp. 37–46). New York: MSS Information.

Khleif, B. (1976). The sociology of the mortuary. In V. Pine et al. (Eds.), *Acute grief and the funeral* (pp. 55–91). Springfield, IL: Thomas.

Kroeber, A. L. (1927). Disposal of the dead. *American Anthropologist, 29,* 308–315.

Kraus, A., & Lilienfeld, A. (1959). Some epidemiologic aspects of the high mortality rate in the young widowed group. *Journal of Chronic Diseases, 10,* 207–217.

Kübler-Ross, E. (1969). *On death and dying.* New York: Macmillan.

Kubey, R. W., & Peluso, T. (1990). Emotional response as a cause of interpersonal news diffusion: The case of the space shuttle tragedy. *Journal of Broadcasting and Electronic Media, 34*(1), 69–76.

Liberman, M. A., & Borman, L. D. (1982). Widows view the helpfulness of the funeral service. *National Reporter, 5,* 2–4.

Lindemann, E. (1944). Symptomatology and management of acute grief. *American Journal of Psychiatry, 101,* 141–148.

Malinowski, B. (1984). Death and the reintegration of the group. In B. Malinowski (Ed.), *Magic, science, and religion and other essays* (pp. 47–53). New York: Doubleday.

Mandelbaum, D. (1959). Social uses of funeral rites. In H. Feifel (Ed.), *The meaning of death* (pp. 189–217). New York: McGraw-Hill.

McReavy, J. (1980). *N.F.D.A. Paid Obituary Notice Survey.* Milwaukee, WI: National Funeral Directors Association.

Mitford, J. (1963). *The American way of death.* New York: Simon & Schuster.

Mole, R. L. (1974). *Next of kin: A study of bereavement, grief and mourning.* Unpublished doctoral dissertation, Howard University, Washington, DC.

The NAMES Project AIDS Memorial Quilt. (1993). San Francisco: The NAMES Project Foundation.

National Park Service. (1984). *Washington: Vietnam Veterans Memorial* (GPO Publication No. 421-609/478). Washington, DC: U.S. Department of the Interior.

Owen, G., Fulton, R., & Markusen, E. (1982). Death at a distance. *Omega, 13,* 191–226.

Parkes, C. M. (1964). Effects of bereavement on physical and mental health—a study of medical records of widows. *British Medical Journal, 2,* 274–279.

Parkes, C. M. (1965). Bereavement and mental illness (part I): A clinical study of the grief of bereaved psychiatric patients. *British Journal of Medical Psychology, 38,* 1–12.

Parsons, T. (1963). Death in American society—a brief working paper. *The American Behavioral Scientist, 6,* 61–65.

Particular criticism reported on birth control. (1968, August 9). *Time,* p. 40.

Particular criticism reported on birth control. (1968, October 4). *Time,* p. 57.

Pope speaks on birth control. (1968, August 2). *Time,* p. 54.

Puckle, B. S. (1926). *Funeral customs: Their origin and development.* London: Laurie.

Quilt facts as of June 5, 1993. (1993). San Francisco: The NAMES Project.

Radcliffe-Brown, A. (1965). Taboo. In A. Radcliffe-Brown (Ed.), *Structure and function in primitive society* (pp. 133–152). New York: Free Press.

Rahe, R., McKean, J., & Arthur, R. J. (1967). A longitudinal study of life-change and illness patterns. *Journal of Psychosomatic Research, 10,* 356.

Rahe, R., Meyer, M., Smith, M., Kjaer, G., & Holmes, T. H. (1964). Social stress and illness onset. *Journal of Psychosomatic Research, 8,* 35–43.

Rees, D. W., & Lutkins, S. (1967). Mortality of bereavement. *British Medical Journal, 4,* 13–26.

Scruggs, J. C., & Swerdlow, J. L. (1985). *To heal a nation.* New York: Harper & Row.

Shand, A. F. (1914). *The foundations of character.* New York: Macmillan.

Sheatsley, P. B., & Feldman, J. J. (1964). The assassination of President Kennedy: A preliminary report on public relations and behavior. *Public Opinion Quarterly, 28,* 189–215.

Solecki, R. S. (1971). *Shanidar.* New York: Knopf.

Stern, G., Winokur, G., Graham, D., and Graham, F. K. (1961). Alterations in physiological measures during experimentally induced attitudes. *Journal of Psychosomatic Research, 5,* 73–82.

Sturken, M. (1992). Conversations with the dead: Bearing witness in the AIDS Memorial Quilt. *Socialist Review, 22*(2), 65–95.

They came to mourn. (1969, April 19). *Time,* pp. 18–19.

U.S. Bureau of the Census. (1960). *Historical statistics of the United States, colonial times to 1957.* Washington, DC: U.S. Government Printing Office.

U.S. Bureau of the Census. (1990). *Census of population* (CPH-L-74). Washington, DC: U.S. Government Printing Office.

Van Gennep, A. (1961). *The rites of passage.* Chicago: University of Chicago Press.

Weisman, A. (1972). *On dying and denying.* New York: Behavioral Publications.

Winn, R. L. (1981). Perceptions of the funeral service and post-bereavement adjustment in widowed individuals. *National Reporter, 4,* 1–8.

Wolfenstein, M., & Kliman, G. (Eds.). (1965). *Children and the death of a president.* Garden City, NY: Doubleday.

Wretmark, G. (1959). A study of grief reactions. *Acta Psychiatrica Neurologica Scandinavica,* (Suppl. 136), 292.

Young, M., Young, M., Benjamin, B., & Wallis, C. (1963). The mortality of widowers. *Lancet, 2,* 454–456.

Chapter 9

Grief and Mourning: Accommodating to Loss

Therese A. Rando

Loss, grief, and mourning. Three inevitabilities of human existence encountered often throughout life. Although typically associated with death and other traumatic events, they are actually inherent aspects of all change, whether it is perceived as positive or negative.

To the extent that a caregiver can identify the elements of loss in a human experience and can respond to and facilitate the attendant grief and mourning, that caregiver possesses knowledge and skill fundamental to intervention in every human condition. Although, certainly, caregivers must be aware of the content, issues, and treatment strategies and techniques specific to particular mental health problems, the dynamics of loss must be recognized within them. For instance, physical and sexual abuse, rape, the problems of adult children of alcoholics and other dysfunctional families, divorce, sexual dysfunction, fear of intimacy, and posttraumatic stress all involve significant amounts of loss, grief, and mourning that need to be addressed.

Similarly, even when change occurs for what is construed to be the betterment of the person, loss is automatically a component of the experience, if for no other reason than change necessarily demands losing the status quo. Hence, loss, grief, and mourning result from normal development and maturation in life (e.g., a couple goes from being a dyad to a triad with the birth of their first child), as well as from competency arising from the attainment of certain abilities, capacities, or functioning (e.g., a teen graduates from high school and leaves home to attend college).

Thus in this chapter, the perspective is taken that loss is a central phenomenon in human existence that must be accommodated in a healthy manner. First, the work of five clinical theorists who have significantly contributed to current thinking about grief and mourning is reviewed. The experiences of and reactions to loss related to death are then examined. The requirements for the appropriate mourning of death are discussed, the seven steps of intervention to facilitate mourning are listed, and the causes and dimensions of complicated mourning are discussed. Some of the material in this chapter has been adopted from an earlier work (Rando, 1993).

This chapter is lovingly dedicated to the memory of Mr. B. Barchstoffales, whose gentle spirit and goodness filled life with special meaning, sweetness, and love, and whose absence darkens the world.

CONCEPTUALIZATIONS OF GRIEF AND MOURNING: CONTRIBUTIONS OF FIVE MAJOR CLINICAL THEORISTS

Before examining current concepts of loss, it is useful to have an understanding of the evolution of thought about grief and mourning that has transpired in the thanatological literature. The following is a brief, noncomprehensive review of five selected clinical authors whose writings have been exceptionally influential in shaping current aspects of thought about responses to loss. One or two of each theorist's many works are referred to to illustrate how his or her particular focus illuminates important realities about grief and mourning today. The chronology is also instructive in revealing the changing foci of interest in the topic as the field has continued to develop.

Freud

The fact that he was not the first to examine bereavement notwithstanding, Sigmund Freud is typically taken as the point of departure when writers attempt to trace the theoretical literature on grief and mourning. His work is helpful in describing the phenomena, purposes, experience, work, and normalcy of mourning and in differentiating mourning from depression.

Freud took up the discussion of mourning in order to elucidate points about clinical depression or, as it was called in those days, melancholia. His most often cited work in the area is "Mourning and Melancholia" (1917/1957), which, despite frequently being misunderstood, misquoted, and mischronicled, delineates eight crucial aspects of mourning (see Rando, 1993, for textual support for and elaboration of each of these elements).

Freud pointed out that mourning is a normal process and that symbolic losses can give rise to it as do actual losses. The distinguishing features of mourning, according to Freud, include profoundly painful dejection, cessation of interest in the outside world, loss of the capacity to love, and inhibition of activity. Mourning is initiated by the need to detach from the lost object, and the reason mourning is such a struggle is that the human being never willingly abandons an emotional attachment, and only does so when he or she learns that it is better to relinquish the object than to try to hold on to it now that it is lost. This process takes time and a great deal of energy and can be accomplished only bit by bit, entailing the review of each one of the memories and expectations associated with the lost object and the experiencing of all of the feelings associated with it before it can be let go. The work of mourning is complete when the ego becomes free from and uninhibited by the lost object. In some people, the same influences produce melancholia instead of mourning, and a disposition toward pathology is suspected in these individuals.

Lorraine Siggins (1966) put Freud's comments in "Mourning and Melancholia" into a helpful perspective by pointing out that in that paper Freud created an account of mourning that is ideal for discussion purposes and that in other writings he supplemented this account with further reflection on the actual course of human mourning. For this reason, Siggins pointed out, it is important that his opinions in this classic work be considered in conjunction with is other works. In these works, one finds critical reversals of some points made in "Mourning and Melancholia." Specifically, in other writings Freud recognized that a lost love object is never totally relinquished (1926/1960), that ambivalence is a normal part of mourning (1913/1955), and that identification with the lost object is a healthy and necessary component of mourning (1923/1961).

Lindemann

Coming from a crisis intervention perspective, itself a somewhat novel approach in the field at the time, and recognizing loss to be a potent factor in psychosomatic disorders, Erich Lindemann added significantly to the understanding of mourning by elucidating the concept of "grief work." His class article "Symptomatology and Management of Acute Grief" (Lindemann, 1944) is the forerunner of subsequent theoretical conceptualizations, operationalizing the three tasks of grief work as emancipation from bondage to the deceased, readjustment to the environment in which the deceased is missing, and formation of new relationships. Asserting that the duration of grief and mourning depends on the success with which the bereaved individual undertakes the grief work, Lindemann observed that persons seek to avoid the intense distress connected with the grief experience and the expression of the emotion necessary to it, creating major obstacles to successful completion of their grief work.

Lindemann found five characteristics to be pathognomonic for grief: somatic distress, preoccupation with the image of the deceased, guilt, hostile reactions, and loss of patterns of conduct. Less frequently, he observed a sixth characteristic in individuals bordering on pathological reactions: the appearance in the bereaved's behavior of traits belonging to the deceased, especially symptoms of the deceased's final illness or behavior the deceased evidenced at the time of the tragedy. Lindemann made a further important clinical contribution by discussing morbid grief reactions as distortions of normal grief, which can be transformed into normal reactions through fairly simple and brief management.

Lindemann discerned two types of morbid reactions: delayed and distorted. The nine indicators of distorted grief, still in use today, include

- Overactivity without a sense of loss;
- The acquisition of symptoms belonging to the last illness of the deceased;
- A medical disease of a psychosomatic nature;
- A conspicuous alteration of relationships to friends and relatives;
- Furious hostility against specific persons;
- A wooden and formal demeanor, with affect and conduct resembling schizophrenic postures;
- A lasting loss of patterns of social interaction;

- Actions detrimental to the individual's own social and economic existence; and
- Agitated depression.

Lindemann believed that proper management of grief reactions by the caregiver could prevent prolonged and serious alterations in the patient's social adjustment, as well as potential medical disease. Lindemann (1944) also wrote about the work of the bereaved individual:

> Comfort alone does not provide adequate assistance in the patient's grief work. He has to accept the pain of the bereavement. He has to review his relationships with the deceased, and has to become acquainted with the alterations in his own modes of emotional reaction. His fear of insanity, his fear of accepting the surprising changes in his feelings, especially the overflow of hostility, have to be worked through. He will have to express his sorrow and sense of loss. He will have to find an acceptable formulation of his future relationship to the deceased. He will have to verbalize his feelings of guilt, and he will have to find persons around him whom he can use as "primers" for the acquisition of new patterns of conduct. (p. 147)

In addition, it was Lindemann who introduced, in a brief note in "Symptomatology and Management of Acute Grief," the concept of anticipatory grief, a topic still hotly debated today (see Rando, 1986).

Bowlby

Probably no one person in the field of thanatology has done more to promote a theory underlying the experience and dynamics of mourning than John Bowlby. As the chief architect of attachment theory, his work has contributed enormously to the literature on attachment, human development, child rearing, separation, loss, mourning, and psychopathology. Although he initially took a psychoanalytic perspective, Bowlby subsequently incorporated into his work on mourning principles from ethology, control theory, and cognitive psychology. Bowlby also rightly can be remembered as being especially persuasive in demonstrating the biological basis for much acute grieving behavior. This, along with his incorporation of principles from other disciplines, permanently broadened the previously exclusively psychoanalytic focus of conceptualizations of grief and mourning. His magnificent three-volume opus on attachment and loss richly explicates numerous aspects of the aforementioned topics, especially, although not exclusively, as they pertain to the responses to loss (Bowlby, 1969, 1973, 1980).

For Bowlby, mourning denoted a wide array of psychological processes, both conscious and unconscious, that are set in train by the loss of a loved person. In uncomplicated responses to the loss of a loved one, the bereaved individual passes through four general phases: (a) numbing, (b) yearning and searching, (c) disorganization and despair, and (d) reorganization (Bowlby, 1980). Bowlby presented compelling evidence that the responses of infants and young children to the loss of a primary attachment figure are, at a descriptive level, substantially the same as those of older children and adults. He argued (against many of his former psychoanalytic colleagues) that these processes constitute mourning and that the subjective experience is one of grief.

Bowlby (1963) further pointed out that the mourning processes commonly seen in infancy and early childhood bear many of the features that are hallmarks of pathological mourning in the adult; including unconscious yearning for the lost person, unconscious reproach against the lost person, combined with conscious and often unremitting self-reproach; compulsive caring for other persons; and persistent disbelief that the loss is permanent. This is important because it alerts caregivers to the similarity between typical mourning in early childhood and pathological mourning in adulthood. In both scenarios, the normal urges to recover and reproach the lost object, along with yearning for and anger at it—which are appropriate biological and psychological adaptations to separation—are not expressed. They become split off and repressed. Pathology results not because defense mechanisms are being used, but because of the scope and intensity of the defense mechanisms, the prematurity of their onset, and their tendency to persist. In essence, processes in childhood and adult pathological mourning are pathological variants of those characterizing healthy mourning, the latter being of lesser degree and later onset.

Among his numerous other contributions, Bowlby (1980) added to the literature through the identification of three groups of individuals whose dispositions to certain affectional relationships predispose them to pathological mourning: those with a disposition to make anxious and ambivalent relationships, those with a disposition toward compulsive caregiving, and those with a disposition to assert independence of affectional ties. In addition, he explicated the selected cognitive biases associated with each of the two main disordered variants he observed in adult mourning—chronic mourning and prolonged absence of conscious grieving—and also pointed out the existence of a minor variant, euphoria. In so doing, Bowlby provided descriptions of and delineated a number of the dynamics behind maladaptive responses to loss.

Parkes

Significantly influenced by Bowlby, and a later associate of his, Colin Murray Parkes has added impressively to the thanatological literature, both individually and with Robert Weiss (Parkes & Weiss, 1983) and Ira Glick (Glick, Weiss & Parkes, 1974). Parkes's early research was especially helpful in revealing that there were no differences between psychiatrically disturbed mourners and individuals appearing to evidence typical reactions, and that there were no symptoms peculiar to pathological grief per se, although extreme guilt, identification symptoms, and delayed grief were seen to indicate that pathology might develop (Parkes, 1987). Dissatisfied with problems in using traditional psychiatric diagnostic categories to obtain an understanding of grief, Parkes and Weiss (1983) identified three main types of pathological grief syndromes associated with failure to recover from bereavement: unanticipated grief, conflicted grief, and chronic grief. Their taxonomy included the etiological, descriptive, and treatment requirement features for each.

In addition to an in-depth analysis and description of the adult's response to the loss of a spouse (Parkes, 1987) and one of the earliest attempts at researching—and proving—the efficacy of intervention for high-risk mourners (Parkes, 1980, 1981), Parkes has made an important contribution to the field of grief and mourning by focusing attention on the concept of psychosocial transitions and explicating the devastating sequelae of invalidated assumptions and expectations about the world after the death of a loved one (Parkes, 1988).

Raphael

Beverley Raphael well may be the consummate thanatologist in bereavement today, integrating theory, research, and practice in her clinical examinations of how individuals cope with, understand, and eventually adapt to many different types of bereavements across the life span. In her unparalleled work *The Anatomy of Bereavement* (Raphael, 1983), she analyzes separation and mourning across all developmental stages, identifying the dynamics, explicating the bereavement experience, and examining future outcomes. She considers special types of bereavements, identifies the factors that affect bereavement outcomes, explains morbid or pathological patterns of grief, and details treatment strategies and specific interventions in this universally acclaimed tome.

Raphael's other contributions to the field are numerous and varied, adding to the interdisciplinary literature. Her work has continued to broaden the focus of bereavement and stimulated thanatologists to expand their vision. She has integrated concepts of grief and mourning with traumatic stress (Raphael, 1986); proposed the concept of personal disaster (Raphael, 1981); critically evaluated the state of research in bereavement (Raphael & Middleton, 1987); and provided what unanimously have been acclaimed as the most well-controlled and methodologically sound investigations of bereavement intervention, offering the first demonstrations of both the importance of identifying high-risk mourners and the efficacy of treatment when offered to this population (Raphael, 1977; Singh & Raphael, 1978). Additionally, Raphael has explained the etiologies of and described three general patterns of morbid or pathological grief—absent, delayed, or inhibited grief; distorted grief; and chronic grief—and has specified interventions for each utilizing her treatment techniques known as "focal psychotherapy" (Raphael, 1975, 1983).

DEFINITIONS AND CONCEPTS PERTAINING TO LOSS
Loss

There are two major categories of loss: physical loss and psychosocial (also known as symbolic) loss. A physical loss is the loss of something that is tangible (e.g., a house burns down, a car is stolen, or a breast is removed in a mastectomy). A psychosocial loss is the loss of something that is intangible or psychosocial in nature (e.g., a person gets a divorce, develops a chronic illness, or has a dream shattered). Often, because physical losses are tangible, people recognize them and are aware that the person who experienced the loss is bereft. Such awareness is necessary so that the bereaved person is given permission and support to mourn. In contrast, in cases of psychosocial loss, others, and often even the bereaved individual him- or herself, fail to recognize that a loss has occurred and must be mourned. When society's failure to recognize a loss culminates in that loss's not being able to be openly acknowledged, publicly mourned, or socially supported, the mourner experiences what is known as disenfranchised grief (Doka, 1989), and mourning becomes complicated.

A concept inherently related to psychosocial loss is that of the assumptive world. The assumptive world is a schema containing everything a person assumes to be true about the world and the self on the basis of previous experience. It consists of all the individual's assumptions (including expectations and beliefs), most of which translate into virtually automatic habits of cognition and behavior. The assumptive world is the person's internal model against which he or she constantly matches incoming sensory data in order to orient the self, recognize what is happening, and plan behavior (Parkes, 1988). It is important with regard to grief and mourning because, in large part, a person's assumptive world determines his or her needs, emotions, and behavior and gives rise to hopes, wishes, fantasies, and dreams—all of which are significantly affected by the death of a loved one.

There are two types of elements in the assumptive world: global and specific. Global assumptions pertain to the self, others, life, or the world in general. The circumstances of a death, the very fact that it occurred, or the sequelae that it engenders can shatter global assumptions the mourner maintains; for example, the mourner no longer believes that the world is a safe, orderly place. In contrast, specific assumptions pertain to loved ones and their continued interactive presence in the individual's world. The death of a loved one always inherently violates a person's specific assumptions, expectations, and beliefs regarding the loved one; for example, the mourner realizes, "My spouse will not be around to grow old with me and see our children's children born."

With the loss of a loved one comes the loss of unique gratification, resources, and meaning. Each of the ties a person has to a loved one is represented in the person's assumptive world. Each is shattered if the loved one dies. For this reason, contending with the death of a loved one inevitably confronts a mourner with psychosocial losses in the assumptive world and ultimately mandates the mourner's revision of his or her assumptive world to accommodate the reality of life in the absence of the deceased.

A secondary loss (Rando, 1984) is a physical or psychosocial loss that coincides with or develops as a consequence of an initial loss. It need not be secondary in terms of impact; it is only secondary in terms of occurrence. For example, with the death of a loved one, a mourner experiences the secondary physical loss of the loved one's presence. If relocation is mandated after the death, the mourner experiences the secondary physical loss of his or her home. Secondary psychosocial losses proliferate the more the mourner was tied or strongly attached to the deceased; the more the deceased played numerous and central roles in the mourner's life; the more meanings the relationship embodied; the more behavior, interaction, and reinforcement patterns involved the deceased; the more the deceased was integrated into the assumptive world of the mourner; and the more the mourner's needs, feelings, thoughts, memories, hopes, wishes, fantasies, dreams, assumptions, expectations, and beliefs were related to the deceased (Rando, 1993). For example, spouses typically play many roles to each other. They are each other's lover, best friend, helpmate, co-parent, social partner, traveling companion, business associate, career supporter, and "other half," among other roles. With the death of a spouse, the mourner loses someone to fill these roles and to gratify the needs, sustain the feelings, generate the meanings, and meet the expectations associated with these roles in the particular way the deceased did.

A mourner may sustain a psychosocial loss without experiencing a secondary physical loss; however, it is impossible to experience a physical loss without a secondary psychosocial loss. At the very least, the significance the mourner assigned to the tangible object is lost when the object is lost. Consequently, every physical loss generates a psychosocial loss. The total bereavement experience of any individual actually represents the accumulated sum of all of the grief and mourning for all the losses—physical and psychosocial, initial and secondary— that have been engendered by the death.

Finally, the term *bereavement* refers to the state of having suffered a loss. It is instructive to know that the words *bereave* and *rob* derive from the same root. Both imply an unwilling deprivation by force, an unjust and injurious stealing of something valuable. This leaves an individual feeling victimized. The concept of victimization is important to bear in mind, because it explains many of the bereaved's reactions to their loss. Not unlike the individual who has been victimized by being physically assaulted and robbed, the bereaved experience anxiety; anger; self-blame; guilt; an assault on their assumptive world; a sense of unfairness; a loss of control, predictability, safety, and security; feelings of helplessness and powerlessness; and posttraumatic stress reactions.

Grief

Grief is the process of experiencing the psychological, behavioral, social, and physical reactions to the perception of loss. This definition has five important implications:

1   Grief is experienced in four major ways;
2   Grief is a continuing development involving many changes over time;
3   Grief is a natural, expectable reaction;
4   Grief is a reaction to all types of loss, not exclusively death; and

5 The experiencing of grief depends on the individual's unique perception of loss, regardless of whether the same perception is held by others (a desirable, but not necessary, condition).

Any particular grief response expresses one or a more of the following four elements: (a) the mourner's feelings about the loss and the deprivation it causes (e.g., sorrow or guilt), (b) the mourner's protest at the loss and wish to undo it and have it not be true (e.g., anger or a preoccupation with the deceased), (c) the effects caused by the assault on the mourner as a result of the loss (e.g., confusion or physical symptoms), and (d) the actions stimulated in the mourner by the preceding elements (e.g., social withdrawal or increased use of psychoactive substances) (Rando, 1993).

However, the healthy mourning of a loss demands more than mere expression of reactions. Active work is required to adapt to the loss. In essence, grief is a response to a stimulus (i.e., loss). It is a complex set of passive reactions to the loss; yet it does not take the individual far enough. The bereaved must make a series of readjustments to compensate for and adjust to the absence of what has been lost. Failure to make the proper adaptations and reorientations necessitated by a loss leaves the survivor unsuitably related to the lost object and the old world. The new reality is not conformed to, and the individual persists in some fashion(s) as if the world is the same when it is not. For this reason, more than grief—that is, the expression of reactions—is required to accommodate a loss healthily. There must be active movement and change if a major loss is to be worked through, reconciled, and integrated into a mourner's life and if the mourner is to continue on in an appropriately healthy manner in the new life without the deceased loved one. Thus, grief is a necessary but not sufficient condition to come to successful accommodation of a loss. It is only the beginning of the process.

Mourning

The active processes of mourning are necessary to take the individual beyond the passive reactions of grief and into the realm of movement and change demanded by major loss. Traditional definitions of mourning have focused on its function as a vehicle for social communication through the cultural and/or public display of grief through behaviors such as attending a funeral or dressing in black garments. The definition of mourning used in this chapter follows the psychoanalytic tradition of focusing on intrapsychic work but expands this focus by including adaptive behaviors necessitated by the loss of the loved one. Thus mourning includes the conscious and unconscious processes and courses of action that promote three operations, each with its own focus. These go beyond the passive reactions of grief and represent the mourner's moving to reorient him- or herself in relation to the deceased, the self, and the external world.

The first operation promoted by mourning is the undoing of the psychosocial ties that bind the mourner to the loved one, with the eventual facilitation of the development of new ties. In this operation, an internal focus on the deceased helps stimulate the acute grief resulting from the separation, as well as the recollection and reexperience of the deceased and the relationship, the ultimate changing of emotional investment in the deceased, and the development of a new relationship with that loved one. In the second operation, mourning processes help the survivor adapt to the loss. Again, in an internal focus, the mourner undertakes the necessary revision of his or her assumptive world; adoption or modification of roles, skills, and behaviors; and development of a new identity. The third and final operation promoted by mourning helps the mourner learn how to live in a healthy way in the new world that does not include the deceased. Taking an external focus, the mourner attempts to move adaptively into the new world through the adoption of new ways of being in that world and the ultimate reinvestment in people, objects, roles, hopes, beliefs, causes, ideals, goals, or pursuits.

The Relationship of Grief to Mourning

As may be seen, grief is actually the beginning part of mourning. It helps the individual recognize the loss and prepare for the later processes of mourning. Without the experiences and learning provided by acute grief, mourning cannot take place. Uncomplicated reactions of acute grief may last a number of months and, in some cases, even longer. In contrast, uncomplicated mourning can last a number of years—forever for some people. This does not mean that the individual is in acute grief all the time. One can mourn but not be in acute grief (i.e., not manifesting psychological, behavioral, social, or physical reactions to the perception of loss). Even though grief reactions may be spent, the mourner still may have to achieve much adaptation and integration before the loss is successfully accommodated (e.g., the widow is no longer in acute grief after the first year or so, but it may take a number of years before she can think about dating again). Also, there will be times when the mourner experiences subsequent temporary upsurges of grief, as discussed later in this chapter. Hence, just as infancy is a part of childhood but childhood is composed of more than that one phase (e.g., toddlerhood, latency stage, early adolescence), grief is a part of mourning, but mourning is not necessarily a part of grief. Mourning encompasses much more than grief.

The distinction between grief and mourning is crucial to treatment. Many caregivers assist the bereaved with the beginning process of acute grief (expressing their reactions to the loss) but not with the important latter processes (reorienting in relation to the deceased, the self, and the external world). As a result, mourners are frequently left alone to reshape themselves and their world after the loss of a loved one, and they suffer additionally as a consequence.

The Concept of Accommodation to the Loss

The goal for any mourner is to find healthy ways to accommodate the loss into his or her life. The term *accommodation* suggests an adaptation to make room for a particular circumstance. Clinical experience suggests that it is to be preferred over the term *resolution,* which insinuates a once-and-for-all closure that typically is not achieved after the death of a dearly loved one, because certain aspects of the loss remain with the mourner until his or her own death. The concept of accommodation captures more accurately the reality that a major loss can be integrated into the rest of life but that a truly final closure usually cannot be obtained and is not even desirable. The term *accommodation* implies making oneself fit with what has happened, as in reconciling the loss. The crucial action-oriented emphasis of mourning is also implied by the term. For healthy accommodation of any loss to occur, six R processes must be completed successfully. These are identified later in this chapter.

FACTORS THAT INFLUENCE GRIEF AND MOURNING

No individual's grief or mourning occurs in a vacuum. It is influenced, shaped, and determined by a constellation of factors that renders each mourner's response as unique as his or her fingerprint. To be able to diagnose and treat grief and mourning, caregivers must know the factors circumscribing the particular loss of a particular mourner at a particular point in time. A response that is perfectly appropriate for one person in one set of circumstances may be pathological for another person in different circumstances. Therefore, no interpretation of appropriateness or pathology can ever be made without careful consideration of these factors. (For a comprehensive discussion of most of these factors, the reader is referred to Rando, 1984.)

The factors that influence grief and mourning include the following:

PSYCHOLOGICAL FACTORS
Characteristics Pertaining to the Nature and Meaning of the Specific Loss
The unique nature and meaning of the loss sustained or relationship severed
Qualities of the relationship lost (psychological character, strength, and security of the attachment)
Roles the deceased occupied in the mourner's family or social system (number of roles, functions served, and their centrality and importance)
Characteristics of the deceased
Amount of unfinished business between the mourner and the deceased
Mourner's perception of the deceased's fulfillment in life
Number, type, and quality of secondary losses
Nature of any ongoing relationship with the deceased

Characteristics of the Mourner
Coping behaviors, personality, and mental health
Level of maturity and intelligence
Assumptive world
Previous life experiences, especially past experiences with loss and death
Expectations about grief and mourning

Social, cultural, ethnic, generational, and religious/philosophical/spiritual back-
    ground
Sex role conditioning
Age
Developmental stage of life, lifestyle, and sense of meaning and fulfillment
Presence of concurrent stresses or crises

Characteristics of the Death
The death surround (location, type of death, reasons for it, mourner's presence at
    it, degree of confirmation of it, and mourner's degree of preparation and partici-
    pation)
Timeliness
Psychosocial context within which the death occurs
Amount of mourner's anticipation of the death
Degree of suddenness
Mourner's perception of preventability
Length of illness prior to the death
Amount, type, and quality of anticipatory grief and involvement with the dying
    person

SOCIAL FACTORS
Mourner's social support system and the recognition, validation, acceptance, and
    assistance provided by its members
Mourner's social, cultural, ethnic, generational, and religious/philosophical/spiri-
    tual background
Mourner's educational, economic, and occupational status
Funerary or memorial rites
Involvement in the legal system
Amount of time since the death

PHYSIOLOGICAL FACTORS
Drugs (including alcohol, caffeine, and nicotine)
Nutrition
Rest and sleep
Exercise
Physical health

Note: Adapted from *Treatment of Complicated Mourning* (pp. 31–32) by T. A. Rando, 1993, Champaign, IL: Research Press. Copyright 1993 by Therese A. Rando. Reprinted by permission.

INSUFFICIENT APPRECIATION OF THE COGNITIVE PROCESSES IN MOURNING

A majority of the writers discussing bereavement have focused almost exclusively
on the affective or emotional aspects of the mourner's journey throughout the
three phases of grief and mourning. Although this domain is of critical importance, the relative neglect of the cognitive aspects of adaptation to loss has resulted in a significant disservice to mourners. Human beings are cognitive animals

and, as such, need to process loss from that perspective as well as from the emotional.

There are two sets of cognitive processes in bereavement. One set of processes is associated more with acute grief than with mourning per se. These processes relate to the mourner's learning about the reality of the loved one's death and appreciating its implications. Much of what traditionally has been viewed as denial or resistance is actually the mourner's disbelief and inability to achieve clarity and comprehend the loss. The mourner gradually learns the reality through the pain, absence of the deceased, and the frustration of desires to reunite with the deceased. Over time, the mourner comes to know that the loved one is dead. It takes a long time and many lessons before the mourner is able to apprehend this fact. The more sudden and unexpected the death, the lengthier this process.

A second set of cognitive processes is associated more with mourning than with acute grief. These processes pertain specifically to the mourner's revision of his or her assumptive world and formation of a new identity to incorporate the specific changes necessitated by the loved one's death and are described by five theories of cognitive adaptation to threatening or traumatic events (Rando, 1993):

• Parkes's (1988) revision of the assumptive world following psychosocial transitions and Woodfield and Viney's (1984–85) personal construct dislocation and adaptation in bereavement;

• Horowitz's (1986) cognitive-processing aspects of the stress response syndrome and integration of memories and responses, meanings, a new assumptive world, and a new sense of self;

• Taylor's (1983) cognitive adjustment to threatening events, centering on the search for meaning in the experience, the attempt to regain mastery over the event in particular and over one's life in general, and the effort to restore self-esteem through self-enhancing evaluations; and

• Janoff-Bulman's (1985) rebuilding of shattered assumptions after victimization, specifically, the belief in personal invulnerability, the perception of the world as meaningful, and the perception of oneself as positive.

Because of many caregivers' exclusive focus on facilitating affective reaction to the perception of loss, many mourners receive insufficient support for and intervention in the critical realm of cognitive readjustment. It is crucial to remember that cognitive adjustment to loss influences affective adjustment, and vice versa, and that it is just as necessary and requires equal clinical attention. Without making appropriate cognitive change, mourners simply cannot go on in a healthy way, regardless of how much affective processing they have completed.

THE EXPERIENCE OF UNCOMPLICATED GRIEF AND MOURNING

The experience of uncomplicated grief and mourning can be broken into three broad phases: avoidance, confrontation, and accommodation. This schema encompasses all other stage and phase theories of loss and divides reactions into three time periods, each characterized by a major response set toward the loss. Although various theorists may give the phases different names and examine diverse populations, these three phases house all the different loss reactions, regardless of number, type, or source (e.g., the reactions of dying patients, divorcing spouses, persons coping with chronic illness, and survivors of disasters).

It is important to bear in mind that people do not always follow uniform or predictable sequences and that it is inappropriate to apply theories rigidly rather than conduct individual assessments. The three phases of avoidance, confrontation, and accommodation are not discrete; the mourner may move back and forth among them, depending on the idiosyncratic issues and factors with which he or she is dealing. For purposes of illustration, in the following discussion the three phases of uncomplicated grief and mourning describe the phases as they would apply to a sudden, unexpected death. To the extent that circumstances differ, responses will differ. For example, in the situation of an expected death from a terminal illness, the avoidance phase may not be as dramatic as portrayed here. Many of the reactions seen in the avoidance phase after a sudden, unexpected death are present at the time of diagnosis in cases of terminal illness. (See Rando, 1986, for a full discussion of losses inherent in terminal illness and the experience of anticipatory grief.) However, it is important to qualify this statement by saying that anticipating and actually encountering the death of a loved one are two different things. Avoidance of the reality of the death certainly may be evident in those who lose loved ones expectedly from terminal illness, although it is usually not seen to the same degree that it is seen in people who have experienced the sudden, unexpected death of a loved one.

Avoidance Phase

The avoidance phase encompasses the period of time in which the news of the death is received and briefly thereafter. The cardinal feature of this phase is the mourner's very understandable need to avoid the terrible acknowledgment that the loved one is dead. The mourner's entire world is shaken. The mourner is traumatized, and his or her psyche goes into a form of shock to avoid the complete emotional flooding that would occur should the entire reality be absorbed all at once. The mourner unconsciously—and sometimes consciously—institutes emergency procedures to avoid becoming overwhelmed. He or she typically becomes numb. The assault of the news, combined with the mourner's need to protect him- or herself from the deluge of anxiety-provoking information, causes many mourners to become confused, dazed, and bewildered, unable to comprehend what has happened and disorganized in thought, emotion, and behavior.

As realization of what has happened starts to seep in, and shock and numbness slowly start to abate, denial immediately arises. It is only natural that the mourner would want to deny the reality of what has happened. Denial is therapeutic at this time. It functions as a buffer, allowing the mourner to absorb the reality of the loss gradually and serving as an emotional anesthesia while the mourner begins to experience the painful awareness of the loss. As is also the case later on in the mourning process, much of what is perceived by others as denial is actually disbelief. After having the loved one in his or her world for so many years, the mourner simply cannot believe that that person is no longer there and will not be there in the future. It is just too much to comprehend immediately.

Many mourners display outbursts of emotions (e.g., rageful protest, intense separation pain, and intense sorrow). There may be hysteria or screaming. Other mourners withdraw quietly or behave mechanically. Some mourners report feeling depersonalized, as if they were witnessing the experience happening to someone else.

Some mourners attempt to regain control by securing information (e.g., determining the events that led to the death) or focusing on making necessary arrangements (e.g., notifying other family members of the death). Such actions may give them structure in the midst of the chaos and may serve to ground them psychologically during the emotional turmoil. Although it is understandable that the mourner may want to do this to minimize the helplessness and trauma he or she feels at the news of the death, such attempts can be counterproductive if they interfere with the mourner's doing other things necessary for ultimate adjustment to the loss (e.g., expressing feelings and viewing the body in the emergency room after resuscitation efforts have been discontinued). Ideally, caregivers gently encourage both the actions known to be facilitative of future positive adjustment and those actions personally important in enabling the mourner to modulate the emotional experience.

Some survivors appear to accept the news of the death readily and begin immediately to comfort others and make arrangements. This may arise not from the previously mentioned need to assert control in the midst of the trauma, but from the desire to take care of others who would be affected by the news or because there exist pressing responsibilities to which the mourner must attend. This kind of temporary delay of the mourner's personal mourning in order to focus on other tasks at hand need not be harmful if it is reversed relatively soon. In many cases, however, complicated mourning can ensue when delay is lengthy or is undertaken for the wrong reasons (Rando, 1993).

Confrontation Phase

The confrontation phase is the painful interval during which the mourner confronts the reality of the loss and gradually absorbs what it means. Grief is experienced most intensely in this phase, and the reactions to the loss are most acute. Separation from the loved one generates alarm in the mourner, which results in heightened autonomic arousal, anger, protest, and biologically based searching behavior as the mourner reacts to the strong urge to find and reunite with the lost loved one (Bowlby, 1980; Parkes, 1987). Pining or yearning becomes prominent and is the emotional component of the biological urge to search.

The confrontation phase is a time in which the most excruciating learning process takes place, one that is necessary if the mourner is to come to see that changes must be made. Even though this critical function moves the mourner ever closer to healthy accommodation of the loss, it does not take away the pain. Indeed, confrontation necessarily involves pain. Each time the mourner is frustrated in the desire to be with the deceased loved one, he or she learns again that the loved one is dead. Each unfulfilled longing to see or hold or touch or smell or be with the loved one in some fashion teaches the mourner that the loved one is gone. Each pang of grief, each stab of pain whenever the mourner's expectation, desire, or need for the loved one is unmet brings the mourner yet another lesson that the loved one is no longer here.

The education continues for some time. The bereaved mother hears the school bus, thinks for a moment that she will be reunited with her daughter when she disembarks, and then experiences searing agony when she remembers again that her daughter is dead and buried. The young widower reaches out in the middle of the night, only to feel the overwhelming loneliness that accompanies recognition that his wife is no longer sharing his bed because she was killed the previous month. It takes a long time and hundreds, perhaps thousands, of these painful experiences before the mourner is able to transfer to the gut what is known in the head— that the loved one is really, truly, irrevocably gone and that the expectation, desire, and need for that loved one to be there as before will have to be relinquished.

Yearning and searching will continue for some time, despite going unrewarded. The repeated frustration of desires for the deceased and the unsuccessful conscious and unconscious attempts to recover the loved one ultimately lead to a gradual diminution of disbelief and denial and then to the depression, disorganization, and despair that signal the mourner's relinquishment of hope for reversing the loss and avoiding the reactions to its reality. This is why the early period after the loss is marked by so much anxiety—the mourner is striving to find and recover the lost loved one and is anxious lest this not occur. Only when he or she recognizes (i.e., learns) the futility of this, does the mourner exhibit the depression that is so common after loss (Bowlby, 1980).

During the confrontation phase, mourners often encounter confusing types, intensities, and vacillations of emotions and conflicting thoughts, desires, and needs, making them lose their sense of self. Confrontation can make mourners question who and what they are and will become and often makes mourners fear they are losing their mind.

Parkes (1987) observed that mourners oscillate between the opposing tendencies of inhibiting their perception of disturbing stimuli and enhancing their perception and thought about it. The reader will note that this process is identical to the denial–intrusion cycle of the stress response syndrome, which develops after traumatic events and regulates the individual's exposure to trauma-related material (Horowitz, 1986). The similarity between these two schemas supports the conceptualization of acute grief as a form of traumatic stress reaction (Rando, 1993).

During the confrontation phase, the mourner may experience a number of psychological, behavioral, social, and physical responses, some of which are as follows:

PSYCHOLOGICAL RESPONSES
Affects
Separation pain, sadness, sorrow, anguish
Anxiety, panic, fear, vulnerability, insecurity
Yearning, pining, longing
Helplessness; powerlessness; feelings of being out of control, victimized, overwhelmed
Anger, hostility, irritability, intolerance, impatience
Guilt, self-reproach, regret
Depression, hopelessness, despair
Anhedonia, apathy, restricted range of affect
Frustration
Fear of going crazy
Emotional lability, hypersensitivity
Deprivation, mutilation, violation
Loneliness
Abandonment
Ambivalence
Relief

Cognitions
Disbelief
Bewilderment
Disorganization, confusion, distractibility
Preoccupation with, obsession with, rumination about the deceased and/or the death
Impaired concentration, comprehension, mental functioning, memory, decision making
Cognitive dissonance, meaninglessness, senselessness, disillusionment, aimlessness
Spiritual confusion, sense of alienation from/rejection by deity, increased spirituality
Lowered self-esteem, feelings of inadequacy
Pessimism
Diminished self-concern
Decreased interest, motivation, initiative, direction

Perceptions
Feelings of unreality, depersonalization, derealization, dissociation
Development of a perceptual set for the deceased
Paranormal experiences pertaining to the deceased (e.g., visual or auditory hallucinations, a sense of the deceased's presence)
The feeling that something is about to happen

Defenses and Attempts at Coping
Shock, numbness, absence of emotions
Avoidance or repression of thoughts, feelings, or memories associated with the
    deceased or painful reactions to the loss
Denial
Search for the deceased
Protest
Regression
Search for meaning
Identification with the deceased
Dreams of the deceased
Feelings of unreality, depersonalization, derealization, dissociation

BEHAVIORAL RESPONSES
Search for the deceased
Restless hyperactivity, search for something to do, heightened arousal, agitation,
    exaggerated startle response, hypervigilance, hypomanic behavior
Social withdrawal
Disorganized activity, absentminded behavior
Increased intake of medicine, psychoactive substances
Loss of patterns of social interaction (e.g., dependency, clinginess, avoidance of
    being alone)
Crying and tearfulness
Anorexia or other appetite disturbance leading to weight loss or gain
Sleep disturbance (too little, too much, interrupted)
Tendency to sigh
Decreased interest, motivation, initiative, direction, and energy for relationships
    and organized patterns of activity
Decreased effectiveness and productivity in functioning (personal, social, work)
Avoidance of or adherence to people, situations, and stimuli reminiscent of the
    deceased
Self-destructive behaviors (e.g., accident-prone behavior, high-risk behavior such
    as fast driving)
Acting-out behaviors, impulsive behaviors
Hyposexuality or hypersexuality
Change in lifestyle
Concealment of grief for fear of driving others away
Clinging behavior
Grief spasms

SOCIAL RESPONSES
Lack of interest in other people and usual activities because of preoccupation with
    the deceased
Social withdrawal
Decreased interest, motivation, initiative, direction, and energy for relationships
    and organized patterns of activity
Boredom
Criticality, other manifestations of anger or irritation with others

Loss of patterns of social interaction
Feeling of alienation from others
Jealousy of others who have not experienced loss
Dependency on others, clinginess, avoidance of being alone

PHYSICAL RESPONSES
Symptoms Indicative of Biological Indices of Depression
Anorexia, appetite disturbance leading to weight loss or gain
Decreased interest, motivation, initiative, direction, energy
Depressed mood
Anhedonia, apathy, restricted range of affect
Impaired concentration, mental functioning, memory, decision making
Decreased sexual interest; hyposexuality, hypersexuality
Sleep disturbance (too little, too much, interrupted)
Crying, tearfulness
Tendency to sigh
Fatique, lethargy
Lack of strength
Physical exhaustion
Feeling of emptiness, heaviness
Psychomotor retardation, agitation

Symptoms Indicative of Anxiety and Hyperarousal

Motor Tension
Trembling, shaking, twitching
Muscle tension, aches, soreness
Fatigability
Headache
Restlessness, search for something to do

Autonomic Hyperactivity
Anxiety, tension, nervousness
Heart palpitations, tachycardia
Shortness of breath
Numbness, tingling sensations
Smothering sensations
Dizziness, unsteady feelings, faintness
Dry mouth
Sweating; cold, clammy hands
Hot flashes, chills
Chest pain, pressure, discomfort
Choking
Nausea, diarrhea, other abdominal distress
Frequent urination
Tightness in throat, trouble swallowing, feeling that something is stuck in throat
Digestive disturbance

Vigilance and Scanning
Heightened arousal
Agitation
Sense of being geared up
Exaggerated startle response
Irritability, outbursts of anger
Difficulty falling asleep, staying asleep
Impaired concentration
Hypervigilance
Physiological reactivity upon exposure to events that symbolize or resemble an
    aspect of the death or events associated with it

Other Symptoms Indicative of Physiological Response to Distress
Hair loss
Constellation of vague, diffuse somatic complaints, sometimes experienced in
    waves lasting minutes to hours
Gastrointestinal symptoms
Cardiopulmonary symptoms
Pseudoneurological symptoms

Note: Adapted from *Treatment of Complicated Mourning* (pp. 36–39) by T. A. Rando, 1993, Champaign, IL: Research Press. Copyright 1993 by Therese A. Rando. Reprinted by permission.

Accommodation Phase

Accommodation of the loss waxes and wanes during the latter part of the confrontation phase and continues slowly thereafter. Many of the reactions that arise in the confrontation phase coexist for some time with the initial aspects of this new phase. Guilt is particularly salient—successful attempts at accommodation can prompt guilt unless the mourner works through such issues as the mistaken belief that the intensity and duration of acute grief are a testimony to love for the deceased or that it is only by experiencing pain that one can maintain a connection with the deceased loved one.

In the accommodation phase, there is a gradual reduction of symptoms of acute grief and the beginning of social and emotional reentry into the everyday world. However, the world is being reconstructed by the mourner, who is responding to the dictates of reality (i.e., the permanent absence of the loved one) and making a number of necessary external and internal changes. Externally, the mourner is called on to alter, relinquish, or adopt ways of being in the world to compensate for the absence of the deceased. Relationships, roles, skills, and behaviors all are subject to change as the mourner struggles to adapt suitably to what the death has wrought.

Internally, the mourner must work on transforming the relationship with the deceased from one of presence to one based on symbolic interaction. Slowly, the mourner is learning to go on without the deceased, yet finding ways to keep the new relationship with the deceased appropriately alive. The deceased is not forgotten; neither is the loss. However, the mourner learns to live with cognizance of the death and its implications in a way that does not preclude healthy, life-affirming growth.

In addition to forming a new relationship with the deceased, the mourner must make other internal changes. There must be a revising of the assumptive world insofar as expectations, assumptions, and beliefs formerly held demanded the interactive presence of the deceased or a way of viewing the world that has been rendered out of date by the loss and the circumstances associated with it. To the extent that the mourner has changed elements of his or her assumptive world to accommodate the reality of the death, and has made numerous external changes to adapt suitably to the loss, the mourner must reform his or her identity to reflect these changes. Ideally, at the appropriate time, the mourner is able to take some of the emotional energy that once went into the former relationship with the deceased and reinvest it in new people, objects, roles, hopes, beliefs, causes, ideals, goals, or pursuits to obtain some of the emotional gratification that was lost when the loved one died.

In essence, the mourner's goal in the accommodation phase is to learn to live with the loss and readjust his or her new life accordingly. Accommodation does not mean that the mourner would have chosen or wanted the loss. It does not mean that the mourner is unmoved by the death of the loved one. It merely means that the mourner no longer has to fight the loss but has learned to live with it as an inescapable fact of life.

Accommodating the loss will leave a psychic scar, similar to a scar that remains after a physical injury. This scar does not necessarily interfere with the mourner's overall functioning, but on certain days and under particular conditions it may ache or throb and require some attention. For instance, healthy accommodation does not mean that in certain events in later life the mourner will not painfully wish that the loved were alive to share his or her joy or that the mourner is spared the bittersweet feelings that the holidays can bring, when he or she rejoices with those still present but mourns the loved one's absence. It does not mean that the mourner no longer mourns. As mentioned earlier, it means only that the person has learned to live with mourning in ways that do not interfere with his or her ongoing healthy functioning in the new life without the loved one. Accommodation centers on learning to live with the fact of the loved one's absence, moving forward in the new world despite the fact that the psychic scar caused by the loss remains and, on occasion, brings pain.

The Six R Processes of Mourning

Running throughout the three phases of avoidance, confrontation, and accommodation are the six R processes of mourning. These are the processes that the mourner must successfully complete in order to accommodate the loss in a healthy manner. Operationalizing mourning in terms of processes rather than tasks is preferable for a number of reasons (see Rando, 1993). Although the processes are interrelated and tend to build on one another, several of them occur simultaneously (i.e., the second, third, and fourth R processes, which occur in the confrontation phase, and the fifth and sixth processes, which occur in the accommodation phase). In addition, some subprocesses may occur in more than one phase. The sequence is not invariant, although the order in which the processes are presented herein reflects the typical course for a majority of mourners. Mourners may move back and forth among the processes; such movement illustrates the nonlinear and fluctuating course of mourning.

Recognize the Loss   If the mourner is to commence active mourning, he or she must acknowledge that the death has occurred (or else there is nothing to mourn) and must come to an understanding of what caused it.

Acknowledge the Death   Initially, the acceptance of the reality of the love one's death occurs on an intellectual level, involving only recognition and concession of the fact of death. It takes much longer to internalize this fact and accept it emotionally. Emotional acceptance of the death can occur only after repeated and painful confrontations with the loved one's absence. In cases where there is no confirmation of the death, such as a mine cave-in or loss of a boat at sea, mourning often becomes complicated. This is why so much time and effort are spent attempting to locate missing bodies. It is also why the prevailing thought is that in almost all situations of sudden death, viewing of the body is to be encouraged.

Understand the Death   After any death, if the world is to continue to maintain some order for the mourner, he or she will also have to come up with some specific reasons for that particular death that make personal sense. These are not philosophical or religious reasons for why the death occurred; rather, they concern the facts contributing to the death and the circumstances around it. Although the explanation needs to make sense intellectually, it does not necessarily have to be acceptable to the mourner. It merely must provide an account that explains how and why the death happened as it did. Furthermore, the explanation need not be the same as that maintained by others; it only needs to suffice for the mourner. For example, the widow may believe her husband's death by hanging was accidental and not a suicide, which is the conclusion reached by everyone else. Whether the mourner's personal understanding of the death is realistic or indicative of mental health is not the issue here. The issue is the need for some sort of an explanation. Lacking an understanding or a rationale for the loved one's death, a mourner tends to become anxious and confused, wondering what happened to the loved one and what potentially could happen to the self. This contributes to problems in recovering from the loss, because it prevents a sense of the world's having meaning, orderliness, and predictability. Tragically, this is often seen after the death of a baby from sudden infant death syndrome, when autopsy results are negative and there is no reason that can be given to the parents for why their apparently healthy baby died.

React to the Separation Once the reality of the death has been recognized, the mourner must react to and cope with that reality. Responses to the recognition of the death and separation from the loved one are myriad and occur on all levels of functioning. To the extent that the mourner grants him- or herself permission to experience and express all of these reactions appropriately, healthy mourning is promoted. Three subprocesses are involved.

Experience the Pain Although it is understandable that the mourner wants to avoid the pain associated with the loss of the loved one, unless that pain is felt the mourner lacks the experiences that ultimately will teach him or her that the loved one is truly gone and that specific adaptations must be made if he or she is to contend with the loss and integrate it appropriately in present and future life. Pain that is not experienced cannot be processed and channeled, leaving the mourner mired in it.

Feel, Identify, Accept, and Give Some Form of Expression to All the Psychological Reactions to the Loss Unacknowledged and unexpressed emotion is a major precipitant of pathology. For this reason, it is crucial that the mourner address personal, social, cultural, ethnic, or religious resistances to the complete processing of all psychological reactions to the loss and its implications, even those that are uncomfortable (which are often associated with feelings of guilt and/or the recognition of significant dependency on the deceased). To do this effectively, the mourner has to identify, label, differentiate, and trace his or her affective experiences and their component parts and work through all of them, while in the process discovering and using personally comfortable and appropriate avenues of verbal and nonverbal expression.

Identify and Mourn Secondary Losses Each secondary loss prompts its own mourning. It demands that at the appropriate time the same type of identification and processing applied to the initial death loss be applied to the secondary loss.

Recollect and Reexperience the Deceased and the Relationship Before the mourner is able to alter emotional attachments to and investment in the deceased loved one in order to respond to the demands of the loss, he or she must engage in two sets of processes that pave the way for letting go of the old and accommodating to the new. Failure to engage in these processes leaves the mourner lacking a realistic composite of the deceased with which to interact and saddled with undone connections to the loved one (i.e., the mourner remains attached to the deceased as if that person were still alive).

Review and Remember Realistically Remembering realistically entails a complete review of all recollections about the deceased and the mourner's relationship with him or her—the full range of memories of experiences, needs, feelings, thoughts, behavior and interaction patterns, hopes, wishes, fantasies, dreams, assumptions, expectations, and beliefs. It also includes all of the aspects of each of these memories and all of the feelings about them—good and bad, happy and sad, fulfilling and unfulfilling, comfortable and uncomfortable, and so forth. This review, which should stretch back to the very beginning of the relationship, is necessary to put the mourner in touch with the entire range of memories and emotions that must be processed. If only some aspects of the person are remembered (e.g., the good things about Uncle Harry, but not the fact that he would get drunk and out of hand at family picnics), those are the only aspects that will get worked through. The fear of confronting anger, guilt, sadness, regret, or embarrassment; the recognition of dependency; or any other impediment to reviewing and remembering realistically leaves aspects of the deceased or the mourner's relationship with the deceased unrecalled realistically, and makes some connections to the deceased unavailable for processing. This predisposes the mourner to remain unhealthily connected to the deceased in those areas. In addition, a realistic composite image of the loved one, required for healthy mourning, is precluded.

Revive and Reexperience the Feelings All of the feelings associated with all of that which is remembered about the deceased and the relationship must be revived and reexperienced. Only in this way, over time, will the emotional charge of each of these ties to the deceased be defused sufficiently so that it no longer attaches the mourner to the loved one as it had in life. Untying these ties does not mean that the deceased is forgotten or unloved; rather, it means that the ties are modified to reflect the change that the loved one is now dead and cannot return the mourner's emotional investment or gratify his or her needs as before. A new relationship with different ties ultimately must be developed, because the old one is unworkable. This cannot occur until the old emotional bonds are loosened sufficiently that the mourner can let go of them. The desire to avoid the pain of letting go and the fear of losing all connection with the deceased must be worked through for this process to succeed.

Relinquish the Old Attachments to the Deceased and the Old Assumptive World Once the bonds to the deceased—as represented in hundreds or thousands of separate needs, feelings, thoughts, memories, behavior and interaction patterns, hopes, wishes, fantasies, dreams, assumptions, expectations, and beliefs—have been loosened sufficiently, they have to be relinquished. The mourner does not want to let go of these connections to the loved one; letting go causes major secondary losses and leaves him or her insecure and anxious in the world without the deceased and fearful of having no further connection with that loved one. Nevertheless, ultimately the mourner must let go of such bonds (e.g., needing to be held by the spouse, attending the daughter's field hockey games, or relying on the parent for guidance).

Similarly, the mourner is called on to let go of those aspects of his or her assumptive world that have been rendered invalid by the loved one's death. All of the specific assumptions, expectations, and beliefs that were predicated on the loved one's continued interactive presence in the mourner's life (e.g., "He will be there for me always" and "We will grow old together") are violated by the death and must be relinquished. Those global assumptions, expectations, and beliefs pertaining to the self, others, life, or the world in general that have been violated through the circumstances, the consequences, or the very fact of the death also must be relinquished (e.g., the murder of a child may shatter the assumption of invulnerability or invalidate the belief that God protects the innocent).

Readjust To Move Adaptively into the New World Without Forgetting the Old When the mourner has released the old connections to the deceased and the old assumptive world, he or she is free to establish new connections appropriate to the changes that have ensued. In this process, the individual actively takes steps to accommodate the loss. Indeed, the name of this mourning process reflects the main criterion for successful adaptation in mourning: Is the mourner able to move adaptively into the new life while simultaneously having a healthy connection with the old? The key word is *adaptively*. There are four areas in which accommodation must take place.

Revise the Assumptive World The mourner must revise his or her assumptive world insofar as elements of it have been violated by the death and its consequences. The extent of the modification is dependent on a number of factors (Rando, 1993) and determines in part additional secondary losses and consequent grief reactions. While some elements are relinquished entirely (e.g., "I can never feel completely and totally safe again"), the new assumptive world still may contain many elements from the prior one. Additional elements may be completely novel (e.g., "I cannot expect my husband to take care of me anymore. I must learn to do it on my own."). Some former assumptions may be melded with new ones based on what the mourner has experienced (e.g., "I was naive when I believed that God protects the good. Now I realize that you can be good and still die from cancer. I still believe in God, but no longer believe that being good assures me of protection from adversity."). In essence, the mourner must make whatever changes are necessary to reduce any cognitive dissonance stimulated by the discrepancy between what was formerly assumed, expected, or believed and what is now assumed, expected, or believed as a consequence of this death. Failure to make revisions required by the current reality results in the mourner's ongoing pain from continual violation of his or her assumptive world.

Develop a New Relationship with the Deceased Mourner fears and caregiver misinterpretations to the contrary, the mourner can have a continued symbolic relationship with the deceased loved one that is healthy as long as it meets two criteria simultaneously (Rando, 1988): (a) The mourner must recognize that the person is dead and fully understand the implications of the death (i.e., the mourner's expectations of and abstract interactions with the deceased must reflect knowledge of this fact), and (b) the mourner must continue to move forward adaptively in the new life. Failure at one or both of these criteria suggests either that it is too soon in the mourning process to have come to this point or that the relationship that exists with the deceased loved one is not healthy. There are myriad ways of maintaining a healthy connection with the deceased and of interacting with that person on an abstract or symbolic level (e.g., healthy identification, ritual, tangible objects, the mourner's own life and actions, active recall of memories, exposure to memorabilia, and forms of communication to the deceased). The reader is referred to Rando (1993) for extensive discussion of this topic.

Adopt New Ways of Being in the World   Over time, the mourner must learn to act in accordance with the reality that the loved one has died. This entails finding ways to fulfill the needs the deceased had filled (i.e., by meeting the need him- or herself, finding someone else to meet the need, or determining other ways of getting the need met) or of changing the desire for what is wanted or needed. To compensate for the loved one's absence and loss of interaction and role-fulfilling behaviors, the mourner often must adopt new roles, skills, behaviors, and relationships. He or she may experience many changes as aspects of the self are gained (e.g., the mastery of new skills may make him or her feel more competent), lost (e.g., passivity is shed), or modified (e.g., the mourner recognizes that he or she can have a career and be a good single parent simultaneously).

Form a New Identity   With a new assumptive world, a new relationship with the deceased, and new ways of being in the world, the mourner is no longer the same person he or she was before the death. The mourner's self-image must change to reflect this reality, as well as to accommodate the loss of the interactional self formed in the relationship with the deceased. A personal reorientation is mandated: That which is changed must be recognized and mourned, that which continues must be affirmed, and that which is new must be incorporated. The old and new selves have to be integrated.

Reinvest   The emotional energy once invested in the relationship with the deceased eventually needs to be reinvested where it can bring some return gratification to the mourner. Although new attachments will not replace the deceased loved one, they can provide the mourner with some of the emotional gratification that was lost with the death. The reinvestment need not be in a person having the same role as the one who died (e.g., a widow does not have to remarry to reinvest), or even in a person at all. New roles, hopes, beliefs, causes, ideals, goals, pursuits, objects, and so forth can bring the mourner satisfaction in return for the investment that is made.

The Duration and Course of Mourning

One of the most frequently asked questions about mourning is how long it lasts. There is no general answer to this question, because grief and mourning are dependent on the unique constellation of factors associated with the individual loss. Contrary to the myth that mourning declines linearly over time, its course fluctuates significantly, often to the chagrin of mourner and caregiver alike.

Fluctuations occur over both the short (e.g., hourly basis) and long (e.g., a period of months or more) terms. Different types of losses may be associated with different patterns of fluctuation. For instance, in a study of parents whose children died from cancer, 78% of bereavement symptoms diminished from Year 1 to Year 2 after the death but rose again from Year 2 to Year 3 (Rando, 1983). Another striking example of fluctuation across populations is seen in the course of many mourners of sudden death, who erroneously assume that they are at a new equilibrium, only to experience a significant increase in acute distress 6–9 months after the death. The three reasons accounting for this escalation of acute grief symptomatology are discussed elsewhere (Rando, 1993).

Certainly, it is much easier to demarcate the end of acute grief than to identify the end of mourning. In fact, many believe that, in some aspects, mourning continues forever (see Pollock, 1961; Siggins, 1966). This observation is one of the key reasons why the distinction between grief and mourning must be made. A person may be long past acute grief yet still be in mourning, that is, be engaged appropriately in later R processes. The cessation of acute grief does not mean that the loss is totally accommodated. By the same token, involvement in later R processes and the occurrence of subsequent temporary upsurges of grief (STUG) reactions (described below) do not necessarily indicate either that the person is still in acute grief or that mourning is complicated. This can be determined only in relation to the amount of time that has passed since the loss and the mourner's status in terms of completion of the six R processes.

Even long after a death, a wide variety of circumstances can produce STUG reactions, that is, brief periods of acute grief for the loss of the loved one that are catalyzed by a precipitant that underscores the absence of the deceased or resurrects memories of the death, the loved one, or feelings about the loss. Although the majority of STUG reactions are part of uncomplicated mourning, some of them can indicate complicated mourning. In addition, a STUG reaction that is appropriate under one set of conditions may not be appropriate under another. At times, a STUG reaction may help the person experiencing complicated mourning to finish unfinished business. At other times it can reveal unfinished aspects of a loss. As with any grief response, a STUG reaction may be manifested in the psychological, behavioral, social, and physical realms. It is common for mourners to be unaware of a precipitant of a STUG reaction or to be oblivious to its connection to the loss until it is pointed out. For an in-depth discussion of meanings and precipitants of STUG reactions and criteria determining the healthiness of any

STUG reaction, the reader is referred to Rando (1993). The following is a classification of precipitants of STUG reactions.

CYCLIC PRECIPITANTS
Anniversary reactions
Holiday reactions
Seasonal reactions
Ritual-prompted reactions (repetitive)

LINEAR PRECIPITANTS
Age-correspondence reactions
Experience-associated reactions
Transition-stimulated reactions
Developmentally determined reactions
Crisis-evoked reactions
Ritual-prompted reactions (single event)

STIMULUS-CUED PRECIPITANTS
Memory-based reactions
Reminder-inspired reactions
Reactions aroused by loss or reunion theme
Music-elicited reactions

Note: Adapted from *Treatment of Complicated Mourning* (p. 67) by T. A. Rando, 1993, Champaign, IL: Research Press. Copyright 1993 by Therese A. Rando. Reprinted by permission.

Seven Steps of Intervention To Facilitate Uncomplicated Grief and Mourning

In cases of uncomplicated grief and mourning, the caregiver's goal is to facilitate
the mourner's completion of the six R processes of mourning. To this end, there
are seven broad steps of intervention, each encompassing a host of therapeutic
perspectives, clinical directives, and specific techniques. The reader is referred to
Rando (1984) for detailed discussions of these steps. Reworded to incorporate
more recent terminology, the steps are as follows:

1   Make contact and assess.
2   Maintain a therapeutic and realistic perspective.
3   Encourage expression of feelings and recollection of the deceased.
4   Help the mourner identify and work through secondary losses and unfinished business.
5   Support the mourner in coping with the mourning processes.
6   Help the mourner accommodate to the loss.
7   Work with the mourner to reinvest in the new life.

COMPLICATED MOURNING

In order to comprehend uncomplicated grief and mourning, it is critical to have
an appreciation for complicated grief and mourning. This section offers a brief

discussion of complicated mourning and is based on Rando (1993), to which the reader is referred for more in-depth discussion of the issues mentioned below and assessment and intervention strategies and techniques.

Complicated mourning is said to occur whenever, given the amount of time that has passed since the death (sufficient time must have passed for the R processes in question to have been reached), there is some compromise, distortion, or failure of one or more of the six R processes of mourning. In all forms of complicated mourning, the mourner is attempting to do two things: (a) to deny, repress, or avoid aspects of the loss, its pain, and its implications and (b) to hold onto, and avoid relinquishing, the lost loved one. These attempts, or some variation thereof, are what cause the complications in the R processes of mourning.

Complicated mourning may take any one or a combination of four forms: (a) complicated mourning symptoms; (b) one or more of seven complicated mourning syndromes, which include three syndromes with problems in expression (absent mourning, delayed mourning, and inhibited mourning), three syndromes with skewed aspects (the distorted mourning of the extremely angry or guilty person, conflicted mourning, and unanticipated mourning), and one syndrome with a problem with closure (chronic mourning); (c) a diagnosable mental or physical disorder; and (d) death.

There are seven generic high-risk factors that can predispose any individual to complicated mourning. Four factors are associated with the specific death. They include (a) a sudden and unanticipated death, especially when it is traumatic, violent, mutilating, or random; (b) death from an overly lengthy illness; (c) loss of a child; and (d) death associated with the mourner's perception of preventability. Three factors are associated with antecedent and subsequent variables. They are (a) a premorbid relationship with the deceased that had been markedly angry or ambivalent, or markedly dependent; (b) the mourner's prior or concurrent unaccommodated losses or stresses, or prior or concurrent mental health problems; and (c) the mourner's perception of lack of social support.

Caregivers should recognize that the prevalence of complicated mourning is increasing today as a result of a number of contemporary sociocultural and technological trends, which have adversely influenced the types of death seen today; the characteristics of personal relationships severed by today's deaths; and the personality and resources of today's mourners, such that there are more individuals contending with more high-risk factors than ever before (Rando, 1992–93). When added to specific problems in both the mental health profession and the field of thanatology, it is easy to see that all of these changes contribute to causing complicated mourning to rise at the precise time when caregivers are unprepared and limited in their abilities to respond.

REFERENCES

Bowlby, J. (1963). Pathological mourning and childhood mourning. *Journal of the American Psychoanalytic Association, 11,* 500–541.

Bowlby, J. (1969). *Attachment and loss: Vol. 1. Attachment.* New York: Basic Books.

Bowlby, J. (1973). *Attachment and loss: Vol. 2. Separation: Anxiety and anger.* New York: Basic Books.

Bowlby, J. (1980). *Attachment and loss: Vol. 3. Loss: Sadness and depression.* New York: Basic Books.

Doka, K. (Ed.). (1989). *Disenfranchised grief: Recognizing hidden sorrow.* Lexington, MA: Lexington Books.

Freud, S. (1955). Totem and taboo. In J. Strachey (Ed. and Trans.), *The standard edition of the complete psychological works of Sigmund Freud* (Vol. 13, pp. 1–61). London: Hogarth Press (Original work published 1913)

Freud, S. (1957). Mourning and melancholia. In J. Strachey (Ed. and Trans.), *The standard edition of the complete psychological works of Sigmund Freud* (Vol. 14, pp. 243–258). London: Hogarth Press. (Original work published 1917)

Freud, S. (1960). Letter to Binswanger (Letter 239). In E. L. Freud (Ed.), *Letters of Sigmund Freud* (p. 386). New York: Basic Books. (Original work published 1926)

Freud, S. (1961). The ego and the id. In J. Strachey (Ed. and Trans.), *The standard edition of the complete psychological works of Sigmund Freud* (Vol. 19, pp. 12–59). London: Hogarth Press. (Original work published 1923)

Glick, I. O., Weiss, R. S., & Parkes, C. M. (1974). *The first year of bereavement.* New York: Wiley.

Horowitz, M. J. (1986). *Stress response syndromes* (2nd ed.). Northvale, NJ: Jason Aronson.

Janoff-Bulman, R. (1985). The aftermath of victimization: Rebuilding shattered assumptions. In C. Figley (Ed.), *Trauma and its wake: The study and treatment of post-traumatic stress disorder.* New York: Brunner/Mazel.

Lindemann, E. (1944). Symptomatology and management of acute grief. *American Journal of Psychiatry, 101,* 141–148.

Parkes, C. M. (1980). Bereavement counseling: Does it work? *British Medical Journal, 281,* 3–6.

Parkes, C. M. (1981). Evaluation of a bereavement service. *Journal of Preventive Psychiatry, 1,* 179–188.

Parkes, C. M. (1987). *Bereavement: Studies of grief in adult life* (2nd ed.). Madison, CT: International Universities Press.

Parkes, C. M. (1988). Bereavement as a psychosocial transition: Processes of adaptation to change. *Journal of Social Issues, 44*(3), 53–65.

Parkes, C. M., & Weiss, R. S. (1983). *Recovery from bereavement.* New York: Basic Books.

Pollock, G. (1961). Mourning and adaptation. *International Journal of Psycho-Analysis, 42,* 341–361.

Rando, T. A. (1983). An investigation of grief and adaptation in parents whose children have died from cancer. *Journal of Pediatric Psychology, 8,* 3–20.

Rando, T. A. (1984). *Grief, dying, and death: Clinical interventions for caregivers.* Champaign, IL: Research Press.

Rando, T. A. (Ed.). (1986). *Loss and anticipatory grief.* Lexington, MA: Lexington Books.

Rando, T. A. (1988). *Grieving: How to go on living when someone you love dies.* Lexington, MA: Lexington Books.

Rando, T. A. (1992–93). The increasing prevalence of complicated mourning: The onslaught is just beginning. *Omega, 26,* 43–59.

Rando, T. A. (1993). *Treatment of complicated mourning.* Champaign, IL: Research Press.

Raphael, B. (1975). The management of pathological grief. *Australian and New Zealand Journal of Psychiatry, 9,* 173–180.

Raphael, B. (1981). Personal disaster. *Australian and New Zealand Journal of Psychiatry, 15,* 183–198.

Raphael, B. (1983). *The anatomy of bereavement.* New York: Basic Books.

Raphael, B. (1986). *When disaster strikes: How individuals and communities cope with catastrophe.* New York: Basic Books.

Raphael, B., & Middleton, W. (1987). Current state of research in the field of bereavement. *Israel Journal of Psychiatry and Related Sciences, 24,* 5–32.

Siggins, L. (1966). Mourning: A critical survey of the literature. *International Journal of Psycho-Analysis, 47,* 14–25.

Taylor, S. (1983). Adjustment to threatening events: A theory of cognitive adaptation. *American Psychologist, 38,* 1161–1173.

Woodfield, R., & Viney, L. (1984–85). A personal construct approach to the conjugally bereaved woman. *Omega, 15,* 1–13.

Chapter 10

Spiritual Aspects of the Resolution of Grief

Dennis Klass

THE NATURE OF THE SPIRITUAL

Almost any scholarship on death and bereavement could be said to be scholarship on spirituality, for the spirit is what is left when the body and mind are gone. But death educators need the lives of real people facing death in a concrete way to focus the issues for them. In this chapter, an attempt is made to describe the spiritual aspects of the resolution of grief by examining the lives of bereaved parents as they resolved their grief.

The Study

The data presented herein are drawn from a long-term ethnographic study of a local chapter of the Compassionate Friends, a self-help group of parents who have experienced the death of a child (Geertz, 1973; Glaser & Strauss, 1967; Hammersley & Atkinson, 1983; Klass, 1988; Powdermaker, 1966; Wax, 1971; Whyte, 1973). As professional advisor of the chapter, this author was able to collect data through several methods, including ongoing conversations with members, open-ended interviews with bereaved parents, and attendance at chapter meetings. An especially valuable source of data was the chapter newsletters, in which members wrote for themselves and for each other. The study began as the chapter was formed. The chapter grew rapidly and formed groups in different parts of the city. Monthly attendance for all the meetings has averaged about 130 for several years. Apart from the author's role within the group, for five years the author wrote summary observations of clinical psychological practice with bereaved parents.

Because of the close association between the researcher and the group, the understandings that emerged from the study are, in reality, collaborations between the bereaved parents, who were the insiders, and the researcher, the outsider. One of the responsibilities of the researcher as the advisor to the chapter was to help the members reflect on their own experiences and on the processes within the group. The researcher shared his developing ideas in articles written for the chapter newsletter and at meetings. Members have read the book and articles the researcher has written about them and have responded with rigorous critiques and encouraging confirmations.

Definitions

It is difficult to define the word *spiritual,* because it so often refers to that which is beyond words. It has become common of late to differentiate spiritual from religious. In a pluralistic and individualistic world, the distinction probably represents a protest against the particularity of most religions and a longing for the universal. The distinction probably also represents the modern split between personal experience and social forms. In modernity, the spiritual is mostly known in transitory present moments, whereas religion, rooted in the past, endures in abiding social forms. But religion and spirituality cannot be fully separated in the individual's experience or in the study of spirituality, because the reality known in spiritual moments is maintained over time by symbols, rituals, and affiliations that have a religious character. Moreover, the reality known in spiritual moments is often perceived using symbols handed down through religious traditions. Thus awareness of some ideas from religious traditions and from the comparative study of religions is helpful in understanding the spiritual.

For an experience to qualify as spiritual, two characteristics would be implied. First, in a way that seems vitally important or, as Tillich (1951, 1957, 1963) said, an ultimate concern, the person encounters or merges with that which was formerly understood as not self or other. The psychological parallel to this may be times when the ego boundaries become permeable so the individual feels at one with another person, with the divine, or with the environment. In such moments, the distinction between inner and outer reality blurs. In most religious traditions, it is the extreme (or supreme) of such moments that are described. In Sufi Islam, it is *Identity;* in Buber's Judaism, it is the *I–Thou;* in Bhakti Hinduism, it is *Dar'san.* People who have not experienced those supreme moments can recall when the sense experience of the music becomes the truth in the soul (Batson, Schoenrade, & Ventis, 1993) or moments when, as Brunner (1946) said, they knew that they were known by that which is unknowable.

Second, in a way that seems vitally important, the person becomes aware of a higher intelligence, purpose, or order that the person does not control but in which he or she can participate and to which the person can conform his or her life. The person experiences the "multifaceted relationships or connection between human and metaphysical systems" (Prest & Keller, 1993, p. 138). When the person participates in or conforms to the higher intelligence, purpose, or order, the person feels his or her life is more authentic, more meaningful, than when the person lives by other norms and standards. Meaningful living has both a cognitive and a moral aspect: The person's thinking is "set straight" or true, and his or her actions toward others are right and true. Because such order can be codified in precept and example, it is the center of religious teaching: *dharma* in Hinduism, *doctrine* in Christianity, *tao* in Chinese religion.

These two characteristics are in constant interplay. Turner (1969) found both elements in religious rituals of passage. He called encounter and merger *liminality,* from the Latin *limen,* meaning door, threshold, or wall. Thus the word signifies both the limits of human existence and also openings between the world of living humans and other worlds. In liminal situations, the usual boundaries are not in effect, so the individual is in touch with the transcendent. Turner's term for order is *communitas*. He stated that in communitas, individual and social boundaries are discovered, altered, or maintained. Turner found an alternation between these two ways of being in religious ritual. The liminality/communitas relationship can be thought of, he stated, as the relationship between *ecstasy*, which literally means standing outside the self and *ideology*, in which the world and self are defined. Maslow (1964) found a similar interplay in the relationship between peak experience and self-actualization. The peak experience is of nonordinary realities; within the peak experience, a person discovers "being values," which are guidelines to living a more integrated and authentic life.

Death, both as the irrefutable reality and as the symbol of imperfection in the human condition, is the motivator of spirituality. It is because humans know that life is finite that they strive to connect with the infinite. It is because they know that life can hurt that they strive to find meaning and comfort. It is because sometimes neither life nor death makes sense that humans strive to find and to conform to a reality in which the contradictions of living and dying, joy and terror, order and absurdity are reconciled.

Spirituality and the Bond with the Deceased

The process of resolving parental bereavement is something like Turner's (1969) ritual passages, because it is a transitional state. When a child dies, the parent experiences an irreparable loss, because the child is an extension of the parent's self (Benedek, 1959, 1975). Although one of the psychological tasks of parenting in modernity is to separate the child from the self, so the child can be experienced as a separate being (Elson, 1984), such separation is seldom complete. When a child dies, a part of the parent's self is cut off. Many bereaved parents find the metaphor of amputation useful. Like amputation, parental bereavement is a permanent condition. Bereaved parents do adjust in the sense that they learn to invest themselves in other tasks and other relationships, but somewhere inside them, they report, there is a sense of loss that cannot be healed. When his daughter died, Freud wrote,

Since I am profoundly irreligious there is no one I can accuse, and I know there is nowhere to which any complaint could be addressed. "The unvarying circle of a soldier's duties" and the "sweet habit of existence" will see to it that things go on as before. Quite deep down I can trace the feeling of a deep narcissistic hurt that is not to be healed. (cited by Jones, 1957, p. 20)

The resolution of parental grief includes experiences that have spiritual qualities. First, the parent finds, renews, or modifies the bond to that which transcends immediate biological and social reality. This liminal connection provides *solace*, or comfort, in a world that is forever diminished. Second, the parent discovers a *worldview* that answers (or modifies his or her previous worldview to answer) the questions of how the world functions and what the parent's place and power are in the world. In the face of the absurdity that the child's death might signify, the parent's new worldview allows life to be meaningful and authentic in a world that still seems to have an underlying order.

A recurring pattern in Compassionate Friends is that finding solace and establishing or maintaining a worldview are intimately intertwined with the parent's continuing interaction with the inner representation of the dead child. Following Fairbairn (1952), inner representation can be defined as (a) those aspects of the self that are actualized in interaction with the deceased, (b) characterizations or thematic memories of the deceased, and (c) the emotional states connected with those parts of the self and those characterizations and memories.

Phenomena that indicate interaction with the inner representation of the deceased are a sense of the deceased's presence, hallucinations in any of the senses, belief in the deceased's continuing active influence on thoughts or events, and incorporation of the characteristics or virtues of the deceased into the self. These phenomena have a sense of awe and mystery about them, because they suggest the child is still active in the parent's world (Dawson, 1989). Although the parent fully knows that the child is dead, the parent also knows that the child remains immortal.

These phenomena may be experienced in altered states of consciousness (bereaved parents often use phrases such as "It was like a dream"), or they may be experienced in ordinary states of consciousness and accepted as part of the everyday world. Interaction with the inner representation of the deceased may be continuous with the self, or it may seem apart from the self-representation, in that the parent says that having such thoughts and feelings is "just not like me."

The inner representation of the dead child has the character of both outer and inner reality. It is not simply an objective presence, because the meaning of the experience is strongly personal. Neither can it be said to be a simply subjective presence. Many parents in the chapter of Compassionate Friends that this author advised argued strongly against reducing the experience to a psychic reality (as one person said, "Don't tell me that this is just in my head"). At the same time, they were usually able to grant that the meaning of the child's presence was very personal and not generalizable to other people's lives.

Inner representations of the deceased are not simply individual phenomena, but are maintained and reinforced within families and other social systems. The dead child is often a part of the bond within the continuing family and is an integral element of the bonds between members of Compassionate Friends. The Compassionate Friends credo suggests the sense of unity that bereaved parents feel in acknowledging one another's bonds to the deceased:

We reach out to each other with love, with understanding and with hope. Our children have died at all ages and from many different causes, but our love for our children unites us. . . . Whatever pain we bring to this gathering of The Compassionate Friends, it is pain we will share just as we share with each other our love for our children.

Interdependent Constructs of the Spiritual

As counselors begin to understand the spiritual experience of solace and worldview, they find themselves dealing with a series of interdependent constructs:

How the universe works
Place and power of the parent in the universe
Bond with the child
Bond with the transcendent
Meaning of the parent's life
Meaning of the child's death
Community/family membership

If any one of these constructs changes, there is a corresponding change in each of the other constructs. For example, the meaning of the child's death must be congruent with the parent's understanding of how the universe works, or else one or the other must be modified. The parents' view of his or her place and power in the universe and the meaning of the parent's life are often defined in terms of a long-standing sense of connectedness in the bond with the transcendent and in terms of community and family membership. The bond with the child is often felt as continuous with the bond with the transcendent. If the parent feels cut off from God, the meaning of the parent's life, the quality of community bonds, the bond with the child, and the parent's view of his or her place and power in the universe and the community must be recast. The interdependence of the constructs is diagrammed in Figure 1.

In the two elements of a spiritual experience—encountering or merging with

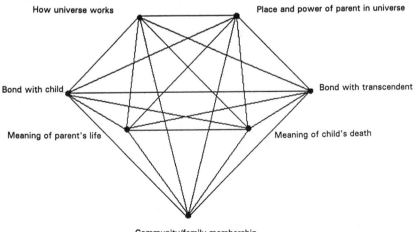

Figure 1   Interdependent constructs of the spiritual experience.

the other and finding order—these seven constructs are in constant interplay. Scholars in different disciplines have looked at some of these constructs, although no one seems to have looked at their interaction, which is the focus of this chapter. Researchers have investigated the meaning of the parent's life and meaning of the child's death in terms of meaning of life, coping styles, and religiosity (Bohannon, 1991; Cook & Wimberley, 1983; Craig, 1977; Edmonds & Hooker, 1992; Feeley & Gottlieb, 1988; Florian, 1989; Hare-Mustin, 1979; Hoekstra-Weebers, Littlewood, Boon, Postma, & Humphrey, 1991; Miles & Crandall, 1983; Peterson & Greil, 1990; Schwab, 1990; Sherkat & Reed, 1992; Smith, Range, & Ulmer, 1991, 1992; Videka-Sherman, 1982; Wilson, 1988). Community and family membership appears in the literature as social support (regarding general bereavement, see Arling, 1976; Bowling & Cartwright, 1982; Lopata, 1973; Maddison & Walker, 1967; Parkes & Weiss, 1983; Rosenblatt et al., 1991; Silverman, 1986; Vachon et al., 1982; regarding bereaved parents, see Bourne, 1968; Carr & Knupp, 1985; Kowalski, 1984; Schreimer, Gresham, & Green, 1979). Although the continuing bond with the child is cited as evidence for pathology in some contemporary grief theory, there is a long tradition of research that indicates that maintaining the bond with the deceased is a healthy part of the resolution of bereavement (Buchsbaum, 1987; Cath & Herzog, 1982; Glick, Weiss, & Parkes, 1974; Goin, Burgoyne, & Goin, 1979; Hogan & DeSantis, 1992; Kalish & Reynolds, 1981; Knapp, 1986; Lehman, Wortman, & Williams, 1987; Lopata, 1973, 1979; Moss & Moss, 1980; Rees, 1975; Rubin, 1985; Silverman, 1986, 1987; Stroebe, 1992; Stroebe, Gergen, Gergen, & Stroebe, 1992; Tessman, 1978; Yamamoto, Okonogi, Iwasaki, & Yoshimura, 1969). The bond with the transcendent, how the world works, and the place and power of the self are largely found in studies of comparative belief systems, philosophies, and artistic expressions (Amato, 1985; Bertman, 1991; Carse, 1980; Chidester, 1990; Doka & Morgan, 1993; Holck, 1974; Huntington & Metcalf, 1979; Sullivan, 1989) and is similar to ideas found in personal construct theory (Nerken, 1993; Woodfield & Viney, 1984). In the remainder of this chapter, solace and the bond with the immortal child—encountering or merging with the other—and the process of maintaining or modifying worldviews—finding order—are examined.

SOLACE

Horton (1981) claimed that the majority of people have a history of solace that they nurture. The defining characteristic of solace is the sense of soothing. To console means to alleviate sorrow or distress. Solace is that which brings pleasure, enjoyment, or delight in the face of hopelessness, despair, sadness, and devastation. Most adults can easily identify a solace-filled object to which they repair when they need soothing—a memory of a special place or person, a piece of music or art, an imagined more perfect world, a sense of divine presence. The earliest form of solace is the child's transitional object (Winnicott, 1953, 1971), such as a security blanket. The security this object provides helps the child explore new situations and adjust to unfamiliar environments (Passman, 1976; Passman & Weisberg, 1975). Winnicott (1971) wrote that humans' ability to participate in cultural, artistic, and religious symbols and myths is an extension of their early transitional objects:

> The task of reality-acceptance is never completed; . . . no human being is free from the strain of relating inner and outer reality, and . . . relief from this strain is provided by an intermediate area of experience which is not challenged (arts, religion, etc.). This intermediate area is in direct continuity with the play area of the small child who is "lost" in play. (p. 13; see Grolnick, Barkin, & Muensterberger, 1978)

Horton made a similar point. He argued that solace is necessary to participate meaningfully in a community. Psychopathic criminals, he claimed, have no solace in their lives.

The Inner Representation of the Child as Solace

How do parents maintain relationships with their dead child? Four common ways that members of the chapter of Compassionate Friends that this author advised maintained their relationships with their dead children through linking objects, religious ideas and devotion, memory, and identification. Note that this typology and the one in the section on worldviews are not empirically validated clusters of variables such as might be generated in quantitative research. In the qualitative research on which this chapter is based, the development of categories is more interactive. That is, the researcher continually refines the question to illuminate best the phenomena being studied. Readers who desire a fuller description of the qualitative research process may consult Glaser and Strauss (1967), Geertz (1973), or Hammersley and Atkinson (1983).

Linking Objects   Linking objects are objects connected with the child's life that evoke his or her presence (Volkan, 1981). Six years after his child's death, a father wrote a birthday letter to him:

> I haven't been able to part with the bicycle cart that I bought for you and your sister a few weeks before you died. It's never used anymore but I keep it in my study at home. . . . I still see your smile as you sat there holding your puppy. . . . Your little wind-up toy, the one of Donald Duck sitting in a shoe, sits on top of the file cabinet in my study. I feel close to you when I'm close to your favorite things.

The linking object need not be small toys or fast fading flowers. A father whose daughter had died 5 years earlier said,

> It's that old pick-up truck. She used to ride around in it with me. She would lean against me on the seat. It has almost 200,000 miles on it, but I am not going to sell it. By now I probably couldn't get anything for it anyway. I told the boys they could work on it and use

it if they got it going. But I'll never sell the truck because I can sit in there and feel my daughter. It's great.

The linking object is a self-validating truth to the parent that although the child is dead, in a sense the child lives. One parent had many memories of being at the beach with her child. They would look for sand dollars, which the boy saved. Her memory of those times also included natural mystical experiences (Hood, 1977) in which her bond with nature and with the child were intertwined. In a newsletter article, she wrote that the child "was especially awed by the setting sun, and as we walked the beaches, always he would stop and watch the sun go down—I did too! I was so happy with him."

In February I went to Padre Island and one lonely evening I walked the beach alone—just the sand, the sea, a beautiful setting sun, the screeching gulls, God and me. It was there I begged Him to show me a sign that E. lives—to "please send me a sand dollar." I knew that it was not the season for sand dollars. Even the local people had told me that they had not seen sand dollars since last summer. But I only wanted just one sand dollar—just one! Watching the fading sunset and listening to the roar of the waves, darkness began to fall, so I turned to go back when, there by my feet, the waves pushed up one lone sand dollar— a small but perfect sand dollar!

That is exactly the way it happened and I cannot begin to tell you the feelings I had. My prayer had been answered.

Now that this woman has had the intense experience of finding the sand dollar, the memory itself can serve as a linking object.

Prayer, Ritual, and Religious Ideation   Linking objects can have a numinous sense (Otto, 1923) about them, because they function like relics of the saints. "Any personal possession or part of a person's body . . . can carry the power or saintliness of the person with whom they were once associated and make him or her 'present' once again" (Sullivan, 1989, p. 51). The numinous feeling is clearer in the many people who sense the presence of their child in their religious experiences of prayer, ritual, and religious ideation. The inner representation of the child is merged with something bigger, but something of which the parent feels a part. Ideas and devotion can be provided by an institutionalized framework. One mother wrote a letter to her dead daughters describing her sense of their presence at Mass.

Every time I attend the sacrifice of the Mass, at the part where our Blessed Lord comes into our hearts, I feel so close to your angelic presence. What a divine experience! The only problem is that it doesn't last long enough. If only the others could share these feelings.

Ideas and devotion can also be outside of churches or theological doctrine—some parents feel the presence of the dead child within their bonds with the whole world. On her child's birthday, one mother wrote a letter to herself as if from the child.

I would have been twenty today, bound by earthly constraints. Do not cry, Mom. I am forever, I am eternal, I am ageless. I am in the blowing wind, the first blades of grass in the spring, the haunting cry of the owl, the shriek of the hawk, the silent soaring of the turkey vulture. I am in the tears of those in mourning, the laughter of little children, the pain of the dying, the hopelessness of the homeless. I am the weightless, floating feeling when you close your eyes at night; I am the heaviness of a broken heart. . . . Like an invisible cocoon I surround you. I am in the moonlight, the sunbeams, the dew at dawn. . . . Do not cry. Remember me with love and laughter and yes, with pain. For I was, I am, and I will always be. Once T., now nameless and free.

The child's presence often comes to the parent within a sense of the uncanny, a feeling often associated with religious belief and practice (Dawson, 1989). In a newsletter account, a woman whose daughter was murdered related how, a few months before she was killed, her daughter had told her of a dream in which she was looking in the window at the family gathered for Christmas.

On Christmas morning, while we were opening the gifts [which the daughter had made] my husband told me to look out the window. There are two rocking chairs on the porch, and one was rocking back and forth. My husband reached over and held my hand, and it was at that moment I remembered what M. had told us about her dream, and I realized then that her dream had become a reality. M. was still with all of us and was indeed content at watching the family she loved so much sharing the joy of Christmas together.

In this account, the uncanny occurs twice, first as a dream that seems a premonition and then as an unaccounted-for physical event.

Knapp (1986) found that bereaved parents could not sustain a belief that there was no afterlife for their child. Almost all the parents in the chapter felt that their child was in heaven. Several people in the chapter felt the child to be with another significant person who had died. One woman whose father had died 4 years before her child reported;

It was hard after my father died because I always had this sense that I didn't know where he was. But I was busy with L. because she was so sick all the time. After L. died I was really bothered that I didn't know where she was and that somehow that meant that I didn't know she was safe. That lasted two years. One day I started crying and I realized I wasn't just crying for L. I was missing my father. And suddenly I just thought, "Daddy is taking care of L. She is OK because she is with him and that's where he is. It is like they are together." That sounds so simple-minded. I don't believe in heaven or afterlife. I think we just live on in memory. But it just feels like I don't have that worry about either of them anymore. I know they are together.

Memories   Bereaved parents can find solace in memory. Unconflicted and peaceful memory is often at the end of a difficult process of separating self-representation from the inner representation of the child. Memories are at first very painful, because they are reminders of the loss. One mother reflected on the discovery that letting go of the pain did not also mean letting go of the child.

You know, I remember being afraid that someday I would wake up and my feeling of being bonded to K. wouldn't be there. I thought that when the pain left, she would be gone too. But now I find that I hope the memories will come. The times in the hospital are not what I remember. I remember the good times, when she was well. Sometimes I just look at her pictures and remember when we took them. I never know when I will look at the pictures, but I feel better afterwards.

This use of memory as solace seems similar to what Tahka (1984) called "remembrance formations." He stated that once the remembrance formation

has been established, its later calling back to mind, reminiscing about it and dismissing it again from the mind are invariably experienced as activities of the self taking place exclusively on the subject's own conditions. Although it is experienced as a fully differentiated object representation, no illusions of its separate and autonomous existence are involved. In contrast to fantasy objects possessing various wish-fulfilling functions, it [the remembrance formation] includes the awareness that nothing more can be expected from it and therefore, in its fully established forms, it has chances for becoming the most realistic of all existing object representations. (Tahka, p. 18)

Reflecting on her life 5 years after her daughter died, a mother wrote:

I still feel the warmth of love when I think of A. I still laugh when I think of some of the witty and wacky things she said or did. I still cry when the loneliness of her absence pierces my heart and I miss her as much as I did at the beginning of this journey.

I have a new relationship with A. It is internal, redefined, relevant, valued. Our relationship and memory are captured within me always to draw upon.

Often it is the emotional states attached to the thematic memories that carry the quality of solace. Writing nearly 20 years after the death of her daughter, a mother reflected on her memory of a beginners' ballet recital:

I can't remember the details of that afternoon. . . . But I remember the feeling, somewhere between laughter and tears. I remember loving that small, beautiful person, my child. I remember my sense of admiration for her, and a fittingly stifled flood of pride. . . . I have forgotten so many things, but I remember the feeling. Always the feeling.

Identification   In identification, the inner representation of the child is integrated into the self-representation in such a way that it is difficult to distinguish the two. Because the inner representation of the child is maintained less as a separate entity, the solace it provides has a somewhat different character. It is found in a sense of reinvigorated life, in renewed feelings of competence.

Identification has a social aspect. With adequate social support, pain is shared, and in that sharing the relationship with the child is shared. As the Compassionate Friends song says, "Our children live on in the love that we share." One parent described the self-help process in a Compassionate Friends meeting as a circle of weavers in which the bonds that were the child now become interwoven with the bonds between the parents in the group.

Often, identification is found in a decision to live fully in spite of the death. One parent wrote,

I came to the decision that I was to try to use my gift of life to the utmost as my son had used his. . . . there is a joy in my life now. . . . We have sought positive ways to remember [him]. Members of our family continue to give books to a memorial shelf of books [at the library] . . . started by [his] friends. . . . Members of our family periodically give blood to the Red Cross, hoping to help others who may need that gift in their struggle for life. . . . Life will never be the same. I will always be disappointed that [he] did not have a longer life, but I will always be proud of him and love him. I continue to search for ways to bring love, home, and meaning in my life as I try to make use of my one gift of life.

Solace and Immortality

In these solace-giving experiences, the child remains immortal in the sense that the inner representation of the child remains a real, living presence in the parent's inner and social worlds. Lifton (1974) claimed the sense of immortality is "man's symbolization of his ties with both his biological fellows and his history, past and future" (p. 685). The parent's bond with the child already symbolizes the parent's ties to his or her biological, personal, and cultural history. Bereaved parents often remind each other, "When your parent dies, you lose your past. When your child dies, you lose your future." Solace is for living in that poorer world. The immortal inner representation of the child maintains the parent's bonds to history and future and biology and culture.

As mentioned earlier, Winnicott (1953, 1971; also see Grolnick et al., 1978) noted that an adult's relationship to culture, including art and religion, is the same blend of inner and outer reality a child sees in his or her transitional object. The language of one mother writing in the newsletter shows that she already knew the part of herself where she now feels connected to her child.

I cannot open my eyes to see his smile. I close my eyes and listen to my heart, for it is there that he lives. I must dig deeper inside myself to a place that I ever knew existed to feel the joy this child brought.

In many of his sonnets, Shakespeare asks how a dead friend or lover can live on. He seems finally to settle on the immortality of his own art, for if he can join the reality of the deceased to the "eternal lines" of the poem, the dead person is made immortal (Hubler, 1952). Shakespeare locates the immortality of the dead in his art much the way bereaved parents locate their dead children in their experience of solace.

And every fair from fair sometime declines,
By chance or nature's changing course untrimm'd;
But thy eternal summer shall not fade
Nor lose possession of that fair thou owest;

> Nor shall Death brag thou wander'st in his shade,
> When in eternal lines to time thou growest:
> So long as men can breath or eyes can see,
> So long lives this and this gives life to thee. (Sonnet 18)

For their parents, dead children do not lose possession of that fairness they embodied; neither do they wander only in Death's shade. They have lived just the summer, but their summer does not fade; it remains eternal in a part of the parent's psyche and in the social system where the parent feels most at home. The parent who has lost a child finds solace in linking objects that evoke the presence of the child; in religious ideas and devotion that merge the child with other death-transcending connections of the parent's life; in memories, through which time drops away and the parent returns to the world when it was a better place; and in identification, by which the child becomes part of a parent's self-representation. So long lives this in the inner and social world of bereaved parents, this gives life to their children who have died.

External symbols of immortality feel less sure, and in the end less meaningful, than the immortality bereaved parents find in the solace-filled bond with their child. To quote Shakespeare,

> Not marble, nor the gilded monuments
> Of princes, shall outlive this powerful rhyme;
> But you shall shine more bright in these contents
> Than unswept stone, besmeared with sluttish time. . . .
> So, til the judgement that yourself arise,
> You live in this, and dwell in lover's eyes. (Sonnet 60)

In a new life, which sometimes feels neither sure nor safe, the immortal child provides a solace-filled reality that feels both inside and outside the self, that does not change, and the truth of which cannot be challenged.

WORLDVIEWS

The death of their child forces parents to reexamine their worldview, that is, to either reaffirm or modify their basic understandings about themselves and the justness and orderliness of their world. The parents' experience of their immortal child is intertwined with their discovery of an underlying order, purpose, or intelligence to which they align their lives.

Worldview is a concept taken from the comparative study of religion (Smart 1983, 1989). Worldviews can be defined as often unarticulated sets of beliefs, myths, rituals, affiliations, altered states of consciousness, and ethical standards by which individuals and communities know how the universe functions and know what station or power the individual holds within the universe (Dershimer, 1990; Shuchter, 1986). Worldviews are experiential in the sense that individuals use them to orient themselves. They are the map of both visible and invisible reality on which individuals locate external and internal events; from which individuals discover or choose religious, political, or ideological affiliations; and on which individuals base their moral judgments and actions. Worldviews allow individuals to "respond to what they see as true, as good, and as sacred in the realities they experience in this ever-changing, puzzling world" (Morgan, 1990, p. 1). Worldviews are not abstractions, but collections of symbols, myths, beliefs, personal experiences, altered states of consciousness, and ritual behaviors that can have varying degrees of internal coherence or intellectual consistency.

Erikson (1963) stated that worldviews rest within the most elementary feelings and earliest human experience, the basic trust developed in the preverbal interactions between mother and child. Fowler (1981) and Wilber (1980, 1981) have shown that worldviews can be maintained at any developmental level and that changing his or her worldview is central in the individual's movement into higher developmental levels. The worldview is given in a culture's heritage and is a central part of the individual's social affiliation (Bellah, Madsen, Sullivan, & Tipton, 1985). Although worldviews throughout the history of humankind show amazing diversity, the range of change available to an individual in a particular time and place is relatively limited.

Effect of Trauma on Worldviews

Traumatic events challenge people's worldviews. According to Janoff-Bulman (1989),

The coping task facing victims is largely a difficult cognitive dilemma. They must integrate the data of their dramatic negative experience and their prior assumptions, which cannot readily assimilate the new information. Victims must rework the new data so as to make it fit and thereby maintain their old assumptions, or they must revise their old assumptions in a way that precludes the breakdown of the entire system and allows them to perceive the world as not wholly threatening. (p. 121)

After a traumatic event, the worldview is like a Piagetian schema in the face of new information. The schema must assimilate the new experience, or, if the experience cannot be fitted into the structure of the schema, the schema must accommodate; that is, the schema must change by developing structures that are adequate to the traumatic experience.

The connection between the solace in the bond to the now-immortal child and the changing of the worldview is illustrated in a clergyman's account in a Compassionate Friends newsletter about how the key to his finding a renewed, albeit changed, faith was a dream of his dead son.

There he was! Walking toward me as if coming out of a mist. There he was—that lanky 17-year-old whose life I loved better than my own. He looked deeply into my eyes and with a grin on his face, the way he used to do when he was "buttering me up." Not a word was spoken, but everything was said that needed to be said for my turning point to come.

It was time to resume life. I would not be bitter, but in loving memory I would be better. I would live again because I knew that my boy lived again. My own Christian faith was to be retrofitted. It offered meaning and purpose within the shadow of my loss. It asserted that though God does not intend my sufferings, He involves himself in them. My pain and loss were not to be the end of life. Rather, it was to be a beginning—a beginning to a more compassionate life of quality and caring.

It may be noted that the boy is not alive in heaven in this account; he is in a dream. The grin on the boy's face renews the bond between father and son and allows the father to renew the bond with the Heavenly Father, who is involved in the father's pain and helps him reestablish his place in the community as the authoritative interpreter of life's meaning. The clergyman finds his faith in a sense of the boy's presence, not in the sacred texts. Indeed, the son's wordless presence marks the occasion for the sacred texts to speak to the father.

Now to be sure, this is a clergyman, who has given his life to the myths, symbols, rituals, and affiliations of a well-defined religious outlook, so perhaps the connection between faith and interaction with the dead child is clearer in this example. Among the parents in Compassionate Friends, a great variety of worldviews and many ways of parents interacting with the deceased are found. But within all the diversity, a strong connection between the solace-filled bond with the dead child and the parent's reaffirming or remolding a meaningful worldview is consistently found.

The Inner Representation in the Restoration of Meaning

Jung's (1953) idea of subjective and objective interpretations of experience is useful as a classification system for the worldviews reported by the parents in the present study, because a worldview is an understanding of how the universe functions (objective interpretation of experience) and an understanding of the station or power of the self within the universe (subjective interpretation of experience). Some parents' worldviews were more subjective, focusing primarily on the continuities and changes within the self. In these worldviews, ideas about how the universe functions were subordinated to the perception of how the self functions. Other worldviews were more objective, focusing primarily on maintaining or modifying a particular understanding of how the universe functions; ideas about the self were subordinated. The majority of the worldviews were objective; the discussion reflects this by focusing more on the objective reports.

Maintaining or Remolding the Sense of Self

Some parents reported primarily on the continuities or developments they saw within themselves. In this section, parents who felt their sense of self stayed the same, that is, who assimilated the experience of the child's death into their preexisting schemas are discussed first, followed by parents who felt their sense of self was changed by the resolution of grief, that is, who changed their schemas to include the experience of the child's death.

Self as Continuous There was a group of parents in the chapter of Compassionate Friends this author advised who maintained the worldview they had held before their child's death by asserting personal competence in their role as bereaved parents, just as they experienced competence in parenting. Because they could maintain the same competence they had felt before, they were able to assimilate the reality of their child's death into the preexisting worldview. These parents' inner representations of their child supported their sense of competence and helped them experience a sense of continuity. This sense of personal competence is especially important in traumatic deaths, because parents are often troubled by thoughts that the death might have been preventable. The assertion of competence is a central dynamic in the group process of Parents of Murdered Children; members of this group resolution of their grief is facilitated by ensuring that the criminal justice systems brings justice in the child's death.

A mother of two children illustrates the important role of sense of competence plays in the bereavement process. Her younger child had learning disabilities and was having many behavioral problems. She had acquired a sense of competence from mothering a bright, normal older child who had been killed as a toddler when a heavily sedated mental patient hit the car she drove. Her sense of competence was not threatened by the accident, because she saw the accident as an occurrence in a random universe. She wanted to testify at the trial:

I agreed with the idea that I'd lost the right of protection for my child. One of our roles as a parent is to protect our child and that right was taken away from me. So I felt I needed to follow through as far as I could in the criminal resolution of what had happened. . . . I just thought we had to get him off the streets.

She lost the trial because the driver pleaded insanity. Therefore, the mother arranged to have information on the driver's medication given to the secretary of state office so that his driver's license was revoked.

Problems with her surviving child often threatened this woman's sense of competence as a parent. When times were hard, the woman reported, the memory of her dead child

reassures me of my abilities as a parent. What I can remember, that I've had success as a parent. As much as relationships are reciprocal and people feed off each other, I still know that what's going on is somehow beyond him [the surviving child] or me.

This woman's account shows how the place and power of the self may be asserted within a nonpredictable universe. The universe may function randomly, but the individual can be competent and so maintain mastery in the random world. Because there is no Holy Other in this worldview, power must reside within the self. Testifying at the trial was a continuation of the competent motherhood this woman had always practiced, and this competence gave meaning to her life. Her memory of her time with her dead child sustained her through the challenges to her competence that were posed by her troubled living child.

Maintaining the Meaning the Child Gave   Becoming a parent can enhance a person's sense of selfhood. Many individuals in the present study had found in their parenting new ways of being and were able to develop those ways of being further as they resolved their grief. Thus the worldview accommodates to include the experience of the child's death.

One mother found that her support system failed her when her child was diagnosed with an inoperable brain tumor.

I found total strangers to be more supportive than the family. In fact, most of the friends we have before P. died are no longer our friends. They disappeared through the illness, and did not come when she died.

Her worldview accommodated this experience, leading her to see herself as quite different from her family and former friends.

I don't think I could ever hear somebody say they felt alone and not feel, "Well, you're not alone, because I'm here." I can't walk away from someone who needs me.

Her bond with the transcendent was immanent, because she now finds goodness in her relationship to others. Her continuing bond with the dead child was central to her new sense of relationship to others, in that the life she now lived was the life that was shown her by the now-dead child.

I value little things that happen with other people; maybe I wouldn't have noticed them before. P. made me aware of the nice things that people can offer. Maybe I pay more attention to those kinds of things than I would have otherwise.

This woman perceived her connectedness with others as a gift the child gave her and experienced it within a sense of connectedness with P.

I'm very aware of her presence; in a sense, she's almost with me more now than when she was ill. I think that she was like a gift and it was almost like maybe she wasn't supposed to be there, that maybe she was just a spirit or something that I was supposed to get, and could have not gotten another way. . . . In my mind, almost somehow, P. and God are almost the same. . . . Even as an infant, there was something different about her, something unusual that I never could quite put my finger on. I knew that it was something that I had never quite seen, and I think in my mind it was like God and P. were inseparable. I feel that I was to be something better because she was here.

This sense of the meaning in the child's life being expressed in the parent's personal growth and significant bonds with others is important in the Compassionate Friend process as a self-help group, because affiliation with the group and becoming a helper within it is within the internalization of the inner representation of the child. The child lives on not simply as a memory or a being in heaven, but in his or her virtues and character, which the parent now takes as his or her own and expresses by helping other bereaved parents. As mentioned earlier, the refrain of the Compassionate Friends song says, "Our children live on in the love that we share."

Maintaining or Remolding Beliefs, Symbols, and Myths

Worldviews were cast more often in terms of objective discussions of religious beliefs, myths, and symbols than in terms of the self. All religions rely primarily on this objective interpretation of experience. It becomes codified in the myth, doctrine, and artistic expressions. In his study of a great many religious systems, East and West, primal and modern, Chidester (1990) identified four characteristic ways of symbolizing transcendence of death: ancestral, experiential, cultural, and mythic. He found that in each religious system, all these ways of transcending are melded into a unified whole. This also seems to be the case for bereaved parents. Each of these ways of symbolizing transcendence was found in the objective worldviews of the parents in the present study. Five subcategories of these objective worldviews emerged: (a) Some parents found a new and compelling worldview during the illness and death of the child, and all their experience fit into that worldview. (b) Some parents interpreted symbols within their worldview in a new and more profound way. (c) Some parents reinterpreted the death of the child in a way that allowed them to maintain their former worldview. (d) When the symbols or affiliation of the parents' worldview were not useful, the parents lived in a divided world. They maintained a bond with the transcendent that was linked to the child, but in other parts of their life they felt cut off from the God in whom they still believed. (e) Some parents changed their worldview. In these objective worldviews, as in the subjective ones, the account of continuing interaction with the inner representation of the dead child was central to maintaining or remolding the worldview.

Increased Religiosity Through Affiliation   For some parents, the world became an authentic and meaningful place during and after the death of their child. In these cases, the parents had found a religious faith prior to the death and that faith had been nurtured in an intense network of interpersonal relationships. Almost all of the children had gone through many months of treatment, and the parents had found a supportive peer and professional group in the hospital. They found in those months of facing death a more authentic way of communicating and living than they had ever known in their lives. That is, the experience of their child's illness and impending death had occasioned a major accommodation in the parents' worldview as they changed their understanding of how the universe works and of both their own and their child's place and power in that universe. Now all experiences could be assimilated into the worldview.

These parents felt a direct bond with the transcendent that seemed to them indistinguishable from the bond with the dead child. The inner representation of the child was part of the religious symbols by which they lived and part of the supportive community in which the symbols were maintained.

One woman reported that in the process of his dying, her teenage son provided the model for her and her husband's present worldview.

I think about the times when B. was so worried about me. His concern was for me. He was strong, a wonderful example for me. He just loved us and we could feel it. B. brought us the example of showing love and now we continue that with our other children. The kids all recognize it too. It is a beautiful experience. We believe in heaven, and that B. is where he should be. We feel that his purpose has been fulfilled; and for us, we are still working on it.

She now experienced her dead son as a saint with the ability to grant favors. "I'll be on the highway in a traffic jam, and I'll say, 'Okay, B., get me out of this.' I'll go by the cemetery and talk to him or I'll be thinking about something, and I'll talk to B." Her husband explained the wide sense of community in which they participated and the place his dead child plays in that community:

I talk about what I call a big circle theory: someone says, "I'm going to pay you back." A helps B and B helps C and they go all around the world, but it will come back. I really believe it.

When asked whether his son was still part of the big circle, the father responded,

He's there to help, and I call on him every once in a while. He's like a saint, like Joseph or Christopher. One of the letters of Corinthians talks about the body of Christ. . . . The dead are still part of that body. I don't hesitate to ask someone to pray for something. And I think that in talking to B., I figure if you are going to get a favor, you might as well get it from someone who has an "in" somewhere.

Reinterpretation of Symbols   Many parents did not find the strength they needed from religious symbols as they perceived these symbols before their child died. These parents reinterpreted symbols from their religious tradition in the light of the new reality. There was some accommodation but no change in the developmental level of the schema. In Wilber's (1981) terms, they translated but did not transform. That is, there was a change in the surface structure of the worldview but no change in the deep structure. Many parents in the study found Kushner's (1981) book *When Bad Things Happen to Good People* helpful, because it allowed them to keep the symbol of a high God, albeit with limited omnipotence.

Several women connected their grief and their mothering to the symbol of Mary, the mother of Jesus. A woman whose retarded child had died wrote,

Since it was God's will for me to have a retarded child, the greatest thing I can say about it is that I thank God He chose me to be B's mother. I feel almost as privileged as Mary must have felt to be chosen as the mother of God.

The parent–child bond is at the core of the central Christian symbol. Usually, believers see themselves as the child of God, the father. But a few parents in the study changed to see God as a parent. Their present reality was assimilated into this paradigmatic symbol. One mother wrote,

Last year, in preparing a Christmas memorial service for our Compassionate Friends group, I had another "faith experience." I always believed God sent his only son to die for us. Last year it hit me that if this is true, this makes God a bereaved parent too! I felt even closer to him, because I realized He knew how I felt (at least sometimes). Whenever I can see human qualities in God, it makes Him more real to me.

This mother and son had not become one, however, as the Heavenly Father and Son did. As she prepared for the holiday, she wrote, she felt both a bond with and a distance from the child. She concluded her newsletter article, "I go on, trying to keep Christmas special for our family, because I know my 'little drummer boy' in heaven wants me to."

Reinterpretation of the Child's Death   If a bad event can be reinterpreted in a way that makes some good come out of it, religious symbols and affiliations can be maintained. The perception of the event is modified so that the event can be assimilated into the worldview with little accommodation. Virtually all the parents forcefully rejected a simple reinterpretation, such as that their child's death was God's will or that any good that comes from the death made the death acceptable. At the same time, they accepted that good may come from a bad thing. A mother struggling with the question "Why?" said,

I just cannot accept that there is no reason for this. There has got to be some purpose. R. was a beautiful girl. She didn't deserve to die. I am a good mother. I cannot accept that God just lets things happen. I feel these changes in me. I see good things happening, like the way the kids at the school responded and the pages in the yearbook. There is a reason for this and good will come out of it.

In this account, the use of the inner representation of child can be seen. The good that came from the death was the expression of shared love for her child. The bond the woman still felt with her daughter was validated in the bond others still feel. She felt changes in herself that were her growth in identification as she began to exemplify some of the admirable traits of her daughter. A few years later, during a social event, the woman sought this author out and spoke at length about the growth her husband had undergone in his grief and about the improvement in their marriage. She said, "You know, it's sad, but this wouldn't have happened if R. hadn't died." Her interpretation of her way of living in the world and of her daughter's continuing influence on her and others allows this woman to maintain her belief in a personal, just God.

Divided World   Some parents were not able to change or maintain the worldview that supported their world, but neither could they abandon it and move to a new one. That is, they seemed unable to either assimilate or accommodate fully. These parents divided the world of their lostness from the parts of the self that still believed in a trustworthy world. For most of these parents, it was the internalized inner representation of their child that connected them with a benevolent world, even as other parts of their psyche felt cut off from it. In a meeting, a father talked of the months of praying during his daughter's illness:

Some of the children would get better and some would not. One night as she was going to sleep N. asked me, "Daddy, how does God decide who gets the miracles?" I didn't know what to answer her. I still don't. I guess I still believe in miracles. How else do you account for the kids I saw get better with no explanation. But we didn't get one. So where am I now?

This father said that although he and his child were passed over in the distribution of miracles, his child was not passed over for heaven. He felt strongly that his daughter was in heaven, a better place than he was. He looked forward to rejoining her when he died. He also felt her presence sometimes, he said. Once as he was making a difficult business decision that had ethical implications, he felt a strong bond with her.

Development of New Meaning   Worldviews are remarkably resilient, even in the face of overwhelming pain, but for some parents, the symbols of their old life do not serve well in the new world of parental bereavement. The old beliefs only bring shame or guilt that prevent the parent from feeling in touch with the inner representation of the child in a way that brings solace. The experience of the child's death and other experiences central to the self cannot be assimilated comfortably into the old worldview. Some of the parents in the study changed their beliefs about themselves and their world, sometimes several years after the death. They accommodated; that is, they transformed (Wilber, 1980, 1981) into a new way of being themselves in a universe that they saw as working quite differently than they used to see it. As they changed their way of being in the world, the role the inner representation of the child played in their life changed.

One woman in the study had had a miscarriage 16 years earlier, and 3 years after the miscarriage, her 2-year-old daughter had died in an accident that she thought she should have been able to prevent. This woman described herself as very religious after a Protestant conversion experience when she was 17 years old. She was in this "religious phase" when she miscarried. Then she had been diagnosed with cancer, and while she was recovering, the toddler had died. After the death and the cancer, she had asked, "What else can happen? Well, I felt like God was saying, 'This is what else can happen and I can do a lot more.'" She had continued to feel inadequate and punished by God for several years. After the miscarriage, she had had a vision or dream of her grandmother standing at the foot of the bed "and this pair of hands just handing the baby to her. It was protective." When the toddler had died, she had used that vision and believed the child was in heaven, so "I can always be sure where she is." But her feeling of being a failure and being punished had persisted, and she would "wonder, in the back of my religious beliefs, if she [the dead child] can see all that we do. If she is ashamed of me as her mother. Would she want me to be her mother again." Thus the inner representation of the child had brought this woman some comfort, but it had also played a role in her strong sense of inadequacy.

About 5 years before the study, this woman had begun slowly to change her worldview. She had developed a mentor relationship with a superior at work who encouraged her to take on new responsibilities and showed that he thought she had admirable qualities. She had gone back to school for her undergraduate degree and was finishing a master's program at the time of the study. In this new self she began to feel that she was worthwhile. She spoke of her hopes for her living daughters:

I've grown to accept maybe it will be and maybe it won't be. But I've tried and I've finally come to the realization that I've done and tried as much as I can. I'm not going to blame myself anymore for the mistakes they make.

When asked whether she still posed the question that she posed to her deceased child—"Would you still want me for a mother?"—the woman responded,

I think I'm not saying "Would you want." I'm saying, "Well, regardless, I am. I was and I am." I have to answer for whatever I am.

Thus the mother no longer felt ashamed when she thought her child was looking down on her from heaven. She accepted herself and believed that the child had to accept the same shortcomings that God and everybody else must. The inner representation of the child, who had died long ago, sometimes did not feel as close as it once did, she said, but when she was in touch with the inner representation, she felt only comfort.

CONCLUSION

The defining characteristics of spirituality are that (a) in a way that feels vitally important, the individual encounters or merges with that which formerly felt like not self or other and (b) in that encounter or merger, the person becomes aware of an underlying order in the world to which the person may harmonize his or her life. In the present study of bereaved parents in a chapter of Compassionate Friends, these characteristics were seen, first, in their finding solace in connections with that which transcended the physical and biological world and, second, in their affirming or modifying their worldviews. Their bonds with their dead children were bound up with their solace in the presence of other unseen realities and with their perception of an underlying order in the world. These spiritual aspects of the resolution of the grief were central elements in the parents' rebuilding of their lives to be able to live in a changed world.

Readers who desired an answer to the question, "How can someone find meaning after such an irreparable loss?", can stop reading here. A larger question may be asked, however: Is what these bereaved parents say applicable to others?

In Compassionate Friends, the relationship of members' solace and worldview to other members has been worked out in a complex and sophisticated way. There is no doubt in the group that the solace and worldview each person finds are meaningful to him or her. But the members of Compassionate Friends also recognize that the solace they find in the presence of their dead children is solace only for them and that others must find that solace for themselves. And they know that the underlying order one person finds is different form the underlying order that another person finds. The statement of principles by which the group is governed says, "We espouse no specific religious or philosophical ideology," and "We never suggest that there is a correct way to grieve or that there is a preferred solution to the emotional and spiritual dilemmas raised by the death of our children." Thus in Compassionate Friends each person's meaning is vitally important to him or her, but not to all; yet the fact that each person finds a reality is one of the bonds that holds the community together. It is at the same time individualistic, pluralistic, and existentially compelling, and it is the socially shared reality around which the community is formed.

Death counselors need as complex and sophisticated an understanding of the nature of shared spirituality as the bereaved parents in the present study have achieved. In a pluralistic world, perhaps spirituality needs to be split from religion. In the closed tribal world in which each person develops the psyche that he or she is now trying to adjust to the global village, communitas could be a shared ontological reality. The objective worldviews of the parents in this chapter of Compassionate Friends are the building materials for myth, symbol, and theological dogma. In modernity, however, the shared reality is no longer a monolithic interpretation of experience. Rather, the shared reality is the human quest for individual meaning and solace. The parents in the present study were forced by the death of their child to undertake that quest in a focused and inescapable way. They illustrate how bereaved parents transcend the human limitations they find in the death of their child. They reveal what people in, as Tillich (1957) called it, "the extreme situation" do and what all persons must do, albeit in less extreme circumstances.

These members of Compassionate Friends are, perhaps, a model for a community of transcendence in the global village. It is not a community of the like-minded. It is a community of the fellow transcenders, of fellow sojourners. In a speech at a holiday candlelight service, a woman summed up her 5 years in Compassionate Friends: "This is what it is about: it is one person stepping back into the darkness to help the next one through." It is not in the light of a shared faith that this community is joined. They have found each other have bonded in the darkness through which they stumble. Perhaps it is not the solace or worldview one finds for oneself that is important. Perhaps the commonality of people's individual searching is the communitas one seeks in the liminal experience of a pluralistic world.

REFERENCES

Amato, J. A. (1985). *Death book: Terrors, consolations, contradictions, and paradoxes*. Marshall, MN: Venti Amati.

Arling, G. (1976). The elderly widow and her family, neighbors, and friends. *Journal of Marriage and the Family, 38*, 757–767.

Batson, C. D., Schoenrade, P., & Ventis, W. L. (1993). *Religion and the individual: A social-psychological perspective*. New York: Oxford University Press.

Bellah, R. N., Madsen, R., Sullivan, A. S., & Tipton, S. M. (1985). *Habits of the heart: Individualism and commitment in American life*. Berkeley: University of California Press.

Benedek, T. (1959). Parenthood as a developmental phase. *American Psychoanalytic Association Journal, 7*, 389–417.

Benedek, T. (1975). Discussion of parenthood as a developmental phase. *Journal of the American Psychoanalytic Association, 23*, 154–165.

Bertman, S. L. (1991). *Facing death: Images, insights, and interventions*. Washington, DC: Hemisphere.

Bohannon, J. R. (1991). Religiosity related to grief levels of bereaved mothers and fathers. *Omega, 23*, 151–159.

Bourne, S. (1968). The psychological effects of stillbirth on women and their doctors. *Journal of the Royal College of General Practice, 16*, 103–112.

Bowling, A., & Cartwright, A. (1982). *Life after death: A study of the elderly widowed*. London: Tavistock.

Brunner, E. (1946). *The mediator*. New York: Butterworth.

Buchsbaum, B. C. (1987). Remembering a parent who has died: A developmental perspective. *The annual of psychoanalysis* (Vol. 15, pp. 99–112). Madison, CT: International Universities Press.

Carr, D., & Knupp, S. F. (1985). Grief and perinatal loss. *Journal of Obstetric, Gynecologic, and Neonatal Nursing, 14*, 130–139.

Carse, J. P. (1980). *Death and existence: A conceptual history of human mortality*. New York: Wiley.

Cath, S. H., & Herzog, J. M. (1982). The dying and death of a father. In S. H. Cath, A. R. Gurwitt, & J. M. Ross (Eds.), *Father and child* (pp. 339–353). Boston: Little, Brown.

Chidester, D. (1990). *Patterns of transcendence: Religion, death, and dying*. Belmont, CA: Wadsworth.

Cook, J. A., & Wimberley, D. W. (1983). If I should die before I wake: Religious commitment and adjustment to the death of a child. *Journal for the Scientific Study of Religion, 22*, 222–238.

Craig, Y. (1977). The bereavement of parents and their search for meaning. *British Journal of Social Work, 7*, 41–54.

Dawson, L. (1989). Otto and Freud on the uncanny and beyond. *Journal of the American Academy of Religion, 58*, 283–311.

Dershimer, R. A. (1990). *Counseling the bereaved*. New York: Pergamon Press.

Doka, K. J., & Morgan, J. D. (Eds.). (1993). *Death and spirituality*. Amityville, NY: Baywood.

Edmonds, S., & Hooker, K. (1992). Perceived changes in life meaning following bereavement. *Omega, 25*, 307–318.

Elson, M. (1984). Parenthood and the transformations of narcissism. In R. S. Cohen, B. J. Cohler, &

S. H. Weissman (Eds.), *Parenthood: A psychodynamic perspective* (pp. 297–314). New York: Guilford Press.

Erikson, E. K. (1963). *Childhood and society* (2nd ed.). New York: W. W. Norton.

Fairbairn, W. D. (1952). *An object-relations theory of the personality.* New York: Basic Books.

Feeley, N., & Gottlieb, L. N. (1988). Parents' coping and communication following their infant's death. *Omega, 19,* 51–67.

Florian, V. (1989). Meaning and purpose in life of bereaved parents whose son fell during active military service. *Omega, 20,* 91–102.

Fowler, J. W. (1981). *Stages of faith.* San Francisco: Harper & Row.

Geertz, C. (1973). *The interpretation of cultures.* New York: Basic Books.

Glaser, B. G., & Strauss, A. L. (1967). *The discovery of grounded theory: Strategies for qualitative research.* Chicago: Aldine.

Glick, I. O., Weiss, R. S., & Parkes, C. M. (1974). *The first year of bereavement.* New York: Wiley.

Goin, M. K., Burgoyne, R. W., & Goin, J. M. (1979). Timeless attachment to a dead relative. *American Journal of Psychiatry, 136,* 988–989.

Grolnick, S. A., Barkin, L., & Muensterberger, W. (Eds.). (1978). *Between reality and fantasy: Transitional objects and phenomena.* New York: Jason Aronson.

Hare-Mustin, R. T. (1979). Family therapy following the death of a child. *Journal of Marriage and Family Therapy, 5,* 51–59.

Hammersley, M., & Atkinson, P. (1983). *Ethnography: Principles in practice.* London: Tavistock.

Hoekstra-Weebers, J. E. H. M., Littlewood, J. L., Boon, C. M. J., Postma, A., & Humphrey, G. B. (1991). A comparison of parental coping styles following the death of adolescent and preadolescent children. *Death Studies, 15,* 565–575.

Hogan, N., & DeSantis, L. (1992). Adolescent sibling bereavement: An ongoing attachment. *Qualitative Health Research, 2,* 159–177.

Holck, F. H. (Ed.). (1974). *Death and Eastern thought.* New York: Abingdon Press.

Hood, R. (1977). Eliciting mystical states of consciousness in semistructured nature experiences. *Journal for the Scientific Study of Religion, 16,* 155–163.

Horton, P. C. (1981). *Solace, the missing dimension in psychiatry.* Chicago: University of Chicago Press.

Hubler, E. (1952). *The sense of Shakespeare's sonnets.* Princeton, NJ: Princeton University Press.

Huntington, R., & Metcalf, P. (1979). *Celebrations of death: The anthropology of mortuary ritual.* New York: Cambridge University Press.

Janoff-Bulman, R. (1985). The aftermath of victimization: Rebuilding shattered assumptions. In C. R. Figley (Ed.), *Trauma and its wake* (pp. 15–35) New York: Brunner/Mazel.

Janoff-Bulman, R. (1989). Assumptive worlds and the stress of traumatic events: Applications of the schema construct. *Social Cognition, 7,* 113–136.

Jones, E. (1957). *The life and work of Sigmund Freud* (Vol. 3). New York: Basic Books.

Jung, C. K. (1953). *Two essays in analytic psychology* (R. C. F. Hull, Trans.). New York: Pantheon Books.

Kalish, R. A., & Reynolds, D. K. (1981). *Death and ethnicity: A psychocultural study.* Amityville, NY: Baywood.

Klass, D. (1988). *Parental grief: Resolution and solace.* New York: Springer Publishing Company.

Knapp, R. (1986). *Beyond endurance: When a child dies.* New York: Schocken.

Kowalski, K. E. M. (1984). *Perinatal death: An ethnomethodological study of factors influencing parental bereavement.* Unpublished doctoral dissertation, University of Colorado at Boulder, Boulder, CO.

Kushner, H. (1981). *When bad things happen to good people.* New York: Schocken.

Lehman, D. R., Wortman, C. B., & Williams, A. F. (1987). Long-term effects of losing a spouse or child in a motor vehicle crash. *Journal of Personality and Social Psychology, 52,* 218–231.

Lifton, R. J. (1974). On death and the continuity of life: A "new" paradigm. *History of Childhood Quarterly, 1,* 681–696.

Lopata, H. Z. (1973). *Widowhood in an American city.* Cambridge, MA: Schenkman.

Lopata, H. Z. (1979). *Women as widows, support systems.* New York: Elsevier.

Maddison, D., & Walker, W. L. (1967). Factors affecting the outcome of conjugal bereavement. *British Journal of Psychiatry, 113,* 1057–1067.

Maslow, A. H. (1964). *Religions, values, and peak-experiences.* Columbus: Ohio State University Press.

Miles, M. S., & Crandall, E. K. B. (1983). The search for meaning and its potential for affecting growth in bereaved parents. *Health Values: Achieving High level Wellness, 7*(1), 19–23.

Morgan, K. W. (1990). *Reaching for the moon on Asian religious paths.* Chambersburg, PA: Anima.

Moss, M. S., & Moss, S. Z. (1980). The image of the deceased spouse in remarriage of elderly widow-(er)s. *Journal of Gerontological Social Work, 3,* 59–70.

Nerken, I. R. (1993). Grief and the reflective self: Toward a clearer model of loss resolution and growth. *Death Studies, 17,* 1–26.

Otto, R. (1923). *The idea of the holy* (J. W. Harvey, Trans.). New York: Oxford University Press. (Original work published 1917)

Passman, R. H. (1976). Arousal reducing properties of attachment objects: Testing the functional limits of the security blanket relative to the mother. *Developmental Psychology, 12,* 468–469.

Passman, R. H., & Weisberg, P. (1975). Mothers and blankets as agents for promoting play and exploration by young children in a novel environment: The effects of social and nonsocial attachment objects. *Developmental Psychology, 11,* 170–177.

Parkes, C. M., & Weiss, R. S. (1983). *Recovery from bereavement.* New York: Basic Books.

Peterson, S. A., & Greil, A. L. (1990). Death experience and religion. *Omega, 21,* 75–82.

Powdermaker, H. (1966). *Stranger and friend: The way of an anthropologist.* New York: W. W. Norton.

Prest, L. A., & Keller, J. F. (1993). Spirituality and family therapy: Spiritual beliefs, myths, and metaphors. *Journal of Marital and Family Therapy, 19,* 137–148.

Rees. W. D. (1975). The bereaved and their hallucinations. In B. Schoenberg, I. Gerber, A. Wiener, A. H. Kutscher, D. Petetz, & A. C. Carr (Eds.), *Bereavement: Its psychosocial aspects* (pp. 66–71). New York: Columbia University Press.

Rosenblatt, P. C., Spoentgen, P., Karis, T. A., Dahl, C., Kaiser, T., & Elde, C. (1991). Difficulties in supporting the bereaved. *Omega, 23,* 119–128.

Rubin, S. S. (1985). The resolution of bereavement: A clinical focus on the relationship to the deceased. *Psychotherapy, 22,* 231–235.

Schreimer, R. L., Gresham, E. L., & Green, M. (1979). Physician's responsibility to parents after the death of an infant: Beneficial outcome of a telephone call. *American Journal of Diseases of Children, 133,* 723–726.

Schwab, R. (1990). Paternal and maternal coping with the death of a child. *Death Studies, 14,* 407–422.

Sherkat, D. E., & Reed, M. D. (1992). The effects of religion and social support on self-esteem and depression among the suddenly bereaved. *Social Indicators Research, 26,* 259–275.

Shuchter, S. R. (1986). *Dimensions of grief: Adjusting to the death of a spouse.* San Francisco: Jossey-Bass.

Silverman, P. R. (1986). *Widow-to-widow.* New York: Springer Publishing Company.

Silverman, P. R. (1987). The impact of parental death on college-age women. *Psychiatric Clinics of North America, 10,* 387–404.

Smart, N. (1983). *Worldviews: Crosscultural exploration of human beliefs.* New York: Charles Scribner's Sons.

Smart, N. (1989). *The world's religions.* Englewood Cliffs, NJ: Prentice-Hall.

Smith, P. C., Range, L. M., & Ulmer, A. (1991). Purpose in life: A moderator of recovery from bereavement. *Omega, 23,* 279–289.

Smith. P. C., Range, L. M., & Ulmer, A. (1992). Belief in afterlife as a buffer in suicidal and other bereavement. *Omega, 23,* 217–225.

Stroebe, M. (1992). Coping with bereavement: A review of the grief work hypothesis. *Omega, 26,* 19–42.

Stroebe, M., Gergen, M. M., Gergen, K. J., & Stroebe, W. (1992). Broken hearts or broken bonds: Love and death in historical perspective. *American Psychologist, 47,* 1205–1212.

Sullivan, L. E. (Ed.). (1989). *Death, afterlife, and the soul: Selections from the encyclopedia of religion.* New York: Macmillan.

Tahka, V. (1984). Dealing with object loss. *Scandinavian Psychoanalytic Review, 7,* 13–33.

Tessman, L. H. (1978). *Children of parting parents.* New York: Jason Aronson.

Tillich, P. (1951, 1957, 1963). *Systematic theology* (Vols. 1–3). Chicago: University of Chicago Press.

Turner, V. (1969). *The ritual process: Structure and anti-structure.* Ithaca, NY: Cornell University Press.

Vachon, M. L. S., Sheldon, A. R., Lance, W. J., Lyall, W. A. L., Rogers, J., & Freeman, S. J. J. (1982). Correlates of enduring distress patterns following bereavement: Social network, life situation and personality. *Psychological Medicine, 12,* 783–788.

Videka-Sherman, L. (1982). Coping with the death of a child: A study over time. *American Journal of Orthopsychiatry, 52,* 688–698.

Volkan, V. D. (1981). *Linking objects and linking phenomena.* New York: International Universities Press.

Wax, R. (1971). *Doing fieldwork: Warnings and advice.* Chicago: University of Chicago Press.

Whyte, W. F. (1973). *Street corner society: The structure of an Italian slum.* Chicago: University of Chicago Press.

Wilber, K. (1980). *The Atman Project.* Wheaton, IL: Theosophical Publishing House.

Wilber, K. (1981). *Up from Eden.* Boulder, CO: Shambhala.

Wilson, D. C. (1988). The ultimate loss. The dying child. *Loss, Grief, and Care, 2,* 125–130.

Winnicott, D. W. (1953). Transitional objects and transitional phenomena. *International Journal of Psychoanalysis, 34,* 89–97.

Winnicott, D. W. (1971). *Playing and reality.* New York: Basic Books.

Woodfield, R. L., & Viney, L. L. (1984). A personal construct approach to the conjugally bereaved woman. *Omega, 15,* 1–13.

Yamamoto, J., Okonogi, K., Iwasaki, T., & Yoshimura, S. (1969). Mourning in Japan. *American Journal of Psychiatry, 125,* 1661–1665.

Chapter 11

Death in the Lives of Children and Adolescents

Hannelore Wass

Youth and death! This association seems inappropriate and contradictory. Youth represents life, growth, and the future. Death marks the end of growth and life. Yet, death in various forms and faces is an integral part of the world that touches everyone, old and young alike. Many adults remain reluctant to talk about death with children and adolescents, however. Some believe young people are not interested in the subject. Others think death is too difficult to understand, and many believe children are too fragile to be able to deal with the fears death arouses.

Ironically, this protective stance persists at a time when children are bombarded with death images not only by the daily news, but in increasing amounts and intensity by fictional entertainment in television, home video, and movies. A pervasive theme in popular culture is the glamorization of violence. Social scientists agree that television influences people's views and has the power to shape both their perception of reality and their behavior. Television is even more influential in childhood, when basic attitudes are formed and the distinction between fact and fantasy is less clear.

At the same time, the war in which the United States was recently involved, the Persian Gulf War, was officially called "Desert Storm," and the civilians killed in it were referred to as "collateral damage." This war became an eerie media show. Those who "watched" it on CNN mostly saw images of fireworks in a dark sky and glowing blips not unlike those in the games adolescents play in the video arcades.

Unfortunately, a significant number of children and adolescents in American inner-city ghettos live in an actual war zone. For them, violent death is very real. Some of them are killed, many are witnesses to violent assaults and murder, and all fear for their lives. Adolescents are also committing violent crimes at increasing rates, including homicide. In addition, an increase in adolescent suicides has occurred in the past decade. All are victims of social ills that urgently need to be addressed.

However, by and large, middle-class children and youth in contemporary American society experience close human deaths far less often than did children in previous eras. In previous eras, death occurred most often in the home and children helped with the care of the dying family member, were present at the moment of death, and participated in the funeral. Today, nearly three fourths of the people who die are 65 years old or older, and most deaths occur in an institution. Grandparents and other relatives often live and die in geographic regions distant from where their grandchildren live, and the grandchildren do not attend the funeral; neither were they especially close to these relatives emotionally while they were alive. Whereas in the 19th century it was common for children to lose a sibling and a parent in their formative years, today more children than ever before will reach adulthood without having experienced a death in the family. This unfamiliarity with death may contribute to the deep sense of inappropriateness people feel about death that occurs in youth. It may also contribute substantially to the sense of separateness and isolation that children and adolescents report who do experience the loss of a loved one or who suffer from life-threatening illness.

In this chapter, findings and insights that have been gained from the study of children's and adolescents' understandings of and encounters with death are discussed. Some of the ways that have been found to be or may potentially be effective in helping youth cope with such experiences are also pointed out.

UNDERSTANDING DEATH

Psychologists have long been interested in children's concepts of death. The observation of animistic thinking by Swiss psychologist Jean Piaget (1929) gave impetus to studies on child animism, on the concepts of "live" and "dead," and the relationships between them, while other studies explored the evolution of death-related understandings. Altogether, the research literature dates back more than half a century (Wass, 1989). Many authors have used Piaget's model of cognitive development as a theoretical basis for their studies or as an explanation of their findings (e.g., Koocher, 1973; Jenkins & Cavanaugh, 1985). Others have reported progressions in the understanding of death consistent with general developmental principles (e.g., Nagy, 1948).

Essentially, the research suggests that the understanding of death progresses from an immature understanding in early childhood to a more mature understanding in older childhood and adolescence, consistent with the stages of cognitive development described by Piaget (1965) (Table 1). The correspondence between the acquisition of a mature understanding of death and progression through the Piagetian developmental stages suggests that children develop their understandings of death not in a random or haphazard fashion, but in a general sequence compatible with their cognitive development.

To this author's knowledge, there have been no studies on infants' cognition about death. It is widely believed that infants have not yet formed concepts, even though they are more advanced in their intellectual development than was earlier thought.

The most consistent findings concern the child's notions of death in early childhood. Studies spanning several generations and cultures have indicated that children in the preschool years have immature concepts of death, understanding death as a temporary restriction, sleep, or departure and believing that the dead

Table 1   Children and Adolescents' Concepts of Death

Developmental/ educational status	Concepts	Piaget's periods/ stages
Infancy	No concepts	I. Sensorimotor Period II. Preparation and Organization
Preschool years	Reversibility, external causation, revival by various means	1. Preoperational Thought (2–7 years)
Early school years to preadolescence	Universality Irreversibility Nonfunctionality	2. Concrete Operations (7–12 years)
Adolescence	Religious and philosophical theories and beliefs about the nature of death and existence after death	III. Formal Operations (12 years and up)

can be brought back to life spontaneously, by administering food, medical treatment, or magic.

During their school years, children come to develop a more mature understanding of death. Such an understanding requires the ability to grasp the abstract concepts of universality, nonfunctionality, and irreversibility. Universality refers to the understanding that all living things die; irreversibility is the understanding that after a living thing has died, its physical body cannot be made alive again; and nonfunctionality refers to the understanding that all life-giving functions cease at death. These three concepts have frequently been used in studies that show wide variations in the chronological ages at which these concepts are acquired (Speece & Brent, 1984). For example, the age at which the understanding of the universality of death is acquired ranges from 4 years in some studies to 10 years and older in others. Such variation may be attributed, in part, to differences in the procedures used or populations sampled in different studies. It appears, however, that they are stable in the sense that once a child grasps the irreversibility of death or understands that all living things will die, he or she will not regress to less mature understandings. Speece and Brent (1992) found that although most of the children in their study acquired one or the other of these three concepts in the early school years, fewer than half achieved all of them, suggesting to the authors that at least a 4-year period is necessary for a child to fully grasp what death means. These findings support earlier work indicating a broad developmental progression in which infants do not have any concepts of death, young children's concepts are immature, and older children acquire more mature concepts in the early school years and preadolescence and formulate abstract ideas about the nature of death and existence in adolescence, consistent with Piaget's stages of development.

Religious Concepts and Beliefs

Consideration of children's concepts of death gives rise to questions about the relationships between cognitive ability and belief. Are children's beliefs about an afterlife dependent on what they can grasp intellectually? When children say that "after you die you go to Heaven," what do they mean? Do young children's religious concepts differ from those of older children and adolescents? Much remains to be learned in this area. For example, researchers need to develop more sophisticated ways of assessing the religious variables and to study the current generation of children and adolescents.

On the basis of past studies, it appears that children's religious beliefs are, to an extent, determined by their cognitive–developmental status. That is, what children mean by concepts such as "Heaven" and "God" reflects their thinking and reasoning modes at the particular developmental level at which they are functioning. According to past studies, young children view God very concretely as a father figure, except that He is much taller, stronger, and older, and has larger hands, than Dad. This God gives out food and lets dead people be angels and fly around (Heller, 1986; Wass & Scott, 1978). Other children think God imposes certain restrictions; for example, you can't play noisy games in Heaven, and there isn't a ladder to climb back down to earth (Gartley & Bernasconi, 1967). Many children offer nonspecific and stereotypical ideas about heaven, are skeptical, or believe there is no afterlife (Koocher, 1973; Lonetto, 1980; Wass & Scott, 1978). In a recent study, young children reported magic or medicine, not God, as the source of power for getting people restored to life (Speece & Brent, 1992).

Adolescents often describe death in abstract concepts as darkness, eternal light, transition, or nothingness (DeMuth, 1979; Wenestam & Wass, 1987). They formulate their own theologies about life after death, which include beliefs in reincarnation, transmigration of souls, spiritual survival on earth, and spiritual existence at another level in a state of peace and beauty, in addition to beliefs about heaven and hell or total annihilation at death.

Studies on the scary television programs and films children watch indicate that besides murderous violence, children also watch dramas depicting ghosts, demons, Satan, and other occult phenomena (Wass, Raup, & Sislet, 1989; Wass, Stillion, & Fattah, 1987). Perhaps such viewing reflects as well as shapes young people's concerns about life, death, and spirituality.

Fears and Anxieties

Death evokes fears and anxieties in most people, children and adolescents included. But death-related emotions in children in ordinary life circumstances have rarely been studied in a systematic way. Psychologists nevertheless have gained insights through clinical observation or in conjunction with other research. For instance, in studies of concepts of death, children have expressed their feelings spontaneously in interviews, in written responses, by overt behavior, or through art and body language. This is not surprising considering that the three major domains of human functioning—cognitive, affective, and overt behavioral—although conceptually distinct, are intricately intertwined in real life.

In the psychological literature, there is, of course, a wealth of clinical data on fears and anxieties in general that may be applied to death. For example, children's fears and anxieties about death may be viewed from a psychoanalytic, cognitive/developmental, or social learning orientation. These perspectives represent distinct and, in some respects, conflicting notions about the nature, sources, and functions or dysfunctions of these emotions (Wass & Cason, 1984). At the same time, each perspective can contribute substantially to conceptualization of, assessment of, or clinical intervention for death-related affect.

Studies and this author's own observations suggest that the catalog of children's fears includes the dark, monsters, werewolves, the Devil, Hell, cemeteries, corpses, bodily mutilation, skeletons, the spirits of deceased persons, and powers of the occult. They fear being abandoned, shot, stabbed, and buried alive. They fear losing their parents as well as their own lives through illness, personal violence, or war. They fear the prospect of getting old and of dying. Some of these fears are more pronounced than others at different ages.

Many psychologists stress the close interaction between cognition and affect in the course of a child's development. Applying this notion to death-related thoughts and feelings, one can hypothesize that children's death-related fears are dependent on their level of cognitive development. Findings suggest that this may indeed be the case, although more study is needed to obtain definitive answers (Furman, 1984; Waechter, 1984). It may be tentatively suggested that the fears and anxieties at each level of cognitive development are as follows.

Unable to conceptualize death, infants are not expected to show any fears. But infants do show anxieties and distress. These have to do with being separated from the nurturing person, dropped, left in the dark, or abandoned (Bowlby, 1960, 1980). Young children seem less fearful of death than do school-age children. This is consistent with the qualitative differences between younger and older children in their understanding of death. There is nothing to worry about when death is not a part of the child's experience and when the concept is meaningless. There is also little to worry about when death is a temporary problem that can be fixed by magic or the doctor. However, death-related fears can also arise directly from an immature understanding of death. For instance, a child frustrated with siblings or parents may wish them dead. In some cases, when a death indeed occurs, the child may feel responsible for the death.

School-age children seem to experience the most fears. At this stage, they know that death is final and happens to everybody. They seem preoccupied cognitively with the scientific details of death, decomposition, and decay and show corresponding fears. They are aware of the many ways a human being can be killed and die. They know there is no magic power to save and protect one, although they may only half-jokingly engage in some superstitious practices, such as holding their breath when passing a cemetery or avoiding the crack in the pavement on the sidewalk.

Adolescents know about the meaning of death and its implications. Adolescents' perception of time is more realistic than school-age children's. Standing at the threshold to adulthood, they are more aware of the years of living that lie ahead, the many experiences yet to have, the relationships yet to establish. One would expect adolescents' fears of death to be intense. Yet, typically, this is not the case, however. Adolescents often say, "Death is a long way off, why worry now?" Researchers can speculate about the possible reasons for such denial and hope that future studies will provide an answer.

Problems with Studies

Problems inherent in the studies on children's concepts of death and death-related fears limit the degree of confidence with which the findings may be generalized to all children. The most serious problem may be the lack of study of the impact of social–cultural factors, such as ethnicity, socioeconomic status, and other demographic factors, and personal experiences on children's death-related understandings and fears. Most researchers have sampled middle-class, white children. Because this population is the most accessible, groups of children living under various circumstances and in various environments typically are not compared systematically with one another in comparison studies. Assessing the influence of social conditions such as poverty, violence in the community, and war on children's death-related concepts and fears is particularly challenging.

The systematic study of fears and anxieties poses professional problems. Clear conceptualizations of death fears and anxieties in childhood and adolescence are lacking. Not surprisingly, no instruments exist for assessing these feelings. But even if such instruments existed, there remains the ethical question, How can these feelings be assessed in children without doing harm, without creating emotional upset? There are no easy answers. Perhaps investigators need to be content with indirect information, as in the past, or rely mostly on casual observation and anecdotal data. More qualitative studies might be performed that invite responses in multiple modes of expression, in a setting of the children's choice, guided by the principles of sympathetic observation, with children in control of their participation at all times.

An understanding of how concepts of death actually develop and what factors influence the process and to what degree is lacking. This should come as no surprise, considering that few of the studies in this area have been longitudinal, examining the development of death-related concepts over a period of time. Typically, the only feasible option for researchers is the cross-sectional approach. In this approach, researchers study a large group of children of differing ages (presumably representing different developmental statuses) at one particular time. Thus any change in an individual, whether it is called development, acquisition, or something else, can only be inferred from comparing that individual with individuals at other ages.

There are other issues as well, such as the approach taken to measuring death-related concepts. By far, the majority of researchers have relied on verbal expression. Younger children may have difficulty articulating their thoughts, however. It has been suggested that younger children's verbal and play expressions about death are discrepant and that the latter more valid (Weiner, 1979). In short, the current research on children's understandings and attitudes toward death is fraught with limitations, and therefore its findings are best viewed as tentative, of value primarily because tentative knowledge is better than stereotyped assumptions.

SOCIETAL FACTORS AND FORCES

Children do not learn to understand and fear death in a vacuum. They grow up in society and learn by absorbing its wisdom, myths, and practices, its ambivalence and anxieties. They adopt many of its values and beliefs from significant adults in their world—parents, teachers, public figures, sports heros, and entertainers. They also learn from their physical and symbolic environments. They learn when they are taking part in a memorial service; when they are listening to adults discussing death, loss, and serious illness; from myriad nonverbal behaviors that accompany speech, such as facial expressions, gestures, and other body language; and by watching animals, the evening news, a drama program, and violent behavior in the home or in the street. This process of enculturation is informal and cumulative. Obviously, children also learn from formal instruction provided in educational institutions. Thus, inevitably, children learn fundamental lessons and develop their basic attitudes about life and death.

Violent Death in Popular Culture

American society is based largely on the Judeo-Christian and humanistic ideology, which affirms the value of life, emphasizes the dignity and worth of each person, and encourages tolerance and peaceful coexistence. In this same society, however, other, conflicting values and attitudes toward death are also present. Ironically, at a time when most children and youth are personally unaffected by death, they are relentlessly bombarded with death through the mass media. Violent death is a preferred theme of entertainment in television, home videos, and movies.

Television Television is by far the most prominent mass medium. About 98% of American households have at least one television set. In its accessibility, television is like no other medium, and thus its power to exert an impact on masses of people is unsurpassed. American children watch 21–28 hr of television per week, primarily programs not designed specifically for them. More than half of all children watch prime-time programs, which contain a great deal of violence, an average of five acts per hour, or 10 times as much violence as occurs in real life (Morgan, 1988).

Violent death on television is spectacular, often shown in graphic detail with close-ups of violent acts and bodily mutilation. In many programs, the plot is not well developed or the victims are criminals, so the viewer is not engaged sufficiently to develop empathy or compassion for the victim. Rarely are the pain and grief that follow death rendered in depth.

Children's programs are even more violent than those for adults. There are about 5 violent acts per hour in prime time, but in children's Saturday morning cartoons there are 20–25 acts per hour involving destruction of property and physical assault that causes injury and death (Gerbner, Gross, Morgan, & Signorelli, 1980). It is little comfort to know that cartoon characters never stay dead very long, because the message is that nobody dies or that whatever death is, it's a temporary condition, neither of which is a helpful message for the young child. In addition, the child learns that violence is the way to handle conflict.

The invention of cable television and the VCR has greatly increased the potential for viewing violent fare. The new fiberoptic capabilities and the electronic information superhighway that is currently evolving increase this potential exponentially.

Violence on television programs has been a concern since broadcasting began. Violence levels were high in the 1970s and have continued to increase, despite accumulating evidence of the negative effects of televised and filmed violence from hundreds of studies over several decades (e.g., National Institute of Mental Health, 1982; Singer, 1983; Surgeon General's Scientific Advisory Committee, 1972).

After a 2-year study involving a review of the literature and recent expert testimony, the American Psychological Association Commission on Violence and Youth (APACVY, 1993) concluded that

1   Frequent viewing of violence on television is correlated with increased acceptance of aggressive attitudes and behavior.
2   Viewing violence increases the fear of becoming a victim.
3   Young children's exposure to television violence can have harmful lifelong consequences.
4   Viewing violence increasingly desensitizes children to violence.
5   Viewing violence increases apathic behavior.

Various professional and citizens groups, such as the American Academy of Pediatrics, the American Psychological Association, and the National Coalition on Television Violence, have testified before Congressional subcommittees and panels during several legislative sessions. This testimony resulted in the passing of the TV Violence Act of 1990. Under this law, broadcasters had until fall of 1993 to lower voluntarily the levels of violence in their prime-time programs. The threat of legislative action by Congress has so far brought promises from industry leaders.

Destructive Themes in Rock and Rap Song   Themes of hate and destruction are also present in the lyrics of certain genres of rock music, especially heavy metal and rap. Rock music has a 40-year tradition as a counterculture forum for adolescent rebellion against parents and other authority figures, and the themes of sex, love, drugs, antiwar protest, and negation of authority that have dominated rock lyrics in the past remain dominant today. However, since the 1980s there has been a new dimension to some rock music, particularly heavy metal and rap, a meanness and crassness not found in previous eras. These songs promote hate, violence, and murder, and the targets are women, ethnic and religious minorities, and authority figures. In one study, although "softer" forms of rock music were the most popular among adolescents, nearly a fifth of the sample were fans of lyrics that promote murder, suicide, or satanic practices or the groups that produce them (Wass, Miller, & Stevenson, 1989). Among residents of juvenile detention centers, the proportion of fans of this music increased to 50% (Wass, Miller, & Redditt, 1991).

Groups that produce hateful and destructive lyrics have become popular. For example, Guns N' Roses sold nearly 9 million copies of their album *Appetite for Destruction*. Professional and advocacy groups such as the National Education Association, the American Academy of Pediatrics, and the Parents' Music Resource Center have worked to inform people about the existence of such lyrics and to persuade the music industry to introduce a system of labeling or rating them on album covers. This is now done by a number of record companies. In addition, record stores and large discount chains have pulled certain albums off their shelves. Other groups have applied pressure with success. For example, when the rapper Ice-T published the song *Copkiller,* police organizations protested, record stores pulled the album that contained it off their shelves, Ice-T removed the song from the album, and Warner-Time released the rapper from his contract, citing "creative differences."

No study has revealed that a rock song or a film was the solitary reason for a young person to kill or commit suicide, and no respectable researcher would make such a claim. But what if a young person who lives in poverty in an unstable family, drinks or takes drugs, and is a failure in school listens to a hundred songs, many times over, and watches a hundred television programs and videos, all with a similar message?

The issue of explicit violence and sex in rock lyrics, and on television and film is deeply controversial. One side argues that a person's right to free speech and free artistic expression is threatened by rating, labeling, and similar constraints. On the opposite side, health professionals and other advocacy groups consider young people's right to personal safety and society's obligation to safeguard and promote it. With these concerns pitted against one another, many decide in favor of social responsibility. Meanwhile, the entertainment industry enjoys its right to profit.

Deadly Violence in Real Life

Unfortunately, for a number of children and youth in American society, violence is not a matter of television drama, rock and rap songs, or news from a distant part of the globe; it happens in their own world. Violent crimes have increased dramatically, especially in the 1980s (see Chapter 1). Increasing violence in the home, on the street, and in the neighborhood affects a substantial number of school-age children, particularly those who live in inner-city ghettos. The rate of death by violence has increased most steeply in the 15- to 24-year-old age group. Homicide is now the second highest cause of death after accidents in this age group (Ewing, 1990). It has been the primary cause of death for African-American males for more than a decade (Hammond & Yung, 1993). A black male is 11 times more likely than a white male to be killed. Homicide is also the primary cause of death for black females ages 15–24, and they are 4 times more likely than white females in this age group to be killed (APACVY, 1993). These racial, gender, and age differences point to troubling problems.

An estimated 40–50% of all American households have firearms, half of them handguns, for a total of about 200 million. With parents armed, it should come as no surprise that children arm themselves also. Most gun-carrying high school students get their guns from home. A recent survey indicated that 1 in 5 high school students had carried a weapon in the 30 days preceding the survey, with 1 in 20 admitting they had carried a gun (Centers for Disease Control, 1991). A 14-year-old recently explained to this author why he carried a gun: "I don't like to fight. With a gun I don't have to fight. I get more respect, and I'm safer." Most large school systems across the country have already installed metal detectors, and smaller schools are asking their states for funding to do likewise. The National Education Association is seeking federal funding to help schools not only obtain security devices, but also hire security guards to patrol grounds, hallways, and cafeterias.

The young people who live in many inner cities are in physical danger, and many have to live with the shock of having witnessed deadly violence. For example, in a study of eighth graders in Chicago, 75% reported they had seen someone robbed, stabbed shot, or killed (APACVY, 1993). Many of these inner-city children show symptoms of posttraumatic stress. All these children and adolescents are victims because they live in constant fear for their lives. Carrying weapons may be a way many young people attempt to deal with their fear.

The Family

As the primary social unit, the family ideally helps the child to learn basic facts and adopt positive attitudes toward him- or herself and others and positive values and orientations toward the world, life, and death. Elkind (1981) and other psychologists have argued that economic change, shifting work patterns, and loss of financial security and their corresponding instabilities in the family have caused a great deal of stress in parents in contemporary American society. Under stress, he suggested, parents become more self-centered and tend to hurry their children. Research indicates that parent–child relationships are often fraught with conflict and alienation, particularly in the adolescent years (Montemeyer, 1986). And adolescents often prefer to discuss important ideas and emotional issues with their peers, rather than their parents. In fact, in an intensive study of parent–adolescent interaction, Csikszentmihalyi and Larson (1984) found that adolescents spent less than one tenth of their time with their parents. In this context, it is understandable that many parents feel uncomfortable talking about death and avoid it if possible. But they have a fundamental role in helping their children understand, evaluate, and manage death experiences by providing guidance and mediation, setting an example, and giving nurturance and comfort. Experiences they provide can serve as powerful antidotes to the violent and destructive acts their children observe in much of the popular culture today. For example, parents may dramatically reduce the potentially negative impact of violence in the media by limiting the types of television programs they allow their children to watch and their frequency and times of television watching and by monitoring their home video viewing.

Toys and Games   Casual perusal of toy stores shows the high number and variety of toys and games designed for imitation of aggression and war. There are many varieties of weapons, toy armies, and fleets of warships, including nuclear submarines and missile-carrying war planes, for the younger age groups. War toys are among the bestselling toys in the United States. For example, the GI Joe Modern Army Action Toys, consisting of more than 50 items, is a leading toy line. Between 1984 and 1990, the sale of war toys rose 500%, and the best-selling single toy during the Christmas season has for a number of years been a war toy (Carlsson-Paige & Levin, 1990). Older children and adolescents favor video games, most of them also violent. Among the recent releases drawing criticism from advocacy groups is the video game Mortal Kombat, made by Acclaim Entertainment. In this game, players use paddles and playsticks to slap, kick, and burn each other. In some versions, winners get to murder losers by ripping out their heart or tearing off their head. Aggressive marketing in television cartoons and MTV contributes to the popularity of such toys.

Toys and games are another means of familiarizing children with the many ways people can kill one another. It also makes such action appear easy, painless, and free of consequences. Thus lethal violence in imaginative play and for amusement is a common aspect of socialization, especially for boys. If "Toys R Us," then "what R we"? It would be naive to think that cultural practice has no influence on children's attitudes and values.

The boom in aggressive toy sales has resulted in responses by peace organizations, psychologists, and educators, who offer suggestions for toys, games, and other activities that promote cooperation, collaboration, conflict resolution, and other prosocial skills (e.g., Carlsson-Paige & Levin, 1990; Leviton, 1991). Peace games may be constructive alternatives to war games.

Keeping Pets   The only direct personal involvement with death many children have throughout childhood and adolescence is the death of animals and pets. Children encounter animal death at a young age. They see dead insects, worms, toads, and birds. Parents can help children learn their first lessons of death by answering questions. Children often form close and tender relationships with pets, and caring for a pet gives a child the opportunity for direct experience with the cycle of life, including dying and death and the feelings of grief they cause. Provided that his or her parents are able to offer sensitive guidance, this may be a valuable experience for a child, preparing him or her to cope effectively with the loss of a close person.

Books   There is a wealth of literature for children and adolescents on the subject of death, written by professional writers who treat the topic with sensitivity and compassion and in a low-key manner (see Chapter 18 for some of them). In some books, death is a subplot of the story; in others, it is the main theme. Research has shown that reading about the feelings and behavior of others is strikingly influential (Bandura & Mischel, 1965). Books can also be sources of comfort. Nonfiction books focus on providing information. Others are written for parents to read with the child. Books may serve as a vehicle for broaching the subject of death.

Talking about Death   Parents may feel uncomfortable talking about death with their children, but it is important that they try. Open and honest communication is far more helpful than silence or evasion. It is best achieved in an atmosphere of mutual trust and respect. Ideally, parents respond to their children's inquiries about death in a calm, straightforward manner and with correct information concerning factual matters. Coming to understand such complex matters as death is an extended process. It cannot be accomplished in one easy session. It is best when parents are prepared to discuss the subject from the perspective of the child's developmental level. A nonthreatening atmosphere in the home makes children more likely to share troubling feelings and ask difficult questions. Children and adolescents inevitably experience fears and concerns about death, in their personal lives, elsewhere in the world, or in fiction. As the most significant people in their lives, parents can comfort and reassure them. They can provide relevant information that may lead to a more optimistic perspective. Perhaps most important, parents can spend time with them in wholesome, family-oriented interactions and activities that teach caring, compassion, and tolerance.

Schools

Long-term, systematic education about dying, death, and bereavement was recommended more than 20 years ago. Schools are logical places for such education. Their purpose is to educate young people in all aspects of life in order to prepare them for future productiveness, well-being, and responsible social behavior. In addition, schools can teach young people skills that will help them cope with loss and grief and manage interpersonal conflicts. Finally, schools can assist children in developing caring attitudes toward themselves, others, and the environment.

Such education may serve as an antidote to misperceptions, distorted views, and destructive attitudes children may acquire from the mass media.

Although schools have been fairly responsive to the need for crisis intervention, especially suicide intervention (one fourth of the nation's public schools report such programs and one fifth report grief support programs), they have, by and large, not included death education courses as part of their regular curriculum offerings. Only about one tenth of the schools offer such courses (Wass et al., 1991).

In systematic death education, wherein death education is not offered in a single course but is worked into other courses, death-related topics may be discussed in many areas. Areas obviously suited for incorporating death-related information and discussion are health sciences/health education and AIDS education. The threat of death can be a powerful motivator for adopting healthy habits of eating, sleeping, sexual behavior, exercise, and personal hygiene and for avoiding activities, no matter how tempting, that threaten health and life. Health sciences/health education can also be an appropriate subject for discussing problems that threaten the health of the entire human community and the globe, as Leviton (1991) suggested. A natural topic for the life sciences would be to study the life cycle of humans, from conception through birth, growth, maturity, old age, and death. Psychology courses or courses on the family are natural contexts for discussions of how people respond to the crises of dying and death, what feelings, thoughts, and behaviors such experiences evoke; and how a person can cope with and transcend them and support others in the process. Discussion of aggression, violence, self-destructive thoughts and behavior, hate, intolerance, and ways to control them may also be incorporated naturally into psychology or related courses.

Teachers at the elementary level can fit death-related topics into their teaching even more easily than can teachers at the secondary level. Because they have more time with students, they have a wider range of possibilities. In the study of the community, for example, younger students often are taken on fieldtrips to city hall, the fire station, the hospital, a supermarket, or the museum. The cemetery and the funeral home could be added to this list. Thoughtful teachers who are comfortable with the subject and have basic knowledge about it find numerous ways to incorporate it naturally into their teaching.

At both the lower and upper levels, school should, first of all, be safe places for children. At present, with few gun control laws for juveniles, it is urgent that schools teach gun safety and discourage young people from carrying guns or other weapons. Informing children about actual homicide rates and about negative bias in news reporting might lessen some of their fears.

Because of the ubiquity of television and the violent tenor of much of the entertainment media, schools need to teach students to become media literate. For example, teachers might present units, modules, or discussions on such topics as program production, types of programs, how networks determine their programs' time slots, the manipulations of television advertising, the relationship between commercials and the programs in which they are shown, product disclaimers, methods of persuasion, and individuals' power to resist. In this way, schools can play an important role in helping young people gain a broader perspective.

PERSONAL ENCOUNTERS WITH DEATH
Terminal and Life-Threatening Illness

A child's or adolescent's being diagnosed with a terminal illness shatters people's faith in the presumed order of life. It is a tragedy that everyone finds difficult to manage—the child, the family, the medical personnel, and society. For more than half of this century, parents' and physicians' protective instincts and their own anxieties, as well as their underestimation of children's competence, caused them to conceal from terminally ill children the truth about their illness. Enormous energies were expended in maintaining a charade, and everyone suffered in silence.

Awareness and Communication   In the 1960s and 1970s, however, studies showed that terminally ill children were aware that something was wrong without being told; that children's reluctance to talk or ask questions about their condition was not a sign of blissful ignorance, but rather reflected the children's perception of the adults' discomfort with the subject (Vernick & Karon, 1965); and, moreover, that terminally ill children experienced greater fears and anxieties than did acutely or chronically ill children (Spinetta & Maloney, 1974). In an extensive ethnographic study of terminally ill hospitalized children ages 3–12 years, Bluebond-Langner (1978) discovered not only that the children were aware of their condition, but also that they come to have quite accurate knowledge about it. She found that the children came by their knowledge and understanding in five progressive steps:

1   Knowledge that "it" was a serious illness.
2   Knowledge of the names and side effects of drugs.
3   Knowledge of the purposes of treatments and procedures.
4   Knowledge that the disease was a series of relapses and remissions.
5   Knowledge that the disease was terminal.

The children developed this knowledge from the cumulative events in their day-to-day experiences, such as various treatment procedures, the behavior of medical staff and family, and observation of other terminally ill children (Bluebond-Langner, 1978). Recent research supports these findings, showing that even when little or no information about the illness is shared with younger children, they experience the same distresses as do older children (Chaflin & Barbarin, 1991). Such knowledge is also reflected in behavior. For example, Bluebond-Langner (1989) found that young children often refused to play with the toys of deceased peers and avoided mentioning their names.

Today, most caregivers recognize the need to communicate openly with the terminally ill child. At the same time, they understand that some children use denial as a way of coping with their own emotions, protecting family members, or maintaining privacy. By and large, however, open communication among the child, family, and caregiving team, including psychological care and therapy, is considered a critical aspect of the child's care.

Psychological Impact Numerous studies have focused on the impact of terminal illness, especially childhood cancer, on the psychological and social functioning of the child and family and on effective interventions to care for and support them. They are difficult to summarize because there are no clear-cut theoretical perspectives on which they are based. It seems clear, however, that the overriding issue is loss: loss of control, of identity, and of relationships. The child's psychological responses may be organized around these issues. The special circumstances of the illness, such as the phase of the illness trajectory (e.g., initial stage or end stage) and other situational factors, contribute to the kinds of responses and their intensity. However, developmental status is perhaps the most important variable affecting children's responses to their terminal illness.

Very young children may experience problems unique to their age. Their immature understanding of death may keep them from having the fears associated with their impending loss, the processes of death and decay, and what happens after death. At the same time, however, their immature reasoning capacity may prevent them from understanding the causal relationships between illness and hospitalization and between illness and painful treatment procedures.

Hospitalized young children experience separation anxiety. In fact, separation anxiety may be the equivalent of death anxiety, because absence from the mother figure is a threat to the child's fundamental safety and eventually to his or her life.

School-age children frequently replace separation anxiety with mutilation anxiety. They have fairly well-developed self-concepts and, therefore, often act with anxiety, anger, and depression to the threats to their body integrity caused by medical treatments. Understanding of illness and treatments in older children can significantly reduce their anxiety and also meet their need for knowledge and information (Susman, Dorn, & Fletcher, 1987).

Adolescents often cope with their condition more effectively than do younger children because they have more problem-solving and coping skills available and have had greater experience for developing them (Susman, Hollenbeck, Nannis, & Strope, 1980). On the other hand, they have a fuller understanding of death. Whereas school-age children are only beginning to have the cognitive ability to grieve the loss of the future, adolescents understand the full implications of this loss (Waechter, 1984). They know that with their death, in addition to their body, consciousness, and loved ones, they lose all hopes, dreams, and possibilities. It is not surprising, then, that terminally ill adolescents are often bitter and depressed (Katz, Kellerman, & Siegel, 1980).

Many children and adolescents face their condition with a courage and strength of spirit that are an inspiration for medical staff and family alike. Sometimes these young people protect their parents in an unusual role reversal. A 15-year-old cancer patient at a university teaching hospital said to her confidante: "My chances on the six-month or one-year chemotherapy aren't good at all. Also, he wants to start right away so I can't go home. . . . I'm just gonna have to be brave and not feel sorry for myself . . . Dad was upset again today. I could tell. I think if I try to keep a good attitude, it'll be a whole lot easier on Mom and Dad."

Care for the Terminally Ill   The hospital is not a good place to die. Even with the most caring and thoughtful medical staff, hospitalization causes hardships. Foremost among them is the separation from the family at a time when their comfort is sorely needed. In addition, there are rules and restrictions that make it difficult for the child and family to maintain some measure of control or carry out normal activities. Hospitalization also separates the child from the comfort of familiar surroundings. Interaction with siblings and peers and their potential support is also very limited, and the child is deprived of the comfort of family pets, music, and natural surroundings. Furthermore, hospitalization disrupts the family system in a major way. It can lead to marital tensions, cause healthy siblings to feel neglected, and make family routines difficult to keep. All these create additional stress and frustration for everyone, including the ill child.

Many of these problems can be eliminated with home or hospice care, although not in all instances. Martinson and her colleagues' pioneering work in developing a model of care in the home has shown that home care under medical supervision and with social support is effective (Martinson et al., 1978) and that parents like it (Carlson, Simacek, Henry, & Martinson, 1984). In addition, it has been shown to facilitate the family's adjustment after the child's death (Mulhern, Lauer, & Hoffman, 1983). Health professionals have also worked to encourage the use of hospice care for terminally ill young people (e.g., Armstrong-Dailey, 1991). However, young patients are not often referred to hospice programs. Understandably, medical professionals try to provide curative treatment as long as there is any chance, even a slight one, that it may succeed. Families usually feel the same way. Recent medical advances in the treatment of certain cancers have indeed been impressive, making physicians and families all the more optimistic. On the other hand, when the prognosis is poor, the treatment is painful, and the child wishes the suffering to end, hospice care may be more appropriate. At this point, physicians and families often have to make decisions about a further course of action for a child. Such decisions are difficult to make. They cut to the core of the right-to-die/obligation-to-treat controversy, but with an additional dimension—the rights of young patients. Although children are legally minors, shouldn't their wishes be respected and shouldn't they be given a voice in decisions affecting their body and being? To assist in the debate of this dilemma, it has been proposed that a distinction be made between consent and assent and that the concept of children's competence to consent be considered (Koocher & DeMaso, 1990).

Long-Term Survival   Because of dramatic treatment advances, childhood malignancies are no longer inevitably fatal. Over the past few decades, survival rates for certain cancers have become increasingly higher, with long periods of remission following initial diagnosis and treatment. What in earlier times was a cancer from which a child was dying is today a cancer with which a child is living. Cancer has, in effect, become a chronic life-threatening illness. This has created a new set of issues for children with cancer and their families. Correspondingly, newer studies have focused on the nature of the problems and ways in which the child and family can be supported (e.g., Dowell, Copeland, & van Eys, 1988; Koocher & O'Malley, 1981).

Children with cancer live in two very different worlds. One is the medical world, in which they must face the threat of relapse and death and endure often painful treatments with side effects (e.g., vomiting, loss of hair, and bodily disfigurement) that may be more difficult to cope with than the illness itself. The other is the social world of home and school, in which the child has to maintain relationships and function successfully. Zeltzer (1988) and others have pointed to the difficulty of moving back and forth between these worlds and trying to integrate them.

A number of factors influence the degree to which such integration is achievable. Obviously, the predictability of the course of illness is an important factor: It is easier to adjust when there is a stable prognosis. How the child perceives the severity of the illness is another factor. At least four major coping tasks for the child can be identified:

1   To create a normal life in the face of uncertainty.
2   To develop effective coping strategies for illness-related distress.
3   To maintain positive self-esteem and personal identity.
4   To maintain positive relationships with parents, caregivers, peers, and teachers.

Each task involves subtasks and challenges. For instance, coping with illness-related problems involves managing the pain of treatment and other medical procedures. Pain may be eased if the child learns skills such as anticipation and mental rehearsal and relaxation exercises.

None of the tasks the child with cancer faces can be easily accomplished without support from family, the medical team, and the community, but the first task may be the most challenging. Creating a new life under conditions of uncertainty involves a search for meaning and purpose. In addition, it requires major life restructurings, such as modifying goals, setting new priorities, and returning to school and as much as possible to normal social activities. The second task involves coping with the pain of medical procedures, disfigurement, and other negative physical consequences; dealing with disruptions and inconveniences; managing negative feelings such as anger, depression, and despair; and maintaining a sense of control. The third task requires looking beyond the body to the mental and spiritual aspects of personhood. This is difficult for young people, in whom personal identity is closely linked with the one concrete aspect of the self, the body. Most children have to overcome a perception of themselves as a freak or at least different, a difficult thing to do in late childhood and adolescence, when the need to be like peers is strong. They also have to learn to accept the body they have. This task is immensely facilitated when the child is able to resume a normal life and receives positive feedback from others. The fourth task requires the young person to learn to interact with divergent sets of people, all probably finding it uncomfortable to talk about the child's condition and all making different demands. Parents often become overbearing in their desire to assist. Peers may be protective, awkward, or insensitive. With respect to medical staff, it is easy for the child to displace his or her anger and hostility onto caregivers. But caregivers are human too, and it is in the child's best interest to maintain positive relationships with the medical care team.

In addition to instrumental and emotional support from the family, a variety of other social supports are needed to help both the child and family. Social support is complex to begin with—to set up and operate several diverse support systems is a considerable challenge. For example, families may need financial assistance and assistance with transportation when frequent visits to the hospital are required. Spiritual support, psychological counseling, and friendship networks are other support systems that may help lighten the child's and family's burden. Chesler and Barbarin (1987) and Chesler (1988) suggested that the key to successful supports is careful communication and coordination among the systems, in which the child's needs and each system's capabilities are assessed and matched. They identified a number of major stressors and the forms of social support that may be useful in alleviating them.

Childhood Bereavement

Next to a child's own impending death, the most hurtful and distressing loss is the death of a parent. Fortunately, psychologists have recognized that children do experience feelings of loss and grief, and, in the past decade or so, researchers have begun to study the dynamics of bereavement in childhood and adolescence. Their findings form the basis for helping young people cope with their grief.

Responses to a Parent's Death   Acute responses commonly seen in bereaved children may be grouped into three categories: somatic, affective, and behavioral. Common somatic symptoms are sleep and digestive disturbances, dizziness, headache, and tightness in chest and throat. The child may develop an actual illness. For example, gastrointestinal symptoms may reflect an early phase of malabsorption, peptic ulcer, or ileitis. Diabetic and thyroid conditions have also been observed occasionally. Uncontrolled sobbing is frequent (Van Eerdewegh, Bieri, Parilla, & Clayton, 1982; Wessel, 1984). Affectively, children are stunned, shocked, and confused and experience feelings of depression, anxiety, anger, and guilt. They report feelings of isolation, embarrassment, and shame. Losses in self-esteem are common. Behaviorally, children often respond to a parent's death with aggression, hostility, or other acting-out behavior or with social withdrawal (boys tend to display the former, and girls tend to display the latter). Academic performance is lower, and children are less able to concentrate and less motivated to study (Kranzler, Shaffer, Wasserman, & Davies, 1990; Silverman & Worden, 1992; Van Eerdewegh et al., 1982).

In the psychoanalytic literature, one of the denial coping mechanisms identified in bereaved children is the fantasy of reunion with the dead parent or hallucination of the dead parent's presence (Elizur & Kaffman, 1983). Although according to traditional psychoanalytic thinking such fantasy is a maladaptive response that prevents proper grief work, new findings suggest differently. In their extensive longitudinal study of parental bereavement in childhood, Silverman, Nickman, and Worden (1992) found that children experienced and maintained active connections with their dead parents. Most of the predominantly Catholic children believed their dead parent to be in heaven watching them or guiding them in a benevolent way. Many dreamed about their dead parents, regularly spoke to them, and felt close to them when visiting the grave. The authors viewed these cognitive constructions of parents as dynamic and interactive and concluded that they facilitated children's coping with their loss and thus may be normal, rather than pathological. Other researchers, such as Klass (see Chapter 10) have reported such connections with the deceased in bereaved adults as well.

Developmental Factors   Early suggestions by psychoanalysts that children are unable to grieve emotionally until adolescence have proved to be incorrect. Children at young ages can and do grieve. Bowlby (1960, 1980) found that even infants experience separation anxiety and respond to separation with protest and despair. Similar responses have been observed in monkeys, suggesting that there may be a biological basis for grief (Laudenslager, Boccia, & Reite, 1993). Even if these behaviors do not fit current theoretical definitions of grief, they are responses to loss in the context of attachment theory.

The child's level of cognitive functioning does, however, contribute significantly to the ability to grieve. Children with immature understandings of death are bewildered and frightened, believing that the parent left voluntarily, perhaps in anger, and will return. The child may fear that the other parent will also disappear, leaving the child alone and abandoned. Furman (1984) and others have stressed the need for careful, repeated explanations and discussions with the child that may extend over a period of weeks and months. These explanations should stress the following: The parent did not die on purpose. He (or she) could not help it. It is not the child's fault (or the other parent's, or the doctor's) that the parent died. The parent did not want to die and was not angry at the child. Such explanations, coupled with caring attention and reassurance, may help the child to realize what happened and learn to cope.

Kranzler et al. (1990) found that children as young as 3 years old, especially girls, were able to express emotions of grief. However, Silverman and Worden

(1992), studying a larger, more representative sample, suggested that children often are not sure what they feel or are unable to articulate their feelings. In discussions with young bereaved children, therefore, it may be helpful to include statements referring to feelings, such as "We are all very, very sad. We will be sad for a long time. We miss Daddy very much. We will always remember him. It's alright to cry, to play and have fun. Daddy would want you to have fun. He loved you very much" (Wass, 1984b). Drawing and painting may be an effective mode for young children for expressing grief-related emotions, such as fear, sadness, and anger (B. B. McIntire, 1990).

The child's level of personality development and life experience are additional factors affecting grief. Obviously, the younger a child, the less likely it is that he or she has had to cope with a loss before and thus the fewer the coping skills available. By this reasoning, adolescents should be able to cope better than children at younger ages. This is not necessarily the case, however. It has been suggested that younger children simply use more "primitive" mechanisms for coping, such as denial and regression. While adolescents may be less able to deny their loss and less able to regress, and thus may have to confront their experiences more directly, they are more likely than young children to have friends and classmates to whom they can turn for support.

The Role of Parents   A number of early studies suggest that losing a parent in childhood may cause or contribute to the development of psychiatric disorders in adulthood. For example, early parental bereavement was identified by Watt and Nicholi (1979) as a causal factor in schizophrenia. Other researchers identified family stability after the death as the critical determinant in the development or prevention of adult psychopathology (Fristad, Jedel, Weller, & Weller, 1993). Similarly, Kranzler et al. (1990), in a prospective study of preschool children, found that the surviving parent's psychiatric status was the significant mediator in the child's adjustment to the loss. In a multiple regression analysis comparing the bereaved group and a nonbereaved control group on a number of measures, the researchers found that once parental depression was controlled for, differences between the bereaved and nonbereaved group were no longer significant.

These findings essentially confirm those obtained by Furman (1974) in her groundbreaking work on bereaved children. She suggested that the child is particularly vulnerable to maladaptation after a parent's death because of the child's dependency on parents for basic security and care. This suggests that the surviving parent's ability to cope successfully with his or her own grief and the parent's capacity to provide for the emotional and instrumental needs of the child are critical factors influencing grief outcome.

On the basis of recent findings it can be concluded that most parental deaths in childhood and adolescence do not lead to psychiatric problems. Young people are hardy and resilient, are able to cope with adversity, and have an innate need to grow and achieve their developmental tasks (Masten, Best, & Garmezy, 1990).

With support from the surviving parent and other caring adults, and otherwise optimal conditions, such as physical health and a stable environment, children may resolve their grief over a parent's death without prolonged difficulties.

Responses to a Sibling's Death The death of a sibling may be as traumatic as the death of a parent. A parent's death threatens the child's sense of security, of being cared for. The death of a sibling informs a child, perhaps for the first time, of his or her own vulnerability, arousing in the child dread and fear for his or her own life. Balk (1983) interviewed adolescents whose sibling had died 4–84 months earlier. Responses reported by these adolescents were similar to those reported by children and adolescents who had lost a parent. Most of the bereaved adolescents reported thinking often about the dead sibling, most reported anniversary reactions, and about half had had experiences in which the dead sibling appeared or spoke to them. Most also reported having problems with schoolwork. Other researchers have found that bereaved siblings frequently feel anger and guilt about being survivors, feel isolated and unable to share their grief, and feel neglected by their parents (Coleman & Coleman, 1984).

In a longitudinal study of children 3 years after the death of a brother or sister, Davies (1987) found that more than half the children were still unhappy, sad, and depressed and preferred to be alone. A third still showed somatic symptoms, such as problems with sleeping, nightmares, and walking or talking in their sleep. And a third did poorly in school. In a follow-up study 7–9 years after the death, Martinson, Davies, and McClowry (1987) found that dreaming about siblings now tended to be comforting, and although loneliness and sorrow persisted, they were no longer problematic issues. Most siblings were still thinking about their deceased siblings at least once a day, and most reported that they had grown in maturity and gained a better appreciation of life as a result of their experience. Taking a closer look at siblings with persistent low self-esteem, these authors found that the parents of these children tended to compare them unfavorably with the deceased child. Parents may be wrapped up in their own grief and pain and may indeed be unavailable to children, unintentionally signaling to the surviving child that he or she is of less worth than the deceased sibling.

The Family System Although parents' important role in helping a child grieve is stressed by most psychologists, the effects of the family system on a child's grieving have not been adequately explored. Hare-Mustin (1979) suggested that the death of a family member may seriously unbalance the role relationships among its members, affecting the entire system. In addition, families have their own characteristic patterns of interaction and unspoken key themes that affect how children respond and adapt to crisis. Raphael (1983) has identified several distinct patterns and themes. For example, in some families, there is no intimacy. When a family member dies, parents keep distant and aloof. Feelings are hidden. The message is "Be brave." In other families, death is taboo. When someone dies, parents are silent and secretive. Expressions of grief are not tolerated. Still other families function with openness and warmth. In such a family, a death is a family crisis. Pain, anger, sadness, and other feelings are shared, and the family pulls together. Obviously, the last pattern generally enhances the grieving process, whereas the former two hinder it. The members of a family also have their own individual patterns of behavior and their own strategies and styles of coping. Different members may cope differently, creating difficulties and confusion for the child.

Support for Parent and Child   Some obvious differences between bereaved children and bereaved adults have implications for helping children cope with bereavement. Children are more dependent; are less mature, with less life experience and fewer coping skills; are less able to articulate their emotions; and often lack resources and a network of social support. In addition, it is important to remember that when a child loses a parent, the surviving parent has to deal with the loss of the spouse. And when a child's sibling dies, the parent has to grieve for a child. An extensive research literature on spousal bereavement attests to the difficulties adults may have in coping with such a loss (e.g., Sanders, 1989; Stroebe & Stroebe, 1993). Likewise, the literature on the death of a child indicates the special hardships these deaths impose (e.g., Rando, 1986; Rubin, 1993). The findings on parents' bereavement alone provide a picture of the potential problems the bereaved child faces. From studies of bereaved children it is apparent that parents, or other caring persons in the family, constitute the child's main source of instrumental and emotional support. Therefore, any support that bereaved parents receive benefits the child as well. Family therapy, self-help groups such as Compassionate Friends and Widow-to-Widow, and hospice-sponsored bereavement follow-up programs for adults have been shown to assist indirectly the bereaved child. More recently, hospice programs, hospitals, and community volunteers have begun to offer group support programs for children. In addition, bereavement support is increasingly offered in schools, either in group sessions or on an individual basis (Wass, Miller, & Thornton, 1990). Individual therapy, of course, is recommended for children with persistent problems. But judging from the studies cited in this chapter, it may be the parent who needs therapy. Often, both parents and child benefit from family therapy.

Often, parents have the emotional strength needed to help their child grieve but lack information about bereaved children's needs. Various organizations and agencies, including hospice programs, can offer practical guidelines and resources. There are also books that parents and other helpers may consult (e.g., Corr & McNeil, 1986; Grollman, 1990; Wass & Corr, 1984). Essentially, at all ages, children need reassurances that they will be cared for and cherished as before the death and demonstrations of such care and love. Open communication in the family, including honest answers and explanations, and open expression and sharing of grief are of critical importance.

Suicide

In the past, most professionals believed that children do not have a mature understanding of the finality and irreversibility of death and therefore cannot commit suicide. When young children died by their own hand, it was thought to be an accident. More recently, however, researchers have found that children experience the same type of depression, hopelessness, and cognitive rigidity that lead to suicidal behavior in adults. Children's suicidal actions most frequently are attempts to escape from psychologically or physically painful life situations, particularly pathological families (Pfeffer, 1984). Orbach and others have proposed that a child is most likely to commit suicide when he or she experiences rejection, is confronted with unsolvable problems, suffers multiple losses, and in other ways develops a generalized negative attitude that Orbach et al. (1981) have called "repulsion by life." When this attitude is accompanied by an immature glorification of death as a condition that will meet more of the child's needs, result in the child's rejoining a dead loved one, or reduce the child's psychological pain, then the child develops an attraction to death, and the inclination toward suicide is increased (Orbach et al., 1981a), even in preschool children (Rosenthal & Rosenthal, 1984). Others point to inherited biological imbalances as causal factors in child and adolescent suicide.

Regardless of the reasons why children attempt and commit suicide, it is a growing phenomenon in American society. In 1990, the suicide rate among children ages 5–14 was 0.7 per 100,000. This is an increase of 133% since 1970, when child suicides were officially reported for the first time. Although completed suicide in children may be seen as relatively rare, other suicidal behavior is not. Pfeffer, Conte, Plutnick, & Jerrett (1980), for example, found that one third of a randomly selected outpatient group had thought about, threatened, or attempted suicide. The actual incidence of all suicidal behavior is believed to be much higher (Berman & Carroll, 1984).

Suicide among adolescents has increased dramatically. The rates for adolescents 15–19 years of age quadrupled from 1950 to 1980. It is currently the third leading cause of death among young people, preceded only by accidents and homicides, and is 5 times more common among young males than among young females (Curran, 1987; Secretary's Task Force, 1989). These rates are all the more disturbing when they are compared with those of older age groups, which have steadily decreased in the past three decades.

Other suicidal behavior is even more frequent in adolescents. The school-based National Youth Risk Behavior Survey indicated that approximately 27% of the high school students surveyed had thought about committing suicide at least once in the 12 months preceding the survey, 16% had made specific plans, 8% had made at least one attempt, and 2% had required medical attention following an attempt (estimated to be more than a quarter of a million students) (Dick, 1992).

Signs and Symptoms of Suicidal Thought

Given this evidence of increasing suicide risk, it is important for caregivers to develop a working knowledge about child and adolescent suicide. It is now widely agreed that most suicide attempts are prefaced by certain changes in the young person. These changes can be grouped into four main categories: physical, cognitive, affective, and behavioral. Physical changes include increased frequency of somatic symptoms, such as headaches and digestive upsets; self-neglect; a general slowing down of movement; and a general appearance of unhappiness and lack of interest. Cognitive changes encompass increased rigidity and negativeness of thoughts, loss of interest in surroundings and activities, preoccupation with suicidal thoughts, and formulation of suicide plans. Affective changes include increased feelings of hopelessness, helplessness, guilt, shame, and remorse, as well as an overall decrease in self-esteem and a general loss of pleasure in life manifested in sadness, crying, and increased irritability. Behavioral changes may take the form of appetite disturbances, sleep difficulties, the giving away of possessions, increased use of alcohol or drugs, discussion of suicide, and increased social isolation. Because late childhood and adolescence are characterized by turbulent change, it is often difficult to distinguish between the painful process of maturing within normal limits and the changes that signal the beginning of suicidal thoughts (Hollinger, 1978; Peck, 1984). Nevertheless, it is widely believed that most suicidal people give friends and family members clear clues about their intention to kill themselves.

Approaches to Intervention

Recent developments in suicide intervention have focused on illuminating the breadth and specificity of young people's suicidal thoughts (see Chapter 14). The old caution against discussing suicide with troubled youth because it might give them ideas has been replaced with an emphasis on discovering the existence of such ideas. Directing specific questions to a young person who exhibits signs of suicidal thinking is now a prescribed approach. Questions should be asked in a supportive, nonjudgmental manner, but they should be direct to shed light on the specificity of the suicidal ideas, such as available methods and ideas about time. A young person who has decided to attempt suicide but has no real plan is less at risk than one who has decided to attempt suicide by taking pills, has collected the pills, and has placed them under the mattress. The persistence of the suicidal thoughts and the young person's ability or inability to control them should also be ascertained. An occasional suicidal thought is far less serious than being flooded with suicidal ideas that will leave the young person feeling vulnerable and helpless. Feelings should also be examined. Young people who feel ashamed of their suicidal thoughts or who admit being ambivalent are easier to work with than those who feel resignation or anticipation when thinking about suicide. Determining whether the young person wants help and what sources of support and help are available to him or her may also alleviate a suicide situation. Finally, it is important to determine whether the young person can envision a personal future. Those who can are at less risk than those who feel hopeless about the future and helpless in the present. Obviously, working with suicidal young people requires patience, the ability to listen and be supportive, and the willingness to engage the help of other professionals in the treatment process.

Fortunately, a great deal of progress has been made in the treatment of suicidal young people. Such psychological approaches as cognitive restructuring and behavioral strategies have been used with good results. Cognitive restructuring involves identifying the persistent thoughts that cause feelings of depression and training the young person to recognize that the thoughts are distortions of reality and to neutralize them by disputing them rationally (Beck, Rush, Shaw, & Emery, 1979). Behavioral strategies frequently involve physical exercise or the monitoring of diet to help ensure change between therapy sessions (Beck, 1970). Biological treatments for depression, such as the tricyclic antidepressants, the monoamine oxidase inhibitors, the serotonin-specific reuptake inhibitors, and the limited electroconvulsive shock therapies, offer promise to severely depressed people who do not respond to psychological approaches (Beck, 1967; Korn, Brown, Apter, & van Praag, 1990). A combination of biological and psychological approaches may well prove to be the most effective approach to reaching suicidal youth (Berman & Jobes, 1991; Lester, 1990).

Another area of research may help professionals understand how children and young people view suicide. Stillion and her associates have studied the extent to which young people sympathize, empathize, and agree with suicidal target figures in a variety of problem situations. Stillion, McDowell, and Shamblin (1984) found that female high school students expressed more sympathy toward suicidal target figures than did males. Females also sympathized, empathized, and agreed more with female target figures than with male target figures. In addition, agreement scores correlated positively with depression scores and negatively with self-esteem scores, indicating that the young people who agreed with the behaviors of the suicidal target figure were more depressed and valued themselves less than did those who did not agree. Comparing attitudes toward suicide among 9th- and 12th-grade students and sophomores in college, Stillion, McDowell, and May (1984) found that the older the adolescent, the less agreement there was with suicidal actions. The overall pattern emerging from these and other studies suggests that older, intellectually brighter, mentally healthy people view suicidal actions more negatively than do younger, less intellectually gifted, and less mentally healthy people and that females are more likely than males to sympathize with suicidal actions (Stillion, McDowell, & May, 1989; Stillion, McDowell, Smith, & McCoy, 1986).

Although much has been written on the topic of suicide, it remains a subject obscured by myth and misunderstanding. Still, it is important to develop education and prevention programs for use in both the home and school. Such programs must recognize that suicidal people generally give warnings about their state of mind and intended actions, that suicide threats must be taken seriously and dealt with in a forthright manner, that intervention in suicide plans is often an effective permanent treatment, and that suicidal young people can frequently be helped by a combination of physical and psychological treatment. Parents and educators dealing with young people can immunize them against suicide by teaching them specific techniques for coping with the inevitably painful and negative experiences of life. Stress reduction and cognitive restructuring techniques are relatively easy to learn. Promoting the use of humor as an aid for maintaining perspective is another approach that can be taught both at home and at school. Encouraging young people to share their frustrations and concerns with supportive, understanding adults who will listen and help them explore options is perhaps the most important method of reaching out to suicidal youth.

A number of programs in crisis intervention and postvention in schools have recently been developed and evaluated (Leenaars & Wenckstern, 1991). Most state departments of education in the United States now mandate suicide intervention programs for public schools, and, according to one recent survey, approximately one fourth of American schools do offer some type of crisis intervention (Wass et al., 1990), although the extent and relative effectiveness of these programs have yet to be determined.

There is also a need to develop school-based prevention programs. Such programs are more difficult to introduce because there is no precipitating event, no crisis to which to respond. Furthermore, prevention education needs to be carried out by regular staff and faculty. There are a number of obstacles to suicide prevention that need to be overcome, as there are to AIDS education in public schools.

It is widely recognized that the rates of suicide attempts, threats, gestures, and ideation are greatly underestimated. One of the problems with many current suicide prevention efforts may be their narrow scope. Large numbers of young people are obviously at risk for suicidal behavior. Similarly, a large number of youths are at risk for drug and alcohol abuse and for becoming HIV infected. Perhaps *all* youth can be considered at some risk and can benefit from preventive measures that ensure positive self-regard; positive and constructive family experiences; and successful social, cultural, academic, and vocational lives for every person.

Homicide

Violent and homicidal behavior among young people has been rising in the United States at accelerated rates as well. Seventeen percent of all people arrested for violent crimes are youths (Cantrowitz, 1993). Between 1985 and 1991, arrests made for homicide among 17-year-olds increased 121%. The rate increase was almost double this for 15- to 16-year-olds. Ewing (1990) reported that, according to FBI statistics, among 13- to 16-year-olds, there were 551 arrests for murder in 1984. This number jumped to 891 in 1988 and 1,500 in 1991—the highest in history.

A disturbing aspect of this phenomenon is that although the statistics are certainly intolerable and clearly demonstrate that a severe social problem exists, the high degree of publicity given to youth homicide by the media distorts the actual incidence, compounding fears and panic reactions. For example, the publicity surrounding the tourist murders in Florida in 1993 resulted in an immediate rise in applications for concealed weapons permits.

Such publicity also has positive consequences. For example, the publicity given to the shooting of tourists in Florida and subsequent arrests of adolescent suspects alerted the public to the fact that in most states it is not illegal for minors to carry guns. In Florida, despite efforts on the part of many, the apparent lobbying power of the National Rifle Association (NRA) was until now strong enough to prevent gun control legislation. The recent shootings and the international attention given to them have made new, powerful enemies for the NRA, such as the Walt Disney Corporation in Orlando and the tourism industry.

The publicity given to adolescent homicide also reveals the problems in the juvenile justice system, which in many states is greatly underfunded. For example, the 13-year-old boy arrested for the killing of a British tourist had a history of 16 prior arrests and more than 50 felony charges. Yet, apparently the nature of his crimes had not qualified him to become a resident in a youth detention center or to receive other therapeutic interventions. Some authorities point out that juvenile crime is not nearly as widespread as it appears, but that a relatively small number of youths are repeat offenders with whom the system is not prepared to deal.

Because of public outrage, an increasing number of state legislators are introducing stricter crime prevention laws. It is time for such action. There is compelling evidence that the accessibility of guns to adolescents is highly correlated with criminal assaults. In fact, three fourths of homicides involving adolescents as either victims or perpetrators involve guns (APACVY, 1993).

Youth violence is also related to the drug business and drug abuse, both of which are prevalent in inner-city ghettos and in groups that live in poverty. In a study of 611 serious juvenile delinquents sponsored by the National Institute of Drug Abuse, Inciardi (1990) found that almost all of the youths had extensive histories of multiple drug use and had begun regular use of crack at age 13. Most carried guns. Their records of criminal behavior were astonishing, an average of about 700 offenses per individual.

Youth gangs flourish primarily in inner-city neighborhoods in poverty conditions. Most gang members are young people under age 24, and some of them are as young as 10 years old. It is widely agreed that abuse, neglect, poverty, and a need to belong cause young people to join gangs.

Considering the broader context, it is obvious that there can be no quick fix for this problem. Gun control is certainly an important interventive measure, as is the provision of facilities and programs such as youth detention centers and community service to get young people off the streets and to halt the upward spiral of antisocial behavior. But to prevent homicidal and other violent behavior in youth from occurring in the first place, the problem must be attacked at its root.

The recommendations for intervention and long-term prevention recently made by the APACVY (1993) include programs directed toward parents, schools, child care and health care providers, police departments, and community leaders. The Centers for Disease Control are funding studies of the efficacy of various prevention programs. Private foundations are establishing grants for programs that combat juvenile violence.

Among primary prevention programs for at-risk children and youth, the APACVY recommended home visitor, preschool, and school-based programs that foster the development of prosocial and cognitive skills. Recommended secondary prevention programs included working with the family to eliminate domestic violence and physical and sexual abuse in the home, treating children with symptoms of posttraumatic stress syndrome, and treating youthful offenders.

Community-based programs to reduce crime in inner-city neighborhoods, such as community revitalization at the grassroots level and private-sector initiatives, have been developed in the past and have been effective. In addition, job programs, in-school training for jobs, senior volunteer programs to prevent school dropout, Head Start, and drug counseling are just some of the initiatives that can improve children's chances for developing prosocial and vocational skills. An important aspect of effective intervention is its multipronged approach, in which components complement and reinforce one another so that all agencies in the child's everyday life—family, school, community, and media—are embraced.

CONCLUSION

Encounters with death in some form and at some level of emotional intensity are inevitable during the formative years. In part because of recognition of this fact, empirical studies and clinical observations focusing on such encounters have increased substantially in the recent past. The results of these efforts have led to better understandings of how young people assimilate, respond to, and cope with death-related experiences. In turn, professional helpers have become more sensitive to young people's needs and have developed various ways of providing effective care and support for those who are directly affected by death, through either life-threatening illness or the loss of a loved one.

Continued efforts are needed to improve early identification of young people at risk for suicidal behaviors and to provide intervention and support at various levels: directly through treatment and support for the involved individuals by community mental health agencies and interventions in the schools, and indirectly through support for the family. Crisis intervention programs in the community, especially in the public schools, remain challenging tasks for the future. An equally important task is to involve school staffs, especially teachers and curriculum specialists, more actively and broadly in efforts to prevent self-destructive behavior. Record increases in juvenile homicidal behavior have become highlighted through the national press. Improved efforts in intervention at the community, state, and federal levels are needed.

The apparent preoccupation with violent death in the popular culture has made social scientists, child advocates, and others more aware of the harmful and potentially harmful effects such indirect experiences have on the young. Professionals and lay persons alike are asking more urgently for preventive measures by parents through mediation and guidance, by schools through educational programs, by the entertainment industry through self-regulation, and by the government through public policy.

Another challenge ahead is the study of young people's death-related emotions, especially death anxiety. Similarly, young people's basic orientations and attitudes toward death, their view of the world, their outlook on life, and how these attitudes affect their behavior still need to be reliably assessed. Better empirical knowledge about children's feelings, thoughts, and views concerning existential matters may aid the development of effective interventions. For example, knowledge of young people's attitudes and orientations toward life and death may point us toward explanations of young people's risk-taking behavior with respect to sex, drug use, and suicidal behaviors.

Also remaining is the challenge for teachers or others who deal with children and adolescents to provide systematic and authoritative education about death, dying, and bereavement appropriate to children's developmental stages. The data show that even at early ages, children are curious about death and dying. Such curiosity is normal and healthy. Evasive answers and silence can be more harmful than the facts. In addition, parents, teachers, and health professionals need to help young people acquire skills for managing fears, anxieties, and other emotions and thoughts related to death and loss.

REFERENCES

American Psychological Association Commission on Violence and Youth. (1993). *Violence and youth: Psychology's response* (Vol. 1). Washington, DC: American Psychological Association.

Armstrong-Dailey, A. (1991). Hospice care for children, their families and health care providers. In D. Papadatou & C. Papadatos (Eds.), *Children and death* (pp. 225–229). Washington, DC: Hemisphere.

Balk, D. (1983). Effects of sibling death on teenagers. *Journal of School Health, 53,* 14–18.

Bandura, A., & Mischel, M. (1965). Modification of self-imposed delay of reward through exposure to live and symbolic models. *Journal of Personality and Social Psychology, 2,* 698–705.

Beck, A. T. (1967). *Depression: Causes and treatment.* Philadelphia: University of Pennsylvania Press.

Beck, A. T. (1970). Cognitive therapy: Nature and relation to behavior therapy. *Behavior Therapy, 1,* 184–200.

Beck, A. T., Rush, J., Shaw, B., & Emery, G. (1979). *Cognitive therapy of depression.* New York: Guilford Press.

Berman, A. L., & Jobes, A. J. (1991). *Adolescent suicide: Assessment and intervention.* Washington, DC: American Psychological Association.

Bluebond-Langner, M. (1978). *The private worlds of dying children.* Princeton, NJ: Princeton University Press.

Bluebond-Langner, M. (1989). Dying children. In R. Kastenbaum & B. Kastenbaum (Eds.), *Encyclopedia of death* (pp. 46–48). Phoenix, AZ: Oryx Press.

Bowlby, J. (1960). Grief and mourning in infancy and early childhood. *Psychoanalytic Study of the Child, 15,* 9–52.

Bowlby, J. (1980). *Attachment and loss. Vol. 3. Loss, sadness and depression.* New York: Basic Books.

Cantrowitz, B. (1993, August 2). Wild in the streets. *Newsweek,* pp. 40–46.

Carlsson-Paige & Levin, D. E. (1990). *Who's calling the shots? How to respond effectively to children's fascination with war play and war toys.* Philadelphia: New Society Publishers.

Carlson, P., Simacek, M., Henry, W. F., & Martinson, I. D. (1984). Helping parents cope: A model home-care program for the dying child. In H. Wass & C. A. Corr (Eds.), *Childhood and death* (pp. 113–127). Washington, DC: Hemisphere.

Centers for Disease Control. (1991). Weapon-carrying among high school students. *Journal of the American Medical Association, 266,* 2342.

Chaflin, C. J., & Barbarin, O. A. (1991). Does "telling" less protect more? Relationship among age, information disclosure, and what children with cancer see and feel. *Journal of Pediatric Psychology, 16,* 169–191.

Chesler, M. (1988). Community support systems. In R. E. Dowell, D. R. Copeland, & J. van Eys (Eds.), *The child with cancer in the community* (pp. 31–44). Springfield, IL: Charles C Thomas.

Chesler, M., & Barbarin, O. (1987). *Childhood cancer in the family.* New York: Brunner/Mazel.

Coleman, F. W., & Coleman, W. S. (1984). Helping siblings and other peers cope with dying. In H. Wass & C. A. Corr (Eds.), *Childhood and death* (pp. 129–150). Washington, DC: Hemisphere.

Corr, C. A., & McNeil, J. (1986). *Adolescence and death.* New York: Springer Publishing Company.

Csikszentmihalyi, M., & Larson, R. (1984). *Being adolescent: Conflict and growth in the teenage years.* New York: Basic Books.

Curran, D. K. (1987). *Adolescent suicidal behavior.* Washington, DC: Hemisphere.

Davies, E. B. (1987). After a sibling dies. In M. A. Morgan (Ed.), *Bereavement: Helping the survivors. Proceedings of the 1987 King's College Conference.* London, Ontario, Canada: King's College.

DeMuth, B. (1979). Life and death drawings in adolescence. *School Arts, 79,* 42–44.

Dick, L. (1992, March/April). Attempted suicide among high school students. *The Forum,* pp. 10–11.

Dowell, R. E., Copeland, D. R., & van Eys, J. (Eds.). (1988). *The child with cancer in the community.* Springfield, IL: Charles C Thomas.

Elizur, E., & Kaffman, M. (1983). Factors influencing the severity of childhood bereavement reactions. *American Journal of Orthopsychiatry, 53,* 668–676.

Elkind, D. (1981). *The hurried child: Growing up too fast too soon.* Reading, MA: Addison-Wesley.

Ewing, C. P. (1990). *Kids who kill.* Lexington, MA: Lexington Press.

Fristad, M., Jedel, R., Weller, R. A., & Weller, E. B. (1993). Psychosocial functioning in children after the death of a parent. *American Journal of Psychiatry, 150,* 511–513.

Furman, E. (1974). *A child's parent dies.* New Haven, CT: Yale University Press.

Furman, E. (1984). Children's patterns in mourning the death of a loved one. In H. Wass & C. A. Corr (Eds.), *Childhood and death* (pp. 185–203). Washington, DC: Hemisphere.

Gartley, W., & Bernasaconi, M. (1967). The concept of death in children. *Journal of Genetic Psychology, 110,* 71–85.

Gerbner, G., Gross, L., Morgan, M., & Signorelli, N. (1980). The "mainstreaming" of America: Violence Profile No. 11. *Journal of Communication, 30,* 10–29.

Grollman, E. A. (1990). *Talking about death: A dialogue between parent and child.* Boston: Beacon Press.

Hammond, W. R., & Yung, B. (1993). Psychology's role in the public health response to assaultive violence among young Afro-American men. *American Psychologist, 48,* 142–154.

Hare-Mustin, R. T. (1979). Family therapy following the death of a child. *Journal of Marital and Family Therapy, 5,* 51–59.

Heller, D. (1986). *The children's God.* Chicago: University of Chicago Press.

Hollinger, P. C. (1978). Adolescent suicide: An epidemiological study of recent trends. *American Journal of Psychology, 135,* 754–756.

Inciardi, J. A. (1990). Drug use can cause youth violence. In D. L. Bender et al. (Eds.), *Youth violence* (pp. 97–102). San Diego, CA: Greenhaven.

Jenkins, R. A., & Cavanaugh, J. C. (1985). Examining the relationship between the development of the concept of death and overall cognitive development. *Omega, 16,* 193–199.

Katz, E. R., Kellerman, J., & Siegel, S. E. (1980). Behavioral distress in children with cancer undergoing medical procedures: Developmental considerations. *Journal of Counseling and Clinical Psychology, 48,* 356–365.

Koocher, G. P. (1973). Childhood, death, and cognitive development. *Developmental Psychology, 9,* 369–375.

Koocher, G. P., & DeMaso, D. R. (1990). Children's competence to consent to medical procedures. *Pediatrician, 17,* 68–73.

Koocher, G. P., & O'Malley, J. E. (1981). *The Damocles syndrome: Psychological consequences of surviving childhood cancer.* New York: McGraw-Hill.

Korn, M. L., Brown, S. L., Apter, A., & van Praag, H. M. (1990). Serotonin and suicide: A functionally dimensional viewpoint. In D. Lester (Ed.), *Current concepts of suicide* (pp. 57–70). Philadelphia: Charles Press.

Kranzler, E. M., Shaffer, D., Wasserman, G., & Davies, M. (1990). Early childhood bereavement. *Journal of the American Academy of Child and Adolescent Psychiatry, 29,* 514–520.

Laudenslager, M. L., Boccia, M. L., & Reite, M. L. (1993). Biobehavioral consequences of loss in nonhuman primates: Individual differences. In M. S. Stroebe, W. Stroebe, & R. O. Hansson (Eds.), *Handbook of bereavement: Theory, research, and intervention* (pp. 129–142). New York: Cambridge University Press.

Leenaars, A. A., & Wenckstern, S. (Eds.). (1991). *Suicide prevention in schools.* Washington, DC: Hemisphere.

Lester, D. (Ed.). (1990). *Current concepts of suicide.* Philadelphia: Charles Press.

Leviton, D. (Ed.). (1991). *Horrendous death and health: Toward action.* Washington, DC: Hemisphere.

Lonetto, R. (1980). *Children's conceptions of death.* New York: Springer Publishing Company.

Lore, R. K., & Schultz, L. A. (1993). Control of human aggression. *American Psychologist, 48,* 1, 16–25.

Martinson, I. M., et al. (1978). Home care for children dying of cancer. *Pediatrics, 62,* 106–113.

Martinson, I. M., Davies, E., & McClowry, S. G. (1987). The long-term effect of sibling death on self concept. *Journal of Pediatric Nursing, 2,* 227–235.

Masten, A., Best, K. M., & Garmezy, N. (1990). Resilience and development: Contributions from the study of children who overcome adversity. *Developmental Psychopathology, 2,* 425–444.

McIntire, B. B. (1990). Art therapy with bereaved youth. *Journal of Palliative Care, 6,* 16–23.

Montemeyer, R. (1986). Family variation in parent-adolescent storm and stress. *Journal of Adolescent Research, 1,* 15–31.

Morgan, M. (1988). Cultivation analysis. In E. Barnow (Ed.), *International encyclopedia of communication* (Vol. 1, pp. 430–433). New York: Oxford University Press.

Mulhern, R. K., Lauer, M. E., & Hoffman, R. G. (1983). Death of a child at home or in the hospital: Subsequent psychological adjustment of the family. *Pediatrics, 71,* 743–747.

Nagy, M. (1948). The child's theories concerning death. *Journal of Genetic Psychology, 73,* 3–27.

National Institute of Mental Health. (1982). *Television and behavior: Ten years of scientific progress and implications for the eighties: Vol. 2. Technical reviews.* Washington, DC: U.S. Government Printing Office.

Orbach, I., Glaubman, H., & Gross, Y. (1981). Some common characteristics of latency age suicidal children. *Suicide and Life-Threatening Behavior, 11,* 180–190.

Orbach, I. (1984). Personality characteristics life circumstances, and dynamics of suicidal children. *Death Education, 8* (Suppl.), 37–52.

Peck, M. (1984). Youth suicide. In H. Wass & C. A. Corr (Eds.), *Childhood and death* (pp. 279–290). Washington, DC: Hemisphere.

Pfeffer, C. R. (1984). Death preoccupation and suicidal behavior in children. In H. Wass & C. A. Corr (Eds.), *Childhood and death* (pp. 261–278). Washington, DC: Hemisphere.

Pfeffer, C. R., Conte, H. R., Plutnick, & Jerrett, I. (1980). Suicidal behavior in latency age children: An outpatient population. *Journal of the American Academy of Child Psychiatry, 19,* 703–711.

Piaget, J. (1965). *The child's conception of the world.* C.K. Ogden (Ed.). Totowa, N.J.: Littlefield, Adams.

Rando, T. A. (Ed.). (1986). *Parental loss of a child.* Champaign, IL: Research Press.

Raphael, B. (1983). *The anatomy of bereavement.* New York: Basic Books.

Rosenthal, P. A., & Rosenthal, S. (1984). Suicidal behavior by preschool children. *American Journal of Psychiatry, 141,* 520–525.

Rubin, S. S. (1993). The death of a child is forever: The life course impact of child loss. In M. S. Stroebe, W. Stroebe, & R. O. Hansson (Eds.), *Handbook of bereavement: Theory, research, and intervention* (pp. 285–299). New York: Cambridge University Press.

Sanders, C. M. (1989). *Grief: The mourning after.* New York: Wiley.

Secretary's Task Force. (1989). *Report of the Task Force on Youth Suicide* (Vol. 1). Washington, DC: U.S. Department of Health and Human Services.

Silverman, P. R., Nickman, S., & Worden, J. W. (1992). Detachment revisited: The child's reconstruction of a dead parent. *American Journal of Orthopsychiatry, 62,* 494–503.

Silverman, P. R., & Worden, J. M. (1992). Children's reactions in the early months after the death of a parent. *American Journal of Orthopsychiatry, 62,* 93–104.

Singer, J. L. (1983). Cognitive and affective aspects of television: Introductory comments. In D. Pearl, L. Bouthilet, & J. Lazar (Eds.), *Television and behavior: Ten years of scientific progress and implications for the eighties* (pp. 2–8). Washington, DC: U.S. Government Printing Office.

Speece, M. W., & Brent, S. B. (1984). Children's understanding of death: A review of review of three components of a death concept. *Child Development, 55,* 1671–1686.

Speece, M. W., & Brent, S. B. (1992). The acquisition of a mature understanding of three components of the concept of death. *Death Studies, 16,* 2, 211–229.

Spinetta, J. J., & Maloney, L. J. (1974). Death anxiety in the outpatient leukemia child. *Pediatrics, 65,* 1034–1037.

Stillion, J. M., McDowell, E. E., & May, J. H. (1984). Developmental trends and sex differences in adolescent attitudes toward suicide. *Death Education, 8* (Suppl.), 81–90.

Stillion, J. M., McDowell, E. E., & May, J. H. (1989). *Suicide across the life span: Premature exits.* Washington, DC: Hemisphere.

Stillion, J. M., McDowell, E. E., & Shamblin, J. R. (1984). The Suicide Attitude Vignette Experience: A method for measuring adolescent attitudes toward suicide. *Death Education, 8* (Suppl.), 65–79.

Stillion, J. M., McDowell, E. E., Smith, R. T., & McCoy, P. A. (1986). Relationships between suicide attitudes and indicators of mental health among adolescents. *Death Studies, 10,* 289–296.

Stroebe, M. S., Stroebe, W., & Hannsson, R. O. (1993). *Handbook of bereavement: Theory, research, and intervention.* New York: Cambridge University Press.

Surgeon General's Scientific Advisory Committee Report on Television and Social Behavior. (1972). *Television and growing up: The impact of televised violence.* Washington, DC: U.S. Government Printing Office.

Susman, E. J., Dorn, L. D., & Fletcher, J. (1987). Reasoning about illness in ill and healthy children and adolescents: Cognitive and emotional developmental aspects. *Journal of Developmental and Behavioral Pediatrics, 8,* 226–273.

Susman, E. J., Hollenbeck, A. R., Nannis, E. D., & Strope, B. E. (1980). A developmental perspective on psychosocial aspects of childhood cancer. In J. L. Schulman & M. J. Kupsts (Eds.), *The child with cancer* (pp. 129–142). Springfield, IL: Charles C Thomas.

Van Eerdewegh, M. M., Bieri, M. D., Parilla, R. H., & Clayton, P. J. (1982). The bereaved child. *American Journal of Psychiatry, 140,* 23–29.

Vernick, J., & Karon, M. (1965). Who's afraid of death on a leukemia ward? *American Journal of Diseases of Children, 109,* 393–397.

Waechter, E. H. (1984). Dying children: Patterns of coping. In H. Wass & C. A. Corr (Eds.), *Childhood and death* (pp. 59–68). Washington, DC: Hemisphere.

Wass, H. (1984a). Concepts of death: A developmental perspective. In H. Wass & C. A. Corr (Eds.), *Childhood and death* (pp. 3–24). Washington, DC: Hemisphere.

Wass, H. (1984b). Parents, teachers, and health professionals as helpers. In H. Wass & C. A. Corr (Eds.), *Helping children cope with death: Guidelines and resources* (2nd ed., pp. 75–130). Washington, DC: Hemisphere.

Wass, H. (1989). Children and death. In R. Kastenbaum & B. Kastenbaum (Eds.), *Encyclopedia of death* (pp. 49–54). Phoenix, AZ: Oryx Press.

Wass, H., & Cason, L. (1984). Fears and anxieties about death. In H. Wass & C. A. Corr (Eds.), *Childhood and death* (pp. 37–38). Washington, DC: Hemisphere.

Wass, H., & Corr, C. A. (1984). *Helping children cope with death: Guidelines and resources* (2nd ed.). Washington, DC: Hemisphere.

Wass, H., Miller, M. D., & Redditt, C. A. (1991). Adolescents and destructive themes in rock music: A follow-up. *Omega, 23,* 199–206.

Wass, H., Miller, M. D., & Stevenson, R. G. (1989). Factor affecting adolescent behavior and attitudes toward destructive rock lyrics. *Death Studies, 13,* 287–303.

Wass, H., Miller, M. D., & Thornton, G. (1990). Death education and grief/suicide intervention in the public schools. *Death Studies, 14,* 253–268.

Wass, H., Raup, J. L., & Sisler, H. H. (1989). Adolescents and death on television: A follow-up. *Death Studies, 13,* 161–173.

Wass, H., & Scott, M. (1978). Middle school students' death concepts and concerns. *Middle School Journal, 9,* 10–12.

Wass, H., Stillion, J. M., & Fattah, A. F. (1987). Exploding images: Gifted children's view of violence and death on television. In C. A. Corr and R. A. Pacholski (Eds.), *Death: Completion and discovery* (pp. 201–208). Lakewood, OH: Association for Death Education and Counseling.

Watt, N. F., & Nicholi, A. (1979). Early death of a parent as an etiological factor in schizophrenia. *American Journal of Orthopsychiatry, 49,* 465–473.

Weininger, O. (1979). Young children's concepts of dying and dead. *Psychological Reports, 44,* 395–407.

Wenestam, C. G., & Wass, H. (1987). Swedish and U.S. children's thinking about death: A qualitative study and cross-cultural comparison. *Death Studies, 11,* 99–121.

Wessel, M. A. (1984). Helping families: Thoughts of a pediatrician. In H. Wass & C. A. Corr (Eds.), *Childhood and death* (pp. 205–217). Washington, DC: Hemisphere.

Zeltzer, L. K. (1988). Self-perceptions of the child with cancer. In R. E. Dowell, D. R. Copeland, & J. van Eys (Eds.), *The child with cancer in the community* (pp. 5–20). Springfield, IL: Charles C Thomas.

Chapter 12

Death in the Lives of Adults: Responding to the Tolling of the Bell

Judith M. Stillion

Death is inevitable, personal, irreversible. To deny this reality has been interpreted as evidence of immature thinking (e.g., Nagy, 1948; Speece & Brent, 1984; Stillion & Wass, 1979; Wass, 1984). Most adults live in the full realization that they will die, and yet, for most, this knowledge is denied or suppressed on a day-to-day basis. Zilboorg (1943) highlighted this seeming contradiction: "In normal times we move about actually without ever believing in our own death, as if we fully believed in our own corporeal immortality. . . . We are suffused with the awareness that our lives will go on forever" (p. 468). And Becker (1973) proclaimed that all of human striving is an effort to deny death:

Everything that man does in his symbolic world is an attempt to deny and overcome his grotesque fate. He literally drives himself into a blind obliviousness with social games, psychological tricks, personal preoccupations so far removed from the reality of his situation that they are forms of madness—agreed madness, shared madness, disguised and dignified madness, but madness all the same. (p. 27)

Because most adults are so skilled in denying death in their own personal lives, their first contact with the death of a person they love or with their own personal mortality may come as a shock.

In this chapter, the impact of death on the lives of adults is examined. After a discussion of the increase in human longevity across the 20th century, each generation of adults currently living is examined in terms of how death-related events occurring during their lifetimes have affected their attitudes toward death. Finally, the special losses likely to occur during each of the periods of the adult life span are reviewed.

CHANGING PATTERNS OF DEATH IN THE 20TH CENTURY

Death is a reality in the lives of adults. In young adulthood, it may still be regarded as a stranger, but by old age, it has come to be viewed as a frequent, if unwelcome, companion on life's journey. Figure 1 makes this point clearly. As shown, after the relatively high death rates during the first year of life, the rate of mortality decreases dramatically. However, after childhood, the rate of mortality increases consistently and in a geometric fashion across the life span.

Although the reality of death remains a constant in the lives of today's adults, much of its substance has changed across the 20th century, including its causes, the timing of its appearance in the lives of most adults, and the way in which its approach is treated both by the medical establishment and by individuals.

In 1900, in the United States, the 10 leading causes of death were influenza and pneumonia; tuberculosis; diseases of the heart; diarrhea and enteritis (under 2 years); nephritis, accident and unspecified causes; cerebral hemorrhage and softening, thrombosis, and embolism; cancer and malignant tumors; diphtheria; and typhoid and paratyphoid fever. Figure 2 shows the death rates for the six major causes of death in 1900 and how they have changed across this century.

It is clear from Figure 2 that the causes of death among adults have changed enormously in the past century. Some causes of death across the adult years, such as tuberculosis, have been nearly vanquished, and others, such as influenza, have become less fatal because of newer treatment approaches. Other causes of death have been reclassified. Thus, in 1991, the six leading causes of death were diseases of the heart, malignant neoplasms (cancer), cerebrovascular diseases, chronic obstructive pulmonary diseases, accidents, and pneumonia and influenza.

In addition to changes in the causes of death, there has been a significant change in life expectancy across the 20th century. The U.S. Department of Health and Human Services has noted that "the average life expectancy at birth has increased by 28 years since 1900 (National Center for Health Statistics, 1992).

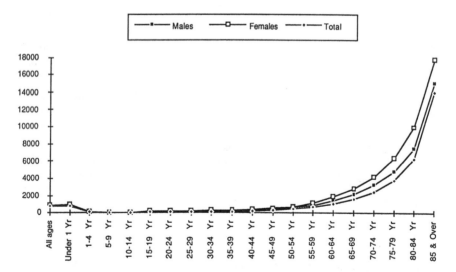

Figure 1   Death rates by age and sex in the United States in 1991 (rates per 100,000 population). Figures for ages not stated are included in "All ages" but are not distributed among age groups. Death rates for infants under 1 year differ from infant mortality rates. The former are based on population estimates, and the latter are based on live births.

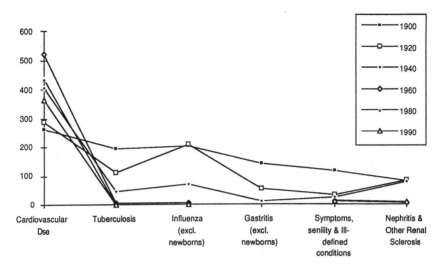

Figure 2   U.S. death rate, 1900 to 1990 (per 100,000 population). Note that the category "nephritis and other renal sclerosis" later became "nephritis, nephrotic syndrome, and nephrosis" and that in 1980 and 1990 "senility" was omitted from its category. Data are from the U.S. Bureau of the Census (1922, 1955, 1992). Dse = disease.

Americans born between 1900 and 1902 could expect to live to be 48 years of age. People born in 1920 could expect to have approximately 56 years of life. People born in 1940 had a life expectancy of nearly 63 years. By 1960, life expectancy had increased to 67.5 and by 1980, it was nearly 71 years (*Information Please Almanac*, 1993). People born in 1990 in the United States can expect to live to approximately 75.4 years of age, depending on their sex.

Females born in 1990 can expect to live to be 78.8, whereas males born in 1990 can expect only 72.0 years of life. The sex differential in life expectancy increased from just 1 year in 1920 to 6.8 years in 1990 in favor of females. The disparity between the sexes is less among whites than among blacks. White males born in 1990 can expect to live to be 72.6, whereas white females can expect to live to 79.3, a difference of 6.7 years. Among blacks, however, the sex disparity is greater. Black males born in 1990 can expect only 68.4 years of life, whereas black females can expect to live 76.3 years, a difference of 7.9 years.

To place the American statistics on longevity in perspective, Table 1 presents the life expectancy figures for 10 developed nations. It is clear that in many countries (e.g., Pakistan) life expectancy has not been extended much beyond turn-of-the-century figures in the United States, but in other countries (e.g., Japan), life expectancy rates exceed the U.S. rates. It is also obvious from Table 1 that people in economically privileged nations enjoy the additional gift of longevity.

Thus the causes of death and life expectancy figures have changed greatly

Table 1   Life Expectancies by Age and Sex for Selected Countries

Country	Time period of most recent report	Males	Females
North America			
U.S.	1988	71.50	78.30
Canada	1985–1987	73.02	79.79
Mexico	1979	62.10	66.00
Central and South America			
Brazil	1985–1990[a]	62.30	67.50
Guatemala	1979–1980	55.11	59.43
Panama	1985–1990[b]	70.15	74.10
Peru	1980–1985[c]	56.77	66.50
Europe			
Austria	1989[d]	72.09	78.78
France	1988[d]	72.33	80.46
Spain	1980–1982[d]	72.52	78.61
Sweden	1988[d]	74.15	79.96
United Kingdom	1986–1989	72.15	77.88
Asia			
Bangladesh	1988	56.91	55.97
India	1976–1980	52.50	52.10
Japan	1989[e]	75.91	81.77
Korea, South	1989	66.92	74.96
Pakistan	1976–1978	59.04	59.20
Africa			
Egypt	1985–1990[a]	57.80	60.30
South Africa	1985–1990[a]	57.50	63.50
Oceania			
Australia	1989[b,f]	73.30	79.55

Note. These figures are the latest available as of August 1992. They are from the United Nations *Demographic Yearbook, 1990* and reprinted in the *Information Please Almanac* (1993).

[a]Estimates prepared by the Population Division of the United Nations.
[b]Excludes tribal Indian population numbering 62,187 in 1960.
[c]Excludes Indian jungle population.
[d]Complete life tables.
[e]For Japanese nationals in Japan only.
[f]Excludes full-blooded aborigines, estimated at 49,036 in June 1966.

across the 20th century in the United States and the life expectancies of Americans differ from those of other nationalities, largely as a result of economic conditions. It is helpful to keep this context in mind when considering the ways in which current generations of adults face the issue of death in their own lives.

GENERATIONAL DIFFERENCES IN DEATH AMONG ADULTS

In a recent historical society, Strauss and Howe (1991) made a strong case for the argument that overlooking generational differences is a serious flaw in much writing within the social sciences. They maintained that only by examining generational effects in conjunction with other influences can researchers begin to understand generational differences in attitudes and values. They further suggested that it is the "coming of age moment" that is critical in influencing the "peer personality," that is, the way generations see and describe themselves and react to the world around them throughout their generational life span. According to Strauss and Howe, generations, like individuals, are marked for their entire life span by what they encountered in the world during their childhood and at the time they came of age. It follows that researchers who want to understand the way in which adults now living think about death must look at the death-related events that shaped the peer personality of the generation to which they belong.

According to Strauss and Howe (1991), there are five generations of adults alive in the 1990s. These include the old old, who were 90 years old or older in 1990. Members of this generation, dubbed the Lost Generation by historians, were born between 1883 and 1900, and thus their coming-of-age moment was influenced by the massive death tolls accumulated during World War I and the outbreak of influenza that followed the war and took more than 20 million lives worldwide, killing more people than the war did (*World Book Encyclopedia,* 1972). This generation's basic way of viewing the world is "reactive," argued Strauss and Howe, and they have come to elderhood as recluses, maintaining respect but having little influence on society. Extrapolating from this, one might expect that this generation's view of death should also be a reactive one, in which they face death stoically, doing comparatively little to prolong their lives. The much-cited finding that elderly people have less fear of death than do younger people may be a reflection of the fact that the studies done to this date with the elderly have focused mainly on members of this elderly generation, rather than a true finding that death acceptance increases with age (Kalish & Reynolds, 1976; Kastenbaum, 1969; Wass, 1979). Only future research can determine whether increased death acceptance is a generation- or age-related factor.

The second oldest generation alive today is what Strauss and Howe (1991) called the G.I. Generation, born between 1901 and 1924. This generation came of age during World War II. Central to their philosophy is the "can-do" attitude that developed as a result of winning the war as well as experiencing the 40 years of unprecedented growth and positive economic conditions that ensued (Strauss & Howe, 1991). One might hypothesize that this "civic" generation has mainly viewed death as just one more enemy to confront. Rather than react to death with resigned acceptance, this generation has developed the technology, chemistry, and medicine that are largely responsible for the increases in life expectancy that younger generations, as well as their own, enjoy. However, this same can-do, never-say-die attitude is largely what is behind the ethical and economic dilemmas facing Americans today as they try to decide whether to limit access to medical technology and medical care in response to the growing realization that resources are limited. It is also this generation who embraced the conspiracy of silence on the subject of death and dying (see Chapter 11 for a brief discussion of this).

The third generation of adults alive today was called the Silent Generation by Strauss and Howe (1991) and was born between 1925 and 1942. The authors characterized this generation as "adaptive." Its members were children and adolescents during the World War II era. They spent their evenings being hushed by adults as families sat around a radio and listened to Franklin Roosevelt and excited newsmen discuss the fortunes of the war that day. They observed the gold stars in the windows of neighbors who had lost sons or husbands in that war and came to know at an early age that life was serious and dangerous, that death could rain from the skies at any moment. As young adults, they were involved in the Korean conflict. Strauss and Howe suggested that the Korean conflict, not a victorious or heroic struggle, showed young Silent Generation members that war does not necessarily solve problems. The peer personality of this generation was forever shaped by that knowledge, and its members bring to their leadership of the country at this time in history a seriousness of purpose and a desire to compromise, rather than to engage in war. They respect the notion of fairness and might be expected to extend that notion to issues surrounding death and dying. Their emphasis on fairness may be seen in the current debates concerning universal health care.

The fourth generation of adults alive today, according to Strauss and Howe (1991), is the baby boom generation. Born between 1943 and 1960, this large generation's coming of age was influenced by the Vietnam War. Although this was not an official war, it did represent the first wholesale, legal death threat, both individually and collectively, to the members of this generation. Thus it might be suggested that they came of age thinking about death as coming from external sources and determined to end the threat by protest. Strauss and Howe described this generation as "idealist" and argued that they have brought to the country a new awakening of the spirit. Now reaching midlife, this generation is demanding better health care and are in the forefront of the fitness movement. It is almost as though their youthful slogan, "Hell, no, We won't go!" is now being directed toward aging and death.

The final generation, just coming into adulthood in the 1990s, was called the 13th generation by Strauss and Howe (1991) because it is the 13th group of Americans to be born since the founding of the United States. Born between 1961 and 1981, it was labeled a new "reactive" generation by Strauss and Howe. Responding negatively to the perceived excesses of the baby boomers, this generation is conservative. Their acquaintance with death is more personal and less glorious than that of the preceding generations. Their conflicts to date have been short (the Persian Gulf War and the invasion of Panama), but more of them have lived in inner cities, where the threat of drive-by shootings and the promise of violent death are part of everyday life. In addition, they are the first generation to come of age knowing that death may come from sexual experimentation. To the 13th generation, then, death is a personal, rather than civic or national concern.

Although Strauss and Howe (1991) did not discuss the various generations' views on death at length, they made an exception in their description of the 13th generation by including among the events that shaped their generational personality several death-related facts, as cited below.

- "The 13th is the most aborted generation in history. . . . Through the birth years of last-wave 13ers, would-be mothers aborted one fetus in three" (Strauss and Howe, p. 324).
- "Thirteener teenagers face a much lower risk of dying from disease than did Silent teenagers 40 years ago. . . . But this 13er advantage has been almost entirely offset by a much higher risk of dying from accidents, murder, and suicide" (Strauss and Howe, p. 326).
- "As teenagers, 13ers are committing suicide more frequently than any generation since the Lost. . . . Through the 1980s, roughly 5,000 children under age 18 committed suicide each year, the largest number and proportion ever recorded for that age bracket" (Strauss and Howe, p. 326).
- "Fear is a perversive reality within a generation of urban schoolchildren that brings an estimated 135,000 guns (and six times as many knives) to the classroom each day" (Strauss and Howe, p. 326).

Although this thumbnail sketch of the peer personalities of each adult generation currently alive in the United States provides a rich background for organizing the discussion of death in adulthood in this chapter, it must be kept in mind that there are individual differences among people within each generation and that it is these differences that require attention in any situation involving death and loss. Every individual encounters the death of others and faces his or her own death uniquely. For example, one person might face the loss of her parents as a preschooler, while another copes with dying parents while he is is his 70s. However, although individual differences need to be acknowledged, losses that tend to be normative events in the lives of adults—that is, death-related events that are more likely to occur at different stages across the adult years and therefore tend to be central marker events for each life stage—can also be identified. For the sake of organization, the following discussion focuses on death-related events most common at various ages, in the full realization that individuals may experience any of these events at any time in their lives.

DEATH IN YOUNG ADULTHOOD

Young adulthood was described generously by Strauss and Howe (1991) as encompassing the ages of 22–43 years of age. Young adults are at their biological and intellectual peaks, and death may seem far away to most of them, especially during the earliest part of this period. In 1991, accidents were the leading cause of death among this age group, according for approximately 26,526 of the 147,750 deaths that occurred in this age group (rate = 32.3 per 100,000 population in this age group). The second major cause of death for both sexes and all races across this age period in 1991 was cancer, which accounted for 22,228 deaths (rate = 27.1). This was followed by HIV infection, which accounted for 21,747 deaths in that year (rate = 26.5); diseases of the heart, accounting for 15,822 deaths (rate = 19.3); homicide, accounting for almost 12,372 deaths (rate = 15.1); and suicide, accounting for 12,281 deaths (rate = 14.9). These figures are taken from the *Advanced Report of Final Mortality Statistics* for 1991 (National Center for Health Statistics, 1993a).

The central role of adults in this period of life is activity, with young adults especially active in establishing families and livelihoods, serving institutions, and testing values (Strauss and Howe, 1991). Because most young adults are investing their energy and identity in families and establishing themselves in vocations, any threat to either of these areas strikes very close to the bone.

It might follow that four types of death are most salient for young adults: abortion, the death of a child, death from AIDS, and death by violence. The death of a grandparent is also a normative event for young adults. However, the deaths of older people do not violate young adults' sense of a just world, because they are perceived as being in the natural order of things. In addition, they do not present a threat to young people's personal sense of mortality, because the age differences between the young and old are still dramatic. Thus, except in special circumstances, these deaths generally do not result in high grief reactions. In contrast, abortion is a special, highly personal, and emotional issue for young adults and may well present the first real encounter with death for many young people. The death of a wanted child after birth not only violates adults' sense of justice, but also strikes at their self-image as competent, caring, and protective parents. AIDS is a threat to young adults because it strikes at the very heart of their ability to work and to procreate, central tasks for this age group, and the increasing violence of our world presents relatively more threat to young adults than to other age groups. A closer examination of each of these types of death is therefore appropriate within the young adult category.

Abortion

Abortion is both a societal and personal issue for young adults. Between 1972 and 1988, the rate of abortions in the U.S. rose from 13.2 per 1,000 women to 27.3 per 1,000 women, and the ratio of abortions to live births rose from 184 per 1,000 live births to 401 per 1,000 live births. Almost all of these abortions were reported by women between the ages of 15 and 44, making this source of death almost entirely a young adult phenomenon. The United States leads the world in the number of abortions performed annually, outstripping its nearest competitor, India, by almost three to one (National Center for Health Statistics, 1992).

Few authoritative studies have been conducted on the effects of abortion on young people's mental and physical health. However, the issue has become an important emotional and legal one in the past two decades, and young adults find themselves struggling to develop their own personal stance on this issue. That struggle, nearly universal among this age group, may well be the first ethical death-related issue that young adults face.

Death of a Child

The death of a child has been characterized as the most difficult death an adult can face. Infant morality has, fortunately, decreased across the last 20 years, dropping from 20 per 1,000 live births in 1970 to 9.8 per 1,000 live births in 1989 (U.S. Bureau of the Census, 1992). However, death from sudden infant death syndrome still claims more than 7,000 lives per year (Rando, 1986b). In addition, a total of 16,200 children between 1 and 14 years of age died in 1989, contributing to a death rate in that age group of 32.4 per 100,000 people (U.S. Bureau of the Census, 1992). After a review of the research, Rando (1986b) identified seven themes that caregivers should be aware of when working with parents confronting the loss of a child.

1   Realizing that there are special grief problems, including guilt and changes in self-concept, after the death of a child.
2   Encouraging parents to share their grief work.
3   Encouraging and facilitating anticipatory grief responses to a child's impending death when possible.
4   Recognizing that bereaved siblings need special consideration.
5   Recognizing that the final disposition of the child's remains should be determined by what is personally best for the parents.
6   Providing the opportunity for professional intervention after the death.
7   Affirming that grief after the death of a child can be resolved.

It should be noted that men and women may react differently to the death of their offspring, particularly if the death occurs before birth (spontaneous abortion) or at birth. Kennell, Slyder, and Klaus (1970) interviewed 18 mothers whose newborns had died and found that they followed a full pattern of mourning. They also interviewed 8 of these women's husbands and found that 2 of them denied grieving because they felt that they had to be strong for their wives's sake. Mothers of dead infants have been shown to grieve for a longer period of time and to express more guilt and yearning to hold and rock their child than fathers, who, although actively grieving the loss, seem to progress to faster resolution of their grief (Helmrath & Steinitz, 1978). Although the death of an older child often is preceded by a period of anticipatory grief, nevertheless, both parents will find that they have grief work to do after the death. This generally includes finding ways to express their grief appropriately, accepting their spouse's grieving pattern and rate, adjusting to the martial relationship without the presence of the child, reestablishing a sense of meaning in their lives now that they are no longer the parents of that child, and learning how to reinvest in other children or other activities and take pleasure again in living (Rando, 1986a). Men especially may have problems resolving guilt over the death, because they often consider the need to keep their offspring safe the core of their parental responsibilities (Stillion, 1985). If this sense of guilt is combined with the traditional male socialization to keep a stiff upper lip and remain emotionally unexpressed, the bereaved father may have a harder time resolving his loss than the bereaved mother, who is permitted to be open and expressive. Compassionate Friends, a support group for parents whose children have died, offers help in resolving the sorrow, loss, anger, depression, hopelessness, and confusion that many young bereaved parents feel.

Death from AIDS

The incidence of AIDS cases grew from 2,920 cases reported between 1981 and 1983 to 43,672 cases reported in 1991 (U.S. Bureau of the Census, 1992). Furthermore, the death rate from AIDS is increasing annually. In 1991, for example, there were 29,555 deaths from HIV infection, a more than 17% increase over the number of deaths from HIV infection in 1990 (National Center for Health Statistics, 1993a). Between 1991 and 1992, the age-adjusted death rate for HIV infection rose from 11.3 to 12.4 deaths per 100,000 population, with the greatest number of deaths reported in the 25–34 and 35–44 age groups (National Center for Health Statistics, 1993b). In 1992, HIV infection was the sixth leading cause of death among those ages 15–24 and the third leading cause of death among those ages 25–44 years of age (National Center for Health Statistics, 1993a). At this time, death from AIDS primarily affects males—88% of those dying from AIDS in 1991 were males.

At present, the diagnosis of AIDS is still regarded as a death sentence, yet the time from diagnosis to death can be as long as a decade. The long dying trajectory inherent in AIDS presents special problems for young adults. They are faced with the fact of their terminality at the very time that they should be investing in jobs and establishing families. Making the situation even more difficult is the stigma attached to the disease by many segments of the population. Finally, for many young people, especially members of the gay community, AIDS presents the special challenge of "bereavement overload" (Kastenbaum, 1969) as well as the spectre of their own mortality. Many young people in the gay community have lost many lovers and friends to this scourge across the last decade. Such multiple losses often deplete the coping reserves of even well-adjusted people, leaving them emotionally unable to work through current losses or face future losses (Rando, 1985).

Violent Death

The final category of death-related behaviors important to young adulthood, especially for males, is violent death. In 1989, for example, the combined death rate for accidents, suicides, and homicides among males ages 25–44 was 199 per 100,000. Those three categories accounted for almost 40% of the deaths from all causes for males in this age group. The equivalent combined rate for these three

causes for females in this age group was 56 per 100,000, with these three categories accounting for only 26% of the deaths from all causes for young adult women.

In addition to sex differences in homicide, there are also significant racial
differences. For example, in 1992, the death rate from homicide for white males
between the ages of 25 and 44 was 14.4 per 100,000 population, whereas that for
black males of the same age was 99.1 per 100,000 population. Comparative figures for white and black females in this age group were 3.8 and 21.4 per 100,000,
respectively (National Center for Health Statistics, 1993b).

It is clear from these figures that males live in a more dangerous world than
females do. Moreover, black young people are approximately 7 times more likely
than young white people to die from homicide. No doubt, biology, socialization,
and environmental risk factors all fuel the gender and racial differences in the
causes of death among young adults (Stillion, 1985). However, the years of potential life lost from these causes, especially among males, should be a major cause
for concern for all age groups in our culture.

Summary

Taken together, the primary death-rleated situations facing young adults, with the
exception of death of a child, all call for personal life choices. Young adults can
choose to live in such a way as to minimize and nearly eradicate their chances of
contracting AIDS or dying from accidents and high-risk behaviors. They can
choose to become pregnant or not and to abort or not, depending on their own
values and life situations. Finally, they can choose not to engage in suicidal behaviors and to address the conditions that increase the incidence of homicidal behaviors. As shall be shown, the element of choice in death-related concerns decreases
with age. In the very act of making choices and coping with the results of them,
young people become increasingly familiar with the reality of death. Moreover,
they have observed the aging process in their parents and themselves and come to
recognize death as a force that affects them personally. From the perspective of
death studies, it may be suggested that young adulthood ends as people come to
understand the eventual inevitability of their own death. That understanding is
accompanied by a change in the way these adults reckon time. Somewhere around
age 40, give or take a few years, most adults stop reckoning time since birth and
start reckoning time left to accomplish their goals (Stillion, McDowell, & May,
1989). That developmental milestone may be the true marker of the passage into
middle age.

DEATH IN MIDDLE AGE

According to Strauss and Howe (1991), middle age extends from approximately
age 44 to age 65, and its central role is leadership, including parenting, teaching,
directing institutions, and using values. People in midlife are more powerful than
at any other stage. They are entering leadership positions in politics, business,

education, and the arts. Their view of the world tends to become the dominant one in society, replacing the worldview of the older generation. However, midlife is also a stressful period. Midlifers have been described by the popular press as "the filling in the sandwich" because they are caught between the needs of parents and adolescent children. Deaths from diseases such as heart disease and cancer, which are believed to be at least partially related to stress, increase exponentially in this age group.

Confronting the Deaths of Peers

The first death-related issue for midlifers, then, is coming to grips with the death of their peers. The total death rate rises from approximately 180 deaths per 100,000 across young adulthood to nearly 790 deaths per 100,000 across the mid-life period (National Center for Health Statistics, 1993a). The reality of death can no longer be defined as midlifers watch their peers die quick deaths from cardiovascular disease and prolonged deaths from cancer, two diseases that together accounted for more than 65% of all deaths in this age group in 1989 (Vital Statistics, p. 83). Deaths from suicide, homicide, and accidents combined recede across this age period, accounting for only 5% of deaths. For people in middle age, fitness becomes not so much a fad as a necessity to help them cope with the increasingly familiar threat of death in their own lives.

Caring for Dying Parents

A second normative death-related issue faced by individuals in midlife is the challenge of caring for their weakening parents and presiding over their deaths. Women tend to bear the brunt of this caregiving, and the extended dying trajectory places special stress on women as they attempt to cope with family responsibilities (perhaps including helping with the care of infant grandchildren), continue their careers, and provide emotional and physical support to their dying or grieving parents. Berezin (1970, 1977) coined the term "partial grief" to refer to the prolonged time before an anticipated death occurs. In such a situation, where the loss is not total because the death is not final, adult children may find themselves grieving the death of their parents while still in the midst of caring for them. When this occurs, adult children are likely to experience feelings of guilt, helplessness, ambivalence, anger, and depression as well as exhaustion and impatience (Kowalski, 1984b).

   Rando (1988) pointed out that even if the death of a parent is expected and accepted as in the proper order of things, it is significant because it represents loss of the possibility of unconditional love, loss of ties to the past and childhood, loss of support in the present and future, loss of the possibility of friendship or resolution of unfinished business with this important authority figure, and loss of the generational buffer between oneself and death. Sanders (1992) added the loss of a grandparent for one's children to the list. Losing the first parent is often the first significant death experienced by middle-aged people. Losing the second parent brings with it the sure knowledge that one is now the cutting-edge generation, the next to face death.

Psychologically, therefore, many people end midlife with the growing realization that their own personal death is becoming ever more imminent and inescapable. By this time, the denial of death that Becker (1973) wrote about cannot be maintained at high levels. Few, if any, people enter elderhood without having examined the face of death intimately and without the deep understanding that they too will die in the not-too-distant future. They may react to this knowledge in a variety of ways: raging against "the dying of the light," embracing death as a release, or accepting it with equanimity. Whatever one's reaction, the true psychological marker of transition into elderhood may be the adoption of a stance toward one's own inevitable and ever-nearer extinction.

DEATH AMONG THE ELDERLY

In elderhood (ages 66–87), the central role becomes one of stewardship, which entails supervising, mentoring, channeling endowments, and passing on values, according to Strauss and Howe (1991). This is the period in life when all but a small minority of extremely long-lived people must face their own death. As in midlife, the two major killers are heart disease and cancer, which again accounted for almost 65% of the total deaths occurring in this age group in 1989 (National Center for Health Statistics, 1992).

Accepting Personal Mortality

The first major normative death-related issue for the elderly is coming to a full sense of acceptance of their own mortality. Several studies have documented lower levels of death anxiety and fear of death among elderly people (Kalish & Reynolds, 1977; Kastenbaum, 1969; Templer, 1971). Thorson and Powell (1988) have suggested that, because people in this stage of life are confronted daily with the deaths of their peers, it may be normative for them to strive to reconcile their understandings of life and death. If successful, this reconciliation may lead to reduced levels of death anxiety in face of the realization that death is approaching. In a study of 346 individuals between the ages of 18 and 88, Thorson and Powell (1990) found that both age and religiosity were negatively associated with death concern. They found that "older respondents in the study scored significantly higher in intrinsic religious motivations and lower in death anxiety" (Thorson & Powell, p. 388). They concluded that although their study presented further cross-sectional evidence that death anxiety is lower and religious motivation higher in later life, further research is needed to understand such issues as how the life review process affects anxiety and how the anxiety of elderly people concerning the pervasive fear of pain and helplessness may be relieved.

Coping with Cumulative Loss

The second major death-related task for the elderly is coping with cumulative loss. Although loss may and does occur at younger ages, for the elderly, losses are normative events (e.g., loss of physical abilities through illness, loss of vocational identity through retirement, and loss of friends and family through death). Moreover, losses tend to occur in such rapid succession in this age group that there is insufficient time for resolution of the grief over each loss (Stillion et al., 1989). Evidence has accumulated that there is a discernible pattern in grieving that must be experienced before individuals can invest time and energy in new relationships and activities (Rando, 1985; Raphael, 1983; Worden, 1982). The elderly do not have the luxury of time between losses or unlimited time to set new directions for their lives. Therefore, coping with cumulative loss becomes a major issue for many elderly adults and may feed into the reality of depression among this age group, which has been called the most common of all illnesses among the aged (Butler & Lewis, 1982).

Coping with the Loss of a Spouse

The loss of a spouse is of such major importance in the lives of elderly people that it deserves special attention. Approximately 51% of women and almost 14% of men over age 65 have been widowed at least once (LaRue, Dessonville, & Jarvik, 1985). In a study of a large sample of elderly in Kentucky, Lund, Caserta, and Dimond (1989) compared subsamples of widowed persons with subsamples of persons who had lost a parent or a child and a subsample reporting no bereavements. They found that the widowed sample was higher in depression than the other bereaved samples and the nonbereaved sample. They suggested that widowhood differs from other losses because "the presence or absence of a spouse defines one's very position in the structure of society" (Lund et al., p. 434).

Much research on widowhood has been conducted in the past two decades, and much of the detail in this research is contradictory. For example, the effect of bereavement on physical health is unclear. Norris and Murrell (1990) have summarized the research on bereavement as indicating that bereavement "has at most minimal effects on physical health" (p. 42), whereas Avis, Brambilla, Vass, and McKinley (1991) concluded from their review of the literature that the "physical effects of widowhood include increased risk of physical symptoms, new illnesses, utilization of medical services, hospitalizations, use of medications, lower perceived health status, and mortality" (p. 1063). In addition, Bowling (1989) found that elderly persons age 75 or older and males were more vulnerable to mortality after bereavement.

There is also controversy in the literature concerning whether the death of a spouse affects men or women more significantly (Bowling 1989; Lund et al., 1989; Stillion, 1984; Umberson, Wortman, & Kessler, 1992). Some researchers cite the fact the men, even very elderly men, are generally in better financial condition and have a better chance of reinvesting in a new relationship than do women as an argument in favor of men's better long-term adjustment. Others cite the fact that women have more continuity in their everyday routines and more domestic skills as evidence that women adjust better. In addition, widows find the support of other widows more easily than widowers find the support of other widowers (Lopata, 1973). Results from a 1986 national survey ($N = 3,614$) show that "having ever been widowed is associated with current levels of depression and that this association is greater for men than women" (Umberson et al., 1992, p. 10).

Regardless of the controversy, the literature is nearly unanimous in documenting widowhood as a problem of major proportions for the elderly. Ulmer, Range, and Smith (1991) suggested that bereavement can induce an existential crisis, especially for people who have not developed a sense of purpose for their own lives. At least two decades of studies have indicated that several months after bereavement, both widows and widowers remain more depressed than control subjects (Clayton, Desmarais, & Winokur, 1968; Clayton, Halikas, & Maurice, 1972; Gilewski, Farberow, Gallagher, & Thompson, 1991; Lund et al., 1989; Murrell & Himmelfarb, 1989; Norris & Murrell, 1990; Parks & Brown, 1972; Umberson et al., 1992). Furthermore, the level of depression and the success of coping with it seem to depend on such things as the individual's level of prebereavement depression, the state of his or her finances, the amount of global stress experienced by the individual, the number of new interests, and the amount of social support available (Norris & Murrell, 1990). The cause of death may also influence the course of mourning. Gilewski et al. (1991) found that survivors of spouses who had committed suicide were at very high risk for depression. In addition to depression, evidence is accumulating that bereaved persons, especially the widowed, may be more subject to anxiety disorders (e.g., Clayton et al., 1972; Parkes & Brown, 1972; Zisook, Mulvihill, & Schuchter, 1990).

Fear of Living Death and Euthanasia

Two other, interconnected death-related issues are salient to the elderly: fear of living death and euthanasia. As noted, Americans' longevity has steadily been increasing, largely as a result of innovations in technology and medical care. In fact, these innovations have made it possible for life to be extended almost indefinitely with the aid of machines, Veatch (1989) has noted that in 1937 only 37% of all deaths in the United States occurred in hospitals or other institutions. In 1983, that figure was 80%. The G.I. Generation and Silent Generations, who are mainly responsible for development of these life-extending technologies, are now being faced with the ethical quandaries that they pose. Society has just begun to address some of the thornier ones, such as the following: Should all individuals have a right to unlimited medical treatment, regardless of their age or physical condition? Should all individuals have the right to decide for themselves the conditions under which they are willing to live? Should the medical establishment help those who no longer wish to live die with dignity? Should the younger members of society have to shoulder the burden of health care for increasing numbers of aging citizens who are living longer after retirement? All of these questions and many more have ramifications for elderly persons living today.

THE ELDEST GENERATION

Members of the Lost Generation, age 90 and older in 1990, although not large in numbers, are subject to all of the death-related concerns of the elderly, but have an additional special concern in facing their own death. These robust survivors have witnessed the loss of most of their peers, coped with cumulative loss, and are faced with meeting their own deaths without the support of people who understand and have shared their personal life histories. Many of these people find it is too late to reconcile past conflicts with others, because most of those they have associated with across their lifetimes have died, including, in many cases, their children. Because of their longevity, the very old have special fears of dying alone and being forgotten. Many are chronically ill and disabled, no longer able to care for themselves, and dependent on strangers in nursing homes to meet their daily needs. Stephenson and Murphy (1986) have pointed out that chronically ill and disabled people must face "separation from the former self" (p. 138); that is, they must grieve the loss of the idealized younger self; must adjust to the stigma of being excluded from society; and must cope with social death, sometimes well before they must face physical extinction. The eldest can teach us lessons about facing helplessness with dignity and struggling to find meaning in existence as physical disability and the threat of death increase.

Coping with Dying

Members of the eldest generation have coped with many deaths and losses across their many years of life. Regardless of their past levels of coping with the deaths of others, they all have the need to confront and prepare for their own deaths. Rando (1984) noted that "it is a gross exaggeration to say that the elderly are all at peace with their coming death. Some are and some are not. The elderly do appear to see death as an important issue, one they often think about and for which they make plans" (p. 247). A psychotherpist who was a member of the Lost Generation clarified the essential ambivalence felt by many as they face their personal mortality, when he wrote in the early 1980s,

If I think that millions of people will greet the sun tomorrow morning and I may not, I get mad. Well, I am old. I had a good and full life. I tried my best, and I should be ready to leave, or at least I should be able to learn how to accept the end and wait quietly. I loved and was loved—and that I shall not take with me? Then I will not go! (Grotjahn, 1984, p. 253).

Caregivers need to remember that the eldest have had more time to develop their own unique personalities than most and that, for this reason, attention to individual differences in facing death may be more important when working with this age group than when working with other age groups.

Fry (1990) suggested that practitioners and clinicians need to assess, as early as possible, the homebound person's thoughts of his or her own gradual and approaching death. Fry measured concerns and ways of coping in 198 elderly persons. He found several themes of fear and anxiety related to death and dying.

Principal among these are the apprehensions of the elderly about physical pain and sensory loss, and the risk to personal safety around the time of death. Other underlying latent themes in the death and dying concerns of the home-bound elderly relate to their self-esteem needs and the fears that they will be easily forgotten after they die or that they will suffer death with indignity and ingratitude. (Fry, p. 746)

The elders also worried about dying alone, being permanently forgotten after death, and the uncertainty of life after death. Fry found that elderly people commonly coped with these concerns by relying on prayer, social support, and internal self-control (e.g., thinking of happier times).

Coping with the Deaths of Adult Children

As difficult as the death of a child may be for parents who are in young or middle adulthood, the death of an adult child brings with it a special, more poignant loss to the eldest generation. Kowalski (1984b) pointed out that "as life expectancy continues to increase, so does the average age of the children of the elderly. Many of these children are facing their own aging-related issues" (p. 190). It is no longer unusual to observe 70-year-old children and 90-year-old parents attempting to help each other deal with death-related issues. Issues faced by the younger generation include widowhood, loss of physical ability, and personal death. For their elderly parents, who are often physically, psychologically, and economically unable to help their children cope, the deaths of their aging children may be the most difficult to accept. Their children may be the only people still alive who knew them when they were younger, in better health, and more productive. The adult children also represent years of loving care invested by the aged parents. In addition, for some, they represent ongoing commitments of friendship and companionship. Schiff (1977) noted that the age of a child at death does not seem to matter. It evokes the same reaction: "How could it be that a parent outlives a child?" This emotional reaction reveals the violation felt by parents who believe that the natural order of things is for parents to die before their children. For the eldest generation, this loss is made even more difficult because the death of their children may deprive them of the very people they thought they could count on to help them through their final illness.

Suicide

The final death-related issue for the eldest generation is suicide. In 1991, the rate of suicide was 16.9 per 100,000 for people ages of 65–74 years. It rose dramatically to 23.5 per 100,000 for people of ages 75–84 and a little higher to 24.0 among those age 85 or older. These rates compare to a rate of 12.2 for all ages in 1991 (National Center for Health Statistics, 1993a). Clearly, suicide, is a threat that increases as age increases, particularly for white males. Much has been written about the causes of suicide among the elderly (for a review, see Stillion et al., 1989). Physical illness has been implicated (Barraclough, 1971; Dorpat, Anderson, & Ripley, 1968; Miller, 1979; Rockwell & O'Brien, 1973; Barraclough,

1987); the use of alcohol is another high-risk factor (Miller, 1979), as is social isolation (Bock & Weber, 1972; Darbonne, 1969). The loss of a spouse has also been shown to increase the risk of suicide, especially among elderly males in the first 6 months of bereavement (Benson & Brodie, 1975; Berardo, 1968). Those widowed by suicide are especially at risk for suicide (Osterweiss, Solomon, & Green, 1984). Not only do the elderly have the highest rate of suicide of all age groups, but also they have the highest attempt/completion rate. That is, elderly people do not threaten suicide—they do it. To them, the present debates over euthanasia, the right to die with dignity, and assisted suicide are merely background noise as they struggle to decide how they will make their personal exit from life.

CONCLUSION

Death is a constant reality in adults' lives. People spend adulthood learning to cope with the deaths of those they love and coming to accept their own mortality. Each stage of adulthood brings different death-related issues to the fore, and each stage requires an individual's best thinking and most positive psychological coping skills. Furthermore, death-related issues increase in number across the adult years, even as people's ability to deny or control death by making positive choices declines. Viorst (1986) pointed out that all people must suffer some "necessary losses" as they move through adulthood. She maintained that growth may come from these losses and that, in the end, people may owe much of their integrity and wisdom to understanding loss from the inside out. If she is right, it follows that death is one of our great teachers throughout the adult years as well as the universal liberator at their close.

REFERENCES

Avis, N. E., Brambilla, D. J., Vass, K., & McKinley, J. B. (1991). The effect of widowhood on health: A prospective analysis from the Massachusetts Women's Health Study. *Social Science and Medicine, 33,* 1063–1070.

Barraclough, B. (1971). Suicide in the elderly. In D. W. Kay & A. Walk (Eds.), *Recent developments in psychogeriatrics* (pp. 89–97). Kent, England: Headly Brothers.

Barraclough, B. (1987). *Suicide: Clinical and epidemiological studies.* London: Croom-Helm.

Becker, E. (1973). *The denial of death.* New York: Free Press.

Benson, R. A., & Brodie, D. C. (1975). Suicide by overdose of medicines among the aged. *Journal of the American Geriatrics Society, 23,* 304–308.

Berardo, F. M. (1968). Widowhood status in the United States: Perspective on a neglected aspect of the family life-cycle. *The Family Co-ordinator, 17,* 191–203.

Berezin, M. A. (1970). The psychiatrist and the geriatric patient. *Journal of Geriatric Psychiatry, 4,* 53–64.

Berezin, M. A. (1977). Partial grief for the aged and their families. In E. M. Pattison (Ed.), *The experience of dying* (pp. 279–286). Englewood Cliffs, NJ: Prentice-Hall.

Bock, E. W., & Weber, I. L. (1972). Suicide among the elderly: Isolating widowhood and mitigating alternatives. *Journal of Marriage and the Family, 34,* 24–31.

Bowling, A. (1989). Who dies after widow(er)hood? A discriminant analysis. *Omega, 19,* 135–153.

Butler, R. N., & Lewis, N. I. (1982). *Aging and mental health: Positive psychosocial and biomedical approaches* (3rd ed.). St. Louis, MO: Mosby.

Clayton, P. J., Desmarais, L., & Winokur, G. (1968). A study of normal bereavement. *American Journal of Psychiatry, 125,* 169–178.

Clayton, P. J., Halikas, J. A., & Maurice, W. L. (1972). The depression of widowhood. *British Journal of Psychiatry, 120,* 71–78.

Darbonne, A. R. (1969). Suicide and age: A suicide note analysis. *Journal of Consulting and Clinical Psychology, 33,* 46–50.

Dorpat, T. L., Anderson, W. F., & Ripley, H. S. (1968). The relationship of physical illness to suicide. In H. L. P. Resnick (Ed.), *Suicide: Diagnosis and management* (pp. 209–219). Boston: Little, Brown.

Fry, P. S. (1990). A factor analytic investigation of home-bound elderly individuals' concerns about death and dying. *Journal of Clinical Psychology, 46,* 737–748.

Gilewski, M. J., Farberow, N. L., Gallagher, D. E., & Thompson, L. W. (1991). Interaction of depression and bereavement on mental health in the elderly. *Psychology and Aging, 6,* 67–75.

Grotjahn, M. (1984). Being sick and facing 80: Observations of an aging therapist. In E. Shneidman (Ed.), *Death: Current perspectives* (3rd ed., pp. 249–257). Palo Alto, CA: Mayfield.

Helmrath, T. A., & Steinitz, E. M. (1978). Death of an infant: Parental grieving and the failure of social support. *Journal of Family Practice, 6,* 758–790.

Information Please Almanac Atlas and Yearbook (46th ed.). (1993). Boston: Houghton Mifflin.

Kalish, R. A., & Reynolds, D. K. (1976). *Death and ethnicity: A psycho-cultural investigation.* Los Angeles: University of Southern California Press.

Kalish, R. A., & Reynolds, D. K. (1977). The role of age in death attitudes. *Death Education, 1,* 205–230.

Kastenbaum, R. (1969). Death and bereavement in later life. In A. H. Kutscher (Ed.), *Death and bereavement.* Springfield, IL: Thomas.

Kennell, J. H., Slyder, H., & Klaus, M. H. (1970). The mourning response to the death of a newborn infant. *New England Journal of Medicine, 283,* 344–349.

Kowalski, N. C. (1984a). The older person's anticipation of her own death. In T. Rando (Ed.), *Loss and anticipatory grief* (pp. 175–186). Lexington, MA: Lexington Books.

Kowalski, N. C. (1984b). Anticipating the death of an elderly parent. In T. Rando (Ed.), *Loss and anticipatory grief* (pp. 187–199). Lexington, MA: Lexington Books.

LaRue, A., Dessonville, C., & Jarvik, L. (1985). Aging and mental disorders. In J. E. Birren & K. W. Schaie (Eds.), *Handbook of the psychology of aging* (2nd ed., pp. 664–702). New York: Van Nostrand Reinhold.

Lopata, H. (1973). *Widowhood in an American city.* Cambridge, MA: Schenkman.

Lund, D. A., Caserta, M. S., & Diamond, M. F. (1989). Impact of spousal bereavement on the subjective well-being of older adults. In D. A. Lund (Ed.), *Older bereaved spouses: Research with practical applications* (pp. 1–15). Washington, DC: Hemisphere.

Miller, M. (1979). *Suicide after sixty: The final alternative.* New York: Springer Publishing Company.

Murrell, S. A., & Himmelfarb, S. (1989). Effects of attachment bereavement and pre-event conditions on subsequent depressive symptoms in older adults. *Psychology and Aging, 4,* 166–172.

Nagy, M. (1948). The child's theories concerning death. *Journal of Genetic Psychology, 73,* 3–27.

National Center for Health Statistics. (1992). *Health, United States.* Hyattsville, MD: Public Health Service.

National Center for Health Statistics. (1993a). Advance report of final mortality statistics, 1991. *Monthly Vital Statistics Report, 42* (Suppl. 2), 1–62.

National Center for Health Statistics. (1993b). Annual summary of births, marriages, divorces, and deaths: United States, 1992. *Monthly Vital Statistics Report, 41* (Suppl. 13), 1–34.

Norris, F. H., & Murrell, S. A. (1990). Social support, life events, and stress as modifiers of adjustment to bereavement by older adults. *Psychology and Aging, 5,* 429–436.

Osterweiss, M., Solomon, F., & Green, M. (1984). *Bereavement: Reactions, consequences, and care.* Washington, DC: National Academy Press.

Parkes, C. M., & Brown, R. J. (1972). Health after bereavement: A controlled study of young Boston widows and widowers. *Psychosomatic Medicine, 34,* 449–461.

Rando, T. A. (1985). *Loss and anticipatory grief.* Lexington, MA: Lexington Books.

Rando, T. A. (1986a). *Grief, dying and death,* Champaign, IL: Research Press.

Rando, T. A. (1986b). *Parental loss of a child.* Champaign, IL: Research Press.

Rando, T. A. (1988). *Grieving: How to go on when someone you love dies.* Lexington, MA: Lexington Books.

Raphael, B. (1983). *The anatomy of bereavement.* New York: Basic Books.

Rockwell, D., & O'Brien, W. (1973). Physicians' knowledge and attitudes about suicide. *Journal of the American Medical Association, 225,* 1347–1349.

Sanders, C. M. (1992). *Surviving grief and learning to live again.* New York: Wiley.

Schiff, H. S. (1977). *The bereaved parent.* New York: Crown.

Speece, M. W., & Brent, S. B. (1984). Children's understanding of death: A review of three components of a death concept. *Child Development, 55,* 1671–1686.

Stephenson, J. S., & Murphy, D. (1986). Existential grief: The special case of the chronically ill and disabled. *Death Studies, 10,* 135–146.

Stillion, J. M. (1984). Women and widowhood: The suffering beyond grief. In J. Freeman (Ed.), *Women: A feminist perspective* (pp. 282–296). Palo Alto, CA: Mayfield.

Stillion, J. M. (1985). *Death and the sexes: An examination of differential longevity, attitudes, behaviors and coping skills.* Washington, DC: Hemisphere and McGraw Hill International.

Stillion, J. M. (in press). The bottom line. In D. Sabo (Ed.), *Men's health and illness: Gender, power, and the body.* Walnut Creek, CA: Sage Publications.

Stillion, J. M., McDowell, E. E., & May, J. H. (1989). *Suicide across the life span: Premature exits.* Washington, DC: Hemisphere.

Stillion, J., & Wass, H. (1979). Children and death. In H. Wass (Ed.), *Dying: Facing the facts* (pp. 208–235). Washington, DC: Hemisphere.

Strauss, B., & Howe, R. (1991). *Generations: The history of America's future 1584 to 2069.* New York: William Morrow.

Templer, D. I. (1971). Death anxiety as related to depression and health of retired persons. *Journal of Gerontology, 26,* 521–523.

Thorson, J. A., & Powell, F. C. (1988). Elements of death anxiety and meanings of death. *Journal of Clinical Psychology, 44,* 691–701.

Thorson, J. A., & Powell, F. C. (1990). Meanings of death and intrinsic religiosity. *Journal of Clinical Psychology, 46,* 379–391.

U.S. Bureau of the Census. (1992). *Statistical abstract of the United States: 1992* (112th ed.). Washington, DC: Author.

Ulmer, A., Range, L., & Smith, P. (1991). Purpose in life: A moderator of recovery from bereavement. *Omega, 23,* 279–289.

Umberson, D., Wortman, C. B., & Kessler, R. C. (1992). Widowhood and depression: Explaining long-term gender differences in vulnerability. *Journal of Health and Social Behavior, 33,* 10–24.

Veatch, R. M. (1989). *Death, dying and the biological revolution: Our last quest for responsibility.* New Haven, CT: Yale University Press.

Viorst, J. (1986). *Necessary losses.* New York: Fawcett.

Wass, H. (1979). Death and the elderly. In H. Wass (Ed.), *Dying: Facing the facts* (pp. 182–207). Washington, DC: Hemisphere.

Wass, H. (1984). Concepts of death: A developmental perspective. In H. Wass & C. Corr (Eds.), *Childhood and death* (pp. 3–24). Washington, DC: Hemisphere.

Worden, W. (1982). *Grief counseling and grief therapy: A handbook for the mental health practitioner.* New York: Springer Publishing Company.

Zilboorg, G. (1943). Fear of death. *Psychoanalytic Quarterly, 12,* 465–475.

Zisook, S., Mulvihill, M., & Shuchter, S. R. (1990). Widowhood and anxiety. *Psychiatric Medicine, 8,* 99–116.

Part Three

Issues and Challenges

Chapter 13

AIDS: The Second Decade

Karen E. Peterson

THE MANY FACES OF AIDS

More than a decade after the onset of the AIDS crisis, researchers and health professionals are still grappling to find a cure as well as effective treatment strategies for those infected. And although HIV, the virus believed by many to be the cause of AIDS, has been found in nearly all cultures around the world, many individuals have maintained an attitude of invincibility regarding this usually fatal syndrome. However, there is no population or subgroup who can claim immunity from this ravaging disease, as is exemplified by the following three case examples.

Case Example 1

Imagine that you're on your first date with a rich and handsome young football star just 1 week after you've started college in Boston. You're an attractive 19-year-old woman from a small town in Indiana, and this evening with this particular man is your first date since the breakup of your engagement back home. Although you had prided yourself on being a virgin, somewhere between the movie and dinner and drinks and dancing, you find yourself unable to fend off this young man's advances, and he rapes you in the front seat of his car.

The next morning you feel upset for a variety of reasons, but mostly because this man has robbed you of your virginity. About a month later, you come down with the flu, which helps to distract you from your feelings about the rape, but this flu won't seem to go away. Hot flashes of fever, night sweats and chills, sore throat, swollen glands, diarrhea, and fatigue continue to plague you for many weeks. Then, almost as quickly as they arose, these symptoms subside, and your life returns to normal.

However, 8 years later, during routine tests related to your first pregnancy, your physician discovers some abnormalities in your immune system functioning and, after further tests, determines that you are HIV positive, meaning that your blood has tested positive for the human immunodeficiency virus, which is believed to cause AIDS. Because your pregnancy will automatically lower the level of your immune system functioning so that your body will not reject the fetus, continuing the pregnancy will greatly increase your vulnerability to opportunistic infections and to the possibility of developing full-blown AIDS.

Your husband, who is HIV negative, has said he will stand by you and help you to decide whether to carry the pregnancy to term, but most of your friends and relatives have abandoned you. Your employer informs you that your position has been terminated, and your insurance policy has been cancelled.

Considering the fact that you were exposed to HIV during the rape, your immune system already has been severely compromised for eight years. Your future is clouded with the imminent possibility of abortion, recurrent pneumonia, painful intestinal problems, disfiguring skin cancer (Kaposi's sarcoma), dementia (HIV infection of the brain), blindness, and a high probability of death.

Case Example 2

You're a 33-year-old successful advertising executive, a male survivor of the gay sexual revolution of the late 1970s, and you know that you were most likely infected with HIV during your college years, when your sexual exploration—like that of your heterosexual counterparts—was at its peak. You've known about your diagnosis of AIDS for nearly 2 years now, and the trips to the hospital for blood transfusions to cope with the anemia induced by AZT treatments are becoming more frequent and more difficult to hide from your employer.

In the event that your diagnosis is discovered, you know that you will be fired, since you've seen it happen to so many of your friends who are either HIV positive or who are struggling with full-blown AIDS. But even though you've tried repeatedly to take out a disability policy, no insurance company will offer you a policy. It will have to be Social Security Disability—you haven't the money to hire a lawyer or the energy to ask the Lambda Legal Defense Fund to help fight your eventual dismissal from the advertising agency or the discrimination from the insurance companies. Most of your HIV-positive friends have been trying to convince you to draw up a living will and a power of attorney contract, but you haven't been able to bring yourself to do it yet, even though you suspect that your parents will exercise their legal rights to override any efforts by your lover to carry out your last wishes.

On the other hand, your psychotherapist is pleased that, in addition to individual therapy, you have been regularly attending a weekly support group, as well as eating healthier foods and taking vitamins and herbal supplements recommended by the Treatment Alternatives Research Project in New York. For several years now, you have also been avoiding caffeine, alcohol, and other drugs that lower your immune system functioning and have been exercising several times a week. But it is becoming increasingly difficult to finish your workouts at the gym, and with the level of fatigue you've been battling lately, you're quite sure that your T-cell count is slipping below 200 again. You've just received news that another friend has died of AIDS—that makes a total of 43 people you know so far. You wonder if you might be next, but you think of your friend Sam, who is completely covered with spots from Kaposi's sarcoma and jokingly calls himself "The Polka Dot King"; you know he's going to die soon. It's a look you've seen before in so many other faces, and on a daily basis you search the mirror for any signs of it in your own reflection.

Case Example 3

You're a pregnant 32-year-old Latina woman with four children living in a small town in Florida. You know that your husband—the only sexual partner you've ever known—has always had sexual relations with other women; your mother always told you to expect this from men. What you don't know is that your are HIV positive and so are two of your husband's three mistresses. Because you have no symptoms of HIV infection—other than that difficult time with the flu you had last year—you are also unaware that you have about a 35–50% chance of transmitting HIV to your unborn child.

What you also don't know is that after you die, your HIV-positive husband will move back to Colombia, completely in denial about his need for medical care, thereby abandoning your 10-month-old baby to an AIDS hospice clinic. Social services caseworkers will then have difficulty adopting out your other four children, because the word around town is that they came from an "AIDS family."

Incidence of AIDS

The foregoing case examples represent the many faces of AIDS in the 1990s: young people, increasingly female and heterosexual, infants and orphans alike, from all socioeconomic and ethnic groups—all of them living lives of quiet desperation in the face of tremendous loss, isolation, and stigmatization. And even though great advances have been made in terms of prolonging life and improving the quality of life for those who are HIV positive, until science comes up with a cure, death is the most likely consequence—regardless of race, creed, gender, color, or sexual perference.

Tables 1–5 illustrate some of the patterns in the AIDS pandemic. Table 1 indicates the number of reported cases of AIDS in the United States. These figures must be viewed with caution, because the Centers for Disease Control and Prevention (CDC) has acknowledged that they may be low: Although 55% of known AIDS cases are reported within 3 months of diagnosis, 20% are not reported until a year or longer after diagnosis (CDC, 1993). Furthermore, the total cumulative

Table 1   Cumulative Numbers of Reported Cases of AIDS in the United States through June 1993

Geographic areas	Adults and adolescents	Children under 13	Total
Metropolitan areas with populations of 500,000 or more	264,665	3,971	268,636
Metropolitan areas with populations of 50,000 to 500,000	29,476	465	29,941
Non-metropolitan areas	15,343	253	15,596
Total	310,680	4,710	315,390

Note. Data are from Centers for Disease Control and Prevention (1993).

estimate of 315,390 known cases of AIDS in the United States does not reflect the number of HIV-infected persons who either are unaware of their status or have not sought medical care and therefore have not been counted in CDC estimates. Because the average incubation period for AIDS is 10 years (from time of infection with HIV until symptoms develop that warrant a diagnosis of full-blown AIDS), the number of cases of HIV-infected individuals worldwide who have not yet shown symptoms of AIDS was probably closer to 14 million than to the 11,799,000 shown in Table 2 ("AIDS Virus Progressing Faster," 1993). The estimates listed in Tables 2 and 3 (Mann, Tarantola, & Netter, 1992) also suggest an alarming rate of future growth: From 1995 to 2000, the number of cases of HIV infection worldwide is likely to double (a low estimate) and may increase as much as sixfold (a high estimate).

Tables 4 and 5 (Mann et al., 1992) illustrate some of the trends in modes of HIV transmission. Cases of HIV transmission are decreasing among homosexuals but are increasing among heterosexuals, and this trend is expected to continue. Indeed, since the discovery of the AIDS crisis in the early 1980s, the majority of HIV-infected individuals worldwide have been heterosexual, rather than homosexual. It is primarily in the United States where the homosexual community has been hit the hardest. That is perhaps why the homosexual community has been among the most highly organized and effective sources of HIV-related support services and prevention in the United States (Lynch, 1992). Ironically, this high level of organization may help to explain why the rate of HIV infection among homosexuals in North America is decreasing, but the myth that HIV infection is a gay person's disease is still present.

In contrast, in one study of African schoolchildren, the majority of the chil-

Table 2   Estimated Cumulative Number of Cases of HIV Infection among Adults Worldwide in 1992 and Projected for 1995

1992	1995	New cases	% Increase
11,799,000	17,454,000	5,655,000	48

Note. These estimates do not include pediatric cases of HIV infection. Data are from Mann, Tarantola, and Netter (1992).

Table 3   Comparison of Two Groups' Projections of Cumulative Number of HIV Infections in Adults Worldwide for 1995 and 2000

Group	1995	2000
AIDS in the World Coalition	17,454,000	38,112,000 (low) 108,748,000 (high)
World Health Organization	15–20 million	30–40 million

Note. These estimates do not include pediatric cases of HIV infection. Data are from Mann, Tarantola, and Netter (1992).

Table 4   Percentage of AIDS Cases among Adults in the United States by Mode of Transmission as Reported by the World Health Organization

Mode of transmission	1985	1990
Heterosexual intercourse	3	7
Homosexual/bisexual intercourse	66	56
Homosexual intercourse and injection drug use	9	6
Blood transfusion and blood products	3	3
Injection drug use	17	24
Other or unidentified	2	4

Note. These estimates do not include pediatric cases of HIV infection. Data are from Mann, Tarantola, and Netter (1992).

Table 5   Average Estimates of Percentage of HIV Infection by Mode of Transmission in North America: 1991 Versus 2000

Mode of transmission	End of 1991	End of 2000
Heterosexual	9	15
Homosexual	56	43
Blood transfusion and blood products	3	Less than 1
Injection drug use	27	35
Other or unidentified	5	7

Note. These estimates do not include pediatric cases of HIV infection. Data are from Mann, Tarantola, and Netter (1992).

dren indicated that they believed that women are the primary source of HIV transmission and that rich men with AIDS intentionally spread the disease to young women (Barnett & Blaikie, 1992). Thus, depending on where one lives, AIDS carries with it a variety of stigmas and myths emanating from ignorance. Regardless of such myths, by 2000, the World Health Organization has estimated, most new infections will be found in women ("Women's AIDS Rate Rising," 1992). Because of "physical discrimination" and sexual discrimination, women are at higher risk for HIV infection. The direction of sexual spread favors male-to-female transmission based on sheer anatomy; in addition, women are usually socialized to please men sexually and fear rejection if safer sex is suggested by the woman, and women in many cultures place a high value on bearing children and thus a low value on wearing condoms (Mann et al., 1992). However, most AIDS educators who seek to prevent the transmission of HIV agree that the phrase "high-risk groups" should be replaced with the phrase "high-risk behaviors."

In light of these dismal statistics, it is important to remember that the primary defense against HIV is currently prevention. For people already infected, treatment strategies are becoming increasingly complex, involving simultaneous administration of strong combinations of drugs (Chow et al., 1993) as well as holistic approaches based in the concepts of psychoneuroimmunology (Kiecolt-Glaser & Glaser, 1988; Temoshok & Dreher, 1992) and psychotherapy (Kain, 1989; Seligson & Peterson, 1992). Given the negative side effects of many medical interventions and the painful emotions often faced in psychotherapy, most

HIV-positive individuals find themselves on an emotional rollercoaster—with their families, friends, and professional caregivers forced along on the tumultuous ride.

Accordingly, this chapter focuses on the medical/psychological treatment of HIV-spectrum disease, the prevention of burnout among lay and professional caregivers, and the prevention of HIV transmission among the currently uninfected.

COPING WITH HIV-SPECTRUM DISEASE
The Course of HIV-Spectrum Disease

Etiology Researchers and theorists have offered numerous possible explanations for the origin of HIV, which actually comprises an extended family of viruses that are known to infect primates; two of these viruses, HIV-1 and HIV-2, are known to infect humans (Cowley, 1993). Many have speculated that humans first became infected from other primates, such as chimps or monkeys, via bites or scratches or possibly through a 1950s African polio vaccine program that employed kidney cells from African green monkeys (Cowley, 1993). Others have suggested that AIDS may in actuality be caused by syphilis (Mitchell, 1988). However, still other researchers have taken a Darwinian perspective, suggesting that HIV may be a very old virus that only recently has begun to survive more effectively by increasing its virulence: The virus can now afford to become so virulent that it kills off many of its hosts, because it can still survive via the transmission of bodily fluids from one human to another, and, as a result of more open sexual mores and the rise in intravenous drug use, the availability of hosts has increased (Cowley, 1993). The implication? Let's kill the virus off by making it less virulent again—by offering it no routes of transmission: Safer sex (there is no such thing as "safe sex" when one is with a partner) may prove to be the primary cure for AIDS, not just a form of prevention (Cowley, 1993).

HIV Infection What most people need to know is that the HIV attaches itself to the helper T-cells, which are the very cells that normally fight off viruses and other deadly invaders of our delicate systems. To make matters worse, HIV not only kills off these helper T-cells, but also uses them as hosts to replicate more HIV, which eventually wipes out an individual's immune system. Without an effective immune system, an individual becomes easy prey for a wide range of opportunistic infections (OIs)—bacterial and viral infections, syndromes, and diseases that ordinarily would be fought off by a healthy immune system. Hence the term "HIV-spectrum disease."

Among the most common OIs are pneumocystis carinii pneumonia, Kaposi's sarcoma (a formerly rare type of cancer), and cytomegalovirus infection (which may cause blindness prior to death) (Jennings, 1993; Mann et al., 1992; Seligson, 1992). Persons with AIDS also face the possibility of HIV-induced dementia, which may entail the loss of memory or cognitive functioning and shifts in mood state and personality, amounting basically to a young person's version of Alzheimer's disease (Rich, 1992).

Symptoms   The symptoms of HIV infection—which usually do not appear until 8–11 years after infection—are usually rather vague: sore throat, fever, swollen glands, diarrhea, fatigue, night sweats and chills, weight loss, and depression (Jennings, 1993; Mann et al., 1992). However, approximately 10–30% of individuals experience a more acute reaction to HIV infection, which may appear 2–4weeks after exposure, wherein the onset and the cessation of symptoms are quick and the symptoms may be quite severe (Jennings, 1993).

Among HIV-infected women, recurring gynecological problems are common (Corea, 1992; Norwood, 1988), as well as invasive cervical cancer (CDC, 1993). In pediatric cases of HIV infection, severe bacterial infections and lung diseases are more commonly seen (Fletcher et al., 1991). However, among adult cases of HIV infection, many persons may go symptom free for as long as 10 years (in some cases, longer) before they are even aware they are carrying the virus, and during this time they may infect others unknowingly (Cowley, 1993; Jennings, 1993). As mentioned, once HIV has depleted an individual's immune system, the body can no longer defend itself against the wide array of infectious diseases present in the environment, and with the presence of OIs an individual begins to develop full-blown AIDS (Seligson, 1992).

Testing   There is no test to detect the presence of AIDS or HIV, only tests to detect the presence of HIV antibodies, which are the human body's reaction to HIV infection. Because it usually takes approximately 3–6 months for the body to manufacture such antibodies, an "HIV test" the day after exposure is worthless—during this "window period," an infected person would test negative (Jennings, 1993; Seligson, 1992). Thus, the minimum amount of time to wait for testing after suspected exposure is 6 months, preferably with tests repeated at 3-month intervals for a year after the suspected exposure.

However, some researchers have found that some individuals may not develop HIV antibodies for as long as 36 months (Imagawa et al., 1989). Thus, it may be prudent for a person to practice safer sex and to continue getting tested for as long as 3 years after the suspected HIV exposure. Furthermore, because neither the ELISA (the initial screening) nor the Western blot test (the confirmatory screening)—which must be used in combination—is 100% accurate, and because labs are not 100% accurate and lab technicians are not 100% accurate ("False Positive," 1993), until science comes up with a cure, it is probably wise for a person to continue to practice safer sex even if he or she is not considered "seropositive" (HIV positive) after a testing series.

If an individual does decide to seek an HIV test, it is essential that the test be performed under *anonymous,* rather than merely confidential, conditions. An anonymous test means that the individual never gives a name, address, social security number, or any identification other than a random number, whereas a confidential test means that an individual is trusting that no one who sees his or her name in the file will be tempted to gossip or leak information. Although this may seem to border on paranoia, the literature and media are replete with examples of individuals who have suffered discrimination not only for being HIV positive, but also simply for getting tested (Harmon, 1992; Terl, 1992, 1993). In other words, even if an individual tests negative, he or she may still face being dropped or disqualified by insurance companies that may view this person as being at high risk. These and other counseling issues that arise before and after testing are discussed below.

The Treatment of HIV-Spectrum Disease

Medical Treatment   Researchers have found that a combination of three drugs—AZT, dideoxyinosine, and pyridinone—has been shown to cripple the virus believed to cause AIDS by preventing its replication (Chow et al., 1993). Furthermore, numerous treatments have been developed for halting the OIs associated with HIV, thereby prolonging patients' lives. Such OIs include pneuomocystis carinii pneumonia, cytomegalovirus infection, Kaposi's sarcoma, toxoplasmosis, candidiasis, cryptococcal meningitis, herpes zoster infection, mycobacterium infection, Epstein-Barr infection, cryptosporidiosis, and tuberculosis (Jennings, 1993; Levy, Van Der Meulen, & Apuzzo, 1993; Mann et al., 1992). For updated information on the latest in medical treatment, research, and prevention, the reader is advised to consult the many journals that focus on AIDS (e.g., *AIDS, AIDS Patient Care,* and *AIDS and Public Policy Journal*) as well as the proceedings from the annual International Conference on AIDS (available in libraries via Medline) and the CDC's National AIDS Clearinghouse hotline (1-800-458-5231).

Holistic Treatment   Just as the mainstream medical world has been sent scrambling for a treatment and cure for AIDS, so has the holistic community of alternative medicine, which is now consulted more often than primary care physicians in the United States for a variety of problems and disorders (Eisenberg et al., 1993). In response to the AIDS crisis, alternative medicine has suggested a variety of possible treatments, ranging from Siberian ginseng to vitamin E to therapeutic massage and meditation. Clinical evaluations conducted by the World Health Organization suggest that numerous Chinese herbs have anti-HIV properties (Mann et al., 1992). Some of the plant extracts, nutritional supplements, and alternative therapies that have been investigated for use with HIV-infected persons in controlled clinical trials include aloe vera extract, licorice, shiitake mushrooms, Compound Q, betacarotene, vitamins B_6 and B_{12}, and acupuncture (Mann et al., 1992). Such groups as the Treatment Alternatives Research Project in New York, a project of the PWA (People with Aids) Health Group in New York, are conducting observational studies of these and other treatments (Mann et al., 1992).

Psychological Treatment Many psychological issues have arisen as a result of the AIDS pandemic, such as grief, loss, and anger. It is important to remember that psychological treatment must be offered not only to HIV-positive individuals, but also to their lay caregivers (family members, friends, and lovers) and professional caregivers.

Counseling must be offered before and after an individual decides to take an HIV-antibody test. Issues to be covered in pretest counseling include reassurance that confidentiality will be maintained and that having an HIV-positive test result does not mean having full-blown AIDS. In addition, the client's physical and emotional states, level of knowledge of HIV and safer sex practices, level and type of high-risk behaviors, and willingness to inform sexual partners or needle-sharing partners if the test result is positive are assessed (Seligson, 1992). During the pretest counseling, the client must provide written consent for the testing procedures. Finally, during the waiting period before the client returns for the test results, the counselor must assess the client's coping resources. The test results are given during a scheduled posttest counseling session (Seligson, 1992), During posttest counseling, clients who are HIV negative must be told that such a test result is not a guarantee of permanent safety and that the result may be invalid if high-risk behaviors occurred within the last few months (the window phase). Repeated testing at 3- or 6-month intervals is recommended, and safer sex should still be practiced.

Clients who must be told they are HIV positive should be carefully assessed, especially for suicidal tendencies. They must also be reassured that being HIV positive does not mean they have AIDS or are about to die. Numerous medical treatments are available to forestall the development of AIDS and to treat OIs, and clients should be given the names of physicians, holistic practitioners, and psychotherapists to ensure that they maintain the highest level of physical and mental health possible in order to boost the immune system. HIV-positive individuals should be counseled to inform their sexual partners and needle-sharing partners of the test results. They should also be advised to practice safer sex, not only to avoid infecting others, but also to avoid reinfecting themselves, because each exposure to HIV elevates viral activity in an already-infected person (Seligson, 1992).

In addition to being told they should maintain a well-balanced regimen of healthy foods and exercise and abstain from alcohol and any other nonprescribed drugs so as not to compromise their immune systems further (Cowart, 1992; Seligson, 1992), HIV-positive clients must also be offered other coping mechanisms within and outside the context of psychotherapy. Numerous 12-step groups are available, such as Alcoholics Anonymous, Narcotics Anonymous, Codependents Anonymous, Incest Survivors Anonymous, and Sex and Love Addicts Anonymous. Support groups run by community-based AIDS organizations are also available (Lynch, 1992).

Once the HIV-positive individual makes the transition from one or more counseling sessions with the posttest counselor to the initial session with the follow-up counselor, care must be taken to instill a sense of hope. Issues to be covered include coping with emotions such as anxiety, fear, stigmatization, shame, sadness, grief, and guilt, as well as coping with life issues such as discrimination, loss of job, and loss of family or friends, many of whom will abandon the HIV-positive person upon learning of the diagnosis (Harmon, 1992; Kübler-Ross, 1987; O'Donnell, 1992; Seligson, 1992; Terl, 1992; Youngstrom, 1991). Of particular importance is the young age at which most persons are diagnosed with AIDS: 60% of men and 61% of women who are diagnosed with AIDS are between the ages of 25 and 39 (CDC, 1993). Thus, the counselor must address the issues that arise when HIV-positive individuals find themselves incapacitated by a critical illness, something they didn't expect to face until old age.

What is perhaps most important to remember in counseling the HIV-positive individual is the sheer unpredictability of HIV-spectrum disease. One day the client may be healthy enough to take a trip to Paris, and a week later he or she may be close to death from a sudden bout of pneumonia. And yet while some HIV-positive persons have fallen prey and died from an OI fairly soon after a diagnosis of full-blown AIDS, others have remained relatively healthy for more than 10 years after being diagnosed with full-blown AIDS—which means they have been HIV-positive for as long as 20 years (Callen, 1990). Thus, although it is important to discuss such issues as anticipatory grief (early stages of grief in anticipation of death), the living will, and power of attorney contracts (O'Donnell, 1992), it is also essential to instill a sense of hope and positive thinking in the minds of those who are HIV positive.

Some of the psychotherapeutic techniques that may be used to help the HIV-positive person maintain some sense of stability and hope include cognitive restructuring (reframing the disease and creating changes in thinking patterns toward irreversible life crises), Gestalt rage work or empty-chair dialogues (allowing the client to "argue" with the virus, to become angry at it rather than being angry at the self, or allowing the client to switch chairs in order to experience his or her empowered side versus his or her victim side), hypnotherapy (to relieve stress and to encourage healthy immune system functioning), and stress management techniques. Poetry therapy may also be helpful (Hadas, 1991; Leedy, 1969; Peterson, 1992c), whether clients create their own poetry (Hadas, 1991) or read the poetry of other AIDS survivors (Hadas, 1991; Monette, 1988).

Increasing HIV-positive individuals' use of humor may also be beneficial, because humor—if used properly—has been shown to enhance psychotherapy (Fry & Salameh, 1987; Peterson, 1992c). Research has also indicated that humor can decrease stress (White & Winzelberg, 1992) and physical pain (Cogan, Cogan, Waltz, & McCue, 1987). Humor has even been shown to bolster the healthy functioning of the immune system (Berk, Tan, Nehlsen-Cannarella, Napier, Lee, et al., 1988; Berk, Tan, Nehlsen-Cannarella, Napier, Lewis, et al., 1988; Dillon, Minchoff, & Baker, 1985–86, as cited by Cousins, 1989). However, it is important that a therapeutic level of humor be used (Salameh, 1983) so that the client is not denigrated in any way. The idea is to make the disease, not the client, the object of humor. For example, in the Humorous Anger Response (Peterson, 1992c), clients are asked to fill in the blank regarding their level of anger by comparing themselves humorously to a character in a play or movie.

Such a technique may also be adapted for use with lay and professional caregivers of HIV-positive individuals (the Humorous Anger Response–Revised, which follows, may be used with caregivers.).

Humorous Anger Response–Revised

Imagine that you are a comedian or humorist—someone like Jay Leno, Whoopi Goldberg, Steve Martin, Paula Poundstone, Quentin Crips, Carol Burnett, Mark Twain—but definitely *your favorite* humorist. Picture yourself sitting at a desk, writing your script for your next monologue, which happens to be about your anger regarding the effects of being a lay or professional caregiver to HIV-positive persons. Below are a few "starter" sentences to help you develop your monologue.

I'm telling you, being a _____ (nurse, physician, friend, etc.) to an HIV-positive person in the 1990s is like _____.
The first time I had to _____
I felt like _____ (main character)
in _____ (movie/play/TV show).
The only difference was that in the original _____
(movie/play/TV show), the main character (does/doesn't) _____,
and in my real life version, I ended up looking like _____ and (thinking/feeling/doing) _____.

Adapted from HAR [Humorous Anger Response; K. E. Peteson (1992). The use of humor in AIDS prevention, in the treatment of HIV-positive persons, and in the remediation of caregiver burnout. In M. R. Seligson & K. E. Peterson (Eds.), *AIDS prevention and treatment: Hope, humor, and healing* (pp. 37–57). New York: Hemisphere.].

A high degree of burnout is to be expected among caregivers, be they family members/friends/lovers or physicians/nurses/mental health practitioners. Support groups may assist these individuals in coping with feelings of helplessness, loss, grief, anger, anxiety, and burnout (Grossman & Silverstein, 1993; Namir & Sherman, 1989; Seligson, 1992; Thomas, 1989).

Thus, just as HIV-positive individuals need to maintain a sense of humor, so do their loved ones and professional caretakers. Cousins (1979, 1989) and Siegel (1986, 1989, 1993), in particular, have recommended a more equal balance of power in the patient–medical practitioner relationship (Ratzan, 1993), including a healthy interchange of humor. This is perhaps most absurdly exemplified by one of Garry Trudeau's *Doonesbury* strips, wherein Andy's doctor tells him that his Kaposi's sarcoma lesions "clash with your jammies." But timing is everthing, and such a humorous response requires a great degree of trust and camaraderie between the HIV-positive individual and the caregiver. The budding humorist would do well to investigate the appropriate and skillful use of humor in psychotherapy before practicing it on a given patient (Peterson, 1992c; Salameh, 1983).

THE PREVENTION OF HIV-TRANSMISSION

Humor may also provide a helpful forum for the AIDS educator who seeks to prevent further HIV infection in any and all populations—for though we try to deny it, we are all at risk. One long-term AIDS survivor has summed up quite accurately the current level of denial: "There's an old Jewish story that applies to AIDS. Right now, most United States citizens are saying, "Oh, don't worry; the leak is in the *back* of the boat, and I'm in the front'" (C. Shihar, cited by Callen, 1990, p. 95).

But in the world of safer sex, one rule of thumb can save a life: Don't exchange bodily fluids. Although this sounds simple enough in theory, it is difficult to put into practice (Peterson, 1992a).

Prerequisites for Prevention

Health educators and prevention experts alike agree that certain conditions must be present if the spread of any disease is to be prevented and that changing group norms is the key to behavior modification (Glaser, 1989). These conditions are clearly articulated in the health belief model developed by Becker in 1974 (cited by Guydish & Ekstrand, 1989) and later adapted to include the effects of perceived norms and Bandura's (1977) model of self-efficacy. According to the health belief model, six factors influence an individual's willingness to modify his or her behaviors and attitudes to prevent disease:

1   Knowledge of the disease and of preventive behavior;
2   Perceived susceptibility to a given disease and beliefs regarding the severity of the consequences;
3   Perceived benefits and costs of engaging in preventive behavior;
4   A cue that triggers preventive behavior, such as the illness of a friend or reading about the disease;
5   Peer and social norms, which may be perceived as supporting or discouraging preventive behavior; and
6   A sense of self-efficacy, or seeing the self as capable of engaging in preventive behavior (Guydish & Ekstrand, 1989, pp. 31–32).

Thus, it is clear that if the spread of AIDS is to be prevented, people must be aware that the disease is a real and present danger, that the benefits of prevention far outweigh the costs of unsafe sex, and that techniques of prevention are readily available. Among gay men in the United States, these precepts have been instilled since the early 1980s, and one result has been a stabilization and subsequent lowering of HIV infection rates among gay men, whereas HIV infection rates are rising among heterosexuals (Mann et al., 1992). Thus, if done effectively, AIDS prevention programs can work, as has been documented in various research projects, such as those with college student populations (Castronovo, 1990; Rhodes & Wolitski, 1989; Silver, Gerrity, & Akman, 1989). However, in some individuals who may be at higher risk of experiencing unsafe sexual encounters, these precepts are particularly difficult to instill (Peterson, 1992b).

Hidden Populations

Preventing AIDS in groups of individuals who may be likely to have unsafe sexual experiences means dealing with a multitude of underlying issues that these persons have traditionally met with denial. For example, such groups include both male and female survivors of childhood sexual abuse (Davis, 1990; Lew, 1988; Mann et al., 1992; Uribe, Ornelas, Valdespino, & Palacios, 1989), who often attempt to regain sexual control via high-risk promiscuity, yet rarely remember or spontaneously disclose their abuse histories (Stinson & Hendrick, 1992). Cases of severe sexual abuse may engender multiple personality disorder (Braun, 1986; Kluft, 1985; Putnam, 1989; Ross, Anderson, Heber, & Norton, 1990), wherein adulthood sexual encounters that appear to be voluntary may not even be remembered by the host or core personality, especially because it is often a naive child alter who emerges during such sexual encounters (Peterson, 1992b). This problem was sadly illustrated by the recent case of the young woman with multiple personality disorder who took her assailant to court after he purposely elicited one of her child alters in order to force sex upon her ("*Woman*: Man Raped My Naive Personality," 1990). Obviously, safer sex practices are not common in such cases.

Even among less clinical populations, to prevent more cases of AIDS, health educators must address the epidemic number of acquaintance rapes among teenagers and adults—10% of which involve male victims (Parrot, 1988). But the majority of survivors of acquaintance rape are women between the ages of 15 and 24 (Parrot & Bohmer, 1993). This problem has been tragically illustrated by the case of a young woman who has chosen to speak out about her experience. A virgin, she became infected with HIV when she was raped on her first date with a male acquaintance ("A Sad Sisterhood," 1990). Indeed, with the rise in gang rapes on college campuses (Parrot & Bohmer, 1993; Sanday, 1990), university administrators are becoming increasingly aware of what has been called the "triple-A phenomenon": alcohol abuse, acquaintance rape, and AIDS (Peterson, 1992a). In one study, 35% of fraternity men reported that they had forced sex on a woman at least once (Parrot & Bohmer, 1993). Similarly, university HIV prevention materials must address such high-risk behaviors as male and female roommates' sharing blood-tainted razors, athletes' sharing needles for injecting illegal steroids, and the use of shared needles for tattooes.

Adolescents and teenagers are particularly at risk for unsafe sexual experiences, because they have a high degree of denial of death and are often at the height of their sexual exploration (Hein, Blair, Ratzan, & Dyson, 1993; Kantrowitz et al., 1992). Homeless youth, who often sell their bodies for sex in exchange for food or money, are also a population in which the HIV rate is increasing (Rotheram-Borus, Koopman, & Ehrhardt, 1991), especially when substance abuse is a factor. Obviously, the abuse of alcohol and other drugs, commonly found among individuals with low self-esteem and dysfunctional family histories (Bradshaw, 1990; Carey, 1993; Thombs, Beck, & Mahoney, 1993), will often cloud individuals' judgment during a sexual encounter, leading to high-risk sexual behaviors.

Other examples of subgroups who have problems with self-esteem and a high need for affection, both of which make it less likely that an individual will insist on a high level of safety during sexual encounters, include men or women suffering from a relationship loss (e.g., through death or divorce) and women with premenstrual syndrome (Frank, Dixon, & Grosz, 1993; Peterson, 1992b). Among many women with premenstrual syndrome, there is a particularly lethal combination of high-risk factors that occur 3–4 days before the onset of menstruation: an increase in sex drive, an increase in cravings for alcohol, and a lowered tolerance for alcohol (Dalton, 1990)—the perfect setup for a one-night stand or an acquaintance rape. Even lesbians are at risk via sexual contact during menstruation (blood contact), as well as via artificial insemination with a potentially HIV-infected donor (Jennings, 1993).

Health Care Workers

The prevention of HIV transmission is a serious issue for health care workers. As of June 1993, the CDC had reported a total of 37 documented cases of occupationally transmitted HIV, with an additional 78 possible cases of occupational transmission (CDC, 1993). To prevent HIV exposure, health care workers must follow the universal precautions set forth by the CDC with all patients at all times. To clean up spills of HIV-infected materials (e.g., blood, vomit, urine, or feces), a worker must use latex gloves and a 10% bleach solution (one part bleach, nine parts water). If human skin is exposed to HIV-infected materials, it must be immediately washed with soap and water. If an open wound is exposed to HIV-infected materials, it must be immediately flushed with large amounts of hydrogen peroxide or a 10% bleach solution, although these two solutions may not be used on mucous membranes or in the eyes, mouth, vagina, anus, urethra, or other body orifices (Jennings, 1993).

Suggestions for Education

Whether one is conducting an AIDS education workshop for health professionals, college students, church groups, or the elderly, it is important to keep in mind that most people do not want to sit through a droning speech about macrophages and retroviruses (although a good reference or two included in the program packet for the intellectually curious may be helpful; e.g., Mann et al., 1992; Rich, 1992; Seligson, 1992). An excellent source for the layperson is Jennings's (1993) *Understanding and Preventing AIDS: A Book for Everyone,* a 30-page booklet that is updated with each printing. A further resource for education and prevention is the CDC AIDS Hotline: 1-800-342-AIDS.

However, once the audience members are keenly aware of just how virulent

HIV can be, they usually need a bit of humor to make the detailed discussion of safer sex practices at least tolerable. Such a balanced approach to persuasion has been shown to be effective in communication research: After the arousal of fear, participants should be given information about how to reduce such fear, and humor is an effective modality (Edgar, Hammond, & Freimuth, 1989).

Why humor? Consider the many ways in which humor may assist in breaking down the high level of denial that most people have about the risk of becoming HIV positive (Catania et al., 1992). Humor has been correlated with increased openness in conversation (Fink & Walker, 1977), higher levels of self-disclosure (Avant, 1982), personal adjustment (Clabby, 1980), and high ego strength (Goldsmith, 1979). Humor can also reduce stress (Dixon, 1980; White & Winzelberg, 1992), anxiety (Ribordy, Holmes, & Buchsbaum, 1980), and aggression (Baron, 1978; Grody, 1976). Numerous programs using humor for AIDS prevention have proven to be successful in changing participants' thoughts and behaviors about HIV risk (Baggaley, 1988; Downer, Kelleigh, Welch, & Purdue, 1989; Edgar et al., 1989; Ramos, Afonso, Gomes, & Ramos, 1989).

But whether one chooses to use a humorous film wherein the use of a condom is demonstrated with a banana (AIDSFILMS, 1987) or a more serious film (e.g., one of those produced by the HIV Center for Clinical and Behavorial Studies in New York) or pamphlet (American College Health Association, 1990) or handouts that combine both the serious and the humorous (Appendixes A–R in Seligson & Peterson, 1992), certain information must be articulated to help people to avoid HIV infection. People must be told that instead of assuming that a partner is telling the truth about his or her past sexual history or current sexual habits, they should become particularly well versed in the truths about safer sex versus "suicidal sex" (Kaplan, 1987), because research indicates that both men and women will lie about their sexual histories in order to have sex (Cochran & Mays, 1990).

In discussing condoms, it is particularly important to remind an audience that although condoms are not 100% effective, they should still be used for any form of intercourse—oral, vaginal, or anal—and from the start of intercourse. (Flavored condoms are now available for oral sex on a man.) Some people believe that as long as the man does not ejaculate into his partner, whether male or female, there is no risk of pregnancy or HIV exposure. However, aside from the fact that without a condom the man is as much at risk as the woman, it is important to remember that the first few drops of semen may be the most potent in terms of sperm count, and if the man is HIV positive, the preejaculatory fluid may contain HIV as well.

Furthermore, some heterosexual couples who use condoms primarily for birth control may engage in vaginal intercourse without a condom while the woman is menstruating, under the mistaken assumption that she cannot become pregnant during the menstrual phase (sperm can remain alive in the woman's body for as long as 3 days, and if she has an early ovulation, pregnancy may result). This is a high-risk behavior that should be avoided, because there may be blood-to-semen contact that puts either partner at risk if the other is infected.

The mistaken belief that a woman cannot become pregnant during the menstrual phase is only one of many reasons why condoms are not always used. Loss of erection—an experience particularly common among those who are not accustomed to using condoms—is another of the reasons given for refusal to use a condom, as are the loss of sensation and perceived loss of romance. Again, it is important to emphasize to people that good partner communication is essential, and assertiveness training is definitely in order (Breitman, Knutson, & Reed, 1987; Whipple & Ogden, 1989). "Let me help you" can be an inviting way of stimulating a partner into not giving up when the penis becomes flaccid. However, manual stimulation should not be given with the same hand that was used on the partner before he put on the condom, when preejaculatory fluid may have been released.

In spite of the fact that condoms are the only protection available for vaginal, anal, and oral intercourse (outside of dental dams or nonmicrowavable plastic food wrap for oral sex on a woman), a recent study of more than 10,000 Americans in the general heterosexual population revealed that only 17% of sexually active persons with multiple partners reported that they use condoms all the time (Catania et al., 1992). Now that the female condom (which protects the inner and outer anatomy of the woman) has been approved for use in the United States, it may be interesting to compare how often women are willing to use them as well ("Female Condoms Expected on Shelves," 1993; Mann et al., 1992). Although less effective than male condoms, the female condom, when used with such products as vaginal contraceptive film (a dissolving translucent wafer of spermicide inserted 5–15 min before intercourse), may prove to be helpful for the woman who is unable or unwilling to convince her male partner to wear a condom. Indeed, many AIDS activists and researchers have called for an HIV prevention method that is more directly under women's control (Corea, 1992; Juffer, 1992).

The troubling dilemma is this, however: After all is said and done, even male condoms are not 100% effective. Their failure rate in terms of preventing pregnancy generally ranges between 2% (nondefective condoms correctly used) and 30% (incorrect use, defective condoms, condom breakage during highly vigorous intercourse). Furthermore, whereas a woman can get pregnant only 1 or 2 days out of 30, either partner can become infected with HIV 30 days out of 30, so although we are still not sure how effective condoms are in preventing HIV, it is possible that they do not have the same effectiveness rate they have in preventing pregnancy. Still, they are the only protection available, and when considering intercourse of any kind, the question people need to ask themselves is quite basic: Is this person worth dying for?

Because one cannot tell by looking at a person is he or she is HIV infected, and because an infected person may not even know he or she is HIV positive for as long as 10 years (or more), it is essential that condoms be used correctly, every time one engages in any form of intercourse.

One should purchase condoms made of latex rubber only (lambskin condoms have microscopic holes that can be penetrated by HIV). After checking the expiration date on the package, one must be sure to purchase condoms that are pre-lubricated (with nonoxynol-9 spermicide) and have a reservoir tip—both charac-teristics help prevent breakage. The condoms must not be exposed to heat or light, and they should be used only with water-based lubricants such as K-Y Jelly. Heat, light, and oil-based lubricants such as hand lotion will destroy a condom.

In light of these cautionary facts about condom use, it is wise to recommend that individuals abstain from any form of intercourse—oral, vaginal, or anal. The fact is, if someone is worth dying for, he or she is also worth living for. Most women are relieved and most men are intrigued when told that the majority of women are orgasmic not through intercourse, but rather through gentle, indirect manual stimulation of the clitoris. The fact is that safer sex is often better sex, because it is more likely to lead to orgasm for many women and to open commu-nication and more intimacy as each partner discusses what he or she likes in terms of physical contact.

But no matter how well-versed an AIDS educator may be in "AIDS 101" and "Safer Sex," nothing will get through to an audience that is too deep in denial to hear the realities of HIV transmission. Thus the AIDS educator not only must be comfortable with the frank discussion of sex, but also must be comfortable enough with him- or herself to get an audience laughing about the foibles of hu-mankind as we grapple with our sexuality, keeping ourselves safe until science comes up with a cure.

Summary

In summary, it may be instructive to cite the words of Reverend Steven Pieters, a long-term AIDS survivor: "I have done lots of laughter therapy, like Norman Cousins recommends. I bought a VCR and have lots of sitcoms on tapes and musical comedy. . . . Now, I want to write a book. I think I'll call it *Tap Dancing Through AIDS*" (Callen, 1990, p. 87). The essential message for caregivers and the HIV-positive person is this: Perhaps we cannot in actuality tap-dance our way through this horrific pandemic, and perhaps we cannot always laugh in the face of the potential death of millions of unique individuals from hundreds of cultures worldwide, and perhaps we cannot ignore the fact that we are faced with what might be our ultimate destruction, but one thing is certain: In conducting preven-tion programs, providing treatment, and engaging in research for the cure of AIDS, we must all be empowered by that which can never die, the hope and humor and healing power of the human spirit.

REFERENCES

A sad sisterhood. (1990, July 30). *People Magazine*, pp. 66–72.

AIDSFILMS. (Producer). (1987). *AIDS: Changing the rules* [videotape]. Franklin Getchell and John Hoffman, directors. (Available from AIDSFILMS, 50 West 34th Street, #6B6, New York, NY, 10001)

AIDS virus progressing faster than research, head of U.S. effort says. (1993, June 13). *Miami Herald*, p. 31A.

American College Health Association. (1990). *Making sex safer.* (Available from American College Health Association, P.O. Box 28937, Baltimore, MD 21240-8937)

Avant, K. M. (1982). Humor and self-disclosure. *Psychological Reports, 50,* 253–254.

Baggaley, J. P. (1988). Perceived effectiveness of international AIDS campaign. *Health Education Research, 3*(1), 7–17.

Bandura, A. (1977). Self-efficacy: Toward a unifying theory of behavioral change. *Psychological Review, 84,* 191–215.

Barnett, T., & Blaikie, P. (1992). *AIDS in Africa: Its present and future impact.* New York: Guilford Press.

Baron, R. A. (1978). Aggression-inhibiting influence of sexual humor. *Journal of Personality and Social Psychology, 36,* 189–197.

Berk, L. S., Tan, S. A., Nehlsen-Cannarella, S. L., Napier, B. J., Lee, J. W., Lewis, J. E., Hubbard, R. W., & Eby, W. C. (1988). Mirth modulates adrenocorticomedullary activity: Suppression of cortisol and epinephrine. *Clinical Research, 36,* 121A.

Berk, L. S., Tan, S. A., Nehlsen-Cannarella, S. L., Napier, B. J., Lewis, J. E., Lee, J. W., & Eby, W. C. (1988). Humor associated laughter decreases cortisol and increases spontaneous lymphocyte blastogenesis. *Clinical Research, 36,* 435A.

Bradshaw, J. (1990). *Homecoming: Reclaiming and championing your inner child.* New York: Bantam.

Braun, B. G. (Ed.). (1986). *Treatment of multiple personality disorder.* Washington, DC: American Psychiatric Press.

Breitman, P., Knutson, K., & Reed, P. (1987). *How to persuade your lover to use a condom . . . and why you should.* Rocklin, CA: Prima.

Callen, M. (1990). *Surviving AIDS.* New York: HarperCollins.

Carey, K. B. (1993). Situational determinants of heavy drinking among college students. *Journal of Counseling Psychology, 40,* 217–220.

Castronovo, N. R. (1990). Acquired immune deficiency syndrome education on the college campus: The mandate and the challenge. *Journal of Counseling and Development, 68,* 578–580.

Catania, J. A., Coates, T. J., Stall, R., Turner, H., Peterson, J., Hearst, N., Dolcini, M. M., Hudes, E., Gagnon, J., Wiley, J., & Groves, R. (1992). Prevalence of AIDS-related risk factors and condom use in the United States. *Science, 258,* 1101–1106.

Centers for Disease Control and Prevention. (1993). *HIV/AIDS Surveillance Report, 5*(2).

Chow, Y. K., Hirsch, M. S., Merrill, D. P., Bechtel, L. J., Eron, J. J., Kaplan, J. C., & D'Aquila, R. T. (1993). Use of evolutionary limitations of HIV-1 multidrug resistance to optimize therapy. *Nature, 361,* 650–654.

Clabby, J. F. (1980). The wit: A personality analysis. *Journal of Personality Assessment, 44,* 307–310.

Cochran, S. D., & Mays, V. M. (1990). Sex, lies, and HIV. *New England Journal of Medicine, 322,* 774–775.

Cogan, R., Cogan, D., Waltz, W., & McCue, M. (1987). Effects of laughter and relaxation on discomfort thresholds. *Journal of Behavioral Medicine, 10,* 139–144.

Corea, G. (1992). *The invisible epidemic: The story of women and AIDS.* New York: HarperCollins.

Cousins, N. (1979). *Anatomy of an illness: As perceived by the patient.* Toronto, Ontario, Canada: Bantam.

Cousins, N. (1989). *Head first: The biology of hope and the healing power of the human spirit.* New York: Penguin.

Cowart, J. (1992). Substance abuse and AIDS. In M. R. Seligson & K. E. Peterson (Eds.), *AIDS prevention and treatment: Hope, humor, and healing* (Pp. 143–152). Washington, DC: Hemisphere.

Cowley, G. (1993, March 22). The future of AIDS. *Newsweek,* pp. 46–52.

Dalton, K. (1990). *Once a month: The original premenstrual syndrome handbook.* Claremont, CA: Hunter House.

Davis, L. (1990). *The courage to heal handbook: For women and men survivors of child sexual abuse.* New York: Harper & Row.

Dixon, N. F. (1980). Humor: A cognitive alternative to stress? In I. Sarason & C. D. Spielberger (Eds.), *Stress and anxiety* (Vol. 7, pp. 281–289). Washington, DC: Hemisphere.

Downer, A., Kelleigh, B., Welch, N., & Purdue, T. (1989, June). *The judicious use of humor in a condom promotion campaign.* Paper presented at the International Conference on AIDS, Montreal, Quebec, Canada.

Edgar, T., Hammond, S. L., & Freimuth, V. S. (1989). The role of the mass media and interpersonal communication in promoting AIDS-related behavioral change. *AIDS & Public Policy Journal, 4,* 3–9.

Eisenberg, D. M., Kessler, R. C., Foster, C., Norlock, F. E., Calkins, D. R., & Delbanco, T. L. (1993). Unconventional medicine in the United States: Prevalence, costs, and patterns of use. *New England Journal of Medicine, 328,* 246–252.

False positive HIV test leads to suit. (1993, February 19). *Miami Herald,* p. 6B.

Female condomd expected on shelves by end of the year. (1993, May 11). *Miami Herald,* p. 5A.

Fink, E. L., & Walker, B. A. (1977). Humorous responses to embarrassment. *Psychological Reports, 40,* 475–485.

Fletcher, J. M., Francis, D. J., Pequegnat, W., Raudenbush, S. W., Bornstein, M. H., Schmitt, F., Brouwers, P., & Stover, E. (1991). Neurobehavioral outcomes in diseases of childhood: Individual change models for pediatric human immunodeficiency viruses. *American Psychologist, 46,* 1267–1277.

Frank, B., Dixon, D. N., & Grosz, H. J. (1993). Conjoint monitoring of symptoms of premenstrual syndrome: Impact on marital satisfaction. *Journal of Counseling Psychology, 40,* 109–114.

Fry, W. F., & Salameh, W. A. (Eds.). (1987). *Handbook of humor and psychotherapy: Advances in the clinical use of humor.* Sarasota, FL: Professional Resource Exchange.

Glaser, V. (1989). Battling AIDS through behavior modification. *New York State Journal of Medicine, 89,* 108.

Goldsmith, L. A. (1979). Adaptive regression, humor, and suicide. *Journal of Consulting and Clinical Psychology, 47,* 628–630.

Grody, G. L. (1976). The effects of exposing derisive humor to juvenile delinquent males as a cathartic tool to reduce aggressive impulse strength. *Dissertation Abstracts International, 37,* 2477B.

Grossman, A. H., & Silverstein, C. (1993). Facilitating support groups for professionals working with people with AIDS. *Social Work, 38,* 144–151.

Guydish, J. R., & Ekstrand, M. (1989). A research update for counselors. In C. D. Kain (Ed.), *No longer immune: A counselor's guide to AIDS* (pp. 29–50). Alexandria, VA: American Association for Counseling and Development.

Hadas, R. (1991). *Unending dialogue: Voices from an AIDS poetry workshop.* Boston: Faber & Faber.

Harmon, L. (1992). AIDS in the workplace. In M. R. Seligson & K. E. Peterson (Eds.), *AIDS prevention and treatment: Hope, humor, and healing* (pp. 175–197). Washington, DC: Hemisphere.

Hein, K. K., Blair, J. F., Ratzan, S. C., & Dyson, D. E. (1993). Adolescents and HIV: Two decades of denial. In S. C. Ratzan (Ed.), *AIDS: Effective health communication for the 90s* (pp. 215–232). Washington, DC: Taylor & Francis.

Imagawa, D. T., Lee, M. H., Wolinsky, S. M., Sano, K., Morales, F., Kwok, S., Sninsky, J. J., Nishanian, P. G., Giorgi, J., Fahey, J. L., Dudley, J., Visscher, B. R., & Detels, R. (1989). Human immunodeficiency virus type 1 infection in homosexual men who remain seronegative for prolonged periods. *New England Journal of Medicine, 320,* 1458–1462.

Jennings, C. (1993). *Understanding and preventing AIDS: A book for everyone.* Cambridge, MA: Health Alert Press.

Juffer, J. (1992, September/October). Spermicides, virucides, and HIV. *Ms.,* pp. 74–75.

Kain, C. D. (Ed.). (1989). *No longer immune: A counselor's guide to AIDS.* Alexandria, VA: American Association for Counseling and Development.

Kantrowitz, B., Hager, M., Cowley, G., Beachy, L., Rossi, M., Craffey, B., Annin, P., & Crandall, R. (1992, August 3). Teenagers and AIDS. *Newsweek,* pp. 44–50.

Kaplan, H. S. (1987). *The real truth about women and AIDS: How to eliminate the risks without giving up love and sex.* New York: Simon & Schuster.

Kiecolt-Glaser, J. K., & Glaser, R. (1988). Psychological influences on immunity: Implications for AIDS. *American Psychologist, 43,* 892–898.

Kluft, R. P. (Ed.). (1985). *Childhood antecedents of multiple personality.* Washington, DC: American Psychiatric Press.

Kübler-Ross, E. (1987). *AIDS: The ultimate challenge.* New York: Macmillan.

Leedy, J. J. (1969). *Poetry therapy.* Philadelphia: J. B. Lippincott.

Levy, M. L., Van Der Meulen, J. P., & Apuzzo, M. L. J. (1993). Neurosurgical professionalism and care in the treatment of patients with symptomatic AIDS. In S. C. Ratzan (Ed.), *AIDS: Effective health communication for the 90s* (pp. 203–214). Washington, DC: Taylor & Francis.

Lew, M. (1988). *Victims no longer: Men recovering from incest and other sexual child abuse.* New York: Harper & Row.

Lynch, M. F. (1992). Social support in men and women with AIDS. In M. R. Seligson & K. E. Peterson (Eds.), *AIDS prevention and treatment: Hope, humor, and healing* (pp. 59–73). Washington, DC: Hemisphere.

Mann, J., Tarantola, D. J. M., & Netter, T. W. (1992). *AIDS in the world.* Cambridge, MA: Harvard University Press.

Mitchell, R. B. (1988). *Syphilis as AIDS.* Austin, TX: Banned Books.

Monette, P. (1988). *Love alone: 18 elegies for Rog.* New York: St. Martin's Press.

Namir, S., & Sherman, S. (1989). Coping with countertransference. In C. D. Kain (Ed.), *No longer immune: A counselor's guide to AIDS* (pp. 263–280). Alexandria, VA: American Association for Counseling and Development.

Norwood, C. (1988, July). Alarming rise in deaths. *Ms.,* pp. 65, 67.

O'Donnell, M. C. (1992). Loss, grief, and growth. In M. R. Seligson & K. E. Peterson (Eds.), *AIDS prevention and treatment: Hope, humor, and healing* (pp. 107–117). Washington, DC: Hemisphere.

Parrot, A. (1988). *Coping with date rape and acquaintance rape.* New York: Rosen.

Parrot, A., & Bohmer, C. (1993). *Sexual assault on campus: The problem and the solution.* Lexington, MA: Lexington Books.

Peterson, K. E. (1992a). AIDS education and prevention at colleges and universities. In M. R. Seligson & K. E. Peterson (Eds.), *AIDS prevention and treatment: Hope, humor, and healing* (pp. 121–141). Washington, DC: Hemisphere.

Peterson, K. E. (1992b). Hidden populations at high risk for HIV infection. In M. R. Seligson & K. E. Peterson (Eds.), *AIDS prevention and treatment: Hope, humor, and healing* (pp. 153–172). Washington, DC: Hemisphere.

Peterson, K. E. (1992c). The use of humor in AIDS prevention, in the treatment of HIV-positive persons, and in the remediation of caregiver burnout. In M. R. Seligson & K. E. Peterson (Eds.), *AIDS prevention and treatment: Hope, humor, and healing* (pp. 37–57). Washington, DC: Hemisphere.

Putnam, F. (1989). *Diagnosis and treatment of multiple personality disorder.* New York: Guilford Press.

Ramos, S., Afonso, C., Gomes, C., & Ramos, M. J. (1989, June). *An AIDS prevention program designed for civil construction workers in Rio de Janeiro.* Paper presented at the International Conference on AIDS, Montreal, Quebec, Canada.

Ratzan, S. (1993). Health communication as negotiation: The COAST model and AIDS. In S. C. Ratzan (Ed.), *AIDS: Effective health communication for the 90s* (pp. 37–53). Washington, DC: Taylor & Francis.

Rhodes, F., & Wolitski, R. (1989). Effect of instructional videotapes on AIDS knowledge and attitudes. *Journal of American College Health, 37,* 266–271.

Ribordy, S. C., Holmes, D. S., & Buchsbaum, H. K. (1980). Effects of affective and cognitive distractions on anxiety reduction. *Journal of Social Psychology, 112,* 121–127.

Rich, L. D. (1992). Central nervous system complications of HIV infection. In M. R. Seligson & K. E. Peterson (Eds.), *AIDS prevention and treatment: Hope, humor, and healing* (pp. 75–105). Washington, DC: Hemisphere.

Ross, C. A., Anderson, G., Heber, S., & Norton, G. R. (1990). Dissociation and abuse among multiple-personality patients, prostitutes, and exotic dancers. *Hospital and Community Psychiatry, 41,* 328–330.

Rotheram-Borus, M. J., Koopman, C., & Ehrhardt, A. A. (1991). Homeless youths and HIV infection. *American Psychologist, 46,* 1188–1197.

Salameh, W. A. (1983). Humor in psychotherapy: Past outlooks, present status, and future frontiers. In P. E. McGhee & J. H. Goldstein (Eds.), *Handbook of humor research* (Vol. 2, pp. 61–88). New York: Springer-Verlag.

Sanday, P. R. (1990). *Fraternity gang rape: Sex, brotherhood, and privilege on campus.* New York: New York University Press.

Seligson, M. R. (1992). Mental health services and HIV-spectrum disease. In M. R. Seligson & K. E. Peterson (Eds.), *AIDS prevention and treatment: Hope, humor, and healing* (pp. 3–35). Washington, DC: Hemisphere.

Seligson, M. R., & Peterson, K. E. (Eds.). (1992). *AIDS prevention and treatment: Hope, humor, and healing.* Washington, DC: Hemisphere.

Siegel, B. S. (1986). *Love, medicine and miracles.* New York: Harper & Row.

Siegel, B. S. (1989). *Peace, love and healing.* New York: Harper & Row.

Siegel, B. S. (1993). *How to live between office visits.* New York: HarperCollins.

Silver, S., Gerrity, E. T., & Akman, J. S. (1989, June). *Comprehensive HIV education for university students in a high incidence area.* Paper presented at the International Conference on AIDS, Montreal, Quebec, Canada.

Stinson, M. H., & Hendrick, S. S. (1992). Reported childhood sexual abuse in university counseling center clients. *Journal of Counseling Psychology, 39,* 370–374.

Temoshok, L., & Dreher, H. (1992). *The type C connection: The behavioral links to cancer and your health.* New York: Random House.

Terl, A. H. (1992). Public policy and discrimination. In M. R. Seligson & K. E. Peterson (Eds.), *AIDS prevention and treatment: Hope, humor, and healing* (pp. 199–217). Washington, DC: Hemisphere.

Terl, A. H. (1993). *AIDS and the law: A basic guide for the nonlawyer.* Washington, DC: Taylor & Francis.

Thomas, B. (1989). Supporting carers of people with AIDS. *Nursing Times, 85*(16), 33–35.

Thombs, D. L., Beck, K. H., & Mahoney, C. A. (1993). Effects of social context and gender on drinking patterns of young adults. *Journal of Counseling Psychology, 40,* 115–119.

Uribe, Z. P., Ornelas, H. G., Valdespino, J. L., & Palacios, N. M. (1989, June). *Sexual abuse in children and HIV infection.* Paper presented at the International Conference on AIDS, Montreal, Quebec, Canada.

Whipple, B., & Ogden, G. (1989). *Safe encounters: How women can say yes to pleasure and no to unsafe sex.* New York: Pocket Books.

White, S., & Winzelberg, A. (1992). Laughter and stress. *Humor: International Journal of Humor Research, 5,* 343–355.

Woman: Man raped my naive personality. (1990, November 8). *Miami Herald,* p. 2A.

Women's AIDS rate rising fast. (1992, July 21). *Miami Herald,* pp. 1A, 7A.

Youngstrom, N. (1991). AIDS training project started. *APA Monitor, 22*(12), 31–32.

Chapter 14

Suicide

Antoon A. Leenaars

Death is difficult to understand. Death is mysterious. It is almost universally feared. And it remains forever elusive. This is especially so with suicide. Almost all of us are perplexed, bewildered, confused, and even overwhelmed when confronted with suicide. Yet, for some it is a final solution. It is actively sought. However, these same people are likely the least aware of the essential reasons for doing so. Understanding suicide—and death—is a complex endeavor.

DEFINITION OF SUICIDE

Briefly defined, suicide is the human act of self-inflicted, self-intentioned cessation (Shneidman, 1973). Suicide is not a disease (although there are many who think so); it is not an immorality (although it has often been treated as such); it is not a biological anomaly (although biological factors may play a role in some suicides); and it is not a neurological dysfunction (although even minimal brain dysfunction may play an additive role in some suicides).

It is unlikely that any one theory will ever define or explain phenomena as varied and as complicated as acts of human self-destruction. Our own initial definition is fraught with complexities and difficulties.

The history of the word *suicide* provides only initial assistance. *Suicide* in fact, is a relatively recent word. According to the *Oxford English Dictionary,* the word was used in 1651 by Walter Charleton when he said, "To vindicate one's self from . . . inevitable Calamity, by Sui-cide is not . . . a Crime." However, the exact date of the first use of the word is open to question. Some claim that it was first used by Sir Thomas Browne in his book, *Religio Medici,* published in 1642. Edward Philips, in his 1662 edition of his dictionary, *A New World of Words,* claimed to have invented the word. The word *suicide* does not appear in the 1652 edition of Robert Burton's *Anatomy of Melancholy* or in Samuel Johnson's *Dictionary,* published in 1755. Before the word was introduced, of course, other terms were used to describe "the act"—among them *self-destruction, self-killing, self-murder,* and *self-slaughter.* Burton's phrases for suicide include "to make way with themselves" and "they offer violence to themselves." The classical (and current) German term—*Selbstmord,* meaning "self-murder"—is in keeping with this tradition.

Present-day individuals who have attempted to define the term (e.g., Beau-

First and foremost, I need to make explicit my debt to Edwin Shneidman. Many of our conversations are reflected in this chapter. These ideas are used with his encouraging permission.

champ, 1978; Frey, 1980; Graber, 1981; Windt, 1980) have given scholarly definitions, but these suffer from intellectual overkill (Shneidman, 1985). An excellent discussion of the problem of definition was offered by Douglas (1967). Douglas outlined the fundamental dimensions of meanings that are required in the formal definition of suicide, including aspects of initiation, willingness, motivation, and knowledge.

Suicide today may be defined differently depending on the purpose of the definition—medical, legal, administrative, etc. In the United States and Canada (and most of the countries reporting to the World Health Organization), suicide is defined (by a medical examiner or coroner) as one of the four possible modes of death. An acronym for the four modes of death is NASH: natural, accidental, suicidal, and homicidal. This fourfold classification of all deaths also has it problem. Its major deficiency is that it treats the human being in a Cartesian fashion, namely, as a biological machine, rather than appropriately treating him or her as a motivated psychosocial organism. It obscures the individual's intentions in relation to his or her own cessation and, furthermore, completely neglects the contemporary concepts of psychodynamic psychology regarding intention, including unconscious motivation.

There is no one definition of suicide today. In fact, there never was one. Varah (1978) collated some of the variety of definitions. Here is a sampling:

From Sarah Dastoor (India):
I vengeful, killer, hate-inspired—so I die.
I guilty, sinner, trapped—escaping life.
I hoping rebirth, forgiveness divine—live again.

From Josef Hes (Israel):

Fruit of illogical action resulting from "funnel" thinking, which prevents a person from perceiving alternatives to self-destruction.

From Maria Luisa Gomezil (Mexico):

Alienation's last word.

From Tadeusz Kielanowski (Poland):

Suicide is the most tragic decision of a man who found nobody to hold out a hand to him.

Soubrier (1993), in his review of this topic, concluded, "A major issue in suicidology is the following: Do we have a common definition of suicide?" (p. 33)

The topic of definition of suicide was the focus of an entire book by Shneidman (1985). His *Definition of Suicide* can be seen as a necessary step to more effective understanding and treatment of suicide. Shneidman argued that a clarification of the definitions of suicide is desperately needed—definitions that can be applied to needful persons. He defined suicide as follows: "Currently in the Western world, suicide is a conscious act of self-induced annihilation, best understood as a multidimensional malaise in a needful individual who defines an issue for which the suicide is perceived as the best solution" (Shneidman, p. 203).

This definition should not be seen as the final word but as a *mnemonic* for understanding the event.

EPIDEMIOLOGY OF SUICIDE

It is generally believed that many actual suicides fail to be certified as suicides. Be that as it may, most suicidologists (e.g., O'Carroll, 1989) agree that official statistics on suicide can validly be used, and, furthermore, Sainsbury and Barraclough (1968) showed that cross-national comparisons can be not only validly, but reliably, made. Suicide rates vary from country to country (Lester, 1992). Table 1 shows suicide rates in various countries of the world based on data from the World Health Organization (WHO; 1992).

Not only do statistics vary between nations, but also substantial variations in suicide rates exist among subgroups (e.g., age, gender, and ethnicity) in each nation. Age is an especially important demographic variable. Both children and adolescents commit suicide. Although suicide is rare in children under 12, it occurs with greater frequency than most people imagine. Suicide is an alarming problem in adolescents in many parts of the world, especially in older boys. The tragedy of adolescent suicide is especially poignant because the life expectancy of these youths is the greatest in terms of both interval of years and the diversity of experiences that await them. Nonetheless, it is young adults (ages, 18–25) and the elderly (age 55 or older) who are most at risk. In the United States, it is the elderly who are at highest risk, again especially the males. However, that trend does not hold in other nations. For example, the suicide rate for young adults is as high as, if not higher than, that for the elderly in Canada. In females, the highest rate occurs in middle adulthood, often the 40s, in many nations. Although space limitations preclude a more detailed discussion of epidemiology, the reader is referred to reviews (e.g., Lester, 1992) on the topic.

HISTORY OF SUICIDE

The modern era of the study of suicide began around the turn of this century, with two main threads of investigation, the sociological and psychological, associated primarily with Emile Durkheim (1858–1917) and Sigmund Freud (1856–1939), respectively. Much earlier, during classical Greek times, suicide was viewed in various ways. Pythagoras of Samos, who introduced the theory of number to understand humans and the universe ("Number is all things and all things are number"), proposed that suicide would upset the spiritual mathematics of all things. All was measurable by number, and to exit by suicide might result in an imbal-

Table 1   Suicide Rates around the World

Country	Year	Total	Male	Female
Argentina	1987	7.4	10.5	4.4
Australia	1988	13.3	21.0	5.6
Austria	1990	23.6	34.8	13.4
Belgium	1986	22.3	30.9	14.1
Bulgaria	1990	14.7	20.7	8.8
Canada	1989	13.3	20.9	6.0
Chile	1987	5.6	9.2	2.0
Colombia	1984	3.8	6.0	1.6
Costa Rica	1988	5.0	8.6	1.3
Czechoslovakia	1990	17.9	27.3	8.9
Denmark	1990	24.1	32.2	16.3
Ecuador	1988	4.6	6.3	2.8
Egypt	1987	0.04	0.1	0.0
El Salvador	1984	10.5	14.8	6.1
Finland	1989	28.5	46.4	11.5
France	1989	20.9	30.5	11.7
East Germany	1989	25.8	36.1	16.3
West Germany	1989	16.5	23.5	10.0
Greece	1989	3.8	5.6	2.1
Hong Kong	1989	10.5	11.8	9.1
Hungary	1990	39.9	59.9	21.4
Iceland	1990	15.7	27.4	3.9
Ireland	1989	7.9	12.1	3.7
Israel	1988	6.8	9.7	4.0
Italy	1988	7.6	11.1	4.4
Jamaica	1984	0.2	0.3	0.1
Japan	1990	16.4	20.4	12.4
Korea	1987	8.0	11.5	4.4
Kuwait	1987	0.8	1.0	0.6
Luxembourg	1989	19.6	30.0	9.8
Malta	1990	2.3	4.6	0.0
Martinique	1985	3.7	4.4	3.0
Mauritius	1987	13.9	17.4	10.5
Mexico	1986	2.2	3.6	0.7
Netherlands	1989	10.2	13.0	7.5
New Zealand	1987	14.0	22.2	6.0
Norway	1989	15.6	23.0	8.4
Panama	1987	3.8	5.6	1.9
Poland	1990	13.0	22.0	4.5
Portugal	1990	8.8	13.5	4.5
Puerto Rico	1989	8.9	16.4	1.9
Singapore	1989	14.3	15.4	13.2
Spain	1987	7.2	10.6	4.0
Srilanka	1985	33.2	46.9	18.9
Surinam	1985	21.6	31.8	11.6
Sweden	1988	18.8	26.4	11.5
Switzerland	1990	21.9	31.5	12.7
Trinidad/Tobago	1988	13.2	19.0	7.4
United Kingdom	1990	8.1	12.6	3.8

Table 1   Suicide Rates around the World (*continued*)

Country	Year	Total	Male	Female
United States	1988	12.4	20.1	5.0
Union of Soviet Socialist Republics	1990	21.1	34.4	9.1
Uruguay	1989	11.1	18.1	4.4
Venezuela	1987	4.1	6.6	1.5
Yugoslavia	1989	16.5	23.2	9.9

Note. Rates given are annual deaths by suicide per 100,000 of population. Years are the latest years suicide rates were available. Data are from World Health Organization (1992).

ance, unlike other deaths, which were in harmony with all things. Plato's position (428–348 B.C.), best expressed in *Phaedo* in his quotation from Socrates, is as follows:

Cebes, I believe . . . that the gods are our keepers, and we men are one of their posses-
sions. Don't you think so?
Yes, I do, said Cebes.
Then take your own case. If one of your possessions were to destroy itself without intimation from you that you wanted it to die, wouldn't you be angry with it and punish it, if you had any means of doing so?
Certainly.
So if you look at it in this way I supposed it is not unreasonable to say that we must not put an end to ourselves . . .

There are however, provisions for exceptions. Socrates continues,

until God sends some compulsion like the one which we are facing now.

The compulsion, of course, was the condemnation by the Athenian court of Socrates for "corrupting the minds of the young and of believing in deities of his own invention instead of the gods recognized by the state." Socrates then drank poison, hemlock.

Aristotle (384–322 B.C.) espoused the view that suicide was against the state and therefore wrong. An individual was answerable for all to the state and thus was to be punished for acts of wrongdoing, including suicide. In *Nicomachean Ethics*, Aristotle further noted that

to die to escape from poverty or love or anything painful is not the mark of a brave man, but rather of a coward; for it is softness to fly from what is troublesome, and such a man endures death not because it is noble but to fly from evil.

In classical Rome, in the centuries just before the Christian era, life was held rather cheap and suicide was viewed either neutrally or, by some, positively. The Roman Stoic Seneca (4 B.C.–65 A.D.) said, "Living is not as long as he can. . . . He will always think of life in terms of quality not quantity. . . . Dying early or late is of no relevance, dying well or ill is. . . . Even if it is true that while there is life there is hope, life is not to be bought at any cost." Zeno, the founder of Stoic philosophy, hanged himself after putting his toe out of joint in a fall at age 98. The history of Rome is filled with such incidences, where life was given up for seemingly trivial reasons. Rome's civilization itself was, indeed, inimical; the life-style in Rome truncated that civilization's very existence.

The Old Testament does not directly forbid suicide, but in Jewish law suicide is wrong. Life had value. In the Old Testament, one finds only six cases of suicide: Abimelech, Samson, Saul, Saul's armor bearer, Ahithapel, and Zimni. The New Testament, like the Old Testament, does not directly forbid suicide. During the early Christian years, in fact, there was excessive martyrdom and tendency toward suicide, resulting in considerable concern on the part of the Church Fathers. Suicide by these early martyrs was seen as redemption, and thus the Fathers began increasingly to associate sin and suicide. In the 4th century, suicide was categorically rejected by St. Augustine (354–430). Suicide was considered a sin because it precluded the possibility of repentance and because it violated the Sixth Commandment, "Thou shalt not kill." Suicide was a greater sin than any sin one might wish to avoid. This view was elaborated by St. Thomas Aquinas (1225–1274), who (echoing the views of Aristotle) emphasized that suicide was not only unnatural and antisocial, but also a mortal sin because it usurped God's power over life and death. By 693, the Church, at the Council of Toledo, proclaimed that individuals who attempted suicide were to be excommunicated. The notion of suicide as sin took firm hold and for hundreds of years played an important part in Western cultures's view of self-destruction. Only during the Renaissance and the Reformation did a different view emerge, although, as Farberow (1972) has documented, the Church's view of Suicide remained powerful among the lower classes into this century.

The writers and philosophers from the 1500s on began to present a variety of different views on suicide. Shakespeare (1564–1616), for example, has provided us with an excellent array of such views. Fourteen suicides occur in his plays.

The French philosopher Jean-Jacques Rousseau (1712–1778) emphasized the natural state of human beings. He transferred sin from the individual to society, making people generally good (and innocent) and asserting that it is society that makes them bad. The disputation as to the locus of blame—the individual or society—is a major theme that dominates the history of thought about suicide. David Hume (1711–1776) was one of the first major Western philosophers to discuss suicide apart from the concept of sin. In "On Suicide" (1777), he refuted the view that suicide is a crime by arguing that suicide is not a transgression of our duties to God, to our fellow citizens, or to ourselves. He asserted that "prudence and courage should engage us to rid ourselves at once of existence when it becomes a burden. . . . If it be no crime in me to divert the Nile or Danube from its course, were I able to effect such purposes, where then is the crime in turning a few ounces of blood from their natural channel?"

Whereas Hume tried to decriminalize suicide and make it the individual's right, others, including Immanuel Kant (1724–1804), wrote that human life was sacred and should be preserved, in an antistoic sense, at any cost. Johann Wolfgang von Goethe (1749–1832) presented the opposite view in his novel *The Sorrows of Young Werther:* Life does not need to be preserved. Werther kills himself in the face of unbearable emotional pain, his intoxication with Lotte, who is betrothed to and marries another.

Werther had a strong impact in Europe; Goethe himself became known only as "the author of *Werther.*" Even the clothes Werther wore became fashionable. A contagious suicide effect seemed to occur, a concern that preoccupies many suicidologists to this day. It should be noted that Goethe himself battled against his own emotional difficulties, for example, working on *Faust* for 60 years until he had completed it.

In more recent times, other main threads of suicidal study have evolved. Existentialism, for example, has brought suicide into sharp focus, best exemplified in Albert Camus's *The Myth of Sisyphus* (1942/1955). In the opening lines, Camus wrote,

There is but one truly serious philosophical problem, and that is suicide. Judging whether life is or is not worth living amounts to answering the fundamental question of philosophy. All the rest and whether or not the world has three dimensions, whether the mind has nine or twelve categories—comes afterwards. (p. 3)

The two giants in the field of suicidal theorizing at the turn of the 20th century were Durkheim and Freud. In *Suicide* (1897/1951), Durkheim focused on society's inimical effects on the individual; Freud, eschewing the notions of either sin or crime, gave suicide back to the individual but put the locus of action in the unconscious. Since around 1900, a host of psychological theories aside from Freud's have focused on the individual, for example, those of Alfred Adler, Ludwig Binswanger, Carl Jung, Karl Menninger, George Kelly, Henry A. Murray, Edwin Shneidman, Harry Stack Sullivan, and Gregory Zilboorg (Leenaars, 1988a). Indeed, the history of suicide shows not only a constant development in defining suicide, but also that suicide is open to various constructions.

CONTEMPORARY DEVELOPMENTS IN SUICIDOLOGY

In the *Oxford English Dictionary,* the arbiter of the English language, we read:

Suicidology [f. SUICIDE *sb.*[2] + -OLOGY] The study of suicide and its prevention. Hence **suici'dologist.**

[**1929** W. A. BONGER in *Psychiatrisch-Juridsch Geselschap* . . . De wetenschap van de zelfmoord, the *suicidologie* (cursivering van mij) zou men haar kunnen noemen, is ruim een eeuw oud.] **1964** E. S. SHNEIDMAN in *Contemp. Psychol.* IX. 371/2, I thank Louis Dublin, the Grand Old Man of suicidology, for this book because in it he . . . has given us all new clues to suicide. **1967**——*Bull. Suicidology* July 7/2, The 10-point program for suicide prevention here outlined is a mutual enterprise whose successful development depends on the active interest, support, and activities of 'suicidologists' (p. 145).

The "fulcrum moment," Shneidman himself called it, of contemporary suicidology occurred several minutes after he discovered several hundred suicide notes in a coroner's vault in 1949 in Los Angeles. At that moment he had a glimmering that the vast potential value of the notes could be immeasurably increased if he did not read them, but rather compared them blindly, in a controlled experiment, with simulated suicide notes, elicited from matched nonsuicidal persons. John Stuart Mill's method of difference came to Shneidman's aid, and the seeds for the study of contemporary suicidal phenomena were sown.

Maris (1993) has recently outlined the evolution of suicidology since that critical event. As one reads Maris's paper, one becomes aware of suicidology's vasteness today. It is a multidisciplinary enterprise. It is the study of psychological, biological, cultural, sociological, interpersonal, intrapsychic, logical, conscious, unconscious, and philosophical elements in the suicidal event. Shneidman has always insisted, and most suicidologists agree, that suicidology is not reducible to any one of its domains.

Maris (1993) provided a long list of subdisciplines, including psychology, medicine, psychiatry, sociology, anthropology, epidemiology, criminology, nursing, biology, philosophy, religion, education, literature, etc., all of which make contributions to suicidology. As Maris noted, that list "could be extended or refined almost indefinitely" (p. 5).

From its embryonic beginnings in the vault, suicidology has become an expanded discipline. It involves survivorship. It involves crisis work on telephone hotlines. It involves research in laboratories and in natural field settings. It involves associations such as the American Association of Suicidology, the Canadian Association Suicide Prevention, and the International Association for Suicide Prevention. It involves a research group, the International Academy of Suicide Research, dedicated to enhancing the research in the field. It involves training and practice. Thus suicidology today includes not only the study of suicide, but also its prevention.

SUICIDE FACTS AND MYTHS

People in general are not only perplexed and bewildered by self-destructive behavior, but also believe a number of misconceptions of suicide. Here are some common fables and facts about suicide, formulated by Shneidman around 1952 and incorporated into a number of publications (e.g., Shneidman & Mandelkorn, 1970):

Fable: People who talk about suicide don't commit suicide.
Fact: Of any 10 persons who kill themselves, 8 have given definite warnings of their suicidal intentions.
Fable: Suicide happens without warning.

Fact: Studies reveal that the suicidal person gives many clues and warnings regarding suicidal intentions.

Fable: Suicidal people are fully intent on dying.

Fact: Most suicidal people are undecided about living or dying, and they "gamble with death," leaving it to others to save them. Almost no one commits suicide without letting others know how he or she is feeling.

Fable: Once a person is suicidal, he or she is suicidal forever.

Fact: Individuals who wish to kill themselves are suicidal only for a limited period of time.

Fable: Improvement following a suicidal crisis means that the suicidal risk is over.

Fact: Most suicides occur within about 3 months following the beginning of "improvement," when the individual has the energy to put his or her morbid thoughts and feelings into effect.

Fable: Suicide strikes much more often among the rich (or, conversely, it occurs most exclusively among the poor).

Fact: Suicide is neither the rich person's disease nor the poor person's curse. Suicide is very democratic and is represented proportionately among all levels of society.

Fable: Suicide is inherited.

Fact: Suicide is not inherited. It is an individual pattern.

Fable: All suicidal individuals are mentally ill, and suicide always is the act of a psychotic person.

Fact: Studies of hundreds of genuine suicide notes indicate that although the suicidal person is extremely unhappy, he or she is not necessarily mentally ill.

There is also the misconception that we talk about "myths" as if we know what people believe. Studies by McIntosh, Hubbard, and Santos (1983) and Leenaars et al. (1988) addressed this topic. Their findings support the belief that people's knowledge regarding some of the above facts is generally well above what was anticipated from the previous anecdotal literature. People with direct experience of suicide seem to know more than those who have not had direct experience with it (Durocher, Leenaars, & Balance, 1989). Older people seem to fare the poorest in their knowledge (Leenaars, Saunders, Balance, Wenckstern, & Galgan, 1991).

ATTEMPTED SUICIDE

Although it is obvious that a person has to attempt suicide in order to commit it, it is equally clear that the event of attempting suicide does not always have death (cessation) as its objective. It is acknowledged that often the goal of attempted suicide (such as cutting oneself or ingesting harmful substances) is to change one's life (or to change the behavior of the significant others around one), rather than to end it. On some rare occasions, death is actually intended and only luckily avoided. However, it should be stressed, as others have pointed out (e.g., Stengel, 1964), that it is useful to think of "attempters" (now often referred to as "parasuicides") and "completers" as overlapping populations: (a) a group of people who attempt suicide, a few of whom go on to commit it, and (b) a group of people who commit suicide, many of whom had previously attempted it. A great deal has to do with the levels of perturbation and lethality associated with the event.

Perturbation refers to how upset (disturbed, agitated, sane–insane) the individual is and is rated as low, medium, or high (alternatively, on a 1-to-9 scale). Perturbation may be measured by various means (e.g., self-reports, biological markers, psychological tests, and observations). *Lethality* is roughly synonymous with the "deathfulness" of the act and is an important dimension in understanding any potentially suicidal individual. Lethality can be rated as low, moderate, or high (alternatively, on a 1-to-9 scale). An example of how lethality may be measured is the following assessment item, derived from Shneidman (1967): "During the last 24 hours, I felt the chances of my actually killing myself (committing suicide and ending my life) were: absent, very low, low-medium, fifty-fifty, high medium, very high, extra high (Came very close to actually killing myself)" (p. 512). A critical distinction in suicide is that lethality—not perturbation—kills. All sorts of people are highly perturbed but are not suicidal. The ratio between suicide attempts and completions is about 8 to 1—one committed suicide for every eight attempts; however, in young people, the ratio is 50 to 1, even 100 to 1.

The "attempter" (along with individuals who engage in self-assaultive and self-mutilative behavior) and the "completer" share some commonalities; however, they are, by and large, operationally quite different. There is a third group, the "contemplators," whose numbers are so vast that it is difficult to begin to highlight their commonalities. The differences between suicide and parasuicide were presented by Shneidman (1985). He suggested, for example that whereas the common stimulus in suicide is unendurable psychological pain, in parasuicide it is intense, potentially endurable, psychological pain. As another example, whereas the common purpose in suicide is to seek a solution to an overbearing problem, in parasuicide it is to reduce tension and to evoke a response. However, there are also similarities, although the content of such characteristics may be quite different. Shneidman, for example, provided the following examples: the common stressor in both is frustrated needs, and the common consistency in both is lifelong adjustment patterns.

A recent study—a rare opportunity to compare attempters and completers—actually found that there may be more similarities than differences between the two groups (Leenaars et al., 1992). That archival research, a comparison of suicide notes written by individuals who killed themselves and notes (called *parasuicide notes*) by individuals who made highly lethal attempts, found only a few differences between attempters and completers. Attempters see their act as a style of life, being too weak to cope with life's ever present difficulties, and lacking in social integration. Suicide attempts become a way of life. The empirical observations on this topic are sparse; Smith and Maris (1986) have called for extensive research in this area.

Suicide attempts have many meanings and, whatever the level of their lethality, ought to be taken seriously. A person who attempts suicide may not necessarily mean to die, but the situation is so intense he or she has to communicate the pain. Words like "manipulation" or "blackmail" or "attention" add only a pejorative emotional tone, revealing our own attitudes and fears.

PARTIAL DEATH AND SUBSTITUTES FOR SUICIDE

Freud (1901/1974), Shneidman (1963), Murray (1967), and others have speculated that beyond intentional suicides, there is a vast array of subintentional inimical behaviors. The very lifestyle of some individuals seems to truncate and demean their life so that they are as good as dead. Freud stated,

It is well known that in the severe cases of psychoneurosis instances of self injury are occasionally found as symptoms and that in such cases suicide can never be ruled out as a possible outcome of the psychical conflict . . . Many apparently accidental injuries that happen to such patients are really instances of self-injury. (1901/1974, pp. 178–179)

Freud further noted that such self-destruction is not rare. Alcoholism, drug addiction, mismanagement of physical disease, auto accidents, and masochistic behavior can often be seen in this light. Farberow (1980) edited a book on "the many faces of suicide." Therein, he asked a number of relevant questions. For example,

Why did a person stop taking insulin when he knew he had to take it regularly to stay well, or even to stay alive?

Why did a person, knowing what drugs can do to you, get hooked?

Why did a person drive so fast on the curving mountain roads when he had known for the last three months how bad his brakes were? (Farberow, p. 1)

In these cases, there may be no intent to kill him- or herself, but the person is as good as dead. Karl Menninger (1938), the chief theorist on the concept of partial death, wrote of (a) chronic suicide—including asceticism, martyrdom, neurotic invalidism, alcohol addiction, antisocial behavior, and psychosis; (b) focal suicide—focusing on a limited part of the body, including self-mutilation, multiple surgery, purposive accidents, impotence, and frigidity; and (c) organic suicide—focusing on the psychological factors in organic disease, especially the self-punishing aggressive and erotic components. Freud (1901/1974) speculated that there is, in fact, a suicidal thread in all persons. The reason why some exhibit chronic, focal, or organic suicide may be related to some or all of those characteristics listed by Shneidman (1985) regarding parasuicide.

A related concept is "subintentioned death" (Shneidman, 1963). This concept

asserts that there are many deaths that are neither clearly suicidal nor clearly accidental or natural, but are deaths in which the decedent played some covert or
unconscious role in permitting his or her death to occur, either "accidentally," by
inviting homicide, or by unconsciously disregarding what could be a life-
extending medical regimen. Freud (1901/1974) speculated,

Anyone who believes in the occurrence of half-intentional self-injury—if I may use a
clumsy expression—will be prepared also to assume that in addition to consciously intentional suicide there is such a thing as half-intentional self-destruction (self-destruction with
an unconscious intention), capable of making skillful use of a threat of life and of disguis-
ing it as a chance mishap. (pp. 180–181)

A PSYCHOLOGICAL THEORY OF SUICIDE

Shneidman (1985) suggested that a psychological theory regarding suicide begins
not with the question "What kind of people commit suicide?" but with the question "What are the interesting common psychological dimensions of committed
suicide?" This question, according to Shneidman, is critical, for the common dimensions are what suicide is. Not necessarily the universal but certainly the most
frequent or common characteristics provide a meaningful conceptualization regarding suicide.

Most frequently, nonprofessionals identify external causes (e.g., ill health,
being abandoned by a lover, or losing one's fortune) as what is common in suicide.
A recent downhill course (e.g., a drop in income, sudden acute alcoholism, a
change in work, or a divorce or separation) can, indeed, be identified in suicide.
However, although there are always situational aspects in every suicidal act, they
are only the precipitating events. Suicide is more complex. Suicide is a multidimensional malaise. How can these psychological complexities be understood?

To begin to answer this question, it is useful to consider Shneidman's proposition that the psychological dimensions of suicide are the "trunk" of suicide.
Shneidman (1985), using an arborial image, wrote,

An individual's biochemical states, for instance, are the roots. An individual's method of
suicide, the contents of the suicide note, the calculated effects on the survivors, and so on,
are the branching limbs, the flawed fruit, and the camouflaging leaves; but the psychological component, the problem-solving choice—the best solution of the perceived problem—
is the main "trunk." (pp. 202–203)

Suicide is an intrapsychic drama on an interpersonal stage. According to this
psychological view (Leenaars, 1988a, 1989a, 1989b, 1994), suicide relates to
the following:

Intrapsychic Drama

Unbearable Psychological Pain   The common stimulus in suicide is unendurable psychological pain (Shneidman, 1985). The enemy of life is pain. The

suicidal person is in a heightened state of perturbation. It is the pain of feeling pain. Although, as Menninger noted in 1938, other motives (elements, wishes) are evident, the person primarily wants to flee from pain—a trauma, a catastrophe. The fear is that the trauma, the crisis, is bottomless, an eternal suffering. The person feels boxed in, rejected, deprived, forlorn, distressed, and especially hopeless and helpless. It is the emotion of impotence, the feeling of hopelessness–helplessness, that is so painful for many suicidal people. The situation is unbearable and the person desperately wants a way out of it. Suicide, as Murray (1967) noted, is functional because it abolishes painful tension for the individual; it provides relief from intolerable suffering.

Cognitive Constriction The common cognitive state in suicide is constriction (Shneidman, 1985), that is, rigidity in thinking, narrowing of focus, tunnel vision, concreteness. Constriction is the major component of the cognitive state in suicide. The person is figuratively intoxicated or drugged by the constriction, resulting in dysfunction in emotions, logic, and perception. The suicidal person exhibits at the moment before death only permutations and combinations of a trauma (e.g., poor health or rejection by spouse) (Sullivan, 1962, 1964). The suicidal mind is in a special state of relatively fixed purpose and of relative constriction. In the face of the trauma—pain—a possible solution becomes *the* solution. This constriction is one of the most dangerous aspects of the suicidal state of mind.

Indirect Expressions Complications, ambivalence, redirected aggression, unconscious implications, and related indirect expressions (or phenomena) are often evident in suicide. The suicidal person is ambivalent (Shneidman, 1985). There are complications, concomitant contradictory feelings, attitudes, and thrusts toward a person or even life (Schneidman, 1985). Not only do love and hate clash, but there may also be a conflict between survival and unbearable pain. The person experiences humility, submission, devotion, subordination, flagellation, and sometimes even masochism (Adler, 1910/1967). Yet, there is much more. What the person is consciously aware of is only a fragment of the suicidal solution. There are more reasons to the act than the suicidal person is consciously aware of when making the final decisions. Suicide is more complicated than the person's conscious mind had been aware (Leenaars, 1993). The driving force may well be unconscious processes.

Inability to Adjust People with all types of problems, pain, losses, etc., are at risk for suicide. Although the majority of suicides may not fit well into any specific nosological classification, depressive disorders, the down phase of manic–depressive disorder, obsessive–compulsive disorder, schizophrenic disorders, panic disorders, hysterical disorders, psychopathic disorders, and other disorders have been related to some suicides (Leenaars, 1988a; Sullivan, 1962, 1964). Indeed, suicidal people see themselves as unable to adjust (Adler, 1910/

1967) Their state of mind is incompatible with discerning recitation of what is going on. Considering themselves too weak to overcome difficulties, these people reject everything except death. They do not survive life's difficulties.

Ego   The suicidal person him- or herself is a critical aspect of the suicidal act. Ego strength, the part of the mind that reacts to reality and has a sense of individuality, is a protective factor against suicide. Suicidal people, however, frequently exhibit a relative weakness in the capacity to develop constructive tendencies and to overcome their personal difficulties (Menninger, 1938). Their egos have likely been weakened by a steady toll of traumatic events (e.g., loss, rejection, abuse, and failure). This implies that a history of traumatic disruptions—PAIN—placed the person at risk for suicide; it likely disrupted the person's ability to develop mechanisms (or ego functions) to cope. The weakened ego correlates positively with suicide risk (Jung, 1921/1974). The ego is thus a critical factor in the suicidal scenario.

Interpersonal Stage

Interpersonal Relations   The suicidal person has problems establishing or maintaining relationships. There is a disturbed, unbearable interpersonal situation (Sullivan, 1962, 1964; Zilboorg, 1936, 1937). A calamitous relation has prevailed. A positive development in those same disturbed relations is held as the only possible way to go on living, but such development is seen as not forthcoming (Sullivan, 1962, 1964). Suicide appears to be often related to unsatisfied or frustrated affiliation (attachment) needs, although other needs may also be evident, such as achievement, autonomy, and dominance. The person's psychological needs are frustrated, exemplified in the often interpersonal trauma. Suicide is committed because of the thwarted or unfulfilled needs, needs that often become frustrated interpersonally (Murray, 1938, 1967).

Rejection–Aggression   The rejection–aggression hypothesis was documented by Stekel in a famous 1910 meeting of the Psychoanalytic Society in Freud's home in Vienna (Friedman 1910/1967). Adler, Jung, Freud, Sullivan, and Zilboorg all expounded variations of this hypothesis. Loss is central to suicide; it is often a rejection that is experienced as an abandonment. It is an unbearable narcissistic injury (Zilboorg, 1936). It is a traumatic event that leads to self-directed aggression. In fact, in the first controlled study of suicide notes, Shneidman and Farberow (1957) reported that both hate directed toward others and self-blame were evident in the notes. The person is deeply ambivalent. A characteristic in some suicides is the turning onto oneself of murderous impulses (wishes, needs) that had previously been directed against a traumatic event, most frequently someone who had rejected them (Freud, 1917/1974). Suicide may be veiled aggression—it may be murder in the 180th degree.

Identification–Egression   Freud (1917/1974, 1920/1974) hypothesized that intense identification with a lost or rejecting person or, as Zilboorg (1936) showed, with any ideal (e.g., health, youth, employment, or freedom) is crucial in understanding the suicidal person. Here, identification is defined as an attachment (bond), based on an important emotional tie with another person (Freud, 1921/ 1974) or any ideal. If this emotional need is not met, the suicidal person experiences a deep discomfort (pain) and wants to egress, that is, to leave, to be gone, to be elsewhere (Murray, 1967). Suicide becomes the only egression or solution, and the person plunges into the abyss.

What these elements mean is a seed for an extensive project. Of course, suicide is more than these elements. However, these common elements highlight that suicide is not due only to external "stress." Each suicide has a history. Consistency in suicides is found within lifelong adjustment patterns (Shneidman, 1985). Yet, this synthesis provides the best perspective of suicide at this time.

THEORETICAL/CLINICAL OBSERVATIONS

This section consists of six parts, all focused on clarifying the relations of suicide and biology, learning disabilities, physical disabilities and illness, depression, specific precipitating events, and the family system.

Biological Roots

Biology is our roots; yet there is relatively little secure knowledge regarding the neurobiology of suicide. Although there has recently been a flood of information regarding biological correlates of suicide, much of it lacks scientific rigor. Indeed, Lester (1992), in a recent review of this area, suggested that the "research has been quite poor" (p. 27). Sample sizes are small. Confounding variables, such as postmorten delay, have added to the confusion. Depression or other psychiatric disorders have rarely been controlled. Studies of biological correlates in the elderly (Rifai, Reynolds, & Mann, 1992) and across the life span (Motto & Reus, 1991) have concluded that biological conjectures about precipitants of suicide are, in fact, premature.

Despite the state of the art, suicide is a biological event (and much more). Possible markers include urinary 17-hydroxycorticosteroids, cortisol in plasma and cerebrospinal fluid, 5-hydroxyindoleacetic acid in cerebrospinal fluid, tritiated impimpromine binding, 3-methoxy-4-hydroxyphenylglycol and homovanillic acid, urinary norepinephrine: epinephrine ratio, and thyroid-stimulating hormone response to thyrotropin-releasing hormone. Slaby (1992), in his comment about this field, was more optimistic, especially regarding the relation of suicide to affective disorders (i.e., manic–depressive disorder) and their neurobiological correlates. At least in some suicides, biological correlates are strikingly relevant.

Learning Disabilities and Brain Dysfunction

The relation between brain dysfunction and learning disabilities in children is well documented. The relation between brain dysfunction and socioemotional problems in people is, however, a more neglected topic in the literature. Not only does a learning disability render a person at risk for socioemotional problems, including suicide, but there are also particular subtypes of learning disabilities, and these different subtypes may result in different levels of risk. Rourke and Fisk (1981) documented that different patterns of cerebral dysfunction and their resulting learning disabilities render a person at risk for different types of socio-emotional disturbances. They reported three major subgroups. The first group has a right brain dysfunction. These people are prone to learning problems with non-verbal, visual information. They may show the following socioemotional problems: not paying attention to visual objects, including other people; rarely expressing emotions appropriately in their facial expressions; having a voice that can be expressionless; being very talkative; talking to themselves; having flow problems in their speech; and being awkward socially. The second group has a left brain dysfunction. These people are prone to learning problems with verbal information. They may show the following socioemotional problems: rarely initiating conversations; having problems paying attention, for example, in conversation; being brief and often concrete in their remarks; and often responding "I don't know" to questions. In addition, some are very impulsive, not thinking before they act. The third group has both left and right brain dysfunction and exhibits a conglomerate of symptoms.

Other more specific cerebral deficits render people at risk for other specific problems, such as in planning, sequencing social events, and so on. Although further empirical studies need to be conducted in the neuropsychology of suicides, these observations clearly warrant attention. Indeed, Rourke, Young, and Lee-naars (1989) found that possible adolescent and adult outcomes of childhood central processing deficiencies are suicidal behavior as well as other socioemotional problems. They suggested that it is especially the first pattern associated with right brain dysfunction that predisposes those afflicted to adolescent (and adult) suicide risk.

Physical Disabilities and Illness

It would be remiss not to note the importance of physical problems in suicidal behavior in some people. Physical illness interacts with an individual's emotional functioning; indeed, some illnesses directly affect a person's emotions. Empirical study on the relation between illness and suicide is urgently needed. Currently, research suggests that some physical illnesses, including anorexia, bulimia, diabetes, epilepsy, traumatic brain injury, and muscular dystrophy (Barraclough, 1986), are associated with suicidal behavior. Some individuals with physical disabilities who are at risk are those with limb amputations or spinal injuries resulting in quadriplegia. Individuals with terminal illness such as AIDS appear also to be at high risk (Fryer, 1986; Marzuk, 1989). However, it is important to realize that not all such people are suicidal and that research is needed to substantiate these views.

Depression

First and foremost, it must be understood that not all suicidal people are depressed, and that not all depressed people are suicidal. Depression and suicide are not equivalent. Yet, Lester (1992) has noted that depression distinguishes many suicidal people from nonsuicidal groups. Depression can be noted in mood and behavior (ranging from feeling dejected and hesitant in social contacts to isolation and serious disturbance of appetite and sleep), verbal expression (ranging from talking about being disappointed, excluded, blamed, etc., to talking about suicide, being killed, abandoned, helpless), and fantasy (ranging from feeling disappointed, excluded, mistreated, etc., to suicide, mutilation, loss of a significant person) (Pfeffer, 1986). Behaviors such as excessive aggressiveness, change in work performance, and expressions of somatic complaints or loss of energy have all been associated with depression. However, not all depression is overt, especially in youth. Some children and especially teenagers (and some adults) exhibit what has been termed *masked depression.* Anorexia, promiscuity, and drug abuse, for example, have been associated with depression. It is important to remember, however, that depression does not equal suicide in a simple one-to-one fashion., Most suicides experience unbearable pain but not necessarily depression (Shneidman, 1985). The unbearable emotion might be hostility, anxiety, despair, shame, guilt, dependency, hopelessness, or helplessness. What is critical is that the emotion—pain—is unbearable. Unendurable psychological pain is the common stimulus in suicide (Shneidman, 1985), not depression alone.

Specific Environmental Precipitating Events

A current popular formulation regarding suicide is that suicide is simply due to an external event: a rejection, the influence of the music of a pop singer, whatever. Although precipitating events (e.g., deprivation of love, sexual abuse, the death of parent, divorce, or a rejection) do occur in the suicides of people, this is less frequent in children. This brings to mind a clinical example, which is quite similar to one reported by Menninger (1938): A 16-year-old was found dead in a car, having died of carbon monoxide poisoning. People were perplexed: "Why did this young person from an upper-middle-class family kill himself?" The parents found out that his girlfriend had rejected him the day of his suicide. That was the reason: when a young person gets rejected and is so in love, he may kill himself. A few friends and his teachers knew that he had been having problems in school. That was the reason. A few others knew that his father was an alcoholic and abusive. That was the reason. His physician knew that he had been adopted and had been recently upset about that. She knew the real reason. And others knew . . .

Shneidman (1985) noted that the common consistency in suicide is not the precipitating event but lifelong coping patterns. One can see a continuity despite developmental changes. People who kill themselves experience a steady toll of threat, stress, failure, challenge, and loss that gradually undermines their adjustment process. Suicide has a history.

One event, however, that has frequently been identified as a possible precipitating event in young people is the death of a parent (Pfeffer, 1986). Indeed, when the death occurs by suicide, everyone in the family is at risk.

This discussion also raises the issue of the contagion (copycat) effect. A few years ago in Japan, an 18-year-old pop idol, Yukiko Okada, after a fight with her lover, leaped to her death from the building that housed her recording company in Tokyo. In the 17 days following her suicide, the suicide toll reached 33 young people. Phillips (1986) recently documented that such cluster suicides do occur in teenagers and adults. Suicide clusters have, in fact, been reported in Japan, North America, and across the world. Brenner (1988), however, showed that a contagion effect in boys (5–14 years old) may not exist. Aside from clustering, the impact of suggestion is also seen in the effect of media coverage of suicide. Most recently, it has been noted that there may be particular characteristics of those suicides (Brent, 1992). This is an area for further study (Lester, 1992).

Family Background

A review of the literature (e.g., Berman & Jobes, 1991; Corder & Haizlip, 1984; Corder, Parker & Corder, 1974; Leenaars, 1988b; Leenaars & Wenckstern, 1991; Maris, 1985; Pfeffer, 1986; Richman, 1993; Seiden, 1984; Toolan, 1981) suggests that certain characteristics of the family system and its functioning are central factors associated with suicide and suicidal behavior in children, adolescents, and even older people, although by no means do all families of suicidal individuals show these characteristics. Nevertheless, a few common observations of families are provided, followed by a few specific additional observations for teenagers.

1   There is, at times, a lack of generational boundaries in suicidal families. There is an insufficient separation of the parent from his or her family of origin. For example, grandparents may take over the parenting role.

2   The family system is often inflexible. Any change is seen as a threat to the survival of the family. Denial, secretiveness, and especially a lack of communication characterize the family's interactions, even in the suicides of the elderly. One 8-year-old boy said to this author, "If I try to kill myself, maybe my dad will listen." In addition, such families have patterns of strong discipline and limit setting that bind the teenager in his or her identity development, which is critical at this time of a person's life. Parents may interfere in the romantic relationships of their children, even in late adolescence.

3   At times, there is a symbiotic parent–child relationship. A parent, usually the mother, is too attached to the youth. Not only is such a relation disturbing, but the parent also does not provide the emotional protection and support that a

parent usually provides intuitively to a youth as he or she grows. Sometimes, the parent treats the child as an adult. One such teenager tried to break this bond by attempting to kill herself in her mother's prized car, while another—a straight A student—intentionally obtained a B, resulting in a parental conflict and a suicide attempt by the youth. In addition, it has been repeatedly found that if such a parent dies, the child may kill him- or herself to be magically reunited with that same parent.

4 Long-term disorganization (malfunctioning) has been noted in these families, for example, the mother's or father's absence, divorce, alcoholism, or mental illness. In teenage girls there is a very high rate of incest, compared with the general population. Even in the suicides of adults, and even more so the elderly, these types of disorganization have been observed. One such 74-year-old female tried to kill herself, stating in a note that she had not seen her children for 20 years.

In addition, three differentiating observations about the families of suicidal teenagers have been made. First, adolescents in such families often feel a lack of control over their environment, stemming from rigid family rules or symbiotic relationships. Second, adolescence is a time of stress and turmoil. It is not, as some believe, a time of simple joys and peace. Often, however, the parents in these families do not allow any conflict, turmoil, and development to occur. Third, recent family disorganization, such as a recent move, unemployment in the home, physical or mental illness, or parental conflict, has been noted in the family.

Berman (1986), by way of critique of some of the literature, argued that much of the current research is not scientifically controlled. For example, the research has not compared suicidal youth and their families with other troubled or nontroubled youth and their families. Thus, the conclusions offered herein about the families of suicidal people should be considered only tentative pending further study.

BEHAVIORAL CLUES

In understanding suicide, therapists need to be aware of behaviors that are potentially predictive of suicide. However, there is no single definitive predictive behavior. Two concepts that have already been discussed that may be helpful are lethality and perturbation. The clues below are applicable to all age groups, although the mode of expression may differ depending on age and numerous other factors.

Previous Attempts

Although it is obvious that a person has to attempt suicide in order to commit it, it is equally clear that the event of attempting suicide need not have death as its objective. As noted earlier, it is useful to think of attempters and completers as overlapping populations: (a) a group of those who attempt suicide, a few of whom go on to commit it, and (b) a group of those who commit suicide, a few of whom previously attempted it. A previous attempt is a good clue to future attempts, especially if no assistance is obtained after the first attempt. However, not all previous attempters go on to attempt again (or kill themselves). All too frequently, such behavior is not taken seriously. One very depressed 11-year-old girl cut her wrists at school, and the principal's response was merely, "She is just trying to get attention." What an extreme way to get attention! The girl was moderately lethal and highly perturbed, requiring considerable intervention.

Verbal Statements

The attitude toward individuals who make verbal threats of suicide, like the attitude toward those who make behavioral threats, is too frequently negative. Suicidal statements are seen as "just for attention." This attitude results in ignoring the behavior of a person who is genuinely perturbed and potentially suicidal. The important question is, "Why is the person using this way of getting attention, when there are so many other constructive ways?"

Examples of direct verbal warnings are "I'm going to kill myself" and "I want to die." Other more indirect examples are "I am going to see my (deceased) wife" and "I know that I'll die at an early age."

Cognitive Clues

The single most frequent state of mind of the suicidal person is constriction (Hughes & Neimeyer, 1990). There is a tunnel vision, a narrowing of the mind's eye. There is a narrowing of the range of perceptions or opinions or options that occur to the mind. Frequently, the person uses words like "only," "always," "never," and "forever." The following are examples: "No one will ever love me. Only mom loved me"; "John was the only one who loved me"; "My boss will always be that way"; and "I'll kill either my husband or myself." A 40-year-old bank manager, who recently had been fired from his job, expressed the constriction as follows: "Either I get my job back or I'll kill myself."

Emotional Clues

The person who is suicidal is often highly perturbed; he or she is disturbed, anxious, perhaps agitated. Depression, as already noted, is frequently evident. Suicidal people may feel boxed in, rejected, harassed, and unsuccessful. A common emotional state in most suicidal people is hopelessness–helplessness. Hopelessness may be signaled by statements such as "Nothing will change. It will always be this way," whereas helplessness may be verbalized as "There is nothing I can do. There is nothing my children can do to make a difference."

Sudden Behavioral Changes

Sudden changes in behavior are also suspect. Both the outgoing individual who suddenly becomes withdrawn and isolated and the normally reserved individual who starts being outgoing and seeking thrills may be at risk. Such changes are of particular concern when a precipitating painful event is apparent. Changed performance in school or work, such as sudden failure, may be an important clue. Giving away a record collection, a favorite watch, or other possessions may be ominous and often not responded to by the receiver; the receiver is simply too pleased to get the gift. A sudden preoccupation with death, such as reading and talking about death, may be a clue. Nonetheless, constructive discussion of this topic such as a class project for a university student may be helpful for the individual and his or her classmates.

Life-Threatening Behavior

In this author's experience, it is not rare for people to engage in life-threatening behaviors over a period of time without explicitly acknowledging they are attempting suicide. A 9-year-old boy who killed himself had previously been seen leaning out of an open window in his apartment as well as, at another time, playing with a gun. A 24-year-old male died in a single-car accident on an isolated road after having had several similar accidents following the rejection by his girlfriend. A 70-year-old female died from drug mismanagement, despite the fact that the nurse in her residence controlled her medication. Self-destruction is not rare. Often, alcoholism, drug addiction, mismanagement of medical treatment, and automobile accidents can be seen in this light, as previously mentioned.

Suicide Notes

Like previous attempts and verbal statements, suicide notes are important clues; however, they are often read but not listened to by the reader. Notes are very rarely written by children, but they are somewhat more frequent among adolescents. About 12–15% of adults leave notes. The topic of notes warrants a book by itself (Leenaars, 1988a); if one wants to understand the event, there is no better source than the words of the suicidal person that he or she wrote minutes before death. A sample of notes appears in the Appendix.

GENDER

The basic sex difference in suicide is that more males than females kill themselves. In contrast, more females than males attempt suicide. This sex difference has been found in almost all nations (Lester, 1988, 1992). The male-to-female ratio of suicide has, in fact, remained fairly stable, even in other eras. The generally accepted male-to-female ratio of completed suicides is 3 to 1.

Explanations in the literature (Leenaars, 1988c, 1988d) have varied. Females use different and less lethal methods (drugs vs. shooting). Individuals with severe psychiatric disorders have higher rates of suicide, and men are more likely to be diagnosed with such disorders. There are alternative social expectations for men and women in trauma, such that males act more catastrophically. Yet Shneidman (1985) argued that genotypic similarities may be more prevalent than differences. This author's own research (Leenaars, 1988c, 1988d) on the suicide notes of males and females concurs. For example, the observations presented in the Theoretical / Clinical Observations section are applicable to both sexes. Pain is pain. Frustrated needs are frustrated needs. Constriction is constriction. Maybe there are phenotypic differences (e.g., method or diagnostic label) in suicide but not genotypic ones across sex? Could the high rates of completed suicide in males be more influenced by gender roles than by psychological factors? As Greenglass (1982) noted,

Since the beginning of recorded history, being male or female has been one of the most significant characteristics of a person. Sex and gender not only determine the kinds of experiences people have, but they also significantly influence the way people perceive and act toward each other. Moreover, socio-cultural expectations have been integrated into elaborate gender-role systems which have an enormous impact on all areas of psychological and social functioning. (p. 256)

Tomlinson-Keasey, Warren, and Elliot's (1986) study of gifted female suicides revealed the same findings as this author's study of suicide notes (Leenaars, 1988c, 1988d). The markers (e.g., mental dysfunction or a history of problems) of suicide were the same in both sexes. Others (e.g., Canetto, 1994) have cited such factors as socioeconomic disadvantage, unemployment, hostile relationships, and a history of suicidal behavior among friends and family as relevant to women's suicides. However, such factors have also been observed in men's suicides (Lester, 1988, 1992; Tomlinson-Keasey et al., 1986). The area is, however, plagued by stereotypes (Canetto, 1994). For example, the division of women's suicides as irrational and men's as rational is not supported in the data (Leenaars, 1988c, 1988d). Reflections on this topic are most relevant (Lester, 1988). Equally, maybe one should ask, "Why are women *not* killing themselves?"

LIFE SPAN PERSPECTIVE ON SUICIDE

There are various ways in which life time lines—including the suicidal person's— can be conceptualized. Although suicide is in many ways the same across the entire life span, understanding suicide from a developmental perspective is productive (Leenaars, 1991). This section presents a brief summary of the area.

Maris (1991) offered a developmental perspective of suicide. He stated, "The suicidal act is a process, a convergence of many factors over time. . . . Suicide is not one thing and is not the simple product of an acute crisis" (p. 36). He argued that the person's history (or "career" as he termed it) is always relevant to his or her self-destruction. Yet, Shneidman (1991) argued that although it may be useful to group suicides under "adolescent or adult, or middle age or old," there is only suicide. "There is only human suicide and all of it is to be understood in terms of the same principles" (p. 40).

An American dies by his or her own hand on the average of every 17 min. However, this differs depending on the time-line/age (as well as other major demographic factors: sex, gender, race/ethnicity, etc.). The rate of suicide varies depending on developmental age. Lester (1991) looked at international trends across the life span and illustrated, as noted earlier, that there are different rates of suicide for different ages in different countries.

Developmental ages (or time lines) have their unique—despite common—psychological issues. In line with the epidemiological findings that there are different rates of completed suicide across the life span and that such rates differ from country to country, research and clinical findings indeed show that there may well be unique psychological issues at different ages for the suicidal person.

Although the "trunk" of suicide (Shneidman, 1985) may be the same, there appear to be differences in such psychological issues as "I love you"; "This is me"; "I am caving in"; "I want to be gone"; "I am weakened"; and "This is the only thing I can do." These may be more quantitative, however, than presence or absence. Richman (1991, 1993) found, for example, that suicide in the elderly is not to be understood primarily as a response to being old. As in other age groups, suicide in the elderly is a multifactored event. Sociological, biological, and cultural correlates may vary with age (Leenaars, 1991).

Stack (1991) presented the social correlates of suicide by age. He stated that "correlates of suicidal behavior that vary by age include the position of the age group in society's institutional structure: the economy, religion, and family" (p. 188). He showed that there are different correlates depending on age, such as the high divorce rates for young adults, the disproportional investment in motherhood by middle-aged women, and physical illness in the elderly. Stack also showed that the impact of the media on the rate of suicide is different for different ages and that it is especially adolescents who are affected by the media and subsequent acts of violence, including suicide.

Thus, the time lines in the suicidal process have a pivotal place in the study of the suicidal person. Much greater attention by clinicians and researchers alike is needed.

CULTURAL VARIATION IN SUICIDE

Suicide is a multifaceted event, and suicidology is a multidisciplinary enterprise. Much of our understanding, including Shneidman's (1985) definition, has a Western orientation. Cultural elements in the suicidal event must be understood.

Shneidman (1985) stated that his proposed definition of suicide is applicable only to the Western world and noted that this caution needed to be given so that researchers making "cross-cultural comparisons do not make the error of assuming that a suicide is a suicide" (p. 203).

The views of suicide (e.g., as portrayed in the media) commonly held in Western cultures are likely not shared by the individual, family, or community outside the Western hemisphere. This may be illustrated with a few examples from different cultures.

In Japan, according to Iga (1993), suicide, though not welcomed, has traditionally been accepted. The Japanese government is not overly concerned with suicide. Suicide is seen as a personal problem (Iga, 1993; Takahashi, 1993). To understand suicide in Japan, Iga wrote, one must especially understand Japanese views of death. These views include the following: Death (even if by suicide) is a philosophical concept based on the idea of *mujo,* the sense of eternal change and the ephemeral nature of all things. Death is welcomed by many Japanese as an emancipation as, for example, illustrated in medieval times, when many priests and their followers drowned themselves in the ocean, believing that they were going to *Saiho Jodo* (Buddha Land). Death is viewed as providing a sense of achievement and a return of the soul to its natural habitat. Death for the group is thought to be the ultimate fulfillment of human potential, in that it reflects devotion to one's group or master. Death is perceived as beautiful, and this beautification of death is promoted by mysticism, a characteristic of Japanese thinking. Death allows one to identify with one's family, to have a continuing life (Shneidman's "post-self") through one's children and their children in an endless chain. Finally, with deep devotion the dead continue to communicate with family members at the *butsudan* (miniature household temple) and even become "angel gods," watching over their family's welfare.

This view of death and, by implication, of suicide, within the larger Japanese cultural framework, may make the well-publicized case of Fumiko K. less baffling. According to Iga (1993), during the period from 1985 through 1989 there were three reported cases of *oyako shinju,* or homicide–suicide, among Japanese Americans in the United States. Fumiko, a gentlewoman and devoted, dedicated mother, who was about to be divorced, walked into the Pacific Ocean off Santa Monica with her infant daughter and 4-year old son. Passers-by intervened, pulling the mother and children from the ocean. Fumiko survived; her children did not. Fumiko was charged with murder; she reportedly told the police she took her children with her because she loved them. It seemed incomprehensible to many Westerners that this woman, who had been in the United States for 14 years, had not become socialized to American attitudes toward divorce, infanticide, and social services. How could she have killed her children? Why would she have tried to kill herself?

Iga (1993) proposed that to understand Fumiko's actions, it is necessary to appreciate not only the Japanese concept of death, but also other Japanese cultural norms/rules. To illustrate, Iga argued that in Japan divorce robs women of their future security; there is little government protection for the divorcee. Marital failure is primarily blamed on the woman, who is viewed as not having been able to satisfy her husband's needs. Japanese people's sense of shame, as well as their reluctance to take problems to others, is strong, leaving Fumiko with limited ability to avail herself of social services and resources.

In Japan, there is also a prejudice against orphans. Without parental love, protection, and supervision, Fumiko knew, her children would suffer excessive hardships if she left them behind. Therefore, by her homicide–suicide, Fumiko would traditionally be viewed as having acted in the best interests of her children.

Other cultures have different meanings. Even within North America, there is a great diversity of peoples, e.g., aboriginal peoples, African Americans, Inuit people, French Canadians, and so on. It is erroneous to assume that there is one commonly held definition or understanding of suicide (or death in general). Suicide is a multidimensional concept that researchers need to understand within the heuristic framework of the dominant culture/society, while appreciating and being sensitive to the specific meanings of suicide held by cultures within the North American mosaic.

Consider an example from one group of aboriginal people. For Native Americans, the loss of their traditional holistic view and the process of forced acculturation to the majority culture and its devastating impact are expressed in the high rate of suicide in these people, a rate that is well above that of the general population. Although the complexity of this problem cannot be addressed here, perhaps a look at the past may assist heuristically. Barter and Weist (1970) extensively investigated patterns of suicide in the Northern Cheyenne Indians in Montana. They reported that, contrary to the belief that suicide was rare in the early history of the Northern Cheyenne, they found documentation of 25 suicide deaths between 1830 and 1884. The majority of these deaths were committed by suicide warriors, who were generally, though not always, young men who had vowed to die in battle. Barter and Weist noted,

If a certain young man wished . . . he could make a vow that in the next battle, when the enemy began to close in, he would drive a pin into the ground and tie himself to it. This meant that he would take a stand there and not retreat, fighting until the enemy was driven back or he was killed. . . . A man who vowed to take such a stand was called a suicide warrior and it was a great thing to die fighting in this way.

This self-sought "glorious" death gave the suicide high prestige, with a corresponding increase in self-esteem—which to someone with a Western perspective must appear to be a denial of death. The suicide pattern shifted dramatically during the first reservation period (1884–1949) and again during the contemporary reservation period (1950–1969) reflecting, according to Barter and Weist (1970), cultural changes in the Northern Cheyennes. Aside from illustrating cultural variation on the meaning of suicide, the example of the suicide warrior also illustrates that cultures are not static. Even if one has some familiarity and comfort with working with people of a certain ethnic group or culture, that that culture is ever evolving and changing.

Simply put, suicide has different meanings for different peoples at different times. Culture is an especially powerful vehicle for meaning. Insensitivity to this fact will likely result not only in problems in knowledge, but also in difficulties in suicide prevention among different cultural groups.

SUICIDE PREVENTION

The classical approach to the prevention of mental health problems and public health problems is that of Caplan (1964), who distinguished the concepts of *primary, secondary,* and *tertiary prevention.* The more commonly used terms for these three modes of prevention are *prevention, intervention,* and *postvention,* respectively. All have a place in preventing suicide.

Prevention relates to the principle of good mental hygiene in general. It consists of strategies to ameliorate the conditions that lead to suicide; "to do"— *venire*—something before the dire event occurs. Prevention is best accomplished through education. Such education, given that suicide is a multidimensional malaise, is enormously complicated, tantamount to preventing human misery.

Intervention relates to the treatment and care of a suicidal crisis or suicidal problem. It involves doing something during the event. A great deal has been learned about how to intervene—in crisis intervention and therapy—with suicidal people. Obviously, suicide is not solely a medical problem, and many persons can serve as life-saving agents. Nonetheless, professionally trained people (psychologists, psychiatrists, social workers, and psychiatric nurses) continue to play the primary roles in intervention. The state of the art in suicide intervention has been reviewed in a recent book by Leenaars, Maltsberger, and Neimeyer (1994).

Postvention, a term introduced by Shneidman in 1971, refers to those things done after the dire event has occurred. Postvention deals with the traumatic aftereffects in the survivors of a person who has committed or attempted suicide. It involves offering psychological services to the bereaved survivors. It includes working with all survivors who are in need—children, parents, teachers, friends, and so on.

Discussion of these approaches in more detail would require a separate chapter. However, a few comments should be made regarding suicide prevention in schools (Leenaars & Wenckstern, 1990). The response to suicide has to be complex, especially when it concerns young people. Schools, as suggested by the Secretary's Task Force on Youth Suicide (1989) of the U.S. Department of Health and Human Services, offer an excellent opportunity of reaching a large number of young people. Staff in schools must act as "reasonably prudent persons." The decision of the Ninth Circuit Court of Appeals in *Kelson v. the City of Springfield,* 1985, supports this view. In that case, the parents of a 14-year-old boy sued the school for negligence, complaining that the school had a duty to provide training in suicide prevention and that it had failed to do so. Though settlement was eventually made out of court, the case was admissible to court because the court held that a person may bring action against a school for nonprudent behavior.

Although prevention efforts should be part of a comprehensive prevention/ intervention/postvention plan, it is generally agreed that the most cost-efficient and potentially constructive avenue in public health problems is prevention. Prevention demands great patience and long-term commitment of resources and should not be confused with the intervention that suicidal people need. Prevention means education, not intervening with lethal people. There are four persistent problems facing prevention programs for youths:

1   The difficulty that suicidologists have in gaining access to the schools. System entry issues are a common concern, highlighting the need to begin the entry and development of such programs with the administration, followed by school staff and other individuals involved. A systemwide and even statewide policy is needed to allow entry.

2   The myth that talking about suicide will cause suicide. In reality, discussion facilitates openness by a suicidal person, leading to intervention. Improving skills, raising self-esteem, and so on may reduce school failure, increase self-control, reduce depression, etc.

3   The belief that such programs are not cost-effective. Such programs, in fact, generate mental health even among low-risk people.

4   The fear that schools can be sued if they have a program. On the contrary, the staff and schools must act in a prudent and competent fashion. Not having a program actually opens a school to liability concerns, as *Kelson v. the City of Springfield* illustrates.

This is not to say that schools should not critically reflect on their programs. Evaluation will have an important place in the prevention of teen suicide, and such programs must be part of a comprehensive program that addresses all aspects of Caplan's (1964) model.

ETHICAL ISSUES IN SUICIDOLOGY: RATIONAL SUICIDE, ASSISTED SUICIDE, AND EUTHANASIA

In August 1991, Derek Humphry's book *Final Exit* (1991) reached the *New York Times* bestseller list for advice books. To date, this book has sold more copies than any other book on suicide. The book highlights a topic that all professionals working in suicidology and thanatology must face. In *Final Exit,* the practicalities for suicide are spelled out. Do people need to have a guide to a method? Humphry says yes. His certainty is not shared by this author. Yet, what is the importance to us of *Final Exit* as well as related efforts, like Dr. Jack Kevorkian's campaign to assist terminally ill individuals to end their lives "with dignity?"

Humphry and the Hemlock Society do not advocate suicide per se. But they believe suicide and assisted suicide carried out in the face of terminal illness causing unbearable suffering should be ethically and legally acceptable. Old age in and of itself is not espoused by the Hemlock Society as cause for suicide. But, like it or not, terminal illness in some people is sufficient cause. It is, in fact, the most rational of such people who choose suicide as a final exit, according to Humphry. However, the views on the right to die are not uniform. Dr. Kevorkian, for example, disassociates himself from the Hemlock Society (and other right-to-die groups). Kevorkian believes that, without further debate, assisted suicide should be provided to those who request it. Indeed, the positions of Humphry and

Kevorkian are quite different, and there are conflicts between them (Humphry, 1993). Humphry and most of the right-to-die advocates argue for democratic reform. Kevorkian has a disregard of the law.

Considering views from different countries may better reveal the issues faced in North America (Battin, 1993). In The Netherlands, lawful euthanasia for the terminally ill is tolerated. Euthanasia refers to a merciful death caused by an intervention, not merely the withdrawal or withholding of treatment. Withdrawing, practiced in America, is the act of retracting life-sustaining treatment, such as in the landmark case of Karen Ann Quinlan. Withholding or refusal also is practiced in America, when a patient declines to undergo medical or surgical procedures. Euthanasia refers to the practice, after treatment has failed, of allowing the person to die, with the physician prepared to ease the suffering (West, 1993). Although legislation stops short of legalization of euthanasia in The Netherlands, it guarantees protection from prosecution for the physician who performs euthanasia, provided a set of guidelines are met. The "carefulness requirements," as they are called, are as follows:

- The request must reflect the person's own will,
- The person must be informed about alternatives,
- The decision must be persistent,
- The person must experience his or her pain as unbearable and perpetual,
- The physician must consult at least one colleague, and
- The physician must write a well-documented report.

Despite ongoing controversy, reports have indicated that Dutch doctors are responsible and are reticent in advising euthanasia.

In Germany, there is an opposition to euthanasia, and the Germans see the Dutch as falling down a slippery slope. Assisted suicide is, however, practiced in Germany. Assisted suicide is performed not by the physician, but by the patient, who is provided the means to end his or her own life. In fact, a support group, the Deutsche Gesellshaft für Humanes Sterben (DGHS) has been established. Even though assisted suicide is not illegal, the DGHS remains controversial in Germany.

Humphry (1992) stated that such options as those available in The Netherlands and Germany should be available to people in North America. Dr. Kevorkian stated that such matters are irrelevant. The real importance of these issues—and these are Humphry's words—is that "society needs now to come to terms with elderly suicide" (Humphry, p. 129).

Suicide by the terminally ill, maybe even the nonterminally ill, requires understanding: Is it rational? What are possible alternatives? Is it legitimate to withhold or withdraw life support? Can a case be made for euthanasia? Should assisted suicide be condoned or approved?

On the issue of "rational" suicide, Diekstra (1992) suggested that the word *rational* should be eliminated from discussion on this topic. "Rational" is a construction. As Diekstra asked, "When is any behavior just 'rational' or not?". It is misleading to ask whether a suicide is rational.

Obviously, old age is not a reason for suicide. Many elderly people, including those who are terminally ill, are suicidal. Their pain has become unbearable. Recovery from the suicidal state is possible, however. Whether such pain ends in recovery or death depends partly on the relationship of the older person to his or her family and society. A person's decision to kill him- or herself is a process. Even in the terminally ill person, it calls into question the person's history, especially his or her attachments. It is often an evaluation that past, present, and future relationships offer some hope, something bearable that stops the exit. Attachments are so crucial: They may alleviate the unbearable pain.

Richman (1992) believed that the foregoing ideas are critical to the topic at hand and argued against the right to die. He and others have argued that suicide, including the terminally ill, is never based only on being ill. Freud is a dramatic example, because his work in mental health is so influential. Freud killed himself. Was it, as he stated, because of his terminal illness? Or was it because he had been severely depressed at the time? He had been overwhelmed by World War II and had notable problems in his adjustment to moving to England. Was Freud's suicide due only to his terminal illness? Does Freud's suicide differ in its essence from other suicides? Humphry would say yes; Richman would say no. There are other questions; for example, was Freud's death really a suicide? Would it be more appropriate to call it self-determined death or a free death or a voluntary death?

There are other issues in considering the legitimacy of suicide as a solution to serious illness: Is there a slippery slope, leading from the condoning of suicide in some terminal ill cases to tacit acceptance of it in a wide range of ills such as mental illness? Humphry says no. Dr. Kevorkian, of course, believes that such considerations are irrelevant; we should simply assist people *now,* without further discussion. Others, however, disagree. For example, is it a trap for the young? Young people often imitate behavior, as in the phenomenon of cluster suicide. When are suicide, assisted suicide, and euthanasia acceptable and when not?

Last May, this author witnessed the afteraffects of a suicide of an elderly male, age 84. His wife had died 3 months earlier, he had cancer, his car was in the shop, he had no family, and he chose to jump 22 stories to his death. That was tragic. What was even more tragic was observing the people in his building, a senior citizen apartment house with no social services. I remember seeing an older woman on the fifth floor look and look, as did others, for 1 1/2 hr at the body. What services had the man needed? Could someone have helped him with his crisis? What about the other people? Is it humane to allow these senior people to be forced to witness such a death, or would euthanasia or assisted suicide (e.g., by a family doctor) be more humane?

The importance of the discussions of euthanasia and assisted suicide is that it raises questions that society must begin to try to answer. Are we willing to support hospice care for those who are dying? Are politicians and the public willing to provide the money for the services that elderly people need? There are many questions regarding euthanasia and assisted suicide. The right-to-die issue must be discussed by society in general, not just suicidologists. It will likely be one of the most critical issues in thanatology in the next decade.

CONCLUDING REMARK

This chapter is a prologue to the understanding of suicide. Suicide is a multifaceted event. Understanding such an event is a complex endeavor. Over the 100-year existence of suicidology, some things have been learned about suicide. Still, there is much left to learn. The need to understand the nature of suicide prompts us to analyze it from various points of view. This is as true about suicide as about death itself.

REFERENCES

Adler, A. (1967). Contributions to discussions of Vienna Psychoanalytic Society—1910. In P. Friedman (Ed.), *On suicide*. New York: International Universities Press. (Original work published 1910)

Barraclough, B. (1986). The relation between mental illness, physical illness and suicide. In J. Morgan (Ed.), *Suicide: Helping those at risk* (pp. 61–66). London, Ontario: King's College.

Barter, J., & Weist, K. (1970). *Historical and contemporary patterns of northern Cheyenne suicide.* Unpublished manuscript.

Battin, M. (1993). Suicidology and the right to die. In A. Leenaars (Ed.), *Suicidology: Essays in honor of Edwin Shneidman* (pp. 377–398). Northvale, NJ: Jason Aronson.

Berman, A. (1986, April). *Suicidal youth.* Paper presented at the annual conference of the American Association of Suicidology, Atlanta, GA.

Berman, A., & Jobes, D. (1991). *Adolescent suicide: Assessment and intervention.* Washington, DC: American Psychological Association.

Beauchamp, T. (1978). What is suicide? In T. Beauchamp & S. Perlin (Eds.), *Ethical issues in death and dying* (pp. 97–102). Englewood Cliffs, NJ: Prentice-Hall.

Brenner, M. (1988, April). *Economic and behavioral risk factors. Accounting for suicide over the life cycle.* Paper presented at the annual conference of the American Association of Suicidology, Washington, DC.

Brent, D. (1992, April). *Psychiatric effects of exposure to suicide among friends and acquaintances.* Paper presented at the annual conference of the American Association of Suicidology, Chicago.

Camus, A. (1955). *The myth of Sisyphus* (J. O'Brien, Trans.). New York: Vintage Books. (Original work published 1945)

Canetto, S. (1994). Gender issues in the treatment of suicidal individuals. In A. Leenaars, J. Maltsberger, & R. Neimeyer (Eds.), *Treatment of suicidal people* (pp. 115–126). Washington, DC: Taylor & Francis.

Caplan, G. (1964). *Principles of preventive psychiatry.* New York: Basic Books.

Corder, B., & Haizlip, T. (1984). Environmental and personality similarities in case histories of suicide and self-poisoning in children under ten. *Suicide and Life-Threatening Behavior, 14,* 59–66.

Corder, B., Parker, P., & Corder, R. (1974). Parental history, family communication, and interaction patterns in adolescent suicide. *Family Therapy, 3,* 185–190.

Diekstra, R. (1992). Suicide and euthanasia. *Giornale Italiano Di Suicidologia, 2,* 71–78.

Douglas, J. (1967). *The social meaning of suicide.* Princeton, NJ: Princeton University Press.

Durocher, J., Leenaars, A., & Balance, W. (1989). Knowledge about suicide as a function of experience. *Perceptual and Motor Skills, 68,* 26.

Durkheim, E. (1951). *Suicide* (J. Spaulding & G. Simpson, Trans.). Glencoe, IL: The Free Press. (Original work published 1897)

Farberow, N. (1972). Cultural history of suicide. In J. Waldenstorm, T. Larsson, & N. Ljeingstedt (Eds.), *Suicide and attempted suicide* (pp. 184–202). Stockholm: Nordiska, Bokhanlelus, Forlag.

Farberow, N. (Ed.). (1980). *The many faces of suicide*. New York: McGraw-Hill.

Freidman, P. (1967). *On suicide*. New York: International Universities Press. (Original work published 1910)

Freud, S. (1974). Psychopathology of everyday life. In J. Strachey (Ed. & Trans.), *The standard edition of the complete psychological works of Sigmund Freud* (Vol. 6, pp. 1–310). London: Hogarth Press. (Original work published 1901)

Freud, S. (1974). Mourning and melancholia. In J. Strachey (Ed. & Trans.), *The standard edition of the complete psychological works of Sigmund Freud* (Vol. 14, pp. 239–260). London: Hogarth Press. (Original work published 1917)

Freud, S. (1974). A case of homosexuality in a woman. In J. Strachey (Ed. & Trans.), *The standard edition of the complete psychological works of Sigmund Freud* (Vol. 18, pp. 147–172). London: Hogarth Press. (Original work published 1920)

Freud, S. (1974). Group psychology and the analysis of the ego. In J. Strachey (Ed. & Trans.), *The standard edition of the complete psychological works of Sigmund Freud* (Vol. 18, pp. 67–147). London: Hogarth Press. (Original work published 1921)

Frey, R. (1980). Did Socrates commit suicide? In M. Battin & D. Mayo (Eds.), *Suicide, the philosophical issues* (pp. 35–38). New York: St. Martin's Press.

Fryer, J. (1986). Aids and suicide. In J. Morgan (Ed.), *Suicide: Helping those at risk* (pp. 193–200). London, Ontario: King's College.

Goethe, J. (1951). *Die leeden des junger Werther, Goethes Werke, Vol. 6.* Hamburg: Christian Wegner Jerlag. (Original work published 1774)

Graber, G. (1981). The rationality of suicide. In S. Wallace & E. Eser (Eds.), *Suicide & euthanasia: The rights of personhood* (pp. 51–65). Knoxville, TN: University of Tennessee Press.

Greenglass, E. (1982). *A world of difference*. New York: Wiley.

Hughes, S., & Neimeyer, R. (1990). A cognitive model of suicidal behavior. In D. Lester (Ed.), *Current concepts of suicide* (pp. 1–28). Philadelphia: Charles Press.

Humphry, D. (1991). *Final exit*. Eugene, OR: Hemlock Society.

Humphry, D. (1992). Rational suicide among the elderly. In A. Leenaars, R. Maris, J. McIntosh, & J. Richman (Eds.), *Suicide and the older adult* (pp. 121–129). New York: Guilford Press.

Humphry, D. (1993). Letter to the editor. *Suicide and Life-Threatening Behavior, 23,* 281.

Iga, M. (1993). Japanese suicide. In A. Leenaars (Ed.), *Suicidology: Essays in honor of Edwin Shneidman* (pp. 301–323). Northvale, NJ: Jason Aronson.

Jung, C. G. (1974). Psychological types. In H. Read, M. Fordan, & G. Adler (Eds.), *The collected works of C. G. Jung, Vol. VI.* London: Routledge & Kegan Paul. (Original work published 1921)

Leenaars, A. (1988a). *Suicide notes*. New York: Human Sciences Press.

Leenaars, A. (1988b, October). Preventing youth suicide: Education is the key. *Dimensions in Health Services,* pp. 22–24.

Leenaars, A. (1988c). Are women's suicides really different from men's? *Women and Health, 14,* 17–33.

Leenaars, A. (1988d). The suicide notes of women. In D. Lester (Ed.), *Why women kill themselves* (pp. 53–71). Springfield, IL: Charles C Thomas.

Leenaars, A. (1989a). Suicide across the adult life-span: An archival study. *Crisis, 10,* 132–151.

Leenaars, A. (1989b). Are young adults' suicides psychologically different from those of other adults? (The Shneidman lecture). *Suicide and Life-Threatening Behavior, 19,* 249–263.

Leenaars, A. (Ed.). (1991). *Life span perspectives of suicide*. New York: Plenum.

Leenaars, A. (1994). Suicide: A multi-dimensional malaise. Paper in progress.

Leenaars, A., Balance, W., Pellarin, S., Aversano, G., Magli, A., & Wenckstern, S. (1988). Facts and myths of suicide in Canada. *Death Studies, 12,* 191–210.

Leenaars, A., Lester, D., Wenckstern, S., McMullin, C., Rudzinski, D., & Brevard, A. (1992). A comparison of suicide notes and parasuicide notes. *Death Studies, 16,* 331–342.

Leenaars, A., Maltsberger, J., & Neimeyer, R. (Eds.). (1994). *Treatment of suicidal people*. Washington, DC: Taylor & Francis.

Leenaars, A., Saunders, M., Balance, W., Wenckstern, S., & Galgan, R. (1991). Knowledge about facts and myths of suicide in the elderly. *Gerontology and Geriatrics Education, 12,* 61–68.

Leenaars, A., & Wenckstern, S. (Eds.). (1990). *Suicide prevention in schools.* Washington, DC: Hemisphere.

Leenaars, A., & Wenckstern, S. (1991). Suicide in the school-age child and adolescent. In A. Leenaars (Ed.), *Life span perspectives of suicide* (pp. 95–107). New York: Plenum.

Lester, D. (Ed.). (1988). *Why women kill themselves.* Springfield, IL: Charles C Thomas.

Lester, D. (1991). Suicide across the life span: A look at international trends. In A. Leenaars (Ed.), *Life span perspectives of suicide* (pp. 71–80). New York: Plenum.

Lester, D. (1992). *Why people kill themselves* (3rd ed.). Springfield, IL: Charles C Thomas.

Maris, R. (1985). The adolescent suicide problem. *Suicide and Life-Threatening Behavior, 15,* 91–109.

Maris, R. (1991). The developmental perspective of suicide. In A. Leenaars (Ed.), *Life span perspectives of suicide* (pp. 25–38). New York: Plenum.

Maris, R. (1993). The evolution of suicidology as a professional discipline. In A. Leenaars (Ed.), *Suicodology: Essays in honor of Edwin Shneidman* (pp. 3–21). Northvale, NJ: Jason Aronson.

Marzuk, P. (1989, April). *AIDS-related suicides.* Paper presented at the annual conference of the American Association of Suicidology, San Diego, CA.

Menninger, K. (1938). *Man against himself.* New York: Harcourt, Brace.

McIntosh, J., Hubbard, R., & Santos, J. (1983, April). *Suicide facts and myths: A compilation and study of prevalence.* Paper presented at the annual conference of the American Association of Suicidology, Dallas, TX.

Motto, J., & Reus, V. (1991). Biological correlates of suicide across the life span. In A. Leenaars (Ed.), *Life span perspectives of suicide* (pp. 171–186). New York: Plenum.

Murray, H. (1938). *Explorations in personality.* New York: Oxford University Press.

Murray, H. (1967). Death to the world: The passions of Herman Melville. In E. Shneidman (Ed.), *Essays in self-destruction* (pp. 7–29). New York: Science House.

O'Carroll, P. (1989). A consideration of the validity and reliability of suicide mortality data. *Suicide and Life-Threatening Behavior, 19,* 1–16.

Oxford English Dictionary (2nd ed., Vol. XVII, pp. 144, 145). (1989). Oxford: Clarendon Press.

Pfeffer, C. (1986). *The suicidal child.* New York: Guilford Press.

Phillips, D. (1986, April). *Effects of the media.* Paper presented at the annual conference of the American Association of Suicidology, Atlanta, GA.

Richman, J. (1991). Suicide and the elderly. In A. Leenaars (Ed.), *Life span perspectives of suicide* (pp. 153–167). New York: Plenum.

Richman, J. (1993). *Preventing elderly suicide.* New York: Springer Publishing Company.

Rifai, A., Reynolds, C., & Mann, J. (1992). Biology of elderly suicide. In A. Leenaars, R. Maris, J. McIntosh, & J. Richman (Eds.), *Suicide and the older adult* (pp. 48–61). New York: Guilford Press.

Rourke, B., & Fisk, J. (1981). Socio-emotional disturbances of learning disabled children: The role of central processing deficits. *Bulletin of Orthopsychiatry Society, 31,* 77–88.

Rourke, B., Young, G., & Leenaars, A. (1989). A childhood learning disability that predisposes those affected to adolescent and adult depression and suicide risk. *Journal of Learning Disabilities, 22,* 169–175.

Sainsbury, P., & Barraclough, B. (1968). Differences between suicide rates. *Nature, 220,* 1252.

Seiden, R. (1984). The youthful suicide epidemic. *Public Affairs Report.* Los Angeles: Regards of the University of California.

Slaby, A. (1992). Creativity, depression and suicide. *Suicide and Life-Threatening Behavior, 22,* 157–166.

Shneidman, E. (1963). Orientations toward suicide. In R. White (Ed.), *The study of lives* (pp. 202–227). New York: Atherton.

Shneidman, E. (1967). Sleep and self-destruction: A phenomenological approach. In E. Shneidman (Ed.), *Essays in self-destruction* (pp. 510–537). New York: Science House.

Shneidman, E. (1973). Suicide. In *Encyclopedia Britannica* (pp. 383–385). Chicago: William Benton.

Shneidman, E. (1985). *Definition of suicide.* New York: Wiley.

Shneidman, E. (1991). The commonalities of suicide across the life span. In A. Leenaars (Ed.), *Life span perspectives of suicide* (pp. 39–52). New York: Plenum.

Shneidman, E., & Farberow, N. (Eds.). (1957). *Clues to suicide.* New York: McGraw-Hill.

Shneidman, E., & Mandelkorn, P. (1970). How to prevent suicide. In E. Shneidman, N. Farberow, & R. Litman (Eds.), *The psychology of suicide* (pp. 125–143). New York: Science House.

Smith, K., & Maris, R. (1986). Suggested recommendations for the study of suicide and other life-threatening behaviors. *Suicide and Life-Threatening Behavior, 16,* 67–69.

Soubrier, J. (1993). Definitions of suicide. In A. Leenaars (Ed.), *Suicidology: Essays in honor of Edwin Shneidman* (pp. 35–41). Northvale, NJ: Jason Aronson.

Stack, S. (1991). Social correlates of suicide by age: Media impacts. In A. Leenaars (Ed.), *Life span perspectives of suicide* (pp. 187–213) New York: Plenum.

Stengel, E. (1964). *Suicide and attempted suicide.* Baltimore: Penguin Books.

Sullivan, H. (1962). Schizophrenia as a human process. In H. Perry, N. Gorvell, & M. Gibbens (Eds.), *The collected works of Harry Stack Sullivan* (Vol. 2). New York: W. W. Norton.

Sullivan, H. (1964). The fusion of psychiatry and social sciences. In H. Perry, N. Gorvell, & M. Gibbens (Eds.), *The collected works of Harry Stack Sullivan* (Vol. 2) New York: W. W. Norton.

Takahashi, Y. (1993). Suicide prevention in Japan. In A. Leenaars (Ed.), *Suicidology: Essays in honor of Edwin Shneidman* (pp. 324–334). Northvale, NJ: Jason Aronson.

Tomlinson-Keasey, C., Warren, L., & Elliot, J. (1986). Suicide among gifted women: A prospective study. *Journal of Abnormal Psychology, 95,* 123–130.

Toolan, J. (1981). Depression and suicide in children: An overview. *American Journal of Psychotherapy, 35,* 311–322.

West, L. (1993). Reflection on the right to die. In A. Leenaars (Ed.), *Suicidology: Essays in honor of Edwin Shneidman* (pp. 359–376) Northvale, NJ: Aronson.

Windt, P. (1980). The concept of suicide. In M. Battin & D. Mayo (eds.), *Suicide: The philosophical issues* (pp. 39–47). New York: St. Martin's Press.

World Health Organization. (1992). *Statistics annual.* Geneva, Switzerland: Author.

U.S. Department of Health and Human Services. (1989). *Report of the Secretary's Task Force on Youth Suicide.* Washington, DC: U.S. Government Printing Office.

Varah, C. (Ed.). (1978). *Answers to suicide.* Landon: Constable.

Zilboorg, G. (1936). Suicide among civilized and primitive races. *American Journal of Psychiatry, 92,* 1347–1369.

Zilboorg, G. (1937). Considerations on suicide, with particular reference to that of the young. *American Journal of Orthopsychiatry, 7,* 15–31.

Appendix

A SAMPLE OF SUICIDE NOTES
1: Adolescent female

Dear Mother & Dad,

Please forgive me. I have tried to be good to you both. I love you both very much and wanted to get along with you both. I have tried.

I have wanted to go out with you & Dad but I was always afraid to ask for I always felt that the answer would be no.

And about Bud, I want to dimiss every idea about him. I don't like any more than a compasion, for a while I though I did but no more, in fact, I am quite tired of him, as you know, I get tired of everyone after a while.

and Mother, I wish you hadn't called me a liar, and said I was just like Hap. as I'm not. It is just that I am afraid of you both at times, but I love you both very much.

> So Long
> Your loving daughter
> That will always
> love you
> Mary

P.S. Please forgive me. I want you to, and don't think for one minute that I haven't appreciated everything you've done.

2: Adolescent male

Mary,

You can have your student card back. Give it to the next guy in line. I'm curious to see who's next. I hope he doesn't get hurt easy. I don't know about you but I find it hard to hurt someone.

Why don't you figure out exactly what you expect from a guy. Then shop around to find one. Good luck at finding one. There aren't too many total jurk-off guys who will tell you that they love you and then let you do whatever you want (and not even tease you once). You had this with John and you made him sound like a fuckin idiot. That's how I felt. How does a guy keep you happy?

Do you enjoy people sucking up to you and do you enjoy fuckin everyone's life up?

I think you're the one who needs to grow up.

See you in Hell.

> Bill

Thanks for the chocolates but you can have them back.
Why do I still love you?

What does it take to Fuckin grow up?
How many times do you have to be Fuckin hurt?
What do you have to do to Fuckin please someone?
Doesn't anyone give a shit?
Don't the words I LOVE YOU mean anything?
I have nothing left to experience in life.
My conclusion is, Life Sucks and I'm getting the fuck out.

One last thing. I hate every fuckin one of you. So creamate me and dump my ashes over the town
dump where I belong with everything else that nobody has a use for. (*I'm so childish.*)
Just give me what I want and I'll be happy, shit.
I don't want fuck all. Okay!

Bill

I knew I'd Die before I got old.
      Ha!   Ha!
I was a drugging teen
          okay
I admit.
I enjoyed it for a while at least.
Bill

3: Young adult female

My dear dear family,

    I do not really know how to word this. Please, I beg of you, do not blame yourselves, please.
You have done everything possible for me. Your love—all of you—has been everything & now I wish
I could hold you all in my arms and kiss you tenderly—for I love you all so.

    I have tried & tried to overcome my unhappiness: but in the end have always failed. It seemed I
always was too heavy or too flashy, or underflashy or too thin or something. I never have really
achieved anything except for Bohemian items like my earrings etc. & we all know that I
am _____ & have not even been loved truly by a boyfriend or husband. Everything I
have desired has been so close—yet so far.

    It has not been anyone's fault—only a quirk of fate or work of God. I hope that God under-
stands & receives me into his Kingdom for is it possible for one to deserve two hells in succession.
Perhaps reincarnation is true, than I shall certainly succeed in my second life.

    Mother, I love you so please do not weep tears of sorrow for me. I would have suffered all my
life & you would have suffered, too. I love you beyond words, be happy that I am at last at peace. You
have never failed me, it is only I that has failed. Keep your love alive for you have a complete and
wonderful family now. I love you so.

    Dad, you have been wonderful and now I know that you have loved me also. Please stay as you
are & never return to you "old way of life." You have now found the "secret" of life, and God bless
you. We have never really been close, but the love has always been there.

    Lindsey you are so beautiful & elegant & sweet & unspoiled by modern trends & influences—
stay that way. I have always loved & admired you & know you will find an excellent place in life.

    Heather, I have no words for you because I love you so. I have even carried your picture every-
where with me. Please, Heather, try your best in school, & make everyone happy. I have always felt so
close to you. We both have similar emotions—a little nervous, very sensitive & you are very handsome
too. I love you very much be good.

    Kristen, you are a little devil. You're darling & fun to be around. Take care of yourself & be good.

    Mom, I love you always remember our love. Dad, don't cry, instead you remember our love too.

    I am much better off as I am because I have only thru the years, become progressively worse &
sick. You have all tried your best, so do not blame yourselves. I love you all.

    I hope you do not cry. You can't understand the pain of fighting & failing time after time. Here,
at the hospital I see people fail & degenerate before my very eyes. to think that someday I would be
one of them. I do not fear for myself, but I can't put you thr pain for years to come. Mother, I love you
too much for that. This, you will overcome someday, my continuing illness you could not.

    I do not regret being my life, only the joy (incomparable) of your company mother, the strength

of yours dad, the pride I have for you Lindsey, the laughter of you Heather & Kristen—the everything of you. I love you all so.
    When you think of my name, think only of love.

Love forever & beyond,
Mary

4: Young adult male

I'm sorry for this and so much else—I have no backbone—have always been weak & lazy—life for me has been a living death—it is my fault—for the few I have been close with & hurt deeply & still hurt just by being a fearful, stupid, self-centered _____ year old crybaby—I'm tired of crying—I'm tired of myself—I'm tired of seeing my closest & oldest friends & having nothing to say but—yes—I must be queer—I am but not in the way it would seem—I am happy when asleep—when alone—I think I've never been happy since my brother was born & whom I tormented constantly throughout our growing up—I always wanted to be spoiled so I went to people who would spoil me—There is no one to blame—no one to feel guilty—no one to blame themselves in any way for what has happened—I fell in love like a little boy—never wanting or able to take responsibility for the words that fell so easily from my lips.

People (all those who love themselves & love their parents & relatives as well) I am a beast . . . for _____ years I felt sorry for myself & made things as easy for me & difficult for others as possible. I never knew who I was or what I was, I never tried & hence took little pride in myself, I never broke loose & had fun . . .
    I am a homosexual who has never wanted to

5: Middle-aged adult female

Hello Sweetie
    I just wanted to tell you i still love you very much
Sweetie I'll always love you very much.
    My God i don't know how all this happen but it did. I wish it never did happen. All i know it hurts real bad just thinking of it makes me cry and say why. I never thought you would do this to me.
    Byi my Lady I love you forever,

P.S.   talk
        Byi
You're always be
part of me and thought
Betty I just want you to know I love you very much You know I still love you sweetie, I don't understand how all this happened, but you know what, I wish this would never have happened. Betty It hurts me very much. Just thinking of what happened makes me wonder why. I never thought you would do this to me! Sweetie I miss you.

respectfully
Mary

PS. I love you Sweetie

Middle-aged adult female

Your wedding band is in my radio, give it to Beverly.
This is the cheepest devoroce you can get

I'm going to wear my wedding band.

Here is all I got take it and be happy

Old adult female

Susanne—
Im heartsick First grnma the Ed—then my home—my car—my eyesight—now my apartment.
The last few days my sight is getting worse. I can only write by [*one word*]

Love
Mary

Thanks for everything to everyone
Alice & George: so long to two good friends.

Mary

8: Old adult male

To all concerned

My brother and sister now living. Brother—Windsor Ave.
I have taken my own life. I can't go on like this. It is the only way out for me. Papers can be found in small cellar in pantry floor. May the lord have mercy on me. Bills have mounted up and I see no way out.

Bill

Information for other relatives by telephone stand.
Actually the main reason is that car in the yard. Just bought it and pad for it at BMW Motors. but I bit off too much and it will o me out of house and home. Nobody is to blame but myself.

Chapter 15

Rights and the Dying

Arthur Zucker

[The Hemlock Society] believe[s] that [how best to commit suicide] should be raised within the physician-patient relationship, and we seek a change in the law to permit physician-aid-in-dying. This would protect the patient, the physician and society and make the actions of a Dr. Kevorkian . . . unnecessary. (Rosoff, 1993, p. 16)

So wrote Sidney Rosoff (1993), in a letter published in the *New York Times Sunday Magazine* on December 3, 1993. This chapter is an attempt to fill out all that is implicit in Mr. Rosoff's statement.

The following five cases revolving around the right to die, each followed by some questions and answers, serve as an introduction to this chapter. Each of the answers represents the actual positions taken by the people involved. The analyses of the actions taken are meant only to be illustrative.

FIVE CASE EXAMPLES ILLUSTRATING THE CONFLICTS REGARDING PATIENTS' RIGHT TO DIE

Case 1   An 82-year-old woman initially refused heart bypass surgery, saying, "It just isn't worth the risk to me." But she relented under pressure from her daughter and grandchildren. During surgery, she suffered some permanent brain damage as a result of a cardiac arrest. She did not do well after surgery. Aware of her new brain dysfunction, she was now vehement about preferring to be dead rather than live the way she seems destined. Her lungs did not clear properly and she was put on a ventilator, a situation she actively disliked. It soon became apparent that it would be difficult to wean her from the respirator. She found her whole situation maddening as well as demeaning. She requested that she be disconnected and allowed to die. Her daughter insisted that everything be done for her mother. The physician in charge was sure that she can be weaned; it would just take a bit more time than usual. He insisted on continuing care. The daughter supported his decision.

Is the elderly woman competent in these circumstances to be allowed to make a decision to die? Which of her previous decisions (first not to have the surgery and then to have the surgery) should be given more weight as indicating her true desires? What should be the role of medical expertise (facts) in a case like this? Should the opinions of the physician—even if they are opinions about facts— override the opinions of patients? Suppose the elderly woman had made some sort of document, properly witnessed, making it clear that if she ever were in such a situation, she would want to be allowed to die. Should all patients be told that making such a document is their right and should be done? Under what circumstances would it be morally and professionally acceptable to ignore such a document?

The woman decided to undergo the surgery to please her family and not because she wanted it for herself. No one should make decisions this important just to please others. If the physician is correct that just a brief amount of extra time is needed for the weaning, it makes sense to try to get the woman to agree to the attempted weaning, especially if the doctor also has good reason to think that she can regain all her previous functions. But even if the doctor is right about the facts, if the woman is competent and still refuses, she ought to be allowed to refuse and she ought to be allowed to die. If this woman had prepared some sort of advance directive and if it were legally recognized in the state, the doctor would be legally protected if he decided to withdraw support.

Case 2   Baby L. was a 2-year-old girl. She was born about 4 weeks premature and in great distress. At birth, she exhibited poor neurological functioning and required resuscitation and mechanical ventilation. Although her breathing improved to the point where the mechanical ventilation was no longer needed, her neurological condition worsened. She often choked when fed, and she suffered numerous seizures. She was responsive only to pain. Baby L. spend 14 months in neonatal and infant intensive care. She was released in the care of her mother and a 24-hr nurse. Two weeks later, Baby L. was readmitted because of pneumonia. A course of antibiotics cleared the pneumonia, and Baby L. was released. However, the pneumonia proved to be recurrent and basically recalcitrant to treatment. She was readmitted at 23 months for severe pneumonia and shock. She needed mechanical ventilation and began showing signs of cardiac failure. She had four cardiac arrests, from each of which she was resuscitated. The baby's mother insisted that everything be done for her child. The nursing staff felt that the baby's condition was hopeless. A consulting pediatric neurologist agreed. She pointed out that the baby could not survive for any length of time (no matter what the level of support) and that the medical interventions were causing the baby pain.

The staff (nurses and physicians) wanted to allow Baby L. to die. The mother refused to allow it and continued to demand that her baby be saved at all costs (Paris, Crone, & Reardon, 1990).

When is further treatment hopeless or futile? Can the concept of medical futility be precisely defined? Is it ever appropriate to override a parent's wishes?

Futility is relative. It is futile for a 45-year-old to want to be 25 years old again. It is not futile for a professional baseball pitcher to train after breaking his arm, in the hopes of regaining previous form. It is not futile to try experimental therapies in the hopes of beating an otherwise terminal disease. It is futile for a patient to expect to get back to his or her original, prediseased-state baseline after requiring many cardiopulmonary resuscitations (CPRs) at the end stages of a condition that has always proved fatal. Physicians should explain to patients what their conditions are and what they can expect. Patients must, however, be allowed to decide for themselves just how much they are willing to undergo; how much or how little care and treatment they want.

But this is a case of an infant. When a patient is incompetent or unknown to those in charge, that patient obviously needs to be spoken for. The person speaking must have the best interests of the patient and only the patient at heart. Sometimes emotional ties blind one to reality. Futility must be faced. In the Baby L. case, either the mother did not believe that the child was feeling pain, or she believed that the pain would be outweighed by ultimate recovery. Neither of these beliefs was warranted. But because of society's desire not to interfere with obviously well-intentioned actions of a parent, the desires of a mother must be followed. Because the rights of well-meaning parents are so important to respect, the cost of the procedures should not be factored into the decision about continuing life-sustaining health care.

Suppose a well-meaning parent wanted to use non-traditional health care in the face of a life-threatening but clearly treatable condition (e.g., Christian Science prayer instead of surgery or distilled water and herbs instead of chemotherapy for leukemia). In this case, the courts in general have found that children must be afforded the advantage of traditional treatment on the grounds that children cannot give the appropriate informed consent to take greater-than-usual risks. However, there is no consensus concerning whether to punish parents whose nontraditional approaches to health care have harmed their children. The state holds that it has a legitimate interest in protecting children's rights and health.

Case 3 Helga W. was started on a respirator on January 1, 1990. It was an emergency measure for pulmonary problems. By May, she was discharged to a chronic care facility because she had yet to be weaned from the respirator. At the chronic care hospital, she required CPR and was revived. She was then transferred to another hospital, where doctors recommended withdrawal of life support because they saw no hope for recovery; after 2 weeks, she was diagnosed as being in a persistent vegetative state. Again, the physicians recommended withdrawing life support. Her husband and her children refused. However, they did accept Do Not Resuscitate orders. Ultimately, the hospital went to court. It wanted to know if it was obliged to render clearly futile treatment.

The head of the ethics committee at the hospital argued that physicians should not always be bound by patients' wishes. He argued that when those wishes fly in the face of medical reality and when carrying out those wishes uses more than a fair share of resources, physicians and hospitals ought to be allowed to say no.

Case 4 Marcella L. recently committed suicide. She had had heart disease, arthritis, and emphysema. Before her death, she had said that she wished that those people who argue against the moral and legal legitimacy of suicide for people like her could have her pain for just one night.

Marcella's physician was more than willing to treat her according to the canons of the medical profession. But those canons did not include helping her to commit suicide. Why shouldn't a physician be allowed by society, the law, and the ethical standards of the medical profession to help some patients commit suicide?

If patients should be allowed to make their own decisions and a decision to end all treatment or never to begin treatment is acceptable, then a decision to commit suicide should also be acceptable. Part of a physician's charge is to reduce suffering related to disease. If certain drugs are the best means for committing suicide and these drugs are controlled by physicians, then sometimes it ought to be their duty to help patients get those drugs and perhaps even to help administer them. In a word, physician-assisted suicide ought to be seen as a legitimate part of medical practice.

Case 5   Howard R., 87 years old, had been confined to a nursing home since he had had a stroke 3 years ago. He was bedridden, aphasic, and incontinent. He currently had all the symptoms of pneumonia. His only visitor was a friend who had mentioned that he hoped that no heroics would be used to keep Howard alive and suffering. Three years ago, on admission, Howard's niece had called and asked that everything be done for her uncle. However, she had never visited.

Should the physician on call in this case order all the usual tests and begin treatment for pneumonia? Or, should he or she temporize just long enough to let the patient die from the pneumonia?

The elderly are often seen as a special economic burden because they are ill more often than the young. Ironically, they suffer more because letting them die seems morally and legally troublesome to many physicians and nursing home administrators. Advance directives are especially important for the elderly who live in nursing homes, because they often have no one to speak for them. If physicians felt more comfortable with letting patients die, cases like Howard's would not arise so often. In Howard's case, the physician chose to treat the condition. An ethics committee asked to examine this case decided that the aggressive treatment given to Howard was appropriate because that is what his next of kin had wanted. The committee pointed out that there would have been no legal protection for the facility had a complaint been brought.

Summary   The answers suggested to the foregoing cases are not unreasonable, but they are unsettling because it is easy to see replies and rejoinders and replies to the rejoinders. There is no way in this chapter to discuss all of the issues raised by these cases and these brief answers. What this chapter offers is a philosophical look at the issues, followed by a more medially oriented examination of the issues. The two perspectives are meant to be complementary.

PHILOSOPHY AND THE RIGHT TO DIE

Some of the moral issues involved in the preceding cases are as follows: What is euthanasia? When is it justified? Should physicians ever be allowed to help patients commit suicide? Is there a difference between suicide and euthanasia? What does it mean to be terminally ill? Who should be allowed to make decisions that will affect a patient's impending death? Sometimes, this issue is described as one that pits autonomy against paternalism. Before these questions are addressed, a brief look at moral theory may be helpful.

Moral Theory

Creating a moral theory is much like house cleaning. What you find was there all the time. But, occasionally, something you hadn't thought about in a long time appears, and you are glad for finding it. Of course, some of what you find gets thrown out. The rest gets rearranged so that it will be easier to find and therefore usable.

Moral theories should do at least the following:

• Limit the range of reasonable answers to what people should do when they are in a moral quandary;
• Tell people what they should do when they are in a moral quandary;
• Allow people to evaluate what they (and others) have done in past moral quandaries;
• Allow people to evaluate others, the intentions of others, the actions of others, and the consequences of the actions of others.

These sorts of evaluations are usually classified as *normative ethics*. To make these sorts of evaluations, a moral theory must also provide some definitions, for example, of *moral quandary, good, bad, responsibility, obligation,* etc. This part of moral theory is called *metaethics*. A full moral theory also answers the question, Why do people do the sorts of things they do? This part of moral theory is similar to what is called personality theory in psychology and is called *moral psychology.*

Theories have in common the appeal to rules or generalizations. The idea is simple. Once people have a rule, they can use it to determine what they should do in a situation. Here is a simple example. Should you lie to your uncle when he says, "Don't I look great in my new suit?" After all, you think he looks absurd. If you can make a simple appeal to the simple moral rule "Don't lie," the answer to what to do is easy. If you appeal to the simple rule "Never hurt the feelings of a loved one," the answer is still easy, but it is different from the other answer. A moral theorist would be careful not to specify rules without making plain when they were applicable and when they were not. (Notice that the two rules that may be invoked in the situation of the uncle in the unattractive suit conflict unless they are stated with riders, such as "Never lie, unless _____." Often, theories offer a ranked hierarchy of rules.

Moral theories that focus on the consequences of actions, called *consequen-*

tialist theories, use a rule something like "Always do that action that leads to the maximization of the good." Moral theories that reject the assessment of consequences and emphasize acting from duty as the only moral course are called *deontological* theories. In general, deontological moral theories use a rule something like "Always do your duty." Naturally, the consequentialist must define the good that is to be maximized, and the deontologist must provide a list of specific duties (or offer some way to get that list). Consequentialists such as John Stuart Mill (1806–1873) defined good as pleasure. The most famous deontologist, Immanuel Kant (1724–1804), listed truth telling, keeping promises, and never committing suicide among the important duties. The history of ethics is often characterized as an ongoing debate between the consequentialists and the deontologists. Each camp has responded to critiques by the other. There is now no one way to look at a contemporary moral theory and say that it is just consequentialist or just deontological.

A third type of moral theory that has become increasingly popular is called *virtue ethics*. It differs from the two types discussed above in that it stresses the fact that certain actions are consistent with being a certain kind of person and that doing certain kinds of things tends to make one a certain kind of person. To give what may be an unfair example, to be successful at selling used cars, a person must be willing and able to deceive customers. Such a salesperson might get into the habit of deceiving and might well turn into a deceptive sort of person. Virtue ethics asks, What sorts of persons are worth having, and what sorts of actions will lead to the development of such persons? The general answer is that society wants and needs virtuous people. Therefore, the general sort of rule used in virtue ethics is "Always act in accord with the virtues." Of course, people need a list of these virtues. The list usually given is not surprising: Honesty, courage, and fairness in treating others are always mentioned.

What is the value of making and using theory in practical ethics? Suppose someone believed that physicians should never assist in a suicide. Critics of this rule could have a field day. The rule is too absolute; real life requires exceptions. The rule is vague. What exactly is it to "assist"? What is to count as "suicide"? Unless all of these questions are answered, the rule cannot even be used. Of course, these questions can be answered. The answers, so clearly needed, would count as the first step in creating a moral theory.

There is another plus to having a moral theory. Theories allow people to categorize. Without some means of categorization, each and every action, each and every moral quandary would be unique. If that were so, people could never learn from a mistake. They could *never grow* ethically. How they reasoned in the past could be no guide to reasoning now or in the future. This leads to yet another advantage to theory. It emphasizes reason over reaction. Ethics is subjective enough without also allowing it to focus primarily on how people react without careful thought. Conflicting reactions will rarely lead to compromise, except perhaps out of fear. Reasoning through (and, one hopes, out of) a conflict appears far more promising a tactic.

The Vocabulary of Euthanasia

Euthanasia has now come to mean the actions taken or not taken that hasten a patient's death. In clear cases of action taken (injecting an overdose of morphine), the euthanasia is classified as *active*. In clear cases of action not taken (or deferred), such as writing Do Not Resuscitate orders, the euthanasia is classified as *passive*. (Sometimes, these actions are referred to as *direct* and *indirect*, respectively.) If the patient asks for and gives competent consent to euthanasia, the euthanasia is called *voluntary*. If the patient cannot give consent at the time of the euthanasia or has not given previous consent (i.e., an advance directive), the euthanasia is called *nonvoluntary*. If euthanasia were ever done against the will of a patient, it would be termed *involuntary* and would clearly be an illegal action.

Voluntary euthanasia is a special case of suicide. Suicide is generally thought of as something done by desperate people on themselves and without the help or approval of others. Indeed, many people believe suicide is committed by individuals whose judgments are clouded by the exigencies of the moment. Hence the listing of suicide hotlines in newspapers. Often, suicide is seen as a waste, and people say things like "What a shame" or "If only someone had been there."

Euthanasia differs from this usual account of suicide in that the people who contemplate euthanasia, although desperate, have very good reason to be desperate. They are patients whose lives are miserable and for whom no end to the misery—except death—is in sight. Often, they are patients who are dealing with a terminal disease. (A disease is considered terminal when it will, in the absence of other factors, lead to death, whether treated or not, in a period of time that is usually shorter than would have been expected of that person without the disease. The length of time from diagnosis to death is irrelevant. Incurability itself does not make a condition terminal. Patients with a terminal disease can die from other causes, e.g., automobile accidents. Also, terminality is a judgment relative to available therapies.) They may be so near the end point of the disease that a few days or weeks of suffering seem pointless. They may be not near the end point of their disease but know what is in store for them and choose not to suffer as the disease progresses (e.g., Lou Gehrig's disease or Alzheimer's disease). Some patients have a condition that is not terminal but is so painful, debilitating, or demeaning to them that they prefer death (e.g., severe and disfiguring burns or quadriplegia).

If there is a right to die, it is clearest in dire medical straits. A full understanding of the right to euthanasia requires understandings of the following concepts: competence, autonomy (the right to self-determination), and paternalism (the limits some may legitimately place on others' right to self-determination).

Competence refers to a person's ability to make rational judgments. A rational judgment is one that is not irrational. An irrational judgment is one that leads to death, pain, disability, or loss of pleasure without an acceptable reason. For example, an acceptable reason for undergoing the pain of a tooth extraction is to avoid possible infection. An acceptable reason for choosing death over long-term therapy is the financial cost; another acceptable reason for choosing death is to avoid great pain. An unacceptable reason for undergoing the amputation of both legs would be to see how one looks without legs. What makes a reason acceptable is a function of the persons and the community involved. For example, it would be acceptable to some people but not to others to undergo the pain and risk of a tattoo. Strictly speaking, following this account, a mentally ill person could still be rational and competent much of the time. (This analysis is modeled after the one offered by Gert, 1988.) The right of a competent person to make binding decisions about health care was ensured by the Supreme Court's decision in *Cruzan v. Director, Missouri Department of Health,* which is discussed below.

The competent person who opts for death does so because it is the only way to avoid other (perhaps greater) evils. In this view, choosing death is not *ipso facto* a sign of incompetence. Neither is it a reason to interfere with the carrying out of the decision.

What are the *limits* of autonomy? Put another way, how is paternalism to be justified? People are justified in limiting the actions of others when

1   Their actions will cause harm to themselves or to others;
2   That harm is easily avoidable;
3   The harm avoided is clearly greater than the harm done in restraining the person in question;
4   Society is willing to advocate that in all similar situations autonomy be restricted.

But what about suicide? It has already been noted that death itself may not be the greatest of all evils. To a libertarian, suicide counts as the most private of all acts. Extended to the medical context of euthanasia, the libertarian argument is this: If it is my life and my life alone that is at stake, and if I am miserable as a living being, then no one should have a right to force me to stay alive in that state of misery.

There are two easy criticisms to make against the libertarian view. One is that no action goes without consequences and some of those consequences do affect others. The libertarian must offer some way of drawing the line between important and trivial effects. But the line is never made clear. Indeed, it is likely that it cannot be made clear. Another critique is that the presumption of a right to be left alone does not make it clear when (if ever) a right to be helped comes into existence. Moreover, the libertarian position ignores the conflicts that often arise between the wishes of an individual and the ethics and traditions of a profession.

The libertarian view assumes that if people should be in charge of anything, it should be their bodies. The only restrictions on what people are allowed to do with their bodies, in this view, is that they should not be allowed to harm others physically. Barring this, people may do as they please with their bodies, including destroy them when they see fit. For example, if a person buys a toaster and it just does not work well and frustrates the person to no end, then it is certainly within the person's right to toss that toaster in the garbage or, in a fit of pique, whack it with a sledge hammer. (If the person tosses the offending toaster out a 23rd-floor window and it kills a passerby, the person is in trouble.) If an individual can do that with a troublesome toaster, then why not with his or her body when it is racked with pain and disease?

There are two replies to this argument. The libertarians' privacy argument disallows behavior that causes physical harm to others. But why not disallow behavior that causes emotional harm to others? Suicides often cause emotional pain to others. Why should this fact be ignored? Another counter to the privacy claim is that some things are not really owned the way that toasters are owned. Some things, for example, great art works, are held in stewardship for others. People's bodies, according to this line of reasoning, while not entirely like the Mona Lisa, are more like it than like a toaster or lawn mower. Thus, we are not nearly as free to do as we please with our bodies. Although stewardship has a religious ring to it, it need not be based on religion at all, just the recognition that some things are rare and valuable.

How would the establishment of a right to die affect the medical profession? Briefly, a right is a legitimized expectation, legitimized by the law or by commonly accepted moral standards. Thus, a person expects to be helped in some circumstances and not to be interfered with in other circumstances. Infants, the unconscious, the comatose, and even the dead have rights. Even if they can have no literal expectations, the relevant community expects them to be treated in certain ways. There are then two sorts of rights: claim rights and liberty rights. If there is a *claim right* to die, if a person wants to die and cannot do it him- or herself, someone has the obligation to help the person. If there is only a *liberty right* to die, no one can stand in the person's way so long as the person can commit suicide him- or herself, but no one is obligated to help the person do so.

It is the view of Dr. Jack Kevorkian (discussed below) and the Hemlock Society that the time and style of a person's death are so important that they must be considered claim rights. Dr. Kevorkian especially sees helping some people commit suicide as a professional obligation of physicians.

If the courts were to find that the right to die is a claim right, physicians would have to rethink what seems to be a professional proscription against directly (actively) killing patients. On the other hand, with the courts holding (so far) that the right to die is no more than a liberty right, doctors are asked only not to interfere with patients, and this is usually spelled out by asking physicians to inform patients of their rights as patients. An interesting example of how this works is provided by the Patient Self-Determination Act.

The Patient Self-Determination Act, in effect since December 1991, applies to all health care institutions that receive Medicare or Medicaid. The act

requires that all individuals receiving medical care be given written information about their rights under state law to make decisions about that care, including the right to accept or refuse medical or surgical treatment. They must also be given information about their rights to formulate advance directives such as living wills and durable power of attorney for health care. . . . The states must develop a written description of their own laws . . . to be given to patients. (Rouse, 1991, p. 52)

This act determines a claim right. But the claim is only to information. The act does not guarantee the carrying out of a living will. The act assumes that a competent patient should determine his or her health care. But it does not define *competent*. The act does not force a physician to act against his or her conscience or provide a remedy for the fact that few physicians (or health care institutions) will follow the advance directive of a very sick patient, who has asked for no further care, over the wishes of a healthy relative (especially a spouse or parent) who asks that the patient be saved. The act does not itself address this basic moral question: Do patient requests bind physicians? Specifically, how should physicians respond to requests for no more treatment and assistance with dying?

The Slippery Slope

Is there no stopping from the registration of some guns to the confiscation of all firearms? Is there no stopping from the performing of amniocentesis for Down's syndrome to the performing of amniocentesis for sex selection? Is there no stopping from letting doctors assist in the suicide of some patients to building Nazi-style concentration camps?

Take a step onto ice-covered stairs, even a tentative one, and you are likely to be unceremoniously to the bottom of the stairs. In this case, there is simply no going back. Can this sort of thing happen with ethical reasoning, especially as it deals with the medical field? The answer seems to be, It depends.

Taking the slippery-slope perspective, Hurley (1993) stated,

If some form of limited euthanasia were allowed by law, it is quite possible that some . . . chain of events would occur [leading to bad consequences]. Deciding the question [would this actually happen?] . . . would require a close study of society's commitment to the value of human life. (p. 180)

Thus the use of the slippery-slope argument has to be watched with care as well as evaluated on a case-by-case basis. There are actually two types of slippery-slope perspectives. One type claims that an argument used in one situation with acceptable consequences will continue to be used in other situations, leading to clearly immoral or unwanted consequences. What makes the argument so eminently repeatable is the existence of some crucial property on a smooth gradation or spectrum. For example, allowing an infant with severe birth defects to die will ultimately lead to allowing less and less severely affected infants to die until all but the healthiest infants are left to die. What makes this argument seem compelling is that there is a smooth gradation from severe through moderate to normal; the gradation is so smooth that there seems to be no way to stop the move from "It's all right to allow the severely affected ones to die" to "It's all right to allow the ones with clubbed feet to die."

The other slippery-slope perspective postulates that accepting one kind of situation sets people up psychologically to accept other types of situations that are unwanted. In this case, it is not the repetition of an argument in a series of situations along a grade, but the transfer of a feeling that seems appropriate in one situation to a situation where it is no longer appropriate. For example, the feeling that it is acceptable to assist in the death of debilitated and terminally ill elderly persons who ask for assistance in dying might lead to the feeling that it is acceptable to assist in the death of debilitated and terminal elderly persons who do not ask for such assistance. The conclusion: Do not allow euthanasia.

Neither form of slippery slope is as slippery as icy stairs. The first type of slope—the logical slope—requires care to avoid. It also requires enough skill to know when to use a different argument. But the very fact that society can recognize a slippery slope indicates that it realizes that some results are to be avoided. Society can dig in its heels and stop at any point it chooses. Will society have the psychological ability to stop; will it want to stop? Certainly, there is no evidence that people run totally on logic. But neither is there evidence that they run totally on feelings.

As Gorovitz (1985) has noted, anyone who skis understands the flaw with slippery-slope arguments. Skiers look for slippery slopes precisely because they give the best ride. This makes them dangerous, but only to beginners. Good skiers know how and when to stop. So it is with people doing ethics.

MEDICINE AND THE RIGHT TO DIE

Although there is no documentation of it, there must have been cases of patients' refusing treatment and physicians' assisting patients in dying before the current interest in euthanasia. It is clear that medical technology has forced the issue of euthanasia on society by making it possible to revive, restore, and otherwise revitalize people who in the past would have died. It is just that sometimes the state of the person after medical restoratives is not at all what that person would have wanted, probably not what anyone would have chosen. Given that the new lifesaving technologies are now a part of the medical profession, how can their use be controlled? Discussion of two important legal decisions, the issue of the definition of death, the economic need for restraining the use of some medical techniques, and recent attempts at incorporating euthanasia into medical practice as well as opposition to such actions will help answer this question.

Two Legal Cases: Quinlan and Cruzan

Karen Ann Quinlan was a young woman maintained on a respirator for many months. She had suffered irreversible brain damage. There was no hope for a return to anything even remotely like normal health. Her father petitioned the courts to have her life support withdrawn. Ultimately, this case was decided by the New Jersey Supreme Court. They held for the father, pointing out that they were sure that Karen herself would have made such a decision and that "no external compelling interest of the State could compel Karen to endure the unendurable, only to vegetate a few measurable months with no realistic possibility of returning to any semblance of cognitive or sapient life" (In re Quinlan, 1975, p. 35). Because of the attendant publicity, this case made the issue of letting a person die an unavoidable one for the public. It also called attention to the need for some sort of documentation, some sort of evidence that a person would not want to be kept alive. This need for evidence was crucial in the next case.

Nancy Cruzan had been in a persistent vegetative state since 1983, the result of an automobile accident. Her parents wanted her feeding tube withdrawn, but the state of Missouri refused. The state pointed out that there was no evidence as to what Ms. Cruzan herself would have wanted, and without such clear and compelling evidence the state believed that treatment was the only moral and legal recourse. The case was decided by the U.S. Supreme Court in 1990. The Court held for the state of Missouri, but it made its general opinion on the topic of a right to die clear. The Court held that when there is clear evidence that a patient does not want or never wanted some treatment—life saving, life sustaining, or otherwise—that treatment may not be started or, if it has already been started, must be withdrawn. The Court explicitly held that this right to die grew out of the liberties protected by the 14th Amendment and not privacy, which some legal scholars still reject as a Constitutionally protected right (*Cruzan v. Director, Missouri Department of Health,* 1990).

What Is Death?

Neither the Quinlan nor the Cruzan lawyers worried about the definition of death. By using some version of a higher-brain-function definition of death, the lawyer in each case could have argued that the patient was already dead. So settling the question of when someone is dead is crucial to putting the right to die into practice.

One truly spectacular case highlighted brain death. In 1967, in South Africa, Dr. Christian Barnard transplanted a heart from a donor who was declared dead despite having a healthy, beating heart. A less spectacular case occurred in the United States. In 1968, Bruce Tucker was brought to the Medical College of Virginia suffering massive head injuries. The next day, he was declared brain dead. After an intensive but unsuccessful search for relatives, Tucker's heart was transplanted. This was technically allowed under the Unclaimed Bodies Act. Four years later, Tucker's brother brought a wrongful death suit against the hospital and the physicians involved. After all, was Tucker not killed when his beating heart was transplanted? At the trial, the judge allowed testimony to the effect that brain death, as the sign of the loss of personal identity, was criterion enough for death. This was also one of the first trials where an ethicist, Joseph Fletcher, testified as an expert witness (Fletcher, 1979). The fear that the medical profession will settle on the criterion for death that will best foster organ transplants has been a concern at least since the first Barnard heart transplant.

When *is* someone dead? In bygone days, a mirror was held up to a dying person's mouth. When the mirror ceased to fog, the person was dead. Later, a stethoscope was used to determine cessation of a heartbeat and therefore death. Now society is toying with definitions of brain death. Because of medical technology, hearts can be kept beating and respiration can be continued, if not indefinitely, then certainly long after patients seem unable to do much other than vegetate. Thus it seems reasonable to revamp the definition of death. The new definition involves the brain. The reason for focusing on the brain is the intuitive idea that to be dead is to be unable to be a person and that to be a person requires a degree of consciousness ensured only by a properly functioning brain. The question was in 1968 (and still is), Should it be the whole brain or just the centers of higher function?

The whole-brain defenders fear that any other less stringent brain-oriented definition will yield to easy misuse. The higher-brain-function defenders reject that claim and argue that what counts as the whole brain is unclear and that what counts as a dead whole brain is just as unclear. Higher-brain-function defenders point out that "the human is essentially the integration of the mind and body and . . . the existence of one without the other is not sufficient to constitute a living human being" (Veatch, 1993, p. 21). These higher-brain-function defenders claim that the integration they refer to provides the physiological basis for determining which part of the brain has to be impaired, and by how much, to justify the declaration that death has occurred. When it comes to a specific recommendation, Veatch (1993) suggested that a person is dead when and only when there is irreversible cessation of the capacity for consciousness.

The higher-brain-function defenders are quick to point out that what is at stake is not biology, but moral and social philosophy. The debate over how to define death is a debate about the moral status of humans; it is not a debate about how the brain (or any other organ) functions. Veatch (1993) stated, "Saying people are alive is simply shorthand for saying that they are bearers of [moral and legal] rights" (p. 21). But what does it mean to bear a right? Cadavers (dead people in general) do have legal and moral rights. These rights are limited by law and custom. But they do exist. For example, when people are dead is precisely when they have both a legal and moral right to have their wills executed. Their next of kin can sue on their behalf if their good name is slandered. The expression "Don't speak ill of the dead" indicates that society believes that the dead have moral rights. The entire issue is clouded by lack of precision regarding the definitions of terms such as *mind* and *consciousness*.

Left open is the possibility that by making death a social and moral characteristic, society might define as dead those people who make society uncomfortable or who cost society too much time and effort. Also what counts as dead might vary from segment to segment of the population. Recognizing this, Veatch (1993) stressed the need for pluralism in society; different definitions of death, depending on deeply held philosophical and religious views, ought to be allowed. But he failed to consider that even a pluralistic society might come to have a need to force a definition on itself. Put another way, even a longstanding pluralistic society might decide that it can no longer afford the luxury of pluralism when it comes to defining death.

The Economics of the Right To Die

It is virtually impossible to separate the right to die from economic issues. Usually, the patients with the most problems, the patients who cost the most, are among the elderly. Whether they are cared for in acute care settings in hospitals or in nursing homes, the elderly cost society more than any other group. How does this relate to the right to die?

Callahan (1987), in *Setting Limits,* argued that there ought to be (indeed, realistically had to be) a cutoff point after which the elderly receive no life-lengthening care. Callahan's suggested program would, however, provide palliative care and support such as eyeglasses, hearing aids, wheelchairs, and food for the very poor. He pointed out that high-tech acute care pays far too little attention to quality-of-life issues. That is, elderly patients are saved but then shunted off to nursing homes, as illustrated in Case 3 earlier in this chapter, where they linger and continue to be a drain on the economy.

There is another clear connection between economics and choosing to die. Some people, elderly or otherwise, might choose to die rather than create a financial burden on their children or relatives. Although the thought that economics would figure into life-or-death decisions is troublesome to some, there is no reason it should not be one factor among many in such decisions. Moreover, the feeling that economics should not be the deciding factor (or should not be a factor at all) may just be a reflection of a society that has never really understood the limits of wealth.

Death in The Netherlands

The Dutch have legalized active, voluntary euthanasia under certain conditions. The request has to be made consistently and clearly by a conscious and competent patient. A consulting physician, who will not assist with the suicide, must examine the patient. Only terminal patients, suffering physical and emotional pain, with no real hope of improvement, may be candidates for active euthanasia. Mental suffering alone is not considered an indication for assisted suicide ("Euthanasia Policy OK'd," 1993). Dutch physicians who abide by these restrictions will be immune from prosecution for 'mercy killing.'

There is no clear evidence that euthanasia is rampant in The Netherlands. But, of course, officially gathered data would be unlikely to reveal cases of violation. Even if there is no blatant abuse of the program yet, it does not follow that there will not be such abuse in the future. Also, the fact that there as yet has been no abuse does not mean that such a program should be institutionalized as a part of the practice of medicine.

The issue of abuse is clouded by the number of patients classified in collected data as "terminated without consent." The Dutch physicians van der Maas et al. (1991) said this:

> Our study suggests that [termination without consent] happens in about .8% of all deaths. . . . In [these cases], possibly with a few exceptions, the patients were near to death and clearly suffering grievously, yet verbal contact had become impossible. The decision to hasten death was then nearly always taken after consultation with the family, nurses, or one or more colleagues. (p. 673)

Kevorkian: A Medical Specialty in Death

Dr. Jack Kevorkian is a retired pathologist who is on a crusade to make assisted suicide for certain terminal patients legal. The case that brought him to national attention concerned Ms. Janet Adkins. She and her husband traveled to Detroit from Portland to use Kevorkian's "suicide machine." The machine consisted of a patient-activated IV drip—drips that were fatal. Ms. Adkins, who had early Alzheimer's disease, went through with the procedure. Dr. Kevorkian notified the authorities. He was charged with murder. Michigan authorities felt that if they allowed his actions, Michigan would become a "magnet for this type of murder," in the words of the prosecutor.

There was a videotape of Ms. Adkins's discussions with Dr. Kevorkian. The tape can be interpreted as showing that she was competent. Although Dr. Kevorkian provided the suicide machine, can there be a murder when the person involved is competent, has good reasons, and actually performs the suicide? Michigan has no antisuicide laws. So the legal question deals with assisted suicide.

The medical–ethical issues are just as unclear as the legal issues. Ms. Adkins's doctor thought that her plan was precipitous; that she had several more years during which "she would be able to . . . enjoy the types of experiences she was currently enjoying" (Lewin, 1990). Almost certainly, Dr. Kevorkian was not fully aware of the details of the case. The medical system works against those like Ms. Adkins who want assisted suicide. What choice was left her except to go to someone like Dr. Kevorkian? He would not know the ins and outs of the case. But this can be seen as irrelevant if Ms. Adkins was competent. Even if she had some good years left, was it for her doctors to decide that she should not have committed suicide? More to the point, was it for her doctors to tell her what she should have accepted as good years? In other words, forcing her to die only after a long bout of Alzheimer's disease can easily be seen as unjustified paternalism. Still, the question remains, should Dr. Kevorkian be the only alternative? Many ethicists see what Dr. Kevorkian did as against the norms of medicine. Medicine should limit itself to healing, counseling, and relief of suffering. Deliberate killing should never be a legitimate part of medicine.

The Oakland County District Court dismissed the charges against Dr. Kevorkian for two reasons: Michigan had no specific law against assisted suicide, and, according to the judge, it was Ms. Adkins who was the cause of her death (Lewin, 1990).

Dr. Kevorkian has never stopped in his work. On August 4, 1993, he assisted Mr. Thomas Hyde in committing suicide. Hyde was suffering from Lou Gehrig's disease. On August 17, 1993, Dr. Kevorkian was charged with violating Michigan's new law banning assisted suicide. The law was put into practice in February 1993 precisely to enable the state to charge Dr. Kevorkian if he continued with his "mercy killings." The Michigan Court of Appeals is reviewing the law, which has already been struck down and then reinstated. The Wayne County prosecutor, John D. O'Hair, believes that Dr. Kevorkian must be prosecuted because he broke the law. O'Hair himself supports the concept of assisted suicide and will propose a bill to legalize assisted suicide. (As of this writing, Michigan's anti-assisted-suicide law has been found unconstitutional by the Wayne County Circuit Court.)

Three Ethicists on Death: Quill, Pellegrino, and Brody

Dr. Timothy Quill (1993) reported a case of his that involved assisted suicide. "Diane" was a patient of Dr. Quill's. She had successfully fought alcoholism and vaginal cancer. Then she was found to have acute leukemia. She surprised her oncologist by deciding not to treat her disease. She called Dr. Quill and asked for a barbiturate. Previously, he had told her to get information from the Hemlock Society. He knew that she planned to use the drug to kill herself and was careful to tell her exactly how much to use. Assisted suicide in New York, where this took place, is illegal. But Dr. Quill believed it was important to bring this case to the public eye—even at risk to himself.

Dr. Quill's case is quite different from that of Dr. Kevorkian in that Dr. Quill knew his patient very well. After reporting the case of Diane, Dr. Quill (1993) published vignettes on six patients who asked to die. His purpose in publishing the vignettes was to show how he believed physicians should relate to patients who make such requests for assisted suicide. Dr. Quill offered the following guidelines: Listen and learn. Be compassionate, caring, and creative. Promise to be there until the end. Be honest about whether you will help with suicide. Have an open heart and an open mind toward intolerable suffering. Have support systems for yourself.

Pellegrino (1992) interpreted Dr. Quill as defending assisted suicide as a legitimate part of medical practice. He highlighted the following comment from Dr. Quill:

If there are no good alternatives [to suicide] what should the patient do? There is often a moment of truth for health care providers and families faced with a patient whom they care about who has no acceptable options. Physicians must not turn their backs, but continue to problem-solve, to be present, to help their patients find dignity in death. (Quill, 1993, p. 873)

What else can this mean except that physicians should be ready to assist in suicide?

Pellegrino (1992) criticized Dr. Quill's use of the case study method of presenting his research. Pellegrino argued that overriding general principles were lacking. In the absence of such principles, Pellegrino argued, how can Dr. Quill claim that these cases are clear examples of morally justified assisted suicide? In other words, Pellegrino was arguing for the legitimacy of a moral theory underlying medical ethics. Such a theory, he claimed, would not allow assisted suicide. In outline form, here is Pellegrino's theory.

1 In passive euthanasia, the disease kills the patient. When there is assisted suicide, the physician kills the patient. Physicians should never kill patients.

2 To choose death is to give up on any possible future options. So how can this be an exercise in autonomy? After all, life is a necessary condition for freedom. Thus the principle of autonomy cannot be used to justify active euthanasia.

3 Dying allows people to reach closure and see their lives for what they really were. A premature death is artificial and lacks true lived-through quality. Only a natural death allows for proper closure. When shared with loved ones, such a natural death can be fulfilling to all involved. Thus the principle of beneficence (do good) cannot be used to support active euthanasia.

4 Even what appears to be a bad death can result in moral growth—of both the person dying and his or her loved ones.

5 The practice of medicine as we know it cannot exist if patients fear that their physicians have an interest in their "early" deaths. This will be the inevitable result if doctors are allowed to kill patients as part of medicine.

Pellegrino (1992) saw a slippery slope on the horizon; he was convinced that society is likely to go from killing patients with unmitigatable pain (if there really is such a thing) to killing nuisance patients. He acknowledged that physicians must do a better job controlling the pain and discomfort of all sorts that many patients experience when they reach the end of their lives.

Pellegrino's second, third, and fourth points deflect the claim that suffering demands immediate alleviation. To be fully appreciated, these points must be seen as constituting a philosophy of life based on virtue ethics, the ancient Greeks, as well as Christian and Jewish ethics and theology. Realizing that his position is highly theoretical, Pellegrino based much of his argument on a need for preserving a medical practice, which he pointed out, has never really allowed the direct taking of life (Pellegrino, 1992).

Yet, one must ask, why can there not be room for different ways to practice medicine, depending on patients' desires and felt needs, which may vary from community to community? Pellegrino (1992) claimed that assisted suicide is premature, helping people reach an ending that was never meant to be. Such views are so theoretical that they are likely to be disputed and unlikely to be shared. They provide shaky grounds at best for legislation or professional regulation.

In contrast to Pellegrino (1992), Brody (1992) argued that although physician-assisted suicide should not be institutionalized as part of the practice of medicine, it does not follow that on a case-to-case basis, a physician cannot justify helping patients to die. Brody pointed out that the medicine field should remain open to change in response to people's needs and desires. Allowing patients a good death is a reasonable goal for medicine; by "good death" Brody meant at least what Pellegrino wanted to ensure in his third and fourth points. Brody argued that denying certain patients help in achieving a good death is a violation of a physician's duty.

Brody (1992) argued for passive over active euthanasia because of the ambivalence people often feel at the moment of death. If the patient is in charge, that ambivalence can be acted on; for example, the patient might say, "Well, I think I'll see how I feel tomorrow." But if the death-bed scene is controlled by the physician, patients may not feel so free to admit their mixed feelings about dying. Worse, they may not be able to express them.

CONCLUSION

Real suffering, not just fleeting pain, isolates people. When pain is the primary cause of people's suffering, they focus on the pain. Worse, they become their pain. When great, abiding fear is the primary cause of people's suffering, people concentrate on that fear. They become nothing more than that fear. Only the diminution of that fear, and hence the suffering, will make them fully human again.

If anything can be said to create an obligation on the part of health professionals, it is the call to help diminish suffering. When the only way to diminish suffering is to let the patient know he or she will not be allowed to die without a fight, that is what ought to be done. But when the only way to diminish suffering is to assist in suicide, it is the refusal to do so that should be seen as requiring justification.

This analysis of suffering, like the analyses of the brief case examples presented at the beginning of this chapter, may or may not be appealing. What should be clear by now is that to take a position on the right to die is to take many positions. The goal of this chapter has been to list some of those positions and their strengths and weaknesses and to provide the traditional philosophical context in which many of these issues have been discussed by professionals in the field.

REFERENCES

Brody, H. (1992). Assisted death—a compassionate response to medical failure. *New England Journal of Medicine, 327,* 1384–1388.

Callahan, D. (1987). *Setting limits.* New York: Simon & Schuster.

Cruzan v. Director, Missouri Department of Health, 110 S.Ct. 2841 (1990).

"Euthanasia Policy OK'd." *Columbus Dispatch,* Dec. 1, 1993, p. 3A.

Fletcher, J. (1979). *Humanhood.* Buffalo, NY: Prometheus Books.

Gert, B. (1988). *Morality.* New York: Oxford University Press.

Gorovitz, S. (1985). *Doctors' dilemmas: moral conflict & medical care.* New York: Oxford University Press.

Hurley, P. (1993). *A concise introduction to logic.* Belmont, CA: Wadsworth.

In re Quinlan, Superior Court of New Jersey, Chancery Division, Docket No. C-201-75 (November 10, 1975), p. 35.

Lewin, T. (1990, December 14). Judge clears doctor of murdering woman with a suicide machine. *New York Times,* p. B6.

Paris, J., Crone, R., & Reardon, F. (1990). Physicians' refusal of requested treatment. *New England Journal of Medicine, 322,* 1012–1015.

Pellegrino, E. (1992). Doctors must not kill. *Journal of Clinical Ethics, 20,* 95–102.

Quill, T. (1993). Doctor, I want to die, will you help me? *Journal of the American Medical Association, 270,* 870–873.

Rosoff, S. (1993). There's no simple suicide [Letter to the editor]. *New York Times Sunday Magazine,* Dec. 3, 1993, p. 16.

Rouse, F. (1991). Patients, providers and the PSDA. *Hastings Center Report, 21*(5), S2.

van der Maas, P., et al. (1991). Euthanasia and other medical decisions concerning the end of life. *Lancet, vol. 338, no. 8768,* 669–674.

Veatch, R. (1993). The impending collapse of the whole-brain definition of death. *Hastings Center Report, 23*(4), 18–24.

Chapter 16

The Definition of Death: Problems for Public Policy

Robert M. Veatch

At 5:41 A.M. on Sunday, November 10, 1985, Philadelphia Flyers hockey star Pelle Lindbergh slammed his 1985 Porsche into the cement wall of a Somerdale, New Jersey, elementary school. The headline for the story in the newspaper the next day read, "Flyers Goalie Is Declared Brain Dead" (Sell, 1985). In spite of the claim that he was "brain dead," the story went on to say that Lindbergh was listed in "critical condition" in the intensive care unit of John F. Kennedy Hospital in Stratford, New Jersey.

Referring to his parents, who were called from Sweden to be at his side, Vicki Santoro, nursing supervisor at the hospital said, "They were just devastated" (Sell, 1985). Dr. Edward Viner, the Flyers's team physician, said that if Lindbergh's situation did not improve, the family would be left with a decision about how long to leave him on the respirator.

That was not the only decision they faced. If some of Lindbergh's vital functions remained even though he was dead, he would be an ideal candidate to be an organ donor. His intact heart and kidneys could provide life-saving help for three other people. Possibly even his liver, lungs, pancreas, and corneas could benefit others. Suddenly it became a very practical, life-saving matter to figure out whether Pelle Lindbergh was dead or alive. The headline said he was "brain dead," but the article spoke of him as if he were still alive. The story referred to him as "near death" (Sell, 1985). Society used to believe that persons with beating hearts were alive even though their brain function was lost irreversibly. Now society is not so sure. The way Pelle Lindbergh was treated, the decisions his parents had to make, the behavior of the physicians and nurses, and the fate of several desperately ill human beings all hinge on figuring out whether Lindbergh was already dead or is only dying.

The public policy discussion of the definition of death began in earnest in the late 1960s. It began in the context of a world that in that same decade had seen the first successful transplantation of an organ from one human being to another, including the first transplant of the human heart in December 1967. It cannot be denied that this sudden infatuation with the usefulness of human organs was the stimulus for the intense discussion of the real meaning of death. What many thought would be a short-lived problem, resolved by the combined wisdom of the health professionals and nonscientists on the Ad Hoc Committee of the Harvard Medical School To Examine the Definition of Brain Death, has lingered as a morass of conflicting technical, legal, conceptual, and moral arguments. Much of this confusion can be avoided, however, by focusing exclusively on the problems for public policy.

Focusing on public policy means avoiding a full linguistic analysis of the term *death*. Although that may be an important philosophical enterprise, and many have undertaken it (Becker, 1975; Cole, 1992; Green & Wikler, 1980; Lamb, 1978; Mayo & Wikler, 1979; Veatch, 1989a, 1989b; Wikler & Weisbard, 1989; Youngner, 1989), this analysis is of only indirect importance for public policy questions. Likewise, a detailed theological account of the meaning of death is not necessary for an examination of the public policy problems created by the uncertain definition of death. Those studies are numerous (Bleich, 1979, 1989; Fletcher, 1969; Haring, 1973; Hauerwas, 1978; Pope Pius XII, 1958; Ramsey, 1970), but they are not of immediate concern in the formation of secular public policy. Most significantly, a scientific description of the biological events in the brain at the time of death is not necessary. This information is of crucial importance for the science of neurology, and a vast literature is available giving such an account (Ashwal & Schneider, 1987a, 1987b; Black, 1978; Collaborative Study, 1977; Cranford, 1979; Harvard Medical School, 1968; O'Brien, 1990; President's Commission for the Study of Ethical Problems in Medicine and Biomedical and Behavioral Research [President's Commission], 1981; Task Force for the Determination of Brain Death in Children, 1987; Shewmon, 1988). The scientific biological and neurological description of precisely what takes place in the human body at the point of death is not a matter that need directly concern public policymakers.

THE PUBLIC POLICY QUESTION

What policymakers are interested in is the question, When should we begin treating an individual the way we treat the newly dead? Is it possible to identify a point in the course of human events at which a new set of social behaviors becomes appropriate, at which because the individual is said to have died, he or she can justifiably be treated in a way that was not previously appropriate either morally or legally? In short, what policymakers are interested in is the social system of *death behaviors*.

Social and cultural changes take place when someone is labeled dead. Some medical treatments may be stopped when an individual is considered dead that would not be stopped if the individual were alive—even if he or she were terminally ill. This of course does not imply that there are treatments that should not be stopped at other times, either before or after the time somebody is labeled dead. Many treatments are stopped before death for technical reasons. According to many, there are other treatments that may justifiably be stopped before death because they are useless or too burdensome. In other cases, if the newly dead body is to be used for research, education, or transplant purposes, it is possible to continue certain interventions after death has been declared. Many have held that this is morally acceptable (Haring, 1973; Ramsey, 1970). It appears, however, that, traditionally, at least, there have been some treatments that are stopped when and only when it is decided that it is time to treat the individual as dead.

Other behaviors also have traditionally taken place at the time the individual is considered dead. The survivors begin mourning in a pattern that is not appropriate in mere anticipatory mourning (Fulton & Fulton, 1972). They start several social processes that would not have been appropriate before the decision was made that death behavior is appropriate. They begin the process that will lead to the reading of a will, to burying or otherwise disposing of what are now taken to be the mortal remains. The survivors assume new social roles, for example, the role of widowhood. If the individual who has been labeled dead happens to have been the president of a country or an organization, the labeling of that individual as dead normally leads to the assumption of the role of president of the one who was formerly vice president. Finally, and perhaps of most immediate relevance to the concern that generated the definition of death discussion, the procedures and justifications for obtaining organs from the body are changed. Before death, organs can be removed only in the interests of the individual or, in rare circumstances, with the consent of the individual or legal guardian (Fellner, 1971; Mahoney, 1975; Robertson, 1976; Simmons & Fulton, 1971). At the moment it is decided a person may be treated as dead, an entirely different set of procedures is called for—the procedures designated in the Uniform Anatomical Gift Act, drawn up in 1968. At that point, if the deceased has donated organs, they may be removed according to the terms of the donation without further consideration of the interest of the deceased or consideration of the wishes of the family members. If the deceased has not so donated and has not expressed opposition to donation, the next of kin or other legitimate guardian in possession of the body assumes both the right and the responsibility for the disposal of the remains. It is clear that at least in Anglo-American law, the one with such a responsibility cannot dispose of the body capriciously in any way he or she sees fit, but bears a responsibility for treating the new corpse with respect and dignity (May, 1973). This, however, has been taken both in law and in morality as permitting the donation of body parts by the one with this responsibility, except when there has been an explicit objection expressed by the deceased during the time of his or her life.

In short, traditionally there has been a radical shift in moral, social, and political standing when someone has been labeled as dead. Until the 1960s, there was not a great deal of controversy over exactly when such a label should be applied. There were deviant philosophical and theological positions and substantial concern about erroneous labeling of someone as dead, but there was little real controversy about what it meant to be dead in this public policy sense.

Now, for the first time, it is a matter of real public policy significance to decide precisely what is meant when someone is labeled dead. In an earlier day, all of the socially significant death-related behaviors were generated at the time of the pronouncement of death. Little was at stake if there was imprecision in sorting the various indicators of the time when this behavior was appropriate.

Virtually all of the plausible events related to death occurred in rapid succession, and none of the behaviors was really contingent on greater precision.

Matters have changed in two important ways. First, several technologies have greatly extended the capacity to prolong the dying process, making it possible to identify several different potential indicators of what should be taken to be the death of the individual as a whole and have separated these points dramatically in time. Second, the usefulness of human organs and tissues for transplantation, research, and education makes precision morally imperative. In an earlier day, the most that was at stake was that an individual could for a few seconds or moments be falsely treated as alive when in fact he or she should have been treated as dead, or vice versa. Of course, it is important, out of a sense of respect for persons, that living individuals not be confused with their corpses, so in theory it has always been important that society be clear about whether someone is dead or alive. Yet, traditionally the very short time span in which the entire series of events took place meant that there was little at stake as a matter of public policy. Death could be pronounced on the basis of the rapid succession of an inevitably linked series of bodily events: heart stoppage, stoppage of respiration, or the death of the brain.

As the period of time over which these events can occur lengthens, permitting much more precision in identifying what it is in the human body that signifies that it ought to be treated as dead, society must ask itself whether a single definable point where all of these social death behaviors should begin can still be identified. It may turn out that as the dying process is extended, all of these behaviors will find their own niches and it really will cease to be important to label someone as dead at a precise moment in time. If so, death itself, as well as dying, may begin to be viewed as a process (Morison, 1971). However, this seems unlikely to happen. Rather, we may want to continue to link at least many of these social events so that we shall continue to say there is a moment when it becomes appropriate to begin the entire series of death behaviors (or at least many of them). If so, the death of the individual as a whole will continue to be viewed as a single event, rather than a process (Kass, 1971). There are several plausible candidates for that critical point at which it can be said the individual as a whole has died: the time when circulatory function ceases, the time when all brain functions cease, and the time when certain important brain functions (e.g., mental function) cease.

The question is therefore not precisely the same as the one the philosopher asks when he or she asks the question of the end point of personhood or personal identity (Green & Wikler, 1980; Tooley, 1979). Analyses of the concept of personhood or personal identity suggest that there may be an identifiable end point at which a human organism should no longer be thought of as a *person*. That analysis by itself, however, never indicates whether it is morally appropriate to begin treating that human the way the dead are traditionally treated, unless personhood is simply defined with reference to death behavior, which it often is not. According to some formulations, such as those of Green and Wikler (1980), for example, it is conceptually possible to talk about a living individual in cases where the person no longer exists. This would be true, for example, if society said that living humans were persons only when they possessed self-awareness or the ability to distinguish themselves from others. Some human individuals could then be alive but not persons. Logically, society would then be pressed to answer the moral and policy question of whether these living bodies that are no longer persons are to be treated differently from the way society is used to treating living persons.

Fortunately, for matters of public policy, if not for philosophical analysis, we need not take up the question of personhood, but can confront directly the question of whether we can identify a point where this series of death behaviors is appropriate. Death thus comes to mean, for public policy purposes, nothing more than the condition of some group of human beings for whom death behavior is appropriate. Can a point be identified at which these behaviors are appropriate? If it can, then, for purposes of law and public policy, that point may be labeled the moment of death. The laws reformulating the definition of death do not go so far as to say they are defining death for all purposes, theological, philosophical, and personal. Some explicitly limit their scope, saying that they define death "for all *legal* purposes."

This formulation makes it clear that when policymakers talk about death, they are talking about death of the entity as a whole. It is with reference to the entire human organism, not some particular body part, that policymakers want to determine appropriate behavior.

Unfortunately, the term *brain death* has emerged in the debate. This is unfortunate in part because policymakers, as just mentioned, are not interested in the death of brains; they are interested in the death of organisms as integrated entities subject to particular kinds of public behavior and control. In contrast, the term *brain death* is systematically ambiguous. It has two potential meanings. The first is not controversial at all; it simply means the destruction of the brain, leaving open the question of whether people with destroyed brains should be treated as dead people. It is better to substitute the phrase *destruction of the brain* for *brain death* in this sense. It clearly refers only to the complete biological collapse of the organ or organs called the brain. Exactly how that is measured is largely a neurological question.

Unfortunately, *brain death* has also taken on a second, very different, and much more controversial, meaning. It can also mean the death of the individual as a whole, based on the fact that the brain has died. The problem is illustrated in the original report of the Ad Hoc Committee of the Harvard Medical School to Examine the Definition of Brain Death (Harvard Medical School, 1968), which has become the most significant technical document in the American debate over the definition of death. The title of that 1968 document is "A Definition of Irreversible Coma." In it, the committee sets out to define "characteristics of irreversible coma" and produces a list of technical criteria that purport to predict that an individual is in a coma that is irreversible. Note, however, that the name of the committee is the Ad Hoc Committee of the Harvard Medical School To Examine *Brain Death*. The presumption apparently was that irreversible coma and brain death were synonymous. We now realize that this is not precisely true. An individual can apparently be in an irreversible coma and still not have a completely dead brain. In any case, the title of the report and the name of the committee, taken in the context of what the committee did, imply that the objective of the committee was to describe the empirical measures of a destroyed brain.

In the opening sentence of the report, however, the committee states, "Our primary purpose is to define irreversible coma as a new criterion for death." It does not claim to be defining the destruction (death) of the brain, but death simpliciter, by which everyone, including the committee members, meant death of the individual for the purposes of death behaviors, clinical practice, and public policy. Yet the report contains no argument that the destruction of the brain (measured by the characteristics of irreversible coma) should be taken as a justification for treating the individual as a whole as dead. The members of the committee and many others believed that this should be so, possibly with good reason, but the reasons were not stated.

Because the term *brain death* has these two radically different meanings, there is often confusion in public and professional discussion of the issues. For instance, neurologists can claim that they have real expertise on brain death, meaning, of course, expertise in measuring the destruction of the brain. Others claim, however, that brain death is exclusively a matter for public policy consideration, meaning that the question of whether an individual should be treated as dead because the brain tissue is dead is outside the scope of neurological expertise. A far better course would be to abandon that language entirely, substituting precise and explicit language that refers either to the destruction of the brain or to the death of the individual as a whole based on brain criteria.

PRELIMINARY ISSUES TO PUBLIC POLICY
DISCUSSION
Allowing Someone to Die Versus Deciding That Someone
Is Dead

In many cases, the public's fascination with the definition of death discussion may be misplaced. There have been several cases in which problems with the care of the critically ill have been addressed by trying to figure out whether the individual has died. Efforts are sometimes made to resolve these critical problems in health care simply by defining the terminally ill patient as dead. For example, some people try to resolve the question of whether it is acceptable to stop providing life-supporting treatment by arguing that the individual is dead.

In the early phase of the discussion of the case of Karen Quinlan—the young woman in New Jersey who suffered irreversible brain damage and was sustained in a chronic vegetative state—the lawyer for her family, the judge, and many others initially cast their arguments in terms of the definition of death (Sullivan, 1975). It was much later in the case that everyone became convinced that Karen was not dead according to brain criteria but might be withdrawn from the respirator even though still alive. Likewise, when a Maryland nurse was prosecuted for disconnecting a respirator on a terminally ill cancer patient, her defense centered on the claim that her patient was dead according to brain criteria (Saperstein, 1979). The jury was sufficiently confused over the definition of death that it was unable to reach a verdict and the charges were eventually dropped.

An alternative to insisting that these problems of clinical care can be resolved only by reformulation of the definition of death is to recognize that it is possible that some living individuals are in such a condition that it would be appropriate to allow them to die. This of course raises moral questions of its own, but it does not force all of the complex problems of ethics concerning the terminally ill into the one potential solution of the redefinition of death. That prolonging life serves no purpose does not establish, by itself, that an individual has died.

There are several unfortunate and tragic situations in which a patient may be stabilized indefinitely and still be considered living for public policy and legal purposes. One of these might turn out to be the condition known as persistent vegetative state (Bernat, 1992b; Council on Scientific Affairs and Council on Ethical and Judicial Affairs, 1990; Cranford & Smith, 1979; Jennett & Plum, 1972; Levy, Knill-Jones, & Plum, 1978). This is the condition in which Karen Quinlan lived for 10 years (In re Quinlan, 1976; Korein, 1978a, 1978b). It is crucial to realize that in order to justify a treatment-stopping decision in a case such as Karen Quinlan's, it is not necessary to reach the judgment that the person is dead. It is logically quite possible to decide simply that the person should be allowed to die because there is no longer any appropriate justification for continuing treatment.

The same argument applies even more forcefully to patients who are terminally ill while perhaps senile or in a semicomatose state, but, nevertheless, retain some limited capacities for mental activity. Society will at some point have to address the very difficult questions of public policy related to the care of such individuals. This is not, however, an appropriate matter for a discussion of the definition of death. The definition-of-death problem is one small subset of the moral and legal issues related to death and dying.

Criteria for Death Versus the Concept of Death

One of the most crucial preliminary issues in public policy consideration of the definition of death grows out of the problem of the systematic ambiguity of the term *brain death*. Some of the questions related to the pronouncement of death based on brain-related criteria are clearly technical and scientific, whereas others are questions of morality, politics, and law. It is crucial that the two be kept separate and the public role in each of these kinds of questions be identified (Biorck, 1967).

Criteria for Death: Largely a Scientific Matter   Virtually no one holds that every body structure and function must be destroyed in order for the individual as a whole to be considered dead for public policy purposes. That would mean that every cell in the body would have to be determined to be dead or at least every organ would have to be destroyed.

It is also generally held that those with appropriate medical skills are capable of developing tests or procedures or criteria for predicting that a particular bodily function or structure is irreversibly destroyed. For example, if heart function is determined to be important in deciding when to treat people as dead, certain measures, such as feeling the pulse or taking an electrocardiogram, are available to diagnose and predict the future status of heart function. If lower brain functions are determined to be critical, neurologists can tell us that certain reflex pathways are good predictors of the status of the lower brain. If cerebral function is determined to be critical, different tests, based on the electroencephalogram (EEG) and cerebral angiography, which measures blood flow, can be useful.

The tests or procedures or criteria for determining that critical bodily structures or functions have been lost must be established by those with scientific skills in biology or medicine, that is, those with the appropriate knowledge and skill (Capron & Kass, 1972; President's Commission, 1981; Veatch, 1976). These tests or procedures or criteria need not be incorporated into public policy or statutory law. In fact, because empirical measures of this sort are likely to change as the status of scientific knowledge changes, many take the view that these tests should not be included in the statutory law. As a general rule, statutes that have been passed have not included any reference to any specific empirical measures or criteria.

Technically, it is not correct to treat even these criteria for measuring the death of the brain as purely scientific, completely lacking in evaluative or other public policy importance. For example, in testing to measure the destruction of the brain, a judgment must be made about how often these tests are to be applied and for how long a period of time they must be satisfied before the pronouncement of death can be made. Different sets of criteria propose different lengths of time. The Harvard criteria (Harvard Medical School, 1968) specify 24 hr; the President's Commission for the Study of Ethical Problems in Medicine and Biomedical and Behavioral Research (1981) suggests 6 hr, or 12 in the absence of confirmatory tests such as an EEG; and other groups have required 12 hr as the minimum time period to be satisfied (Mohandas & Chou, 1971). If the tests are not applied over a long enough period, some individuals may be declared to have irreversibly lost brain function when, in fact, such function could return. On the other hand, if the tests are applied for too long a period of time, some individuals will be treated as if brain function has not irreversibly disappeared when, in fact, it has. Deciding on the correct length of time will depend on how one assesses the moral risks of falsely considering the brain to be dead and falsely considering it still to be alive. The best neurological science can do is tell us the probabilities of each kind of error after different time periods. It cannot tell us how to trade off the two kinds of errors. That is fundamentally a moral or policy issue.

If neurologists' intuitions about the relative moral risks of these two kinds of error were the same as those of others in society, then little would be at stake in asking the neurologists to specify the balance between the errors for the rest of society. There is reason to doubt, however, that neurologists balance the two kinds of errors the same way that other people do. If they differed significantly—if, for example, they worried more than most people about falsely treating people as alive and less than most people about falsely treating people as dead—they would systematically recommend the wrong time period for repeating tests. Logically, deciding the mix of the two kinds of errors is not a scientific question; it is a policy question for lay-persons to decide, even though most people do not see it that way (Veatch, 1989a).

The Concept of Death: Essentially a Policy Matter   A more obvious policy question is which structures or functions should be tested, which changes in the body should signal the time when death-related behavior is appropriate. Should it be loss of heart function or brain function? If it is the brain, just which functions are critical? The goal is to determine when it is appropriate to treat the organism as a whole as dead. The loss of certain essential bodily structures or functions will almost certainly signal the time when such treatment is appropriate. These potential end points are normally called the "concepts of death" or "standards of death." Picking among them, in principle, cannot be done scientifically. It is essentially a policy matter.

For example, some people take the position that the organism as a whole should be considered dead if there is irreversible cessation of spontaneous respiratory and/or circulatory functions. Other people take the position that the organism should be considered dead if there is irreversible loss of all spontaneous brain functions. Still others maintain that the organism should be considered dead if there is irreversible loss of spontaneous cerebral functions. Behind each of these formulations is some implicit view of what is essential in the human being's nature.

Although society might choose to specify precisely what that philosophical or religious understanding is, that may not be either necessary or possible. It might turn out that different people would formulate the precise underlying concept somewhat differently but still be able to agree at the level of the standard of death that is to be specified in the law. They might be able to agree that death should be pronounced when the functions of the circulatory and respiratory system are irreversibly lost. Or they might agree that it is the functions of the entire brain that count.

The selection of these basic standards of death is now generally agreed to be a matter of public policy, a task for the broader public. The only real question is the method that will be used to express public policy. Traditionally, there was such an overwhelming consensus on an apparent concept and standard of death that there was no need for explicit public policy formulation. Society relied on the common law and saw very little dispute, except perhaps in the question of inheritance in cases of almost simultaneous death. An example would be an inheritance following the death of spouses in an automobile accident, where a different pattern of inheritance would result if either spouse survived the other.

There is in principle no scientific basis for choosing one set of standards or underlying concepts over another, although once a particular concept or standard is chosen, there may be good scientific reasons for selecting a set of criteria or tests or measures that correspond to the standard or concept. This does not necessarily mean, however, that the choice is entirely an arbitrary one. It is possible, in fact it is widely held, that such choices have foundations in objective reality. In deciding to make slavery or murder illegal, there is no scientific proof that either of these activities is wrong. It is not even clear what a scientific proof of such an evaluation would look like. Nevertheless, society can feel sufficiently sure that slavery and murder are wrong that it can choose to make them illegal without any suggestion that such a decision is arbitrary or capricious. Thus, Henry Beecher (1970), the Harvard physician and chair of the Harvard Ad Hoc Committee, was not speaking precisely when he said that the choice of a definition of death is arbitrary. He probably meant that there is no basis in the natural sciences for making such a choice, although it is likely he would have conceded that some choices are better than others and some might be so persuasive that it is meaningful to call them the correct choices.

If this is true, selecting a point when it is appropriate to treat people as dead must be a matter for public policy. In an earlier time, the public judgment reflected such a wide consensus that common law was sufficient for expressing that policy judgment. Now, however, when many possible, plausible end points of life have been identified, the public policy question may have to be resolved more explicitly. For this reason, many hold that the policy question should be resolved legislatively (Mills, 1971; Richardson, 1976; Skegg, 1976). Others see it as more appropriately derived from case law, that is, in the courts. The disadvantage of using the courts is that judges deciding many cases will potentially formulate the policy differently.

Still others appear to believe that the policy question can be resolved without any formal expression of policy (Frenkel, 1978; Friloux, 1975; Kennedy, 1971, 1975, 1977; Mackert, 1979; Potter, 1968). Some kind of resolution to the policy question must be reached, however. Deciding what changes in bodily structure or function justify treating an individual as dead is logically prior to and independent of the question of what tests, measures, or criteria should be used for determining whether those changes have taken place.

There is no need to resolve all of the philosophical problems pertaining to the definition of death in order to reach public policy resolution of the question of when people are to be treated as dead. General agreements on the standards may be reached as a matter of public policy even though the philosophical disagreement remains at the most abstract conceptual level.

The Reason for Selecting a Standard for Death   Some have suggested that a new standard for pronouncing death should be selected, because if one is selected that is based on the use of brain criteria for death pronouncement, new organs will be available for transplantation and other worthwhile purposes (Fletcher, 1969). Others, however, have questioned whether this constitutes an adequate reason for adopting a particular reformulation of the notion of death (e.g., Forrester, 1976). Jonas (1974) doubted that others' interests in body parts can be a legitimate basis for deciding when someone has died. Ramsey (1970) expressed similar concern over using the usefulness of organs as a reason for choosing a new definition of death, arguing "If no person's death should for this purpose be hastened, then the definition of death should not for this purpose be updated" (p. 103). Still others have argued that although it would be wrong to choose a new concept of death for this reason, the newfound potential usefulness to others of being clear on what being dead means might justify the effort at clarification (Veatch, 1976).

THE ISSUES OF THE DEBATE PROPER
The Problem of Irreversibility

There are several questions that any public policy debate over the definition of death must resolve if that policy is to be clear and complete. One is whether irreversibility is a requirement in the public policy related to the definition of death. The problem is whether society wants to speak of people who have temporarily lost some critical body structure or function as dead, even though such functions or structures can be restored and thus the individual will be alive at some point in the future. In the past, it was common in folk discussion of death to talk about someone having died on the operating table or in some other setting, only to be resuscitated and returned to life. This may simply be an imprecise use of language, however. (See Cole, 1992, for a philosophical argument to the contrary.) Many would hold that irreversibility is inherent in the notion of what it means to be dead (Lamb, 1992). At least for public policy purposes, people who have temporarily lost a critical function such as heart function really cannot be thought of as dead. Those mentioned in such an individual's will do not inherit his or her possessions. The President of the United States would not have been removed from office because of such a temporary stoppage. The provisions of the Uniform Anatomical Gift Act giving the next of kin authority over the use of organs would not take effect. Irreversibility is an essential requirement for public policies related to treating people as dead (Ladd, 1979). If that is the case, it is incorrect to talk about people dying temporarily and then coming back to life. Rather, in such cases, it may be said that the individual continues to live but would have died had not certain critical features been restored.

Is the Critical Bodily Loss One of Function or Structure?

Recently, some commentators have argued that the loss that is critical for treating people as dead is not necessarily a functional loss. It may be anatomical. That is, an individual may continue to live until certain anatomical structures are destroyed (Becker, 1975; Byrne, O'Reilly, & Quay, 1979).

There is no decisive argument for or against such a view. Should a society want to hold that the shape or form of the body is what is critical, rather than its activity, such a policy could be adopted. However, most people continue to maintain that the critical loss is a functional one. It may be that those who talk as if the loss is anatomical rather than functional are really just seeking greater certainty of the irreversibility of the loss. Such individuals might take the position that what is essential is irreversible functional loss but the only empirically certain way to demonstrate irreversible functional loss is to show anatomical destruction. If so, the anatomical destruction is merely a test or measure or a criterion of irreversible functional loss and probably should not be incorporated into a formally articulated public policy. However, it is possible that some people actually believe that the critical loss is structural, in which case that notion should be made a matter of the public policy formulation.

Is the Critical Loss One at the Cellular Level or Some Higher Level of Function (or Structure)?

The human organism operates at many levels, including cellular and supercellular levels of organization. It is possible to insist that each cell, or at least each cell of a critical organ, be destroyed. After all, as long as one cell remains alive, it is possible to say there is life in the particular tissue or organ. However, many would take the position that mere cellular level activity is of no significance when it comes to determining when people should be treated as dead. If, for example, one is concerned about the irreversible loss of brain function, one may not really mean the firing of an isolated neuron within the brain, but only the organ-level integrated functioning at the supercellular level.

This has potential importance because certain tests or measures may actually indicate the presence of cellular life even though organ-level functioning has irreversibly been lost. For instance, the technical literature pertaining to the use of the EEG for the measure of the loss of brain function makes clear that what is normally referred to as a flat EEG in fact is one that shows very low microvolt levels of activity. To the uninitiated, it seems certain that if electrical activity is coming from the brain, it is not totally dead. If, however, neurologists are able to determine with certainty that certain low levels of activity are really only signs of cellular activity and not consistent with continued capacity for organ-level functioning, it is quite appropriate to exclude such activity if one has adopted a policy of pronouncing death on the basis of the irreversible loss of total brain function at the supercellular level (Collaborative Study, 1977). This appears to be what the state of Wyoming had in mind when it passed a statute based on the Uniform Brain Death Act but added the sentence, "Total brain function shall mean purposeful activities of the brain as distinguished from random activity." This still raises the question of what counts as purposeful activity, but at least it excludes random cellular-level activity. Others make a similar distinction by talking of "integrated" (Grenvik et al., 1978) or "clinical" (Cranford, 1979) functioning. Recently, neurologists have conceded that groups or "nests" of cells may continue to function in brains that are considered dead (Bernat, 1992a). These brains, of course, are not literally dead, but, in the opinion of some individuals, the remaining functions, even if they are above the cellular level, may be insignificant (Bernat, 1992a). The real problem with this position, as shall be revealed, is that if individuals use their own idiosyncratic judgments to decide what is insignificant, countless disputes and personal variations in opinion can be expected. Society will have abandoned its commitment to the position that literally the whole brain and all its functions must be lost for an individual to be dead (Veatch, 1992).

Which Functions (or Structures) Are Critical for Determining That an Individual Should Be Considered Dead?

The most fundamental and important public policy question still remains: Which functions or structures should be identified as critical for deciding that the individual as a whole should be treated as dead? The debate has taken place in several stages.

The Late 1960s   The first stage of the debate began in the late 1960s, especially with the Harvard Ad Hoc Committees report (1968). At this point, virtually everyone formulated the question in terms of a struggle between two alternatives. One group believed that the critical activity that should be measured is the capacity of the heart and lungs (Jonas, 1969; Potter, 1968). This seems to be included in the early common-law definition of death, which says that an individual shall be considered dead when there is "a total stoppage . . . of all animal and vital functions" (*Black's Law Dictionary,* 1968, p. 488).

Precisely what it was about heart and lung activity that was considered critical is not clear. It seems certain that it was not the functioning of the heart and lungs per se, but rather the activities they cause in the body. This is made apparent by the recognition that an individual whose lungs have been destroyed but whose blood is oxygenated by a machine is obviously still alive. Likewise, an individual whose heart had been destroyed but whose blood was pumped by a machine would also be considered alive. In fact, an individual who might be maintained indefinitely on a heart/lung machine or artificial heart would obviously be alive according to this formulation. Thus, it seems probable that people taking this position held a concept of death that emphasized the importance of the flowing of vital bodily fluids, that is, the blood and breath. According to this notion, an individual should be considered dead when there is the irreversible loss of the capacity for the flowing of these vital fluids.

This is a rather vitalistic notion of the nature of the human being, one that sees the human as merely physicochemical forces. It totally excludes any concern for integrated functioning or for mental processes. Yet many have apparently believed that anyone who has the capacity for the flowing of these fluids ought to be treated as alive.

During this period, the alternative position was that the critical loss that signaled the point at which people ought to be treated as dead was the loss of the capacities of the brain (Beecher, 1970; Collins, 1971; Fletcher, 1969; Task Force on Death and Dying, 1972; Toole, 1971; Wasmuth, 1969). Defenders of this position were frequently not very precise about exactly what it was in the brain that was considered critical. The empirical measures that were performed implied that the critical functions were quite diverse and inclusive. They included a large number of integrating activities, such as reflex pathways in the lower brain as well as the centers that control respiration. Thus, it has been suggested that holders of this view might have been taking the position at the conceptual level that people should be treated as dead when they have irreversibly lost the neurological capacity to integrate bodily activities. At this point, according to this view, the individual no longer functions as a whole and can therefore legitimately be treated as dead.

Some people have continued to favor the use of heart-and-lung-oriented standards for pronouncing death. Some even explicitly affirm such standards when they are given the alternative of pronouncing death based on the concepts underlying the use of brain-oriented standards (Arnold & Younger, 1993; Charron, 1975). Nevertheless, the number of defenders of standards related to heart and lung function seems to have decreased substantially.

The Early 1970s   In the early 1970s, a new and more complicated question emerged, that is, which brain functions (or structures) are so critical that their loss ought to be considered the death of the individual as a whole. Two major camps emerged in this debate. One held fast to the position that all brain function (at least at the supercellular level) must be lost (Black, 1977; "Diagnosis of Death," 1979; Horan, 1978; Stickel, 1979). The second group held that some functions, even at the supercellular level, might remain intact but it would still be appropriate to treat an individual as dead (Haring, 1973; Olinger, 1975; Sweet, 1978; Veatch, 1975). The choice was dramatically illustrated in two case reports presented by Brierley, Adam, Graham, and Simpson (1979) in *The Lancet*.

The first case was that of a 58-year-old man who had suffered cardiac arrest related to bronchospasm. He was resuscitated with cardiac massage and placed on a respirator. The EEG was flat from the third day on. He maintained reflexes after the first day and respired without the aid of the respirator from Day 20 on. He died (based on cardiac criteria) after 5 months.

The second case involved a 48-year-old man who suffered a massive allergic reaction. He was resuscitated with cardiac massage and mouth-to-mouth breathing. He also had reflexes after the first day, but he had a flat EEG from the second day. He also died after 5 months (based on cardiac criteria). In both cases, upon examination after death, it was found that tissues in the higher brain (neocortex) were dead while lower brain centers were intact, showing slight to moderate neuronal loss. The patients at no time met the Harvard criteria purported to measure irreversible coma, yet they clearly seemed to be irreversibly comatose (Van Till, 1975).

These cases revealed that there are at least two quite different positions, each reflecting a different concept of death. Those insisting on the destruction of total supercellular brain function would consider these patients alive. They breathed spontaneously. Defenders of this view would probably hold fast to a concept that death is something like the irreversible loss of the capacity for bodily integration. They would specifically recognize that integrated activities mediated through the lower brain, such as respiratory control mechanisms or the cough reflex, represent a level of bodily integration that would be taken as sufficient to justify treating the individual as still alive.

Others, however, would consider these patients dead. They have abandoned the whole-brain view, making it clear that a very different concept of death is operating. They focus on the activities of the higher brain centers, including such capacities as remembering, reasoning, feeling, and thinking. One underlying concept of human nature that might be implied is that the human is essentially a combination of mental and physical activity, both of which must be present in order for the individual to be alive. According to this view, any capacity for consciousness would be sufficient to treat the individual as alive.

Closely related to this view is a notion having both Greek and Judeo-Christian roots, the notion that the human is essentially a social animal. According to this view, it is appropriate to treat individuals as dead whenever they have irreversibly lost the capacity for social interaction. It is important to understand that what is meant here is not that an individual is dead merely when he or she is not interacting socially. That would make being dead or alive dependent on one's fellow human beings' willingness to interact. Rather, what is meant is the *capacity* for such interaction.

A standard might be chosen that focuses on higher brain function, rather than total brain function. This standard is often articulated as the irreversible loss of total cerebral or neocortical function. The exact specification would depend on exactly what functional loss was considered crucial and where that function was localized in the brain. There is substantial debate over whether there can be any exact identification between mental functions and brain functions (Burnham, 1977; Feigl, 1967; Globus, 1973; Wilson, 1976). Probably, society shall never be able to identify precisely which tissues are responsible for the functions often identified, such as consciousness or thinking or feeling or interacting with one's fellow humans. There is general agreement, however, that, without cerebral tissue, these functions are all impossible. To the extent this is true empirically, the standard for death according to a holder of this position would be the irreversible loss of cerebral function. Some, however, are purposely avoiding speaking of "*cerebral*" or "*neocortical*" definitions of death, because they realize that some cerebral or neocortical functions may survive even if the critical functions are completely lost. They are now speaking in purposely vague language of the "*higher brain definition of death*" (Veatch, 1988). For holders of this view, in contrast with the whole-brain standard, quite clearly a different set of empirical measures or tests would be appropriate for confirming death, measures that single out these higher, presumably cerebral functions.

Since the Late 1970s   This reformulation of the question of the definition of death so as to ask which brain functions are critical has begun to raise additional questions. For instance, once one has moved to a concept of death based on higher brain function, rather than total brain function, one might appropriately ask whether an individual could be considered dead even though certain higher brain functions remain intact. If, for example, a person retains motor capacities in certain brain centers but has no capacity to feel or think, should he or she be considered alive? There is no particular reason why this progressive narrowing of the criteria needs to stop at this point. For instance, one might ask whether an individual could be considered dead solely on the basis of deterioration of mental function even though many higher brain centers remain intact. It is apparent that one of the dangers of the move from total brain function to higher brain function is that there may be no obvious and clear point to stop the progression to narrower and narrower formulations of higher brain function. Thus, there is the potential that gradually more and more people will literally be defined out of the category of human existence. Some critics of the move to higher brain function have opposed it less on the grounds that lower brain activity is an essential component of life than on the grounds that once society moves beyond total brain activity it will be impossible to find a point for a public policy to stop the regression. They claim that the defenders of the higher-brain-function position are on a slippery slope and will not be able to avoid sliding into morally untenable positions that would treat mentally impaired but conscious humans as dead (Bernat, 1992a).

Defenders of the move to higher-brain-function notions of death reject this slippery-slope or wedge argument (Veatch, 1992). They maintain that it is possible to hold firmly to the notion that an individual should be considered dead when there is irreversible loss of consciousness, but they insist that no compromise be made beyond that point. In fact, they have recently turned the slippery-slope argument against those who are apparently defending the whole-brain formulations. They argue that there is no principled reason why a line can be drawn between the top of the spinal cord and the base of the brain stem. This means that the defenders of the whole-brain formulations must either acknowledge that activity of the spinal cord should be taken as a sign of life (because it provides integrated nervous system activity not distinguishable from that of the brain stem) or concede that some "insignificant" brain functions, even supercellular functions, should be discounted, thereby abandoning the true whole-brain position that insists that *all* functions of the *entire* brain must be gone for a person to be dead. As has been shown, Bernat (1992a) and others apparently defending the whole-brain position have done precisely this in conceding that certain functioning of "nests of cells" is "insignificant" (Bernat, p. xxx). They abandon the literal whole-brain definition without providing any principled way of explaining which nests of cells are significant. The defenders of the higher-brain-function position at least offer a basis for distinguishing by insisting that the functions that are significant are those that provide integration of mental and organic function.

Still others (e.g., President's Commission, 1981) may accept the idea in principle that death can be related to the irreversible loss of higher brain function but believe empirically that there are no solid grounds for measuring such loss. Logically, as a matter of public policy, such people should be willing to adopt a policy that individuals should be treated as dead when their higher brain function has irreversibly ceased, leaving to those with competency in the neurological sciences to determine whether there is any empirical way to measure the mere loss of a higher brain function. It might turn out empirically that the only reliable test would be one that measures the loss of total brain function. That would seem to be conceptually the correct way to articulate public policy. However, policymakers may be made uncomfortable enough by the possibility of some practitioners' prematurely attempting to measure the loss of merely higher brain function that they would feel it necessary to specify in law that death should be pronounced only when total brain function is lost, even though in principle they would be willing to accept death pronouncement even when certain lower brain functions remain intact but all higher function has irreversibly ceased.

The concern about whether irreversible loss of mental function or consciousness can be measured may be resolved. At least two major groups have now concluded that, at least in some cases, some irreversible loss of consciousness can be diagnosed with great accuracy (Council on Scientific Affairs and Council on Ethical and Judicial Affairs, 1990; President's Commission, 1981).

These practical and theoretical concerns with the attempt to move to a higher-brain-oriented formulation of death have characterized the debate over the definition of death since the later part of the 1970s. Advocates of higher brain standards have differed among themselves over exactly which tissues and functions are critical. Other concerns have also emerged, some of which have been mentioned previously. The difference between cellular-level function and more complex function has become increasingly apparent. The tension between those who formulate a concept of death functionally and those who formulate it anatomically has also become recognized. The net effect has been that the public has increasingly become aware that there are many different formulations that are plausible and seen as acceptable by different people. It is no longer a debate between two clearly contrasting camps, as it was between the heart and brain camps in the earliest days of the discussion or between the whole-brain and higher-brain-function camps, as it was in the early part of the 1970s. It is clearly impossible to reach any consensus on the underlying theological and philosophical issues.

It is probably even impossible to specify clearly what counts as a change in a human so significant that that human can begin to be treated as if he or she were dead. At best, society must come to some common understanding of some general area of bodily structure or function that is so significant that its destruction justifies treating the individual as dead (Veatch, 1979). Society may be able to agree that an individual is dead when, say, all brain function is lost, even if it cannot agree on exactly what the critical function is.

The question is one that really cannot be reduced any further. Society must determine what bodily conditions make treating an individual as dead acceptable. It will probably be sufficient to express public policy in terms of general standards for death. Even though those standards have some concept implicit in them, it is clear that greater consensus can be reached on the standards than on the concepts themselves. The three primary candidates are those that have been identified herein: the irreversible cessation of spontaneous respiratory and circulatory functions, the irreversible loss of all spontaneous brain functions, and the irreversible loss of all spontaneous cerebral or higher brain functions.

SOME REMAINING ISSUES
Should Safer-Course Arguments Prevail?

It is clear that controversy will remain over which of the several plausible concepts or standards for pronouncing death ought to be adopted for public policy. Some standard or combination of standards must be chosen for public policy purposes. This raises the question of whether, as a matter of public policy, society ought not to play it safe and choose the policy that will satisfy the most people that an individual is dead. Some have argued that when society is in doubt about which of several public policies to adopt, it should take the safer course, especially in matters that are literally life and death. The safer-course argument is presumably the one that will avoid treating people as dead who ought to be considered alive (Currie, 1978; Jonas, 1969).

This safer-course argument might justify abandoning efforts to incorporate concepts or standards of death related exclusively to higher brain function, because many people hold that an individual can be alive even though higher brain function is lost. There is real doubt in our society over the use of such a standard for death pronouncement. Under a safer-course argument, society would move to the more conservative, now older, definition of death that requires that the whole brain be destroyed.

The problem with this safer-course argument is that it would be even safer and more inclusive to insist that not only the whole brain but also the heart and lung activity be irreversibly destroyed. In fact, it would be safer still to insist that not only these functions but the anatomical structures as well be destroyed. If society adopted the position that all heart, lung, and brain function and structure must be destroyed, it would satisfy virtually everyone that an individual is indeed dead before being treated as such.

The difficulties with the safer-course argument may now be apparent. If there were no practical or theoretical problems with treating people as alive who are in fact dead, society could safely continue a policy of erring on the side of treating people as alive, but it is clear there are good reasons not to do so. There are bad consequences from treating a dead individual as alive. Some of these consequences are very practical. There are the financial costs of medical care as well as the cost in terms of human agony. There are organs and tissues that would be lost. None of these concerns about consequences would justify treating someone as dead who was really alive, but they do, at least, justify striving for precision in the understanding of what it means to be dead. And they give sufficient reason to avoid the extreme applications of the safer-course arguments. At the very least, this means that society can set some conservative limit on when people ought to be treated as dead. The majority of the population now seems prepared to move at least as far as the whole-brain formulations, that is, treating people as dead when there has been total destruction of supercellular-level brain function.

Can There Be Variation in the Public Definition of Death?

Because there is such disagreement among people over a definition of death, many have speculated on the difficulty of reaching a policy consensus. In many cases in a pluralistic society, the resolution of this apparent problem is found in pluralism, that is, permitting individual variation based on individual or group preferences. However, the idea of permitting variation in the definition of death raises serious problems, each of which should be explored. Three kinds of variation have been considered.

Variation by Expected Use of the Body The first variation might be based on the expected use of the body. Society could endorse varying definitions of death, depending, in part, on whether the body will be used for transplant, research, therapy, or other important purposes. In fact, a law passed in Kansas (Kansas State Ann., 1974) appears to do just that. The Kansas statute includes two alternative definitions of death, one based on respiratory and cardiac function and the other based on brain function. The same alternative definitions appear in the Uniform Determination of Death Act (President's Commission, 1981), although that law does not specifically state when a particular definition should be used. The implication, however, is that the latter should be used when transplantation is anticipated and the brain is destroyed and the heart continues to beat (because of mechanical support).

Critics of such a variation argue that it seems that whether a person is treated as dead or alive should not be contingent on the anticipated use of the corpse. In fact, one could envision bizarre circumstances were alternative standards permitted. A transplant might be anticipated and death pronounced on that basis. But in the interim before the organ is removed from the newly deceased, if the planned recipient dies suddenly, there may no longer be an anticipated transplant. If so, there would be confusion over whether the individual continued to be dead according to the original alternative or should suddenly have the other alternative applied.

Variation Depending on the Physician's Preference   The second potential kind of variation is variation based on the physicians' preference. The policy
question is whether physicians should be required or only permitted to use brain-
oriented standards when pronouncing death. Should the physician have the choice
of whether to use a brain-oriented definition? As a practical matter, this reduces
to the question of whether laws should say that a physician *shall* pronounce death
or that a physician *may* pronounce death when all functions of the brain are irreversibly lost. A model bill by the American Medical Association (AMA) dated
January 1979 says, for example, "A physician, in the exercise of his professional
judgment, may declare an individual dead in accordance with accepted medical
standards." The immediate bizarre implication is that a physician need not declare
an individual dead in accordance with accepted medical standards. He or she
might use discretion and choose some other standard. At the very least, this leads
to policy confusion. Different physicians seeing the same patient could use different standards for pronouncing death. Thus, a physician who sees a patient one
afternoon might decide not to use brain-oriented standards, whereas another
physician who sees the same patient that evening in exactly the same condition
that evening might decide to use brain-oriented standards and pronounce
death. In December 1979, the AMA amended its model bill by removing the term
may.

   In an effort to overcome the ambiguity generated by having several different
proposed statutes, the President's Commission for the Study of Ethical Problems
in Medicine and Biomedical and Behavioral Research (1981) worked with the
AMA, the American Bar Association, and the National Conference of Commis-
sioners on Uniform State Laws to develop what is referred to as the Uniform
Determination of Death Act, which all of these groups have endorsed in place of
their previous proposals. It states that:

An individual who has sustained either (1) irreversible cessation of circulatory and respiratory functions, or (2) irreversible cessation of all functions of the entire brain, including
the brain stem, is dead. A determination of death must be made in accordance with accepted medical standards. (President's Commission, 1981)

   As long as this is interpreted as requiring that death must be pronounced if
either of these conditions is met, there is no problem of variation from physician
to physician. This formulation relies on "accepted medical standards," which
could create a problem if the consensus of professionals about the relative significance of different types of errors is significantly different from the consensus
of nonprofessionals.

   The potential for difficulty if variation by physician is permitted is great. For
example, if standards based on loss of total supercellular brain function are
adopted but then physicians are given discretion, as in the original AMA model
bill, physicians could presumably opt either for more conservative or more liberal
interpretations. Thus, a physician, at his or her discretion, could use traditional
heart and lung standards, higher-brain-function standards, or even more permis-

sive criteria. It seems strange that citizens should be considered dead or alive depending on the preferences of their physician. Many have concluded that such discretion is not acceptable. Physicians should not be permitted to refrain from pronouncing death in a jurisdiction specifying a whole-brain definition of death. By the same token, it is an even more serious offense if physicians in jurisdictions such as Japan or Denmark that have not adopted a brain-oriented definition of death take it upon themselves to pronounce death on the basis of loss of brain function. There is some empirical evidence that physicians have, in fact, taken it upon themselves to use their own standards, pronouncing death based on brain criteria when states had not authorized such pronouncements (Black & Zervas, 1984).

In fact, individuals with dead brains in the few jurisdictions that have no legal authorization for death pronouncements based on brain criteria should be treated as still living. If a patient then really dies (based on heart and lung function appropriate in that jurisdiction) because treatment was stopped because of an erroneous death pronouncement based on brain criteria, a physician might appropriately be prosecuted for homicide.

Variation Based on the Patient's Preferences   There is a final kind of variation to be considered: variation based on the views of individual patients or their agents. There is overwhelming evidence that citizens differ over precisely what standards should be used for pronouncing death. These differences are rooted in underlying conceptual philosophical and theological differences over the definition of death that have nothing to do with matters requiring knowledge of neurological science. It now seems clear that if any single policy is adopted, some citizens will have their personal convictions about something as basic as the meaning of life and death violated. Some have proposed that limited discretion be given to individuals to exercise conscientious objection to a state's chosen definition of death.

In 1968, Halley and Harvey proposed a very early version of a redefinition of death. It contained a provision for pronouncing death in "special circumstances" using standards other than cardiac and respiratory standards, provided that "valid consent" has been given by the appropriate relative or legal guardian. They were criticized for the consent requirement on the grounds that they had apparently made the state of being dead contingent on consent when critics thought they must have intended to make the withholding of treatment from a dying person dependent on consent (Capron & Kass, 1972).

It does appear that Halley and Harvey (1968) confused two quite different questions. Certainly, it is more obvious that the decision to withhold treatment might be contingent on the patient's or guardian's consent. Yet a case can be made that even the choice of a standard for pronouncing death could incorporate the discretion of the individual or his or her legal agent. What is at stake is not whether a person's heart or brain had lost function. That presumably is a fact independent of the views of the individual or others. The question is when the person should be treated as dead, that is, when death behaviors become appropriate. Some limited discretion could be given to the individual or others in answering that question. Whether it *should* be given is, of course, another question.

In New York in the early 1970s, efforts to pass a bill redefining death met with opposition from certain minority groups, some Orthodox Jews and others, who were strongly opposed to any change. These groups included people who felt strongly that an individual should be treated as alive as long as the heart beats, regardless of the condition of the brain. In response, the governor proposed a bill in 1976 incorporating a standard based on "total and irreversible cessation of brain function." The proviso was added in the draft, however, that this brain-oriented standard would be used "unless the physician receives written notice from a parent, spouse, next of kin of such individual that such pronouncement conflicts with such individual's beliefs." It is not clear why written notice from the individual him- or herself written in advance while competent was not included. It is also not clear why parents were not given such veto power in cases where the individual him- or herself has not developed views on the subject (e.g., because of infancy or mental deficiency). In any case, this bill was never passed (Guthrie, 1979).

A New York State Task Force on Life and the Law was appointed to study and make recommendations concerning the ethical, legal, and medical issues related to the determination of death. It recommended that "both the traditional standard cessation of heart and lung activity and the standard of total and irreversible cessation of brain function, including brain stem function, should be recognized as the legal standards for determining death in the State of New York" (New York State Task Force on Life and the Law, 1986, p. 1). Although the 1984 New York Court of Appeals decision in *People v. Eub* negates the necessity for legislation to adopt the brain death standard, the Task Force recommended the issuing of a Department of Health regulation to ensure that the brain death standard is uniformly applied throughout the state. The Task Force endorsed a uniform determination of death standard, although it believed that "where feasible, an effort should be made to respect the deeply held religious or moral beliefs of individuals who object to the brain death standard for determining death" (New York State Task Force on Life and the Law, 1986, p. 19).

Along these lines, one member of the Task Force, Rabbi J. David Bleich, rejected the Task Force's recommendations. He suggested that the "adoption of a brain death statute is nothing other than a moral judgment to the effect that there is no human value which argues in favor of the preservation of the life of an irreversibly comatose patient or that there are other values which must be accorded priority" (New York State Task Force on Life and the Law, 1986, p. 32). Bleich argued that despite the apparent majority in favor of brain death standards, other individuals exist, especially within certain religious traditions, who do not hold the same values. To impose brain-based criteria for determining death on these individuals would be a violation of their autonomy and their religious and civil liberties. Bleich suggested, "The simplest, most expedient and most honest method of resolving the problem is not by redefining death, but by enacting a statute providing for the withholding of life support mechanisms from irreversibly comatose patients without at all disturbing the classical definition of death" (New York State Task Force on Life and the Law, 1986, p. 34).

Because of the philosophical and theological disagreement underlying the debate and the absolute necessity of having some policy for initiating death behaviors, some have advocated limited discretion for individuals or their agents in selecting the standard of death to be used (Veatch, 1976).

It is clear that there cannot be unlimited individual discretion. That would permit individuals to choose to be pronounced dead and treated as dead when heart, lungs, lower brain, higher brain, and capacities for consciousness and thinking all remain intact. No matter how strongly some deviant member of this society might think he or she is dead under such circumstances, as a matter of public policy society cannot permit the full range of death behaviors in such circumstances. Likewise, if some person holds the firm conviction that he is not dead until every cell in his body ceases to function, society probably cannot tolerate treating such a person as alive until every cell dies.

It is possible, however, to adopt a public policy that would permit limited individual discretion. If choice is to be permitted, it would have to be from a limited range of alternatives in cases where those who dissent from the state's definition were motivated so strongly that they would go through the necessary procedures to reject it. Assuming that all people who had strong feelings on the matter would exercise such an option, it would make little difference which of the plausible definitions of death were adopted for public policy purposes: one focusing on the heart, whole brain, or higher brain function. It would be efficient to adopt the policy that appeared to be held by the largest number of people. Alternatively, policy might be formulated under the assumption that many people would not take the initiative to exercise such judgment even if they did have rather strong feelings on the matter. In such a case, it might be a prudent policy option to adopt a rather conservative definition of death, perhaps even one based on irreversible loss of heart and lung function, and then permitting individuals to opt for formulations based on total brain function and possibly higher brain function.

In 1991, New Jersey became the first jurisdiction in the world to adopt a limited form of individual discretion in choosing a definition of death. On the basis of the work of the New Jersey Commission on Legal and Ethical Problems in the Delivery of Health Care, the state adopted a whole-brain definition of death while permitting individuals who have religious objection to exercise a document opting for use of a heart-oriented definition of death for their own death pronouncement (New Jersey Determination of Death Act, 1991; Olick, 1991).

It seems bizarre that the definition of death should be left to such individual discretion. Society has always considered death to be an objective fact. For policy purposes, however, society is not interested in biological or even philosophical or theological formulations, but rather is interested in the much more practical question of when people ought to be treated as dead (Ladd, 1979). That clearly is an evaluative question where, traditionally, individual discretion has been tolerated within limits. The mechanics of tolerating such limited objections or basic philosophical concerns may make the option of permitting variations seem infeasible to some (Ramsey, 1978), but the alternative of insisting that all operate under the same uniform definition of death regardless of their most deeply held religious and philosophical beliefs is also alien to American tradition. While the President's Commission (1981) recommended the adoption of the Uniform Determination of Death Act in all jurisdictions in the United States and specifically rejected a "conscience clause" permitting an individual (or family member where the individual is incompetent) to specify the standard to be used for determining death, it also urged "those acting under the statute to apply it with sensitivity to the emotional and religious needs of those for whom the new standards mark a departure from traditional practice" (p. 43), implying possible physician variation in selecting standards (Olinger, 1975).

By 1993, all states of the United States and almost all other jurisdictions of the world (except Denmark and Japan) had adopted a whole-brain definition of death, but only New Jersey has permitted conscientious objection. New Jersey's conscience clause may be exercised only by the individual, not by the next of kin. The objection must be based on religious conviction, and objectors may choose only a heart-oriented definition as an alternative, not a higher-brain-function definition. Still no jurisdiction has seen fit to adopt a definition of death based on higher brain function even as an option that can be chosen by those whose religious or philosophical convictions support that option. These individuals can legally choose to exercise an advance directive refusing life-supporting medical treatment once their higher brain function is permanently lost so that they will be dead soon in any case, but they cannot presently choose the definition of death that would treat them as dead under these circumstances.

The public policy issues raised by the definition of death are more complex than they appear. There is a growing consensus that some form of brain-oriented definition fits the religious and philosophical convictions of the majority of the population, at least of Western societies. But there is growing doubt about the present whole-brain definition that requires that literally all functions of the entire brain must be lost before death is pronounced. A minority holds religious convictions that support the traditional heart-oriented definition, whereas others favor some form of a newer higher-brain-function definition. The choice among the alternative definitions is fundamentally a religious or philosophical one based on personally held beliefs and values. It is for that reason that the dispute is likely to continue.

REFERENCES

Arnold, R. M., & Youngner, S. J. (1993). Ethical, psychological, and public policy implications of procuring organs from non-heart-beating cadavers [Special issue]. *Kennedy Institute of Ethics Journal, 3.*

Ashwal, S., & Schneider, S. (1987a). Brain death in children, I. *Pediatric Neurology, 3,* 5–10.

Ashwal, S., & Schneider, S. (1987b). Brain death in children, II. *Pediatric Neurology, 3,* 69–78.

Becker, L. C. (1975). Human being: The boundaries of the concept. *Philosophy and Public Affairs, 4,* 334–359.

Beecher, H. K. (1970). *The new definition of death, some opposing views.* Paper presented at the annual meeting of the American Association for the Advancement of Science.

Bernat, J. L. (1992a). How much of the brain must die on brain death? *Journal of Clinical Ethics, 3,* 21–26.

Bernat, J. L. (1992b). The boundaries of the persistent vegetative state. *Journal of Clinical Ethics, 3,* 176–180.

Biorck, G. (1967). On the definition of death. *World Medical Journal, 14,* 137–139.

Black, P. M. (1978). Brain death. *New England Journal of Medicine, 299,* 338–344, 393–401.

Black, P. M. (1977). Three definitions of death. *The Monist, 60,* 136–146.

Black, P. M., & Zervas, N. T. (1984). Declaration of brain death in neurosurgical and neurological practice. *Neurosurgery, 15,* 170–174.

Black's law dictionary (4th ed., rev.). (1968). St. Paul, MN: West.

Bleich, J. D. (1979). Neurological criteria of death and time of death status. In J. D. Bleich & F. Rosner (Eds.), *Jewish bioethics* (pp. 303–316). New York: Sanhedrin Press.

Bleich, J. D. (1989). Of cerebral, respiratory, and cardiac death. *Tradition: A Journal of Orthodox Jewish Thought, 24*(3), 44–66.

Brierley, J. B., Adam, J. A. H., Graham, D. I., & Simpson, J. A. (1971). Neocortical death after cardiac arrest. *Lancet, 2,* 560–565.

Burnham, J. C. (1977). The mind-body problem in the early twentieth century. *Perspectives in Biology and Medicine, 20,* 271–284.

Byrne, P. A., O'Reilly, S., & Quay, P. M. (1979). Brain death: An opposing viewpoint. *Journal of the American Medical Association, 242,* 1985–1990.

Capron, A. M., & Kass, L. (1972). A statutory definition of the standards for determining human death: An appraisal and a proposal. *University of Pennsylvania Law Review, 121,* 87–118.

Charron, W. C. (1975). Death: A philosophical perspective on the legal definitions. *Washington University Law Quarterly, 4,* 979–1008.

Cole, David J. (1992). The reversibility of death. *Journal of Medical Ethics, 18,* 26–30.

Collaborative Study. (1977). An appraisal of the criteria of cerebral death—A summary statement. *Journal of the American Medical Association, 237,* 982–986.

Collins, V. (1971). Considerations in defining death. *Linacre Quarterly,* pp. 94–101.

Council on Scientific Affairs and Council on Ethical and Judicial Affairs. (1990). Persistent vegetative state and the decision to withdraw or withhold life support. *Journal of the American Medical Association, 263,* 426–430.

Cranford, R. B., & Smith, H. L. (1979). Some critical distinctions between brain death and the persistent vegetative state. *Ethics in Science and Medicine, 6,* 199–209.

Cranford, R., et al. (1979). Uniform Brain Death Act. *Neurology, 29,* 417–418.

Currie, B. (1978). The redefinition of death. In S. F. Spicker (Ed.), *Organism, medicine and metaphysics* (pp. 177–197). Boston: D. Reidel.

Diagnosis of death. (1979). *Lancet, 1,* 261–262.

Feigl, H. (1967). *The "mental" and the "physical."* Minneapolis, MN: University of Minnesota Press.

Fellner, C. H. (1971). Selection of living kidney donors and the problem of informed consent. *Seminars in Psychiatry, 3,* 70–85.

Fletcher, J. (1969). Our shameful waste of human tissue. In D. R. Cutler (Ed.), *Updating life and death* (pp. 1–27). Boston: Beacon Press.

Forrester, A. C. (1976). Brain death and the donation of cadaver kidneys. *Health Bulletin, 34,* 199–204.

Friloux, C. A. (1975). Death? When does it occur? *Baylor Law Review, 27,* 10–21.

Frenkel, D. A. (1978). Establishing the cessation of life. *Legal Medical Quarterly, 2,* 162–168.

Fulton, R., & Fulton, J. (1972). Anticipatory grief: A psychosocial aspect of terminal care. In B. Schoenberg, A. C. Carr, D. Peretz, & A. H. Kutscher (Eds.), *Psychosocial aspects of terminal care* (pp. 227–242). New York: Columbia University Press.

Globus, G. G. (1973). Consciousness and brain I: The identity thesis. *Archives of General Psychiatry, 29,* 153ff.

Green, M. B., & Wikler, D. (1980). Brain death and personal identity. *Philosophy and Public Affairs, 9,* 105–133.

Grenvik, A., Pawner, D. J., Snyder, J. V., Jastremski, M. S., Babcock, R. A., & Loughhead, M. G. (1978). Cessation of therapy in terminal illness and brain death. *Critical Care Medicine, 6,* 284–291.

Guthrie, L. B. (1979). Brain death and criminal liability. *Criminal Law Bulletin, 15,* 40–61.

Halley, M. M., & Harvey, W. F. (1968). Medical and legal definitions of death. *Journal of the American Medical Association, 204,* 423–425.

Haring, B. (1973). *Medical ethics.* Notre Dame, IN: Fides Press.

Harvard Medical School. (1968). A definition of irreversible coma. Report of the Ad Hoc Committee of the Harvard Medical School To Examine the Definition of Brain Death. *Journal of the American Medical Association, 205,* 337–340.

Hauerwas, S. (1978). Religious concepts of brain death and associated problems. In J. Korein (Ed.), *Brain death: Interrelated medical and social issues* (pp. 329–338). New York: New York Academy of Sciences.

Horan, D. J. (1978). Euthanasia and brain death: Ethical and legal considerations. *Linacre Quarterly, 45,* 284–296.

In re Quinlan, 70 N.J. 10,355 A2d 647(1976).

Jennett, B., & Plum, F. (1972). Persistent vegetative state after brain damage. *Lancet, 1,* 734–737.

Jonas, H. (1969). Philosophical reflections on experimenting with human subjects. *Daedalus, 98,* 219–247.

Jonas, H. (1974). Against the stream: Comments on the definition and redefinition of death. In *Philosophical essays: From ancient creed to technological man* (pp. 132–140). Englewood Cliffs, NJ: Prentice-Hall.

Kansas State Ann. 77–202 (Supp. 1974).

Kass, L. (1971). Death as an event: A commentary on Robert Morison. *Science, 173,* 698–702.

Kennedy, I. M. (1971). The Kansas state statute on death—An appraisal. *New England Journal of Medicine, 285,* 946–949.

Kennedy, I. M. (1975). A legal perspective on determining death. *The Month, 8,* 46–51.

Kennedy, I. M. (1977). The definition of death. *Journal of Medical Ethics, 3,* 5–6.

Korein, J. (1978a). Editor's comment. In J. Korein (Ed.), *Brain death: Interrelated medical and social issues* (pp. 320–321). New York: New York Academy of Sciences.

Korein, J. (1978b). Terminology, definitions, and usage. In J. Korein (Ed.), *Brain death: Interrelated medical and social issues* (pp. 6–10). New York: New York Academy of Sciences.

Ladd, J. (1979). The definition of death and the right to die. In J. Ladd (Ed.), *Ethical issues relating to life and death* (pp. 118–145). New York: Oxford University Press.

Lamb, D. (1978). Diagnosing death. *Philosophy and Public Affairs, 7,* 144–153.

Lamb, (1992). Reversibility and death: A reply to David Cole. *Journal of Medical Ethics, 18,* 31–33.

Levy, D. E., Knill-Jones, R. P., & Plum, F. (1978). The vegetative state and its prognosis following nontraumatic coma. In J. Korein (Ed.), *Brain death: Interrelated medical and social issues* (pp. 293–304). New York: New York Academy of Sciences.

Mackert, J. F. (1979). Should the law define brain death? *Hospital Progress, 60*(3), 6ff.

Mahoney, J. (1975). Ethical aspects of donor consent in transplantation. *Journal of Medical Ethics, 1,* 67–70.

May, W. F. (1973). Attitudes toward the newly dyed. *Hastings Center Studies, 1,* 3–13.

Mayo, D., & Wikler, D. I. (1979). Euthanasia and the transition from life to death. In W. Robinson & M. S. Pritchard (Eds.), *Medical responsibility: Paternalism, informed consent, and euthanasia.* Clifton, NJ: The Humane Press.

Mills, D. H. (1971). The Kansas death statute: Bold and innovative. *New England Journal of Medicine, 285,* 968–969.

Mohandas, A., & Chou, S. N. (1971). Brain death: A clinical and pathological study. *Journal of Neurosurgery, 35,* 211–218.

Morison, R. (1971). Death–Process of event? *Science, 173,* 694–698.

New Jersey Declaration of Death Act. (1991). *New Jersey Statutes Annotated.* Title 26, 6A-1-8.

New York State Task Force on Life and the Law. (1986). *The determination of death: Proposed report.*

O'Brien, M. D. (1990). Criteria for diagnosing brain stem death. *British Medical Journal, 301,* 108–109.

Olick, R. S. (1991). Brain death, religious freedom, and public policy. *Kennedy Institute of Ethics Journal, 1,* 275–288.

Olinger, S. D. (1975). Medical death. *Baylor Law Review, 27,* 22–26.

Pope Pius XII. (1958). The prolongation of life: An address of Pope Pius XII to an International Congress of Anesthesiologists. *The Pope Speaks, 4,* 393–398.

Potter, R. B. (1968). The paradoxical preservation of a principle. *Villanova Law Review, 13,* 784–792.

President's Commission for the Study of Ethical Problems in Medicine and Biomedical and Behavioral Research. (1981). *Defining death: Medical, legal, and ethical issues in the definition of death.* Washington, DC: U.S. Government Printing Office.

Ramsey, P. (1970). *The patient as person.* New Haven, CT: Yale University Press.

Ramsey, P. (1978). *Ethics at the edges of life.* New Haven, CT: Yale University Press.

Richardson, D. R. (1976). A matter of life and death: A definition of death: Judicial resolution of a medical responsibility. *Harvard Law Journal, 19,* 138–148.

Robertson, J. A. (1976). Organ donations by incompetents and the substituted judgment doctrine. *Columbia Law Review, 76,* 48ff.

Saperstein, S. (1979, March 22). Maryland law on brain death was unclear to jurors. *The Washington Post.*

Sell, D. (1985, November 11). Flyers goalie Lindbergh is declared brain dead. *The Washington Post,* pp. D1, D13.

Shewmon, D. A. (1988). Commentary on guidelines for the determination of brain death in children. *Annals of Neurology, 24,* 789–791.

Simmons, R. G., & Fulton, J. (1971). Ethical issues in kidney transplantation. *Omega, 2,* 179–190.

Skegg, P. D. G. (1976). Case for a statutory "definition of death." *Journal of Medical Ethics, 2,* 190–192.

Stickel, D. L. (1979). The brain death criterion of human death. *Ethics in Science and Medicine, 6,* 177–197.

Sullivan, J. F. (1975, October 3). Lawyer outlines arguments he'll use in coma case. *New York Times.*

Sweet, W. H. (1978). Brain death. *New England Journal of Medicine, 299,* 410–411.

Task Force for the Determination of Brain Death in Children. (1987). Guidelines for the determination of brain death in children. *Neurology, 37,* 1077–1078.

Task Force on Death and Dying, Institute of Society, Ethics and the Life Sciences. (1972). Refinements in criteria for the determination of death: An appraisal. *Journal of the American Medical Association, 221,* 48–53.

Toole, J. F. (1971). The neurologist and the concept of brain death. *Perspectives in Biology and Medicine, 14,* 599–607.

Tooley, M. (1979). Decisions to terminate life and the concept of person. In J. Ladd (Ed.), *Ethical issues relating to life and death* (pp. 62–93). New York: Oxford University Press.

Van Till, D'Aulnis de Bourouill, A. (1975). How dead can you be? *Medical Science Law, 15,* 133–147.

Veatch, R. M. (1975). The whole-brain-oriented concept of death: An outmoded philosophical formulation. *Journal of Thanatology, 3,* 13–30.

Veatch, R. M. (1976). *Death, dying and the biological revolution.* New Haven, CT: Yale University Press.

Veatch, R. M. (1978). The definition of death: Ethical, philosophical, and policy confusion. In J. Korein (Ed.), *Brain death: Interrelated medical and social issues* (pp. 307–321). New York: New York Academy of Sciences.

Veatch, R. M. (1988). Whole-brain, neocortical, and higher brain related concepts. In R. M. Zaner (Ed.), *Death: Beyond whole-brain criteria* (pp. 171–186). Dordrecht, The Netherlands: D. Reidel.

Veatch, R. M. (1989a). *Death, dying, and the biological revolution* (Rev. ed.). New Haven, CT: Yale University Press.

Veatch, R. M. (1989b). The definition of death: Unresolved controversies. In H. H. Kaufman (Ed.), *Pediatric brain death and organ/tissue retrieval* (pp. 207–218). New York: Plenum.

Veatch, R. M. (1992). Brain death and slippery slopes. *Journal of Clinical Ethics, 3,* 181–187.

Wasmuth, C. E. (1969). The concept of death. *Ohio State Law Journal, 30,* 32–60.

Wikler, D., & Weisbard, A. J. (1989). Appropriate confusion over "brain death." *Journal of the American Medical Association, 261,* 2246.

Wilson, D. L. (1976). On the nature of consciousness and of physical reality. *Perspectives in Biology and Medicine, 19,* 569ff.

Youngner, S. J., et al. (1989). "Brain death" and organ retrieval. *Journal of the American Medical Association, 261,* 2205–2210.

Part Four

Conclusion

Chapter 17

Closing Reflections

Hannelore Wass and Robert A. Neimeyer

Given the complexity and scope of contemporary thanatology, even the most authoritative volume on death and dying serves more as a gateway to an evolving
field than as a comprehensive repository of secure knowledge. It is hoped that this
third edition of *Dying: Facing the Facts* will also function as an invitation to the
reader to participate actively in both the scholarly and humanitarian aspects of
working with death and loss. In this concluding chapter of the book, a few personal reflections on the current state of thanatology are offered, and areas of research and application that deserve greater attention are identified. Because this
book itself represents an educational effort (at the university and professional levels), particular consideration is given to death education; some of its problems as
well as prospects are pointed out.

THE SCOPE OF CONTEMPORARY THANATOLOGY

A cursory review of the table of contents of this or other books on death and dying
suggests the remarkable scope and range of the contemporary study of death,
which cuts across conventional disciplinary boundaries while also making contributions not easily accommodated within any typical academic discipline. Thus,
this edition of *Dying: Facing the Facts* spans such fields as psychology, philosophy, nursing, medicine, ethics, law, political science, theology, suicidology, education, history, and cultural anthropology, with varying degrees of emphasis. Moreover, many of the contributors necessarily operate at the boundaries of traditional
disciplines, drawing on knowledge in two or more domains in order to treat particular thanatological problems with greater adequacy. For example, explorations of
the complex ethical issues surrounding various forms of euthanasia (ranging from
the withholding of life-extending measures to physician-assisted suicide) require
a multidisciplinary grounding in the ethics of health care, the changing medical
definition of death, and even the clinical application of suicidology. Similarly, an
understanding of the functions of the inner representation of a lost child for grieving parents in a mutual-support network like Compassionate Friends is enriched
by psychological, spiritual, and perhaps sociological perspectives. This transdis-
ciplinary character of the field accounts for much of the excitement of death studies, but it also raises important questions about its status as a specialty vis-à-vis
more established areas of study.

One such question concerns the centrality or marginality of thanatological
knowledge within existing disciplines. For example, despite the immense output
of studies on death attitudes and bereavement and grief that has occurred for the

better part of two decades, such research rarely receives a mention in standard course work or textbooks in the psychology of attitude measurement or in clinical and counseling psychology, while these same courses and texts devote significant attention to a number of other topics that have generated a far less voluminous literature. Likewise, death-related content is often strangely absent even in specialty courses and textbooks in which such content would be essential, such as gerontology. Gerontology texts give extensive coverage to the losses experienced in the course of aging (e.g., loss of memory, sensory function, motor control, stamina, and health), while omitting discussion of the most fundamental losses of all, namely, of loved ones or one's own life.

How can we account for these omissions? In all probability, the lack of integration of thanatological content into mainstream disciplines results not only from trends and biases within those disciplines, but also from trends within thanatology itself. On one hand, academic specialties, like other established social institutions, are essentially conservative. With occasional exceptions (e.g., the development of radical social theory within sociology, critical legal studies within law, and social constructionism within psychology), such disciplines tend to reflect dominant cultural values (e.g., the denial of death) and objectivist modes of analysis, which can be inimical to at least the more personal or subjective aspects of death and dying. But thanatologists also participate in their own marginalization, to the extent that they tend to insulate themselves from mainstream developments and create an alternative literature that disregards both the theoretical formulations and the issues and problems given attention within their parent disciplines. Research on death anxiety, for instance, is largely atheoretical, and for the most part has failed to benefit from more recent cognitive psychological formulations that could give the study of attitudes of any kind a more secure grounding. Grief counselors and therapists have been similarly insular, only recently beginning to articulate theories of loss with developments in research and practice in such areas as posttraumatic stress or interpersonal attachment. Fortunately, thanatologists are beginning to participate in broader ranging discussions with representatives of traditional disciplines, making it more likely that the perspectives will inform one another in the future.

The growing interface between thanatology and other disciplines raises the question of the proper or ideal role of the former in relation to the latter. Usually, thanatologists seem to aspire to play a *contributory* role in relation to their parent fields, adding to the base of accredited knowledge the data on death and dying that they have generated. From this perspective, pedagogical programs of study would incorporate essential material on loss and grief into educational curricula, medical and nursing schools would offer coherent training in the unique needs of the dying, family studies would examine the impact of the death of a family member on others in the family system, and so on. In this contributory role, death and loss might even become a recognized specialty within the parent discipline, much as medical ethics has become an established field of study and estate planning and inheritance has become a recognized concentration within law.

Although playing this contributory role is a feasible and even desirable goal in many areas, at least two other outcomes are possible as thanatology negotiates its identity in relation to conventional fields of study. One is a *complementary* role, in which thanatologists would not so much seek assimilation within other disciplines as attempt to provide an alternative to them. This path of development offers unique advantages insofar as it permits the continued refinement of a distinctive knowledge base concerning death and dying generated from the multidisciplinary matrix from which thanatology has emerged. This course minimizes the likelihood that thanatology will fall prey to the assumptions of biases inherent in any single parent discipline, but risks thanatology's remaining insular from advances in other areas. In many ways, this is the path taken by suicidology, an adolescent sibling of thanatology, which has also faced the challenge of fostering a continued interchange with mainstream areas after having differentiated itself as a legitimate specialty in its own right.

Finally, a third developmental trajectory seems possible for thanatology in relation to traditional disciplines, namely, to play a *revolutionary* role. This is clearly a prospect within political science, where a thanatological perspective can provide a critique of hegemonic power interests within a given society in a way that more conservative and conventional political perspectives cannot. Although this possibility may have strong intellectual and social activist appeal to some thanatologists, the developmental trajectory of the hospice movement should provide at least a cautionary note for would-be revolutionaries. Originally conceived as an alternative to mainstream medical treatment of the dying, contemporary hospices have in some ways been victims of their own success. That is, as they have made inroads into the increasingly bureaucratized health care delivery system, they have had to grapple with the mundane realities of third-party reimbursement, administrative review by accrediting commissions and associations, and coordination of services with the very institutions (hospitals and nursing homes) from which they have distinguished themselves. This is not to minimize the substantial gains in both the quantity and quality of care for the dying and their families offered by hospice programs, but merely to point out that as revolutionary programs become institutionalized, revolutionary fervor becomes tempered by the establishment of new conventions and inevitable accommodation to old ones.

Which of these three paths—the contributory, the complementary, or the revolutionary—will thanatology take as it continues to mature as a discipline? Any attempt at social forecasting relies on a somewhat dusty crystal ball, but it is likely that death studies will pursue all three routes, though with varying degrees of emphasis. That is, scholars, researchers, educators, and practitioners concerned with issues of death and loss will continue to make inroads into their mainstream disciplines, and they will do so successfully to the extent that they are cognizant of the theoretical and methodological advances in those fields of study. Of course, some areas are more receptive to such contributions than others, typically those that are closer to the domain of practice (e.g., nursing, medicine, clinical psychology, applied ethics, and family and estate law). Playing this contributory role in

relation to existing specialties could also be facilitated by the proper balance between publishing in mainstream outlets (e.g., the *Journal of Personality and Social Psychology* and the *Journal of the American Medical Association*) that bring
thanatological work to the attention of a wide readership and publishing in specialty journals (e.g., *Death Studies* and *Omega*) that provide a focal point for readers and researchers attracted to the field.

But developments in thanatology over the last 15 years also indicate that the
field will continue in a trajectory toward emergence as a complementary discipline in its own right. It is important to remember that academic disciplines are
comprised of people and that people organize their work and relationships
through the establishment of structures that facilitate their joint objectives. In the
case of thanatology, these structures have emerged in the form of successful organizations (e.g., the Association for Death Education and Counseling [ADEC]
and the International Work Group on Death, Dying, and Bereavement [IWG]) and
publications (both books and journals) that promote more intensive communication among group members and mutual recognition and validation of their work.
Although the individuals who participate in the conferences and publications resulting from these efforts typically also contribute to the conferences and publications of their parent disciplines, the emergence of distinctively thanatological
groups, books, and journals should foster the coherence of the "movement" and
its differentiation as an identifiable specialty.

And what of the revolutionary character of contemporary thanatology? Although bold new expressions of thanatological theory that perturb existing specialties are worth supporting, the likelihood that death studies will remain a form
of permanent revolution is not great. As alluded to earlier, the most successful
revolutions in any field tend to pay for their success with increasing conservatism
and institutionalization, until a new revolutionary perspective arises to oppose
them. In a sense, this has already begun to happen to the death awareness movement as a whole, as it has made important cultural inroads into the death-denying
societal trends that inspired it. Thus, it is likely that the further institutionalization
and differentiation of thanatology as a distinctive specialty in the future will provide a secure base from which participants in this multidisciplinary field will
gradually transform their respective disciplines, albeit in limited ways. Occasional
revolutionary scholarship will draw attention to the presence and potential of thanatological research, although it will be adulterated and softened in the course of
its assimilation into mainstream disciplines.

NEGLECTED AREAS OF STUDY

Despite the range and depth of contemporary scholarship in death studies, thanatologists ultimately should be humbled by the intransigence of ancient and fundamental questions concerning the meaning of death, as well as the urgent new
death-related challenges that confront society. Although research alone will not
resolve these problems, it can contribute to the knowledge base required to formu-

late an intelligent response to at least some of these problems at the level of social action.

At a general level, such research could benefit from greater attention to the historical and local factors that shape our unique cultural arrangements regarding death. Like other macroscopic aspects of our social lives (e.g., language and ethnicity), the pervasive influence of our unique "death system" may remain invisible until the system is contrasted with systems originating in other times and places. It was in part this historical view of care for the dying in technologically simpler times that fueled the contemporary hospice movement and the contrast provided by other Western cultural arrangements for disposing of the dead that motivated attempts at critique and reform of the American funeral industry. Yet most researchers in the field of death studies tend intuitively to operate from a rather individualized perspective, leading to general inattention to the broader social parameters that influence death-related behaviors. For instance, most of the research on death, dying, and bereavement has tended to ignore the critical influence of ethnic variation and cultural diversity in affecting preferred and actual ways of dying and grieving, important recent exceptions to the contrary notwithstanding (e.g., Irish, Lundquist, & Nelson, 1993).

At least as pressing as this general neglect of cultural and subcultural factors is the specific neglect of particular problems that resist conventional methods of analysis and problem solving. While several of these problems, such as AIDS and adolescent suicide, have been highlighted in this book, two death-related problems have received even less attention by researchers, practitioners, and policymakers, although they have reached epidemic proportions. The first is the rate of individual homicide, which has reached shocking proportions, especially in the United States. For the most part, the official federal and organizational response to the outbreak of lethal violence has been statistical, compiling ever more discouraging data on the increasing frequency of homicides, drive-by shootings, and random murders, particularly in large cities. In contrast, relatively few serious studies have been conducted on the psychosocial causes and dynamics of homicidal behavior, in effect relegating the whole problem to a criminal justice system that is ill equipped to handle it. For example, it was not until 1985 that the FBI established a clearinghouse for data on serial murder that was made available to researchers. As a result of this inattention, traditional models for homicidal behavior, which rely on such concepts as passion or killer instincts, may be seriously dated and in need of revision. Fortunately, homicidal and less lethal forms of violent behavior on the part of children and adolescents is beginning to receive long-overdue attention, and some responsible groups (e.g., the American Psychological Association) are beginning to advocate preventive action on the basis of the existing research findings.

Of course, homicide is another example of the complex, multidimensional problems faced by thanatologists, which resist reduction to a single (motivational) aspect. Murder obviously affects not only its victim and perpetrator, but also survivors and the larger community in which they live. Whole communities can be traumatized by a murder or mass murder, in ways that are poorly understood by psychologists, sociologists, and other relevant professionals. Likewise, there are unique stressors involved in homicide investigation that are insufficiently appreciated within the institutional structure of law enforcement (Sewell, in press). Clearly, this cluster of problems—which call for improved understanding as well as more enlightened efforts at treatment and prevention—requires a more aggressive response on the part of thanatologists, among others.

A second problem concerns the phenomenon of horrendous death, whether natural or caused by humans. Despite the grounding of thanatology in Lindemann's (1944) investigation of the impact of the Coconut Grove fire on the Boston community, few contemporary thanatologists have conducted in-depth ethnographic or field studies of the impact of natural disasters, of which there unfortunately has been no shortage. Still, some research is being done on trauma and its aftermath, even if primarily from an individual rather than family systemic or community perspective, giving at least some guidance to psychologists and others involved in disaster relief teams and other postvention efforts.

Perhaps the most neglected form of horrendous or traumatic death is that which is systematically inflicted or tolerated by governments and other organized groups, including international aggression, civil war, genocide, starvation of whole communities, and all manner of atrocities against civilian populations. In the main, these forms of "megadeath" have been relegated to journalistic reportage and political analysis, conveniently exempting those in the social and behavioral sciences from the responsibility for understanding their consequences for human individuals and communities. The occasional exceptions to this neglect (e.g., Bettelheim, 1960; Leviton, 1991a, 1991b; Lifton, 1986) have made a substantial contribution to our understanding of some forms of organized killing, and these pioneering efforts deserve to be emulated and extended by more thanatologists. Death studies might even provide an integrative framework for weaving a more complete picture from the disparate strands of literature on war, the holocaust, starvation, and other forms of organized large-scale killing, in a way that illuminates both classical and contemporary causes of conflict triggering these all-too-human forms of dying.

Among the many questions surrounding violent and horrendous death that deserve consideration is the question of the relationship between particular sanctioned forms of social control (e.g., capital punishment) and the lethal behaviors they are designed to suppress. For example, the use of the death penalty and the incidence of individual homicide in the United States have risen in tandem over the last 15–20 years, reaching their highest point in two decades. Yet the meaning of this correlation is unclear: Does the increased frequency of capital punishment represent simply an insufficient response to the higher incidence of homicide in the population, or are some forms of homicide (e.g., murder of police) an aggravated response to perceived injustices in a criminal justice system seen as prejudicial to whole races or communities? Or are both statistics merely reflections of some third variable, such as the disintegration of family structures or the glorification of violence in the media, entertainment, and society in general? What seems called for are studies that assist in the *interpretation* of the data on death and dying, so that statistical trends can be meaningfully understood and used by decision makers.

Other questions concerning horrendous and large-scale death also beg for answers. What are the effects on people—and particularly children—of being in harm's way merely by being in the street or schoolyard in the life-threatening environments in which they are forced to live? What are the effects of witnessing widespread death and violence personally or through instant news reportage via satellite, all too often in the absence of any serious evaluative commentary? What is the effect of describing organized efforts to kill hundreds of thousands of people or of sophisticated weapons technologies given sanitized and romanticized titles more appropriate to movies (e.g., Desert Storm, Star Wars) than to campaigns or instruments of destruction? For that matter, how are people's attitudes toward death shaped by other linguistic conventions, such as the substitute of terms like *terminal* for *dying, homicide* for *murder,* and *trauma* for *death and grief* or the use of other euphemisms? Such issues go beyond semantics, insofar as people's conceptions of reality (as threatening or safe, immediate or distant, painful or painless) are shaped by the way they think and speak about it.

But even if definitive answers to such questions were available, this knowledge would be of little use unless it were appropriately disseminated in a form that it becomes usable by people in real-world contexts.

EDUCATION ABOUT DEATH, DYING, AND BEREAVEMENT

Curiously, death education represents another relatively neglected area in thanatology, despite its critical significance in making the results of basic research and scholarship accessible to the broader public. However, it would be unfair to conclude that there has been a lack of effort in this direction. Intelligent discussion of the goals and methods of death education date to the very beginning of the field and have since been reiterated, refined, and revised to adapt them to different constituencies (e.g., professionals and young children) in a range of settings (e.g., medical, nursing, and graduate schools; secondary schools; grade schools; and hospitals). Numerous books, chapters, and articles have been published that describe specific curricula, educational guidelines, and resources. But despite this impressive outpouring of effort, death education remains diverse and fractionated. It varies in scope, form, level of intensity, and pedagogical approach—from the occasional broadcast of a single item of public health information via the media to a systematic course of academic study and clinical experience for professionals. Precisely because of this diversity and the potential sensitivity of the subject matter, there is a need for the establishment of general standards for death education, perhaps combined with some form of accountability and quality control. Important steps toward the establishment of such standards have been taken by the two major professional organizations in the field, the IWG and ADEC. Over a period of several years the IWG (1994) has worked to articulate the basic assumptions and principles for education concerning death, dying, and bereavement in general and for the training of health care professionals and volunteers in particular. Similarly, ADEC (1993) has published a Code of Ethics and standards for educators and counselors, which it disseminates to an expanding membership numbering in the thousands. The cumulative effect of these efforts should be the development of greater consensus on the core content of death education in various contexts, as well as standards for distinguishing between those programs that are truly innovative and those that are merely idiosyncratic.

In order to appreciate the challenges confronting death education, it is critical to place it in the various contexts in which it is, or could be, practiced. Three such contexts are the education of children and adolescents, postsecondary (college and university) education, and postgraduate or professional training.

Education for Children and Adolescents

Setting standards for death education is nowhere more important than in programs for children and adolescents. Although only a minority of public schools offer death education as part of their regular curricula, existing programs affect thousands of students. Moreover, related programs in such areas as crisis intervention, suicide prevention, and health and wellness are increasing in number, providing students with at least some exposure to materials concerning death, loss, and coping with serious illness or other forms of adversity. Thus, these courses as well need to conform to standards of professional behavior on the part of teachers or program coordinators, as well as defensible and clear instructional goals and coordinated activities for achieving them.

This dual focus on the behavior of the teacher and the nature of the program requires more attention in primary and secondary education contexts. Some qualities of effective death educators have been identified, including thorough knowledge of the subject matter, sensitivity and responsiveness to students, an understanding of group dynamics, skills in interpersonal communication, and the ability to counsel students in distress (Durlak, 1994; Wass, 1987). Likewise, research has begun to identify those aspects of programs that contribute to their effectiveness in promoting attitude change on the part of students, such as an experiential emphasis (Durlak, 1994; Durlak & Reisenberg, 1991) or delicate attunement to the individual student's experience and construction of death (Warren, 1989). Still, far more work is needed, particularly in terms of extending such research to younger children. This extension should be done with care, however. Currently, most models of human development that influence pedagogy are based on universalist assumptions of homogeneity in the tasks or stages people face at various points in their lives, suggesting a lockstep progression that is often disconfirmed in individual cases. As implied in the previous section, what seems required is the development of educational objectives for various settings that are responsive to the distinctive historical, (sub)cultural, and individual concerns and resources of students.

The urgency of primary prevention efforts (e.g., AIDS education and suicide prevention) with younger groups of students also suggests the need for educational reform or revision to heighten the impact of potentially life-saving or life-enhancing educational interventions. For example, there is a need for more creativity in the implementation of AIDS education programs, to avoid the poorly founded assumption that providing clinically or scientifically correct information by itself will produce the desired attitudinal change (e.g., greater understanding of high-risk groups) or behavior modification (e.g., promotion of safer sex practices). In these respects, when education is attempting to modify fundamental values and forms of relating to others, educators would do well to consult the substantial literature on conditions that promote change in the course of psychotherapy or counseling (e.g., Bergin & Garfield, 1994). This suggests the importance of promoting more cross-fertilization of findings and methods between psychology and other disciplines sharing common problems, issues, and methods, so that the knowledge base in one area can be used to enrich that in another.

Postsecondary College or University Education

With the advent of hundreds of college-level courses on death and dying over the last 15 years, one might assume that postsecondary death education would be securely institutionalized, having established its niche in both the intellectual marketplace of ideas and the commercial marketplace of textbook publishing. Indeed, there are clear signs that this is the case, ranging from the differentiation of general course work in death and loss into specialty courses such as Children and Death (Corr, 1992), and the increasing availability of high-quality texts appropriate for both beginning or advanced undergraduate students. But postsecondary death education also confronts its own challenges, particularly in terms of its role vis-à-vis more established academic specialties, as mentioned at the beginning of this chapter. For example, should death-related curricular material be presented in a free-standing interdisciplinary or integrative course, or should it be subsumed by specialty courses in existing departments (e.g., psychology, sociology, and philosophy)? Alternatively, should such content be mainstreamed by incorporation into more general core courses focusing on life span development, clinical psychology, or family studies? Naturally, the degree and kind of attention given to thanatological content under these various pedagogical conditions vary widely, entailing some inevitable trade-offs between offering at least some acquaintance with death studies to the majority of students and providing more satisfying and comprehensive coverage for a few. Unfortunately, the most obvious and appealing alternative—to do all of the above—is probably untenable given current administrative demands on faculty to eliminate perceived curricular redundancy and therefore ensure adequate class enrollments for funding purposes.

A second factor that deserves special consideration in the postsecondary context is interdisciplinary exchange. By their very design, colleges and universities are settings that promote critical exchange, between students and faculty, between researchers and reviewers, and between adherents to different theoretical or disciplinary perspectives. Yet, in spite of their interdisciplinary characters, such exchange is fairly limited in most college-level course work in death and dying as currently institutionalized. For example, a constructively critical exchange between psychologists and sociologists in the context of thanatological course work might benefit the former by exposing hidden biases deriving from a largely individual level of analysis, just as it might benefit the latter by adding a concrete and personal dimension to the otherwise abstract study of broad social forces. Likewise, psychologists might have much to offer educators in terms of knowledge of student motivations that influence their readiness for certain kinds of affective, cognitive, or behavioral learning in the context of death education (e.g., Durlak, 1994), and educators might reciprocate by familiarizing psychologists with the functioning and performance of students in a real-world classroom context. This kind of cross-fertilization is notoriously difficult to sustain in practice, however, given internal pressures toward insularity within academic departments and even within educational institutions. Indeed, the attempt to overcome the distortions and limitations associated with adherence to traditional academic lines of distinction may be one of the healthy reasons that thanatologists have struggled to establish their work as a coherent and independent field of study. Still, particularly in the multiperspective climate of higher education, the death education of the future could benefit from the kind of intellectual exchange that the university was designed to offer.

Professional Education

Perhaps the context for death education that has the most immediate impact is professional education, particularly in core clinical specialties such as medicine, psychology, nursing, counseling, and the other helping professions. Students and trainees in such programs typically are enrolled in practicum experiences with people in distress and therefore have frequent contact with issues of death, loss, suicide, serious illness, and other broadly thanatological problems. Moreover, with or without appropriate preparation, graduates of such programs will embark on careers that repeatedly confront them with such problems, typically in the absence of ongoing supervision and support. Thus, for the sake of both the new professional and his or her clients or patients, adequate training in issues of death, dying, and loss should be an indispensable part of such course work.

Unfortunately, the data on the availability and comprehensiveness of such training are ambiguous at best. On one hand, less than 50% of graduate programs in clinical psychology and related professions provide coverage of even the most common and urgent death-related problems, such as suicide (Bongar & Harmatz, 1991), and there is empirical evidence that beginning counselors feel intensely uncomfortable when faced with client complaints concerning grief, impending death, and life-threatening illness, even more uncomfortable than when they are presented other serious problems, such as rape, spouse abuse, or alcohol dependence (Kirchberg & Neimeyer, 1991). On the other hand, recent studies have indicated that from 40–80% of medical, nursing, and other health-related professions offer at least some coverage of topics concerning death and grief (Dickinson, Summer, & Frederick, 1992), up from mere fractions of these figures in the 1970s. However, these relatively optimistic projections should be tempered by the recognition that most of these courses are elective and therefore remain outside of core professional training experiences for most students.

To some extent, these deficiencies in graduate and professional education can be remedied by continuing professional education experiences in death-related issues (e.g., at workshops, in conferences, and in home-study programs), and the popularity of such continuing education is itself one index of its perceived value by its consumers. But these offerings are no substitute for systematic training that incorporates not only integrative theoretical frameworks for organizing the results of empirical research, but also practicum opportunities for honing professional helping skills in the context of an ongoing relationship with supervising faculty. Because professional thanatology is still fluid and the quality of the knowledge bases in different disciplines is variable and evolving, it is important to develop systematic professional education that provides structure, focus, continuity, guidance, and appropriate resources for today's students, who will become tomorrow's helping professionals (Wass, 1992).

SUMMARY

The vast scope and complexity of the contemporary study of death presents thanatologists with both problems and prospects, at the level of self-definition as a legitimate field of study vis-à-vis other disciplines, in terms of pressing social problems that require urgent response, and in the eventual educational dissemination of death-related knowledge and insights to a diverse public. In a sense, each of the contributors to this third edition of *Dying: Facing the Facts* has invited the reader to enter the complex, ethical, legal, medical, and psychosocial debates that surround society's ways of living its dying. We hope that the reader has accepted this invitation and will join in developing more satisfying scholarly and personal responses to the human encounter with death.

REFERENCES

Association for Death Education and Counseling. (1993). *1993–94 Directory of members.* Hartford, CT: Author.

Bergin, A., & Garfield, S. (1994). *Handbook of psychotherapy and behavior change.* New York: Wiley.

Bettelheim, B. (1960). *The informed heart.* Glencoe, IL: Free Press.

Bongar, B., & Harmatz, M. (1991). Clinical psychology graduate education in the study of suicide: Availability, resources, and importance. *Suicide and Life-Threatening Behavior, 21,* 231–245.

Corr, C. A. (1992). Teaching a college course on children and death. *Death Studies, 16,* 343–356.

Dickinson, G. E., Summer, E. D., & Frederick, L. M. (1992). Death education in selected health professions. *Death Studies, 16,* 281–289.

Durlak, J. A. (1994). Changing death attitudes through death education. In R. A. Neimeyer (Ed.), *Death anxiety handbook: Research, instrumentation, and application* (pp. 243–260). Washington, DC: Taylor & Francis.

Durlak, J. A., & Reisenberg, L. A. (1991). The impact of death education. *Death Studies, 15,* 39–58.

Irish, D. P., Lundquist, K. J., & Nelson, V. J. (Eds.). (1993). *Ethnic variations in dying, death, and grief.* Washington, DC: Taylor & Francis.

IWG (International Work Group on Death, Dying and Bereavement). (1994). *Statements on Death, Dying and Bereavement.* London, Ontario, Canada: King's College.

Kirchberg, T. M., & Neimeyer, R. A. (1991). Reactions of beginning counselors to situations involving death and dying. *Death Studies, 15,* 603–610.

Leviton, D. (Ed.). (1991a). *Horrendous death, health, and well-being.* Washington, DC: Hemisphere.

Leviton, D. (Ed.). (1991b). *Horrendous death and health: Toward action.* Washington, DC: Hemisphere.

Lifton, R. J. (1986). *The Nazi doctors: Medical killing and the psychology of genocide.* New York: Basic Books.

Lindemann, E. (1944). Symptomatology and management of acute grief. *American Journal of Psychiatry, 101,* 141–148.

Sewell, J. (1994). The stress of homicide investigation. *Death Studies, 18,* 565–582.

Warren, W. G. (1989). *Death education and research: Critical perspectives.* New York: Haworth.

Wass, H. (1987). Visions in death education. In C. A. Corr & R. A. Pacholski (Eds.), *Death: Completion and discovery* (pp. 5–16). Lakewood, OH: Association for Death Education and Counseling.

Wass, H. (1992). Disseminating our thanatology knowledge. In E. J. Clark & A. H. Kutscher (Eds.), *The thanatology community and the needs of the movement* (pp. 37–49). New York: Haworth.

Chapter 18

Resources

Hannelore Wass and David E. Balk

This chapter provides a selection of three types of resources—print, audiovisual, and organizational—that may be useful to the reader. In the preparation of this chapter, the second edition of *Dying: Facing the Facts,* published in 1988, was used as the departure point. However, most of the printed materials listed herein became available since then, the majority of them between 1990 and 1994. In addition to recent publications, the list of books for professionals includes a number of classic works, and the list of books for children and adolescents includes several long-time favorites from the juvenile literature.

The professional books are organized under five headings: Life-Threatening Illness, Dying, and AIDS; Bereavement; Death Attitudes: Cultural and Individual; Suicide, Homicide, and Horrendous Death; and Ethical, Social, and Medical Issues.

There is a voluminous journal literature in this field. It would be difficult to achieve a fair representation of this literature, even if there were no space limitations. Therefore, bibliographies of this important group of resources are not included; the journals likely to be of greatest interest to readers are merely noted. The individual contributors to this book refer to many journal articles in their chapters. For additional work, the reader may find the Psychlit, Medline, Sociofile, and Eric computer databases helpful.

The majority of the audiovisual resources listed were released after 1989 and a third after 1990. They are grouped into audiotapes and videotapes and into three audience groups: general adult/professional, adolescents/youth, and children.

This list of organizations, although not comprehensive, provides up-to-date addresses and includes brief descriptions of their purposes. It should be noted that, upon request, many of these organizations make available their own bibliographies and other informational material.

In addition to personal libraries, the following reference works were consulted: the *Encyclopedia of Associations* (1993), the *Film & Video Finder* (1989), *Words on Cassette* (1993), *Video Source Book* (1994), and *Bowker's Complete Video Directory* (1993).

BOOKS FOR PROFESSIONALS
Life-Threatening Illness, Dying, and AIDS

Adams, D. W., & Deveau, E. J. (1988). *Coping with childhood cancer.* Hamilton, Ontario, Canada: Kinbridge Publications.

We express appreciation to Lynn Edgar, Nancy Hall Sanders, Wendy Thornton, Molly Rose, and Phyllis Erickson for their assistance.

Ahmed, P. I., & Ahmed, N. S. (Eds.). (1992). *Living and dying with AIDS.* New York: Plenum Press.

Amenta, M. O., & Tehan, C. D. (Eds.). (1991). *AIDS and the hospice community.* New York: Haworth.

Bertman, S. L. (1991). *Facing death: Images, insights, and interventions.* Washington, DC: Hemisphere.

Bluebond-Langner, M. (1978). *The private worlds of dying children.* Princeton, NJ: Princeton University Press.

Corless, I. B., & Pittman-Lindeman, M. (1988). *AIDS: Principles, practices, and politics.* Washington, DC: Hemisphere.

Davidson, G. W. (Ed.). (1985). *The hospice: Development and administration* (2nd ed.). Washington, DC: Hemisphere.

Doka, K. J. (Ed.). (1993). *Death and spirituality.* Amityville, NY: Baywood.

Feigenberg, L. (1980). *Terminal care: Friendship contracts with dying cancer patients.* New York: Brunner/Mazel.

Glaser, B. G., & Strauss, A. L. (Eds.). (1968). *Time for dying.* Chicago: Aldine.

Koocher, G. P., & O'Malley, J. E. (1981). *The Damocles syndrome: Psychosocial consequences of surviving childhood cancer.* New York: McGraw-Hill.

Kübler-Ross, E. (1969). *On death and dying.* New York: Macmillan.

Lindeman, D. A., Corby, N. H., Downing, R., & Sanborn, B. (1991). *Alzheimer's day care: A basic guide.* Washington, DC: Hemisphere.

Papadatou, D., & Papadatos, C. (Eds.). (1991). *Children and death.* Washington, DC: Hemisphere.

Parry, J. K. (Ed.). (1990). *Social work practice with the terminally ill: A transcultural perspective.* Springfield, IL: Charles C Thomas.

Pattison, E. M. (1977). *The experience of dying.* Englewood Cliffs, NJ: Prentice-Hall.

Piel, J. (Ed). (1989). *The science of AIDS.* New York: W. H. Freeman.

Samarel, N. (1991). *Caring for life and death.* Washington, DC: Hemisphere.

Sudnow, D. (1967). *Passing on: The social organization of dying.* Englewood Cliffs, NJ: Prentice-Hall.

Vachon, M. L. S. (1987). *Occupational stress in the care of the critically ill, the dying, and the bereaved.* Washington, DC: Hemisphere.

Viney, L. L. (1989). *Images of illness* (2nd ed.). Malabar, FL: Krieger.

Weismann, A. (1972). *On dying and denying.* New York: Behavioral Publications.

Bereavement

Angel, M. D. (1987). *The orphaned adult.* New York: Human Sciences Press.

Bertman, S. L. (1991). *Facing death: Images, insights, and interventions.* Washington, DC: Hemisphere.

Burnell, G. M., & Burnell, A. L. (1989). *Clinical management of bereavement: A handbook for healthcare professionals.* New York: Human Sciences Press.

Cleiren, M. P. (1993). *Bereavement and adaptation: A comparative study of the aftermath of death.* Washington, DC: Hemisphere.

Doka, K. J. (Ed.). (1989). *Disenfranchised grief: Recognizing hidden sorrow.* Lexington, MA: Lexington Books.

Gilbert, K. R., & Smart, L. S. (1992). *Coping with infant or fetal loss: The couple's healing process.* New York: Brunner/Mazel.

Haig, R. W. (1990). *The anatomy of grief: Biopsychosocial and therapeutic perspectives.* Springfield, IL: Charles C Thomas.

Klass, D. (1988). *Parental grief: Solace and resolution.* New York: Springer Publishing Company.

Leon, I. G. (1990). *When a baby dies: Psychotherapy for pregnancy and newborn loss.* New Haven, CT: Yale University Press.

Lund, D. A. (Ed.). (1989). *Older bereaved spouses: Research with practical applications.* Washington, DC: Hemisphere.

Morgan, J. D. (Ed.). (1993). *Personal care in an impersonal world: A multidimensional look at bereavement.* Amityville, NY: Baywood.

Parkes, C. M. (1987). *Bereavement: Studies of grief in adult life.* Madison, CT: International Universities Press.

Rando, T. A. (1993). *Treatment of complicated mourning.* Champaign, IL: Research Press.

Raphael, B. (1983). *The anatomy of bereavement.* New York: Basic Books.

Redmond, L. M. (1989). *Surviving when someone you love was murdered.* Clearwater, FL: Psychological Consultation and Education Services.

Rosenblatt, R. (1984). *Children of war.* Garden City, NY: Anchor Press/Doubleday.

Sanders, C. M. (1989). *Grief: The mourning after: Dealing with adult bereavement.* New York: Wiley.

Stroebe, M. S., Stroebe, W., & Hansson, R. O. (Eds.). (1993). *Handbook of bereavement: Theory, research, and intervention.* New York: Cambridge University Press.

Walsh, F., & McGoldrick, M. (Eds.). (1991). *Living beyond loss: Death in the family.* New York: W. W. Norton.

Worden, J. W. (1991). *Grief counseling and grief therapy: A handbook for the mental health practitioner.* New York: Springer Publishing Company.

Death Attitudes: Cultural and Individual

Aries, P. (1981). *The hour of our death.* New York: Knopf.

Becker, E. (1973). *The denial of death.* New York: Free Press.

Choron, J. (1963). *Death and Western thought.* New York: Collier.

Feifel, H. (Ed.). (1959). *The meaning of death.* New York: McGraw-Hill.

Feifel, H. (Ed.). (1977). *New meanings of death.* New York: McGraw-Hill.

Fischer, J. M. (Ed.). (1993). *The metaphysics of death.* Stanford, CA: Stanford University Press.

Fulton, R., & Bendiksen, R. (Eds.). (1994). *Death and identity* (3rd ed.). Philadelphia: Charles Press.

Irish, D. P., Lundquist, K. F., & Nelsen, V. J. (1993). *Ethnic variations in dying, death, and grief.* Washington, DC: Taylor & Francis.

Kastenbaum, R. (1992). *The psychology of death* (2nd ed.). New York: Springer Publishing Company.

Kübler-Ross, E. (1969). *On death and dying.* New York: Macmillan.

Neimeyer, R. A. (Ed.). (1994). *Death anxiety handbook: Research, instrumentation, and application.* Washington, DC: Taylor & Francis.

Pine, V. R. (1975). *Caretaker of the dead: The American funeral.* New York: Halstead.

Weisman, A. (1972). *On dying and denying.* New York: Behavioral Publications.

Weisman, A. D. (1984). *The coping capacity.* New York: Human Sciences Press.

Suicide, Homicide, and Horrendous Death

Barnaby, F. (1986). *The automated battlefield.* New York: Free Press.

Bauer, Y. (1982). *A history of the holocaust.* New York: Franklin Watts.

Curran, D. K. (1987). *Adolescent suicidal behavior.* Washington, DC: Hemisphere.

Des Pres, T. (1976). *The survivor: An anatomy of life in the death camps.* New York: Oxford University Press.

Gore, A. (1992). *Earth in the balance: Ecology and the human spirit.* Boston: Houghton Mifflin.

Kuper, L. (1985). *The prevention of genocide.* New Haven, CT: Yale University Press.

Leenaars, A., Maltsberger, T. & Neimeyer, R. A. (Eds.). (1994). *The treatment of suicidal people.* Washington, DC: Taylor & Francis.

Leenaars, A. A., & Wenckstern, S. (1990). *Suicide prevention in schools.* Washington, DC: Hemisphere.

Lester, D. (Ed.). (1990). *Current concepts of suicide.* Philadelphia: Charles Press.

Leviton, D. (Ed.). (1991). *Horrendous death and health: Toward action.* Washington, DC: Hemisphere.

Leviton, D. (Ed.). (1991). *Horrendous death, health, and well-being.* Washington, DC: Hemisphere.

Lifton, R. J. (1986). *The Nazi doctors: Medical killing and the psychology of genocide.* New York: Basic Books.

Orbach, I. (1988). *Children who don't want to live: Understanding and treating the suicidal child.* San Francisco: Jossey-Bass.

Osgood, N. J. (1992). *Suicide in later life: Recognizing the warning signs.* Lexington, MA: Lexington Books.

Schell, J. (1982). *The fate of the earth.* New York: Avon.

Schneidman, E. S. (1982). *Voices of death.* New York: Bantam.

Shneidman, E. S. (1985). *Definition of suicide.* New York: Wiley.

Shneidman, E. (1993). *Suicide as psychache.* Northvale, NJ: Jason Aronson.

Stillion, J. M., McDowell, E. E., & May, J. H. (1989). *Suicide across the life span—Premature exits.* Washington, DC: Hemisphere.

Westing, A. H. (1985). *Warfare in a fragile world: Military impact on the human environment.* London: Taylor & Francis.

Ethical, Social, and Medical Issues

Anspach, R. R. (1993). *Deciding who lives: Fateful choices in the intensive care nursery.* Berkeley: University of California Press.

Callahan, D. (1993). *The troubled dream of life: Living with mortality.* New York: Simon & Schuster.

Degner, L. F., & Beaton, J. I. (1987). *Life-death decisions in health care.* Washington, DC: Hemisphere.

Levine, C. (Ed.) (1993). *Taking sides: Clashing views on controversial bioethical issues* (5th ed.). Guilford, CT: Dushkin Publishing Group.

Moller, D. W. (1989). *On death without dignity: The human impact of technological dying.* Amityville, NY: Baywood.

Veatch, R. M. (1989). *Death, dying and the biological revolution* (Rev. ed.). New Haven, CT: Yale University Press.

BOOKS FOR CHILDREN AND ADOLESCENTS

Arrick, F. (1980). *Tunnel vision.* Scarsdale, NY: Bradbury. Middle school age and adolescence.

Breebaart, J., & Breebaart, P. (1993). *When I die, will I get better?* New York: Peter Bedrick. Adolescence.

Dudley, W. (Ed.). (1992). *Death and dying: Opposing viewpoints.* San Diego, CA: Greenhaven. Adolescence.

Carrick, C. (1981). *The accident.* New York: Clarion. Elementary and middle school ages.

Clifton, L. (1983). *Everett Anderson's goodbye.* New York: Henry Holt. Elementary and middle school ages.

Cohn, J. (1987). *I had a friend named Peter.* New York: William Morrow. Middle school ages.

Daisaku, I. (1991). *The cherry tree.* New York: Knopf. Elementary and middle school ages.

Deaver, J. R. (1988). *Say goodnight, Gracie.* New York: Harper & Row. Adolescence.

DePaola, T. (1973). *Nana upstairs and Nana downstairs.* New York: Putnam's. Preschool and elementary grades.

Dodge, N. C. (1986). *Thumpy's story: A story of love and grief shared by Thumpy, the Bunny.* Springfield, IL: Prairie Lark. Preschool.

Gravelle, K., & Haskins, C. (1989). *Teenagers face to face with bereavement.* New York: Simon & Schuster. Adolescence.

Greene, C. C. (1976). *Beat the turtle drum.* New York: Viking. Elementary and middle school ages.

Grollman, E. A. (1993). *Straight talk about suicide for teenagers.* Boston: Beacon. Adolescence.

Grollman, S. (1988). *Shira: A legacy of courage.* New York: Doubleday. Middle school age.

Hazen, B. S. (1985). *Why did Grandpa die?* New York: Golden. Elementary school age.

Hitchcock, R. (1988). *Tim's dad: A story about a boy whose father dies.* Springfield, IL: Human Services. Elementary and middle school ages.

Holden, L. D. (1989). *Gran-Gran's best trick: A story for children who have lost someone they love.* New York: Magination. Elementary school age.

Hughes, M. C. (1984). *Hunter in the dark.* New York: Atheneum. Adolescence.

Levine, J. (1992). *Forever in my heart: A story to help children participate in life as a parent dies.* Burnsville, NC: Mountain Rainbow. Elementary school age.

Krementz, J. (1989). *How it feels to fight for your life.* New York: Simon & Schuster. Middle school age and adolescence.

Maple, M. (1992). *On the wings of a butterfly.* Seattle: Parenting Press. Preschool and elementary grades.

McDaniel, L. (1992). *Sixteen and dying.* New York: Bantam. Adolescence.

Mellone, B., & Ingpen, R. (1983). *Lifetimes: The beautiful way to explain death to children.* New York: Bantam. Middle school age.

Orgel, D. (1971). *Mulberry music.* New York: Harper & Row. Elementary and middle school ages.

O'Toole, D. (1989). *Aarvy Aardvark finds hope: A read-aloud story for people of all ages* (with tape recording). Burnsville, NC: Rainbow Connection. Elementary and middle school ages.

Powell, E. S. (1990). *Geranium mourning.* Minneapolis: Carolrhoda B. Middle school age and adolescence.

Richter, E. (1986). *Losing someone you love: When a brother or sister dies.* New York: Putnam's. Middle school age.

Simon, N. (1989). *I am not a crybaby.* Morton Grove, IL: Albert Whitman. Elementary and middle school ages.

Smith, D. B. (1973). *A taste of blackberries.* New York: Crowell. Elementary and middle school ages.

Stiles, N. (1984). *I'll miss you, Mr. Hooper.* New York: Random House. Elementary school age.

Tott-Rizzuti, K. (1992). *Mommy, what does dying mean?* Pittsburgh, PA: Dorrance. Elementary and middle school ages.

Varley, S. (1984). *Badger's parting gifts.* New York: William Morrow. Elementary school age.

Vigna, J. (1991). *Saying goodbye to daddy.* Morton Grove, IL: Albert Whitman. Elementary school age.

Weir, A. B. (1992). *Am I still a big sister?* Newton, PA: Fallen Leaf Press. Elementary school age.

White, E. B. (1952). *Charlotte's web.* New York, Harper & Row. Elementary and middle school ages.

Young, A. E. (1991). *Is my sister dying?* St. Petersburg, FL: Willowisp. Elementary and middle school ages.

JOURNALS AND PERIODICALS

A great many journals in psychology, medicine, the allied health sciences, and the social sciences publish occasional articles on issues of death and loss. However, the following publications are wholly or substantially devoted to the latest developments in thanatological theory, research, and practice.

Bereavement (magazine)

Death Studies

Hospice Journal

Illness, Crises and Loss

Journal of Near Death Studies

Journal of Palliative Care

Journal of Psychosocial Oncology

Omega: Journal of Death and Dying

Suicide and Life-Threatening Behavior

AUDIOVISUAL RESOURCES
Audiotapes for a General Adult Audience and Professionals

Aging & dying: A positive view. C. Hayward et al. 4 hr. New Dimensions Foundation, P.O. Box 410510, San Francisco, CA 94141.
Cancer. 30 min. National Center for Audio Tapes, University of Colorado, 348 Stadium Boulevard, Boulder, CO 80309.
Care of a dying person. (1989). Elder Care Solutions, 1220 Bardstown Road, Louisville, KY 40204.
Care of dying children. 52 min. National Public Radio, 635 Massachusetts Ave. NW, Washington, DC 20001.
Circle of healing: Suicide prevention for young Native Americans. 30 min. National Public Radio, 635 Massachusetts Ave. NW, Washington, DC 20001.
Euthanasia. 59 min. National Public Radio, 635 Massachusetts Ave. NW, Washington, DC 20001.
Facing death. 59 min. National Public Radio, 635 Massachusetts Ave. NW, Washington, DC 20001.
Grief man. (1992). L. Elmer. 60 min. New Dimensions Foundation, P.O. Box 410510, San Francisco, CA 94141.
Hospice care for the terminally ill and their families. (1986). E. Dobihal et al. College of Chaplains, Suite 311, 1701 East Woodfield Road, Shaumburg, IL.
How to survive the loss of a love. (1991). M. Colgrove & P. McWilliams. 90 min. Bantam Audio, 414 East Gold Road, Des Plains, IL 60016.
Learning to live. 29 min. National Public Radio, 635 Massachusetts Ave. NW, Washington, DC 20001.
No time for goodbyes—Death of a son or a daughter. (1991). J. H. Lord. Pathfinder, CA, 458 Dorothy Avenue, Ventura, CA 93003.
Suicide prevention: You've got a friend. 30 min. National Public Radio, 635 Massachusetts Ave. NW, Washington, DC 20001.
Teenage suicide: A shared secret. 25 min. National Public Radio, 635 Massachusetts Ave. NW, Washington, DC 20001.
Understanding and preventing suicide. L. D. Hankoff. Soundwords, 56-11, 217th Street, Bayside, NY 11364-1999.
Waiting around to die. 29 min. National Public Radio, 635 Massachusetts Ave. NW, Washington, DC 20001.
When should life end? 59 min. National Public Radio, 635 Massachusetts Ave. NW, Washington, DC 20001.
Widowed: How to cope with loss. (1991). J. Brothers. 3 hr. Dove Audio, c/o Time-Warner, Suite 203, 301 North Canon Drive, Beverly Hills, CA 90210.

Videotapes for a General Adult Audience and Professionals

A child dies. (1989). 28 min. American Journal of Nursing, Educational Services Division, 555 West 57th Street, New York, NY 10019-2961.
A cradle song: The families of SIDS. (1989). 26 min. Fanlight Productions, 47 Halifax Street, Boston, MA 02130.
AIDS: A family experience. (1988). 33 min. Baxley Media Group, 110 West Main Street, Urbana, IL 61801.
Alive again. (1985). 30 min. Health Services Consortium, 201 Silver Cedar Court, Chapel Hill, NC 27514-1517.

Angels don't wear headlights. (1992). 25 min. Kidsrights, 10100 Park Cedar Drive, Charlotte, NY 28210.

Born dying. (1989). 20 min. Baxley Media Group, 110 West Main Street, Urbana, IL 61801.

Buffer zone: The mental health professional in the AIDS epidemic. (1989). 25 min. Baxley Media Group, 110 West Main Street, Urbana, IL 61801.

Care for the caregiver: Coping with perinatal death. (1988). 15 min. Altschul Group Corporation, 930 Pitner Avenue, Evanston, IL 60202.

Death in the family. Individual and systemic responses to loss. (1994). R. A. Neimeyer. 1 hr., 10 min. PsychoEducational Resources, P.O. Box 14123, Gainesville, FL 32614.

Dialogues on death and dying. (1991). E. Kübler-Ross. 3 hr. Audio-Renaissance/St. Martin's Press, 175 Fifth Avenue, New York, NY 10010.

Death in the family. (1987). 52 min. Wombat Film & Video, Division of Cortech Communications, Suite 2421, 250 West 57th Street, New York, NY 10019.

Dynamics of crisis intervention: The suicidal person. (1986). K. Reed et al. College of Chaplains, Suite 311, 1701 East Woodfield Road, Shaumburg, IL 60173.

Euthanasia in the '90s. (1990). 45 min. Ignatius Press, 15 Oakland Avenue, Harrison, NY 10528-9974.

Euthanasia: Murder or mercy? (1988). 30 min. Churchill Media, 12210 Nebraska Avenue, Los Angeles, CA 90025.

Family response to death. (1990). 30 min. for abridged edition, 50 min. for unabridged edition. Michigan State University, IMC Marketing Division, Instructional Medial Center, P.O. Box 710, East Lansing, MI 48826-0710.

Guns: A day in the death of America. (1990). 60 min. Ambrose Video Publishing, Suite 2245, 1290 Avenue of the Americas, New York, NY 10104.

Heart of the new age hospice. (1991). 28 min. Baxley Media Group, 100 West Main Street, Urbana, IL 61801.

Interview with a dying patient. (1988). 44 min. Professionals. Pennsylvania State University Audio-Visual Services, University Division of Media and Learning, Resources Special Services Building, University Park, PA 16802.

One of our own: Dealing with AIDS in the workplace. (1990). 30 min. Cambridge Career Products, P.O. Box 2153, Charleston, WV 25328-2153.

Suicide: A teenage dilemma. (1987). 30 min. Health Services Consortium, 201 Silver Cedar Court, Chapel Hill, NC 27514-1517.

Suzi's story. (1988). 58 min. Films Incorporated Video, 5547 North Ravenwood Avenue, Chicago, IL 60640-1199.

Talking with young children about death. 30 min. Family Communications, 4802 Fifth Avenue, Pittsburgh, PA 15213.

The Awakening of Nancy Kaye (1986). 46 min. Filmmakers Library, No. 901, 124 East 40th Street, New York, NY 10016.

The grieving family. (1989). 28 min. American Journal of Nursing, Educational Services Division, 555 West 57th Street, New York, NY 10019-2961.

The pitch of grief. (1985). 32 min. Fanlight Productions, 47 Halifax Street, Boston, MA 02130.

The right to die. (1993). 23 min. Lucerne Media, 37 Ground Pine Road, Morris Plains, NJ 07950.

There was a child. (1989). 28 min. Fanlight Productions, 47 Halifax Street, Boston, MA 02130.

When children grieve. (1988). 20 min. Churchill Media, 12210 Nebraska Avenue, Los Angeles, CA 90025.

When the bough breaks. 71 min. Fanlight Productions, 47 Halifax Street, Boston, MA 02130.

Winnie. (1989). 45 min. Wombat Film & Video, Division of Cortech Communications, Suite 2421, 250 West 75th Street, New York, NY 10019.

Videotapes for Adolescents and Youth

Good kids die too. (1989). 25 min. Learning Corporation of America, Division of New World Video, Suite 600, 4640 Lankashim Boulevard, North Hollywood, CA 91602.

In the midst of winter. (1992). 46 min. Pyramid Film & Video, P.O. Box 1048, 2801 Colorado Avenue, Santa Monica, CA 90406.

Living with AIDS. (1987). 24 min. Baxley Media Group, 110 West Main Street, Urbana, IL 61801.

Nothing to fear. (1989). 30 min. Direct Cinema, P.O. Box 10003, Santa Monica, CA 90410.

Taking charge: You and AIDS. (1988). 17 min. Pyramid Film & Video, P.O. Box 1048, 2081 Colorado Avenue, Santa Monica, CA 90406.

To whom it may concern: A program confronting teen suicide. (1990). 25 min. Kidsrights, 10100 Park Ceder Drive, Charlotte, NC 28210 or United Learning, 6633 West Howard Street, P.O. Box 48718, Niles, IL 60648.

Understanding AIDS. (1988). 45 min. Cambridge Career Products, P.O. Box 2153, Charleston, WV 25328-2153.

Understanding and coping with death. (1990). 60 min. Wishing Well Distributing, P.O. Box 1008, Silver Lake, WI 53170.

Videotapes for Children

All in its proper time. 29 min. In Spanish and English. PBS Video, 1320 Braddock Place, Alexandria, VA 22314-1698.

Death of a friend: Helping children cope with grief and loss. (1988). 15 min. New Dimension Media, 85803 Lorane Highway, Eugene, OR 97405.

Death of a goldfish. (1989). 30 min. PBS Video, 1320 Braddock Place, Alexandria, VA 22314-1698.

Echoes. (1991). 10 min. Media, P.O. Box 496, Media, PA 19063.

Grampa. (1992). Supplemental materials available. 27 min. Weston Woods, 289 Newtown Turnpike, Weston, CT 06883.

Losing hurts. But not forever. (1988). 45 min. Marshfilm/Marshmedia, P.O. Box 8082, Shawnee Mission, KS 66208.

The accident. (1988). 40 min. Barr Films, 12801 Schabarum Avenue, P.O. Box 7878, Irwindale, CA 91107.

The letter on the light blue stationery. (1989). 30 min. Cornell University, Audio Visual Resource Center, 8 Business and Technology Park, Ithaca, NY 14850.

Uncle elephant. (1991). 26 min. Churchill Media, 12210 Nebraska Avenue, Los Angeles, CA 90025.

ORGANIZATIONS

AIDS Resource Foundation for Children, 182 Roseville Avenue, Newark, NJ 07107. Foundation that operates homes for children with HIV, AIDS, or AIDS-related complex.

American Association of Suicidology, 2459 South Ash, Denver, CO 80222. Organization of professionals from various disciplines that promotes studies of suicide prevention, and life-threatening behaviors.

American Cancer Society, 1599 Clifton Road NE, Atlanta, GA 30329. Association supporting education and research programs pertinent to cancer prevention, recognition, diagnosis, and care.

American Foundation for AIDS Research, Second Floor, East Satellite, 5900 Wilshire Boulevard, Los Angeles, CA 90036. Fund-raising organization for conducting AIDS research.

American Hospital Association, 840 North Lake Shore Drive, Chicago, IL 60611.

American Institute of Life Threatening Illness and Loss, 630 West 168th Street, New York, NY 10032. Association promoting improved care for critically and terminally ill persons and assistance for their families.

American Medical Association, 515 North State Street, Chicago, IL 60610.

American Sudden Infant Death Syndrome Institute, Suite 100, 275 Carpenter Drive NE, Atlanta, GA 30328. Organization working to identify the cause of and find a cure for sudden infant death syndrome.

Association for Death Education and Counseling, 638 Prospect Avenue, Hartford, CT 06105-4298.

Association of individuals and institutions interested in responsible, effective education and counseling regarding death and bereavement.

Association of Nurses in AIDS Care, Suite 106, 704 Stony Hill Road, Yardley, PA 19067. Association providing leadership and educational services for its members and working to develop national standards for AIDS care.

Association of SIDS Program Professionals, Massachusetts Center for SIDS, Boston City Hospital, 818 Harrison Avenue, Boston, MA 02118. Association that organizes activities for professional development, produces practice standards, and connects practitioners who work with families who lost a child to sudden infant death syndrome.

Bereaved Parents, P.O. Box 3147, Scottsdale, AZ 85271. Association of parents grieving the deaths of children from autoerotic asphyxiation that provides counseling to families and supports research.

Candlelighters Foundation, Suite 460, 7910 Woodmont Avenue, Bethesda, MD 20814. Self-help organization for families with dying children.

Center for Loss in Multiple Births, c/o Jean Kollantai, P.O. Box 1064, Palmer, AK 99645. Provides peer support for parents bereaved over the death of one or more multiple-birth children during pregnancy, labor, or childhood.

Center for the Rights of the Terminally Ill, P.O. Box 54246, Hurst, TX 76054-2064. Advocates against euthanasia, assisted suicide, and abortion.

Centers for Disease Control, National AIDS Clearinghouse, P.O. Box 6003, Rockville, MD 20849-6003. Collects, analyzes, and disseminates information on HIV/AIDS.

Children's Hospice International, Suite 700, 901 North Washington Street, Alexandria, VA 22314. Organization promoting the inclusion of hospice care in pediatric facilities.

Choice in Dying—The National Council for the Right to Die, 200 Varkk Street, New York, NY 10014. Organization providing education about the legal, ethical, and psychological implications of decisions concerned with terminal care.

Concerned Relations of Nursing Home Patients. P.O. Box 18820, Cleveland Heights, OH 44128. Association promoting nursing home care that offers dignity and comfort regardless of ability to pay.

Foundation for Hospice and Homecare, 519 C Street NE, Washington, DC 20002. Focuses on improving the quality of life of the dying, the disabled, and the elderly, particularly as related to health care.

Helping Other Parents in Normal Grieving, Sparrow Hospital, 1215 East Michigan Avenue, P.O. Box 30480, Lansing, MI 48909. Self-help group for newly bereaved parents.

Hemlock Society, P.O. Box 11830, Eugene, OR 97440-4030. Organization that advocates voluntary euthanasia and assisted suicide for persons with advanced terminal diseases.

Hospice Association of America, 519 C Street NE, Washington, DC 20002. Promotes the concepts of hospice, provides forums for nurses, offers hospice start-up programs, and consults on hospice-related matters such as Medicare payments.

Hospice Education Institute, 5 Essex Square, Suite 3-B, P.O. Box 713, Essex, CT 06426. Offers education on hospice, death and dying, and bereavement.

Hospice Nurses Association, P.O. Box 8166, Van Nuys, CA 91409-8166. Association of registered nurses who provide hospice care.

International Anti-Euthanasia Task Force, P.O. Box 760, Steubenville, OH 43952. Opposes voluntary euthanasia and assisted suicide.

International Association for Near-Death Studies, P.O. Box 7767, Philadelphia, PA 19101-7767. Supports the scientific study of phenomena associated with near-death experiences.

International Workgroup on Death, Dying and Bereavement, c/o John Morgan, King's College, 266 Epworth Avenue, London, Ontario, Canada N6A 2M3. Association of professionals concerned with care for the terminally ill and bereaved and with issues of research and education in health care.

Leukemia Society of America, 600 East 3rd Avenue, New York, NY 10016. Organization that raises funds to fight leukemia by means of research, health care, and education.

Make-A-Wish Foundation of America, Suite 936, 2600 North Central Avenue, Phoenix, AZ 85004. Grants the wishes of terminally ill children up to 18 years of age.

Make Today Count, P.O. Box 6063, Kansas City, KS 66106-0063. Self-help organization for persons with life-threatening illnesses and for their families.

Mothers of AIDS Patients, 1811 Field Drive NE, Albuquerque, NM 87112–2833. Association providing support for families of AIDS patients during the illness and after the death.

National Association of People with AIDS, 1413 K Street NW, Washington, DC 20005. Association promoting local groups of persons diagnosed with AIDS, AIDS-related complex, or HIV to develop greater community awareness and to promote greater participation of local organizations in AIDS-related health care and social services.

National Citizens' Coalition for Nursing Home Reform, Suite 301, 1224 M Street NW, Washington, DC 20005. Organization devoted to reforming long-term care in nursing homes and related systems.

National Council of Guilds for Infant Survival, P.O. Box 3586, Davenport, IA 52808. Group providing consolation to parents who lost a child to sudden infant death syndrome (SIDS), supplying information about SIDS, and raising funds for medical research.

National Hospice Organization, Suite 901, 1901 North Moore Street, Arlington, VA 22209. Organization promoting standards of care for hospice programs, monitoring legislation pertinent to hospice care, and conducting educational programs about hospice.

National Institute for Jewish Hospice, Suite 652, 8723 Alden Drive, Los Angeles, CA 90048. Association of individuals, businesses, and organizations interested in helping terminally ill Jewish persons and their families.

National Right to Life Committee, Suite 500, 419 7th Street NW, Washington, DC 20004. Organization opposing abortion and euthanasia.

National Self-Help Clearinghouse, Room 620, 25 West 43rd Street, New York, NY 10036. Organization that maintains up-to-date information on self-help groups.

National SIDS Resource Center, Suite 600, 8201 Greensboro Drive, McLean, VA 22102. Organization that develops materials on sudden infant death syndrome (SIDS), apnea [temporary cessation of breathing], methods to monitor apnea, and grief over SIDS death.

Pregnancy and Infant Loss Center, 1421 West Wayzata Boulevard, Wayzata, MN 55391. Organization working to increase public understanding about perinatal death and to establish support groups for persons grieving such deaths.

Pregnancy and Infant Loss Support, St. Joseph's Health Center, 300 1st Capitol Drive, St. Charles, MO 63301. Self-help group of parents who have suffered a perinatal loss.

Project Inform, Suite 220, 1965 Market Street, San Francisco, CA 94103. Information clearinghouse on experimental drug treatments for persons with HIV or AIDS.

Samaritans, 500 Commonwealth Avenue, Kenmore Square, Boston, MA 02215. Association providing daily walk-in service for the suicidal and the depressed.

SEASONS: Suicide Bereavements, c/o Tina Larson, P.O. Box 187, Park City, UT 84060. Self-help group of persons grieving a suicide.

SIDS Alliance, Suite 420, 10500 Little Patuxent Parkway, Columbia, MD 21044. Clearinghouse that provides medical and other scientific information about sudden infant death syndrome (SIDS), offers bereavement support, and promotes SIDS research.

Society of Compassionate Friends, P.O. Box 3696, Oak Brook, IL 60522-3696. Self-help organization for bereaved parents.

UNITE, c/o Jeanes Hospital, 7600 Central Avenue, Philadelphia, PA 19111-2499. Self-help support group for persons bereaved after miscarriage or infant death.

Youth Suicide National Center, 445 Virginia Avenue, San Mateo, CA 94402. Educational organization that develops and distributes materials about youth suicide and youth suicide prevention programs.

Youth Suicide Prevention, 65 Essex Road, Chestnut Hill, MA 02167. Volunteer association of parents, professionals, and civil service workers concerned with preventing youth suicide.

Index